T0297919

Lecture Notes in Computer Science 6436

Commenced Publication in 1973
Founding and Former Series Editors:
Gerhard Goos, Juris Hartmanis, and Jan van Leeuwen

Marinos Ioannides   Dieter Fellner
Andreas Georgopoulos
Diofantos G. Hadjimitsis (Eds.)

Digital Heritage

Third International Conference, EuroMed 2010
Lemessos, Cyprus, November 8-13, 2010
Proceedings

 Springer

Volume Editors

Marinos Ioannides
Higher Technical Institute, Computer Department
P.O. Box 20423, 2152 Nicosia, Cyprus
E-mail: gammat@cytanet.com.cy

Dieter Fellner
TU Darmstadt, Tu Graz, Fraunhofer IGD,
Fraunhoferstraße 5, 64283 Darmstadt, Germany
E-mail: d.fellner@igd.fraunhofer.de

Andreas Georgopoulos
National Technical University of Athens
Iroon Polytechniou 9, 15773 Zografos, Athens, Greece
E-mail: drag@central.ntua.gr

Diofantos G. Hadjimitsis
Cyprus University of Technology, Faculty of Engineering and Technology
Department of Civil Engineering and Geomatics
P.O. Box 50329, 3603 Lemessos, Cyprus
E-mail: d.hadjimitsis@cut.ac.cy

Library of Congress Control Number: 2010938004

CR Subject Classification (1998): H.5.1, H.3, H.5, I.3-4, C.2, K.4

LNCS Sublibrary: SL 3 – Information Systems and Application, incl. Internet/Web
and HCI

ISSN   0302-9743
ISBN   978-3-642-16872-7 Springer Berlin Heidelberg New York

Typesetting: Camera-ready by author, data conversion by Scientific Publishing Services, Chennai, India
Printed on acid-free paper   06/3180

Preface

This volume comprises the proceedings of the Third International Euro-Mediterranean Conference (EuroMed 2010) on the historical island of Cyprus.

The focal point of this conference was digital heritage, which all of us involved in the documentation of cultural heritage continually strive to implement. The excellent selection of papers published in the proceedings reflects in the best possible way the benefits of exploiting modern technological advances for the restoration, preservation and e-documentation of any kind of cultural heritage. Above all, we should always bear in mind that what we do now may be used by people in another century to repair, rebuild or conserve the buildings, monuments, artifacts and landscapes that seem important. Recent events like earthquakes, tsunamis, volcanic eruptions, fires and insurrections show that we can never be too prepared for damage to, and loss of, the physical and, non-tangible elements of our past and, in general, our cultural heritage.

To reach this ambitious goal, the topics covered included experiences in the use of innovative recording technologies and methods, and how to take best advantage of the results obtained to build up new instruments and improved methodologies for documenting in multimedia formats, archiving in digital libraries and managing a cultural heritage.

Technological advances are very often reported in detail in specialized fora. This volume of proceedings establishes bridges of communication and channels of cooperation between the various disciplines involved in cultural heritage preservation. Furthermore, the contributions presented at this conference and included herein can assist all experts involved in the cultural heritage area in restoring, renovating, protecting, documenting, archiving, and monitoring the history of humanity in order to secure this information for the years to come. It is evident and clear that a worldwide collaboration in this area will help make our "hi-tech-story" accessible to the present and the future.

This important event and the proceedings you are holding in your hands contribute decisively to providing a forum for scientists and professionals to share ideas, experiences, needs and problems.

In this volume you will find all the submitted and reviewed contributions to the full and project papers.

We gratefully acknowledge that this task would not be possible without the support from our sponsors.

November 2010

Marinos Ioannides
Dieter Fellner
Andreas Georgopoulos
Diofantos G. Hadjimitsis

Conference Organization

Chairs

Marinos Ioannides	Cyprus
Dieter Fellner	Germany

Co-chairs

Andreas Georgopoulos	Greece
Diofantos G. Hadjimitsis	Cyprus

Local Organizing Committee

Agapiou, Athos	Hadjigavriel, Loukia	Philimis, Panayiotis
Christodoulou, Andreas	Lambrias, Christos	Skarlatos, Demitrios
Chrysanthou, Yiorgos	Lanitis, Andreas	Stylianou, George
Chrysostomou, Christis	Louka, Andreas	Themistokleous, Kyriakos
Eliades, Ioannis	Marangou, Anna	Tsimpoglou, Filippos
Fillipou, Filippos	Maratheftis, Antonis	Zervas, Marios
Flourenzos, Pavlos	Papachristodoulou, Andreas	

International Scientific Committee

Agapiou, Athos	Cyprus
Amditis, Angelos	Greece
Andia, Alfredo	USA
Arnold, David	United Kingdom
Artusi, Alessandro	Italy
Baltsavias, Manos	Switzerland
Barcelo, Juan A.	Spain
Beacham, Richard	United Kingdom
Beraldin, J-Angelo	Canada
Bernsen, Niels Ole	Denmark
Bertoncini, Massimo	Italy
Blas, Nicoletta	Italy
Boehm, Jan	Germany
Bourke, Paul	Australia
Brantl, Markus	Germany
Catalano, Chiara Eva	Italy
Chrysanthou, Yiorgos	Cyprus

Chrysostomou, Christis	Cyprus
Chrysoulakis, Nektarios	Greece
Cignoni, Paolo	Italy
Clayton, Chris	United Kingdom
Coquillart, Sabine	France
D'Andrea, Andrea	Italy
Dahari, Uzi	Israel
Dallas, Costis	Canada
Davies, Rob	United Kingdom
Day, Andy	United Kingdom
Dikomitou, Maria	Cyprus
Doerr, Martin,	Greece
Doneus, Michael,	Austria
Duguet, Florent,	France
Eckes, Georg,	Germany
El-Hakim, Sabry,	Canada
Eliades, Ioannis,	Cyprus
Falcidieno, Bianca,	Italy
Forte, Maurizio,	USA
Gaitatzis, Sakis,	Cyprus
Gebhardt, Andreas,	Germany
Griffin, Stephen M.,	USA
Grussenmeyer, Pierre,	France
Haala, Norbert,	Germany
Hagedorn-Saupe, Monika,	Germany
Hanke, Klaus,	Austria
Havemann, Sven,	Austria
Heliadi, Hesperia,	Cyprus
Huggett, Jeremy,	United Kingdom
Ioannidis, Charalambos,	Greece
Ioannidis, Yiannis,	Greece
Jabi, Wassim,	USA
Jerem, Elizabeth,	Hungary
Kenderdine, Sarah,	Australia
Kolias, Stefanos,	Greece
Krizova, Romana	Czech Republic
Kunkel, Timo,	United Kingdom
Kyza, Eleni A.,	Cyprus
Lanitis, Andreas,	Cyprus
León, A. Grande	Spain
Lerma, Jose Luis	Spain
Loscos, Céline	Spain
Madija, Lidija	Russia
Malzbender, Tom	USA
Mania, Katerina	Greece
Maratheftis, A.	Cyprus
Martin, Kathi	USA

May, Keith	Greece
Michael, Despina	Cyprus
Mullins, David	Ireland
Oudenaren, John	USA
Owen, John M.	The Netherlands
Papagiannakis, G.	Greece
Pattanaik, S.	USA
Pechlivanidou, L.	Greece
Philimis, Panayioti	Cyprus
Pitikakis, Marios	Greece
Pletinckx, Daniel	Belgium
Quak, Ewald	Estonia
Quintero, M. S.	Belgium
Remondino, Fabio	Italy
Renaud, C.	France
Retalis, Adrianos	Greece
Richards, Julian D.	United Kingdom
Rinaudo, Fulvio	Italy
Ross, Seamus	United Kingdom
Roussou, Maria	Greece
Rushmeier, Holly	United Kingdom
Ryan, Nick	United Kingdom
Sablatnig, Robert	France
Saleh, Fathi	EG
Sanders, Donald	United Kingdom
Sarris, Apostolos	Greece
Savino, Pasquale	Italy
Schlaumeier, Holly	United Kingdom
Scopigno, Roberto	Italy
Segond, Frederique	France
Skarlatos, Dimitrios	Cyprus
Stylianides, Stratos	Cyprus
Stylianou, Georgos	Cyprus
Tapinaki, Sevasti	Greece
Thalmann, Nadia	Switzerland
Themistokleous, K.	Cyprus
Torres, JuanCarlos	Spain
Troyer, Olga	Belgium
Tsapatsoulis, N.	Cyprus
Vavalis, Manolis	Greece
Verdiani, Giorgio	Italy
Walczak, Krzysztof	Poland
Wehr, Aloysius	Germany
White, Martin	United Kingdom
Zaphiris, Panayiotis	Cyprus
Zervas, Marios	Cyprus

Table of Contents

2D and 3D Data Capture Methodologies and Data Processing in Cultural Heritage

Digital Data Acquisition Technologies and Data Processing in Cultural Heritage

Long Term Availability of Content and Its Long Term Accessibility

Digital Cultural Heritage Applications and Their Impact

Standards, Metadata, Ontologies and Semantic Processing in Cultural Heritage

Remote Sensing for Archaeology and Cultural Heritage Management and Monitoring

2D and 3D Data Capture Methodologies and Data Processing in Cultural Heritage

3D-Reconstruction and Virtual Reality in Archaeology

2D and 3D in Digital Libraries

e-Libraries and e-Archives in Cultural Heritage

2D and 3D GIS in Cultural Heritage

A Processing for Digitizing Historical Architecture

Hung-Ming Cheng, Ya-Ning Yen, Min-Bin Chen, and Wun-Bin Yang

China University of Technology, 56 Sec. 3 ShingLong Rd., 116 Taipei, Taiwan
{hungmc,alexyen,cmb,wunbin}@cute.edu.tw

Abstract. This study describes a process for digitizing 3D documentation with 3d laser scanner tools. The process of capturing 3D data is mainly for as-built environment in reconstruction and documentation of historical scenes. For retrieving the 3d shape of historical building, the workflow needs to be developed in terms of 3D data acquisition, 3D modeling, documentation and web-based representation. For practical demonstration, several cases present the reconstructed results and the application of virtual scene. These practical cases were applied the technique solution to approach digitizing tasks of preservation for cultural heritage, which could evoke more heritage preservation issues.

Keywords: 3D Documentation computing, Digital archive, Digital cultural heritage, 3D Laser scanner, Heritage preservation.

1 Introduction

Digital archiving and 3D digitizing technology apply in several fields, including manufacturing industry, medical sciences, entertainment industry and, cultural heritage [1], [3], [11]. In application of manufacturing industry, inspection probes and survey are substituted by non-contact laser scanning equipment that are often used for aero industry and automotive parts design and testing [17]. Otherwise computer aided design and manufacture in reverse engineering is employed in a wide range of applications in the field of science and industry, together with animation techniques and WEB application [9], [12], [15].

Cultural heritage, ancestors' historical assets, transmits conventional environment and craftsman's experience in the civilization and cultural progress [2], [16], [19]. However, owing to the longer process of confirming and the limitation of budget and timing, the preservation of historical architecture is not efficiently executed preservation. Moreover, natural disaster, such as earthquake, fire and accident collapse, caused historical architecture disappeared in one moment. For these reasons, we are seeking an integrating technique to help building preserved works at the limited opportunity.

Traditional methods are slow, time-consuming and present a number of evident limitations [19]. The way of survey and measuring of historical architecture are using photographing and manual tape method, then manually transferring these discrete numbers into engineering drawings in AutoCAD [8], [19]. Although 2-dimensional drawings and graphics provide some support documents to rebuild historical architecture. They are no way to complete these information but truly 3-dimensional model.

M. Ioannides (Ed.): EuroMed 2010, LNCS 6436, pp. 1–12, 2010.
© Springer-Verlag Berlin Heidelberg 2010

Cultural heritage needs more advanced techniques to support preservation and conversation in cultural heritage [2].

Digitizing historical cultural architecture is a trend on international preservation. Traditional tools using survey and probing in manuals couldn't correspond to preservation procedure in effective and efficient [9], [12] . Therefore, we consider an integrating mechanism in tool and procedure. Laser scanner is using the reflection and projection of laser beam and probing the difference of time. As the objects scanned by laser beam, the scanner machine calculates the distant of machine and objects. And by calibrating the ejection angle of laser beam, the laser scanner records the spatial data as data of point clouds. This study is employed 3D laser scanner with the high quality digital camera that can reach more than 1000 meters. And the inaccuracy of survey result is less than 5mm. Acquiring surface data of building are the first step of the heritage preservation [8], [14].

In this paper, we concentrate on extracting 3D models of cultural heritage for 3d document application. Hence, our techniques are considerably procedure in systematic and reasonable than those isolating in machine body or limited to people training. We start from an investigation of survey technology and reverse engineering which is more mature field to utilize laser scanning technology. After comparing the techniques of laser scanner and photogrammetry application, we realize laser scanner with more accurate, efficient, faster and reliable than other documentation techniques.

2 Survey Process

Heritage preservation is a continuous process which are the many data need to integrate, acquire and analysis which mean a lot of construction data to be recorded. There are a serial of process and operation that include engineering surveying, drafting and design, monitoring for post-construction analysis [3], [17]. Recorded data are made by discrete manual 2D drawings have limitations in describing the allocation of geometries in 3D space. 3D data are intuitive, visualizing and continuous representation to simulate space characteristics which will be the best way to manipulate with architectural and historical senses. As such, we choose the 3D laser scanner of survey manner to reach our objective directly.

Cultural heritage protection is an important issue in the world. The sustainable concept in public awareness and these kinds of monuments constitute an important part of our past. Digital 3d documentation presents a process of restore and protection which integrate the survey technique and building computing between reality and virtual world.

2.1 Laser Scanner with Operation System

For reconstructing a 3D environment and architecture, we choose Riegl LMS-Z420i of LiDAR system which offers the most powerful in distant effective to capture the spatial data with point clouds format acquire clouds data (Fig. 1). The machine scan the surface of object to receive spatial data about 11,000 points per second with high precision up to 4 mm. The field of view is 80° x 360° and the range is up to 1000m.

For each scanning mission, scanner machine also needs laptop-computer with bundled operation software package "RiSCAN PRO" to operate the scanner for acquiring high-quality 3D data in the field [10]. By mechanically scanning the surface of object with the laser set, different sections of the object are sequentially acquired and cloud data are therefore generated. For the specific parts and detailed objects, they need a concentrated shot on these specific details with condense scanning of laser points.

The laser scanner can take advantage in the territorial field with reference points to connect difference station data. However, Target site have some obstacle views to disable cross scanning. The scanning plan therefore adopts higher view point to solve these limitations.

Fig. 1. Riegl LMS-Z420i & software RiSCAN PRO

2.2 Survey Planning and Scan Works

Supported by National Science Council, We selected 10 experimental sites for the experiments, which located at Taipei County. They are with several different types of archaeological objects and historical buildings. For acquiring the 3D data of real environments, we have to integrate scan whole archaeological objects from several different scan stations. The stations with difficult accessing problem, we have developed such device in view of high and wide to overcome and take the 3d data with scanning machine.

For development of 3D scanner supports 360 degrees field-of-view, the scanner has to move around archaeological objects to complete exterior scan views with registration targets. The laser scanner is difficult to work at those buildings placed closely without appropriate station-locations on scanning and registration entire surroundings. Therefore, we select several higher locations among those buildings nearby. Basically, higher scanning locations are used to avoid obstructions problems and reduce numbers of scanning station. (Fig. 2)

For those objects to be scanned in a well-controlled environment (for example: indoor space and no obstruction problem), objects can be oriented scan completely without extra registration targets. However, ranged scanning is often incomplete for obstructions or lack of controlled-high-view scans at outdoor site. There is no way to solve such as problems until we build a lift-able car and movable support.

Fig. 2. Mobile car working with lift-able device

The device provides a carrier of 3D laser scanner with lift-able and stable character. It is not only fixing on the ground but also avoid to vibration. Furthermore, it can be controlled in height by expert experience for the best survey. The device with platform on the top can fixed scanner on the lift-pole. The each of multi-supported legs implement dynamic device for lift-up the truck that is for stable survey implementation without shaking by rubber tires. The lift-able device includes scissors-like instrument and platform, which includes a space for 3d laser scanner instrument and multi-action kinematics extending the range of survey and reach proper height for advantage process. Therefore, the creative work includes lift-able and stable character that is not only stability of scanner and also convenient adjusting height for the best survey efficiently. (Fig. 3).

Fig.3. Lift-able car and movable support

2.3   Registration and Data Process

The operation software integrates data from different stations with different coordinate systems. Therefore, merging range data into a single coordinate system is necessary for creating a complete 3D model [2], [7], [14]. In the operation procedure, we analyze at least three overlapping fields of target points for software to calculate the rough transformation between two different scan world systems [16]. Then the

Fig. 4. Environmental scanning result: Jing-Tung Train Station

software system will minimize the registration error between the overlapping coordinate system. After all scanned worlds processed, they are merged to an integrated model. Figure 4 shows the integrated point clouds model of Jing-Tung Train Station.

2.4 Registration and Data Process

The modeling operation starts to capture the feature of object. These features (for example, points, lines or components) will be extracted from images, enhancing the spatial characteristics and representing the coherence of geometry with mesh or solid of computer graphics algorithm [6], [12]. The proposed feature extractors are adapted to solution softwares that are CATIA and Rapidform XOR2. (Fig. 5) The softwares are based on the similarity of directional feature vector. For the 3D modeling (shape, surface and volume), there are some other options so called middleware of Reverse Engineering in order to develop Rapid Prototyping in design application [9], [13], [14].

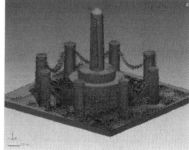

Fig. 5. Software Rapidform XOR2 processes the point cloud as mesh modeling

3 The Application of Digital Archiving

3.1 The Procedure of 3D Scanning

For the work flows of 3D data acquisition of cultural heritage, the quantity and density of point cloud control the detail of 3d modelling by reverse engineering. In the registration of laser scanning, both software and hardware influence the representation and accurate of point cloud. Therefore, we develop a procedure and method for different size and distant of heritage's objects. In 3d data acquisition of laser scanning, we not only process specific machine on manual to acquire 3D data but also attempt to integrate different machine and software to registration point cloud. For the digital archiving of cultural heritage, these precious 3d data can provide an original digital format to reconstruct e physical heritage in future.

On the post operation phase, 3D modeling depends on the software of reverse engineering which is a from the survey technology for production. We manipulate the software of reverse engineering for modeling the digital building which is a key process of industry utilization in physical form design. The whole processes are through surface analysis, holes filling, and rebuild the mesh models. The purpose of 3d modeling is building up the same size of physical heritage in digital form that can export as visualization and virtual reality on the Internet.

For the web representation, we proceed proprietary VR authoring tool is introduced to demonstrate the reconstructed results. The comprehensive virtual scene is then laid out in VR tool that is the web-base browser for navigating in 3d virtual world. For more application of VR, we knew the point file is not replaced in original representation. Therefore we adopt the point cloud into virtual reality for representing point in 3D space. As a result, we can freely walk through the virtual historical site. And, further rich illustrations are also readily carried out through interactive manipulation in the Web. (Fig. 6).

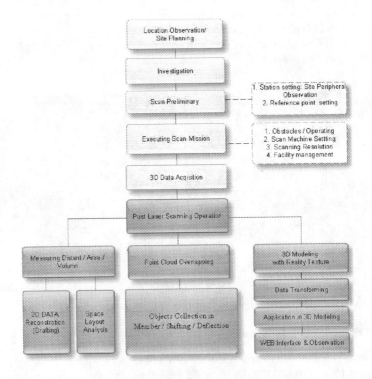

Fig. 6. Workflow of digitizing

3.2 The Result of Works

In this project, we used 3D laser scanner techniques to rebuild the objects of heritage, which includes an upright stone tablet, pavilion, bridge and historical building. According to our experiments, we found that this integrated approach is efficient and

Table 1. Five Types of digitizing cultural heritages

Interior of Fort San Domingo, Danshui			
Real picture	Image of point clouds	Image of 3d modeling	Stations and point clouds (statistics)
			Stations: 8 40 Million Points
Lin Family Gardens			
Real picture	Image of point clouds	Image of 3d modeling	Stations and point clouds (statistics)
			Stations: 9 17 Million Points
Tomb of Dr. Mackay			
Real picture	Image of point clouds	Image of 3d modeling	Stations and point clouds (statistics)
			Stations: 4 2 Million Points
Shanchia Station			
Real picture	Image of point clouds	Image of 3d modeling	Stations and point clouds (statistics)
			Stations: 18 168 Million Points
Shanhsia Arch Bridge			
Real picture	Image of point clouds	Image of 3d modeling	Stations and point clouds (statistics)
			Stations: 7 12 Million Points

accurate. LiDAR technology could precisely digitize fine details and sculpted surfaces which are essential for modeling those monuments and historical buildings. We process these raw data which are real picture, image of point clouds, image of 3d modeling and some statistics numbers of stations and points. And we present several types of heritages which are interior, garden, monuments, building and bridge.

4   Application in Scanning Technology

Digital archiving has been applied on several purposes in heritage preservation recently. We selected two issues for this digitizing project. The first is monitoring of cultural which is following currently reconstruction work. The second is trying to find out the data characters for decision supported making

4.1   Documentation and Monitoring of Cultural Heritage

Virtual preservation takes advantage of the expansion and long-term saving. Cultural heritage needs these data for continuous monitoring. In particular, the heritages in real environment are irreversibly damaged by environmental disaster or atmospheric damages. Those damages sometime were discovered too late. High accuracy 3D scanning, at regular times, could detect deformations and cracks. The data for monitoring could be the fundamental of reconstructing heritage.

The 3D documentation archives the spatial data of cultural heritage. Documentation should be considered as an integral part of a greater action in general documentation of the cultural heritage. Those data includes text, picture, music, and more other format media. These multi-format media with historical documentation, architectural documentation store a whole picture of cultural heritage.

On the other hand, cultural heritage protection is a key issue around the world today. Those issues evoke public awareness over recent years which address some important monuments of our past. The documentation and display of ancient artifacts and antiquities is an essential task in the field of cultural heritage preservation [19]. Digital archive of high quality three-dimensional models would give improvement in the restoration science field. Digital archives thus can be used as reference for monitoring and restoration of cultural heritages [15]. (Fig. 7)

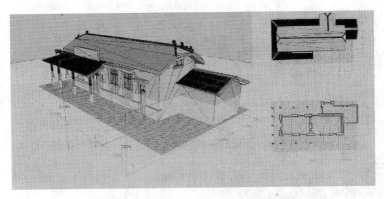

Fig. 7. 3D Documentation (Jing-Tong Train Station)

4.2 Multimedia and Data Management as Decision-Support

Multimedia (such as 3D scenes navigation, animation) has developed for two purposes. The first offers in showing the sequence of possibilities image sequences,
where each image represents an option based on a set of parameters. As architects are
interested in specific image, that shows the closest match between model and the
virtual measurement. The 3D navigation also reveals an insight of spatial design
thinking that cannot possibly be revealed through flat and analogue representation.

This project produces heritages in Taipei County establish archive of all the survey
material combined with the work, that are integrated in the digital format for next
application. Heritage materials are combined with historical document, physical situation and contemporary observation. Digitally managing materials have been essential
programs that need to organize comprehensive representation in terms of the web
environment to display accurate information (Fig. 8). On the other hand, text, image
and drawings are importance in design studio for reconstruction issues. Consulted
these data through the digital archives, the design can continuously work. Multimedia
has been used to assemble these data for specific purposes including reconstruction or
VR tour. These could improve design teamwork for design decision making.

Fig. 8. Photo Picture and Texts Present in Webpage and GIS Applying Google Map

5 Discussion

Preserving and representing cultural heritage motivates the new technology for producing complex and heterogeneous data. For managing these data, digitalizing is
essential task for the use and the diffusion of the information gathered on the field.
We discuss these issues in terms of the concepts of digital archiving, 3D documentation and WEB application for the emergence of digitalization in recent years.

5.1 Digital Archiving in Cultural Heritage

The jobs of digital archiving include several phases of the preserving, organizing and
retrieving on the cultural heritage. 3D laser scanning technology evolves in the most
diverse fields, an increasing number of cultural institutions take into consideration the
need to capture 3D datasets of heritage assets. However, the digitizing procedures
with 3d laser scanning are very heterogeneous and complex, including not only the

economic management and the logistic activities which take place in the offices, but also on-stage artistic production and craft-made activities in workshops.

The whole process involves the three-dimensional digitization, digital data processing and storage, archival and management, representation and reproduction. In this paper, we briefly review methods for three-dimensional digitization that are applicable to cultural heritage recording.

5.2 Survey Technologies and Other Applications

With recent developments in computer and information technologies, this well-known traditional method has been replaced with digital survey and Internet technology.

These new methods offer us new opportunities such as automatic orientation and measurement procedures, generation of 3D point-clouds data, digital surface modeling and WEB representation in cultural heritage. These methods and equipments commonly used for digitalizing buildings are: traditional manual surveying methods, photogrammetric methods, scanning methods and WEB database application. These methods determine the main data representation, the instruments limitation and the key points of each cultural heritage.

On the other hand, 3D laser scanning is an essential technology for territory survey that has become increasingly popular for 3D documentation. These techniques provide very dense 3D points on an object surface with high accuracy. In addition, the 3D model within digital image can be easily generated using generated 3D point cloud and recorded as vector measured drawing data. These large data must be processed by proper procedures for solving the work flow in order to connect human-machine interface and operation software.

Current digital archiving has been carried out for the digital preservation and treatment of Cultural Heritage information. The development of computerized data management systems to store and make use of archaeological datasets is a significant task. For such application in the Internet, 3D WEB representation is a broadcasting platform for highlighting 3D spatial information browsing which should be processed on the phases of captured, structured, and retrieved in order to transform multimedia performances in cultural heritage for other application. The whole digital system need to compliant to every kind of Cultural Heritage site and allows management of heterogeneous data.

6   Conclusion

This project develops three phases to initialize digitizing works. (1) 3D data acquisition: using the 3d laser scanner to rebuild the surfaces of environment which are several stations of view to registration. (2) 3D modeling: using the reverse engineering software to process those raw data (points of cloud). This phase mainly is data transformation and 3D geometry rebuild. (3) Web representation and others application: We procedure digitizing process to integrate 3D data and others media format (i.e. text, picture...) for navigating in World Wide Web. These 3D data are integrating into 2D graphic drawing and specific derails to present rich culture heritage.

Concluding current works, we plan a roadmap of digital archiving for proposing 3 possible directions: The first direction considers Web visualization is an essential communication platform to represent 3D data in the world. These data are easy access and retrieve by Internet technology which also are unlimited time and place. The second direction is 3D laser scanners become an essential application from industry engineering to cultural heritage. The tools and theory are contributed to the heritage preservation and conservation. We will try to develop strategic application of heritage preservation. For the last direction is digital archiving, these data are formed a kind of "3D documentation of digital heritage". In the wide definition of conservation and preservation, 3D laser scanners grab the most part of heritage form which include primitives of geometry, shape, color and texture.

For the future works, the handicap scanning tools of lift-able car and movable support for the 3D laser scanning of historical architecture is a useful way to overcome many obstacles. We will develop more mechanism in scanning processes and physical tools. In the process of digital archiving, we manage and preserve the 3D data information system for digital museum in heritage preservation. These raw data with 3D character of culture heritage become virtual heritage in future.

Acknowledgements

This study is sponsored by the National Science Council for 2007-2008 National Digital Archive Program (NSC-96-2422-H-163-001, NSC-97-2631-H-163-001) and 2010 (NSC-99-2632-H-163-001), Taiwan.

References

1. Addison, A.C., Alonzo, C.: The Vanishing Virtual: Safeguarding Heritage's Endangered Digital Record. In: Kvan, T., Kalay, Y. (eds.) New Heritage: Beyond Verisimilitude: Proc., of the New Heritage Conference, pp. 36–48. University of Hong Kong (2006)
2. Arayici, Y.: An approach for real world data modelling with the 3D terrestrial laser scanner for built environment. Automation in Construction 16(6), 816–829 (2007)
3. Berndt, E., Carlos, J.: Cultural heritage in the mature era of computer graphics. IEEE Computer Graphics and Applications 20(1), 36–37 (2000)
4. Bhatti, A., Nahavandi, S., Frayman, Y.: 3D depth estimation for visual inspection using wavelet transform modulus maxima. Computers and Electrical Engineering 33(1), 48–57 (2007)
5. Bosche, F., Haas, C.: Automated retrieval of 3D CAD model objects in construction range images. Automation in Construction 17(4), 499–512 (2008)
6. Datta, S.: Digital reconstructions and the geometry of temple fragments. In: The Proceedings of the 2007 International Conference on Digital Applications in Cultural Heritage, National center for research and preservation of cultural properties, Tainan, Taiwan, pp. 443–452 (2001)
7. Dorai, C., Weng, J., Jain, A.K., Mercer, C.: Registration and integration of multiple object views for 3D model construction. IEEE Transactions on Pattern analysis and Machine Intelligence 20(1), 83–89 (1998)

8. Fischer, A., Manor, A.: Utilizing image Processing Techniques for 3D Reconstruction of Laser-Scanned Data. CIRP Annals - Manufacturing Technology 48(1), 99–102 (1999)
9. Fontana, R., Greco, M., Materazzi, M., Pampaloni, E., Pezzati, L., et al.: Three-dimensional modelling of statues: the Minerva of Arezzo. Journal of Cultural Heritage 3(4), 325–331 (2002)
10. Goldberg, H.E.: Scan Your Would with 3D Lasers. CADALYST Magazine, 20–28 (2001)
11. Levoy, M.A.: The Digital Michelangelo Project. Computer Graphics Forum 18(3), xiii-xvi(4) (1999)
12. Li, J., Guo, Y., Zhu, J., Lin, X., Xin, Y., Duan, K., Tang, Q.: Large depth-of-view portable three-dimensional laser scanner and its segmental calibration for robot vision. Optics and Lasers in Engineering 45(11), 1077–1087 (2007)
13. Marschallinger, R.: A method for three-dimensional reconstruction of macroscopic features in geological materials. Computers & Geosciences 24(9), 875–883 (1998)
14. Monga, O., Benayoun, S.: Using Partial Derivatives of 3D Images to Extract Typical Surface Features. Computer Vision and Image Understanding 61(2), 171–189 (1995)
15. Pieraccini, M., Guidi, G., Atzeni, C.: 3D digitizing of cultural heritage. Journal of Cultural Heritage 2(1), 63–70 (2001)
16. Shih, N.J., Wang, H.J., Lin, C.Y., Liau, C.Y.: 3D scan for the digital preservation of a historical temple in Taiwan. Advances in Engineering Software 38(7), 501–512 (2007)
17. Shih, N.J., Wang, P.H.: Point-cloud-based comparison between construction schedule and as-built progress - a long-range 3D laser scanner's approach. Journal of Architectural Engineering 10(3), 98–102 (2004)
18. Willis, A., Speicher, J., Cooper, D.B.: Rapid prototyping 3D objects from scanned measurement data. Image and Vision Computing 25(7), 1174–1184 (2007)
19. Yilmaz, H.M., Yakar, M., Yildiz, F.: Documentation of historical caravansaries by digital close range photogrammetry. Automation in Construction 17(4), 489–498 (2008)

Calculation Methods for Digital Model Creation Based on Integrated Shape, Color and Angular Reflectivity Measurement

Robert Sitnik, Grzegorz Mączkowski, and Jakub Krzesłowski

WUT, Institute of Micromechanics and Photonics, 8 Boboli, 02-525 Warsaw, Poland
{r.sitnik,g.maczkowski,j.krzeslowski}@mchtr.pw.edu.pl

Abstract. The paper presents a complete methodology for processing sets of data registered by the means of a measurement system providing integrated 3D shape, multispectral color and angular reflectance characteristic. The data comprise of clouds of points representing the shape of the measured object, a set of intensity responses as a function of wavelength of incident light used for color calculation and a set of distributions of reflected intensity as a function of illumination and observation angles. Presented approach allows to create a complete 3D model of the measured object which preserves the object's shape, color and reflectivity properties. It is developed specifically for application in the digitization of cultural heritage objects for storing and visualization purposes, as well as duplication by the means of 3D printing technology.

Keywords: cultural heritage digitization, structured light projection, multispectral color, BRDF, cloud of points, triangle mesh, texture, calculation methods.

1 Integrated System for Cultural Heritage Objects Digitization

1.1 Introduction

Recently, different techniques for digitization of many classes of objects have emerged. They usually require specific data processing methods and vary greatly because of different technologies involved, different accuracy and applications. A review of different approaches to shape digitization depending on object's size, material and complexity was given by Pavlidis et al. [1]. There also exist several studies involving multispectral color measurements of oil paintings [2]. Different implementations of such devices vary in the number of registered spectral bands and data processing algorithms depending on specific application [3], [4]. Consequently, there are different possibilities of registering angular reflectance, either by time consuming gonio-reflectometry or a kind of simplified bidirectional reflectance distribution function (BRDF) estimation similar to extended photometric stereo [5]. Nevertheless, combining these kinds of data together to create a more precise representation of the object usually requires some manual processing to fit the data from different measurement devices into a single, complete model.

M. Ioannides (Ed.): EuroMed 2010, LNCS 6436, pp. 13–27, 2010.
© Springer-Verlag Berlin Heidelberg 2010

In this paper we would like to focus on digital measurements of cultural heritage objects based on the measurement of integrated shape, multispectral color and angular reflectance characteristic [6]. In this case, directional illumination is used for BRDF estimation, but with additional knowledge of surface position and its normal vectors. The main purpose of this research is the registration of object's appearance with good accuracy for storing in a digital archive, visualization and duplication. We propose a set of calculation methods which allow to obtain a complete virtual model from raw data acquired with the 3D scanner.

At the beginning of the paper the measurement system is presented along with the data format used in calculation methods. It is followed by the description of the concept of data processing methodology and its implementation, after which detailed descriptions of implemented algorithms are provided along with exemplary results of their application in experimental measurements.

1.2 Measurement System Description

The system incorporates a 3D scanner, a multispectral camera for color measurement and a custom designed angular reflectance measurement device. The fact that all the components use the same detector eliminates the need for manual alignment of the acquired data, as all the necessary information is provided for every point registered on the measured surface unambiguously.

The shape measurement system comprises of a digital light projector and a CCD camera which are calibrated together. Its operation relies on structured light projection [7] and it allows for registering shape of the investigated surface within a 200 x 300 x 200mm measurement volume with 0.1mm resolution and 0.03mm accuracy (Fig. 1).

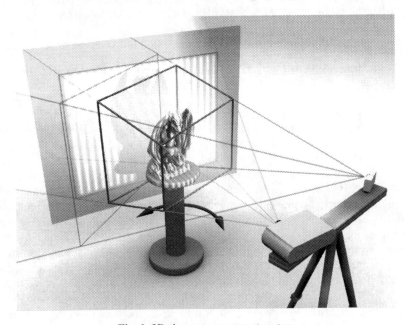

Fig. 1. 3D shape measurement system

The color measurement system [6] uses a multispectral approach based on capturing images of the object in several different spectral bands under specified, known illumination. The system measures spectral reflectance distribution in every point registered by the camera. In the described setup a custom built multispectral camera with 20 spectral bands and flash as a light source was used (Fig. 2)

Fig. 2. Multispectral camera integrated with the 3D shape measurement system

For angular reflection measurement [6] a specially designed setup was used, which supports controlled directional illumination of the investigated surface from several known positions relative to the direction of observation. Eleven uniformly distributed white light emitting diodes with additional diffusers were used as light sources.

1.3 Raw Data from the Measurement

Data registered in the integrated measurement include space coordinates of the surface. Additionally, a set of reflected energy responses in several spectral bands within the visible spectrum and a set of luminous energy responses from several angles of illumination are independently acquired for every point. Other data resulting from the measurement include spectral emission characteristic of a light source, optical setup attenuation and geometry of angular light sources distribution.

The data are organized in a structure in order to simplify further processing. The basic structure is a cloud of points with normal vectors calculated in every point based on its local neighbourhood. The rest of the data is assigned to the cloud of points as additional layers in such a way, that each point in the cloud can have a vector of properties attached. In the case of integrated measurement, the previously described information containing energy responses from spectral and angular measurements is stored in this vector. The whole structure can be extended to make it possible to add other data layers and increase the dimension of the attached vector of properties. The data structure is stored in several binary files with a single XML interface, which makes it easy to manage and extend. The scheme of the data structure is shown in Fig. 3.

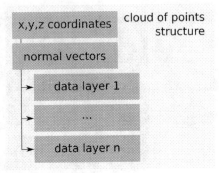

Fig. 3. Diagram of a basic data structure for storing cloud of points geometrical data with additional per point information

2. Data Processing Path

2.1 The Concept

Data registered in a single measurement process can be divided into three separate categories, as mentioned in the previous section. The first category is shape in the form of cloud of points, the second is spectral reflectance and the third – angular reflectance (Fig. 4).

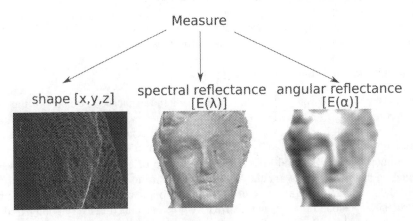

Fig. 4. Categories of surface measurement data, which can be processed by various calculation methods and combined into a 3D model

We propose three final stages for the processed data depending on their application – storing in a digital archive, displaying in a virtual scene and duplication by the means of 3D printing technology. It is therefore necessary to propose different processing paths for each implementation. In order to use intermediate processing stages efficiently, applied operations are designed in a way which allows them to make use of results from previous processing stages. A flowchart in Fig. 5 shows relations between the processing stages.

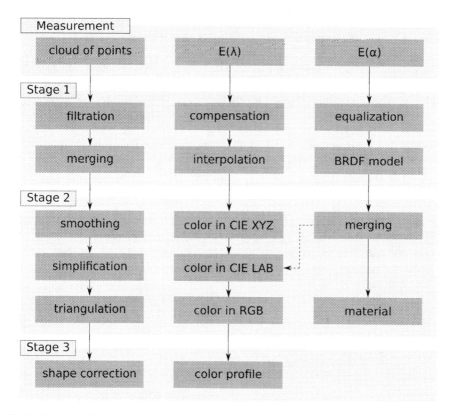

Fig. 5. Diagram of three data processing stages and three main processing paths (one for each data category). It should be noted that even though the processing paths are not joint, some calculation methods use a portion of output from the other paths.

In the first stage, data are processed for storing in a digital archive. Clouds of points are filtered in order to eliminate noise and errors caused by incorrect phase calculation. Next, the clouds acquired from several different directions are merged with the use of ICP algorithms [8] in order to create a full model of the measured object. At this stage the shape data are considered sufficient for storage purposes.

Color measurement data are interpolated over the visible spectrum domain, so that spectral reflectance for each point in the cloud of points can be estimated. Other calibration data, including emission spectrum characteristic of the light source used in the measurement, correction coefficients of the field's of view uniformity and spectral filters' energy compensation factors are necessary for this operation.

Angular reflectance measurement data are used for a BRDF derivation according to Phong model [9]. Additional calibration data used include black component compensation factors and information about the distribution of light sources in space.

The second stage of operations is used for obtaining a model adequate for display in a virtual environment. It is based on the data received from the previous stage rather than on the raw measurement data.

At this moment the complete 3D model represented as a set of dense clouds of points constitute the input shape measurement data. First it is smoothed to eliminate noise and improve the quality of clouds' fit. Next the clouds are simplified in order to decrease the amount of superfluous data while preserving the curvature of model's surfaces. Finally comes the triangulation procedure which produces a triangle mesh, which then needs to be filtered and smoothed.

Color data processing for visualisation relies on the calculation of color coordinates from estimated spectral reflectance. First the colors are represented in the CIE XYZ color space for a chosen standard illuminant, and then transformed into the CIE $L^*a^*b^*$ color space, where the L^* coordinate can be exchanged for the intensity value calculated from Phong parameters based on the angular reflectance measurement. This allows to include material properties directly in the texture of objects with lambertian angular reflectance characteristic. Afterwards color profile in RGB color space necessary for the displaying device color is calculated. This data, along with mapping coordinates assigned to the triangle mesh, create the texture for the model. The Phong parameters, modelling the BRDF of the surface can be used to determine material properties for realistic rendering with the use of arbitrary illumination conditions of the virtual scene.

Consequently, the result of the second stage of data processing is a model represented as a triangle mesh with mapped texture along with material reflectivity characteristic. It can be exported to VRML format for use in a variety of renderings software to create static or animated renderings for online, as well as offline visualisation.

The purpose of the third stage of processing is the preparation of data for a color 3D printer in order to produce copies of digitized objects. As before, the data from previous stage (in this case the triangle mesh and $L^*a^*b^*$ color coordinates) are used as input.

As for the printing technology, 3DP is assumed, which requires application of a procedure for compensating shape deviation of the model due to shrinkage of material during the printing process. Therefore an analytical model is applied to the triangle mesh which enhances its shape in order to get more precise correspondence between the original object and its copy.

Additionally a color profile for the 3D printer based on local interpolation of a set of representative reference color samples is applied. This allows to take into account limited color resolution of the color 3D printer.

2.2 Integration with 3DMADMAC Environment

All mentioned operations are implemented as separate calculation methods which work within the 3DMADMAC environment [10]. The calculation methods can be exchanged easily, as well as combined into more complicated calculation patterns, as they work as independent plug-ins supplied in DLL libraries. This allows the user to customize the processing path to meet the needs of a specific application and even extend the functionality of the system by adding new calculation methods.

3 Implementation

3.1 3D Shape Calculation Methods

Clouds of Points Filtering. Usually a cloud of points registered in a shape measurement has uniform density distribution of points in the middle of the measurement volume, whereas on borders and in parts with sharp edges points are more sparse and more prone to noise. Such points need to be filtered out and replaced by data acquired from other directions. The filtration procedure [11] relies on finding small groups of points separated from each other farther than the average distance between points in the cloud multiplied by a predefined constant, which are then deleted from the cloud.

Merging Clouds of Points. The procedure of fitting directional clouds of points [12] can be divided into two steps. First, a coarse fitting algorithm is applied, which calculates an additional data layer with curvature coefficients of a surface. After that segmentation is performed on the curvature data layer and similar segments from adjacent clouds of points are merged together. The second step of clouds' fitting incorporates the ICP algorithm [8], which minimizes the root mean square error between corresponding points in roughly fitted clouds by applying small orientation and translation adjustments to the position of one of the clouds.

Smoothing Clouds of Points. In order to minimize the noise resulting from phase calculation as well as small imprecision of fitting the clouds a smoothing algorithm [11] is applied, which fits a plane to a small neighbourhood of every point and changes its position based on the neighbourhood if the distance to such plane is bigger than a specified threshold.

Simplification of Clouds of Points. In most cases clouds of points taken directly from a measurement are too dense to be the source of a triangle mesh, because the procedure would create unreasonably many triangles, which would be very difficult to manage with restricted software resources. Clouds of points therefore usually require simplification – which can be either a uniform process or done using an adaptive algorithm which varies the number of points left according to local curvature [13]. When the surface's shape is more complicated i.e. has higher curvature, more points are left for more precise triangle mesh construction. The parameter which constrains the simplification procedure describes maximum deviation of mesh compared to the simplified surface.

Triangulation. Visualisation of a 3D model in an arbitrary virtual scene requires representing the object as a mesh of triangles which can be textured and rendered. Among many triangulation algorithms the one chosen for this stage of processing is the algorithm developed specifically for creating meshes from clouds of points generated in 3D shape measurements [14]. It generates the mesh in several steps including sharp edges detection, edges triangulation, creation of seed triangles and triangulation of the remaining area. It has very good performance in triangulation of noisy and irregular clouds of points thanks to its optimization in the direction of processing this kind of data.

3.2 Color Calculation Methods

Before interpolation of the spectral reflectance data over the domain covering the visible range of wavelengths, a compensation of the optical setup characteristic is necessary. The proposed system does not distinguish emission spectrum characteristic from detector's sensitivity characteristic, but it is able to compensate them together through calibration using a photographic white reference plate. The reference plate scatters all wavelengths within the visible spectrum uniformly, so its spectral reflectance can be assumed constant. It is possible to prove this through a measurement with a spectrophotometer. Knowing intensity responses from the white reference plate as a function of wavelength, it is possible to perform the compensation. Additionally, transmission characteristics of the spectral filters used for spectrum sampling are energetically normalized according to formula (1) and (2):

$$I(x, y, z) = \frac{I_d(x, y, z)}{t} \tag{1}$$

$$t = \frac{\int_{\lambda_i - \frac{\Delta\lambda}{2}}^{\lambda_i + \frac{\Delta\lambda}{2}} T(\lambda)d\lambda}{\Delta\lambda \cdot 100\%} \tag{2}$$

Where $I_d(x,y,z)$ is the intensity registered by the detector for a specific point and $T(\lambda)$ is the transmission characteristic of a spectral filter as a function of wavelength.

Finally input data for interpolation can be described by the formula (3):

$$I_s(r, \lambda) = I(r, \lambda)\frac{C}{I_{max}}\frac{1}{I_i(r, \lambda)I_a(r, \lambda)T(\lambda)} \tag{3}$$

where r denotes point's x, y, z coordinates in space, C is a constant corresponding to the intensity level of white reference plate; I_i is the illumination intensity and I_a is the attenuation characteristic of the optical setup. Both I_i and I_a are specified using the calibration data.

Having I_s calculated, an interpolation algorithm is introduced. It interpolates data with $\Delta\lambda$ increments of 5nm and relies on fitting a cubic spline to the sparsely sampled data [15]. This approach is justified by the assumption that the spectral reflectance characteristic of common surfaces is smooth and has a continuous first derivative within its domain.

Color Spaces Calculation. After calculating the spectral reflectance characteristic, it is possible to derive the color in the CIE XYZ color space, assuming spectral characteristic of specific standard illuminant and color matching functions for chosen standard observer. These procedures are widely known and can be found in [16].

Additionally, color values in the CIE $L^*a^*b^*$ color space are possible to derive [17], which allows to apply a procedure for equalization of intensity on clouds of points registered from different directions. One approach takes advantage of normal vectors orientation on a surface and normalizes L^* coordinate for each point in the cloud. The normalization procedure considers neighbourhood of the investigated point which includes points from all clouds overlapping in this neighbourhood. It calculates L^* as a weighted average of its values L_i from different points from the neighbourhood, where the weight factor is a dot product between normal vector n in the chosen point and the observation direction o, which is constant and parallel to the detector's optical axis (equation 4).

$$L_{norm}(x, y, z) = \frac{\sum_{i=1}^{N} L_i(x, y, z)\cos(\angle \vec{n}, \vec{o})}{\sum_{i=1}^{N} \cos(\angle \vec{n}, \vec{o})} \qquad (4)$$

This solution favours parts of the surface which are oriented perpendicularly to the observation direction and therefore have higher signal to noise ratio. Apart from this, the influence of specular reflection component on color calculation is diminished. It is also possible to derive an alternative L^* coordinate values from Phong BRDF parameters estimated from angular reflection measurement.

Having calculated the color in CIE XYZ or $L^*a^*b^*$ coordinates allows for further processing in order to apply a color profile for a specific display device, such as an LCD monitor or a 3D printer, to reproduce colors faithfully. These operations can be implemented as separate calculation methods.

The color profile for a color 3D printer is based on a series of 729 predefined samples' color values spaced uniformly within the printer's dynamic range, which had

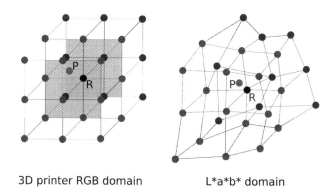

3D printer RGB domain   L*a*b* domain

Fig. 6. Local interpolation of color values for a 3D printer color profile

been measured by a reference spectrophotometer to determine their $L^*a^*b^*$ values. The profile should enable to transform from arbitrary $L^*a^*b^*$ color values into printer specific RGB coordinates. To achieve this a local interpolation algorithm is proposed (Fig. 6). For each specific input $L^*a^*b^*$ color coordinates (point P), it searches for the nearest neighbour R within the reference color samples and it calculates the printer RGB values as a weighted average of RGB values from direct neighbours of the R color point with distances between the point P and these neighbours in the $L^*a^*B^*$ domain as the weights.

3.3 Angular Reflectance Calculation Methods

To estimate the intrinsic angular reflectance [18] properties of the investigated surface, several steps are taken before creating a parameterized BRDF representation.

By the use of a reference plate mentioned above, the illuminating setup is calibrated for inequalities of light source intensities for a given geometrical model of their spatial distribution. Based on the geometrical relation between reference lambertian surface, the camera and every light source, compensation coefficients are derived and saved within the calibration framework.

From every directional illumination frame, a dark frame is subtracted for eliminating background bias. After the intensity of directional illumination frames is compensated, for every point a set of halfway versors is derived. The halfway versor h lies on the angle bisector between the reflection and viewing directional vectors (r and v, respectively), and is calculated according to equations (5) and (6).

$$\vec{r} = m(\vec{i},\vec{n}),\tag{5}$$

$$\vec{h} = \frac{\vec{r} + \vec{v}}{|\vec{r} + \vec{v}|}\tag{6}$$

To calculate the ratio between luminance and illuminance, the photometric law is applied. The incident intensity is multiplied by the inverse product of square distance from the light source and the cosine of incident angle. Both x, y, z coordinates and normal vector are taken from the previously calculated cloud of points structure. The halfway angles [19] are calculated as the dot product of every halfway versor in array and the unit length normal vector at the analysed point. Then the array of reflectance ratios ordered by ascending halfway angle, referred to as the response array, is used for BRDF model fitting (Fig. 7).

BRDF Estimation. Two methods were implemented for retrieving Phong components based on such prepared measurement data. First method incorporates the use of a nonlinear solver, where diffuse, specular and shininess terms are controlled by the RMS value of the overall BRDF slice fitted to data samples. This method produces best results, but it is time consuming and inappropriate for processing the whole cloud of points.

The second method was designed for speed of calculation and takes consecutive steps in order to calculate the three components. Starting from estimation of the diffusive component, the last term of response array is assumed to have the least contribution from specular reflection. This value is then subtracted from all the other higher values. Then, the specular coefficient is taken from the highest value in the array. The shininess is estimated based on the highest slope of remaining values.

This method is fast but introduces several limitations. For ill positioned points of measured surface, the halfway angle is never equal zero, and so the specular parameter is lower than expected. For this purpose a method of further data processing is introduced, based on the premise, that data merged from several directions introduce different error of angular reflection estimation.

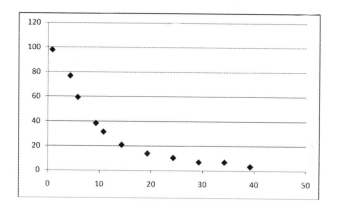

Fig. 7. Depiction of a response array of ordered reflectance values in a descending fashion

Reflectance Quality Factors. Apart from three data layers of Phong parameters created by the means of single directional measurement calculation, an additional data layer of quality factors is saved for every directional cloud of points. These quality factors are inverse values of the lowest halfway angle calculated in the previous methods. The data layer of quality factors correlates to the systematic error of specular reflection estimation at every point of the surface geometrical model.

BRDF Data Merging. For clouds of points measured from different directions and fitted using the ICP algorithm, the quality factors of locally corresponding points may have higher values and manifest better estimation of specular and shininess components. By the means of local averaging of these components, quality factors are used as weights. This way for every point P_i and a set of neighbouring points P_i within radius r coming from different directional measurements, specular k_s and shininess k_e components are corrected in the following relation (equation 7):

$$k_{s,e}(P_1)^{(new)} = \frac{k_{s,e}(P_1)^{(old)} \cdot q(P_1) + \sum k_{s,e}(P_i)^{(old)} \cdot q(P_i) \cdot (r_i - r)}{q(P_1) + \sum q(P_i) \cdot (r_i - r)} \quad (7)$$

In this manner points with lower quality values enhance with more probable estimates of intrinsic reflection properties, allowing to compensate the drawbacks of a time efficient calculation method.

The parameters of BRDF describing the specular lobe can be used in computer generated images of the object illuminated in an arbitrary way. However, the diffusive component, which relates to the lambertian surface model common in colorimetry, may also be used at the stage of calculating $L^*a^*b^*$ color space as the value of L^* – simulating a perfectly ambient object illumination.

Virtual 3D Model. For use in 3D visualisation a simplified geometrical surface model is created. After geometrical data processing and triangulation described in [14], a material map with spatially varying BRDF parameters is created using adaptive texturing algorithm. Similarly as in the case of diffusive color map, a bitmap of Phong material patches is created with analogous size and texture mapping coordinates for vertices in the triangle mesh structure.

Such model can be easily imported into several 3D modelling environments and further processed. The surface can be simplified and segmented into parts of similar material properties. Finally the object can be recreated in virtual reality in real time using hardware acceleration of Phong's illumination model.

4   Exemplary Results

Procedures described above were successfully applied for processing measurement data from several test measurements. They allowed to create digital models of exemplary objects which are visible in Fig. 8. The first is a result of measurement of a figure of ancient Greek goddess Kybele, presented as a cloud of points with RGB texture. It consists of 2,8 million points. The second example is a digital model of a plaster figure of a dog, represented as a textured triangle mesh with over 40 thousand triangles.

Fig. 8. Exemplary results of digital reconstruction based on the integrated measurement

Several referential measurements have been performed to determine the limitations of described processing algorithms as well as to estimate the overall error of calculated reflectance values. To verify the results, other techniques were used together with objects of well defined properties.

A spectrophotometer was used for comparison with the multispectral camera. The reflectance spectrum obtained from both devices was compared directly rather than L* a* b* coordinates, however both cases were investigated. GretagMakbeth Color Checker patches were used as a target for calculating spectral reflectance. The same patches were measured using the multispectral camera and their reflectance spectrum was independently estimated. After that it was possible to compare every two measured spectra and infer about quality of color measurement system. Example characteristic of the color patches measured by both devices are shown in the Fig. 9.

To verify the angular reflectance characteristics, several samples of surfaces with distinguishable reflective properties were chosen and measured independently by the

Table 1. RMS error of calculated angular reflectance characteristics compared with gonioreflectometric data

Material	Class	RMS error (%)
paper	diffusive	2,8
unruffled cardboard	semi-specular	7.0
polished aluminum	shiny	1.8

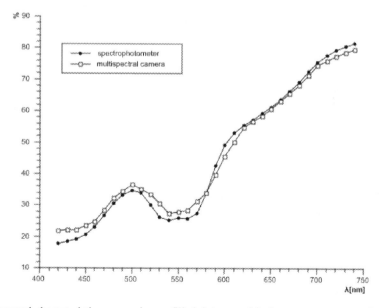

Fig. 9. Spectral characteristics comparison – filled dots resemble the measurement results from a spectrofotmeter, hollow dots from a multispectral camera

measurement system and a gonioreflectometric device. The objects have been grouped in classes of different BRDF profiles. Table 1 shows a collation of the estimated errors between two methods for exemplary surfaces based on RMS difference between BRDF slices. While it is still difficult to compare measurement data from different 3D measurement techniques, the overall error is less than 10% compared to reference methods, which brings a satisfactory result.

5 Summary

The paper describes data processing procedures which can be used for managing data from an integrated measurement of 3D shape, multispectral color and angular reflectance characteristic. The algorithms mentioned are divided into three stages depending on the final destination of the results. The first one serves as a digital archive and is meant to preserve as much information about object's appearance as is possible with a given measurement setup. The second stage covers procedures used for displaying purposes and allows for a creation of a digital model in a form of a triangle mesh with texture which can be exported to an independent visualisation software. The third stage produces a model which can be sent directly to a 3D printer in order to produce a faithful copy of the measured object.

The implementation of mentioned calculation methods as independent plug-ins in the 3DMADMAC calculation environment allows users to modify or exchange these procedures for custom applications.

Acknowledgements. This work was performed under the grant No. PL0097 financed by the Norwegian Financial Mechanism and EOG Financial Mechanism (2004-2009).

References

1. Pavlidis, G., Koutsoudis, A., Arnaoutoglou, F., Tsioukas, V., Chamzas, C.: Methods for 3D digitization of Cultural Heritage. Journal of Cultural Heritage 8(1), 93–98 (2007)
2. Imai, F.H., Rosen, M.R., Berns, R.S.: Multi-spectral imaging of Van Gogh's Self-portrait at the National Gallery of Art. In: Proceedings of IS&T PICS Conference, Washington, D.C, pp. 185–189. IS&T, Springfield, VA (2001)
3. Imai, F.H., Rosen, M.R., Berns, R.S.: Comparison of Spectrally Narrow-Band capture versus wide-band with a priori sample analysis for spectral reflectance estimation. In: Proceedings of IS&T's, pp. 234–241 (2000)
4. Conde, J., Haneishi, H., Yamaguchi, M., Ohyama, N., Baez, J.: Spectral Reflectance Estimation of Ancient Mexican Codices, Multispectral Images Approach. Revista Mexicana de Fisica 50, 484–489 (2004)
5. Georghiades, A.S.: Recovering 3-D Shape and Reflectance from a Small Number of Photographs. ACM International Conference Proceeding Series, vol. 44, pp. 230–240 (2003)
6. Sitnik, R., Mączkowski, G., Krzesłowski, J.: Integrated Shape, Color, and Reflectivity Measurement Method for 3D Digitization of Cultural Heritage Objects. In: Proceedings of SPIE, vol. 7526, p. 75260Q (2010)

7. Sitnik, R.: New Method of Structure Light Measurement System Calibration Based on Adaptive and Effective Evaluation of 3D-Phase Distribution. In: Proceedings of SPIE, vol. 5856, p. 109 (2005)
8. Besl, P.J., McKay, N.D.: A Method for Registration of 3-D Shapes. IEEE Transactions on Pattern Analysis and Machine Intelligence 14(2), 239–256 (1992)
9. Phong, B.T.: Illumination for Computer Generated Pictures. Communications of the ACM 18, 311–317 (1975)
10. Sitnik, R., Kujawińska, M., Woźnicki, J.: Digital Fringe Projection System for Large-Volume 360-deg Shape Measurement. Optical Engineering 41, 443–449 (2002)
11. Sitnik, R., Kujawińska, M., Załuski, W.: 3DMADMAC System: Optical 3D Shape Acquisition and Processing Path for VR Applications. In: Proceedings of SPIE, vol. 5857, pp. 106–117 (2005)
12. Sitnik, R., Kujawińska, M.: From Reality to Virtual Reality: 3D Object Imaging Techniques and Algorithms. In: Proceedings of SPIE, vol. 5146, pp. 54–61 (2003)
13. Sitnik, R., Kujawińska, M.: From Cloud of Point Co-ordinates to 3D Virtual Environment: The Data Conversion System. Optical Engineering 41(2), 416–427 (2002)
14. Sitnik, R., Karaszewski, M.: Optimized Point Cloud Triangulation for 3D Scanning Systems. Machine Graphics & Vision 17, 349–371 (2008)
15. Press, W.H., Flannery, B.P., Teukolsky, S.A., Vetterling, W.T.: Numerical Recipes in C: The Art of Scientific Computing. Cambridge University Press, Cambridge (1992)
16. Wyszecki, G., Stiles, W.S.: Color Science: Concepts and Methods, Quantitative Data and Formulae. John Wiley & Sons, New York (2000)
17. Malacara, D.: Color Vision and Colorimetry: Theory and Applications. SPIE Press, Bellingham (2002)
18. Nicodemus, F.E., Richmond, J.C., Hsia, J.J., Ginsber, I.W., Limperis, T.: Geometrical Considerations and Nomenclature for Reflectance, NBS Monograph 160, U. S. Dept. of Commerce (1977)
19. Rusinkiewicz, S.: A New Change of Variables for Efficient BRDF Representation. In: Drettakis, G., Max, N. (eds.) Rendering Techniques 1998 (Proceedings of Eurographics Rendering Workshop 1998), pp. 11–22. Springer, New York (1998)

Automated Processing of Data from 3D Scanning of Cultural Heritage Objects

Robert Sitnik and Maciej Karaszewski

Warsaw University of Technology, Mechatronics Faculty, Sw. Andrzeja Boboli 8,
02-525 Warsaw
{r.sitnik,m.karaszewski}@mchtr.pw.edu.pl

Abstract. In this paper, the concept of computational environment for processing of very large datasets (clouds of points with amount up to 10^{11} measurement points) obtained from 3D shape measurement systems, is presented. The software design is directed at maximum automation of processing, allows for defining scripts describing complicated calculations which make user interaction and attendance during operations unnecessary. The following paper describes main postulates of the environment along with its practical exemplary implementation as the application controlling fully automated 3D shape measurement system, 3DMADMAC AUTO, designed for precise, autonomous digitization of cultural heritage objects.

Keywords: automated 3D data processing, cultural heritage 3D digitization, automated view integration.

1 Introduction

With the rapid development of scanning devices [1], 3D digitization of cultural heritages is becoming more and more popular [2], [3], [4], transferring from experimental operations into normal, standardized documentation techniques. Very important issue which makes this transition possible is the automation of measurement [5], [6], [7] which allows for obtaining objective (because no user interaction is needed) and repeatable results, while shortening the time and reducing costs of digitization. Systems for automatic measurement, beside special mechanical devices (robots, rotational stages etc) also need specialized software. This software must be designed to cope with very large datasets, because single directional measurement can easily contain 10 million points amounting to roughly 500 MB of memory (10 000 000 points * [24 bytes of XYZ coordinates, double precision + 24 bytes of NxNyNz normal vector coordinates, double precision + 3 bytes of color - RGB + 4 bytes of quality, single precision] = 524 MB). Resolution of the measurement along with physical dimensions of scanned object determine number of sampled points and therefore size of obtained dataset.

To allow for automatic processing of data, all calculations and operations have to be performed without any user intervention (of course setting of some parameters is allowable at the beginning of measurement).

M. Ioannides (Ed.): EuroMed 2010, LNCS 6436, pp. 28–41, 2010.

Pursuing the need of development of software for automatic digitization of 3D objects, especially cultural heritage ones, authors of this paper formulated the concept of computational environment attuned to processing very large datasets (clouds of points) which is presented in the next chapter of this work. Exemplary implementation, in the form of application controlling 3DMADMAC AUTO system [6], [7] is described in Chapter 3 and 4 along with some processing results. Presented application was already tested and used for processing of datasets containing roughly 1 billion points (10^9 measurement points). It can be also used without automated measuring system for general cloud of points processing. The software itself does not limit scanned object physical size or complexity, it can be also used for processing data obtained from small details scanning as well as entire archeological sites.

2 Software Concept

Like it was said in the Introduction, the main aim of designed environment was its ability to process very large datasets. Nowadays, the size of data obtained from average multidirectional measurement is greater than memory capacity available in typical PC-class computers. As it is widely known, computer architecture limits the maximum size of useable operational memory [8]. In 32bit systems theoretically this limit is set at 4GB, but for single application it shrinks to 2 or 3 GB, depending on operating system used. It is clear than, that with this memory limit one can load only about four directional measurements (each one about 500MB) into RAM, what is in general not enough. The 64bit architecture allows for addressing much more memory space (in AMD64 there are 48 addressing bits which results in 256TB limit), but in reality the limits are sharper and in typical systems they are about 24GB (desktop systems) and 192GB (servers), not mentioning the cost of this amount of RAM modules. Because of this, the designed calculation environment should implement some mechanisms allowing to use other kind of memory (for example hard disks) cooperating with operational memory. Those mechanisms should be heavily optimized with respect to the nature of the processed data because mass memory (like hard disks) is much slower in access and read-write performance than RAM.

Present-day trends in evolution of computer hardware determine the need of making applications able to run in multithreaded mode [9]. Running calculations in parallel allows for better utilization of computational power shortening processing time but requires additional programming skills and tools, which should be provided by computing environment (such as thread management mechanisms, synchronization objects etc).

The projected software should be as universal as possible, particularly able to process clouds of points obtained from measurement of different classes of objects. This assumption implies modular structure of computing environment, because monolithic designs are suitable only when the input parameters of data are perfectly defined. In contrast, when the data is varied, some methods usable for one class of objects are completely useless for the other (initial adjustment of clouds of points from manual measurements is a good example – for some objects those calculations can be based on local curvature of object, but for planar-like objects other algorithm has to be used, for example identifying unique features in texture of measured object). In monolithic application, any modification is complicated, while in modular one it

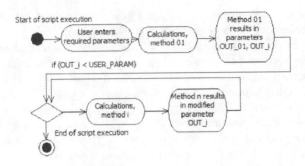

Fig. 1. Script processing path

requires only changing or adding a library with new functionality. Therefore, the developed software should be based on exo-kernel principle [10], where only basic functionalities are closed in application core and any other ones – available as plugins (dynamic libraries, loaded when needed).

To obtain maximum automation of data processing, the application should require no interaction with user during the calculations. It is also very advantageous if it can be used in the manner similar to batch processing, running selected calculation methods in defined order, especially when they can pass some calculated parameters to each other and running calculations in conditional loops. This may be achieved by creating some kind of scripting language which can be later compiled and run by application. Scripting can also be used to perform calculations one by one on all measurements in selected directory etc. Generally speaking, the processing path of application running script should be similar to one presented in Fig. 1.

3   Conceptual Model

The concept of software, presented in previous chapter was realized as an application for controlling automated measuring system 3DMADMAC AUTO, developed in cooperation with Museum Palace at Wilanow [6], [7]. This system is built from measurement head (structured-light scanner) [11], [12] mounted on industrial robot which is placed on the vertically-moveable column to extend its motion range. Measured object is placed on the rotational stage Fig. 2). All of those devices are used for automated positioning of scanning head in measurement volume and they are controlled by specialized software which calculates collision-free transition paths of scanning head between subsequent measurement positions.

Subsequent places, in which scanning head should be placed, are calculated by specialized module (called NBV from Next Best View) of controlling software which is used for data processing [7].

The main functions of this application are: receiving the data obtained by scanner head, along with position and orientation of the scanner head, filtering and removing erroneous data (for example small groups of points which are result of light reflections on objects in the environment), noise filtering, initial cloud stitching (in the case of automated measurement this function is realized by applying the transformations returned by robotized system to received cloud of points), fine clouds stitching, mostly by running ICP algorithms [5], [13], global relaxation of clouds (running global ICP), re-coloring overexposed clouds etc (see Chapter 4).

The following subchapters present internal organization of implemented software, and briefly describe most important modules.

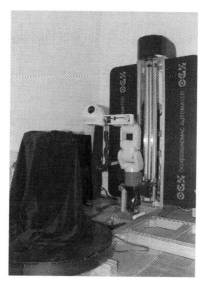

Fig. 2. Automated 3D shape measurement system

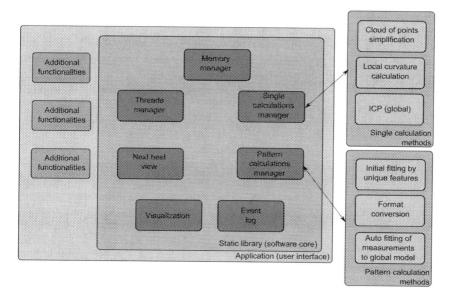

Fig. 3. Internal structure of application

3.1 Internal Software Architecture

3DMADMAC software was designed and implemented as a package of easily exchangeable modules (Fig. 3), each of which realizes specific function and is connected with others by mechanism of generalized interfaces [14], which allow to standardize method of information exchange between modules.

The core of the software is build as static library containing basic functionalities like memory and thread manager, event log, single and pattern calculations manager, 3D visualization etc. This library is the basis of the whole application, which in reality is responsible for user interfacing. Additionally, various calculation methods (for example filtration, simplifying, etc) are attached in runtime as dynamically loaded libraries (DLLs in Microsoft Windows systems).

Most important modules of core library are presented in consecutive subchapters.

3.1.1 Memory Manager

As stated before, one of the main challenges which the software must cope with, is the size of processed data. Because of this, the implementation of system core contains a module for managing memory utilization. Its working principle is simple – the whole computer memory subsystem (RAM and selected hard disk) is presented to application as unified, continuous memory space. Any module which wants to allocate, deallocate, write or read any memory block uses manager's functions (*AllocateMemory, DeallocateMemory, ReadBlock, WriteBlock*) which govern the rules of using RAM and hard disk storage space. In general, in operational memory, only currently used data is held, all other blocks are written to disk (Fig. 4). This technique is similar to swap files used in operating systems, however its implementation is optimized with regard to nature of processed data. As a result of existence of memory manager, the application is theoretically able to process virtually any number of directional measurements, limited only by available hard disk space.

Implemented application was used with measurements greater than 1 billion points (over 50GB). Of course, the time required to process data with storing part of it on hard disk is much longer because relatively low data transfer rates and long access times of disks in comparison with RAM Average access time for RAM memory is about 10 ns, transfer rate 10667 MB/s for DDR3-1600 memory modules, for magnetic hard disk 9 ms and 70 MB/s, solid state drive: 10 µs, 200 MB/s respectively.

RAM

Hard disk

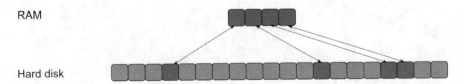

Fig. 4. Large cloud of points data stored in temporary file no hard disk and currently analyzed fragments loaded into main memory (RAM)

3.1.1.1 Internal Data Organization. Each point of each cloud is stored in memory as a group of attributes. The basic ones are its Cartesian coordinates (XYZ), color (RGB), surface normal vector (NxNyNz) and state flags (F). Additionally, for each dataset, any number of attributes can be added in the form of so called data-layers (DL) which are one-dimensional, floating point typed arrays with one cell bound to each point in clouds. In those data-layers various parameters can be stored, most often results of performed calculations (for example value of spherical curvature, deviation of point from locally fitted plane, etc). Schematic of data organization (with two data-layers) is presented in Fig. 5.

Content of data-layer can be visualized on clouds of points in gray or topographical scale.

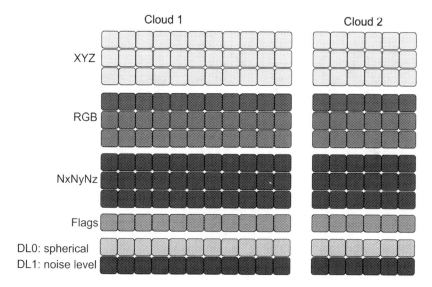

Fig. 5. Data organization

Exemplary cloud of points with pseudocoloring based on data-layer (distance of vertex to best fitted plane) is shown in Fig. 6.

Fig. 6. Cloud of points pseudocoloring basing on data-layer content

3.1.2 Threads Manager

Nowadays, almost every modern computer is equipped with multicore processor which allows to run multiple operations in parallel [9]. This feature can however be only used when application is optimized for multithreaded operations. The presented software was designed to support multicore hardware, and the process of running calculations in multithreaded mode is governed by thread manager. This module is an overlay on operating system functions allowing to start, stop, terminate thread, get its

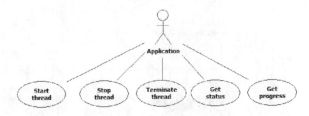

Fig. 7. Thread manager functions

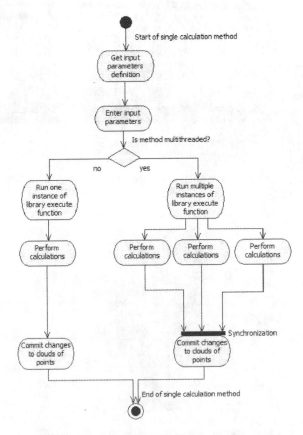

Fig. 8. Running calculations by thread manager

progress and state (Fig. 7). It also provides tools for synchronizing access to shared data. Typical process of running calculation method with respect to its multithreaded abilities is presented in Fig. 8.

It is worth mentioning, that while thread manager automatically runs selected calculations in multithreaded mode, software engineer designing calculation library must be familiar with techniques for creating efficient and error-free parallel applications.

3.1.3 Calculations Manager

The main module of presented software is calculation manager. This module is used for automatic identification of libraries containing calculation methods, obtaining information about parameters they require, asking operator about values of those parameters, entering them into the methods and running calculations. Presented application uses two types of calculations – single and pattern ones.

3.1.3.1 Single Calculations. Single calculations can be defined as atomic, from the operator's point of view, operations which are started each time by user (or automatically) after their required parameters are entered. It is important to state, that presented application does not limit any functionality of those methods, they may even perform some tasks not related to clouds of points (for example list files in directory).

Authors of the presented software adopted an approach that all calculation methods are build as dynamically loaded libraries (plug-ins) which allow for easy exchange or add new calculations without the need of any changes in the application.

As previously stated, the calculation methods can be defined as single or multithreaded. Basing on this definition, the application via thread manager runs single or multiple instances of the method.

Data importers and exporters are designed in the same way as calculation methods (as dynamically linked libraries) which allows for easy enhancement of supported file formats. Currently, presented application can import data from 3DMADMAC scanner as well as text files and can export it after calculations to application's native format, VRML and IGES files. This functionality can be widened to any format as long as its documentation is provided. Furthermore, output data does not need to be stored in files, it can be sent directly to databases or archiving systems via network.

3.1.3.2 Pattern Calculations. When processing numerous datasets, or even small ones, but with complicated calculation scheme, the chance of operator's mistake is very high. Sometimes results of this mistake are easy to spot, but nevertheless time consuming and disrupting. Errors in values of entered parameters are quite frequent, especially when number of operations or number of parameters is high. Above all, controlling repetitious operations is tiresome and leads to routine which is often a source of mistakes and errors.

In the concept of software (presented in Chapter 2), authors propose implementation of simple scripting to allow for automated executing of a series of calculation methods, with ability to transfer parameters between themselves. This scripting language and interpreter should be capable of coping with conditional and looped executions of calculation methods.

Manager of pattern calculations implemented in presented software has all of above mentioned functionalities. Scripts are defined via user interface and stored as xml files. They can contain loops and conditional variables, and the designer can define which parameters returned by used calculation methods are used as input ones for the other, either directly or after some mathematical operations (multiplication, division, min, max, sum or difference). User creates script by selecting available calculation methods, parameters, operations and so on, and the xml definition is created automatically. After the script is designed it can be run by pattern calculation manager. Upon start of script, operator fills every required parameter and the execution proceeds autonomously.

Exemplary script realizing automatic integration of directional clouds loaded one by one from selected directory to global model (which grows larger and larger with each loaded measurement) is presented in Fig. 9.

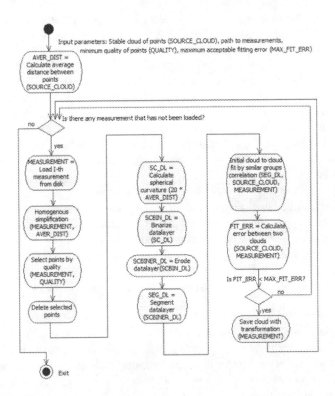

Fig. 9. Exemplary script integrating views from selected directory

3.1.4 Next Best View

Among software modules, the one intended to calculate next positions of scanning head during measurements, is implemented (it is called Next Best View module – NBV). It is generally used in connection with automated scanner positioning system (like 3DMADMAC AUTO), but can also be utilized in manual measurements during which operator wants to receive suggestions where to place scanning device before subsequent scans. It is worth noting that NBV is designed to minimize number of scans required to fully digitize surface of unknown measured object. It works by analyzing already measured part of object and calculating places in which the possibility of object's surface presence is largest. This is the first mode of operation – rapid measurement. In the second one, algorithm searches for discontinuities in obtained cloud of points and tries to calculate such placement of scanner that ensures successful scanning of those areas [7]. In reality implemented algorithm calculates the required position and orientation of device's measurement volume, however having the model of a scanner (i.e. placement of physical device in relation to its measurement volume), the NBV module can define where to put the scanning head to measure interesting part of an object.

4   Application of Software

The presented software is used in various projects and tasks performed by authors, especially during automated measurements of objects, but also for integrating multiple

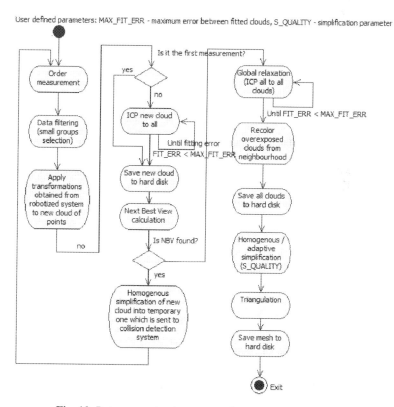

Fig. 10. Data processing in automated measurement mode

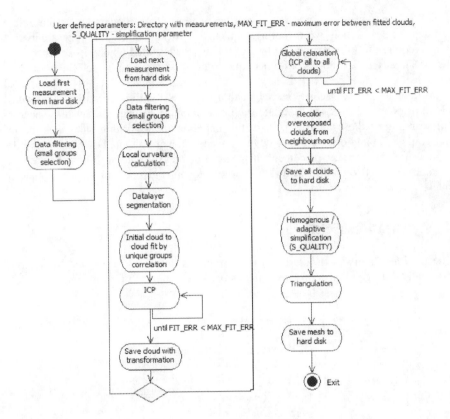

Fig. 11. Data processing in manual measurement mode

measurements done with manual scanner positioning. Typical data processing paths of the automatic and manual mode is presented in Fig. 10 and in Fig. 11 respectively.

Exemplary stages of automated measurement are presented in Fig. 12. After the first measurement is made, the data is filtered and analyzed by NBV module (Fig. 12a). Selected views (scanner positions) are sent to application which calculates the transitions of positioning devices' nodes required to place scanning head in desired point of space. After this, the next measurement is made and the data is also filtered, initially transformed (by transformation matrix obtained from positioning device) and then iteratively adjusted to existing measurement by ICP algorithm (Fig. 12b, c). The process continues until the whole measureable surface of an object is scanned (Fig. 13a). After each scan, the information about obtained points is transferred to collision detection module of positioning application.

When the whole object is digitized, the resultant cloud of points is saved to hard disk and then optionally simplified with user defined quality and method (homogenously or adaptively). It can be further used as a eternal copy of object or as a VR

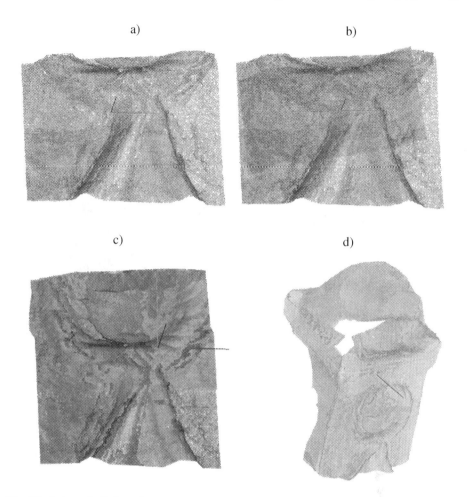

Fig. 12. Automatic fitting of next measurement into the existing model: a) first measurement, b) two measured clouds, c) clouds after initial and precise fitting, d) partially digitized object

model for visualization. After simplification the model can be converted to triangle mesh by triangulation algorithm (Fig. 13b).

The presented object (Roman votive altar, Lower Moesia) was scanned with resolution of 170 points per mm^2 (273 mln points) with 42 directional measurements, which took 5 hours and 30 minutes. Processing time for one directional cloud of points during measurements is about 7 minutes, while processing the whole model (global relaxation, re-coloring, saving) took additional 42 minutes. Simplification to homogenous cloud of points with average distance between points about 0.8 mm took 1 minute 20 seconds and the triangulation of resultant cloud (0.5 mln points) – about 10 minutes. The final triangle mesh has 1.2 mln triangles.

a)   b)

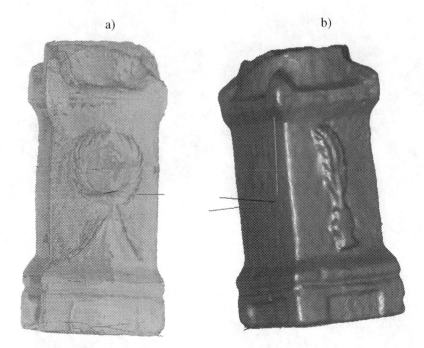

Fig. 13. Digitized object a) cloud of points, b)triangle mesh after simplification)

5 Conclusions and Future Work

The concept of software aimed at automatic processing of very large datasets was presented in the article. Its implementation allows to perform unrestrictedly complicated calculations on data obtained with 3D measurement systems like structured light or laser scanners or any other, which generates results in the form of clouds of points. Those calculations can be run as single or multithreaded, as a part of greater calculation pattern (script), for one or all loaded clouds. There is also a possibility to convert clouds of points into triangle meshes by means of triangulation algorithms. As for calculation methods, the greatest emphasis was put on methods used for integration of multiple measurements of the same object taken from different viewpoints without any knowledge on those viewpoints' positions. Those methods allow for automatic and repeatable stitching of measurements without any user intervention what makes them dispassionate and impartial. Thanks to presence of module which calculates next scanner position, the application can be also used for supporting manual scanning with results of those calculations serving as guidance for operator of the scanner. The measurement object shown as an example in Chapter 4 is medium sized, however presented software can be used for objects of any size and shape complexity as long as they can be measured by available scanners.

Future works will be aimed at distributed calculations (i.e. parallel cloud of points processing on many computers), as well as further calculation method development, especially regarding initial clouds of points stitching (for automatic fitting of clouds

of points obtained in manual measurements). Authors plan to implement new triangulation methods along with some operations on meshes aimed mostly at preparation of
this meshes for printing on 3D printers.

Acknowledgments

This work was performed under the grant No. R17 001 02 financed by the Polish
Ministry of Science and Higher Education.

References

1. Blais, F.: Review of 20 years of range sensor development. J. Electron. Imaging, 13 (2004)
2. Parry, R.: Recording the Museum. Routledge, London (2007)
3. Wojciechowski, R., Walczak, K., White, M., Cellary, W.: Building Virtual and Augmented
   Reality museum exhibitions. In: Proceedings of the Ninth International Conference on 3D
   Web Technology, pp. 135–144 (2004)
4. Baltsavias, M., Gruen, A., Van Gool, L., Pateraki, M.: Recording, Modeling and Visualization of Cultural Heritage. Taylor & Francis, London (2006)
5. Ikeuchi, K., Miyazaki, D.: Digitally Archiving Cultural Objects. Springer, Boston (2007)
6. Sitnik, R., Karaszewski, M., Załuski, W., Bolewicki, P.: Automated full-3D shape measurement of cultural heritage objects. In: Proc. SPIE, 73910K-1-10 (2009)
7. Sitnik, R., Karaszewski, M., Załuski, W., Rutkiewicz, J.: Automation of 3D scan data capturing and processing. In: Proc. SPIE, p. 75260Y (2010)
8. AMD: AMD64 Programmer's Manual Volume 2: System Programming, Advanced Micro
   Devices (2007)
9. Walmsley, M.: Multi-Threaded Programming in C++. Springer, Berlin (1999)
10. Engler, D.R., Kaashoek, M.F., O'Toole Jr., J.: Exokernel: An Operating System Architec-
    ture for Application-Level Resource Management. In: Proceedings of the Fifteenth ACM
    Symposium on Operating Systems Principles, pp. 251–266 (1995)
11. Sitnik, R., Kujawinska, M., Woźnicki, J.: Digital fringe projection system for large-volume
    360-deg shape measurement. Opt. Eng. 41, 443–449 (2002)
12. Sitnik, R.: New method of structure light measurement system calibration based on adap-
    tive and effective evaluation of 3D-phase distribution. In: Proc. SPIE, vol. 5856, pp. 109–
    117 (2005)
13. Curless, B., Levoy, M.: A Volumetric Method for Building Complex Models from Range
    Images. In: SIGGRAPH 1996 Conference, New Orleans, pp. 303–312 (1996)
14. Headington, M.R., Riley, D.D.: Data abstraction and structures using C++. D. C. Heath,
    Lexington (1994)

From Laser Data to Parametric Models:
Towards an Automatic Method
for Building Façade Modelling

Hakim Boulaassal[1], Christine Chevrier[2], and Tania Landes[1]

[1] The Images Sciences, Computer Sciences and Remote Sensing Laboratory (LSIIT)–
Photogrammetry and Geomatics Group, INSA Strasbourg, 24, Boulevard de la Victoire
67000 Strasbourg, France
{hakim.boulaassal,tania.landes}@insa-strasbourg.fr
[2] MAP-CRAI, School of Architecture of Nancy, 2, rue Bastien Lepage, 54000 Nancy, France
christine.chevrier@crai.archi.fr

Abstract. The interest in the generation of 3D façade models is increasing more and more. TLS data have introduced other visions to deal with this topic. This paper proposes a new approach to façade modelling using TLS data. Geometric relevant features of façades are first extracted via a segmentation algorithm. Then, based on the segmentation results, the automatic extraction of edges has been carried out. Afterwards, the edges are decomposed into straight segments and arcs, based on the criterion of the collinearity of points. Then, the intersection points are calculated based on the study of their geometric characteristics, as well as their topological relationships. These points allow us to construct the parametric objects that can be correctly sized and completed via an interactive graphical user interface.

Keywords: Algorithm, Architectural modelling, Laser scanning data, Parametric models.

1 Introduction

The production of 3D urban models is of high interest in the photogrammetric and computer vision fields. The recent developments made for terrestrial laser scanners (TLS), especially in terms of acquisition speed and measurement accuracy, lead to new research topics like for instance the modelling of 3D building façades. If the TLS data acquisition is relatively easy, their automatic processing, however, is particularly difficult and requires many skills.

The point cloud acquired by a TLS is a model in itself, since the set of points provides a primary description of the façade geometry. However, integration and management of these raw data in databases is problematic because of the huge amount of points. That's why it is necessary to generate another kind of model which enables us to describe the object in a lighter way. The 3D geometric modelling seems to be a good solution to this issue. It enables the passage from a model composed of points to a model composed of a small number of geometric shapes. In this form, the

M. Ioannides (Ed.): EuroMed 2010, LNCS 6436, pp. 42–55, 2010.

model constitutes a support for other types of information, such as semantic and architectural information. Obviously, the quality of the obtained geometrical models of façades depends closely on the quality and the completeness of the TLS data.

The aim of this work is to use the geometrical information automatically extracted from the raw point clouds for creating parametric components. A new method has therefore been developed. It starts by detecting automatically the façade geometric features. Then, it transforms them to parametric objects that can be easily controlled and completed via an interactive GUI (Graphical User Interface). The parametric objects are constructed based on semantic architectural information. In this context, this paper contributes to filling the gap between two research fields: lasergrammetry and architectural 3D modelling of complex environments.

Before going on to describe the new method, we would like to present some works related to building façades modelling (part 2). Then the automatic edge extraction of the façade's relevant components is explained in part 3. Part 4 deals with the automatic classification of the extracted components. Part 5 introduces the automatic creation of the parametric components. Based on these parameters, an interactive GUI is developed in order to improve the model (part 6). Finally, we conclude and present the future work (part 7).

2 Related Work

Considering laser scanning data, façades can be modelled based on meshing techniques and/or geometric primitives recognition. Meshing techniques allow us to pass from a discontinuous space (point cloud) into a continuous space (surface model). They are rather used for complex objects modelling such as cultural heritage structures (statues, castles...) that are difficult to be mathematically modelled ([1] and [2]). Meshing techniques are not sufficient if they are limited to simple triangulations of raw point clouds. They should also deal, among others, with measurement noise, holes and occlusions, isolated points, reflection from windows. [3] propose a solution by applying a set of data processing techniques on building facade meshes. Firstly, data is divided into easy-to-handle segments which are transformed into depth images. In these depth images, building structures are detected. Then, large holes caused by occlusions are filled in by planar interpolation and isolated points are removed by processing the depth image. Main disadvantage of meshing techniques is that they require a large amount of memory and disk space. For this reason, they are frequently substituted by models based on geometric primitives.

Modelling techniques based on geometric primitives start by segmenting the cloud of points into homogeneous subsets of points. Then the reconstruction occurs. Regarding the segmentation of TLS data, many methods have been proposed. Most of them were originally developed on aerial LiDAR data. Segmentation methods can be classified in two families: methods based on growing and fusion principles ([4], [5], [6]) and methods based on geometric primitives detection ([7] and [8]). Only a few works are published on the reconstruction techniques. For instance, [9] and [10] propose a modelling approach using linear features detected in TLS data in a semi-automatic way. The reconstruction of the façades in this way is often a difficult task if it is exclusively based on a point cloud. To overcome these difficulties [11], [12] and

[13] propose a semi-automatic modelling of facades by combining TLS data and photographs.

Most of the models obtained through meshing or through primitives extractions do not take semantic information into account. This is harmful, because the architectural knowledge on the building façade and of its components is of great interest, especially in the case of gaps in the point cloud (due to objects hiding the façade).

As far as the architectural domain is concerned, there are many research projects dealing with 3D modelling, i.e. 3D models for conception goals [14] and 3D models for patrimonial and archaeological goals [15]. In both cases a parametric modelling based on semantic knowledge ([15] and [16]) is of great help compared to a non parametric way of modelling, as it is done in modelers such as SketchUp (Google), Wings 3D (Izware).

Procedural modelling with shape grammars allows either the quick creation of virtual coherent cities or the modelling of existing buildings ([17] and [18]). In [19] Gothic rose windows are studied in order to generate parametric models. [20] has conceived a low level interpretive language called Generative Modelling Language (GML) for the description of procedural shapes. The GML can be used by developers to create domain-specific modelling tools. After the authors, the goal of the GML architecture is to facilitate the composition of high level tools for 3D modelling. They show examples of architectural objects, car components, furniture, but no library of architectural parametric components exists. There is no software to handle architectural components nor to adjust them to measured data.

The use of architectural 3D parametric components allows a quick and accurate modelling. However the adjustment of the parameters of the virtual 3D model in order to fit the real one is tedious. In [21] we explain that we can load existing data (2D plans, pictures and point clouds) to help the adjustment step. Until now, this latter step is performed mostly manually. To overcome this defect, parameters provided by relevant elements - automatically extracted from point clouds - are used. The following parts explain the developed process.

3   Extraction of Facade's Edges

3.1   Extraction of Planar Clusters

A geometric approach for segmentation and modelling of building façades using terrestrial laser scanner data is proposed. The processing sequence consists of a segmentation step followed by a modelling step. Firstly, by assuming that façades are mainly composed of planar surfaces, an automatic segmentation proceeds to the decomposition of the point cloud into a set of planar clusters. A "planar cluster" means a set of points located in a buffer zone around the calculated plane using the RANSAC algorithm (RANdom SAmple Consensus). Since real façade planes are not always adjustable by mathematical models, the RANSAC algorithm has been optimized at several stages.

As explained in [22], the algorithm is applied sequentially and removes the inliers from the original dataset every time one plane is detected. As shown in [23], the raw point cloud has a thickness which is usually generated by noise coming from the surface roughness, from the object colours, from the TLS resolution capacities and from the registration operation. Therefore, a tolerance value describing the authorized thickness around a plane has been set. The planes are thus described by planar clusters having some specific thickness.

Obviously, the quality of plane detection depends strongly on the tolerance value applied. On the other hand, the quality of planes is also related to the architectural complexity of the façade. Fig. 1 shows results obtained for a portion of façade segmented by the algorithm described above. In this case, the tolerance value has been set to 2cm.

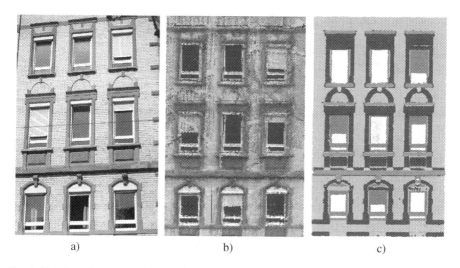

a)   b)   c)

Fig. 1. Results of segmentation: a) façade picture; b) colorized point cloud of the façade; c) segmentation results. Each colour depicts a planar cluster on the façade.

3.2 Extraction of Edge Points

Once planar clusters are extracted by the developed segmentation approach, the extraction of their contours is carried out. An efficient algorithm based on Delaunay triangulation has been developed. The main idea is based on the hypothesis stipulating that edge points belong to the long sides of Delaunay triangles. More explanations can be found in [22]. Fig. 2 presents edge points extracted from a triangulated planar cluster. The window belongs to the façade presented in Fig. 1.

3.3 Edge Decomposition

Now it is time to generate a geometric model from the edge points extracted previously. To do this, a method based on the extraction of simple geometric elements is proposed. The edge points are initially decomposed into straight and curved edges according the linearity criterion of points. The points representing the straight edges

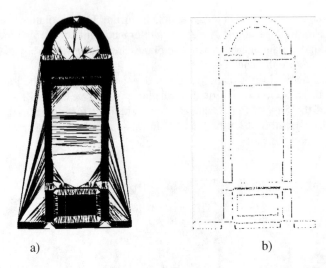

a)   b)

Fig. 2. Edge points detected by the developed algorithm; a) results of segmentation and triangulation; b) extracted edge points

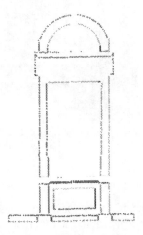

Fig. 3. Edges decomposed into arcs and straight segments

are extracted using the RANSAC algorithm applied to the geometric primitive "line".The remaining points are classified as curved edges. The segment must contain a number of points which is higher than a predefined threshold. Fig. 3 shows an example of edge points classified in arcs and straight segments.

3.4 Determination of Intersection Points

Since corners are captured with difficulty by TLS, it is necessary to deduce them from the existing cloud. In order to identify points of intersection between straight edges and / or arcs, the algorithm calculates the intersection of two curves in two dimensions. Only the intersection points representing nodes must be preserved (Fig. 4). To do this, topological constraints have been integrated into the algorithm. In this way, only the intersections between neighbouring segments are kept. These points constitute nodes and allow the transition from edge points to well connected line segments and arcs.

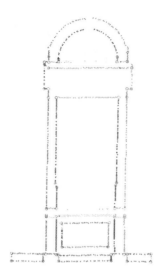

Fig. 4. Nodes created at the intersection of segments (red circles)

4   Classification of Relevant Elements

4.1   Wall and Openings

Wall of the main façade is considered as a reference for the features describing the façade (doors, windows, architectural elements). The planar cluster corresponding to the wall is generally the first cluster extracted in the segmentation step since it is the best plane in the sense of RANSAC paradigm. The openings are the set of holes lying on the wall. They are characterised by a lack of points. Fig. 5 illustrates the definition of openings (here windows) on the wall.

4.2   Components Which Are in Juxtaposition with an Opening

Once the openings have been identified, the relevant geometrical elements extracted from the point clouds are analyzed and assigned to the opening it belongs to. For this purpose, a distance criterion is used, i.e. the remoteness of the components to the opening, whatever the opening size and the distance between the other openings. This step allows us to affect to each opening the relevant elements which are in juxtaposition with it.

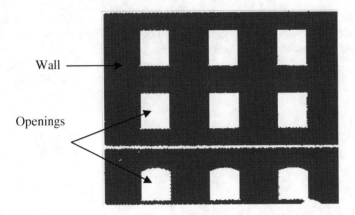

Fig. 5. Openings characterized by a lack of points in the planar cluster describing a wall

The second step consists of categorizing these geometrical elements in four groups: relevant components belonging to the upper part (Upper) of the opening (lintel, cornices, pediment, key, …), relevant elements belonging to the lower part (Low) of the opening (support, balcony, …), relevant components belonging to the right-hand side (Right) of the opening (jamb, columns, …) and finally relevant components belonging to the left-hand side (Left) of the opening which are not necessarily identical to the right-hand side (see Fig. 6).

All relevant elements above the opening (including the overflowing to the sides) are considered in this step belonging to the upper components. Note that if the upper shape is an arch, a triangle or another shape, the separation line is created with the upper shape extended horizontally on both sides. The same is done for the lower part.

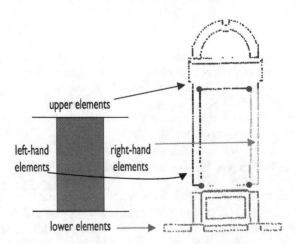

Fig. 6. Classification of the opening elements into upper components (in blue), lower components (in red), left-hand components (in black) and right-hand components (in green) of the opening defined by brown points

It is then easy to determine the left-hand and the right-hand components among the rest of elements. The elements that are on the separation line (segments) belong to the two sets of components.

5 Automatic Creation and Adjustment of the Parametric Objects

5.1 Parametric Adjustment of Wall and Openings

The parameters of a wall are the normal of the plane, the width and the height of the wall. In order to position the objects easier, the lower left corner of the wall is chosen as the frame origin. The parameters of an opening are its relative position on the fa-çade defined by the lower left corner of the opening, its width and its height.

To get such parameters, it is important to assign to each opening the segments of points surrounding it. The process applied is the following: the edge points of the planar cluster describing the wall plane are firstly extracted. Then, they are classified regarding their directions and decomposed into vertical, horizontal, tilted straight or curved edges as explained in part 3. Results are presented in Fig. 7a. Then, edge points are grouped into segments regarding the distance separating two successive points. A predefined threshold is introduced for this step (Fig. 7b). Finally, based on the distance computed between these segments, they are assigned or not to the same opening regarding the neighbourhood criterion. In the same time, the edges of an opening are classified into upper, lower, left-hand and right-hand edges. Fig. 7c shows the result of this assignment.

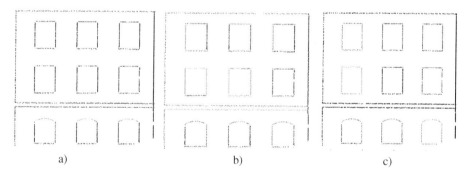

Fig. 7. Edge points of wall and openings; a) decomposition and classification of edges regarding their directions; b) decomposition of segments into contiguous segments; c) Assignment of neighbouring edges to compose the openings

Afterwards, the neighbouring edges are regrouped in order to get separately the wall contour (exterior contour) and the opening contours (inner contours). The width of an opening is estimated by computing the mean distance between the left-hand and the right-hand edges of an opening. The height of an opening is the mean distance computed between the upper and the lower edges.

Architectural components which are juxtaposed with an opening are very various and can have very complex shapes (see Fig. 8 for examples of openings). Furthermore

Fig. 8. Various kinds of opening components

each architectural style has its own specificities. Lots of components in ancient styles are sculpted. In this case, it is impossible firstly to automatically recognize components in the relevant geometrical elements and secondly to adjust parameters. Note that it is also impossible to generate parametric models for all existing cases. So we first have begun our research with simple shapes and we will try to detail as we go along.

5.2 Parametric Objects Creation

At this stage, a 3D model of the wall and its openings is automatically created based on the parameters delivered by the previous processing step. Fig. 9 shows the result of the parametric model of the façade presented in Fig. 1.

In a first stage, only boxes are automatically created and dimensioned. For instance, Fig. 10a represents the automatically computed window, already studied in Fig. 2. Fig. 10b represents the boxes created with the relevant components extracted from the laser point cloud. Then a manual refinement is performed to create the components surrounding the window.

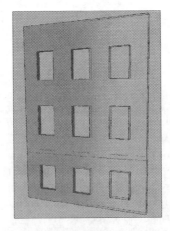

Fig. 9. 3D model of a wall and its openings. In blue, the parametric model; in red, the automatically extracted relevant elements (straight segments and arcs) and the points of the cloud.

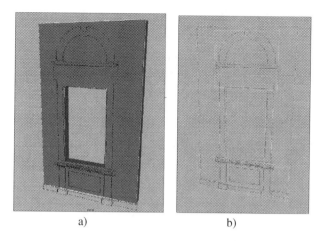

a)   b)

Fig. 10. Relevant points extracted from the cloud and bounding boxes; a) automatically computed window; b) boxes of the upper, lower, right and left-hand components

Software development for automatic extraction and creation of edges is performed with Matlab. For the parametric modelling, software development is performed in C++ and Mel (Maya embedded Language), in order to create some plug-ins and a graphical user interface for Maya. The parametric model is exported from Matlab in a file format allowing its import into Maya software [24] for further uses.

6   Manual Refinement and Adding of Other Components

A Maya object is described via a set of attributes displayed in a window (the attribute editor). When an attribute is modified, the object is regenerated with the new parameters'

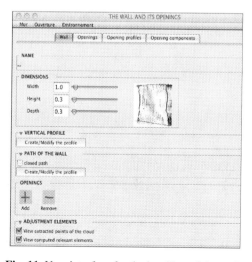

Fig. 11. User interface for the handling of the walls

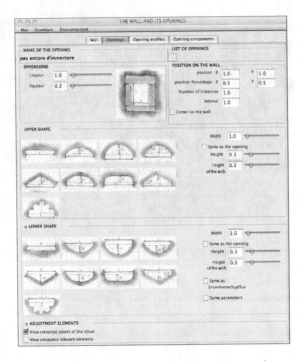

Fig. 12. User interface for the handling of the openings

values. To each architectural component (for instance an opening or a lintel) corresponds a Maya object; to each parameter (for instance the height) corresponds a Maya attribute.

When creating automatically the components, the values of some parameters are specified and others cannot be determined. In the component parameters, we store not only the corresponding relevant components but also the 3D points of the laser data that have been used to determine them. These points and components can be visualized in the scene. This is done for two reasons. Firstly it allows the user to check if the

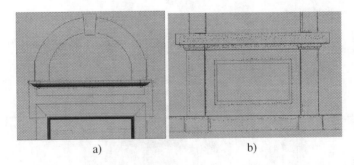

a)   b)

Fig. 13. Relevant points (in black) extracted from the cloud and corresponding architectural parametric components (in blue); a) for the upper part; b) for the lower part

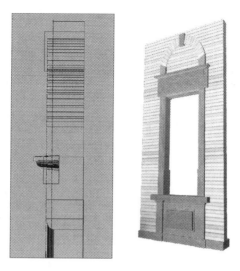

Fig. 14. Adjustment of the components according to the relevant points (in green) and 3D textured model of the window

Fig. 15. The final 3D textured and illuminated model of the façade depicted in Fig. 1

automatic process has chosen the right kind of component. For example the automatic detection could have decided the upper shape was a semi-cylinder but in fact it is a more complicated shape: arches with rounded corners. The user can also check if the values affected to the parameters are correct. Secondly, the user can use the relevant components to visually adjust the other parameters or create new components (bricks, keys, corbels, abutment, etc.), to position and adjust them. Fig. 11 and Fig. 12 represent the user interface for the handling of the walls and the openings.

The user can now examine the results of the automatic process. We first notice that the height of the window is not right: from the point cloud the line extracted was in fact the shutter (see Fig. 13). With the help of the other relevant components, we can adjust the height of the window. We have also created new parametric components (lintels, key, cornices, profiles…) that are automatically positioned around the window as they are described as belonging to that specific window. Fig. 14 shows the adjustment step in perspective and the textured 3D model of the window. Fig. 15 shows the final 3D textured and illuminated model of the façade.

7 Conclusion and Future Work

In this paper a new method for the creation of 3D parametric models has been presented. It is based exclusively on laser data. The developed workflow automatically extracts lines and curves in the point data to create the main architectural components of the scene (walls and openings). This method uses parametric models allowing easy further handling of components and further adding of other parametric components (lintels, balconies…) to the scene.

In the future, the automatic process will be completed and improved. Also the implementation of semi-automatic creation is forecasted: the user will have the possibility of choosing a component and of selecting relevant elements to automatically create the component and adjust its parameters. The user will also be able to fix some predefined values (such as thresholds needed in adjustment) and launch the automatic adjustment on other parameters.

Acknowledgments. The authors would like to thank "The Region Alsace" for supporting the LSIIT-Photogrammetry and Geomatics Group, INSA Strasbourg especially in the field of Terrestrial Laser Scanning. Thanks are also due to Autodesk for providing us Maya licences.

References

1. Stamos, I., Yu, G., Wolberg, G., Zokai, S.: 3D Modeling Using Planar Segments And Mesh Elements. In: 3rd International Symposium on 3D Data Processing, Visualization & Transmission, pp. 599–606. IEEEXplore (2006)
2. Yokoyama, H., Chikatsu, H.: Efficient Corner Detector for 3D point Crowd Data and application to 3D modeling of Structures. In: Proceedings of Electric Imaging Science and Technology "Videometrics VIII", vol. 5013, pp. 208–215 (2004)
3. Frueh, C., Jain, S., Zakhor, A.: Data Processing Algorithms for Generating Textured 3D Building Facade Meshes From Laser Scans and Camera Images. International Journal of Computer Vision 61(2), 159–184 (2005)

4. Pu, S., Vosselman, G.: Automatic extraction of building features from terrestrial laser scanning. In: IAPRS, vol. 36, part 5, p. 5 (2006)
5. Stamos, I., Allen, P.K.: Geometry and texture recovery of scenes of large scale. CVIU 88(2), 94–118 (2002)
6. Wang, M., Tseng, Y.-H.: LIDAR data segmentation and classification based on octree structure. In: 20th ISPRS Congress, Commission 3 (2004)
7. Fischler, M.A., Bolles, R.C.: Random Sample Consensus: A Paradigm for Model fitting with application to Image Analysis and Automated Cartography. Communications of the ACM 24(6), 381–395 (1981)
8. Hough, P.V.C.: Method and Means for Recognizing Complex Patterns. U.S. Patent 3.069.654 (1962)
9. Belton, D., Lichti, D.: Classification and segmentation of terrestrial laser scanner point clouds using local variance information. In: IAPRS, vol. 36, part 5, pp. 44–49 (2006)
10. Briese, C., Pfeifer, N.: Line based reconstruction from terrestrial laser scanning data. Journal of Applied Geodesy 2(2), 85–95 (2008) ISSN 1862-9016
11. Haala, N., Becker, S., Kada, M.: Cell Decomposition for the Generation of Building Models at Multiple Scales. In: IAPRS, Symposium Photogrammetric Computer Vision, vol. 36, part 3, pp. 19–24 (2006)
12. Böhm, J., Becker, S., Haala, N.: Model refinement by integrated processing of laser scanning and photogrammetry. In: Proceedings of the 2nd ISPRS International Workshop 3D-ARCH (2007)
13. Pu, S., Vosselman, G.: Building facade reconstruction by fusing terrestrial laser points and images. Sensors 9(6), 4525–4542 (2009) ISSN 1424-8220
14. Wetzel, J.P., Belblidia, S., Bignon, J.C.: Specification of an operator for the design of architectural forms: "Pleating". In: eCAADe (2007)
15. Chevrier, C., Maillard, Y., Perrin, J.P.: A method for the 3D modelling of historic monuments: the case study of a Gothic abbey. In: Proceedings of ISPRS Workshop 3D ARCH, International Archives of Photogrammetry, Remote Sensing and Spatial Information Sciences (2009)
16. ArchiCad, http://www.aricad-cao.com (accessed April 2010)
17. Müller, P., Wonka, P., Haegler, S., Ulmer, A., Van Gool, L.: Procedural Modeling of Buildings. In: Proceedings of ACM SIGGRAPH 2006 / ACM Transactions on Graphics (TOG), vol. 25(3), pp. 614–623. ACM Press, New York (2006)
18. Chen, G., Esch, G., Wonka, P., Müller, P., Zhang, E.: Interactive Procedural Street Modeling. In: Proceedings of ACM SIGGRAPH 2008 / ACM Transactions on Graphics (TOG), vol. 29(3), 9 pages. ACM Press, New York (2008)
19. Havemann, S., Fellner, D.W.: Generative Parametric Design of Gothic Window Tracery. In: Proceedings of the Shape Modeling International, The 5th International Symposium on Virtual Reality, Archaeology and Cultural Heritage VAST (2004)
20. GML (2008), http://www.generative-modelling.org (accessed January 12, 2008)
21. Chevrier, C., Perrin, J.P.: Generation of architectural parametric components. In: Proceedings of CAAD Future conference, pp. 105–118 (2009)
22. Boulaassal, H., Landes, T., Grussenmeyer, P.: Automatic extraction of planar clusters and their contours on building façades recorded by terrestrial laser scanner. International Journal of Architectural Computing (IJAC) 7(1), 1–20 (2009)
23. Vögtle, T., Schwab, I., Landes, T.: Influences of Different Materials on the Measurements of a Terrestrial Laser Scanner (TLS). In: The 21th ISPRS Congress (2008)
24. Maya (2009), http://www.autodesk.com (accessed April 2010)

New Instruments and Technologies for Cultural Heritage Survey: Full Integration between Point Clouds and Digital Photogrammetry

F. Rinaudo[1], F. Chiabrando[2], F. Nex[1], and D. Piatti[1]

[1] DITAG/POLITECNICO DI TORINO, Corso Duca degli Abruzzi, 24, 10129 Torino, Italy
`(fulvio.rinaudo,francesco.nex,dario.piatti)@polito.it`
[2] DINSE/POLITECNICO DI TORINO - Viale Mattioli 39, 10125 Torino, Italy
`filiberto.chiabrando@polito.it`

Abstract. In the last years the Geomatic Research Group of the Politecnico di Torino faced some new research topics about new instruments for point cloud generation (e.g. Time of Flight cameras) and strong integration between multi-image matching techniques and 3D Point Cloud information in order to solve the ambiguities of the already known matching algorithms. ToF cameras can be a good low cost alternative to LiDAR instruments for the generation of precise and accurate point clouds: up to now the application range is still limited but in a near future they will be able to satisfy the most part of the Cultural Heritage metric survey requirements. On the other hand multi-image matching techniques with a correct and deep integration of the point cloud information can give the correct solution for an "intelligent" survey of the geometric object break-lines, which are the correct starting point for a complete survey. These two research topics are strictly connected to a modern Cultural Heritage 3D survey approach. In this paper after a short analysis of the achieved results, an alternative possible scenario for the development of the metric survey approach inside the wider topic of Cultural Heritage Documentation is reported.

Keywords: ToF camera, calibration, matching, multi-image, digital photogrammetry, LiDAR.

1 Introduction

The close range metric survey approach has been completely renovated thanks to the developments of LiDAR and multi-image matching (digital photogrammetry) techniques. While in the past a metric survey was an intelligent, rational, and manual selection of the points needed to describe the shape of the surveyed object, today the above mentioned techniques force the surveyors to work with point clouds acquired without any understanding of the object shape. Starting from this "not-intelligent" geometry the user has to interpret and describe the searched shapes.

The rapid development of the research studies in the fields of point cloud management and interpretation, by using segmentation and modeling algorithms and/or by using some of the information extracted from oriented images, has allowed the

M. Ioannides (Ed.): EuroMed 2010, LNCS 6436, pp. 56–70, 2010.

production of traditional (technical drawings such as plans and sections) and innovative (true orthophoto, solid images, 3D realistic models) representation instruments. In the last few years, the research group of Geomatics of the Politecnico di Torino has developed specific research projects considering two different aspects: testing and calibration of new instruments able to generate 3D point clouds and a full integration between point clouds and multi-image matching techniques.

The first topic aims to reduce the time needed to acquire dense point clouds and the costs of the needed instrumentation on the survey budget; the second topic aims to re-evaluate digital photogrammetry as the more suitable technique to produce dense and affordable information if helped by a rough shape model of the surveyed object especially in Cultural Heritage applications.

2 ToF Cameras

Time of Flight (ToF) cameras (also known as 3D cameras or Range cameras) represent a rather new way to obtain 3D point clouds, which are almost comparable with those of traditional LiDAR acquisitions. Using these cameras, a bundle of distances is determined simultaneously (at video frame rates) for each pixel of a two-dimensional sensor array. Although ToF cameras are usually characterized by no more than a few thousands of tens of pixels, a maximum unambiguous measurement range up to 30 m can be reached and complete 3D point clouds of the analyzed objects can be quickly acquired (the sampling rate can reach more than 50 frames/s).

These devices allow to generate point clouds such as in the case of the LiDAR technique and photogrammetric matching but with the great advantage of real time acquisition, low cost (approximately 1/10th of the standard price of a LiDAR equipment) and handiness. Unlike photogrammetric techniques, 3D cameras allow a point cloud to be obtained of the object which has to be surveyed from even only one point of view, without the need of any particular lighting conditions, since these cameras are active sensors that work outside of the visible spectrum.

Two main variations of the ToF principle have been implemented above all in 3D cameras: one measures distances by means of direct measurement of the runtime of a travelled light pulse using arrays of single-photon avalanche diodes (SPADs) [1] [16]; the other method uses amplitude modulated light and obtains distance information by measuring the phase difference between a reference signal and the reflected signal [8] [9]. While complex readout schemes and low frame rates have prevented the use of SPAD arrays in commercial 3D-imaging products up to now, the second category has already been implemented successfully in several commercially available 3D camera systems. More information about pixel structures and performance limitations of these sensors can be found for instance in [3].

ToF cameras usually deliver a range image and an amplitude image with infrared modulation intensities: the range image (or depth image) contains for each pixel the radial measured distance between the considered pixel and its projection on the surveyed object, while the amplitude image contains for each pixel the strength of the reflected signal. In some cases an intensity image is also delivered, which represents the mean of the total light incident on the sensor (reflected modulated signal and background light of the observed scene).

Each 3D camera is usually equipped with a standard calibration but, as reported in different works [14][16] and in our previous tests [16] the distance measurements of ToF cameras are still affected by some residual systematic errors which can have the same extent of the precision of the instrument.

In Table 1 the main technical specifications of some commercial ToF cameras are reported.

Table 1. Technical specification of some commercial ToF cameras

Camera	Sensor [px x px]	Meas. range [m]	Accuracy [m]	Weight [kg]
CAM CUBE 2.0	204 x 204	0.3 ÷ 7	± 0.01÷0.03	1.438
SR-4000	176 x 144	0.3 ÷ 10	± 0.015	0.470
OPTRICAM DS10K-A	120 x 90	0.3 ÷ 10	± 0.03	n.a.
FOTONIC B70	160 x 120	0.1 ÷ 7	± 0.015	1.049

Table 2. SR-4000 camera specifications (http://www.mesa-imaging.ch – accessed 10th June 2010)

Pixel array size [-]	176 (h) × 144 (v)
Field of view [°]	43.6 (h) × 34.6 (v)
Pixel pitch [µm]	40
Illumination wavelength [nm]	850
Working range [m]	0.3 ÷ 5.0
Maximum frame rate [fps]	54
Dimensions [mm]	65 × 65 × 68
Weight [g]	470

In the following sections some of the tests performed by our Research Group on the SR-4000 camera are summarized.

2.1 ToF Camera Calibration

The more recent 3D cameras are usually provided with a calibration model of the measured distances in order to correct most of the biases related to their electronic components. In order to check the measurement accuracy which can be obtained on a real object, the following test has been performed.

An architectural artifact (a decorated frame) has been surveyed by using a triangulation based scanner (MENSI S10) which guarantees an accuracy of about 0.1 mm at a taking distance of 2 m (see Fig. 1 left). The obtained 3D point cloud can be considered as the "truth" since the MENSI S10 accuracy is less than 1/10th of the expected accuracy of the SR-4000 camera. The same object has been surveyed by using the SR-4000 camera (see Fig. 1 right), acquiring and averaging thirty frames in order to reduce the measurements noises of the single frame acquisition. Then, the obtained

3D point cloud has been compared with the previous one. Before the acquisition, the camera has been used for a continuous acquisition of about 40 minutes (warm up time) in order to reach a good measurement stability [16].

Fig. 1. The MENSI S10 and SR-4000 camera record the decoration

In order to compare the two point clouds, they have to be defined in a unique coordinate system: therefore, seven control points (the white cubes visible in Fig. 1) have been positioned inside the acquired scene and used to register the SR-4000 point cloud in the same coordinate system of the MENSI S10 point cloud. The estimated discrepancies can be interpreted as a residual variable that, by theory, has a null mean and a mean square error equal to the measurement precision if the measurements are accurate and precise. In Fig. 3 (RIGHT top) a representation of the estimated discrepancies on the architectural decoration is reported with an arbitrary color scale. In this case, a mean value and a standard deviation value of the differences of 0.006 m and 0.011 m have been obtained respectively. Therefore, a residual systematic effect is still present inside the camera measurements. Its amount is not acceptable since it is very close to the declared measurement precision of 5 mm: the calibrated 3D camera is precise but not accurate enough. In order to overcome this problem, an extra self-calibration model has been developed, which increases the SR-4000 measurement accuracy.

The model is described by the following equation:

$$e = \lambda_0 + \lambda_1 \cdot d \cdot \sin(\lambda_2 \cdot d + \lambda_3) \tag{1}$$

where: d is the pixel measured distance, λ_0 is a constant error, λ_1 represents a scale factor which multiplies a "wiggling error" modeled by a sinusoidal function (λ_2 = angular frequency, λ_3 = phase shift).

The values of the calibration model parameters have to be estimated by using a reference plain placed at know distances [16]. These parameters can be considered stable for the camera, however the calibration should be repeated every year in order to check the stability of the instrument. Coming back to the previously described test, the 3D point cloud acquired with the SR-4000 camera has been corrected by using the proposed calibration model and a new estimation of the discrepancies against the 3D point cloud of the MENSI S10 has been performed.

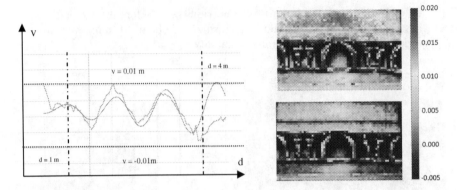

Fig. 2. LEFT: Experimental discrepancies v (green line) and proposed calibration model (blue line) – RIGHT: Discrepancies between the MENSI S10 point cloud and the SR-4000 point cloud before (top) and after (bottom) applying the extra calibration model (scale bar in meters)

In this case the mean value of the discrepancies falls down to 0.001 m, while the standard deviation is the same of the previous one. In Fig. 2 (RIGHT bottom) a representation of the estimated discrepancies on the architectural decoration after applying the calibration model is reported with an arbitrary color scale.

Considering the theory of the residual variable, it is possible to state that, after the proposed self-calibration, the SR-4000 camera is able to produce more accurate measurements with a precision that is close to the declared technical specification (see Tab. 2).

2.2 A Complete Survey

The SR-4000 camera has been used in a standard survey procedure to generate a realistic 3D model of a window, applying the self-calibration model on the four acquired point clouds.

A digital image has been acquired by means of a calibrated CANON EOS 5D MARKII camera: this image has been oriented in the same coordinate system of the ToF point cloud by using some reference points.

Fig. 3. Point cloud (left), mesh model (centre), textured final model (right)

The processing of the point cloud necessary to reach the mesh model of the window has been performed by using the *Geomagic Studio*® software; the model has been finally coloured by using the radiometric information extracted from the digital image. Fig. 3 shows the obtained results.

2.3 First Conclusions

3D cameras represent an affordable solution to be used instead of the traditional LiDAR approach to produce point clouds useful to provide the primary data for modeling small and medium sized objects.

The proposed self-calibration model refines the distance measurement accuracy between 0.5 m and 4.0 m of the camera to object distance, therefore only small objects can be surveyed with a static acquisition.

The high sampling rate of the SR-4000 camera allows to conceive a possible use as a 3D video-camera in order to record data on larger objects (e.g. a room, a statue, etc.): in this case a real-time ICP based registration of the video frames could be developed in order to allow an easy and self controlling acquisition.

In any case, the ToF point clouds have to be corrected by using a self-calibration model whose parameters can be estimated with a suitable calibration procedure like the one adopted by the authors [16].

3 Lidar/Digital Photogrammetry Integration

When we talk about LiDAR and digital photogrammetry integration we actually mean the possibility to overcome the limits of LiDAR technology by using some information coming from digital photogrammetry (e.g. realistic 3D model, manual understanding of break-lines, etc.) or to extend the photogrammetric procedure thanks to the information coming from LiDAR data (e.g. true orthophoto generation).

These applications define the lowest level of possible integrations: it can be stated that digital photogrammetry, especially in Cultural Heritage applications, can provide useful results (by paying many manual interventions) even without LiDAR integration. On the other hand, LiDAR without any help from digital photogrammetry cannot give satisfactory solutions to the 3D metric survey.

In addition, LiDAR technology uses a not self-controlled survey strategy: the three coordinates of a generic point are estimated by using just three independent measurements, therefore, a correct estimation of the achieved accuracy is not possible. On the contrary, photogrammetry estimates 3D coordinates of a generic point by using at least four independent measurements (in the case that only two overlapping images are used). Then, in a modern approach of digital photogrammetry the multi-image matching allows the estimation of the 3D coordinates of a generic point also by using three or more overlapping images: this means that the three unknown coordinates are estimated in a least squares approach with at least six independent equations. Therefore, the redundancy that a multi-image approach allows is equal to the number of the unknowns and, from a statistical point of view, this is the best condition for a correct estimation of the precision.

3.1 Multi-image Matching

The automated extraction of objects from photogrammetric images has been a topic of research for decades. Nowadays, image-matching techniques allow a great number of points to be extracted in a quick way. In particular, multi-image techniques allowed obtaining a point cloud density comparable to the LiDAR one. Then, they allow an improvement in the geometric precision and the reliability with respect to image pairs, by extracting points and edges from images and projecting their match in the space [17]. Actually, this kind of solution requires an approximate DSM in order to "drive" the solution to the correct match; the more accurate is this model, the more correct (without blunders) is the solution.

These techniques consider the epipolar geometry between images in order to reduce the search area in adjacent images, and, thus, decreasing the number of blunders to a great extent. The run along the epipolar line is further reduced by the z-value that is provided by an approximate 3D model. The needed approximation increases with the ratio between the depth differences (Z-values) and the taking distance and with the decreasing of the base/taking distance ratio of the overlapping used images.

Therefore in Cultural Heritage applications, where large values of the Z/taking-distance are present (e.g. façades are usually rough with balconies, columns or decorations that protrude of several meters), these variations are more relevant as they can be greater than 1/5 of the taking distance. In these conditions, multi-image matching can have the right help just by using dense and accurate 3D models.

These 3D models can be produced by LiDAR instruments or, as we demonstrated in the previous sections, by means of the ToF cameras. Therefore, instead of talking about LiDAR and digital photogrammetry integration, it is possible to generalize the concept saying that digital photogrammetry needs a closed Point-Cloud integration.

3.2 Point Clouds and Digital Photogrammetry Integration

Fig.4 shows the flow-chart of a standard multi-image matching process integrated with a correct use of an approximate point cloud in order to overcome the ambiguity of the standard matching procedure. The point cloud can be produced by using LiDAR or ToF cameras, as mentioned before.

The goal of this approach is to try to satisfy the needs of the final users (photogrammetrists, surveyor, architects, engineers, archaeologists) reducing the time needed to reach the final products. In particular, façade break-lines are automatically extracted in the space in order to ease and limit the manual intervention in the post processing phases.

The images are acquired according to an *ad hoc* taking configuration (Figure 9): several images are acquired and the most central one is considered as reference image during the matching process [17]. The point cloud is acquired from a central position with respect to the image acquisition in order to have approximately the same occluded areas in the Point Cloud data and in the reference image.

The acquired images are pre-processed according to an auto-adaptive smoothing. Then, they are enhanced using a Wallis filter; this filter is able to sharpen the radiometric boundaries and to enhance the edges.

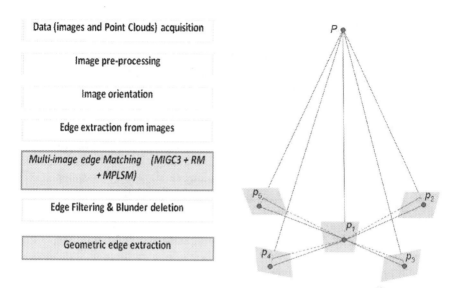

Fig. 4. Multi-Image matching process enhanced by Point Cloud integration (colored boxes) and suggested image taking strategy

The orientation is performed in a local coordinate system. In this step, the A^2SIFT (Auto-Adaptive Scale Invariant Feature Transform) operator [16] is adopted in the tie-point extraction and a robust (Least Median Square) relative orientation is then performed in order to eliminate the mismatches [16]. Finally, a bundle block adjustment is performed.

After that, the edge extraction is performed by the Canny operator on the reference image. The extracted edges are then approximated, by identifying the pixels where the edge changes in direction (e.g. knots) and linking these dominant points by straight edges.

The edges are only extracted in the regions of interest: façade glass is always excluded as it could create mismatches and blunders due to reflection.

The point cloud is registered in the photogrammetric coordinate system. In this way, the information between the images and the point cloud are shared.

Then, a multi-image matching algorithm is set up: this step can be divided in three different algorithms. The first algorithm (MIGC^3) is similar to the Geometrically Constrained Cross Correlation (GC^3) [17] and it is used to define a pixel accuracy location of the homologous points.

The images are preliminarily corrected (using the camera inner calibration) in order to ease them into a central perspective.

Then, the algorithm uses a multi-image approach by considering a reference image and projecting the image patch of each dominant point of the reference image onto the point cloud. Using the approximate Z-value achieved by the point cloud interpolation, it back-projects the image patch onto the other images, giving an approximate position of the homologous points.

The epipolar constraint limits the search space in the images. The length of this line could be achieved considering the Z-value given by the point cloud; then, in order to find the homologous points in all the images, this value is varied into a range (Δz). This work can be further enforced and improved through the position of the already matched points: the Z-value of two adjacent dominant points being on the same edge must be similar. In this way, it is possible to reduce the length of the epipolar line on the object to few centimeters [14].

Through this algorithm, the dominants points of each edge are matched in all the images in order to reconstruct the break-line 3D position.

Even if MIGC[3] is able to match a high percentage of the extracted dominant points, some dominant points can have more than one possible match in terms of cross correlation. In order to solve these ambiguous matching and to improve the rate of the successfully matched points, the relational matching (RM) has been developed. This algorithm has allowed several ambiguities to be solved during the matching phases by imposing a smoothness constraint.

Finally, a Multi-Image Least Square Matching (MILSM) [16] has been performed for each extracted point. The MILSM has been implemented in order to improve the accuracy up to a sub-pixel dimension.

During the matching process, some blunders can be generated. These blunders are firstly deleted from the extracted edges using a filter that considers the relative point positions on the same edge: in particular, the position of a point is predicted considering the neighboring points of the edge and, then, the difference between the predicted and the real position of the point is evaluated. If the difference value is higher than a predefined threshold, the point is deleted. This filter is not robust: it will work well if the blunders are isolated from each other. For this reason, a second filter could be used to clean the edges when several blunders are present in a narrow space: this algorithm uses the point cloud information to verify the correctness of each dominant point: when it is out of a defined threshold from the point cloud, it is deleted.

Fig. 5. Radiometric edges extracted before the point cloud validation (left) and geometrically validated and smoothed edges (Torino Valentino Castle test site)

Image matching allows radiometric edges to be extracted. Some of these edges are due to shadows or radiometric changes but they do not have a geometric correspondence. Only geometric boundaries are of interest in the survey for modeling purposes. For this reason, the position of each dominant point on the extracted edges is considered with respect to the point cloud: it is verified whether a geometric discontinuity occurs in the 3D model to the projected edge point.

The edges extracted by the matching algorithm are random noise affected and they cannot be directly used in the drawing production. For this reason, the noisy edges are split in basic elements (linear and curved elements), each element is smoothed and eased, in an automatic way, into lines, and second order curves by means of a polynomial fitting. Then, the basic elements are recollected in a unique smoothed edge [17].

Finally, geometric edges are exported in CAD environment in order to give preliminary data for the graphic drawing realization of the survey and for a rough evaluation of the achieved results.

3.3 First Conclusions

Multi-image matching, if correctly integrated by the point cloud data, can give more affordable information than LiDAR technology for a modern Cultural Heritage 3D survey.

In the photogrammetric approach, the radiometric content is directly used to extract the geometric information while in the case of LiDAR techniques the color information is added as external information. In some way, the link between geometric and radiometric data is more effective in photogrammetry than in Point Cloud generation techniques such as LiDAR and ToF cameras.

The automation level offered by photogrammetry is higher than the one achievable by using traditional point cloud segmentation techniques. The manual intervention is reduced to few steps and the results are more complete and reliable than using only the point cloud information.

4 ToF Camera Point Clouds and Digital Photogrammetry Integration

Following the achieved results explained in the previous sections, and the same workflow, a practical test of break-line extraction by using the multi-image matching approach integrated with a ToF camera point cloud has been realized on a decorated window of the Valentino Castle test site (Torino, Italy).

Considering the technical characteristics of the SR-4000 camera, the test is limited to an architectural object that can be acquired with a limited number of ToF camera acquisitions.

The façades are painted and the texture is generally not good enough for the traditional image matching approach to be performed.

4.1 ToF Data Acquisition

After the camera warm-up, the SR-4000 camera was positioned on a photographic tripod and moved to different positions in order to achieve a complete coverage of the window to be surveyed (Fig.6).

According to the SR-4000 specifications, since the average distance between the camera and the window was about 3.5 m, the acquired area dimensions for each range image were about 3.00 m x 2.50 m.

Fig. 6. Three views of the surveyed window of the test site and SR-4000 data acquisition

Fig. 7. Complete 3D ToF point cloud

In order to obtain a complete 3D model of the window (3 m large, 5 m high), the ToF data was acquired from six different positions, with an overlap of about 70% between the acquired range images.

4.2 ToF Data Processing

The distance of each pixel of the averaged frames was corrected with the distance error model proposed in [16], using a custom-made *Matlab*® application.

The obtained point clouds were registered using the ICP algorithm implemented in the *Geomagic Studio*® software in order to obtain a unique 3D model of the window.

In this way a dense Point Cloud (168551 points) was generated and then employed for the multi-image matching approach in order to extract the needed break-lines.

4.3 Image Acquisition

The image acquisition was performed using the CANON EOS-5D MARK II digital camera equipped with a 24 mm lens. The taking distance was about 6 m. Five images were acquired according to an *ad hoc* configuration [17]. In Fig.8 an example of epipolar lines and correlation patches on the five images employed for the multi-image matching approach is reported.

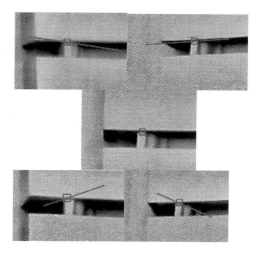

Fig. 8. Epipolar geometry of the acquired digital images

According to this particular configuration the epipolar lines run in tilted direction with respect to the main lines of the façade (horizontal and vertical), and the homologous points can be determined in an unambiguous way. Thanks to the image dimension (5616 x 3744 pixels) and the short taking distance, an excellent image resolution was reached (less than 2 mm of Ground Sample Distance (GSD)).

4.4 Data Integration and Results

The edge extraction allowed a complete set of lines to be defined from the reference image: Fig. 9 (left) shows the extracted edges, which are described by 45636 dominant points.

After the matching process, the position in the space of 32566 dominant points was defined. Only a percentage of 3% of these points was deleted after the blunder detection process. The resulting data was smoothed in order to ease the edges in lines and curves.

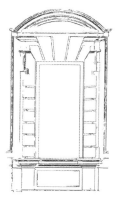

Fig. 9. Extracted and smoothed edges on the reference image

The result of this work is reported in Fig. 9 (right): it can be noticed that the window geometry is complete and only some parts of the arcs are missing.

The smoothing correctly eased all the elements of the façade. In Fig.9 (right) a zoom of the final result is shown.

Obviously to produce useful representation drawings and/or 3D models a lot of works have to be done. Fig. 10 shows a 3D realistic model produced by using a LiDAR and Digital photogrammetry integration and the final drawing of a section.

5 Conclusions

The results of the researches carried out in the last few years by the Geomatics Research Group of the Politecnico di Torino for Cultural Heritage metric survey allow some final considerations to be outlined.

Fig. 10. From the results of a metric survey to the final drawing

Cultural Heritage metric survey essentially requires a geometric break-line definition. Point clouds of regular surfaces are generally not useful: the point clouds can give a proper answer to the metric survey requirements only when irregular and smoothed surfaces have to be described.

In the past the selection of points performed by a human operator using total stations, distance measurements and photogrammetric plotting forced the user to select the only necessary information during the acquisition and processing phases: the geometric points and break-lines which delimitate the surveyed objects were usually selected.

The new trend started with the LiDAR technique (and today with the ToF cameras), which changed the starting point of the process: the acquisition is made without any logic criteria, collecting millions of points and only the surveyor work allows useful information to be extracted. Unfortunately, as it is well known, the processing of point clouds in order to extract break-lines and affordable geometric descriptions (the true goal of a metric survey!) is not an easy task and a lot of work has to be still completed.

Multi-image matching is able to directly extract the geometry of the radiometric edges of a set of images but it usually finds a lot of troubles when high Z variations occur. The knowledge of an approximate 3D model of the surveyed object allows this problem to be overcome. Then, the point cloud (provided by LiDAR or ToF camera) is a good solution in order to distinguish between radiometric and geometric edges (the needed break-lines for a complete metric survey).

The ToF cameras represent a good alternative to LiDAR techniques to quickly produce point clouds with the same accuracy and precision.

Therefore, we can state that in the near future the 3D metric survey of Cultural Heritage will probably be performed by using multi-image matching and ToF point clouds: today technology allows this approach to be employed for object surveys where the taking distance is less than a tens of meters but in the near future the limitations in using these cameras will probably be solved.

Finally, considering the costs of digital and ToF cameras and their on-the-field easy management, the proposed approach will speed-up and simplify (from an economical point of view) the Cultural Heritage 3D metric survey.

References

1. Albota, M.A., Heinrichs, R.M., Kocher, D.G., Fouche, D.G., Player, B.E., Obrien, M.E., Aull, G.F., Zayhowski, J.J., Mooney, J., Willard, B.C., Carlson, R.R.: Three-dimensional imaging laser radar with a photon-counting avalanche photodiode array and microchip laser. Appl. Opt. 41, 7671–7678 (2002)
2. Baltsavias, E.: Multiphoto Geometrically Constrained Matching. Phd. dissertation, ETH Zurich, Switzerland (1991)
3. Büttgen, B., Seitz, P.: Robust optical Time-of-Flight range imaging based on smart pixel structures. Trans. Circ. Sys. 1, 1512–1525 (2008)
4. Chiabrando, F., Chiabrando, R., Piatti, D., Rinaudo, F.: Sensors for 3D Imaging: Metric Evaluation and Calibration of a CCD/CMOS Time-of-Flight Camera. Sensors 9, 10080–10096 (2009)
5. Falie, D., Buzuloiu, V.: Noise characteristics of 3D Time-of-Flight cameras. In: Proceedings of IEEE Symposium on Signals Circuits & Systems (ISSCS), Iasi, Romania, pp. 229–232 (2007)
6. Habib, A.F., Ghanma, M.S., Tait, M.: Integration of LIDAR and photogrammetry for close range applications. In: International Archives of Photogrammetry and Remote Sensing, Istanbul, Turkey, vol. XXXIV/B2 (2004)
7. Kahlmann, T., Remondino, F., Ingensand, H.: Calibration for increased accuracy of the range imaging camera Swiss Ranger. In: Int. Soc. Photogramm. Remote Sens. 2006, vol. XXXVI, pp. 136–141 (2007)
8. Lange, R.: Time-of-Flight range imaging with a custom solid-state image sensor. In: Proceedings of SPIE, Munich, Germany, vol. 3823, pp. 180–191 (1999)
9. Lange, R.: 3D Time-of-Flight distance measurement with custom solid state image sensors in CMOS/CCD-technology. Ph.D. Thesis, University of Siegen, Siegen, Germany (2000)
10. Lingua, A., Marenchino, D., Nex, F.: Performance Analysis of the SIFT Operator for Automatic Feature Extraction and Matching in Photogrammetric Applications. Sensors 9, 3745–3766 (2009)

11. Lichti, D.: Self-Calibration of a 3D Range Camera. In: The International Archives of the Photogrammetry, Remote Sensing and Spatial Information Sciences, Beijing, China, vol. XXXVII, part B5, pp. 927–932 (2008)
12. Lindner, M., Kolb, A.: Lateral and depth calibration of PMD-distance sensors. In: Bebis, G., Boyle, R., Parvin, B., Koracin, D., Remagnino, P., Nefian, A., Meenakshisundaram, G., Pascucci, V., Zara, J., Molineros, J., Theisel, H., Malzbender, T. (eds.) ISVC 2006. LNCS, vol. 4292, pp. 524–533. Springer, Heidelberg (2006)
13. Lingua, A., Rinaudo, F.: Aerial triangulation data acquisition using a low cost digital photogrammetric system. In: The International Archives of Photogrammetry and Remote Sensing, vol. XXXIII/B2, pp. 449–454 (2000)
14. Nex, F.: Multi-Image Matching and LiDAR data new integration approach. PhD Thesis, Politecnico di Torino, Torino, Italy (2010)
15. Nex, F., Rinaudo, F.: New integration approach of Photogrammetric and LIDAR techniques for architectural surveys. In: Laserscanning 2009, Paris, France (2009)
16. Rochas, A., Gösch, M., Serov, A., Besse, P.A., Popovic, R.S.: First Fully Integrated 2-D Array of Single-Photon Detectors in Standard CMOS Technology. IEEE Photonic. Technol. Lett. 15, 963–965 (2003)
17. Weyer, C.A., Bae, K., Lim, K., Lichti, D.: Extensive metric performance evaluation of a 3D range camera. In: Int. Soc. Photogramm. Remote Sens., vol. XXXVII, pp. 939–944 (2008)
18. Zhang, L.: Automatic Digital Surface Model (DSM) generation from linear array images. Phd. dissertation, ETH Zurich, Switzerland (2005)

Digital Image Processing in Weathering Damage Analysis and Recovery Treatments Monitoring

Fulvio Zezza

Faculty of Architecture, University IUAV of Venice,
Convento delle Terese - Dorsoduro 2206, Venice, Italy
fulvio.zezza@iuav.it

Abstract. Scientists and conservators, involved in cultural heritage documentation management, have to furnish not only qualitative but also quantitative
description of the assessment of state of conservation that is incomplete without
a realistic estimation of degradation conditions. Scientists and technicians,
involved in analytical analysis, are able to satisfy these needs through stone or
paints sampling analysis, often destructive when approaching a monument. The
paper refers to the application of the Digital Image Processing and non-invasive
damage analysis (ICAW technique) employed to verify in qualitative and quantitative way the decay of stone and rock paintings.

Keywords: Digital Image Processing, Non Destructive Technique, Salt damage, Recovery treatments, Monuments Conservation.

1 Introduction

Non destructive techniques (NDT) were widely applied on cultural heritage. The non
invasive analysis of weathering damages and the non destructive monitoring of degradation evolution, especially in case of recovery treatment, brought to the development of the ICAW technique (Integrated Computer Analysis for Weathering, F. Zezza
1989). This technique, widely applied in several Mediterranean Basin monuments,
covers entirely the most critical aspects of monuments conservation, permitting a non
destructive Digital Image Processing of the weathering conditions, the time monitoring evolution of degradation, and the non invasive monitoring of the efficiency and
the limits of recovery treatments. The methodology was applied to stone building,
sculpture and paints, and permits to lead and to orient the recovery treatments. ICAW
was born for a new cultural heritage documentation approach; it is able to avoid, or at
least to limit, the laboratory invasive sampling, under the awareness that the future
scientific development of monuments quantitative documentation must be related to
the available non invasive technology. The non destructive technique (ICAW) here
presented is an answer to the pressing needs of conservators, nowadays always more
engaged into a wide global sharing knowledge on cultural heritage.

2 Digital Image Processing and Cultural Heritage

An efficient diffusion and multidiscipline exchange of global know-how in the areas of
cultural heritage could be reached through modern information and communication

M. Ioannides (Ed.): EuroMed 2010, LNCS 6436, pp. 71–84, 2010.
© Springer-Verlag Berlin Heidelberg 2010

technology (ICT) focusing on multimedia technologies. Every data diffusion, however, could not elude from an accurate documentation on the knowledge we need to share (M.Ioannidis, 2003). The assessment of state of conservation is an essential aspect that has to precede knowledge diffusion. On the other hand, the state of conservation is incomplete without a realistic estimation of degradation conditions, obtained through analytical analysis that suffers several operating limitations when approaching a monument. Answering this needs implies that scientists and conservators must work together to focus on the most non invasive technique applicable to the cultural heritage under investigation, due to the uniqueness of the assets they are treating.

For these reasons non destructive technique (NDT) finds wide applications worldwide to satisfy the analytical assets description essential for conservation and maintenance of the monuments (F.Mallouchou-Tufano, Y.Alexopoulus 2003, C.Borg, 2004, A. Adriaens, 2004). On-site and remotely sensed data collection are particularly indicated where the collection of samples, also micro-destructive, finalized to laboratory analysis, could be damaging for the monument, especially in case of architectural elements or delicate paints. Moreover the punctual results by samples analysis, necessary for a preliminary quantification of the damage, are often non-representative of the entire asset. Instead, the remotely sensed techniques, especially in the prediffusion cultural assets documentation steps, seems to be more appropriate to obtain a global and areal evaluation of the monuments characteristics. A fundamental aspects of every physical evaluation on a monument is also the time monitoring control of the parameters adopted. These on site remotely sensed techniques, thanks to their relatively easy repeatability, due to the absolute non invasive operations and relatively low onerous logistic and economical efforts, seems to be preferable for these aims.

Between non destructive on site techniques, Digital Images Processing are widely applied, and involve techniques that range from laser-scanning to infra-red visualizations or colorimetry. Between images analysis, the ICAW technique was successfully applied on monuments conservation description. Integrated Computerized Analysis for Weathering (ICAW, F. Zezza 1989) is a non destructive technique, employable in situ, which offers the possibility of determining the state of conservation of stone material exposed to atmospheric agents, both of natural and anthropogenic origin, and to evaluate the rate of weathering in time, describing quantitatively the decay distribution on the studied surfaces. ICAW, performed in several monuments of the Mediterranean basins for his absolute non-invasive applicability to describe the state of conservation, was progressively implemented considering different environmental conditions and different building material (e.g. F.Zezza 1996, 1997, 2002), proving to be particularly useful to monitor the decay distribution in time, both before and especially after recovery treatments, of paints, monuments, architectonical elements, sculpture and historical buildings. This innovative and unique technique, able to avoid invasive sampling analysis, or in the worst cases to limit them, is directly useful for the cultural heritage documentation and knowledge sharing.

3   Methodology

The ICAW analysis (Integrated Computerised Analysis of Weathering, F. Zezza 1989) consists in a digital image processing complemented by NDT techniques. The basics lie in the level of restitution of light energy from the surfaces exposed: the initial analysis of the image is addressed to establish the chromatic characteristic of the stone depending on colour, structure and state of conservation of the material; in this way the stone surface corresponds to different levels of returned light.

Illustration, quantitative evaluation of damage and information can be reached through a methodological approach which gives back in an objective way the scientific rating of stone damage. The ICAW technique, fixing the rate of weathering through the degree of stone decay considered both as digital images of the weathering forms and related buried structure, allows detecting the weathering on surface and in depth.

The process to determine the weathering forms and the thickness of the decayed layer consists in the transformation of the pictorial images into digital images and in the employment of ultrasonic pulses (Fig.1).

With reference to the exposed surfaces, the quality of the image must allow to perceive the properties of the object. In digital image processing a black and white image (pictorial image) may be considered as a continuous dimensional function in two variable planes x and y able to supply a representative value of the luminosity for every pair of coordinates. This f(x,y) function is representative of a certain distribution of luminosity in a planar domain internally connected and without singularity. Each image pixel will contribute through a different level of grey with which it is associated, to the formation of a digital image, these individual spatial samples (pixels) are represented by a value (Lg) indicating the level of luminosity relative to an appropriate scale. As regards the tonal range associated to images processed in false colour, the 256 gradations allowed for each of the three basic colours used (red, blue and green), practically a limitless number of combinations. As fig 2 shows in schematic form, the grey levels histograms reflect both the restitution of light energy determined by the chromatic variations of the rock (fig.2) and the textural and structural properties of the stone (exfoliation, lamination, fossils, fissuring, graded bedding etc.). The stone decay, as degree, is showed in abscissa by the interval of grey levels which tend towards 0 increasing in width.

Considering the variations of luminosity recorded in a series of images of rock of different colour and composition as well as different states of conservation, and supplying histograms from freshly quarried rock to severely damaged stone, it is possible to make the following observations: a) the gradual move towards the start of the abscissa, or rather towards the dark shades of grey, of the intervals relative to images of fresh of weathered stone; b) the dispersion of luminosity levels due to the presence of structures of organic or inorganic origin; c) the increase of the dispersion of these levels accompanied by a wider interval of the grey levels in which are included those of severely weathered stone and those of the fresh one.

The ICAW technique can be applied to assess above all the deterioration degree of buildings materials and paints. In addition the ultrasonic measurements, through the indirect method, allowed to detect changes in physical conditions of the stone material and to calculate the depth of decayed layer with their laying and interrelations. The decay patterns which can be obtained in relation to the distance-time diagrams represent the buried structures. The surfaces on which the technique is applied are generally flat. However, during the processing of the time-distance diagrams (homeosurface or indirect method), it is considered that the irregularity of the damaged stone surface corresponds to different levels of light returned from different parts.

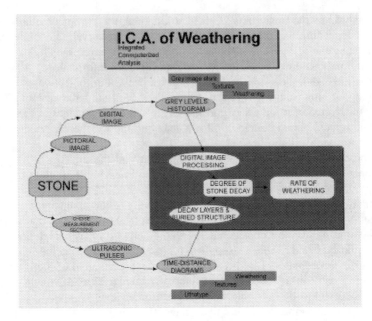

Fig. 1. ICAW technique: analytical approach to detect the rate of weathering (from F.Zezza 1996)

Therefore, the different grey intervals indicate the stone properties, the weathering forms and the state of conservation of the material. The intervals of grey levels content, interpreted as above and collected in different block of colour, outline as digital maps the weathering in an objective way.

Daily, monthly and seasonal data can be elaborated to produce digital images and maps of different kinds of substrates before and after treatment application, or simply to monitor the natural decay condition. Also, before and after treatment, the areal distribution of the decay patterns with the surface change forms can be detected;

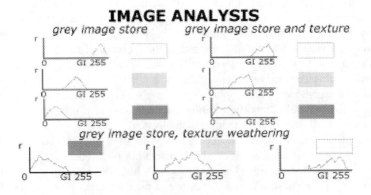

Fig. 2. The grey levels histograms allow to identify chromatic variations, textural characteristics and weathering degree of building material (from F.Zezza 1989)

therefore, in case of recovery treatments, using image analysis, it is possible to obtain a micro-morphological evaluation of the untreated and treated surfaces.

4   Weathering Damage Analysis

4.1   Assessment of the State of Conservation

In fig.3 is assessed the deterioration degree and the thickness of the weathered layer of the marble portal (Cathedral of San Nicola, Bari) built in XII century. For the ancient marbles the ultrasonic measurements show the overlap of different weathered layers as the reproduced example (fig.3), referred to the marble of the Temple of

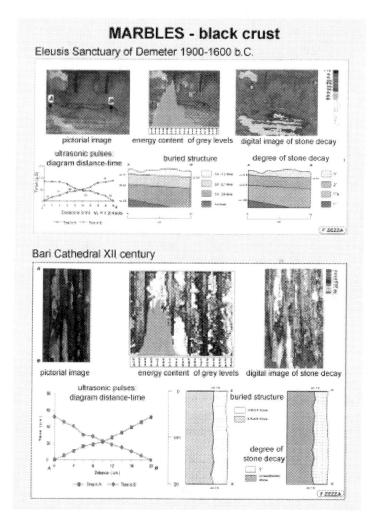

Fig. 3. Damage assessment determined by ICAW: qualitative and quantitative evaluation of the weathering (damage categories), from F.Zezza 1996

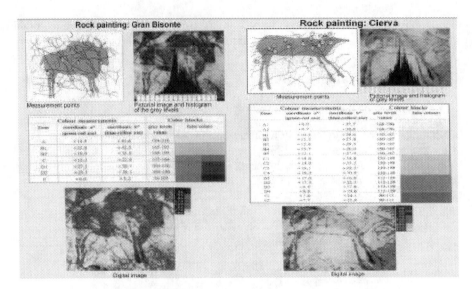

Fig. 4. Chromatic coordinates, grey levels histogram and digital image analysis (ICAW) used to determine the fading of 'Bisonte' and 'Cierva' paintings, Altamira Cave, Spain, (from F.Zezza 2002)

Eleusis dated between 1900-1600 B.C., indicates. The quantitative evaluation of stone decay degree depends by the damage indexes that express the rating of the weathering: their calculation is related to ultrasonic velocities which in turn mark the strength classification and the values of indexes as compactness, porosity and imbibitions of the building material (F.Zezza, 1996).

Stone decay degree and damage indexes reveal the overall need of preservation measures for stone monuments or individual stones structures.

The colorimetric measurements performed in the CIELAB system, collected in selected points of the paintings, can be converted into computerized maps. The technique, applied to determine the conservation state of the Palaeolithic paintings in Altamira Cave (Spain), refers to the surface extension of weathering. Colour changes due to chemical processes of dissolution, neoformation salts, biological and anthropogenic processes (F. Zezza, 2002), indicate a significant degree of weathering. Therefore, the determination of the colour parameters and their monitoring in time is extremely important to assess the state of conservation of the paintings.

The colorimetric determinations provide reproducible mathematical information that allows the verification, by comparative means, of the effects produced by the action of the natural and anthropogenic pollution, like the occurrence and the superficial distribution of black crusts. The extrapolation of punctual values into processed image involves the transformation of chromatic coordinates in the corresponding grey levels considering the values of the chromatic coordinates as a criterion for the definition of zones of distinct colour (fig.4). This method, which investigates the visible optical spectrum images, lends itself to detailed examination of the images in the near infrared spectrum.

4.2 Weathering Damage Time Monitoring

To be able to document the state of conservation in time is fundamental for monuments conservation practice and for the correlations concerning decay, anthropogenic interventions and environmental conditions. The assessment of these processes can be based on NDT techniques. The control of the evolution in time of decay processes or that of the effectiveness of the treatment is extremely important to define the plan of maintenance interventions or to improve the environmental conditions.

The ICAW methodology, basing on its non invasive approach and on its logistic repeatability, allows controlling the evolution in time of the decay processes. The fig. 5 reproduces, as examples, the results of some comparative analysis regarding the fading which affects the paintings of the Altamira Cave.

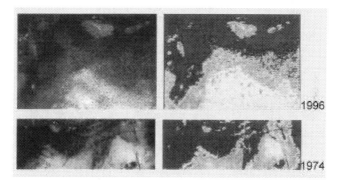

Fig. 5. 'Cabajo' painting of Altamira Cave (Spain). Fading monitoring in time by digital images collected on 1974 (bottom) and 1996 (top), from F.Zezza 2002.

The same ICAW methodology can be suitable to evaluate the threshold that indicates the risk to lose a painting due to fading as the fig.6 related to the paintings of the Grotta dei Cervi (Badisco, Italy) shows. Therefore the computerized analysis of the damage can be positively employed to plan the maintenance interventions.

4.3 Recovery Treatments Monitoring

Conservative interventions. The comparison of digital images elaborated before and after treatment application enables the evaluation of the effectiveness in time. For example, the computerized mapping utilized for the control of the conservative treatments effectiveness carried out for the 'Basilica of San Nicola' in Bari, Italy (fig.7), highlighted the existence of black crusts before the intervention (areas in blue, fig.7a, June 1986). The church portal digital image after treatment showed the total removal of black crusts (fig.7b). After six years the digital image has been able to reveal the reappearance of new weathering forms (areas in blue and dark green, fig.7c).

In particular, the digital images revealed a worsening of marble properties with the reappearance of black crusts and the reopening of cemented fractures, as well as the intercrystallyne decohesion.

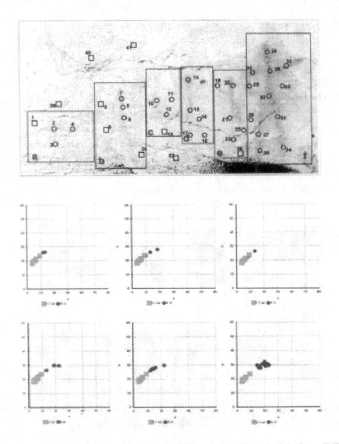

Fig. 6. Fading threshold evaluation for Grotta dei Cervi, (Badisco, Italy), from F.Zezza 2003

Fig. 7. Assessment of treatment by ICAW technique: monitoring in time of the Basilica of Bari, Italy. State of conservation: before treatment (8a, 1986), after treatment (8b, 1986) and after 6 years from treatment (8c, 1992,) from F.Zezza 1996.

Laser cleaning control. The analytical techniques currently used to evaluate the laser cleaning effects are based on stereomicroscopic and polarizing observations, XRD analysis, FTIR and SEM-EDAX analyses, artificial ageing tests and further colorimetric measurements. For some monuments and particularly for those of great esteem to control the laser cleaning effects it exists objectively the difficulty to collect the stone material directly by the exposed surfaces or to have at disposal samples of size suitable to carry out the wide spectrum of the tests which are useful to validity of the reached results.

To supply the data concerning the structural properties of the stone materials, the weathering and the micro-morphology of the surfaces and, in the specific case, the effects of the laser cleaning, the non-destructive computerized analysis can be applied. To assess the results of the laser cleaning concerning the preliminary application performed on samples of Penthelic marble utilized for the Blocks of the Parthenon West

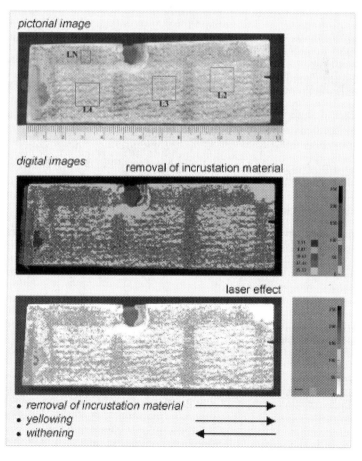

Fig. 8. Digital image analysis: chromatic variations of a Penthelic marble sample, after removal of incrustation material, treated with different infrared (IR) and ultraviolet (UV) radiation combination at relatively low energy fluencies

Frieze, the author has developed, in collaboration with the Department of Surface Conservation of the Monument of YSMA, under the auspices of the Committee for the Conservation of the Acropolis Monument, some demonstrative applications of the ICAW technique.

The tests regarded a fragment of a Penthelic marble slab which, within the experimental stage, was also utilized for the quantitative and qualitative tests to evaluate the effects of the preliminary applications of the cleaning methods above mentioned initially performed on newer marble additions (dating to the 1960's) from the West Frieze.

Three cleaned areas (L2, L3, L4, fig.8) have been interested by a simultaneous action of two discrete laser – based removal mechanism, characterized by different parameters as: i) the infrared (IR) and ultraviolet (UV) radiation combination at relatively low energy fluencies, ii) the number of pulses and iii) energy density (P.Pouli, V. Zafiropulos, 2003). The digital images analysis regarding the effects of removal of the incrustations (fig.8) clearly shows that the selected area L3 is located between two opposite conditions, the former (area L4) characterized by lower removal of crust with whitening effects, the latter (area L2) with higher removal of crust and yellowing effects.

On the other hand, the digital image analysis has been focused on the control performed accordingly to the following criteria selected within the laser cleaning techniques: i) to allow the widest possible preservation of the noble patina which preserves details of the relief; ii) do not cause direct or indirect damage to the substrata; iii) do not generate by –products; iiii) to consider the chemical and mineralogical structure of the marble, the state of decay as well as the stratigraphy of the incrustation.

As Tab.1 shows, different aspects of the laser cleaning method have been considered for the elaboration of the computerized images of the treated surfaces.

Table 1. Laser cleaning effects on treated surfaces

A. *Removal of crusts*	1) chromatic variations
	2) homogeneity of the treated surface
	3) preservation of the noble patina
B. *Evaluation of the aggressiveness*	1) fissuring
	2) decohesion
	3) loss of crystals
	4) loss of material
	5) cratering
	6) by-products
C. *Roughness*	1) deviation of the profile by mean line

The degree and the efficiency of the laser cleaning method (figg.9-10) have been tested taking into account the cases (E. Papakonstantinou, 2003) evaluating the points A, B and C outlined in Tab.1:

- loose deposits (of soot and dirt particles) on the marble substratum
- black crusts (homogeneous compact crust and dendritic crust) on the marble surface
- black crusts on the monochromatic surface layer (beige layer)
- black crusts on the monochromatic surface layers (orange-brown layer with beige layer traces)

Fig. 9. Parthenon West Frieze Block – BIII

Fig. 10. Laser cleaning of the West Frieze Block - BVIII

82   F. Zezza

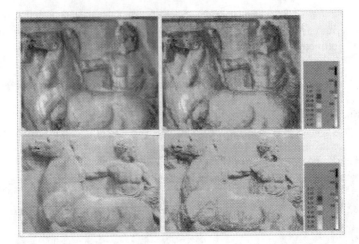

Fig. 11. Pictorial and digital images of the West Frieze - Block III before and after laser cleaning treatment

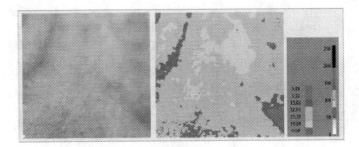

Fig. 12.

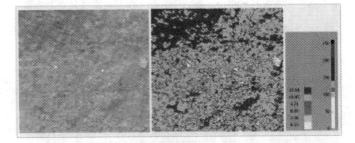

Fig. 13. Laser cleaning control: pictorial and digital images showing crystals broken (fig.12, yellow and beige colour) and cratering (fig.13, yellow and beige colour); in the last case the micro-morphology of the surface can appear also as consequence of a coalescence of laser spots

The comparisons of the pictorial and digital images certificate the homogeneity of the treatment which has preserved the monochromatic surface layers, verifying the good effectiveness of the cleaning process (fig.11). The black crusts have been removed as well as the loose deposits. The homogeneity of the orange colour indicates that the block surface has not suffered, in this case, chromatic variations, indicating the good cleaning result obtained by operators. The presence of the yellow colour is linked with washed zones during the exposition of the marble to the weathering and the blue-red colour indicates traces of monochromatic layers or primary and secondary structural characteristics (i.e. veins, cracks) of the Penthelic marble.

Preliminary tests can allow improving the treatment. Further details of digital image analysis areas, enlarged 22x (fig.12) and 8x (fig.13), indicate the possibility to avoid loss of material induced by crystal broken or cratering. By this point of view, the digital image analysis constitutes a control on-line of the laser cleaned objects.

5 Conclusion

ICAW image analysis improves the quality and the quantity of cultural heritage documentation and appears nowadays a new goal to safeguard monuments and to document the state of conservation.

The technique offers the possibility to avoid invasive sampling, often non representative of the entire monuments surface studied, and the possibility of a constant time monitoring remotely sensed, low demanding in term of cost and logistic efforts. ICAW found many application in several EC projects concerning the conservation of monuments and recovery treatment monitoring, from 1989 up to now, concerning stone, paints and sculptures, and suggests the best conservation approach for museums pieces.

These kinds of knowledge within an efficient exchange and sharing of know-how in the areas of cultural heritage, represent one of the next future scientific challenges, in an integrated collaboration operating system.

References

1. Adriaens, A.: COST Action G8: Non-destructive analysis and testing of museum objects. In: Proc. of COST Action G8 Workshop, Benefits of non-desctructive analytical techniques for conservation, January 8, pp. 5–8 (2004)
2. Borg, C.: Documentation in relation to non-destructive analysis in conservation. In: Proc. of COST Action G8 Workshop, Benefits of non-desctructive analytical techniques for conservation, January 8, pp. 13–19 (2004)
3. Ioannidis, M.: 3d reconstruction and e-documentation in cultural heritage: a challenge for standardization. In: Proc. of the ITECOM European Conf. 'Innovative technologies and materials for the protection of Cultural Heritage. Industry, Research, Education: European Acts and Perspectives, Athens, Greece, December 16-17, pp. 73–76 (2003)
4. Mallouchou-Tufano, F., Alexopoulus, Y.: The documentation of the Acropolis restoration works and the use of information technology. In: Gangemi (ed.) Quad. ARCo Restoration of the Athenian Acropolis (1975-2003), Roma, pp. 176–180 (2003)

5. Papakonstantinou, E.: The conservation of the West Frieze of the Parthenon. In: Gangemi (ed.) Quad. ARCo Restoration of the Athenian Acropolis (1975-2003), Roma, pp. 172–175 (2003)
6. Pouli, P., Zafiropulos, V.: Combination of ultraviolet and infrared laser pulses for sculpture cleaning: the application of this innovative methodology on the surface of the Acropolis monuments and sculptures. In: Papakonstantinou et al (2002)
7. Zezza, F.: Computerized analysis of stone decay material. In: Proc. of the 1st International Symposium for the Conservation of Monuments in the Mediterranean Basin, Bari, Italy, June 7-10, pp. 163–184 (1989)
8. Zezza, F.: Integrated Computerized Analysis of Weathering. Perfecting and experimentation on Pilot Monuments damaged by Aerosol and Pollution. In: Proc. of the EC Workshop 'Non Destructive Testing to evaluate damage due to the environmental effects on historic monuments, Trieste, February 15-17, paper 3 (1996)
9. Zezza, F.: Decay patterns of weathered stones in marine environment. In: Proc. of Origin, Mechanisms & Effects of Salts on Degradation of Monuments in Marine and Continental Environments, Bari, pp. 99–130 (1996)
10. Zezza, F.: Non destructive technique for the assessment of the deterioration process of prehistoric rock art in karstic caves: the paleolithic paintings of Altamira (Spain). In: Galan, E., Zezza, F. (eds.) Protetcion and conservation on the Cultural Heritage of the Mediterranean Cities, Swetz & Zeitlinger, Lisse, pp. 377–388 (2002)
11. Zezza, F.: La Grotta dei Cervi sul Canale d'Otranto. In: Capone (ed.) L'ambiente carsico ipogeo e lo stato di conservazione delle pitture parietali, Lecce, pp. 1–103 (2003)
12. Zezza, F.: Balance and perspectives of research line to control the contaminated substrates. In: Proc. of the 7th International Symposiun on the Conservation of Monuments in the Mediterranean Basin, Orleans, France, June 6-9, pp. XIV–XXVI (2007)

Photogrammetric Measurement of the Classic Marathon Course

Ino Papageorgaki, Sevi Tapinaki, Andreas Georgopoulos, and Charalambos Ioannidis

Laboratory of Photogrammetry, National Technical University of Athens, Greece
inw20@hotmail.com, sevi@survey.ntua.gr, drag@central.ntua.gr,
cioannid@survey.ntua.gr

Abstract. In this paper an alternative method for measuring the Classic Marathon Course using photogrammetric methodology is presented and examined. The course is surveyed in stereoscopic environment and therefore the measurement is performed directly in 3D space. The produced elevation data after the processing procedure are presented in the section plan at a scale of 1:5.000. The Digital Surface Model, with a step of 5m, and the orthophotomap at a scale 1:2.000 of a corridor area, with width of 100m on either side of the course represents an additional product of the photogrammetric method. At the end, in this thesis the photogrammetric methodology is being assessed and evaluated, but also it is being compared with the conventional method of the calibrated bicycle and finally are conclusions drawn and proposals are attempted.

Keywords: Orthophotography, Photogrammetric Measurement, GPS, Cultural Heritage.

1 Introduction

One of the more important events of modern Olympic Games is the Marathon Run, which is run on a course, usually outside the main stadium, with a total length of 42.195 m. This event was included in the Olympic program since the first modern Olympics in 1896 in recollection of the heroic achievement of the warrior - messenger who first announced to the Athenians the victory of the Greeks in the battle of Marathon in 490 B.C. The Classic Marathon Course (Fig. 1) is the route from Marathon, Attica up to the Panathinaikon stadium (Fig. 2) and it measures 42.195m. This is also the distance that marathon runners cover in the event of the Marathon Run in all modern Olympic Games, but also in all other national or international Marathon Runs. Although the marathon run was one of the first modern Olympic Games events its length was not strictly determined until 1924. In 1896, Spyros Louis, the first Gold medal winner ran 40.000m (http://www.sport.gr/default.asp?pid=52&aid=51139). Ten years later, the runners who took part in the marathon run of the "Half" Olympiad) in Athens in 1906, ran 41.860m. In 1908, in the Olympic Games of London the length changed to 42.195m so that the runners would pass in front of the Royal Palaces. It took another 16 years before the differentiations of the distance of the marathon run stopped. The length was officially decided to be 42.195m in the Olympic Games of Paris in 1924 (http://www.sport.gr/default.asp?pid=52&aid=17305).

M. Ioannides (Ed.): EuroMed 2010, LNCS 6436, pp. 85–98, 2010.
© Springer-Verlag Berlin Heidelberg 2010

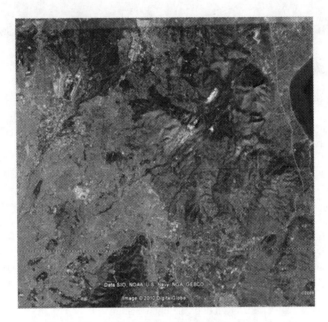

Fig. 1. The Classic Marathon Course

Fig. 2. The Panathinaikon Satdium (Kallimarmaro) in Athens

For the validation of a record time, the length of a course must be measured with certain accuracy. This of course is the case not only for Marathon runs, but for all other events, be it inside or outside the track of a stadium. Over the time widely accepted rules have been developed, in order to ensure the validation both of the organized event and the record times of the winners. As of 1.1.2004 a commonly accepted regulation for the road race courses out of stadium is in effect, compiled by the IAAF (World Federation of Track and Field) and the AIMS (World Union of of Street Runs). This regulation, among other issues, dictates how a street course should be measured, in order to ensure that the athletes will run at least the predetermined length.

Over the years several methods for measuring street course have been proposed, tested and applied. Topographic methods, using all sorts of measuring techniques (staves, steel tapes, EDM's etc) have been used in the Seoul Olympics (Seoul Olympic Organizing Committee, 1988). Other efforts include the application of a DGPS system (Gordon, 2005), the use of a terrestrial Laser scanner (Tsakiri et al, 2004), measuring the distance on a map and odometers adapted on cars. However the only method nowadays recognized as valid by the IAAF/AIMS (IAAF, 2004) for measuring a street course, is that of the calibrated bicycle.

In the present paper an alternative method for measuring the length of the Classic Marathon Course using photogrammetric methodology is described and assessed. The basic argument for using photogrammetry in the measurement of a Marathon Course is based on the fact that the photogrammetric procedure for length measurement can be as effective as the conventional method of the calibrated bicycle. However, careful selection of the suitable photogrammetric method should be carried out, in order to achieve the required result, mainly in terms of accuracy and cost. Photogrammetric methods are actually non-contact methods and in this way tedious fieldwork may be minimized.

2 The Method of the Calibrated Bicycle

2.1 Requirements and Specifications of IAAF/AIMS

Every measurement technique proposed for measuring road courses should comply by the requirements and specifications set by IAAF, independently of the methodology employed.

These specifications are briefly as follows:

- The distance of the Marathon Course should be between 42.195m and 42.237m, that is +0.1% overshooting from the usual distance and only additive.
- The distance should be measured with precision better than a part in the 1000 (0.1%). This means that the whole distance should be measures with an ambiguity of 42 m over the whole length.
- The measured course should follow the ideal path which the athletes will decide to run or walk.
- If the calibrated bicycle method is to be used, the bicycles should be calibrated before and after the process of measurement.
- The process of measurement should be applied twice and the results of these two independent measurements should not differ more than 0.8%. Otherwise a third measurement should be carried out.
- The shortest possible route is defined as the one which runs 0.30m away from the curb, or the end of road surface when a curb does not exist. If constructions are present at the side of the road, such as walls, the shortest possible route should be considered a path 0.61m away from them.

2.2 Analysis of the Conventional Method

The basic idea of the conventional method of measurement is to determine the ratio of the course length covered by a complete revolution of the bicycle wheel and then to count the number of revolutions necessary to cover the whole course. The calibration of this system consists of determining the "bicycle constant" by determining the number of wheel revolutions needed to cover a length known with sufficient accuracy. The method is simple and direct, but a lot of important details are involved and certain steps should be followed so that it results to an acceptable and complete measurement of a course (IAAF, 2004).

For the determination of the length of the Marathon course the line of departure, the finishing line and the shortest possible route should be first of all established and fixed. The final product with the results of the described processes is a document which includes a map of the entire marathon course and all characteristics of the route.

For the choice and the measurement of the calibration length several considerations should be taken into account. Firstly a straight and level part of a paved road should be chosen as the calibration field. It should be approximately 300-500m in length and it is desired not to have any parked vehicles. Secondly, the length of the calibration field should be accurately measured using a steel tape with maximum length of 30m, with practically no change of length at 20°C. The measurement should be executed twice and if the difference is more than 0.8%, a third measurement is repeated. The bicycle used for the course measurement is fitted with a special device called Jones counter (Fig. 3). It actually converts the wheel revolutions to a five or six digit number, which, after careful calibration, provides the bicycle constant. For the calibration of the bicycle the cyclist should cover the calibration field, four times before and four times after the measurement, in both directions.

The bicycle constant is the mean of the four values from the four calibration runs, divided by the calibration distance (in km). The result is the number of units of Jones

Fig. 3. Various types of Jones Counters

Counter per kilometer, which is further multiplied by 1.001, the factor SCPV (short course prevention value), in order to ensure that the final course measurement result is definitely not less (by 0.001) than the desired distance. This results to a total distance for the Marathon course between the values 42.195m 42.237m. In this way, runners are prevented from covering a distance shorter than 42.195m.

The actual measurement of the road race course is determined by the measurement of the shortest possible route (SPR). The shortest possible route is theoretically determined with clarity and precision following the IAAF/AIMS specifications. The determination of road race course in this way ensures that all runners will run at least the predefined distance of the road race course. The shortest possible route in various road configurations is presented Fig. 4.

After the actual course length measurement, the bicycle calibration process is repeated. The objective of this re-calibration after the measurement is to make sure that no change in the bicycle constant has occurred. The re-calibration of the bicycle is essential to be carried out immediately after the actual measurements.

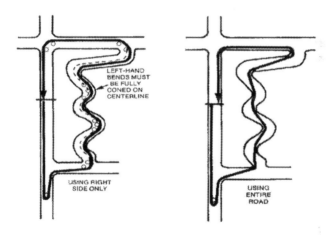

Fig. 4. The SPR in various cases

To calculate the length of the road race course, the *Constant for the Day* must be determined first. This is the average of the two values resulting from the two calibrations. Then the actual course is run by the bicycle, following of course the shortest possible route, and the total number of counts is recorded. This value is then divided by the constant for the day. The result obtained is the length of the road race course. If the measurements last more than one day, the final lengths of each day are added. The measurement process described above should be applied twice, where the second time serves for checking. In the event that a few meters are either surplus or missing from the final result, adequate adaptations are made using simple steel tape measurements, usually by appropriately shifting the start or finishing line. The whole measurement process, as described above, and for it to be officially recognized, should be properly documented (Fig. 5). The documentation of the measurement involves the production of a map of the course, which contains all necessary details used for the measurement process.

90 I. Papageorgaki et al.

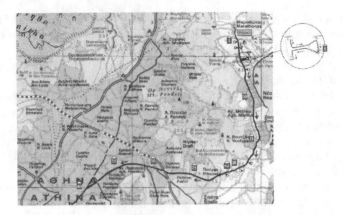

Fig. 5. General map of the Classic Marathon Course measurement documentation

The documentation must be sufficient to allow the course to be checked if a re-measurement is for any reason required, e.g. after a world best performance has been recorded. In the documentation folder all necessary details of the road race course should be included, which are adequate for the race director to re-establish the course even after major construction works on the roads.

3 Photogrammetric Methodology

Photogrammetry is the art, science and technique for the acquisition of reliable metric information on natural objects and the environment, via processes of recording, measuring and interpreting, photographic images, electromagnetic radiation recordings and other phenomena (McGlone, 2004). The basic idea for the use of photogrammetry in the measurement of the Marathon course is based on the fact that photogrammetric measurements could perhaps be as effective as the conventional method of the calibrated bicycle, which is normally used for the measurement of road race courses. It is proposed that photogrammetric methodology should be used to enhance, and not necessarily to replace, the existing methods, especially in cases of long distances as a Marathon Course.

Before the application of any photogrammetric methodology, several considerations are necessary, concerning the data characteristics and the various parameters of the methods that will be used in order to achieve the required objective. The small scale of aerial images used by Photogrammetry, enables the measurement of the whole course, contrary to the conventional surveying methods, i.e. use of total stations or terrestrial scanners, which are unable to cover of whole object at once. Although photogrammetry may be somewhat dependent on topographic measurements, the length of an object may be determined either stereoscopically, by directly measuring in the 3D model, or monoscopically, by measuring on an orthogonal projection (i.e. orthophotograph) and indirectly taking into account the elevation via the existing DTM (Fig. 6). An orthophotograph is a photographic picture that has been reduced differentially to an orthogonal projection, which has no perspective deformations.

Its main advantage is the standard scale, similar to a conventional map, it contains however all qualitative information of a photographic image. For the production of an orthophotograph it is necessary to have oriented images and a sufficient description of the relief.

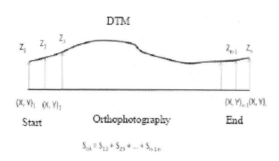

Fig. 6. Monoscopic measurement of course length

Finally the calculation of the length is given by the equation:

$$D = \sqrt{\Delta X^2 + \Delta Y^2 + \Delta Z^2} \qquad (1)$$

Where X, Y, Z are the three-dimensional coordinates of the vertices.

4   Implementation and Results

The proposed photogrammetric methodology for the measurement of Classic Marathon Course includes five main stages:

Determination, acquisition and preparation of the necessary data: First of all aerial photographs of suitable scale are required, imaging the whole course. A total of 34 aerial photographs (diapositives) of scale 1:15.000 and taken in 2005 were obtained from the Hellenic Cadastral and Mapping Organization. The aerial camera used was ZEISS RMK TOP 15 with focal length 153,120mm, format 230x230mm and eight fiducial marks (Fig. 7). The available scale of aerial photographs was considered suitable in order to ensure the specified accuracy for the measurement of Classic Marathon Course. The initial coloured aerial photographs were scanned with Photoscan PS1 by Z/I, a digital photogrammetric scanner of large accuracy, with spatial resolution, i.e. pixel size, 21μm. In this way the recognition of objects larger than 0,15m on the digital images is possible.

Photogrammetric processing: All necessary photogrammetric processing, such as interior and exterior orientation, stereoscopic observations and plotting, were carried out with the digital photogrammetric station PHOTOMOD v.4.4 by Racurs. All 34 images with 60% overlap were imported in the digital photogrammetric workstation

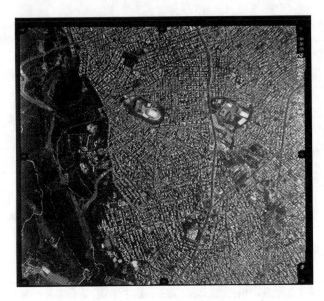

Fig. 7. One of the coloured aerial photographs

and created a block of twelve strips (ten strips of two images each, one of nine and one of six images) with 30% side overlap. The parameters of the interior orientation were given by the calibration report accompanying the aerial photographs.

For the exterior orientation of the images a standard bundle adjustment was applied. For this process control points are essential, as they are necessary to connect the block of images with the geodetic reference system. Control points materialize the reference system of the object and contribute to the absolute orientation of models. The position of the control points influences considerably the course of photogrammetric processing as well as the quality of the final products. The final positions of the control points were determined with stereoscopic observation of the stereo models in order to fulfil the following conditions:

- Uniform distribution of control points, so that control points are situated along the perimeter of the region of interest and to establish strong geometry of the system.
- Ensure that control points exist at least every five stereo models (approximately 10km),
- Control points should be visible and recognizable on the images,
- Ensure high contrast between the point and the surrounding environment,
- If control points are visible in more than two images, economy is accomplished,
- Control points must be in the overlapping part of the images
- Control points should be easily visited and ensure open horizon vision, because it is essential that no obstacles exist (buildings, bridges, trees, antennas etc.) that would interrupt the reception of the satellite signal during the GPS measurements.

The measurement and determination of geodetic coordinates of control points was executed with the use of GPS measurements. 34 points were measured in total, 17 of which were used as control points for the bundle adjustment of the triangulation and the rest were reserved as check points (Fig. 8). Static differential measurements were used and each base less than 8 km was measured for 20 minutes, in such a way the accuracy of every measurement was estimated at 0,06m. The block of all images with the distribution of points, after bundle adjustment, is shown in Figure 9.

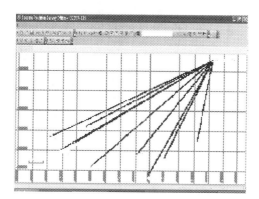

Fig. 8. Screenshot of the computation of several measured bases with GPS

Three-dimensional surveying of Classic Marathon Course using stereoscopic observation: The whole procedure of mapping the course was carried out using the stereoscopic environment of PHOTOMOD, according to the IAAF/AIMS specifications (IAAF 2004). Utmost attention was paid so that the shortest possible route was followed by the floating mark. Whenever possible large straight lines were used (up to 200m), while in cases where circular arcs were needed, the distance between successive vertices was reduced to approximately 20m. The result of the above process was a 3D polyline that is composed of individual 3D lines and constitutes the total classic Marathon course, as determined by the operator. Drawing of the shortest possible route is a difficult process for individuals that come in contact with this task for the first time and have no experience in this whatsoever. Hence, the final course mapped was also examined and approved by an IAAF certified race course measurer.

Measurement of the length directly in 3D space: For measuring the mapped course the following procedure was applied. The 3D polyline was exported to dxf format for the measurement to be carried out in a CAD program. The measurement of the total length of the Classic Marathon Course was carried out within the AutoCAD 3D® environment. Each individual line was measured using the appropriate CAD tools and the total length of the course was calculated by simply adding all these lengths together. The three dimensional line ensures that the measured length corresponds to the real length of the course.

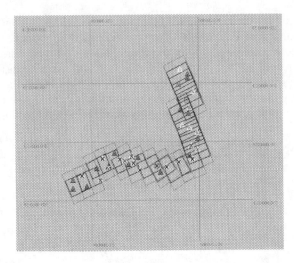

Fig. 9. The block of images with the distribution of points

Evaluation of methodology and results. The photogrammetric methodology is thoroughly evaluated, through the evaluation of the measurement results and the final products as far as effectiveness, accuracy, required time and cost are concerned.

Fig. 10. Documented measurements of the 10th kilometer. (Grall, 2008)

For this purpose the length resulting from the photogrammetric method was compared with the length between the characteristic points which correspond to each kilometre of the course, as documented in the relevant Documentation Folder. The locations of these points are well known and their exact position is recorded both by coloured photos and with accurate measurements, which took place at the same time as the measurement of course with the calibrated bicycle (Fig. 10).

Table 1. Distance check between certain kilometres

Calibrated Bicycle		Photogrammetric Measurement	
Distance from Start (km)	Distance between (m)	Distance between (m)	Distance from Start (m)
4	4.000,00	3.819,83	3.819,83
5	1.000,00	1.180,43	5.000,27
8	3.000,00	3.147,70	8.147,96
12	4.000,00	3.852,11	12.000,07
18	6.000,00	6.004,02	18.004,09
25	7.000,00	7.047,24	25.051,33
28	3.000,00	2.978,14	28.029,46
29	1.000,00	1.045,56	29.075,02
30	1.000,00	1.000,90	30.075,92
35	5.000,00	4.966,95	35.042,87
39	4.000,00	3.978,39	39.021,27
42,195 km	3.195,00	3.208,43	**42.229,69**

Difference between the two methods = 34,69 m (0.08%)

Table 1 shows that, for certain parts of the course, the difference between the distance that was measured with the photogrammetric method and the one that results from the conventional method could be as high as 148m, but the total difference is only 34,69m. This large difference occurs between the 5th and the 8th kilometre, where from the fifth up to the sixth kilometre the athletes are obliged to follow a circular course around the Marathon Tomb, commemorating the battle in 460B.C. This is, obviously, due to the fact that the definition of the shortest possible route (SPR) along an arc demands the use of more points (vertices), while for the large straight lines two points are enough, thus ensuring smaller discrepancies. Although, the use of large straight parts ensures more accurate length measurement, part of the elevation information is lost. However, this does not influence the resulting length for small distances.

The average length from vertex to vertex of the 3D polyline, as mapped within the digital photogrammetric workstation environment, is approximately 50m. The error corresponding to the measurement of each part is estimated to 25 mm. Also, the photogrammetric processing propagates errors to each point determined photogrammetrically. For the determination of the standard deviations σ_x, σ_y, σ_z of the measurements of the coordinates of each vertex of the 3D polyline, with the photogrammetric process, four check points were measured 20 times each in stereoscopic mode. The average of the residuals of each coordinate from the measured ones with the GPS, determines the requested standard deviations: $\sigma_x =\pm 0,119m$, $\sigma_y =\pm 0,112m$ $\sigma_z =\pm 0,179m$. The mathematical relation which was used for the calculation of the total error of the measured distance D with vertices of known coordinates (X, Y, Z) in the reference system (GGRS' 87) and the error of the determination of each coordinate (σ_{xi}, σ_{yi}, σ_{zi}) with the above method is:

$$\sigma^2{}_{D_{ij}} = \sigma^2{}_{xj}(\frac{x_j - x_i}{D_{ij}})^2 + \sigma^2{}_{xi}(\frac{x_j - x_i}{D_{ij}})^2 + \sigma^2{}_{yj}(\frac{y_j - y_i}{D_{ij}})^2 + \sigma^2{}_{yi}(\frac{y_j - y_i}{D_{ij}})^2 +$$

$$\sigma^2{}_{zj}(\frac{z_j - z_i}{D_{ij}})^2 + \sigma^2{}_{zi}(\frac{z_j - z_i}{D_{ij}})^2$$

(2)

Where $D = \sqrt{(\Delta x^2 + \Delta y^2 + \Delta H^2)}$ and $\sigma_{xi} = 0,119m$, $\sigma_{yi} = 0,112m$, $\sigma_{zi} = 0,179m$.

$$\sigma^2{}_D = \Sigma\sigma^2{}_{D_{ij}} \text{ and } \sigma_D = \pm\sqrt{\sigma^2{}_D}$$

$$\sigma_D = \pm 4,69m$$

On the whole, the distance was calculated 42.229 m ± 4,69m. This deviation is better than 0,1% required by the IAAF regulations (42.216m±21m). It is also observed that the larger error is in the determination of the Z coordinate. This was expected since during stereoscopic observation the step of the floating point movement along Z axis is approximately 0,15m, consequently each surface was approached with this uncertainty.

5 Conclusions

The recent technological developments have definitely affected all related disciplines. Especially in the case of digital photogrammetry combined with the contemporary aerial photography progress, the ideal conditions have been created for the production of exceptionally highly accurate base maps, or indeed documents, either in vector or in raster format. With the use of photogrammetric methodology the measurement of any size of object is possible. In cases of large areas or objects the application of conventional survey measurement methods is considered inefficient. On the contrary with photogrammetry where the scales of aerial photographs or satellite images are small, without affecting the final accuracy, raster products with metric attributes may be easily produced.

It has been shown that digital photogrammetric methodology may be a sound alternative to classical measuring techniques, as far as road race course measurement tasks is concerned. Firstly in terms of accuracy, the use of relatively small scale (1:15.000) aerial images with a medium scanning resolution (21μm pixel size) is more than adequate to ensure stereoscopic measurements within the IAAF regulations, both as far as the absolute accuracy of each measurement is concerned, but also for determining the Shortest Possible Route. The use of simple GPS measurements for the control points is fast -only 20 minutes measuring time for each base- accurate -accuracy of a few centimetres is more than enough for such an application- and, of course, it is simpler than any conventional survey technique.

Contemporary Digital Photogrammetric Workstations, as indeed the one used in this project (PHOTOMOD v. 4.4), are generally easy to learn and provide all necessary computational tools for adjusting the photogrammetric networks, thus ensuring the required accuracy and reliability in the results. The conventional method for the Classic Marathon Course measurement requires that the length of the course is never measured less than 42.195m and never greater than 42.237m or otherwise

42.195m+42m. That could equivalently be expressed as 42.216m±21m and in this form it may be compared with the result of the photogrammetric process which is 42.229 m ±4,7m. It may be concluded that in terms of accuracy, the result of the photogrammetric methodology, as implemented in this project, presents a small deviation and the final result is acceptable and within the IAAF regulations.

In terms of time and related cost, photogrammetric methodology is definitely more demanding. Usually conventional official measurers work voluntarily, hence their cost is minimal. The full Marathon Race Course measurement procedure lasts for about two days, including bicycle calibration. On the contrary, aerial photo acquisition, preparation for GCPs measurement, GPS measurements, photogrammetric adjustments and stereo mapping take longer and demand more cost. Hence, as set out at the beginning, photogrammetry is not proposed to replace conventional methodology for the task, if the course measurement is needed once.

The benefits, however, are becoming obvious if the course should be measured repeatedly, or if there are slight alterations to the course and a re-measure is desperately needed. Moreover, it is possible to have a 3D visualization of the course, in order to use it for any kind of simulations. The results of this research, such as the three dimensional data of the surroundings of the whole course could be used as the background for the development of a three dimensional system, which will be targeted to athletes and trainers and will provide a 3D tour of the race course and virtual training. The Classic Marathon Course is considered to be a very difficult course because of the elevation differences. With this system the runners participating to the race will have the opportunity to study the course wherever they are. Alternatively, the 3D visualization of the course could be projected with special monitors in front of exercise treadmills. The runners, during training, will watch in real time the landscape variations of the Classic Marathon Course.

Acknowledgements

We would like to thank Mr. George Doussis, for the very useful information and data he provided, the detailed description of the conventional method of measurement of Marathon courses and the time that he devoted to us. Mr. George Doussis is an active amateur runner and trainer. He participated in the organisation and measurement of several courses during the Olympic Games of Athens, among them the Classic Marathon Course.

References

1. Doussis, G.: The "unmeasured" courses (May 2007),
   http://www.runningnews.gr/?id=2821 (accessed April 5, 2007)
2. Free Encyclopedia,
   http://el.wikipedia.org/wiki/M••••••••#.CE.99.CF.83.CF.84.
   CE.BF.CF.81.CE.AF.CE.B1 (accessed September 11, 2009)
3. Ioannidis, C.: Photogrammetry II. Lecture Notes. National Technical University of Athens, Athens (2006) (in Greek)

98   I. Papageorgaki et al.

4. Gordon, S.: Course Measurement (February 2005),
   http://www.runscore.com/coursemeasurement/Articles/
   Spac%20Meas.pdf (accessed 06/04/2009)
5. Grall, J.-M.: Dossier de Measurage Athens Classic Marathon (November 2008)
6. IAAF (International Association of Athletics Federations) 2004, The Measurement Of RoadRace Courses, second edition (updated 2008)
7. Kraus, K.: Photogrammetry, Technical Chamber of Greece, 2nd edn., Athens, vol. 1, p. 361 (2003) (in Greek) ISBN 960-7018-90-7
8. Racurs, PhotoMod 4.4 User Manual, Moscow, Russia (2007)
9. Seoul Olympic Organizing Committee, Marathon / Race Walks Courses Study and Measurement, Seoul, p. 231 (1998)
10. The variation of Marathon course (27/04/2008),
    http://www.sport.gr/default.asp?pid=52&aid=17305
    (accessed 2/11/2009)
11. The distance of Marathon course (04/11/2009),
    http://www.sport.gr/default.asp?pid=52&aid=51139
    (accessed 05/11/2009)
12. Tsakiri, M., Stathas, D., Arabatzi, O.: Advanced Surveying Techniques for Measuring the Marathon Course. In: Proc. of FIG Working Week 2004, Athens, Greece, May 22-27 (2004)

Analysis of Lacunae and Retouching Areas in Panel Paintings Using Landscape Metrics

Frederico Henriques[1] and Alexandre Gonçalves[2]

[1] Escola das Artes / CITAR, Universidade Católica Portuguesa, Porto, Portugal
[2] Dep. Civil Eng. & Arch. / ICIST, Inst. Sup. Técnico, Tech. Univ. Lisbon, Lisboa, Portugal
frederico.painting.conservator@gmail.com, alexg@civil.ist.utl.pt

Abstract. This paper explores a novel use of Geographic Information Systems and Landscape Metrics in the characterization of lacunae and retouching areas on panel paintings. The aim is to understand some spatial properties of original and non-original areas and contribute to the documentation of conservation and restoration treatments with valuable information. The study uses an orthophoto of the analysed artwork in a GIS program to produce polygons with a direct visual interpretation, corresponding to the major colour zones, the lacunae and the retouching areas. Over these areas landscape metrics are applied and interpreted. The result is a useful set of values describing spatial properties and relations between lacunae, retouching areas and the unaffected zones in the painting. These quantified parameters extend the traditional qualitative diagnosis reports on the state of conservation of artworks and contribute to support the evaluation of conservation and restoration projects.

Keywords: Painting, conservation and restoration, lacunae, retouching, GIS, landscape metrics.

1 Introduction

1.1 General Introduction

The interpretation of the state of conservation of artworks is an issue in conservation and restoration. Its documentation is generally made by empirical observations, sometimes supported by analytical methods that help to qualify and characterize the major pathologies [1][2]. It is thus possible to classify and quantify important items in the diagnosis process, such as tears in linen paintings [3], or the area of lacunae, overpaints, detachments, cracks and other detectable features in the artwork surface.

However, there are other spatial properties in the distribution of pathologies that might be interesting to evaluate the complexity and feasibility of an intervention in the artwork. The production of these properties requires the application of spatial analytical methodologies, such as the evaluation through Landscape Metrics, suggested and described in this work.

Although the method of Landscape Metrics is only used in the characterization of land-use planning and analysis, and specifically in scenarios of territorial evolution, in this work a correlation with such spatial analyses of land surface is used to bridge the

M. Ioannides (Ed.): EuroMed 2010, LNCS 6436, pp. 99–109, 2010.
© Springer-Verlag Berlin Heidelberg 2010

application of the same concept into the analysis of the pictorial surface. Despite the evident difference in the metric scale between the two fields of study, we assume that there is a similarity between land use classes and the elements in the painting surfaces. An explanation of this is related with the pictorial surface, which can be seen as a fragmented territory where, at a specific location, a value (land use/colour or pathology) might be assigned.

The purpose of this study is to evaluate and interpret the application of Landscape Metrics as an analytical methodology that helps to clarify some questions arising in conservation: how extent are significant lacunae/retouching areas in a painting; what their average size is; how irregular their geometry is; what is the spatial pattern of their distribution; and if a tendency to locate in specific chromatic areas is noticed.

1.2 GIS, Spatial Analysis Operations and Landscape Metrics

A geographic information system (GIS) is a computer based information system that enables the capture, modelling, storage, retrieval, sharing, manipulation, analysis and presentation of geographically referenced data [4]. There are several types of models associated to information: databases with georeferenced information (such as addresses), raster (such as images) and vector models (points, lines and areas). A raster image file is a grid of cells, also designated as an array of pixels, structured with columns and lines and with a value associated with each cell [5]. Spatial analysis is a field of study which concerns the manipulation of spatial information and the extraction of spatial relations and properties. The analysis answers questions about the geographic features, such as distance, adjacency, interaction and neighbourhood-induced characteristics between events or spatially distributed objects.

Landscape metrics (LM) are a set of spatial analytical measures and indicators widely applied in territorial analysis. LM has been used to understand the landscape structures in ecology, landscape architecture and land use planning [6]. Several of such metrics allow a quantitative description of spatial patterns, helping the decision makers to define, with respect to the natural environment, agricultural, rural, coastal and transportation policies. Some examples of its application are the 3D LM methodologies used to support forest structure discrimination, mapping and monitoring of the National Park Bavarian Forest [7], the spatial analysis of land occupation in Mainland Portugal [8] and the analysis of vegetation dynamics in Amazon forest [9].

1.3 Case Study

The case study involves the application of GIS-based tools to extract LM values for the lacunae and retouching areas in a wood painting made by an unknown Master, probably of 16th century Portuguese origin. The iconographic representation is attributed to *St. John the Evangelist* because his specific attributes are represented: the figure wears a red drape, and a winged snake emerging from the chalice is present. The panel has a *Castanea sp.* support with 4 cm thickness, tangential cut in a single ca. 145 cm high by ca. 51 cm wide plank and is painted with the common material (pigments, dyes and binders) of the production in the 16th century. Photographs of the painting were taken during the conservation and restoration treatment, after removing varnish and repaints and before the filling and retouching operations.

2 Methodology

2.1 Generic Description

The first operation in the methodology was to acquire digital photographs of the art-work. These images are processed with a close-range photogrammetric program which creates an orthophotograph combining the original imagery. This operation is followed by the use of a GIS to extract features (corresponding to the visually identi-fied most significant colour patches and pathologies). Then the metrics are applicable. These steps are described in detail in the following sections.

2.2 Image Capture and Orthophotograph Processing

Photographic records of the painting were made in digital mode with a 5.0 Mpixel camera, *Sony Cybershot F-717*™. Digital images in JPEG/EXIF 2.2 image format were used to create an orthophotograph with close-range photogrammetry software.

This operation can be presented in three stages: a calibration to determine the geo-metric characteristics of the camera and to set parameters for it; the use of a set of images from different viewpoints to produce, by bundle adjustment, a digital surface model (DSM) with four points located at the vertices; and the production of an ortho-photo [10]. In all the steps of the exercise *Photomodeler 4.0*™ software was used.

An orthophoto image is a document that might be produced from perspective pho-tos, in which all perspective-related distortions have been removed. It is similar to obtain a photograph of a surface where the camera is placed perpendicularly to this surface at an infinite distance. Because orthophotographs are planimetrically correct, they can be used as base maps for direct measurements of distances, angles, positions and areas [11]. Orthophotographs are also used as a base for measuring spatial proper-ties, since the distortion ("barrel effect") of the photographic lens and the relief of the represented surface are considered.

Despite the fact that the panel planks present a negligible warp, an orthographic photo was produced to minimize errors in the measured spatial properties. The ortho-photo produced was a TIFF format file with 542 columns by 1519 rows (823,298 pixels), three bands, uncompressed size of 2,26 MB using 8 bits pixel depth.

2.3 Data Processing in GIS

After the orthophotograph production, the image was georeferenced in a GIS program, *ArcGIS*™, version 9.3, from ESRI®. In this operation a metric scale is assigned and the image is subject to a georeferentiation, with local coordinates being applied. The image layer has a fixed pixel size of 0.095 cm, an empirical value considered to be adequate to represent with detail the artwork. Following this, polygons were drawn to delimit the main regions of colours in the painting and the lacunae/retouching areas.

Eight areas were created in a layer to characterize the zones of *light red drape*, *dark red drape*, *sky*, *flesh*, *winged snake*, *earth pigments* (covering the ground and the figure's hair), *chalice* and *water* (Fig. 1). Lacunae or retouching areas were edited manually and represented in a distinct vector layer, but could also be produced by the application of automatic classification (e.g., via supervised classification). The main reason for the manual classification was the ability to interpret by visual inspection the most adequate of the eight zones for each lacunae/retouching area. Both datasets of lacunae/retouching areas were then converted to the raster format, producing grids with the same detailed resolution as the orthophoto (0.095 cm), which facilitates eventual overlay operations with the original image, within the GIS.

LM analyses could also have been performed with vector data, and the choice of the data model depends on the intended type of metric indices. If the operator chooses to analyse raster datasets, the choice of the spatial resolution influences most metrics, so an adequate value should be selected. After the conversion (lacunae/retouching area and regions of colours) both raster layers were added to result in a single grid with a combination of all data. This dataset represents all the various combinations of pigments and presence or absence of lacunae or retouching, such as "light red drape" or "lacunae on light red drape".

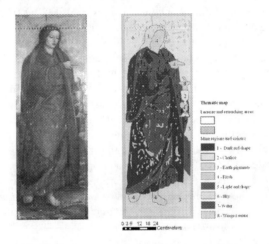

Fig. 1. Orthophotograph of the *St. John the Evangelist* panel painting and the corresponding thematic map of lacunae, retouching areas and main colours

2.4 Application and Interpretation of Landscape Metrics

LM are available to *ESRI® ArcGIS^{TM}* users as an extension named *Patch Analyst* (version 0.9.5) (and also *Patch Analyst for Grids*) developed for version 9.1 or later by the Geomatics Services Group, Ontario Ministry of Natural Resources. The use of the extension is straightforward and requires only the identification of the raster layer with the classified cells.

To apply the landscape metrics there are six categories of statistics in Patch Analyst: *Area Metrics, Patch Density and Size Metrics, Edge Metrics, Shape Metrics, Diversity & Interspersion Metrics* and *Core Area Metrics*.

Landscape metrics are classified into three types, relating with the level at which they apply to: *patches* (individual homogeneous regions), *classes* (set of all patches with the same classification), and *landscape* (all the elements): *patch-level metrics* are defined for individual patches, characterizing their spatial properties. In most applications they are used basically in the calculation of other level metrics, such as the average patch area for a class of in the entire landscape; the computed values for each individual patch may have little interpretive value [12]; *class-level metrics* describe the geometric properties of all patches assigned to the same type or class. Examples are the average values of patches for a specific class, such as the average area, perimeter, and number of distinct neighbour classes, among others; and *landscape-level metrics* describe properties for the entirety of the tessellation of classes/patches in the landscape, reflecting its geometric and topological quantitative properties.

Not all these metrics share the same importance or significance in the particular analysis of a painting. For instance, patch-level metrics will only apply if an individualization of the patches makes sense, which is not the case of the patches in the painting, since no individual value is assigned to it. Class-level metrics express for each colour and type of pathology its geometric and dispersion properties. Landscape-level metrics provide general quantifications on the distribution of the classes (colours and pathologies) in the painting.

The following metrics were selected: *Class Area* (CA), *Number of Patches* (NumP), *Mean Patch Size* (MPS), *Patch Size Coefficient of Variance* (PSCoV), *Patch Size Standard Deviation* (PSSD), *Edge Density* (ED), *Landscape Shape Index* (LSI), *Mean Nearest Neighbour Distance* (MNN) and *Total Core Area* (TCA), because they directly represent properties that might be useful in the characterization and interpretation of the extent and spatial distribution of pathologies.

CA is an area metric, useful to assess the extent of each pathology and defined colour region in the painting, providing valuable information for the diagnosing process.

NumP directly expresses the number of patches in each class. This number is a measure of the landscape configuration which gives an insight on the level of division or fragmentation in each class. It is defined by dividing the class area by the total area of the landscape.

MPS is a measure that informs on the average covered area per class, which gives an insight on the heterogeneity of size in relation with class. It could also be compared between colours and between areas of the same pathology.

PSSD and *PSCoV* are the standard deviation and the coefficient of variation of patch areas, where PSCoV = PSSD/MPS.

ED is the total length of the boundary between patches with different classes divided by the total class area, and gives a measure that expresses the level of fragmentation of each class.

LSI is interesting in expressing, for each class and for the total landscape, the total value of the boundary lengths of its patches divided by the square root of their total area. It is a measure of the average irregularity of each class: the higher the value of LSI, the less circular are the patches. Such measure is useful when applied to patches representing pathologies, since irregularity may be related with a higher volume of retouching work in conservation and restoration interventions. This metric expresses the dissimilarity between the sizes of patches, per class.

ED is the total length of the boundary between patches with different classes divided by the total class area, expressing the level of fragmentation of each class.

MNN is a measure that expresses the isolation of patches, since for each patch the distance to its nearest neighbour in the same class is calculated. For all patches in the same class, the average value of this measure is calculated.

TCA is a shape and core measure. Core areas are comprised of pixels that are entirely surrounded by pixels of the same type. TCA estimates the total area, per class, occupied by these pixels.

The previously mentioned Landscape Metrics were applied to the classified grid. Results are presented in Tables 1 and 2. The classes are: *dark red drape* (DRD); *chalice* (Ch); *earth pigments* (EP); *flesh* (Fl); *light red drape* (LRD); *sky* (Sk); *water* (Wa); and *winged snake* (WS). A dagger (†) following a class name is a correlated area of lacunae.

Table 1. Area Metrics (*) and Patch Density & Size Metrics (**)

	CA*	NumP**	MPS**	PSCoV**	PSSD**
DRD	241,304	33	7,312	76,231	36,572
DRD†	20,537	185	111	28,741	210
Ch	7,060	2	3,530	6,897	1,598
EP	125,893	3	41,964	16,269	41,791
EP†	37,537	31	1,211	71,759	5,701
Fl	31,893	5	6,379	8,264	3,458
Fl†	959	14	68	20,073	90
LRD	156,540	40	3,914	49,694	12,759
LRD†	8,132	93	88	25,886	148
Sk	123,931	5	24,786	18,267	29,705
Sk†	48,228	66	731	88,421	4,240
Wa	12,722	1	12,722	0	0
Wa†	4,481	1	4,481	0	0
WS	3,223	2	1,612	14,438	1,527
WS†	699	16	43	11,210	32

Table 2. Edge Metrics (*), Shape Metrics (**), Diversity & Interspersion Metrics (***) and Core Area Metrics (****)

	ED*	LSI**	MNN***	TCA****
DRD	3,918	834	4,229	221,900
DRD†	1,516	392	11,888	13,551
Ch	94	131	43,417	6,575
EP	961	291	305,310	120,616
EP†	730	197	28,760	33,088
Fl	403	188	127,010	29,931
Fl†	79	128	14,121	621
LRD	3,088	681	2,364	141,461
LRD†	716	245	16,782	4,810
Sk	1,391	370	4,400	116,486
Sk†	1,432	321	8,493	40,352
Wa	108	134	1	12,091
Wa†	83	123	1	3,943
WS	128	137	2,000	2,619
WS†	79	129	4,989	337

The total area of the pictorial surface has 823,740 cells. Using this value as a basis, the statistical analysis is mainly focused in the lacunae areas. The number of cells is given by Patch Analyst as the *Total Landscape Area* (TLA) metric.

The *CA* metric indicates that the largest areas of the original paint layer are the figure's drape, namely the dark red and light red. The sky and earth pigment zones also evidence a significant value. The largest area of lacunae is in the sky and earth pigment regions. To that extension a decisive contribution from the peripheral overpainting, shaped as a frame, in the panel's outer edge.

In the zones of original painting, specifically in both red-hue drape areas, the value of the *NumP* metric is higher. For the lacunae distribution, the highest number of patches is noticed in the areas over the dark red tints, followed by the presence over the light red and sky areas. In the earth colour zones of ground and the figure's hair a lower number of lacunae patches is observed. In the remaining regions the value is negligible. *NumP* is an interesting parameter in the moment of performing a chromatic reintegration as it is directly related with the number of lacunae. In these cases, the higher the number of lacunae, the largest the quantity of matching colours needed and most prolonged the operation is. The fact of the highest values show up in specific regions might express an index on the required amount of work. In the case study, the highest values are noticed in both *drape* regions and in the *sky* (Fig. 2). As such, lower values will translate into less work, and this is verified in the *winged snake* and *flesh* regions.

The *MPS* metric has higher values in the *water*, *earth pigments* and *sky*. For the lacunae in the *St John the Evangelist* panel, a high value occurs in the border since there is a large and continuous area of overpainting (see Fig. 1), significantly raising the average patch size in some classes. Without this specific area, the highest value of this metric would occur in the *dark red drape* and *light red drape* classes, and the lowest in the *winged snake*.

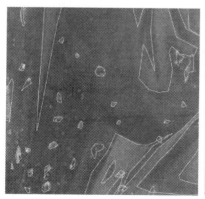

Fig. 2. Detail of lacunae and overpaint regions in the *dark red drape* and *sky* zones. The represented areas were defined with manually edited polygons, and later the information was converted to the raster format.

PSCoV estimates the variance in the region size. As referred, it expresses an assessment directly proportional to the standard deviation of size and inversely proportional to the average size. As such, it suggests a classification on the level of asymmetry on lacunae size. In the artwork it is noticeable that the regions of lacunae over *earth pigments* have the largest difference and those of *red drape* (both *light* and *dark*) are very similar.

Interpretations of Area and Patch Density & Size Metrics are only based on the size of lacunae/retouching areas and not on the many complex shape-related characteristics that might complicate an intervention, such as the proximity and interspertion between zones. Thus, other indicators, such as the metrics presented in Table 2, are needed to complement the analysis:

ED analysis documents the extension of the lacunae borders. As listed in Table 2, the highest values belong to the *dark red* and *light red drape* lacunae areas, which suggest a longer division line between adjacent regions.

The *LSI* metric is a parameter on the lacunae typology: if it shaped like a circle it has a high value, and if it is very irregular the opposite occurs. The highest values are in the *dark red drape*, *sky* and *light red drape*. This analysis also suggest to provide useful information to the conservator-restorer as in the chromatic reintegration operations, besides the matching colour operations, the sinuous shape of the lacunae is the most demanding technical challenge. In practice, it is in these zones that the conservator-restorer's skills and capacities are put to the test. In such irregular zones, in mimetic-type interventions, it is often necessary to execute small and sensitive brush strokes in the border areas between lacunae and the original chromatic layer, to dissimulate the intervention. In the interventions of intentionally non-dissimulate characteristics (*rin-granatura, tratteggio, selezzione cromatica* and *astrazione cromatica*), there is the need to thoroughly respect the border lines between the original layer and the lacunae subject to the chromatic reintegration [13, 14, 15]. The above mentioned *ED* metric also can be considered in the analytical considerations on the required level of expertise.

The *MNN* metric expresses region separation. On one hand it gives a quantification on the isolation level, and on the other hand indicates a measure on the concentration of lacunae. The highest densities and proximity of lacunae occurs in the *sky* and *winged snake* classes. The larger the value of the lacunae density, the larger is the difficulty of an intervention. However, the fact of the lacunae being too close to each other might translate into an operational added value. This is valid in the sense of the proportionality between the proximity of lacunae and a lower number of matching colours required in the intervention. In practice, a colour produced in the palette, with some small adjustments, can be used sometimes as an homogeneous cover for several close lacunae.

TCA metric indicates, for each class, which is its core area. In the table, the large lacunae regions on the border are noticed to have an impact on the high values of this metric. The interpretation is similar to some of the previous metric indicators, and expresses the ease of intervention in these regions.

The entirety of lacunae can also be considered as a single entity, without classifications by regions of colours. Table 3 displays the values of some metrics for the merged lacunae patches. Note that adjacent patches might be combined in a single continuous patch, and the total number of patches (317) is less than the count of lacunae patches in Table 1 (406).

Table 3. Landscape metrics (LM) of the lacunae patches without division by colour regions

Metric	Value
CA	120,573
NumP	317
MPS	380
TCA	79,019

CA indicates that lacunae occupy 14.6% (120,573/823,140) of the entire surface of the panel painting. The number of patches where chromatic reintegration is required is 317, with a mean size of 380 units. Table 3 does not list some LM shown on previous tables since the set of statistics of a single class of lacunae patches did not suggest to be capable of providing additional useful information. However, the unused LM might be considered in the qualitative analysis of collections of artworks by the same artist, or in a set of pieces with aesthetic or style similarities.

3 Conclusions

This paper presented a novel application of spatial analysis operations, namely Landscape Metrics (LM), to the characterization of surface phenomena in paintings. The variety and complexity of LM proved to be very helpful in assessing and describing the shape characteristics of painting detectable features, such as lacunae or overpainting areas, and might be extended to other cases. Such techniques, usually applied in territorial analysis, can also be applied in very distinct domain of conservation of paintings, being useful in the quantitative diagnosis needed in the documentation of artwork conservation status and in the support of the chromatic reintegration phase.

The interpretation of some Landscape Metric parameters, after georeferencing an image of the artwork, supports the use of this quantitative approach, extending human perception in the capability of evaluating important elements, such as lacunae/retouching areas and main colour-regions characteristics, and improving the quality of the diagnostic procedures made by the conservator-restorers.

Some LM are easily interpretable and correspond to important measurable characteristics: for instance, CA, NumP, ED and LSI metrics suggest being good indicators of the skill required in the intervention of chromatic reintegration. Very useful information on the number of lacunae to reintegrate, on the fragmentation level and on the variety and irregularity on their shapes is expressed by these metrics.

All the presented statistics depend on the initial delimitation process of the lacunae and/or colour zones over the orthophotograph, which was performed via manual vectorization and visual inspection. Very small patches were not considered in this exercise, but all the interpretations and assumptions of the significance of Landscape Metrics in the characterization and diagnostic of surface phenomena on artworks were not affected by our generalization. The application of the proposed methodology could be detailed and further assessed with the use of high resolution digital imagery. The possible use of the *velatura* technique, which might be executed in the chromatic reintegration, was also not considered in the evaluation of the patches detected in the analysed painting.

The process of analysis is not fully automatic. It depends on the intrinsic characteristics of the artwork, and on the initial photo-interpretations, to identify on surface the main patches. The accuracy and quality of the presented methodologies strongly depend on the expertise of the GIS operator in perceiving and modelling phenomena and transmitting his interpretation of the statistical data produced and expressed by the Landscape Metrics.

Acknowledgements. This work has been supported by "Fundação para a Ciência e a Tecnologia" and "Programa Operacional Ciência e Inovação 2010" (POCI 2010), cofunded by the Portuguese Government and European Union by FEDER Program. This research was also supported in part by the "Fundação para a Ciência e a Tecnologia" training grant SFRH/BD/42488/2007. The analysed painting is property of Zarco Antiquários, Lda., and we thank the opportunity to use images of the conservation-restoration treatment. We also appreciate the collaboration of Ana Bailão, conservator-restorer of paintings, on the technical information about the state of conservation of the panel painting.

References

1. Letellier, R.: Recording, Documentation, and Information Management for the Conservation of Heritage Places. Guiding Principles, vol. I,
   http://www.getty.edu/conservation/publications/
   pdf_publications/recordim.html
2. Eppich, R., Chabbi, A.: Recording, Documentation, and Information Management for the Conservation of Heritage Places. Illustrated Examples, vol. II,
   http://www.getty.edu/conservation/publications/
   pdf_publicatio/recordim.html
3. Henriques, F., Gonçalves, A., Bailão, A.: Tear Feature Extraction with Spatial Analysis: A Thangka Case Study. Estudos de Conservação e Restauro 1, 11–23 (2009)
4. Worboys, M., Duckham, M.: GIS. A Computing Perspective. CRC Press, Boca Raton (2004)
5. Longley, P.A., Goodchild, M.F., Maguire, D.J., Rhind, D.W.: Geographic Information Systems and Science. John Wiley & Sons, Chichester (2001)
6. Leitão, A.B., Miller, J., Ahern, J., McGarigal, K.: Measuring Landscapes. A Planner's Handbook. Island Press, London (2006)
7. Blaschke, T., Tiede, D., Heurichb, M.: 3D Landscape Metrics to Modelling Forest Structure and Diversity Based on Laser Scanning Data. In: Thies, M., Koch, B., Spiecker, H., Weinacker, H. (eds.) Proceedings of the ISPRS working group VIII/2 'Laser-Scanners for Forest and Landscape Assessment' Freiburg, Germany, October 3-6, vol. XXXVI-8/W2, pp. 129–132 (2004)
8. Couto, P.: Análise Factorial Aplicada a Métricas da Paisagem Definidas em FRAGSTATS. Revista Investigação Operacional 24, 109–137 (2004)
9. Watrin, O.S., Venturieri, A.: Métricas de Paisagem na Avaliação da Dinâmica do Uso da Terra em Projetos de Assentamento no Sudeste Paraense. In: Anais do XII Simpósio Brasileiro de Sensoriamento Remoto, INPE, Goiânia, Brazil, pp. 3433–3440 (2005)
10. Waldhäusl, P., Ogleby, C.: 3-by-3 Rules for Simple Photogrammetric Documentation of Architecture. In: Fryer, J.G. (ed.) Close Range Techniques and Machine Vision. Symposium of Commission V of ISPRS, IAPRS XXX/5, Melbourne, Australia, pp. 426–429 (1994)

11. Wolf, P.R.: Elements of Photogrammetry, 2nd edn. McGraw-Hill International Editions, Singapore (1983)
12. Smith, M., Goodchild, M., Longley, P.: Geospatial Analysis - a comprehensive guide. 3rd edn.,
    http://www.spatialanalysisonline.com/output/html/
    LandscapeMetrics.html
13. Casazza, O.: Il Restauro Pittorico nell'Unità di Metodologia. Nardini Editore, Florence (1981)
14. Bergeon, S.: Science et Patience ou la Restauration des Peintures. Éditions de la Réunion des Musées Nationaux, Paris (1990)
15. Althofer, H.: La questione del ritocco nel restauro pittorico. Il Prato, Padova (2002)

Reality-Based 3D Modeling, Segmentation and Web-Based Visualization

Anna Maria Manferdini[1] and Fabio Remondino[2]

[1] DAPT Department, University of Bologna, Italy
am.manferdini@unibo.it
[2] 3D Optical Metrology Unit, FBK Trento, Italy
remondino@fbk.eu

Abstract. One of the most significant consequences of the introduction of digital 3D modeling in the Cultural Heritage field is the possibility to use 3D models as highly effective and intuitive means of communication as well as interface to share and visualize information collected in databases. Due to the usual complexity of architectural and archaeological artifacts or sites, their digital models need be subdivided in sub-components and organized following semantic definitions in order to facilitate data retrieval. This paper outlines a methodology to semantically segment complex reality-based 3D models, annotate information and share the results within online open-source tools. The segmentation stage to subdivide and organize 3D models is based on both automated and manual methods, giving priority to automated procedures that can ease and speed these steps but not neglecting the user intervention to achieve accurate results. The segmented 3D models are then visualized in web-based systems to allow data access to a wider range of users and enlarge knowledge. The methodology is presented and tested on large and complex reality-based 3D models of architectural and archaeological heritage structures.

Keywords: 3D modeling, photogrammetry, laser scanning, semantic, segmentation, web-based visualization.

1 Introduction

During the last years, in the Cultural Heritage field, the availability of digital collections of 3D data acquired and returned in form of 3D reproductions has represented a fundamental change in our cognitive model and working approach. Indeed the availability of 3D digital replicas, compared to standard 2D photos or video or drawings, generally communicate in a more effective way information about scenes or objects that have intrinsic 3D characteristics. Moreover if metric, accuracy and photo-realism are also taken into consideration, the 3D models are of course a powerful tool in particular for archaeological and architectural applications. Indeed the opportunity given by the 3D world changes the way we can access and exchange knowledge, leads us to the recognition of connections and enlarges the possibilities to interpret and analyze the past. The trend of digitally and faithfully model in three dimensions visual Cultural Heritages helps to simulate reality in a more objective and reliable way and

M. Ioannides (Ed.): EuroMed 2010, LNCS 6436, pp. 110–124, 2010.

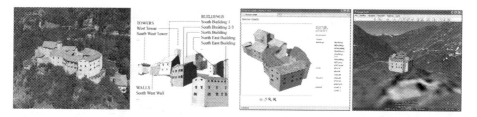

Fig. 1. The developed pipeline to (i) create reality-based 3D models, (ii) segment the geometry according to its sub-elements, (iii) define the hierarchical organization and (iv) visualize the results with an open-source 3D web-based tool

provides the opportunity to use digital 3D models for different purposes that can change through time. Recently an interesting opportunity offered by 3D models is to use them either as visualization container or as highly intuitive interface between different kinds of information. Given their usual geometric complexity and the possibility to link them to a wide range of data, 3D models can be analyzed in detail, split in their sub-components and organized following semantic rules in order to ease data retrieval. For example, following this idea, the Building Information Model (BIM) and CityGML concept were created to describe building components with respect to their geometry, topology and semantic information.

The aim of the paper is to show a research pipeline (Fig. 1) developed to allow the use of reality-based 3D digital models as highly intuitive and effective graphic interface to access, share and communicate different kinds of information related to Cultural Heritage. The reality-based 3D models are produced with range-based, image-based or CAD modeling techniques. Each 3D model can contains different levels of geometry and need therefore to be semantically segmented and organized in different ways. As we employ real 3D models of complex scenes, the segmentation is often user-assisted to better recognize sub-elements and define their hierarchical organization. The semantic models and their components are then visualized in a 3D web-based open-source system to allow geo-referencing, querying and data sharing.

The developed methodology was tested on different digital models (Fig. 2) produced within previous research projects undertaken for different aims. Results are shown throughout the article in order to explain recurrent problems and adopted solutions.

2 Reality-Based 3D Modeling

The continuous development of new sensors, data capture methodologies, multi-resolution 3D representations and the improvement of existing ones are contributing significantly to the documentation, conservation and presentation of heritage information and to the growth of research in the Cultural Heritage field. This is also driven by the increasing requests and needs for digital documentation of heritage sites at different scales and resolutions for successive applications like conservation, restoration, visualization, education, data sharing, 3D GIS, etc. 3D surveying and modeling of scenes or objects should be intended as the entire procedure that starts with the data acquisition, geometric and radiometric data processing, 3D information generation

112   A.M. Manferdini and F. Remondino

Fig. 2. Typical examples of reality-based 3D polygonal models realized for documentation, conservation and analyses purpose: a) range-based 3D reconstruction of an underground frescoed Etruscan tomb in the UNESCO site of Tarquinia, Italy; b) range-based 3D model of a corner mask in the UNESCO archaeological area of Copan, Honduras; c) CAD 3D model of the House of the Surveyors of Claude-Nicolas Ledoux; d) aerial image-based 3D reconstruction of the Angkor Wat temple, Cambodia; e) image- and range-based 3D model of the law code inscription in Gortyna, Crete; range-based 3D survey of a medieval castle in Trentino, Italy

and digital model visualization. A technique is intended as a scientific procedure (e.g. image processing) to accomplish a specific task while a methodology is a combination of techniques and activities joined to achieve a particular task in a better way.

Reality-based surveying techniques (e.g. photogrammetry, laser scanning, etc.) [1] employ hardware and software to metrically survey the reality as it is, documenting in 3D the actual visible situation of a site by means of images [2], range-data [3, 4],

CAD drawing and maps (5), classical surveying (GPS, total station, etc.) or an integration of the aforementioned techniques [6, 7, 8]. Non-real approaches are instead based on computer graphics software (3D Studio, Maya, Sketchup, etc.) or procedural modeling [9, 10] and they allow the generation of 3D data without any metric survey as input or knowledge of the site.

2.1 Range-Based 3D Reconstruction

Optical range sensors like pulsed (TOF), phase-shift or triangulation-based laser scanners and stripe projection systems have received in the last years a great attention, also from non-experts, for 3D documentation and modeling purposes. These active sensors deliver directly ranges (i.e. distances thus 3D information in form of unstructured point clouds) and are getting quite common in the heritage field, despite their high costs, weight and the usual lack of good texture. During the surveying, the instrument should be placed in different locations or the object needs to be moved in a way that the instrument can see it under different viewpoints. Successively, the 3D raw data needs errors and outliers removal, noise reduction and the registration into a unique reference system to produce a single point cloud of the surveyed scene or object. The registration is generally done in two steps: (i) manual or automatic raw alignment using targets or the data itself and (ii) final global alignment based on Iterative Closest Points (ICP) or Least Squares method procedures. After the global alignment, redundant points should be removed before a surface model is produced and textured. Generally range-based 3D models are very rich of geometric details and contain a large number of polygonal elements, producing problems for further (automated) segmentation procedures.

2.2 Image-Based 3D Reconstruction

Image data require a mathematical formulation to transform the two-dimensional image measurements into three-dimensional information. Generally at least two images are required and 3D data can be derived using perspective or projective geometry formulations. Image-based modeling techniques (mainly photogrammetry and computer vision) are generally preferred in cases of lost objects, monuments or architectures with regular geometric shapes, small objects with free-form shape, low-budget project, mapping applications, deformation analyses, etc. Photogrammetry is the primary technique for the processing of image data. Photogrammetry, starting from some measured image correspondences, is able to deliver at any scale of application metric, accurate and detailed 3D information with estimates of precision and reliability of the unknown parameters. The image-based pipeline steps can be performed in an automated or interactive way, according to the user requirements and project specifications. Accurate feature extraction from satellite and aerial images is still a manually driven procedure while in terrestrial applications more automation is available for scene 3D reconstruction. Fully automated 3D modeling methods based on a 'structure from motion' approach [11, 11, ARC 3D Webservice, Microsoft Photosynth, Autodesk Photofly) are getting quite common in the 3D heritage community, although primarily useful for visualization, object-based navigation, annotation transfer or image browsing purposes and not for metric and accurate 3D modeling purposes. The dense 3D reconstruction step can instead be performed in a fully automated mode with satisfactory results [13, 14, 15]. But the complete automation in image-based modeling is still an open research's topic, in particular in case of complex heritage scenes and man-made objects [16] although the latest researches reported quite promising results [17].

2.2 CAD-Based 3D Reconstruction

This is the traditional approach and remains the most common method in particular for architectural structures, constituted by simple geometries. These kinds of digital models are generally created using drawings or predefined primitives with 2D orthogonal projections to interactively build volumes. In addition, each volume can be either considered as part of adjacent ones or considered separated from the others by non-visible contact surfaces. Using CAD packages, the information can be arranged in separate layers, each containing different type of elements, which help the successive segmentation phase. The segmentation, organization and naming of CAD models and their related sub-components generally require the user's intervention to define the geometry and location of subdivision surfaces, as well as to recognize rules derived e.g. from classical orders.

3   3D Model Segmentation

The segmentation of a polygonal model consists in the decomposition of the 3D geometry into sub-elements which have generally uniform properties. The semantic segmentation should be ideally performed fully automatically to imitate the human visual perception and the decision intents. But in most of the applications (Cultural Heritage, 3D city models, etc.) the user intervention is still mandatory to achieve more accurate results. Following [17], the main reasons that limit the automatic reconstruction of semantic models are related to:

- the definition of a target model which restricts object configurations to sensible building structures and their components, but which is still flexible enough to cover (nearly) all existing buildings in reality;
- the geometric and radiometric complexity of the input data and reconstructed 3D models;
- data errors and inaccuracies, uncertainty or ambiguities in the automatic interpretation and segmentation;
- the reduction of the search space during the interpretation process.

The interpretation and segmentation of a 3D model allow to generate a topologically and semantically correct model with structured boundary. The 3D geometry and the related semantic information have to be structured coherently in order to provide a convenient basis for simulations, urban data analyses and mining, facility management, thematic inquiries, archaeological analyses, policies planning, etc. The CityGML, conceived as target data format, fulfills all these requirements and became the standard approach for 3D city models [18].

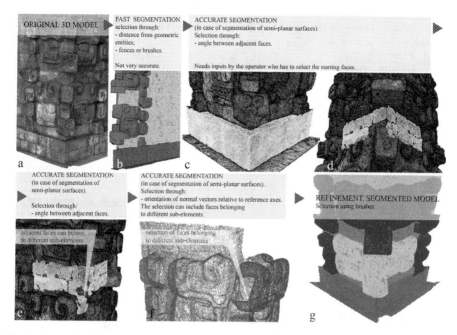

Fig. 3. Example of automated segmentation of complex and detailed polygonal model: a fast but inaccurate segmentation can be improved with geometric constraints and manual refinements to separate the narrative elements

In the literature, the most effective automated segmentation algorithms are based on 3D volumetric approaches, primitive fitting or geometric segmentation methods. While the former two approaches segment meshes by identifying polygons that correspond to relevant feature of the 3D shape, the latter segments the mesh according to the local geometrical properties of 3D surface. In the field of Cultural Heritage, the segmentation of digital 3D models is useful for a large number of applications. For example, segmented models and their sub-elements can be used in searchable databases or can be labeled and used in knowledge ontology contexts [20]. Moreover, segmentation of restored archaeological finds can suggest different locations of sub-elements and therefore can help to review facts and interpret history [21]. A comparative study between some segmentation algorithms and related applications have been presented in [22], where only visual results were presented, without any quantitative evaluation of the algorithm's effectiveness. In [23] a more complete and to-date review of mesh segmentation techniques is presented. A fully automatic protocol for the quantitative evaluation of 3D mesh segmentation algorithms aimed at reaching an objective evaluation of their effects are shown in [24, 25]. In particular, they provided 3D mesh segmentation benchmark in order to help researchers to develop or improve automatic mesh segmentation algorithms. But the offered case studies were rather different and simpler from the wide range of possible cases usually encountered in Cultural Heritage applications. As automation cannot provide for satisfactory results in all the possible dataset, [26] developed a methodology which combines different automatic segmentation algorithms with an interactive interface to adjust and correct the segmented polygonal models.

Our methodology follow also these concepts and uses a combination of automated and interactive segmentation tools according to the 3D model and its complexity (Fig. 3). The methodology is not aiming at the fully automation as reality-based 3D models are generally very complex and detailed and there is no automated procedure able to deal successfully with all these models. Furthermore the segmentation is generally performed according to rules or specifications given by archaeologists or architects and differs for each project. Therefore the user intervention is generally not neglected in order to derive correct subdivisions of the polygonal models.

The segmentation procedure performs:

- an automatic geometric separation of the different mesh portions using surface geometric information and texture attributes;
- a manual intervention to adjust the boundaries of the segmented elements
- an assisted annotation of the sub-elements that constitute the segmented 3D model.

Fig. 4. Segmentation of a stone wall of a castle (Fig.2-f) with small surface irregularities. a) result derived aggregating the main surface orientations; b) result of the segmentation following planar adjacent faces.

The geometric segmentation requires recognizing the transition between the different geometric elements of a 3D model. Automatic procedures to select and group faces of 3D models are available in common modeling packages (Maya, 3DS Max, Rhino, Meshlab, etc.). Faces can be separated and grouped using constraints such as inclination of adjacent faces, lighting or shading values. The surface normals are generally a good indicator to separate different sub-elements , when semi-planar faces need to be separated from reliefs (Fig. 4 and Fig. 5).

The detection of lighting or texture transitions can be instead eased applying filters or using edge detector algorithms. This can be quite useful in flat areas with very low geometric discontinuities where the texture information allow to extract, classify and segment figures or relevant features for further uses (Fig. 6).

For the correct hierarchical organization and visualization of the segmented sub-elements, a precise identification of the transition borders in the segmented meshes is required. For complex geometric models constituted by detailed and dense meshes, the manual intervention is generally required. Another aspect that has to be considered during the geometric segmentation of complex and fully 3D models is related to the possibility of subdividing only visible surfaces or to build complete volumes of sub-element models, modeling also non- visible closure or transition surfaces.

Fig. 5. a) Image of the law code in Gortyna (Fig.2-e) with symbols of ca 3-4 mm depth; b) close view of the 3D textured polygonal model; c) automatic identification of the letters using geometric constraints; d) final segmentation and vectorialization of the letters

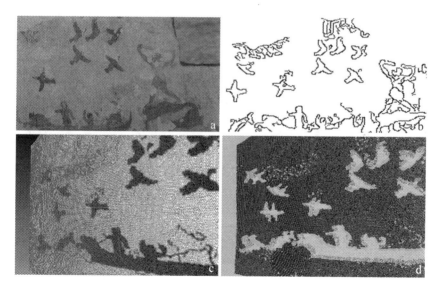

Fig. 6. a) The 3D model of an underground frescoed Etruscan tomb (Fig.2-a); b) filters to detect edges on the texture information of the 3D model; c,d) ease of lighting transitions and final segmentation of the polygonal model

This is for example the case of architectural buildings where interior rooms need to be divided from other geometric elements to fully semantically segment the available 3D model.

The semantic segmentation of a geometric 3D model is followed by the assignation to each sub-element of characteristics and information which need to be represented, organized and managed using advanced repository of geometric and appearance components to allow visualization and interaction with the digital models as well as database queries.

4   3D Model Visualization and 3D Web-GIS

3D models can be used as graphical interfaces and containers for different kinds of information that are usually organized and collected in 2D databases. This is also one of the most interesting need and requirements of 3D geo-browser where the simple visualization should be associated to query functionalities and data retrieval. These would be the typical functions of actual GIS packages which are no more sufficient when dealing with detailed and complex 3D data. A "3D repository" can be considered an informatic tool able to:

- handle geographical features (e.g. landscapes) as well as data more complex than a 2.5D surface (e.g. architectural or archaeological 3D models);
- allow queries and spatial data analyses, possibly via web;
- support multi-users access and interaction, multi-resolution data (LOD) and multi-representation.

In the literature different authors presented possible solutions for 3D data management and visualization [27, 28, 29, 30, 31, 32, 33]. Despite the great research work, nowadays almost no powerful, reliable and flexible package with all the aforementioned capabilities is available. In the video-games domain some packages or development tools are present, adaptable to 3D geo-data and web-based applications (e.g. Unity3D, OSG, OGRE3D, OpenSG, 3DVIA Virtools, etc.) but with limited capabilities for loading and displaying large and complex 3D models. In [34] Google Earth has been used as 3D GIS web-based solution for architectural 3D models while [35] uses the NASA World Wind to deliver a web-based 3D and OGC compliant solution capable to provide interoperable access to geographical information and geospatial processing services. Nowadays a common information model is also the City Geography Markup Language (CityGML), a concept for the modeling, visualization and exchange of 3D city and landscape models that is quickly being adopted on an international level [19]. Unfortunately at the moment CityGML seems to be unable to support high-resolution architectural and archaeological 3D models as the supported geometric entities are still limited to more simple and standard representations although some Application Domain Extensions (ADE) are available or under development.

The aim of enlarging knowledge and allow access to a wide range of users has guided our work towards web-based open source tools which represents a cost effective solution for both servers and clients. Moreover, the possibility to geo-reference digital models and make them available online in order to increase the coverage on virtual globes (i.e. using Google Earth) has encouraged our work towards a cooperation system. The developed visualization methodology is based on the O3D technology, a web-based application which allows a completely free interactive exploration of segmented 3D models. The O3D technology is an open-source JavaScript implementation launched in 2009 by Google in order to create interactive 3D applications inside a web browser. O3D is actually evolving as a library that runs on WebGL, a 3D graphics API based on OpenGL, recently improved thanks to the development of some projects (as, for example, the Angle Project, http://code.google.com/ p/angleproject/) aimed at running WebGL also on computers without OpenGL drivers installed. The O3D choice was reinforced by the awareness of the possible developments of Google's services due to its widespread and to its efforts towards content sharing. Indeed the development of projects like Google Earth and SketchUp demonstrates the wish to let users create and interact with 3D contents in a single context (the virtual globe). Using O3D the user has the possibility to geo-reference 3D models upon the most well-known free geographic information program (i.e. Google Earth) which is constantly improved and enriched with 3D contents. O3D provides also a solution to reduce 3D models file size and speed up the transmission of 3D data. Indeed, when dealing with reality-based 3D models, geometry and texture are generally very heavy, with large memory consumption. Their loading via web can therefore constitute a bottleneck during the online visualization. Despite the fact that O3D is not supporting many 3D file formats, its proprietary format (o3dtgz) allows a compression rate up to 1/3 of the original file size and so the possibility to interactively display even large and complex textured 3D models via web. The typical pipeline to import and visualize segmented 3D models is based on the COL-LADA format which is then converted into the O3D gzipped tar file (o3dtgz) with a JSON file describing the scene and the textures. The model is finally loaded inside the O3D viewer for visualization, interaction and database (DB) queries. Indeed O3D allow to link the segmented 3D models with any kind of information (like drawings, maps, images, videos, text, databases, etc.) and query external DB system (PostgreSQL, ORACLE, etc.).

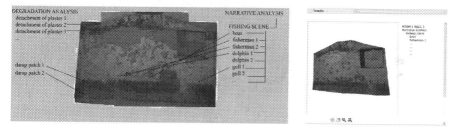

Fig. 7. A segmented 3D model of the frescoed tomb in Tarquinia (Fig.2-a) and its visualization in O3D

5   Further Experiments

The idea of choosing a Claude-Nicolas Ledoux's architecture (Fig. 2-c) as case study is primary due to the important role of this architecture within the debate upon the use of classical orders in architectural composition and the consequent possibility of a semantic organization of these kinds of digital models. Both in Ledoux's built and non-built visionary architectures, it is possible to recognise clear proportions and composition codes derived from the classical orders, so that each architecture is ruled following a specific hierarchy.

120   A.M. Manferdini and F. Remondino

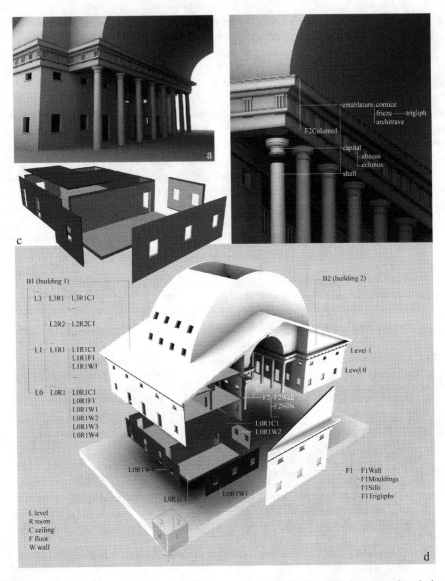

Fig. 8. CAD model of the House of the Surveyors by C.-N. Ledoux (a). Segmentation derived from classical orders and architectural information (b). Detail of the segmented level 0 of the house (c). Main organization of the segmented model with its sub-elements: for each level, the corresponding rooms with ceiling, floor and walls (d).

The semantic organization of these kinds of buildings can therefore take these rules into consideration in order to subdivide and name each single sub-element or groups of elements. The Ledoux's building model was subdivided both following geo-location rules based upon a local reference system and principles derived from classical architectural orders. The complexity of this model also required the numbering of

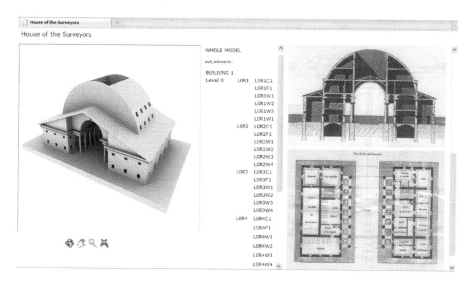

Fig. 9. Visualization of the House of the Surveyors inside a web-browser using the O3D technology. The digital model is accessible through the hierarchical graph that shows the sub-elements in which the CAD model has been semantically segmented. On the right, 2D drawings and other information are linked to the model.

sub-elements that corresponds to their orientation related to the reference system (Fig. 8). Within the O3D web viewer, the segmented model of Ledoux's building was linked to text documents and drawings for consultation and fruition (Fig. 9).

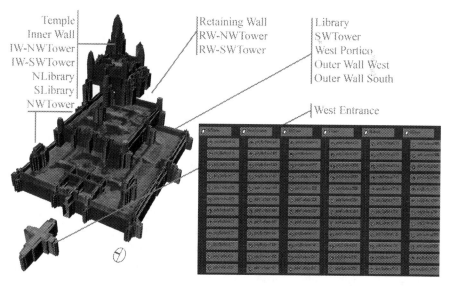

Fig. 10. Manual segmentation and naming of portions of the image-based Angkor Wat temple with its hierarchical graph

The Angkor Wat temple (Cambodia), was digitally reconstructed using aerial images. The successive semantic classification was performed selecting homologues areas based upon the naming of single buildings or their functions (Fig. 10). The model can be then visualized as entire entity or as single sub-elements thanks to the hierarchical graph that shows its semantic organization. The geo-referenced and segmented 3D model is finally display using O3D, which allow also a link to Google Earth or Google Maps or to any kind of external database (Fig. 11).

Fig. 11. Visualization and geo-referencing of the Angkor Wat temple inside O3D, Google Earth and Google Maps, with its related sub-elements and attributes

6 Conclusions

Despite the great development and widespread use of reality-based 3D models, the heritage community is still missing precious and reliable tools to semantically segment, connect, analyze, visualize and share different kinds of information related and belonging to 3D heritages.

In this article the semantic organization of 3D information and its access through an online graphical interface was realized with a collaborative work to realize reliable, efficient and flexible tool usable by different and non-expert users. Besides the management of information through digital models, this paper showed the possibility to interact with complex and detailed 3D models, segment them and visualize the results with an online viewer. The tendency to use automatic procedures in order to subdivide geometric entities is generally not very appropriate when dealing with complex reality-based 3D models, therefore the user interaction should not be neglected. The use of O3D, an open-source web API for creating rich and interactive 3D applications inside browsers, clearly showed the purpose of sharing information with other users or project partners and to contribute to the building of a whole virtual globe conceived as a single graphic interface to various databases.

Further developments of our methodology are represented by the insertion of a tool to query external database (DB) containing scene attributes and visualize the results through the same interface. Planned to be realized are (i) the implementation of tools for the metric evaluation of the segmentation procedure, (ii) a GUI for the direct selection of single sub-elements inside the web viewer and (iii) a procedure for the dynamic visualization of large models using different levels of detail (LOD).

References

1. Gruen, A.: Reality-based generation of virtual environments for digital earth. International Journal of Digital Earth 1(1) (2008)
2. Remondino, F., El-Hakim, S.: Image-based 3d modelling: a review. The Photogrammetric Record 21(115), 269–291 (2006)
3. Blais, F.: A review of 20 years of range sensors development. Journal of Electronic Imaging 13(1), 231–240 (2004)
4. Vosselman, G., Maas, H.-G.: Airborne and terrestrial laser scanning, p. 320. CRC Press, Boca Raton (2010)
5. Yin, X., Wonka, P., Razdan, A.: Generating 3d building models from architectural drawings: A survey. IEEE Computer Graphics and Applications 29(1), 20–30 (2009)
6. Stamos, I., Liu, L., Chen, C., Woldberg, G., Yu, G., Zokai, S.: Integrating automated range registration with multiview geometry for photorealistic modelling of large-scale scenes. International Journal of Computer Vision 78(2-3), 237–260 (2008)
7. Guidi, G., Remondino, F., Russo, M., Menna, F., Rizzi, A., Ercoli, S.: A multi-resolution methodology for the 3d modeling of large and complex archaeological areas. International Journal of Architectural Computing 7(1), 40–55 (2009)
8. Remondino, F., El-Hakim, S., Girardi, S., Rizzi, A., Benedetti, S., Gonzo, L.: 3D virtual reconstruction and visualization of complex architectures - The 3d-arch project. In: International Archives of the Photogrammetry, Remote Sensing and Spatial Information Sciences, 38(5/W10), on CD-ROM (2009)
9. Mueller, P., Wonka, P., Haegler, S., Ulmer, A., Van Gool, L.: Procedural modeling of buildings. ACM Transactions on Graphics 25(3), 614–623 (2006)
10. Whiting, E., Ochsendorf, J., Durand, F.: Procedural Modeling of Structurally-Sound Masonry Buildings. In: Proc. ACM SIGGRAPH, Asia (2009)
11. Goesele, M., Snavely, N., Curless, R., Hoppe, H., Seitz, S.M.: Multi-view stereo for community photo collections. In: Proc. ICCV, Rio de Janeiro, Brazil (2007)
12. Agarwal, S., Snavely, N., Simon, I., Seitz, S., Szelinski, R.: Building Rome in a day. In: Proc. ICCV 2009, Kyoto, Japan (2009)
13. Remondino, F., El-Hakim, S., Gruen, A., Zhang, L.: Development and performance analysis of image matching for detailed surface reconstruction of heritage objects. IEEE Signal Processing Magazine 25(4), 55–65 (2008)
14. Hirschmueller, H.: Stereo processing by semi-global matching and mutual information. IEEE Transactions on Pattern Analysis and Machine Intelligence 30(2), 328–341 (2008)
15. Hiep, V.H., Keriven, R., Labatut, P., Pons, J.P.: Towards high-resolution large-scale multiview stereo. In: Proc. CVPR 2009, Kyoto, Japan (2009)
16. Patias, P., Grussenmeyer, P., Hanke, K.: Applications in cultural heritage documentation. Advances in Photogrammetry, Remote Sensing and Spatial Information Sciences. In: 2008 ISPRS Congress Book, vol. 7, pp. 363–384 (2008)
17. Barazzetti, L., Remondino, F., Scaioni, M.: Automation in 3D reconstruction: results on different kinds of close-range blocks. In: ISPRS Commission V Symposium Int. Archives of Photogrammetry, Remote Sensing and Spatial Information Sciences, Newcastle upon Tyne, UK, vol. 38(5) (2010)
18. Nagel, C., Stadler, A., Kolbe, T.H.: Conceptual Requirements for the Automatic Reconstruction of Building Information Models from Uninterpreted 3D Models. In: International Archives of the Photogrammetry, Remote Sensing and Spatial Information Sciences, vol. 38(3-4/C3) (2009)

19. Kolbe, T.H.: Representing and Echanging 3D City Models with CityGML. In: Lee, J., Zlatanova, S. (eds.) 3D Geo-Information Sciences. Springer, Heidelberg (2009)

20. Attene, M., Robbiano, F., Spagnolo, M., Falcidieno, B.: Semantic Annotation of 3D Surface Meshes based on Feature Characterization. In: Falcidieno, B., Spagnuolo, M., Avrithis, Y., Kompatsiaris, I., Buitelaar, P. (eds.) SAMT 2007. LNCS, vol. 4816, pp. 126–139. Springer, Heidelberg (2007)

21. Manferdini, A.M., Remondino, F., Baldissini, S., Gaiani, M., Benedetti, B.: 3D Modeling and Semantic Classification of Archaeological Finds for Management and Visualization in 3D Archaeological Databases. In: Proc. 14th VSMM, pp. 221–228 (2008)

22. Attene, M., Katz, S., Mortara, M., Patané, G., Spagnuolo, M., Tal, A.: Mesh segmentation - a comparative study. In: Proc. IEEE International Conference on Shape Modeling and Applications 2006, p. 12. IEEE Computer Society, Washington (2006)

23. Shamir, A.: A survey on mesh segmentation techniques. Computer Graphics Forum 27(6), 1539–1556 (2008)

24. Benhabiles, H., Vandeborre, J.-P., Lavoué, G., Daoudi, M.: A framework for the objective evaluation of segmentation algorithms using a ground-truth of human segmented 3D-models. In: Proc. IEEE Intern. Conference on Shape Modeling and Applications 2009, p. 8. IEEE Computer Society, Washington (2009)

25. Chen, X., Golovinskiy, A., Funkhouser, T.: A Benchmark for 3D Mesh Segmentation. Proc. ACM Transactions on Graphics 28(3), 12 (2009)

26. Robbiano, F., Attene, M., Spagnuolo, M., Falcidieno, B.: Part-based annotation of virtual 3d shapes. In: Proc. of the International Conference on Cyberworlds, pp. 427–436. IEEE Computer Society, Washington (2007)

27. Wang, X., Gruen, A.: A Hybrid GIS for 3-D City Models. International Archives of Photogrammetry and Remote Sensing 33(B4), 1165–1172 (2000)

28. Pfund, M.: Topological Data Structure for a 3D GIS. International Archives of Photogrammetry and Remote Sensing 34(2W2), 233–237 (2001)

29. Nebiker, S.: Design and implementation of the high-performance 3D digital landscape server 'DILAS'. In: Joint ISPRS, IGU, CIG Symposium on Geospatial Theory, Processing and Applications, Ottawa, Canada (2002)

30. Shi, W.Z., Yang, B.S., Li, Q.Q.: An Object-Oriented Data Model For Complex Objects in three-dimensional Geographic Information Systems. International Journal of Geographic Information Science 17(5), 411–430 (2003)

31. Calori, L., Forte, M., Pescarin, S.: Real-time interactive reconstruction of archaeological landscapes: an opensource approach - From GIS to virtual reality. In: Proc. Italy-Canada Workshop (2005)

32. Khuan, T.C., Abdul-Rahman, A., Zlatanova, S.: 3D Spatial Operations in Geo DBMS Environment for 3D GIS. In: Gervasi, O., Gavrilova, M.L. (eds.) ICCSA 2007, Part I. LNCS, vol. 4705, pp. 151–163. Springer, Heidelberg (2007)

33. Kibria, M.S., Zlatanova, S., Itard, L., Van Dorst, M.: GeoVEs as tools to communicate in urban projects: requirements for functionality and visualisation. In: Lee, Zlatanova (eds.) 3D Geo-Information Sciences. LNG&C, pp. 379–412. Springer, Heidelberg (2009)

34. Apollonio, F.I., Corsi, C., Gaiani, M., Baldissini, S.: An integrated 3D geodatabase for Palladio's work. International Journal of Architectural Computing 2(8) (2010)

35. Conti, G., Simões, B., Piffer, S., De Amicis, R.: Interactive Processing Service Orchestration of Environmental Information within a 3D web client. In: Proc. GSDI 11th World Conference on Spatial Data Infrastructure Convergence, Rotterdam, The Netherlands (2009)

Capture and Processing of High Resolution 3D-Data of Sutra Inscriptions in China

Natalie Schmidt, Frank Boochs, and Rainer Schütze

i3mainz, Institute for Spatial Information and Surveying Technology
University of Applied Sciences Mainz, Germany
{schmidt,boochs,schuetze}@geoinform.fh-mainz.de

Abstract. Modern high resolution 3D-measuring techniques are widely used in quality control and industrial production, because they allow precise and reliable inspection of objects. Their potential to monitor surfaces, however, must not be restricted to industrial objects. Also in cultural heritage applications a detailed and reliable spatial description of surfaces is often useful and opens up new possibilities for conservation, analysis or presentation of objects.

In the actual work we have considered Buddhistic stone inscriptions (8th-12th centuries) which are important cultural assets of China. They need to be documented, analyzed, interpreted and visualized archaeologically, art-historically and text-scientifically. On one hand such buddhistic stone inscriptions have to be conserved for future generations but on the other hand further possibilities for analyzing the data could be enabled when the inscriptions would be accessible to a larger community, for instance the understanding of the historical growth of Buddhism in China.

In this article we show innovative techniques for the documentation and analysis of stone inscriptions located in the province of Sichuan - south-west of china. The stone inscriptions have been captured using high precision 3D-measuring techniques what produces exact copies of the original inscriptions serving as base for further processing tasks. Typical processing might be directed towards an improvement of the legibility of characters or may try to automatically detect individual letters, to automatically identify certain text passages or even to characterize the written elements with respect to a potential style of the monk or the executing stonemason. All these processing steps will support the interpretation of the inscriptions by the sinologists involved with the analysis and evaluation of the texts. The concept and features of the image processing applied on the captured inscription as well as the aims and the effect of an interpretation based on algorithms for identifying and analyzing the inscriptions are demonstrated. In order to present the outcome to a large community, the results of the stone inscription reconstruction, the done interpretation and additional 2D / 3D maps are published within an interactive web platform.

Keywords: 3D scanning, 3D computer graphics, image processing, Sutra, template matching.

1 Introduction

The development of culture in eastern Asiatic countries, especially china, has been widely influenced by Buddhism, why knowledge about his dissemination over time

M. Ioannides (Ed.): EuroMed 2010, LNCS 6436, pp. 125–139, 2010.
© Springer-Verlag Berlin Heidelberg 2010

and space is an important factor for historical investigations. Unfortunately buddhistic teachings were originally based on verbal communications and cannot be directly observed from today's viewpoint. This changed over time and the monks started to write down their texts, which are called Sutra. A Sutra is usually concerned with a certain topic as for example with the perfection of the wisdom, which is brought out as a central theme in the Diamond Sutra and in the Heart Sutra.

Sutras are already published in the 1st century AD using wood panel printing techniques. For a permanent preservation buddhistic monks began to engrave the Sutras into stones. These Sutras give an incomparable view into the groves of the Buddhism [1], why our project "3D-Sutra" tries to document the texts and to present them to the scientific public. The goal of our research project is the documentation, improvement, analysis and interpretation of these important Chinese inscriptions on an archaeological, art-historical and text-scientifical base. This project is an interdisciplinary cooperation of experts from different disciplines like sinology, cartography, geoinformatics and surveying.

Inside this cooperation we have three different parts. The central one is the sinological research dedicated to interpret and evaluate selected buddhistic texts. This will be supported by modern techniques for data collection, presentation and dissemination. Therefore it is the task of the two other parts to develop, integrate and apply the technological base to collect and process data captured for the Sutras. Here we distinguish between the capture of precise and detailed digital 3D copies of texts, their processing for enhancement and analysis and, as a third part, their integration into a web based geographical information system, what allows to visualize, disseminate and present the results to the scientific public.

The main objects can be found in the province Sichuan, where approximate 80 Sutras with more than 600,000 characters are located at six different sites. These Sutras light up the history of the Buddhism in China from another side and clarify its growth, thus its adaptation to the Chinese culture and its conflict with the secularized state [2], but are so far not very well studied by Chinese side.

In order to document the buddhistic stone inscriptions high resolution structured light 3D scanning will be used. Such scanning data provides precise virtual copies and makes the texts accessible to computer based treatments. Especially due to the spatial characteristics, the digital models might be virtually analyzed using 3D computer graphics based processes as texture, lighting and shading. This allows a close-to-reality presentation of the Sutra and individual analysis steps without the need to access the original, but with quality potential close to a real work in front of the rocks.

The original 3D data needs to be processed in order to optimize the value for the user. This comprises some preprocessing which is indispensable due to structure and volume of the data, and also conversions into special products are necessary to support subsequent interactive analysis steps. Also special processing algorithms are required to improve the legibility of the texts and to allow an acceleration of the text decoding or to contribute by structural analysis procedures, which might allow an analysis of certain characteristics of individual characters.

Finally algorithms could support and assist the interpretation of the buddhistic inscriptions by the sinologist. Each Sutra character within the processed 3D data will then be automatically transformed into machine-encoded character. Additionally the sutra characters will be analyzed under calligraphic aspects. The calligraphic analyses allow the sinologists to distinguish different authors and manufacturers and therefore to conduce to recent conclusions concerning the buddhistic inscriptions.

2 Precise 3D-Data as Base for the Documentation of Inscriptions

Until now stone inscriptions have been documented by manually prepared copies (rubbings), which represent an analogue copy of the stones surface and its features, done on paper [2]. These copies are realized by stitching a paper on the stone and by use of a carbon pencil which is smoothly moved over it. Like this, the engraved inscriptions are copied onto the sheet of paper. As a result, all parts in contact to the wall appear in black, while the engraved inscriptions remain white. The disadvantage of this technique is that the physical impact damages the stone and its inscriptions.

These problems will be avoided by non-contact 3D measuring techniques, like fringe projection, for example. But the advantages of modern 3D techniques are not limited to an objective documentation capability. Simple changes of the equipment may change scale and resolution comparably and allow further documentation approaches. So, precise detailed models might be complemented by local and regional models permitting further analysis processes and spatial considerations thus extending the potential for art-historian research.

With respect to the high resolution 3D technique the data collection provides an exact geometrical copy of the original inscription offering better results in legibility of each character compared to the traditional rubbing (see Fig. 1). Moreover it gives a

Fig. 1. Comparison of rubbing (left) and processed results of the fringe projection (right)

more objective base for analysis and has less impact onto the sometimes sensitive and eroded surfaces. Furthermore the 3D data of the Sutras allows more and other possibilities in processing and gives better preconditions for the interpretation, which might use the knowledge about the position of individual text passages inside a Sutra and its geometrical relation to other text parts. Such local analysis steps can simply be developed based on precise geometrical information to the texts and the signs inside as provided by a 3D-scanning.

In addition to such narrow and local geometrical and relational investigations the content of Sutra might also be connected in a more global scale. That is why it is of general value to use further measuring techniques in the field in order to optimize the framework for the documentation and analysis of art-historical objects [3].

Local and regional investigations can easily be realized based on terrestrial laser scanning. In our context it is used to capture the 3D geometry of the environment around the inscriptions. The resulting 3D point cloud documents the topography so that the relative position of larger texts can be expressed. Also precise 3D models can be created (e.g. Fig. 2), which might be used to analyze the spatial relationships of the sites and allow to visualize the objects in a virtually environment.

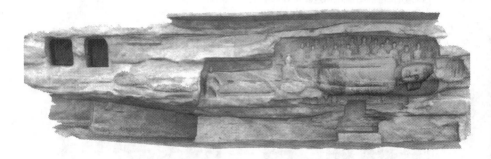

Fig. 2. 3D model of the topography - the laying Buddha in Wofoyuan, Sichuan

As best solution for high resolution scans fringe projecting system have to be selected. They allow to capture 3D geometries in sizes of less than 1 m³. It offers a close-to-detail 3D point cloud of the inscriptions [4] and provides various possibilities in data processing and supports the interpretation by different methods of 3D visualization [5] as shown in Figure 3.

In our case the stone inscriptions have an extension of up to 3x4 m each, why the lateral resolution has to be restricted to about 0.25 mm. With respect to the typical size of characters (~1 cm²) this gives about 1500 to 2500 3D pixel for an individual letter. A more detailed capture would considerably increase the effort for the field work and also produce really huge data sets. Nevertheless it is of interest, to monitor some exemplary parts with higher resolution, to show the improvement of the potential for structural analysis steps dedicated to find individual characteristics correlated with the monks or stonemason responsible for the gravure.

Fig. 3. 3D model of the inscription wall with Buddha figures

Beside laser scanning and structured-light 3D scanning other techniques like Polynomial Texture Mapping (PTM), Stereo Photogrammetry and Panoramic Photography have been used for the documentation of the inscriptions and their environment. They represent an alternative with different information content and use [6]. These techniques can be an alternative if an object is not accessible with the high-tech equipment. In that case Stereo Photogrammetry offers good visual information and a precise basis for measuring, but needs good contrast for optimal results. This might not be the case for damaged and eroded characters. Also, the spatial information is only implicitly included, why it might be necessary to apply manual or automatically post processing when the spatial information of the character is explicitly needed.

Polynomial Texture Mapping (PTM) mainly provides a plastic visualization which is used for the manual interpretation [7]. PTM is used for displaying an object under various lighting direction. The PTM is created by photographing an object multiple times with various lighting directions. These PTMs provides a deeper look onto each character which supports the interpretation of the inscription in an additional way. However, this kind of data is only two-dimensional.

The outcome of the different types of datasets (e.g. terrestrial laser scanning, fringe projection, etc.) is published within an interactive web application [8]. A large community gain access to the results of the reconstructed stone inscriptions and its interpretations as well as to additional 2D / 3D map.

3 3D – Processing of Digital Sutras

As result from the data capture the digital Sutra will be represented as a really detailed and fine 3D-mesh of points expressed in a triangulated irregular network (TIN). This might give some complications for further processing steps. On the one hand the data format of TIN's is not very storage efficient as it needs to model the relation between individual points and thus integrates link data pushing the storage volume upward, on the other hand algorithms available mainly originate from the field of terrain processing and then focus more on morphological treatments which are not of interest here.

That is why an effective use of these data needs to integrate an initial processing which tries to condense the data and to prepare it for further analysis steps. Such a pre-processing comprises reducing of the data volume, minimizing disturbing influences and emphasizing relevant information. The preparation of the data should offer a good base for a manual interpretation performed by the sinologist and also serve as base for an automated interpretation achieved by algorithms like template matching [9]. On the other hand the data should be prepared for a presentation to a wider community via internet with a good performance.

3.1 Volume Reduction

Due to the high resolution – the texts will be represented by spatial elements of fractions of millimeter in size - areas of some square meter will generate millions of spatial elements, which have to be handled and processed. Thus it is essential to have a closer look into aspects of data reduction and / or efficient data handling. Therefore additional processes have been applied allowing reducing the data volume, to minimize interfering influences as well as to enhance the relevant information.

As additional aspect, the size of the data has to be checked with respect to the needs of a web based publication. A native 3D model of an inscription of 2x2 m² may result in a data volume of ~4.32 GByte, when a spatial resolution of 0.25 mm will be used. This amount of data cannot be transferred over the internet in an acceptable manner. The data volume has to be reduced considerably before it might be transferred to the client in a common rate.

As conventional compression algorithms result in a loss of information, more intelligent strategies are necessary. In this context only the individual letters are important for us. As the spatial characteristics of the rock itself has many times higher variations than the texts themselves only special approaches lead to considerable improvements [10]: The spatial background information has to be eliminated leaving only spatial variations for each individual element of the inscription. This will be achieved by planes fitted into the model and the projection of the original 3D points onto this reference plane. In principle, this corresponds to a transformation of the complex 3D data into a 2½D space. Based on the 2½D data we can apply common image processing tools and generate a raster based model, called Digital Elevation Mode (DEM), without having a substantial information loss. The possibility to use procedures from digital image processing furthermore simplifies following steps and avoids the handling of a complex vector based 3D model. Furthermore we are able to reduce the volume of raster data by a factor 100 (4.3 GByte to 40 MByte) which is impossible to be achieved by other compression strategies.

3.2 Structural Enhancement

From the prior step mainly the data volume has been considerably reduced, however the storage of 2.5D DEM image data does not provide an ideal base for the interpretation because the small spatial structures as to be found for the characters will be suppressed by the overall morphological structure inside a Sutra (see Fig. 4). Thus the characters are represented by less information, why the influence of the walls surface has to be removed by further processing steps.

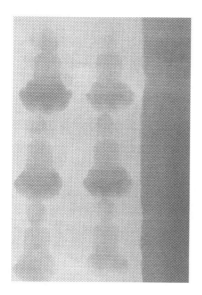 

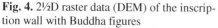

Fig. 4. 2½D raster data (DEM) of the inscription wall with Buddha figures

Fig. 5. Processed DEM of the inscription wall with Buddha figures

Inside this further treatment we distinguish three main image processing steps. These comprise a) the transformation of the 2½D data into a local height system, b) the elimination of the surface topography and c) a further compression of the data set.

By the unevenness of the walls and sometimes existing fractures in the walls large differences in height are present. Most imaging applications are just able to handle 8bit per image channel. This leads in the raster based DEM to the fact that the substantial information of the engraved characters on the walls are not recognizable. For this reason an image normalization algorithm is accomplished, whereby a smoothed variant of the raster-based DEM is subtracted from the original.

A very important part of this step is the filtering algorithm used for the smoothing operation. The intention of the smoothing operation is to get a model of the wall within all its characteristics but without the engraved character. Thus it separates the characters from the wall by subtracting the original and smoothed images. The properties of the filtering algorithm are clearly defined. The type of the filter is a low-pass filter with a small size so that it filters the image in a local way. Furthermore it has to be applied several times to even all characters the weathered one as well as the well-preserved one. In different analysis it clarifies that the size and number of appliances which provides best results is a low-pass filter with size 11x11 pixel and number of appliance of 6 (cp. Fig. 6 and Fig. 7). The high number of appliances (in our case 6) can also be replaced by using a large combined filter and applying it once. However the combined filter is not used because the other proceeding is less complicated to create and implement. These properties conduce to highly smoothed characters and less smoothed sites of fracture.

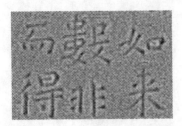   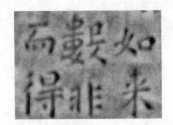

Fig. 6. 3x3 filter applied two times   **Fig. 7.** 11x11 filter applied six times

By subtracting both images, the original and the smoothed one, the heights are transferred on the basis of absolute heights related to the local coordinate system of the cave into relative heights related to the smoothed raster based DEM. Thus it is reached that mainly the small differences in height are left which contains the well-preserved and weathered characters as well as the roughness of the surface. Caused by the bad handling of boundary pixels in the smoothing operation some large differences in height still exist but without containing any substantial information. As an intermediate result the improvement of the legibility of the characters can be emphasized, but at this point a huge amount of gray scale values got lost for displaying irrelevant information.

This fact requires the second processing step. With the help of a histogram clamping the engraved characters are extracted as relevant information whereas the difference in height of the wall is limited. This limitation of the height range goes back on limit values, which are defined by means of statistic values.

Defining the limits of the second processing step influences the appearance of the image and therefore the legibility of the characters. Thus the tasks are to define the extent or the placement of the substantial information in the histogram of the images so that an extraction of the characters is enabled. The analysis of the histogram and statistics of the images leads to a definition of the limits based on statistic values, because of adapting best to the properties and characteristics of each image. The standard deviation is an appropriate value to define the limits but it separates a range of height still being to large. By reducing the standard deviation to a fraction a range of height can be defined representing only the relevant information. This conduces to an upper limit accepting a value of plus an eighth of the standard deviation and a lower limit receiving a value of minus an eighth of the standard deviation.

The application of these defined limit values reduces the complete height differences to a representation of the characters and the surface of the wall. All heights lower and higher than the limits are replaced by the limits itself so that these areas in the raster based DEM are flattened. The raster based DEM is limited to a difference in height from before approx. 100 cm to now approx. 3 cm. Thereby the influences resulted from subtracting the original and smoothed image are minimized and the characters are emphasized, the well received and the weathered ones.

Finally by a histogram stretching it is reached that the extracted height range of the raster-based DEM is transferred on the grey value range of an 8-bit and/or 16 bit image (see Fig. 5 and cp. Fig. 4). This process step allows a reduction of the data volume and the color depth.

The implementation of the histogram stretching is based on the standard function for transferring grey values. By using the minimal and maximal grey value of the image all grey value are stretched to the required range of grey values from 0 to 255 / 0 to 65536. This conduces to the fact that differences in height less than 1 mm can be differentiated and so the characters itself are rich in contrast. The general problem resulting is that not only the well-preserved and the weathered characters are emphasized but also the roughness of the walls surface. Because of their differences in height which contain the same range in the weathered characters and the roughness of the walls surface these characters can barely be differentiated.

However the processing steps provide an enormous increase of the legibility of the characters and a good base for the manual and automated interpretation and for the visualization of the data via internet. Because of the data structure and the quality of data a further processing can be accomplished using simple image processing libraries for implementing the algorithms for automated interpretation and for realizing the planned web application.

4 Data Analysis Based on Image Matching Steps

Due to the fact, that the digital Sutra are finally expressed by 2½D raster data the whole list of algorithms and concepts useful to analyze and automatically evaluate such image data are accessible for further processing steps. Such steps might be directed towards an automation of manual interactions like character identification or may serve for an automated interpretation of text passages or even perform an analysis of individual characteristics within written letters, which find their expression in geometrical or structural features. All these strategies try to simplify or accelerate the process of interpretation by the user or help to derive information, which cannot be generated by a visual inspection and therefore enriches or extends the base for an evaluation of the texts found.

4.1 Automatic Character Recognition

Automatic character recognition is especially of interest, because the manual interpretation of the inscription, which is the main task of the sinologists, produces large effort. This manual process is divided into reading, translating and extracting the information of each character like size and position in the documented inscription. According to the mass of inscriptions (approx. 80 Sutra) and characters (approx. 600,000) this procedure is almost impossible to be solved within reasonable time. That is why a more automatic interpretation would largely speed up the evaluation of the texts.

Having in mind, that the raster images of the texts represent 2½D data the selection of an algorithmic strategy is strait forward. 2½D data which result from a transformation onto the global surface geometry of the walls containing the characters can be seen as an orthophoto with the engraved structures as object information. This is free from any kind of geometrical bias, why it is sufficient to find an appropriate algorithm for the comparison of the engraved structures. Consequently simple template matching can already serve for the processing required.

One general advantage of template matching is its robustness with respect to radiometric influences leading to a reduction of the uniqueness of individual letters. As shown in Figure 8 results are satisfying even in case of lower thresholds. In the upper left an image window is shown which has be manually selected as a representative template for this letter. Below the graphical representation of this sign as derived from the Unicode value is shown. These two representations correspond very well, although small structural differences with respect to length and orientation of the graphical elements forming the sign have to be noted. They express individual characteristics of the hand writing for the person having engraved the signs. These differences may cause difficulties for the matching process as far as they are not as small as shown in this example. It is therefore better to rely the matching process on real data selected by an operator prior to the matching step.

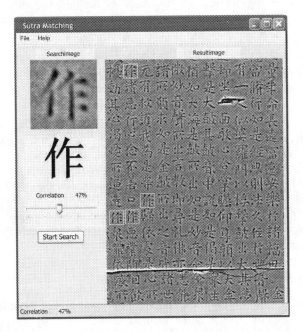

Fig. 8. Automatic character extraction using template matching (e.g. for the character 作, "create")

Other risks for an eventual failure of a template matching arise from potential losses of structural information inside the windows. This might primarily happen due to surface degradations caused by erosion of the surface. This occurs easily, when the walls with the texts are exposed to environmental factors like water or when the stone itself is composed of soft material (e.g. sandstone). But even then, a template matching helps to find characters, as can be found from figure 9. This graphic shows results for a search of the sign for Buddha (佛) and gives an impression of the degradation, which is accepted by the matching. It is clear, that the robustness is correlated with the number of elements inside a character. The more characteristic is the structural information, the higher is the tolerance and robustness of matching.

Fig. 9. Group of extracted characters using template matching for the Buddha (佛) character; Top: DEM image. Bottom: slope model

4.2 Automatic Extraction of Text Passages

The previous shown recognition process allows to locate individual letters, what already largely helps to reduce manual interaction. Nevertheless there is at least human interaction necessary, when the reference window has to be selected. In addition, this step has to be done for each letter within the alphabet represented in the text passage under treatment. As the number of different letter inside text passages of some hundred letters is limited this might be tolerable.

However, there is an improvement of this process possible, when existing additional information is used. This additional information is located inside a database called "Taisho", which contains a digital library of those Sutra texts already having been found and translated from other sources. As monks in general made use of common buddhistic knowledge and teaching during their missionary work, they mainly distributed known texts with their engravings, aiming to communicate these texts into foreign regions. That is why such libraries serve as a good first base for the interpretation and many of the texts found on the walls have their correspondence inside the libraries.

This leads to a second kind of processing, which integrates the information from "Taisho". This is done in an iterative mapping of text sequences found onto the libraries. This mapping tries to identify text streams inside the libraries, which have been found on the wall. It stops, as soon as the subsequent passages from "Taisho" and wall correspond also, showing that the right text inside the libraries has been selected for the comparison.

Therefore, the matching process locates in a first step some individual characters and searches for their counterparts within the reference library. A comparably small number of connected letters already defines unique text passages, which then can definitely be found in the reference. The idea of this processing is to merge the power of matching algorithm applied to well-preserved characters with the knowledge contained in the reference library. The matching might be based on natural templates extracted from the processed data or onto generic templates provided by Unicode characters defined in the Chinese alphabet (see Fig. 8).

After the right text passage could be identified from "Taisho" the comparison continues in order to find differences between the library and the engraved texts. These differences are very important for the interpretation process, because they tell about individual messages integrated by the monk and give a deep view into changes and/or individual characteristics of buddhistic teaching.

4.3 Computer Based Identification of Individual Text Characteristics

As individual modifications of text passages give spot lights onto the monks and their teaching, texts may also contain individual optical characteristics just allowing to group text passages into common areas belonging to different monks or stonemasons. It is similar to individual styles in hand writings for European cultures.

Such individual characteristics could be found in structural changes of individual letters and therefore will be open for template matching also, as long as the changes are significant and provide sufficient information for a reliable grouping of different instances of a letter. But as these changes are unknown beforehand, they have to be found based on a search dividing individual letters into characteristic structural elements.

Such structural elements can be derived from the knowledge about the process of engraving, which tells, that these sign consists of a limited number of lines with varying length and orientation.

Thus a calligraphic feature space will be constructed which has to be filled with the information of each letter. This information is generated by a structural analysis. The construction of the feature space is based on grouping the character strokes under calligraphic criteria and analysis its properties. The properties of each character can be for example its centre of gravity or the form, width, length and slope of its different strokes. After extracting all defined properties for best signification character they can be compared with the properties of this character matched in other data.

The construction of the feature space is based on separated matches of each character type within an inscription. These matches are represented by region images bounded by the characters dimension. For the derivation of features and its comparison the contour of each character or rather of each stroke must be isolated. Therefore a binarisation (see Fig. 10) is accomplished separating the character itself from the background. By means of an edge detection filter, the resulting image still contains the edge of the strokes which have to be connected to closed lines.

This procedure is necessary due to the fact, that crossing strokes can not be separated. For that reason a minimal bounding box is generated around the individual parts of the character (see Fig. 11). Inside this minimal bounding box the parts of the character are polygonized with the analysis of the polygons shape in mind. The shape of the polygons is inspected whether it is convex or concave. In case it is concave this part of the character may consist of more than one stroke. In addition, the corners of the characters are extracted by using the Harris corner detection algorithm [11]. These corners represent feature points and allow to divide the detected parts of characters in its separated strokes. Furthermore this subdivision is also supported by general information to each individual letter contained in the Unicode character table, what helps to formulate appropriate division rules.

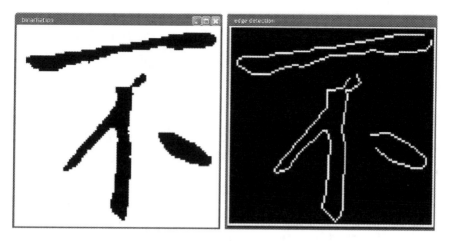

Fig. 10. Binarisation and edge detection applied to the extracted character 不, "no"

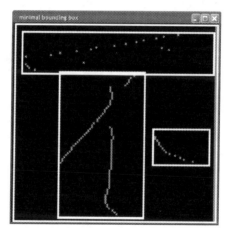

Fig. 11. Minimal bounding boxes (cp Fig. 10)

After the subdivision of all strokes of the character they can be polygonized and compared with each other. The comparison itself concerns with form, width, length and slope of the several strokes or the centre of gravity of the whole character.

All determined and extracted properties are placed in a database. The usage of a database for saving the image information and the segmented matches of each character combined with its feature spaces offers the advantage to analyze the calligraphic properties of the characters with systematically requests and to derive new possibilities for the interpretation.

5   Conclusion

High precision 3D digitization techniques developed for industrial applications show also a large potential for archaeological and art-historical questions. It is obvious, that the objects have to be accessible for the equipment and have to be co-operative for a successful and precise 3D data capture. Based on such digital copies various processing chains can be implemented allowing to analyze and to evaluate the objects collected.

In the present example of buddhistic stone inscriptions we used fringe projection technique to document the inscriptions. Compared to the traditional rubbing this high resolution scanning allows us to create a non-destructive virtual copies of the stone inscriptions and to establish special processing chains.

The processing applied is structured into a pre-processing necessary to reduce the amount of data, to eliminate the impact of the surface topography, to transform the data into a 2½D raster description and to improve the appearance of the character and a following analysis.

Within the final analysis we could show, that already conventional template matching might be useful to automate the process of character identification, what reduces the manual effort. When a data base containing known Sutra texts is integrated, the analysis can be extended to a more complete and automated extraction of text passages. Finally image processing allows also to do some calligraphic analysis, which tries to separate structural elements inside individual representations of a single letter and might give hints to the monk or the stonemason responsible for the engraving of the texts.

In total it could be shown, that simple image processing steps linked with high resolution 3D data give completely new opportunities to support art historical work on buddhistic Sutra texts.

Acknowledgements. This work is funded by the "Bundesministerium für Bildung und Forschung" (BMBF)" - Germany within the "Wechselwirkungen zwischen Natur- und Geisteswissenschaften" research activity program 01UA0814, what is highly appreciated by the authors.

References

1. Ledderose, L.: The Stones resembled printing blocks. The engraved Buddhist stone scriptures at Yúnjū monastery of Fāngshan and the Qìdān canon. In: Anderl, C., Eifring, H. (eds.) Studies in Chinese Language and Culture, pp. 319–329. Hermes Publishing, Oslo (2006)
2. Ledderose, L.: Rubbings in Art History. In: Walravens, H. (ed.) Catalogue of Chinese Rubbings from Field Museum, Field Museum of Natural History, Chicago, USA. Fieldiana Anthropology New Series, vol. 3, pp. XXVIII–XXXVI (1981)
3. Boochs, F., Heinz, G., Huxhagen, U., Müller, H.: Digital Documentation of Cultural Heritage Objects using hybrid recording techniques. In: Ioannides, M., Niccolucci, F., Mania, K. (eds.) The e-volution of Information Communication Technology in Cultural Heritage. part 2, pp. 258–262. EPOCH Publishing, Nicosia (2006)
4. Böhler, W., Bordas Vicent, M., Heinz, G., Marbs, A., Müller, H.: High Quality Scanning and Modeling of Monuments and Artifacts. In: Proceedings of the FIG Working Week 2004, Athens, Greece, May 22-27. FIG (2004)
5. Hanke, K., Böhler, W.: Recording and Visualizing the Cenotaph of German Emperor Maximilian I. In: Int. Archives of Photogrammetry & Remote Sensing, vol. XXXV, B5 (2004)

6. Hoffmann, A., Huxhagen, U., Welter, D., Boochs, F.: Digital reconstruction archaeological objects using hybrid sensing techniques - the example Porta Nigra. In: 2nd International Conference on Remote Sensing Archaeology, Rome, Italy (2006)
7. Malzbender, T., Gelb, D., Wolters, H.: Polynomial texture maps. In: Proceedings of SIG-GRAPH 2001 Computer Graphics, pp. 519–528 (2001)
8. Schmidt, N., Schütze, R., Boochs, F.: 3D-Sutra - Interactive Analysis Tool for a Web-Atlas of Scanned Sutra Inscriptions in China. In: Proceedings of the ISPRS Commission V Mid-Term Symposium Close Range Image Measurement Techniques, Newcastle upon Tyne, United Kingdom (2010)
9. Steinke, K.-H.: Lokalisierung von Schrift in komplexer Umgebung. In: Tagungsband der Jahrestagung der deutschen Gesellschaft für Photogrammetrie, Jena, Germany, pp. 165–173 (2009)
10. Schmidt, N.: 3D-Sutren - Konzeptionierung und Entwicklung eines Prozessierungsmoduls und einer Webapplikation für den Anwendungsbereich Sinologie. Master thesis, FH Mainz (2009) (unpublished)
11. Derpanis, K.G.: The Harris corner detector. York University (2004), http://www.cse.yorku.ca/~kosta/CompVis_Notes/harris_detector.pdf (accessed May 28, 2010)

Same Same But Different – Comparing Rendering Environments for Interactive Digital Objects

M. Guttenbrunner[1,2], J. Wieners[3], A. Rauber[1], and M. Thaller[3]

[1] Vienna University of Technology, 1040 Vienna, Austria
{guttenbrunner,rauber}@ifs.tuwien.ac.at
[2] Secure Business Austria, 1040 Vienna, Austria
mguttenbrunner@sba-research.org
[3] University of Cologne, Cologne, Germany
{jan.wieners,manfred.thaller}@uni-koeln.de

Abstract. Digital cultural heritage in interactive form can take different shapes. It can be either in the form of interactive virtual representations of non-digital objects like buildings or nature, but also as born digital materials like interactive art and video games. To preserve these materials for a long term, we need to perform preservation actions on them. To check the validity of these actions, the original and the preserved form have to be compared. While static information like images or text documents can be migrated to new formats, especially digital objects which are interactive have to be preserved using new rendering environments.

In this paper we show how the results of rendering an object in different environments can be compared. We present a workflow with three stages that supports the execution of digital objects in a rendering environment, the application of interactive actions in a standardized way to ensure no deviations due to different interactions, and the XCL Layout processor application that extends the characterized screenshots of the rendering results by adding information about significant areas in the screenshot allowing us to compare the rendering results. We present case studies on interactive fiction and a chess program that show that the approach is valid and that the rendering results can be successfully compared.

Keywords: Digital Preservation, Rendering, Preservation Planning, Characterization, Emulation, Image Segmentation.

1 Introduction

As more and more representations of our cultural heritage are recreated in digital and interactive form (e.g. interactive models of buildings [1], nature areas [2] or ancient cities [3], we have to ensure, that these representations can be accessed in future rendering environments as well. Also born digital materials like interactive art and video games have to be preserved as part of our digital cultural heritage.

Most recent digital preservation projects concentrated on migration of documents as a main strategy for preserving images and documents. Automatic evaluation of the

M. Ioannides (Ed.): EuroMed 2010, LNCS 6436, pp. 140–152, 2010.

results of migration processes, e.g. for evaluating the validity of tools, compares characteristics of the original and the migrated files. Previous work on characterization of digital objects made clear, that the separation between the properties of digital objects which reside in their persistently stored form and the properties which are inherent in the rendering software is not always sufficiently clear. While for some types of objects most of the information about the rendering can be found stored in the object (e.g. text files, image files) and the rendering software just interprets these properties. On the other hand e.g. 3D objects stored in the resource files of a computer game describe the object but are put into context with the game environment, the player actions, the view-point or lightning only due to the game logic (=the rendering software). In this case it is not possible to deduce the rendering properties from a stored version of the object. Having the object rendered and comparing the outcome of rendering processes from different environments (e.g. the original and an emulated environment) makes it possible to evaluate, if the interaction properties, i.e. the reaction of a digital object to interaction, stay intact. Similar principles apply also to all static objects, as preservation always needs to focus on the intellectual object (the object as conceived by the observer), rather than the stored representation, which always has to include the view path, requiring us to compare rendered forms.

In this paper we describe how the XCL Layout Processor [4] as an extension to the Extensible Characterization Language (XCL) [5] is used to compare different renderings of a digital object. We present a workflow for applying interaction to the same digital object in different rendering environments and measuring the results of comparing significant states of interactive objects. We describe how interaction can be applied to digital objects by using a tool that captures and replays input to the different environments and how the outcome can be compared by taking a screenshot at a certain point in execution time. Using this approach we show how the effects of interaction on a digital object can be measured comparing screenshots of the environment taken from a target state or different intermediary states of the object. This allows for automatic comparison of rendering results and thus supports the evaluation of rendering environments.

The paper is structured as follows. First we give an overview on related work on the subject. In Section 3 we explain how we apply interaction and when we measure the results. Then Section 4 shows how the screenshots we take as a result of the rendering process are analyzed and mapped in the characterization language. In Section 5 the workflow for comparing different rendering environments is shown and in Section 6 we present a case study on interactive fiction and a chess program. Finally the conclusions are presented and an outlook to future work is given.

2   Related Work

The UNESCO guidelines for the preservation of digital heritage [6] list migration [7] and emulation [8] [9] as the main strategies for digital preservation. Migration is the strategy to keep a digital object accessible by converting it to a non-obsolete format, while emulation refers to the capability of a device or software to replicate the behaviour of a different device or software. With emulation the object is kept accessible in its original environment. Previous research has concentrated on methods for evaluating the effects of migration on documents. A preservation planning workflow is described in [10] and allows repeatable evaluation of preservation alternatives. An implementation of this workflow has been done in the preservation planning tool Plato [11], utilizing automatic characterization of migrated objects with tools like Droid [12] to identify files. The significant properties of migrated objects can be compared automatically using the eXtensible Characterisation Language (XCL) [5] to measure the effects of migration on the object.

While the preservation planning tool can be used to compare rendering environments as shown in a case study in [13], the comparison has to be done manually. In [14] the information contained within a file is distinguished from the rendering of this information. Thaller shows that the rendering process can produce different outcomes for the same file if a different view-path for rendering a digital object is used. This makes it necessary to not only compare properties of the file but also properties of the outcome after a rendering process (e.g. output on a screen).

In [15] van Diessen describes the view-path as "a full set of functionality for rendering the information contained in a digital object". The view-path contains the hardware and all the secondary digital objects needed to render an object along with their configuration. It is possible to use different view-paths to display the same object. On various hardware-configurations different operating systems (e.g. WinXP, Linux) can be used to run different applications (e.g. Word, Open Office) to render the same object (e.g. Word-97 Document).

In [16] the levels on which significant properties can be extracted are described and it is shown, what continuity has to be considered when extracting properties with regards to a defined view-path and standardized interaction to expect the same results. In [4] Wieners describes how the XCL Layout Processor was developed as an extension to the XCL tools to extract significant coordinates of areas in an image such as a screenshot of a rendered digital object. For the image segmentation the screenshots of the rendering outcomes are first reduced to monochrome images to facilitate the edge detection. Otsu's global thresholding method as described in [17] is used for this. Then these monochrome images are segmented using an image segmentation algorithm described in [18].

3   Identifying Interaction Properties

Previous tests with different interactive digital objects presented in [13] and [16] made it clear, that some significant properties concerning interaction have to be defined for every interactive digital object. It is necessary to research to what types of input (e.g. certain keys on a keyboard, mouse pointer movement or mouse clicks, joystick input) a digital object responds, but also to the timing in which this input has to occur. While the same interactive response of an action game relies very strong on the exact same timing of the input, in interactive fiction like text adventures or point-and-click adventures the timing is usually not as critical.

By having a user manually interact with the digital object and recording the user input to the digital object as well as the times relative to the object execution start we are able to replay the same input automatically. Using a separate tool this can be done independent of the object execution environment (e.g. a video game rendered in different emulation environments). This approach allows us the use not only on emulation environments but also on other execution environments (e.g. source ports of a software or using game engine interpreters like ScummVM[1] or Frotz[2] for video games). By defining an "end point" where the user finishes the input actions and the interactive object finishes responding to these actions we can take a screenshot of the rendering at a certain point of execution both when recording the user action but also after replaying the user action to a different (or even the same) rendering environment. In the next section we describe the process of analysing the image and placing the significant properties of identified segments in the image in the corresponding XCDL of the screenshot.

4 Image Segmentation and Mapping in XCL

The central analysis task of the method described in this chapter is to identify specific regions in the rendered digital object, which can – in a final step – be compared with the rendering of the same object, using another rendering environment. Those specific regions reflect characteristic layout properties: regions with a high frequency of pixels that could refer to a significant area. To identify and isolate such regions of interest in the prepared, cut to size and binarized image, the image is segmented by the Efficient Graph-Based Image Segmentation Algorithm as presented in (Felzenszwalb, 2004).

For each black pixel in the binarized image, the algorithm determines the affiliation of the processed pixel to a specific region by using three different parameters that influence the operation-mode of the segmentation algorithm:

- σ (Sigma) indicates how strongly the image is smoothed by the Gaussian filter. The higher σ, the more the image gets smoothed.
- k influences the "scale of observation" : the larger k, the larger the components identified by the segmentation algorithm are.
- min determines the minimum component size: the smaller the size of min, the more objects will be identified by the segmentation algorithm.

To facilitate comparison between two screenshots, the proposed solution sets the upper leftmost pixel and the bottom rightmost pixel of a layout-screenshot in relation to the pixel dimensions of the image by dividing both pixel values by the width, respectively the height, of the processed image. Finally, these relative values are embedded into XCDL files, which are connected to the screenshots, to enable a comparison of the objects through the XCL Comparator (Becker et.al., 2008b).

The structure of the input XCDL is supplemented by a new property with a unique identifier: A new property with the id "p15381" (fixed value) is inserted into the XCDL and represents the significant points of the isolated objects in the screenshot file through different valueSet Tags. It is inserted after the XML header, the XCDL Schema and the normData part of the XCDL file, and is visualized in the code snippet shown in Figure 1.

---

[1] ScummVM - Graphical point-and-click adventure game engine interpreter:
    http://www.scummvm.org/
[2] Frotz – Game Engine Interpreter for Infocom and other Z-machine games:
    http://frotz.sourceforge.net/

```
<property id="p15381" source="raw" cat="descr">
    <name id="id9998">significantCoordinates</name>
    <valueSet id="i_i1_i2xx_s1_1">
        <labValue>
            <val>0.118727 0.113586 0.232558 0.335189</val>
            <type>rational</type>
        </labValue>
    </valueSet>
</property>
```

Fig. 1. Code snippet of XCDL enhancement for significant coordinates of identified areas

The four floating point numbers in the first valueSet of the generated XCDL (<val>*leftupper_X leftupper_Y rightlower_X rightlower_Y*</val>) represent the relative pixel position of the significant points, identified through the segmentation process. Therefore, the value *leftupper_X* (0.118727 in the example in Figure 1) indicates the position of the relative x coordinate of the topmost left pixel of the identified object; the second value, *leftupper_Y*, (0.113586 in the example in Figure 1) indicates the relative y coordinate of the topmost left pixel of the identified object. The next two values refer to the relative x and y coordinates of the bottommost right pixel values of the identified object.

An application that accomplishes the described tasks was created as the XCL Layout Processor. A screenshot of the application in use for comparing screenshots of two renderings of a text document (on the one side rendered with Microsoft Word 2007, on the other side rendered with Adobe Reader) can be seen in Figure 2. The screenshot as well as the corresponding XCDL characterization file are loaded into one region of the application of the application's GUI. The XCDL is then enhanced as described above with the significant coordinates of the recognized areas. For a visual comparison a second screenshot and XCDL file can be loaded into the second region and processed likewise.

5 Applying Interaction to Digital Objects and Comparing Rendering Results

To evaluate if the interactive properties of a digital object are preserved properly in a different rendering environment than the one originally intended for the object it is necessary to ensure that the same kind of input is applied to the object at the same point in time. By keeping the secondary digital objects in the view-path for the object as well as external influences like user input unchanged, differences in the rendering are caused by a change in the rendering environment.

A conceptual workflow for comparing the interactive properties of a digital object in different rendering environments is drafted below. It consists of 3 stages with different steps in the stages as shown in Figure 3.

Stage 1: Recording the Original Environment. In this stage the user actions are recorded in the original environment and screenshots of the original rendering process are taken as "ground truth" against which other environments are evaluated. The following steps are followed:

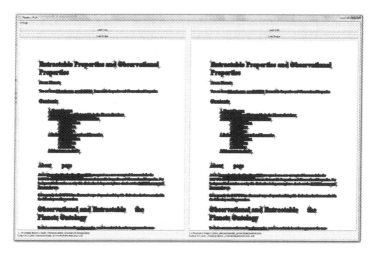

Fig. 2. Comparison of two renderings of a text document in the XCL Layout Processor. Identified areas are shown in blue, identified coordinates as red crosses.

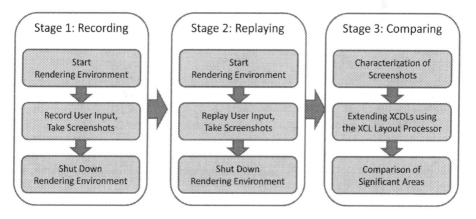

Fig. 3. Conceptual workflow for comparing rendering results of interactive digital objects

1. start the rendering environment with the digital object
2. record the user actions (e.g. in a standardized XML-Format) and take screenshots at predefined intervals or one screenshot after a certain amount of time
3. shut down the rendering environment

Stage 2: Replaying. In this stage the recorded user actions are applied to the alternative rendering environment. The same settings for screenshot interval etc. are used as when recording in the original environment. These steps in this stage are carried out for every alternative rendering environment that is evaluated:

1. start the rendering environment with the digital object (e.g. different emulation environment)

2. replay the user actions from a recorded session and take screenshots at the same predefined intervals or one screenshot after a certain amount of time as in the original recording session
3. shut down the rendering environment

Stage 3: Comparing. Finally in this step the rendering process are compared. Therefore the screenshots need to be characterized and the following steps to be taken to compare the screenshots taken during the rendering processes. The steps in this stage have to be repeated for every alternative rendering environment that is evaluated.

1. Characterization of the screenshot images
2. Extending the XCDL for the screenshots with the coordinates of the identified significant areas using the XCL Layout Processor
3. Pair wise comparison of the screenshots taken at the same object execution time using the XCL comparator to identify differences in the rendering

Using the workflow drafted above, we have established a formalized way to compare the rendering results for the same digital object in different rendering environments. The workflow can be implemented in a tool to support the automatic comparison of rendering of interactive digital objects.

6   Case Study on Interactive Objects

We evaluated the proposed workflow for testing interactive properties of digital objects by comparing the rendered outputs on two case studies. We used the XCL comparator to compare XCDL files of the rendering outcome screenshots. These XCDL files were extended by coordinates of significant areas using the XCL Layout Processor introduced in Section 4.

For the first case study we used the video game "The Secret of Monkey Island". This game was developed by Lucasfilm Games and released on various platforms from October 1990. The game is a typical point and click adventure game, thus not requiring interaction timing that is exact down to millisecond level. It was also chosen because conceptually different rendering engines exist, that are usable for digital preservation purposes:

- ScummVM: a game engine interpreter available for various non-obsolete platforms
- Emulation/Virtualization of the original hardware (e.g. DOSBox[3])

Various tools for recording interaction and replaying it in the form of a macro were evaluated but failed especially in recording/applying interaction in the game running in the original environment (as a Full-Screen DOS-application). As no tool for automating the process described in the previous chapter exists yet, the steps were performed manually. First the game was executed on a workstation running Windows XP. The movements of the mouse pointer as well as the keystrokes and times of these events were manually noted and the game was played up to a point where the character in the game that is controlled by the player enters the SCUMM Bar and talks to

---

[3] DOSBox: http://www.dosbox.com/

pirates sitting on a table telling "I want to be a pirate." At that point in the game a screenshot was taken.

Subsequently the same actions were then performed by trying to replicate the same timing by running the game under a virtualized environment using DOSBox 0.72 and using the ScummVM 1.1.148874 Engine (using also the game data files from the DOS Version of the game). For ScummVM an unscaled rendering replicating the "EGA" settings that were similar to the options of the real DOS-Version of the game were used.

The screenshots taken in the three different rendering environments were then characterized using the XCL tools. Then the XCL Layout Processor was used to binarize and segment the screenshots and extend the XCDLs of the images. Figure 4 shows a screenshot from the original DOS-version of the scene defined as "endpoint" for this scenario on the left. On the right the same screenshot as segmented by the XCL Layout Processor is shown. The image is binarized to black/white to identify areas. Different greyscales present in the segmented image are just a visualization of the different segments in the picture. The following values were used for the segmentation algorithm: $\sigma=0.8$, $k=1000$ and min$=100$. Figure 5 and Figure 6 show the segmentation for the screenshots of the other two rendering environments of the game. A visual comparison of the segmentations shows, that the game running in the DOSBox environment is segmented to very similar areas as in the original version, whereas in the ScummVM version a lot more differences can be found.

The XCL Layout Processor enhances the original XCDL which was created by using the XCL extractor on the screenshots taken in the different environments. Table 1 shows the number of significant areas identified per screenshot.

Table 1. Significant areas recognized in different renderings of the same scene in "The Secret of Monkey Island"

Rendering Environment	Original	ScummVM	DOSBox
Significant Areas in XCDL	**62**	**66**	**62**

Fig. 4. Screenshot of original DOS-Version of "The Secret of Monkey Island" (left). Significant areas in the same screenshot as a result of binarization and segmentation are shown on the right.

Fig. 5. Screenshot of "The Secret of Monkey Island" running in the DOSBox Environment (left). Significant areas in the same screenshot as a result of binarization and segmentation are shown on the right.

Fig. 6. Screenshot of "The Secret of Monkey Island" using ScummVM as a rendering engine (left). Significant areas in the same screenshot as a result of binarization and segmentation are shown on the right.

Using the XCL comparator we then compared the XCDLs of the different screenshots. The comparator reported failure for both comparisons. On closer inspection of the XCDLs of the screenshots the following facts were observed:

- The original and the DOSBox version differed in significant areas that were recognized (e.g. a fire burning in the chimney, pirate's heads moving). The reason are animations in the picture which lead to slightly different images and thus to different areas that are recognized by the segmentation algorithm. Blocks not animated and without other animated blocks overlapping do have the same coordinates.
- The original and the ScummVM version differed in that the colour spaces of the screenshots were different. While the original version was rendered in an 8bit colour space (palette mode), ScummVM rendered the image in a 24bit colour space (true-colour mode). Even though the number of significant areas was coincidental equal, the coordinates differed throughout all areas.

Based on these differences we can draw the following conclusions:

- Timing of screenshots together with the input is important, as animations in interactive dynamic digital objects that occur continuously (e.g. changes in the environment or in small movements of characters) changes the screenshot and thus leads to different coordinates of significant areas and also to different areas that might be recognized as significant.

- This in turn leads to the fact that the values for the segmentation algorithm have to be balanced accordingly to detect the same significant areas even when slight changes in objects occur. The algorithm has to be configured sensitive enough to recognize enough areas to compare two screenshots and detect differences, but in-sensitive to minor differences in an image that lead to changes in recognizing a significant area as being exactly that.

To validate the outcome of the XCL Layout Processor on a digital object which would not pose the problems of animations and need an exact timing of key presses and screenshots taken, we made a second case study on the game "Chessmaster 2100" published for the DOS platform in 1988. Again the original software running in DOS was compared to the same program running in DOSBox in Windows XP. A few beginning moves in a game of chess were played with trying to keep the timing of the moves intact manually. The screenshots taken as well as the segmentations of the screenshots can be seen in Figures 7 and 8 respectively. For all the elements on screen to be correctly visible on the segmented image (e.g. the numbers left and below the board, all the figures in the squares) the following values were used for the segmentation algorithm: $\sigma=1.0$, k=1000 and min=100.

A first inspection of the images shows that the colour depth in DOSBox was increased to 8bit compared to 4bit in the original image. This is also reflected in the extracted XCDL of the images. Visually this also results in slightly different colour shades in the extracted images and is also reported when comparing the images using the XCL comparator as difference in the colour palette. Comparing the XCDL files enhanced with coordinates for significant areas by the XCL Layout Processor, we can see that the identified areas in the images are exactly the same in number (153 recognized areas) and coordinates.

If we compare the results to the case study on "The Secret of Money Island" we can see that depending on the digital object and on the fact that no animations change the image in the evaluated chess program, the timing of screenshots and interaction is less crucial and allows us to manually evaluate the rendering results for certain interactive digital objects like "Chessmaster 2100", thus confirming the validity of the approach of using the XCL Layout processor for comparing rendering outcomes after applying interaction to the object.

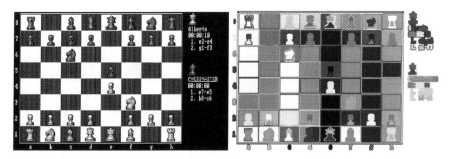

Fig. 7. Screenshot of "Chessmaster 2100" running under DOS on the left and the segmented screenshot showing significant areas on the right

Fig. 8. Screenshot of "Chessmaster 2100" running under DOSBox in Windows XP on the left and the segmented screenshot showing significant areas on the right

7 Conclusions and Future Work

The work presented in this paper showed an approach to identify characteristic objects of rendered digital objects based on screenshots in certain stages during the lifetime of the object. Identification of significant areas in the screenshot is done using pre-processing methods like cutting and reducing the image information through binarization and, finally, the Graph-Based Image Segmentation Algorithm. By comparing the rendering results of one or more pre-determined states during the runtime of a digital object that responds to user input it is possible to evaluate, if a digital object reacts to interactive actions as expected and in the same way over various different rendering environments. The conditions for the rendering must not change over different environments. Different lighting conditions or a different view-point in the new rendering environment will result in a change in rendering, thus producing a different image even though an object behaves similar in two different rendering environments.

We introduced a conceptual workflow for recording user interaction in an original environment along with screenshots along the path, with applying the same interaction and taking screenshots in the same points in execution in other rendering environments. Using the extensible Characterization Language (XCL) properties of the screenshots along with the identified significant areas in the images are compared to evaluate, if a rendering environment is creating the same result as the original rendering environment.

We carried out case studies on interactive fiction using the game "The Secret of Monkey Island" and one on the chess playing program "Chessmaster 2100". The result of the case studies showed:

- It is important to consider exact timing both of interaction but also of the time when the screenshot is taken, to compare the same rendering results, as changes in the image that do not occur due to interaction (e.g. animations of the game environment or characters) influence the result of the segmentation algorithm. If the resulting image is constant exact timing is less crucial.
- Identifying the accurate segmentation parameters (σ, k, min) for a certain digital object is crucial for correctly recognizing the significant areas over different

screenshots, especially if the rendering environments use different colour depth or image resolution for rendering the digital object.

The case study on "Chessmaster 2100" also confirmed that comparison of different rendering environments using the XCL Layout Processor and the XCL Tools can actually be used to evaluate if interactive properties of digital objects are preserved in different rendering environments by comparing rendering outcomes after applying interaction to the digital objects.

For future work it is necessary to implement the proposed workflow in a tool, as exact timing is not possible with manual interactions. Preliminary tests with various keyboard recording and screenshot tools also showed that depending on the environment it is not always possible to record/interact from outside the rendering environment, making it necessary to support the process inside the rendering environment (e.g. an emulator). Additional work has to be done on the segmentation process and the determination of the segmentation parameters for different types of digital objects.

Acknoledgements

Part of this work was supported by the European Union in the 6th Framework Program, IST, through the PLANETS project, contract 033789.

References

1. Foni, A., Papagiannakis, G., Magnenat-Thalmann, N.: Virtual Hagia Sophia: Restitution, Visualization and Virtual Life Simulation. Presented at the UNESCO World Heritage Congress (2002)
2. DeLeon, V., Berry, R.: Bringing VR to the Desktop: Are You Game? IEEE MultiMedia 2000, 68–72 (2008)
3. Maïm, J., Haegler, S., Yersin, B., Mueller, P., Thalmann, D., Vangool, L.: Populating ancient pompeii with crowds of virtual romans. In: Proceedings of the 8th International Symposium on Virtual Reality, Archaeology and Cultural Heritage (VAST 2007), pp. 26–30 (2007)
4. Wieners, J.: Extend the capabilities of the extraction tools to extract layout characteristics. PC/4 - D13. Internal Deliverable, EU Project Planets (2010)
5. Becker, C., Rauber, A., Heydegger, V., Schnasse, J., Thaller, M.: Systematic characterisation of objects in digital preservation: The extensible characterisation languages. Journal of Universal Computer Science 14(18), 2936–2952 (2008)
6. Webb, C.: Guidelines for the Preservation of the Digital Heritage. In: Information Society Division United Nations Educational, Scientific and Cultural Organization (UNESCO) – National Library of Australia,
http://unesdoc.unesco.org/images/0013/001300/130071e.pdf
7. Slats, J.: The Digital Preservation Testbed - Migration: Context and current status. Whitepaper, National Archives and Ministry of the Interior and Kingdom Relations (2001)
8. Rothenberg, J.: Avoiding Technological Quicksand: Finding a Viable Technical Foundation for Digital Preservation. In: Council on Library and Information Resources (1999),
http://www.clir.org/pubs/reports/rothenberg/contents.html

9. Van der Hoeven, J., Lohman, B., Verdegem, R.: Emulation for digital preservation in practice: The results. International Journal of Digital Curation 2(2), 123–132 (2008)
10. Becker, C., Kulovits, H., Guttenbrunner, M., Strodl, S., Rauber, A., Hofman, H.: Systematic planning for digital preservation: Evaluating potential strategies and building preservation plans. International Journal on Digital Libraries (IJDL) (December 2009)
11. Becker, C., Kulovits, H., Rauber, A., Hofman, H.: Plato: a service-oriented decision support system for preservation planning. In: Proceedings of the ACM/IEEE Joint Conference on Digital Libraries (JCDL 2008), Pittsburgh, Pennsylvania, June 16-20 (2008)
12. Brown, A.: Automatic format identification using pronom and droid. Digital Preservation Technical Paper 1 (2008),
http://www.nationalarchives.gov.uk/aboutapps/fileformat/pdf/automatic_format_identification.pdf
13. Guttenbrunner, M., Becker, C., Rauber, A.: Keeping the game alive: Evaluating strategies for the preservation of console video games. International Journal of Digital Curation (IJDC) 5(1), 64–90 (2010)
14. Thaller, M.: Interaction testing benchmark deliverable PC/2 - D6. Internal Deliverable, EU Project Planets (2008)
15. Van Diessen, R.J.: Preservation requirements in a deposit system. IBM/KB Long-Term Preservation Study Report Series, vol. 3, ch. 3 (2002),
http://www-05.ibm.com/nl/dias/resource/preservation.pdf
16. Guttenbrunner, M.: Evaluating the effects of emulation environments on rendering digital objects. Internal Deliverable PP5/D2, EU Project Planets (2009)
17. Otsu, N.: A Threshold Selection Method from Gray-Level Histograms. IEEE Transactions on Systems, Man, and Cybernetics 9(1), 62–66 (1979)
18. Felzenszwalb, P.F., Huttenlocher, D.P.: Efficient Graph-Based Image Segmentation. International Journal of Computer Vision 59(2), 167–181 (2004)

Modeling Procedural Knowledge: A Generative Modeler for Cultural Heritage

Christoph Schinko[1], Martin Strobl[1],Torsten Ullrich[2], and Dieter W. Fellner[1,2,3]

[1] Institut für ComputerGraphik und WissensVisualisierung (CGV),
Technische Universität Graz
{c.schinko,m.strobl}@cgv.tugraz.at
[2] Fraunhofer Austria Research GmbH, Visual Computing, Graz, Austria
torsten.ullrich@fraunhofer.at
[3] Fraunhofer IGD/Technische Universität Darmstadt, Germany

Abstract. Within the last few years generative modeling techniques have gained attention especially in the context of cultural heritage. As a generative model describes a rather ideal object than a real one, generative techniques are a basis for object description and classification. This procedural knowledge differs from other kinds of knowledge, such as declarative knowledge, in a significant way. It can be applied to a task. This similarity to algorithms is reflected in the way generative models are designed: they are programmed. In order to make generative modeling accessible to cultural heritage experts, we created a generative modeling framework which accounts for their special needs. The result is a generative modeler (http://www.cgv.tugraz.at/euclides) based on an easy-to-use scripting language (JavaScript). The generative model meets the demands on documentation standards and fulfils sustainability conditions. Its integrated meta-modeler approach makes it independent from hardware, software and platforms.

Keywords: Generative Modeling, Procedural Knowledge, Content Creation, Documentation and Archival.

1 Motivation

1.1 Generative Modeling

Generative modeling techniques have rapidly gained attention throughout the past few years. Many researchers enforced the creation of generative models due to its many advantages. All objects with well-organized structures and repetitive forms can be described procedurally. In these cases generative modeling is superior to conventional approaches.

Its strength lies in the compact description [1] compared to conventional approaches, which does not depend on the counter of primitives but on the model's complexity itself. Particularly large scale models and scenes – such as plants, buildings, cities, and landscapes – can be described efficiently. Therefore generative descriptions make complex models manageable as they allow identifying a shape's high-level parameters [2].

M. Ioannides (Ed.): EuroMed 2010, LNCS 6436, pp. 153–165, 2010.

Another advantage of procedural modeling techniques is the included expert knowledge within an object description; e.g. classification schemes used in architecture, archaeology, civil engineering, etc. can be mapped to procedures. For a specific object only its type and its instantiation parameters have to be identified. This identification is required by digital library services: markup, indexing, and retrieval [3]. The importance of semantic meta data becomes obvious in the context of electronic product data management, product life cycle management, data exchange and storage or, more general, of digital libraries.

Fig. 1. The combination of various stages during object reconstruction (photos – left part of the temple, generated point clouds – middle, and resulting CAD models – right) offers many advantages for object analysis and documentation

1.2   Cultural Heritage

In the field of computer-aided design and computer-aided engineering, the generative and procedural modeling techniques are well studied. Unfortunately, the context of cultural heritage distinguishes itself by model complexity, model size, and imperfection to an extent unknown to most fields of application.

Complexity. Cultural heritage artifacts represent a masterpiece of human creative genius. Hence, many cultural heritage artifacts have a high inherent complexity.

Size. The UNESCO lists 644 cultural sites in over 130 states. An archaeological excavation may have an extent on the scale of kilometers and miles with a richness of detail on the scale of millimeters or small fractions of an inch.

Domain knowledge by cultural heritage experts and generative modeling techniques are keys to cope with this complexity and size. The advantages of procedural modeling arise from the generative approach. It scales with the object's complexity and does not depend on the object's number of vertices. Furthermore, generative models normally have perfect shapes which do not suffer from wear and tear effects. Therefore they represent an ideal object rather than a real one. The enrichment of measured data with an ideal description enhances the range of potential applications, not only in the field of cultural heritage. A nominal/actual value comparison may indicate wear and tear effects as well as changes in style (see Figure 1). But how are these generative models created?

2 Related Work

2.1 CGA-Shape

In today's procedural modeling systems, grammars are often used as a set of rules to achieve a description. Parish and Müller presented a system for procedural modeling of cities [4] that is based on L-systems and shape grammars. Given a number of image maps as input, it generates a street map including geometry for buildings. For that purpose L-systems have been extended to allow the definition of global objectives as well as local constraints. However, the use of procedurally generated textures to represent facades of buildings limits the level of detail in the results. In later work, Müller et al. describe a system [5] to create detailed facades based on the split grammar called CGA-Shape. A framework called CityEngine provides a modeling environment for CGA-Shape. It relies on different views to guide an iterative modeling process.

Another modeling approach presented by [6] following the notation of Müller [7] deals with the aspects of more direct local control of the underlying grammar by introducing visual editing. The idea is to allow modification of elements selected directly in a 3D-view, rather than editing rules in a text based environment. Therefore principles of semantic and geometric selection are combined as well as functionality to store local changes persistently over global modifications.

2.2 Generative Modeling Language

Havemann proposes a stack based language for creating polygonal meshes called Generative Modeling Language (GML) [8]. The postfix notation of the language is very similar to that of Adobe's Postscript. It allows the creation of high-level shape operators from low-level shape operators. The GML serves as a platform for a number of applications because it is extensible and comes with an integrated visualization engine.

2.3 Scripted Modelers

3D modeling software packages like Autodesk Maya™ provide a variety of tools for the modeling process. In addition to a graphical user interface, a scripting language is supplied to extend its functionality. It enables tasks that cannot be achieved easily using the GUI and speeds up complicated or repetitive tasks.

When using parametric tools in modern CAD software products, geometric validity is a subject. For a given parametric model certain combinations of parameter values may not result in valid shapes. Hoffmann and Kim propose an algorithm [9] that computes valid parameter ranges for geometric elements in a plane, given a set of constraints.

2.4 Processing

Processing is a programming language and development environment initially created to serve as a software sketchbook and to teach fundamentals of computer programming [10]. It quickly developed into a tool that is used for creating visual arts. Processing is basically a Java-like interpreter, but with a new graphics and utility API together with some usability simplifications. A large community behind the tool produced over seventy libraries to facilitate computer vision, data visualization, music, networking, and electronics.

Besides Processing, each of these tools is designed for computer graphics experts. Furthermore, all of them provide a platform, which cannot be changed afterwards.

3 Requirements in the Context of Cultural Heritage

3.1 Documentation

The digitization and content creation process in the field of cultural heritage is confronted with various challenges. Each digitized object needs semantic information [11]. Without semantic information, scanned objects are nothing more than a heap of primitives. As the scanning process itself is now available to a wide audience and the amount of scanned data increases rapidly, the importance of semantic metadata becomes obvious, especially in the context of electronic data exchange and storage or, more general, of digital libraries. For a heap of primitives without valuable metadata, it is hard to realize the mandatory services required by a digital library, namely, markup, indexing, and retrieval [12]. In a very restricted and simple approach, this information may consist of attributes like title, creator/ author, time of creation, and original place of the objects. But for many tasks, this is not enough. In order to allow navigation through the datasets (in 3D as well as on a semantic level), detailed information and semantic markup within the dataset is required, that is, a column of a temple has to be identified as a column. Analyzing the column, it might be necessary to find other artifacts, for example, of the same time period. In general, relations between objects are an essential aspect when working with cultural heritage [13]. In 2000, the International Committee for Documentation of the International Council of Museums released the Conceptual Reference Model (CIDOC-CRM), a standard for representing such relational semantic networks in cultural heritage. The first step to support a user in defining these relations is the identification of artifacts with respect to shapes.

Procedural modeling can help to close this semantic gap due to the naming of functions and operator sequences. Therefore, procedural model libraries are the perfect basis for semantic enrichment [14].

3.2 Sustainability

Another important challenge is the issue of digital sustainability [15]. As long-term data storage is a serious problem on a worldwide scale [16], we restricted our approach to techniques, which meet the sustainability conditions (formulated by the Library of Congress[1]). Seven factors influence the feasibility and cost of preserving content in the face of future changes to the technological environment. These factors are significant whatever strategy is adopted as the basis for future preservation actions.

3.3 Visualization

The digitization process as well as generative 3D models (a.k.a. knowledge descriptions) are not an end in itself. They have a purpose and need visualization. Furthermore they should be published and distributed. According to the European Union Culture program, the aim of cultural heritage digitization and online distribution should (amongst others) promote the awareness and the preservation of cultural items of European significance, encourage the transnational circulation of works and cultural as well as artistic products, and stimulate an intercultural dialogue. Web technologies help to achieve this objective.

3.4 Cultural Heritage Experts

A negative characteristic of generative modeling is its explicit analogy of 3D modeling and programming. As cultural heritage professionals – such as architects, archaeologist, etc. – are seldom experts in computer science and programming, the inhibition threshold to use a programming language should be reduced by beginner-friendly tools with a high degree of usability.

4 Generative Modeling for Cultural Heritage Experts

4.1 JavaScript

We present a new meta-modeler approach for procedural modeling based on the programming language JavaScript. The choice of the programming language was a process of carefully considering pros and cons. JavaScript has a variety of important aspects and features we would like to refer to.

It is a structured programming language featuring a rather intuitive syntax, which is easy to read and to understand. As source code is more often read than written, a comprehensible, well-arranged syntax is useful - which is provided by JavaScript. It also incorporates features like dynamic typing and first-class functions. The most important feature of JavaScript is that it is already in use by many non-computer scientists –namely designers

---

[1] http://www.digitalpreservation.gov/formats

and creative coders [10]. JavaScript and its dialects are widely used in applications and on the Internet: in Adobe Flash (called ActionScript), in the Adobe Creative Suite, in interactive PDF files, in Apple's Dashboard Widgets, in Microsoft's Active Scripting technology, in the VRML97, in the Re-Animator framework, etc. Consequently, a lot of documentation and tutorials to introduce the language exist [17]. In order to be used for procedural modeling, JavaScript is missing some functionality, which we added via libraries.

Our meta-modeler approach Euclides differs from other modeling environments in a very important aspect: target independence. Usually, a generative modeling environment consists of a script interpreter and a 3D rendering engine. A generative model (3D data structures with functionality) is interpreted directly to generate geometry, which is then visualized by the rendering engine. In our system a model's source code is not interpreted but parsed into an intermediate representation, an abstract syntax tree (AST). After a validation process it is translated into a target language [18]. The process of

$$parsing \rightarrow validating \rightarrow translating$$

offers many advantages as illustrated in Figure 2. The validation step involves syntax and consistency checks. These checks are performed to ensure the generation of a correct intermediate representation and to provide meaningful error messages as early as possible within the processing pipeline. The integrated development environment (IDE) is shown in Figure 3. Meaningful error messages are one of the most – if not the most – important aspect of a beginner-friendly development environment.

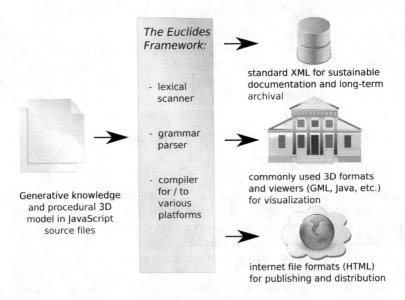

Fig. 2. The overview of the meta-modeler approach shows its advantages: platform/target independence with various exporters for different purposes

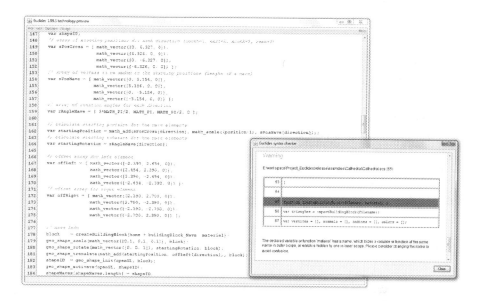

Fig. 3. The integrated development environment (IDE) consists of a syntax-highlighted editor and a syntax checker. Its sensible error messages are one of the most – if not the most – important aspect of a beginner-friendly development environment.

The consistent intermediate representation serves as a basis for back-end exporters to different languages, different targets/platforms and for different purposes [19]. These exporters will be discussed in detail in the next paragraphs. As our compiler has been designed to translate and export JavaScript to other languages, it includes mechanisms to map JavaScript methods and data types to the target language as well as mechanisms to wrap already existing libraries. The Euclides compiler uses annotation techniques to control this mapping and wrapping process.

These annotations are placed in JavaScript comments to ensure 100% compliance with the JavaScript standard. In this way low-level, platform dependent functions – such as a method to draw a single shape – are wrapped platform independently. During the bootstrapping process of a new exporter a few low-level functions need to be wrapped in this way. All other functions, methods, etc are built upon these low-level routines. Consequently, they can be converted and translated automatically.

4.2 Documentation and Source Analysis

The Euclides documentation target (Figure 4) aims to make an important step towards sustainability in procedural modeling by providing a XML representation. For that purpose JavaScript source code is represented as XML structure. Key advantages of the XML format are that it is well-organized, searchable and human readable [20]. Meaningful information needed to perform a source code analysis is also generated during the translation.

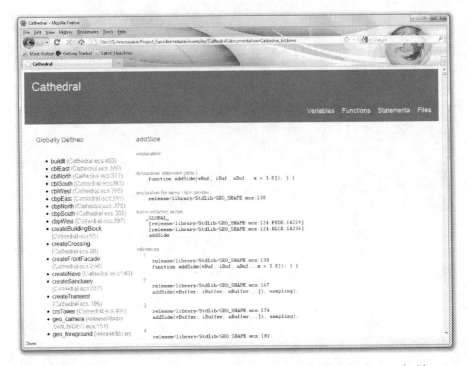

Fig. 4. The Euclides documentation target which represents JavaScript as a sustainable, standard-conform XML document can be displayed in an arbitrary web browser

Based on this data representation four integrated views are available: Variables, Functions, Statements and Files. All globally and locally defined variables are listed in the Variables view. Several properties are available for each variable:

1. Comments. Any comments associated with a variable are preserved and included.
2. Location. The line of code (source, its line number and file name) where the variable is declared.
3. Visibility. The name together with the scope, in which the variable is available.
4. References. All references and uses of the variable in the source code including file name, line number and declaration statement.

Similarly to the Variables view, the Functions view is a collection of all functions defined in the source code and consists of the same four properties mentioned above. The Statements view is a collection of all statements of the source code together with filename and line number which allows, for example, identifying duplicate code snippets. Also it gives a nice overview of the complexity of the source code. In the files view, the source code is available as XML document.

4.3 Sustainability

Euclides meets the sustainability conditions defined by the Library of Congress. These conditions are:

1. Disclosure. The Euclides framework has a complete specification and documentation as well as tools for validating technical integrity.
2. Adoption. The degree to which the format is already used by the primary creators is a dissemination problem which cannot be tackled on a technical level.
3. Transparency. All Euclides source files and documentation files are open to direct analysis with basic tools, such as human readability using a text-only editor.
4. Self-documentation. Each generative model created with Euclides contains basic metadata.
5. External Dependencies. Euclides external dependencies are limited to Java [21], JavaScript (ECMAScript, ECMA-262, ISO/IEC 16262) and standard XML techniques.

Furthermore, all techniques, algorithms, etc. are neither protected by law (6. Impact of Patents) nor by encryption techniques (7. Technical Protection Mechanisms).

4.4 Visualization

During the procedural development process, a major aspect is visualization. Therefore, Euclides is equipped with a flexible visualization library. This library is available for all target platforms. Because visualization depends on low level functionality

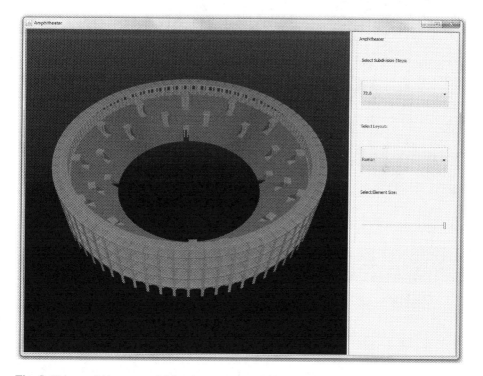

Fig. 5. This amphitheater model has been created in Euclides. Due to its highly regular structure the procedural model only consists of 355 lines of code. This figure shows its visualization using the Java target platform. Using this target it is possible to distribute a generative model as an executable jar file.

like creating a canvas to be used for displaying user interface elements, or creating an OpenGL context, it is mostly target dependent code and therefore needs to be separately written for all target languages. However, the library allows the creation of user interfaces including common user interface elements like sliders, check-boxes and text-fields. Such user interface elements are needed to control a model's high level parameters. A canvas housing a 3D context for all visualization purposes is also available. In order to keep the library as lightweight as possible, no positioning or scaling parameters need to be provided. The library uses predefined layouts to arrange all user interface elements in a meaningful way.

4.5 Publishing

Publishing procedural models represents another important aspect. We favor relying on plugin-free standards like JavaScript, WebGL and HTML5. As JavaScript has been mentioned exhaustively in the previous paragraphs, we concentrate on WebGL and HTML5.

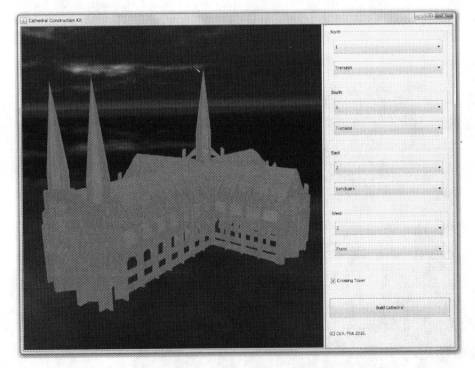

Fig. 6. This example shows a cathedral construction kit. Its main building blocks have been created by thingiverse[2]. They can be arranged arbitrarily using a few lines of code. In this example the arrangement is controlled by nine high level parameters which are exposed in the user interface. The whole cathedral construction kit is realized in 456 lines of JavaScript code. This figure shows its visualization using the Java target platform.

---

[2] http://www.thingiverse.com/thing:2030

WebGL is a JavaScript binding to OpenGL ES 2.0 which enables rich 3D graphics within browsers on platforms supporting the OpenGL or OpenGL ES graphics standards. A main advantage of this upcoming standard is its plugin-free realization within the browser. The WebGL standard will benefit from recent developments in Web technology like the HTML5 specification or the JavaScript performance increases across all major browsers [22], [23], [24].

HTML5 is currently being developed as the next major revision of HTML. One of its goals is to reduce the need for proprietary plug-in-based rich internet application technologies such as Adobe Flash, and Microsoft Silverlight.

Both techniques are still under development so that they can hardly be discussed in detail. However, due to the fact that JavaScript is used as scripting environment, we will support these techniques as soon as they reach a stable status.

5 Conclusion

An analysis of existing procedural modeling tools shows similarities and differences. While some approaches are all-purpose modelers, others are specialized on certain subjects. Based on this analysis we extracted a common subset of data types and language constructs to describe 3D geometry. We integrated this common subset in the scripting language JavaScript and developed a corresponding compiler called Euclides. It is suited for procedural modeling, has a beginner-friendly syntax and is able to generate and export procedural code for various, different generative modeling or rendering engines.

This innovative meta-modeler concept allows a user to export generative models to other platforms without losing its main feature – the procedural paradigm. In contrast to other modelers, the source code does not need to be interpreted or unfolded, it is translated. Therefore it can still be a very compact representation of a complex model.

Additionally, Euclides meets the sustainability conditions defined by the Library of Congress – which is an important aspect in the domain of cultural heritage. The target audience of this approach consists of beginners and intermediate learners of procedural modeling techniques and addresses cultural heritage experts who are seldom computer scientists. These experts are needed to tap the full potential of generative techniques.

6 Future Work

Currently the Euclides modeler is in a public test phase and is available at: http://www.cgv.tugraz.at/euclides.

Future work includes the implementation of a publishing target using HML5 and WebGL technologies, as soon as they become available. Additionally we will incorporate feedback from the public test phase into the final release. The development of infrastructure and incentive models for users, as well as horizontal dissemination through cultural heritage experts, is surely a sensible future task.

Furthermore, the implementation of a larger number of translation targets – possibly including other languages as well as modeling environments – are possible further developments. Additional libraries (e.g. networking) may also be added, if requested by public testers.

Acknowledgements

Figure 1 has been kindly provided by Volker Settgast. In addition the authors gratefully acknowledge the generous support from the European Commission for the integrated project 3D-COFORM (3D COllection FORMation, www.3D-coform.eu) under grant number FP7 ICT 231809, from the Austrian Research Promotion Agency (FFG) for the research project METADESIGNER (Meta-Design Builder: A framework for the definition of end user interfaces for product mass-customization), grant number 820925/18236, as well as from the German Research Foundation DFG for the research project PROBADO (PROtotypischer Betrieb Allgemeiner DOkumente) under grant INST 9055/1-1 (http://www.probado.de/).

References

1. Berndt, R., Fellner, D.W., Havemann, S.: Generative 3D Models: a Key to More Information within less Bandwidth at Higher Quality. In: Proceeding of the 10th International Conference on 3D Web Technology, vol. 1, pp. 111–121 (2005)
2. Havemann, S., Fellner, D.W.: Generative Parametric Design of Gothic Window Tracery. In: Proceedings of the 5th International Symposium on Virtual Reality, Archeology, and Cultural Heritage, vol. 1, pp. 193–201 (2004)
3. Fellner, D.W., Havemann, S.: Striving for an adequate vocabulary: Next generation metadata. In: Proceedings of the 29th Annual Conference of the German Classification Society, vol. 29, pp. 13–20 (2005)
4. Parish, Y., Müller, P.: Procedural Modeling of Cities. In: Proceedings of the 28th Annual Conference on Computer Graphics and Interactive Techniques, vol. 28, pp. 301–308 (2001)
5. Müller, P., Zeng, G., Wonka, P., Van Gool, L.: Image-based Procedural Modeling of Facades. ACM Transactions on Graphics 28(3), 1–9 (2007)
6. Lipp, M., Wonka, P., Wimmer, M.: Interactive Visual Editing of Grammars for Procedural Architecture. ACM Transactions on Graphics 27(3), 1–10 (2008)
7. Müller, P., Wonka, P., Haegler, S., Andreas, U., Van Gool, L.: Procedural Modeling of Buildings. In: Proceedings of 2006 ACM Siggraph, vol. 25(3), pp. 614–623 (2006)
8. Havemann, S.: Generative Mesh Modeling. PhD-Thesis, Technische Universität Braunschweig, Germany 1, 1-303 (2005)
9. Hoffmann, C.M., Kim, K.-J.: Towards valid parametric CAD models. Computer Aided Design 33, 81–90 (2001)
10. Reas, C., Fry, B., Maeda, J.: Processing: A Programming Handbook for Visual Designers and Artists. The MIT Press, Cambridge (2007)
11. Settgast, V., Ullrich, T., Fellner, D.W.: Information Technology for Cultural Heritage. IEEE Potentials 26(4), 38–43 (2007)
12. Ullrich, T., Settgast, V., Berndt, R.: Semantic Enrichment for 3D Documents: Techniques and Open Problems. In: Proceedings of the International Conference on Electronic Publishing, Publishing in the Networked World: Transforming the Nature of Communication, vol. 14, pp. 374–384 (2010)

13. Havemann, S., Ullrich, T., Fellner, D.W.: The Meaning of Shape and some Techniques to Extract It. In: Multimedia Information Extraction (to appear, 2010)
14. Ullrich, T., Settgast, V., Fellner, D.W.: Semantic Fitting and Reconstuction. Journal on Computing and Cultural Heritage 1(2), 1201–1220 (2008)
15. Zorich, D.M.: A Survey of Digital Cultural Heritage Initiatives and Their Sustainability Concerns. In: Council on Library and Information Resources (2003)
16. Bradley, K.: Digital sustainability and digital repositories. In: Proceedings of the Victorian Association for Library Automation (VALA) biennial conference, vol. 13, pp. 1–14 (2006)
17. Vander Veer, E.A.: JavaScript for Dummies. For Dummies (2004)
18. Ullrich, T., Schinko, C., Fellner, D.W.: Procedural Modeling in Theory and Practice. In: Proceeding of the 18th WSCG International Conference on Computer Graphics, Visualization and Computer Vision, vol. 18, pp. 5–8 (2010)
19. Strobl, M., Schinko, C., Ullrich, T., Fellner, D.W.: Euclides – A JavaScript to PostScript Translator. In: Proceedings of the International Conference on Computational Logics, Algebras, Programming, Tools, and Benchmarking, Computation Tools 1 (to appear, 2010)
20. Niccolucci, F.: XML and the future of humanities computing. In: SPECIAL ISSUE: First European Workshop on XML and Knowledge Management, vol. 10, pp. 43–47 (2002)
21. Lindholm, T., Yellin, F.: The Java(TM) Virtual Machine Specification. Prentice Hall, Englewood Cliffs (1999)
22. Di Benedetto, M., Ponchio, F., Ganovelli, F., Scopigno, R.: SpiderGL: A JavaScript 3D Graphics Library for Next-Generation WWW. In: Proceedings of International Conference on 3D Web Technology, vol. 15, pp. 165–174 (2010)
23. Sons, K., Klein, F., Rubinstein, D., Byelozyorov, S., Slusallek, P.: XML3D - Interactive 3D Graphics for the Web. In: Proceedings of International Conference on 3D Web Technology, vol. 15, pp. 175–184 (2010)
24. Behr, J., Jung, Y., Keil, J., Drevensek, T., Zoellner, M., Eschler, P., Fellner, D.W.: A Scalable Architecture of the HTML5/ X3D Integration Model X3DOM. In: Proceedings of International Conference on 3D Web Technology, vol. 15, pp. 185–194 (2010)

A Publishing Workflow for Cultural Heritage Artifacts from 3D-Reconstruction to Internet Presentation

René Berndt[1], Gerald Buchgraber[1], Sven Havemann[1], Volker Settgast[2],
and Dieter W. Fellner[1,3]

[1] Institute of Computer Graphics and Knowledge Visualization,
Graz University of Technology, 8010 Graz, Austria
{r.berndt,g.buchgraber,s.havemann}@cgv.tugraz.at
[2] Fraunhofer Austria Research GmbH, Visual Computing, 8010 Graz, Austria
volker.settgast@fraunhofer.at
[3] Fraunhofer IGD & Technische Universität Darmstadt, 64283 Darmstadt, Germany

Abstract. Publishing cultural heritage as 3D models with embedded annotations and additional information on the web is still a major challenge. This includes the acquisition of the digital 3D model, the authoring and editing of the additional information to be attached to the digital model as well as publishing it in a suitable format. These steps usually require very expensive hardware and software tools. Especially small museums cannot afford an expensive scanning campaign in order to generate the 3D models from the real artifacts. In this paper we propose an affordable publishing workflow from acquisition of the data to authoring and enriching it with the related metadata and information to finally publish it in a way suitable for access by means of a web browser over the internet. All parts of the workflow are based on open source solutions and free services.

Keywords: PDF, XSL-FO, FO3D, Virtual Museum.

1 Introduction

Many cultural heritage artifacts carve out a miserable existence. In an archaeological excavation campaign historic artifacts are typically excavated for scientific reasons, but the majority of them are not considered to be attractive enough to be shown in an exhibition. These artifacts are deposited in some museum archive and are rarely, or never, shown to the public; nor are they accessible to cultural heritage professionals – historians, archaeologists, art historians. The artifacts that are visible to the visitors, and appear in museum catalogues, represent only the tip of the iceberg; and still there is no common comprehensive catalogue of historic artifacts. Even artifacts that are not buried for a second time in some museum deposit gain less attention than they could because they are physically bound to a specific location. Digital media can overcome these physical boundaries, allowing people from all over the world to visit and explore cultural artifacts.

The *Europeana* project (www.europeana.eu) is a large-scale initiative triggered by the European Commission to provide a catalogue of European cultural heritage (*CH*), currently (2010) containing 6 million digital items: *Images*, *texts*, *sounds*, and *videos*.

M. Ioannides (Ed.): EuroMed 2010, LNCS 6436, pp. 166–178, 2010.

But despite the fact that our past, and in particular excavated artifacts, are three-dimensional, there are no *3D datasets* of any kind among those items. The CARARE network of excellence (www.carare.eu) aims to add 3D and Virtual Reality content but for now 3D does not belong to the media types supported by Europeana. We argue that this is mainly due to shortcoming of current 3D technology:

- 3D digitization is labor-intensive and costly,
- 3D datasets are storage intensive,
- 3D is difficult to integrate with other media types,
- lack of standardized formats and viewers, in particular
- lack of archival-quality data formats

For a more thorough treatment see [1]. To change this situation is desirable because of the undeniable benefits of three-dimensional *digital artifacts* over their physical counterparts, the *real artifacts*:

- **Democratization of the past** by public access to CH
- **Immediate engaging experience**: interactive detailed 3D exploration, keep precious object "in your hands"
- **Virtual restoration**: Digital artifact can be restored in different ways, physical artifacts only in one way
- **Protection of the real**: Access to digital artifact is in many cases sufficient, so less usage of the real artifact
- **Ease of manipulation**: No weight, no collisions, so much easier creation of assemblies (scenes)
- **Scale matters less**: Very large or very small digital artifacts are much easier to handle than real ones
- **Re-contextualization**: A digital artifact can be shown in a scanned excavation site or in a 3D-reconstruction
- **Geometric measurements** are much easier to perform
- **Documentation**: Digital conservation and damage can reports link to surface areas of digital artifact
- **Information integration**: The digital 3D object could serve as the master model to which all other data sources refer (text documents, images, annotations).

Because of this versatility a digital artifact is sometimes also called a *digital replica*. However, it is important to emphasize that the digital artifact shall by no means replace the real one. The idea of a complementary *digital exhibition* is to enhance a museum exhibition by placing next to a display cabinet showing a precious real artifact, a 3D kiosk showing its digital counterpart. A successful example is, e.g., the Arrigo showcase [2] where visitors could discover surprising details, i.e., a hollow back which would normally not be seen, of heavy stone statues shown in the same room.

Another possibility is to create *digital museum catalogues* with embedded interactive 3D media that can be viewed by the visitors using a portable device. The new class of *iPad-devices* combines a very intuitive user interface with an excellent large display and is ideal for personalized guided tours that are tuned with respect to the specific visitor – since, e.g., children require additional information that is different from that for adults or for experts.

Another possibility is to create *digital museum catalogues* with embedded interactive 3D media that can be viewed by the visitors using a portable device. The new class of *iPad-devices* combines a very intuitive user interface with an excellent large display and is ideal for personalized guided tours that are tuned with respect to the specific visitor – since, e.g., children require additional information that is different from that for adults or for experts.

Technology that is sufficient for such location-based scenarios, however, has typically only very limited *sustainability*. Sustainability requires a level of interoperability that can only be achieved using *standards*. But the lack of suitable standards is maybe the greatest problem of 3D technology today. So answers to the following questions must be found:

- Which 3D format to choose?
- How to link from a digital artifact to a web resource?
- How to link from a web resource to a digital artifact?
- How can all this information be created?
- How can it be archived?
- And how can it be deployed, i.e., using web delivery?

Today it is not at all trivial to deliver 3D content to a web browser. All currently available solutions use some sort of plugin (Java, JavaScript, or platform dependent solutions like ActiveX, etc.) in order to display 3D content within the browser. Although these limitations might be overcome in the future with HTML5/WebGL, there are still some robustness issues when, e.g., saving a local copy of a web page with embedded images, CSS style sheets, together with a 3D object shown on the page. This solution is especially brittle when saving multi-page documents, i.e., a set of interlinked web pages that describe a set of digital 3D artifacts.

To overcome these problems, this paper presents a completely different solution. We propose the following solutions to the above problems:

- **COLLADA** as extensible XML format for 3D scenes, annotations, and metadata
- **U3D** as 3D format for textured triangle meshes
- **PDF** as delivery format for multi-page text documents with embedded 3D objects
- **XSLT** to describe the conversion of COLLADA to PDF, in particular of the embedded metadata.

COLLADA is described in [3]. We describe the complete workflow, ranging from the acquisition of the 3D model over 3D reconstruction to annotating and enriching the digital artifact with metadata, to finally publishing it to a wide audience through the web. All parts of the workflow that we describe in fact use open source software and services. So this workflow is also manageable for small museums that cannot afford expensive 3D scanning equipment. In the following we will describe the different stages of the workflow in detail.

Section 3 explains the process of 3D acquisition, Section 4 shows the authoring application for 3D annotations, and Section 5 explains the generation of a PDF document with embedded 3D artifacts. Section 6 shows some resulting products and a short discussion.

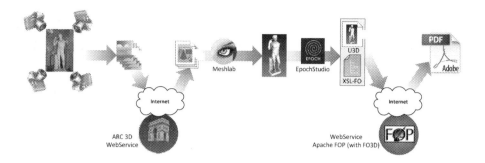

Fig. 1. Schematic visualization of the workflow from acquisition of the 3D model from the artefact over the information authoring to finally the production of the PDF with embedded 3D content

1.1 Contribution

To the best of our knowledge we are the first to describe the complete workflow from 3D acquisition over markup and annotation to web delivery. A schematic overview of the proposed workflow is shown in Figure 1. Furthermore, our solution is particularly flexible in two respects: First, our system allows some flexibility with respect to the markup method. Three ingredients must match: The XML notation for a markup, the user interface to define it, and the XSLT transformation that converts the markup into a 3D object in a PDF document.

Second, our workflow provides great flexibility with respect to the usage scenario. Basically the same methods work irrespective whether a sustainable workflow needs to be defined for a very particular CH domain or sub-domain, whether the annotations are created manually ("interpretation of shape") or automatically ("shape matching"), or whether used in a stand-alone fashion in a remote excavation campaign or integrated into a web server infrastructure that delivers PDF with embedded 3D, e.g., as the result of a query request like "give me a 3D scene containing all Greek statues of male individuals that are holding a spear".

1.2 Benefit

We consider our solution to serve as a model for solving a whole range of practical 3D content creation and dissemination problems. In order to benefit from the aforementioned advantages of 3D technology, we are facing a hen-and-egg situation today: 3D is not widely used because of a lack of tools, and the tools are not developed because of a lack of interest in 3D. We hope we can break this vicious circle by offering a light-weight possibility to create, annotate, and disseminate 3D artifacts. At the same time, it is flexible and can be custom-tailored to accommodate for specific use cases and sets of requirements.

2 Related Work

Since 3D data without any kind of additional information is pleasant but rather useless, most 3D objects are related to further metadata, describing the 3D content or its context more precisely. Especially in the area of cultural heritage, 3D related information is essential. Hence, users benefit from both a 3D visualization and additional information related to the presented 3D content, as it can be done by using X3D embedded in a HTML web page. For example, Kadobayashi [4] proposed an automatic blogging system, where users can share annotations made to 3D content, enabling collaborative experiencing.

In contrast to the X3D/HTML example and the automatic blogging system, PDF documents can contain both, the 3D content and the related metadata within one file, which enables the user to save this file locally, archive it or send it to another interested person. Therefore, a flexible method for generating PDF documents that contain rich 3D content is desirable, but has apparently not yet received much research attention. Barnes and Fluke [5] proposed the incorporation of 3D content in PDF documents as a substantial improvement for the visualization of multi-dimensional data in astronomy research papers. Since multi-dimensional data is no astronomical phenomenon, their ideas for a more appropriate knowledge transfer by using 3D visualizations is of course also applicable in numerous other fields. Nevertheless, their approach just uses 3D content in a quite static way and just for visualization purposes.

Strobl et al. [6] published a workflow for the generation of PDF documents that contain 3D objects, which are dynamically enriched with embedded annotations to provide additional information on some specific parts of the 3D content. Although the proposed workflow greatly shows how 3D content can on-the-fly be enriched to provide additional information, it has several drawbacks. The major limitation of this approach is that it is based on the commercial software Adobe Acrobat Extended.

Concerning the PDF standard, PDF/A-1 has been approved in 2005 as the standard for long-term archival of textual PDF documents [7]. The next version PDF/A-2, is expected for 2011 and will be based on PDF 1.7, which includes support for multimedia content e.g. movies, sounds and 3D. This would make PDF indeed the preferential format for the sustainable publishing of 3D content mixed with other data like text, sounds or videos.

3 Acquisition – The "Gipsmuseum" Campaign

The Gipsmuseum in Graz (http://gipsmuseum.uni-graz.at) is a collection of mostly plaster statues held by the Institute of Archeology, University of Graz. The creation of replica of statues and other decorated objects has a long tradition. At first the plaster copies were mainly used by sculptors to serve as masters for copies of the original works. With the appearance of the modern universities in the 18th century they also served another purpose. The plaster sculptures were and are still used as a three dimensional reference of the ancient art in lectures and studies of arts and history. Some of the exhibits are quite old and a few are the only remains because the original statues were damaged or destroyed. There are enough reasons to digitalize and preserve the plaster copies.

Fig. 2. The acquisition process taking place in the "Gipsmuseum Graz"; summer interns shooting photos of an exhibit

In 2008 our group started to reconstruct some of the exhibits of the museum. The goal was always to generate precise digital models in a cost efficient way. We decided to reconstruct the statues using the ARC 3D Webservice[1] of the University of Leuven (see also in [8]). This service is freely available for the task of preserving cultural heritage. It uses a sequence of photographs to calculate depth images. Those depth images can be used to create a 3D model.

A group of four summer interns was trained to shot photos of high quality. The photos were taken with a Nikon D60, a 6 megapixel single-lens reflex camera. A tripod and a remote-control release were used to avoid camera shake.

Because of the homogeneous color of the statues a photogrammetric reconstruction is not trivial even for good algorithms. We decided to use a random color pattern which was projected onto the plaster using a projector. We tried to match the size of a pixel of the projected pattern with the size of a pixel on the photo. To also capture the correct color of the surface it would be necessary to shoot a second photo without the projected pattern. Due to lack of time this was not done for all photos but only for three shots (start, middle, end) of a sequence.

To get good results, the process of taking photos has to meet some special demands. For example a sequence of photos has to be shot focusing on one spot while moving the camera in a half circle around the object. The movement of the camera has to be planned in advance to make sure, the object of interest is fully visible in all

---

[1] http://www.arc3d.be/

shots. Adjustments of the zoom are not allowed during a sequence. It is important to use the same camera settings for all shots of a sequence, therefore keeping the same distance. Measuring the distance with a piece of string can be seen in Figure 2.

Within the time of the internship we managed to shoot 25 exhibits. For each statue an average of 8 sequences was taken with approximately 20 photos per sequence. For the more complex statues we had to take more sequences. Also sometimes it was hard to move around the exhibits so we had to take more sequences with only a few photos. In total we generated about 4300 photos and sent them to the ARC 3D Webservice.

The resulting depth maps were then processed using Meshlab[2]. In the first step, the resulting 3D fractures of each photo sequence were created using the filter called "Surface Reconstruction: Poisson".

To get a single model for each statue, the factures were then registered to each other. In this step it was necessary to scale the parts of the model according to measurements taken from the real statues. In contrast to a laser scan, the photo reconstruction is not creating accurate measurements. Manual corrections were needed to generate exact digital copies.

The scaling and the final assembling of the parts can also be done in Meshlab. But because of some stability issues we used GeoMagic Studio[3], a commercial solution for the depth map registration. An example statue is shown in Figure 3 and described in Section 6.

Fig. 3. A photo of a plaster statue and the reconstructed 3D model in Meshlab

---

[2] http://meshlab.sourceforge.net
[3] http://www.geomagic.com

4 Authoring

This Section describes the authoring process of combining the 3D model with the additional information, in our case mostly text and images.

For this workflow a modified version of the authoring tool EpochStudio[9] is used. The original version of this authoring tool allowed annotating the 3D model by adding markup geometry which is linked to an internet resource.

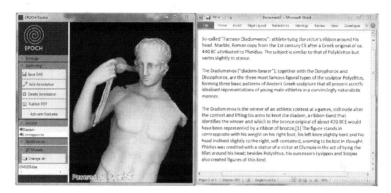

Fig. 4. The diadem of the "Anadumenos Farnese" is annotated using the EpochStudio

The 3D model is loaded from the local disk or from a remote data source. The user can select "Add Annotation" from the menu by clicking on the authoring tab on the left. Annotations can be added by clicking directly on the surface of the 3D object. A dialog pops up and lets the user choose an anchor name. This name can be used later to create a reference to the annotation. Anchors are visualized as spheres in the 3D view and they also appear on the left in the list of anchors. An arbitrary number of URLs can be attached to each annotation. With the included browser it is possible to search for suitable material without the need to switch between the EpochStudio and a web browser. After all annotations are added the user can export a lightweight COLLADA file (COLLADA Lite) by clicking on "Save DAE". This COLLADA file holds the scene graph hierarchy and the annotations. The 3D models, however, are not contained in the COLLADA file. They are only referenced using a link. To generate a PDF, the user selects another export option, "Publish PDF". A PDF file containing the 3D model as well as the annotations is then written to disk.

While it would be possible to download the resource and insert it into the resulting PDF, this may result in a visual clutter because of different layout of the web resource. In order to enable direct editing the information and to edit the page layout, the EpochStudio has been enhanced with direct text editing. The editor allows the user to create the XSL-FO document, in which the 3D model will be embedded. Parts of the text can either be converted to a link into the 3D content or as the target of a annotation markup of the 3D model.

Figure 4 shows the authoring process of the "Farnese Diadumenos". The user defines the area of interest in 3D by creating a sphere, in this example the diadem and one leg as a placeholder for explaining the "contrapposto". For each sphere the user can add the additional text and images in the attached text editor to the right.

```
01  <?xml version="1.0" encoding="utf-8" ?>
02  <COLLADAlite>
03    <library_nodes>
04      <node id="gm100">
05        <instance_geometry url="gm100_200k.osb" />
06      </node>
07    </library_nodes>
08    <scene>
09      <visual_scene>
10        <node name="StatueGM100">
11          <instance_node url="#gm100" />
12          <extra>
13            <annotation title="Diadem"
14                        id="Diadem">
15              <annotation_geometry>
16                <annotation_sphere>
17    <center>7317.4 -825.2 12788.6</center>
18    <radius>282.051</radius>
19                </annotation_sphere>
20              </annotation_geometry>
21              <annotation_camera>
22    <from>8900.1 8586.3 4917.3</from>
23    <at>6927.60 -769.3 12798.6<at>
24    <up>0.9 -0.09 0.13</up>
25              </annotation_camera>
26            </annotation>
27            <annotation title="Contrapposta"
28                        id="Contrapposta">
29              ...
30            </annotation>
31          </extra>
32        </node>
33      </visual_scene>
34    </scene>
35  </COLLADAlite>
```

Listing 1. The Collada Lite file generated by the EpochStudio

5   PDF Publishing

In this section we describe the publishing step for generating the PDF with embedded 3D content in detail. The output from the previous step - the 3d model (U3D) and the XML data - is now combined into a single PDF file using FO3D. The technical details of FO3D are described in the following.

5.1   XSL-FO and FO3D

FO3D is an extension to the XSL Formatting Objects (XSL-FO) standard. XSL-FO [11] was designed for formatting and presenting XML documents. The purpose of XSL-FO is to transform XML documents containing data into other XML documents containing both the data and the XSL-FO elements describing the visual presentation. This transformation makes use of XSLT and XPath. A XSL-FO document is converted by a FO processor (FOP) to a target format. In practice, XSL-FO is primarily used for generating PDF documents, but it is designed as a general formatting system for various render targets, depending on the implementation of the FO processor.

Since the XSL-FO is designed for rendering two dimensional layouts, the FO vocabulary lacks support for embedding 3D content. However support for arbitrary objects is already included within the XSL standard. FO3D utilizes the fo:instream-foreign-object element, which is "is used for an inline graphic or other 'generic' object where the object data resides as descendants of the fo:instream foreign-object, typically as an XML element subtree in a non-XSL namespace" [10]. The most popular example for the use of an fo:instream-foreign-object element is the embedding of SVG, which is a file format for describing two-dimensional vector graphics on the basis of XML. FO3D primarily target is the integration of 3D content and related metadata in PDF documents, therefore the proposed FO3D vocabulary contains various settings and concepts following the ISO-standardized PDF-1.7 specification (ISO-32000-1).

The current version of FO3D supports the following PDF 3D features:

- Multiple views for inspecting different parts of the 3D content. Various aspects like rendermode (e.g. solid, transparent, wireframe, etc.), camera position, lightmode,projection, and background color can be specifies.
- Additional resources that are not part of the original 3D content itself, e.g. additional 3D geometry or 2D graphics
- Support for 3D JavaScript and document-level JavaScript

A more detailed overview of the available FO3D elements can be found in [11].

The prototype of FO3D has been implemented for Apache FOP (The Apache Software Foundation, 2010). Apache FOP is an open-source project licensed under the Apache License version 2.0. It is implemented in the Java programming language and therefore by default available for multiple platforms, including desktop and (web) server environments. The most recent stable version is 0.95, which implements a large subset of the XSL-FO 1.1 W3C Recommendation. FO3D is available for download at http://fo3d.sourceforge.net

5.2 FO3D Extension: Annotations

Though the combination of XSLT, FO, and FO3D offers a wide range of rich interactive PDF 3D visualizations, it might still not be powerful enough, for example, by means of XSLT and JavaScript it is not possible to generate an image that is to be used as a texture, or to load an arbitrary external file that is referenced from the XML input in order to affect the visual appearance of the 3D content. Therefore, additional support during the PDF generation process is needed.

Similar to the FO3D which extends the XSL-FO vocabulary, it is also possible to extend the vocabulary of FO3D. The FO3D extensions element provides the ability of storing custom XML elements, without specifying any structural or content-related restrictions. In general, the purpose of this element is similar to the fo:instream-foreign-object element, which also provides a method for extending the FO document with custom XML data, such as SVG or FO3D.

```
01 <fo:instream-foreign-object>
02     <object-3d
03         xmlns="http://fo3d.sourceforge.net/ns"
04         name="relief"
05         src="Statue10_100k.u3d"
06         width="5cm" height="5cm">
07         ...
08
09         <extensions>
10             <annotations scale="" color="lime">
11                 <link href="http://..."
12                     at="-43.6,134.8,1324.0"
13                     scale="1.34583" color="lime" />
14                 <link href="http://..."
15                     at="-112.9,140.6,906.4"
16                     scale="0.690188" color="red" />
17             </annotations>
18         </extensions>
19
20     </object-3d>
21 </fo:instream-foreign-object>
```

Listing 2. The FO document with two annotation definitions

The functionality for adding the markup geometry into the 3D object is encapsulated in a special FO3D extension "annotations", which adds the element annotations to the FO3D vocabulary. The annotations element can contain one or more link elements defining. Table 1 shows the various types of attributes for this element. Listing 2 shows the usage of the extension within an XSL-FO document.

When the XSL-FO document is processed, the extension adds an addition resource for the markup geometry and adds the necessary JavaScript code for handling the mouse-click on the sphere.

Table 1. Overview of the **link** attribute types and their meaning

Type	Description
href	Unique identifier to the additional data. This can either by a web resource or an internal anchor within the XSL-FO document.
at	Specifies the position of the annotation
scale	Scaling factor for the markup geometry.
color	Specifies the color of the markup geometry.

The results of the previous authoring step are the 3D model in the U3D format, and a XSL-FO document. The XSLT conversion for merging the COLLADAlite information into the XSL-FO is already done by the EpochStudio. Listing 2 shows the resulting FO3D document. The two files are then processed by the Apache FOP (with FO3D included), which was configured to run as a web service. The result is then the final PDF document with the 3D content embedded.

6 Example

The described workflow was exemplarily applied to the statue of a Diadoumenos, a typical type of Greek sculpture. It is showing the winner of an athletic contest knotting a ribbon-band, the diadem, to his head. The plaster statue is a copy of a roman marble copy, the "Farnese Diadumenos". The original Greek statue was made of bronze in the end of the 5th century B.C.

For the large plaster statue (about 2.5 meters high) we created twenty sequences of photos. Ten sequences cover the legs with four of them shot from a higher position targeting the feet. The upper part of the statue was shot from below and straight. Unfortunately it was not possible to create sequences from an elevated position. Because of this the shoulders and the head are not yet reconstructed on the top.

Figure 5 shows the resulting PDF document viewed with Adobe Reader. The 3D content is displayed within a floating window so that the model is always visible independent from the displayed page. Clicking on the links in the text (here diadem or contrapposto) will select the corresponding view in the 3D model. Clicking on the markup geometry in the 3D window causes the document to jump to the corresponding anchor within the text.

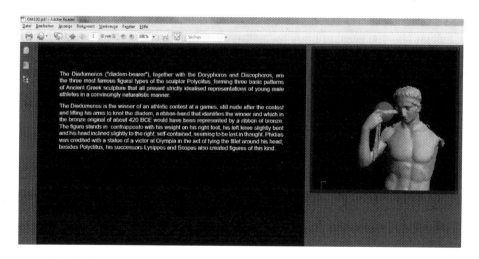

Fig. 5. The resulting PDF; the 3D content is viewed within the floating window

7 Conclusion

We presented a complete prototype workflow from the artifact to a digital interactive museum catalogue.

The proposed workflow is completely based on open source projects. This makes it affordable even for small museums. Since PDF is an ISO standard (ISO 32000-1:2008) and the Acrobat Reader is available on a variety of platforms, it is an ideal format for bringing rich and interactive 3D culture heritage to a large audience.

Currently the tools for the workflow (with except of the ARC 3D Web service) need to be locally installed. Future work will concentrate of establishing parts of workflows as a web service solution, e.g. FO3D. Additional FO3D extension will enhance the possibilities for enriching the 3D content for cultural heritage (e.g. animations or video/audio clips).

Acknowledgments

The authors would like to thank the Gipsmuseum Graz for providing the statues used in this paper. The work presented in this paper was partially supported by the German Research Foundation DFG under grant INST 9055/1-1 (PROBADO project http://www.probado.de/).

And the authors wish to acknowledge the funding from the Seventh Framework Programme of the European Commission (FP7/2007-2013) under grant agreement no. 231809 (IP project "3D-COFORM").

References

1. Havemann, S., Fellner, D.: Seven Research Challenges of Generalized 3D Documents. IEEE Computer Graphics and Applications (Special Issue on 3D Documents) 27(3), 70–76 (2007)
2. Callieri, M., Ponchio, F., Cignoni, P., Scopigno, R.: Virtual Inspector: a flexible visualizer for dense 3D scanned models. IEEE Computer Graphics and Applications 28(1), 44–55 (2008)
3. Arnaud, M., Barnes, M.C.: COLLADA: Sailing the Gulf of 3D Digital Content Creation. AK Peters Ltd., Wellesley (2006)
4. Kadobayashi, R.: Automatic 3D Blogging to Support the Collaborative Experience of 3D Digital Archives. In: Fox, E.A., Neuhold, E.J., Premsmit, P., Wuwongse, V. (eds.) ICADL 2005. LNCS, vol. 3815, pp. 109–118. Springer, Heidelberg (2005)
5. Barnes, D.G., Fluke, C.J.: Incorporating interactive 3-dimensional graphics in astronomy research papers. New Astronomy 13(8), 599–605 (2008)
6. Strobl, M., Berndt, R., Settgast, V., Havemann, S., Fellner, D.W.: Publishing 3D Content as PDF in Cultural Heritage. In: Proceedings of the 10th International Symposium on Virtual Reality, Archaeology and Intelligent Cultural Heritage (VAST), vol. 6, pp. 117–124 (2009)
7. ISO, ISO 19005 - Electronic document file format for long-term preservation, International Organization for Standardization, Technical report, International Organization for Standardization (2005)
8. Vergauwen, M., Gool, L.V.: Web-Based 3D Reconstruction Service. Machine Vision Applications, 411–426 (2006)
9. Havemann, S., Settgast, V., Berndt, R., Eide, Ø.: The Arrigo Showcase Reloaded – towards a sustainable link between 3D and semantics. In: Proceedings of the 9th International Symposium on Virtual Reality and Cultural Heritage (VAST), vol. 9, pp. 125–132 (2008)
10. The Apache Software Foundation, Formatting Objects Processor – Apache FOP (2010), http://xmlgraphics.apache.org/fop/
11. Buchgraber, G., Berndt, R., Havemann, S., Fellner, D.W.: FO3D – Formatting Objects for PDF3D. To appear in Proceedings of the 15th International Conference on 3D Web Technology (2010)
12. W3C, Extensible Stylesheet Language (XSL) version 1.1 (2006), http://www.w3.org/TR/xsl11/

3D Scanning and Modelling of the Bismarck Monument by Terrestrial Laser Scanning for Integration into a 3D City Model of Hamburg

Thomas P. Kersten

HafenCity University Hamburg, Photogrammetry & Laser Scanning Lab
Hebebrandstrasse 1, 22297 Hamburg, Germany
Thomas.Kersten@hcu-hamburg.de

Abstract. In the context of an integrated pilot study between the HafenCity University Hamburg, the Jade University of Applied Sciences in Oldenburg and the Agency for Geo-Information and Surveying Hamburg the Bismarck monument in Hamburg has been scanned with the Z+F IMAGER 5006 3D laser scanning system to generate a virtual 3D model of the monument from the laser scanning data using different programs. A substantial aspect for modelling was data reduction, since the generated 3D model has to be integrated into the city model of Hamburg with the smallest possible data volume. Therefore a combination of triangle meshing and CAD turned out to be an optimal solution. Furthermore, the extent to which the modelled data can be reduced by appropriate polygon decimation, in order to derive a geometrically correct and visually attractive result (virtual 3D model), has been investigated. The geometrical quality of the model was evaluated on the basis of reference values. As well as the integration of the virtual model into the city model of Hamburg the generated virtual model was also prepared for interactive visualisations. For the entire processing of the project time management of the individual work procedures has been calculated, in order to derive statements about the economy of the project. Thus conclusions/recommendations for further projects on object recording, modelling and visualization of such historical buildings and monuments using this procedure with this technology could be provided.

Keywords: 3D modelling, 3D triangulation, cultural heritage, meshing, terrestrial laser scanning.

1 Introduction

While these days world-wide computer networking and the self-evident use of the internet is standard as far as possible, presentation in this medium could become important for a city with tourism value such as Hamburg. So the characteristic cityscape of the Hanseatic city, which is also characterised by a vast number of monuments, could be presented multi-medially as a virtual 3D city model. In the listing of the recognised monuments currently 2800 individual architectural monuments, 2100 ensembles as well as 3000 ground monuments are listed. The protection of historical

M. Ioannides (Ed.): EuroMed 2010, LNCS 6436, pp. 179–192, 2010.

buildings and monuments and the preservation of monuments in the Hanseatic city are described by Hamburg's monument protection law, however a detailed documentation of these objects is often missing.

For geometrical 3D object recording of complex objects such as monuments terrestrial laser scanning is now suitable as an efficient survey procedure. With their ability to scan a very large number of 3D points in seconds without signalisation laser scanning offers high application potential, especially in archaeology, architecture and cultural heritage, as has already been illustrated in numerous publications (see among others [1], [2], [3], [4], [5], [6], [7], [8], [9]).

In this paper 3D object recording and modelling of the Bismarck monument in Hamburg by terrestrial laser scanning are presented as a cooperative pilot study of the HafenCity University Hamburg, the Jade University of Applied Sciences in Oldenburg and the Agency for Geo-Information and Surveying Hamburg. For the production of a virtual 3D model the aspect of data reduction is the main focus in order to merge the geometrically and visually correct model with the smallest data volume as possible into the 3D city model of Hamburg.

Fig. 1. Bismarck monument in an aerial photo (left) and statue (right)

2 The Bismarck Monument in Hamburg

Even during his own lifetime Bismarck monuments were constructed in numerous German cities as well as in other countries in honours of the first German Imperial Chancellor Prince Otto von Bismarck. Born on 1 April 1815 in Schönhausen in the district Stendal Otto von Bismarck became increasingly active in politics after completion of his legal studies in Göttingen and Berlin in 1835. In 1862 he was appointed the Prussian Prime Minister; five years later in 1867 he became chancellor

of the North German federation and after a four further years he became the first
Imperial Chancellor of the German empire. When in 1888 emperor Wilhelm II
ascended to the throne, Bismarck came increasingly into conflict with the young
emperor, so that „the iron chancellor" resigned in the year 1890. On 30 July 1898
Otto von Bismarck died on his estate Friedrichsruh in the Saxonia forest close to the
gates of Hamburg.

One of the most famous statues was built in the Free and Hanseatic City of
Hamburg in the former Elbe Park (Fig. 1). This monument is the largest monument
in Hamburg and has consequently a special meaning for the Hanseatic city. The
building of the monument was controversial at that time. Initially agreement could
not be reached on a location and later the historical Elbe pavilion had to yield for
the final location of the huge statue. The architect Johann Emil Schaudt and the
sculptor and art nouveau artist Hugo Lederer planned the building project and also
implemented it. However, with a height of 34.3 meters and a weight of 625 tons its
gigantic size required further agreements. The construction costs aggregated to
approximately 500,000 Gold marks. The monument shows Bismarck in form of a
Roland statue, a so-called statue of a knight, which was considered as a symbol of
municipal rights. The eight figures at the foot of the object (base) symbolised the
Germanic tribes. The inauguration of the monument took place on 2 June 1906
after a three-year construction period. More than 100 years at the slope of the river
Elbe has not passed without effect on the Bismarck statue. Monitoring activities
have found that the listed building has stability problems - at present nine centimetres of inclination on the overall height. Therefore, it must inevitably be renovated
in the near future.

Fig. 2. Building of 3D city model of Hamburg in level of detail 1 to 3 (© LGV Hamburg)

3   The 3D City Model of Hamburg

The 3D city model of Hamburg is available in three different levels of detail (LoD)
and quality. The level of detail 1 (block model) was completed in 2001 for the entire
area of Hamburg (755 km^2) and consists of 320,000 buildings [10] For the automatic
generation of the block models a sketch from the digital basic city map (DSGK) and
the respective storey height from the Hamburg official land registers (real estate
map and real estate book) for extrusion of the model was used. For LoD 2 the roof

landscapes were measured in large-scale aerial photographs in detail and blended with
the digital terrain model, so that the model consists of roof and wall surfaces (Boundary Representation). This LoD 2 was finished in 2003 for an area of 250km^2 in the
city centre and in Bergedorf and enclosed approx. 130,000 buildings. From LoD 3
(architectural model) texture-mapped buildings are available only in selected areas of
the city Hamburg. In Figure 2 the above described levels of detail 1-3 are represented
for the city model of Hamburg using the example of one building.

4 Object Recording

Object recording was carried out using the IMAGER 5006 terrestrial laser scanner
from Zoller + Fröhlich on 13th August 2008 during very windy weather conditions.
Technical specification and accuracy potential of the laser scanner are described in
[11]. During scanning GPS measurements were acquired using a Leica GPS system
500 for the geodetic network (five additional points), while the targets were measured
by total stations. In total 16 black-and-white targets and four white spheres, which
were used as control points for the registration and geo-referencing of the 17 scan
stations (Fig. 3 left), were attached to the monument at different heights as well as
being set around the viewing platform on tripods. Moreover photographic images
with a Nikon D70 were acquired for later possible texture mapping of the 3D model.
The object recording was carried out by a three-person team of the cooperation partners involved.

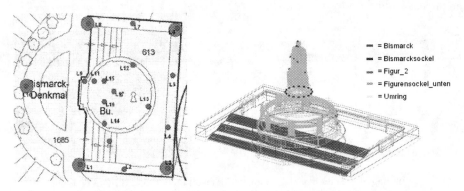

Fig. 3. Scan stations (L1-L17) and five geodetic control points (large circles, left), check points
determined by total station (right)

For later quality control of the 3D model 74 check points were determined by total
station on three stations around the object during an additional day in the field. The
distribution of these check points is represented in Fig. 3 (right). As a check of the
heights of the geodetic network distance levelling was carried out on a further field
survey day.

5 Data Processing

The data processing was performed in several work procedures, which are described in the following.

5.1 Geo-referencing, Filtering and Segmentation of Scans

In total 180 million points were scanned, which had to be processed efficiently. The registration of 17 scan stations was accomplished with the software LaserControl from Zoller + Fröhlich, in which registration and geo-referencing were accomplished in one processing step. All b/w targets and spheres (127 measurements) were semi-automatically measured in the different scans and later transformed into a common coordinate system using the control point coordinates from a bundle adjustment. The average deviation at the control points was 13mm (standard deviation 6.5mm), whereby 13 measurements of the control points with a deviation over 30mm were excluded from the computation. The poor result can be justified by explaining that the spheres were frequently knocked over by wind causing discrepancies in the geodetic network. However, this result is completely sufficient for this task, although a result better by a factor two was expected.

Fig. 4. Single scan of the Bismarck statue (left), quality control of the registration at the head of the statue (centre), segmentation of a figure at the socket (right)

The registration and geo-referencing of the scans was subsequently examined by forming cuts in different levels in the Trimble software RealWorks Survey (e.g. see Fig. 4 centre). The upper scan areas were not evenly supported by control points due to the spatial distribution of the targets. Thus discrepancies of up to 40mm were revealed between the scans but only in the head area of the statue. This difference was not yet critical for the further modelling of the data to meet the requirements of this task. The complete data set was divided into the three areas, platform, socket and statue, segmented and exported accordingly. During export the data were corrected using standard filter parameters in LaserControl and consequently volumes were already reduced (see also [12]). Subsequently, the unnecessary points were eliminated in the segmented point clouds using RealWorks Survey (see Fig. 4 right).

5.2 Modelling

Due to size and complexity of the object a combination of CAD modelling and triangle meshing offers an optimal solution for the 3D modelling of the Bismarck monument. The use of the CAD model is suitable for simple geometrical bodies such as the platform and the socket of the monument, while triangle meshing proves useful for irregular geometry such as the Bismarck statue and the eight figures surrounding the socket. Thus a significant data reduction is already obtained in this stage of the processing by CAD modelling of essential parts of the monument, which also permits more efficient handling of the data for the visualisation of the object at a later stage. Fitting of geometrical primitives such as plane, circle and cylinder into the appropriate positions of the point clouds was not as successful as expected, so that much manual post-processing would have been necessary. Therefore the generation of essential cross-sections in the segmented point clouds (Fig. 5 right top) with the software PointCloud, a plug-in for AutoCAD from the company Kubit, was selected as a successful approach for the creation of a CAD model. However, the manual digitisation in polylines was found to be too labour intensive. Subsequently, the cuts were extruded on their height accordingly, so that one CAD model each has been developed for the socket (Fig. 5 right bottom) and for the platform. Tentative experimentation also showed very quickly that modelling of free form surfaces by cuts is too time-consuming and too inaccurate (see Fig. 6 left).

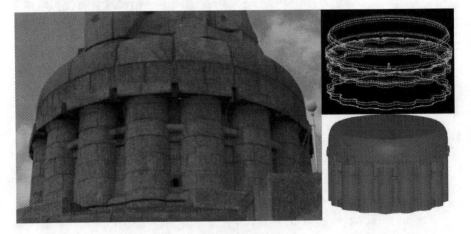

Fig. 5. Part of the socket of the Bismarck statue (left), generated cross-sections of the geometric object (right top), CAD model of the socket (right bottom)

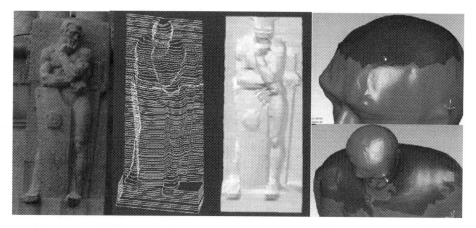

Fig. 6. Modelling of a figure at the socket by cross-sections (left) and curvature-based filling of holes (red) for shoulder and head areas of the Bismarck statue (right)

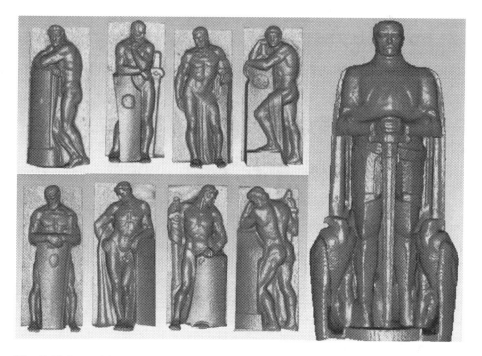

Fig. 7. Eight modelled figures of the monument socket (left) and modelled Bismarck statue (right)

The more complex surfaces of the eight figures around the socket and the Bismarck statue were modelled by 3D triangulation (triangle meshing) in Geomagic (version 10). However, before actual meshing different filter functions were still deployed by Geomagic, in order to eliminate still further outliers and scanning noise from the segmented point clouds (approx. ½ million points of per small figure). The computation of the triangle meshing is performed automatically; however the result can still be optimized afterwards, in which existing holes are filled and the surfaces are smoothed. The large holes within the upper areas of the Bismarck figure, which could not be scanned due to shadowing by the statue height (34.3 meters), were later filled by a curvature-based computation; however bridging points were manually set before due to the size of large holes. The complete result is represented in Fig. 6 (right), while all figures modelled by triangle meshing, are arranged in Fig. 7 (left). During the smoothing of the surfaces one had to proceed very carefully in Geomagic, since important details and intricacies of the surface are quickly lost by over-regulation of the parameter settings. Generally while handling this dataset with Geomagic it was revealed that experience was necessary for optimal parameter control. But a geometrically correct 3D model of the statue (Fig. 7 right) has been generated by processing of the complex object areas (free form surfaces) with Geomagic, which demonstrates a very high visual recognition value.

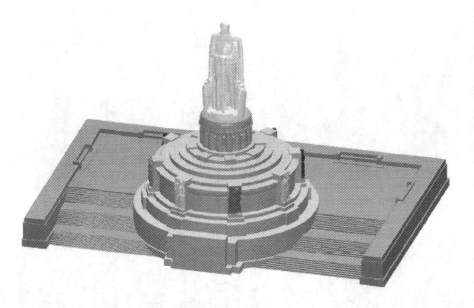

Fig. 8. Colour-coded parts of the Bismarck monument

Finally, all modelled parts of the monument from AutoCAD/PointCloud (CAD) and from Geomagic (triangle meshing) were combined into a entire 3D model using the software MicroStation V8 (Fig. 8). According to the format this entire 3D model has a data volume of 108 MB (DXF), 21 MB (DWG) and 18 MB (DGN), which was transferred into the 3D city model of Hamburg as generated for the integration into the 3D city model of Hamburg, but it is still too large.

5.3   Data Reduction and Accuracy Analysis

In order to be able to reduce the data significantly, a polygon decimation of the meshed object had to be accomplished, which supplies a geometrical and visually correct result. Investigations with Geomagic showed that maximum curvature-based polygon decimation down to 10% supplies a result for the Bismarck figure, which fulfils both mentioned criteria. Thus, the original data volume of the Bismarck figure could be reduced from 800,000 to 80,000 polygons, which corresponds to a reduction of the file size by a factor 10 from 140 MB to 14 MB (DXF). In Fig. 9 differences between the version with 100% and 10% are barely noticeable, while the changes are clearly visible in the figure with the reduction to 3% compared to the full version. The average deviation of 1mm between original and 10% version was calculated in a 3D comparison, while the maximum deviation was 15mm. In the 3D comparison between original and 3% versions the deviations were already higher by a factor of 4 than with the version with 10%. On the other hand polygon decimation down to 5% could be achieved for the figures on the socket without significantly losing geometrical and visual quality.

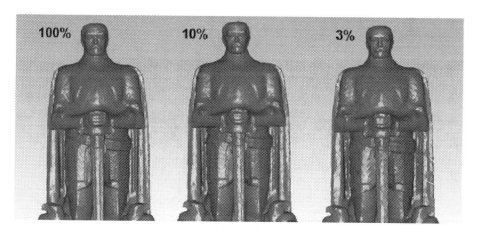

Fig. 9. Visual impression of different levels of polygon decimation in Geomagic for the 3D model of the Bismarck statue

For the accuracy analysis of the modelled 3D monument 74 check points, which were well distributed at the platform, at the socket, at the figures and at the Bismarck statue (see Fig. 3 right), were determined with a total station. The deviations between model and reference were on average between 3-10 cm in XY and in height, which is appropriate for the 3D city model and clearly fulfil the accuracy requirements of 30 cm. The analysis demonstrated the difficulty of identifying and measuring checks points especially on free form surfaces, which could explain larger deviations at several points. However, the re-created geometry of the statue shoulder and head could only be checked visually in the model. A detailed accuracy analysis is documented in [13].

5.4 Visualisation

The generated 3D model of the Bismarck monument was visualized in different formats and with different tools. A simple interactive representation was provided in the VRML format in different resolution stages (including figures at the socket 38 MB, without figures 9 MB) (see Fig. 10). But due to the uniform grey colour of the monument no texture mapping has been carried out. Only Bump Mapping was used as a test, in order to obtain a better depth effect in the model. A further easy-to-use independent viewer is the software AECVIZ from Tornado Technologies Inc., in which the model was imported as DXF (108 MB) and visualised interactively as an executable program (*.exe with 4 MB). In addition the model was converted into the common format 3D PDF (9 MB), which can be represented with each Acrobat Reader starting from version 8 (Fig. 11). The integration of the monument into the 3D city model of Hamburg is shown in Fig. 12. Several video sequences as flights around the virtual monument were generated with the program Cinema 4D (Fig. 13 top). For the integration of the model into Google Earth the quality of this existing geo data could be seen, since situation and height did not fit to the precisely generated virtual monument for a few meters (Fig. 13 bottom). But a Google Earth version of this monument is not planned.

Fig. 10. Presentation of the 3D model in the VRML format

Fig. 11. Visualisation of the Bismarck monument as 3D PDF

Fig. 12. Bismarck monument integrated into the 3D city model of Hamburg (in the background is the St. Michaelis church visible)

Fig. 13. Visualisation of the Bismarck monument in Cinema 4D (top) and in Google Earth (bottom)

6 Conclusions and Outlook

This integrated pilot study showed that complex objects such as the Bismarck monument can be recorded in detail by terrestrial laser scanning within a short time. However, the 3D modelling has been carried out using mostly manual methods; consequently this is time and cost-intensive. In total 210 hours were estimated for the entire project work, which partitioned themselves on the different work procedures: data acquisition 14h, adjustment geodetic net 16h, processing scanning data 30h, 3D modelling 130h, data reduction 8h, texture mapping 4h and visualization 8h. Since 61% of the entire working time was used for modelling, the biggest potential for optimisation can be achieved there by increasing automation. The ratio of object recording to data processing with 1:14 is slightly higher that other practical projects carried out at HCU Hamburg (1:10 for e.g. Kornhaus bridge Hamburg, Holstentor Lübeck). If one calculates a rate of €50 per hour for an engineer in the whole project, as a result costs of € 10,500 can be estimated for the whole project volume, which appears quite expensive for the object recording and modelling of monuments and which might not correspond to real market conditions. There is still substantial optimisation potential in all work procedures. The obtained accuracy of approx. 3 – 10cm for the 3D model of the Bismarck monument fulfils the requirements for the integration into the 3D city model of Hamburg and even for further visualisation applications without any problems. Thus, despite significant data reduction, which was achieved by curvature-based polygon decimation in triangle meshing of the complex structures (figures) and by CAD modelling with volume bodies for simple objects (platform and basement), a geometrically and visually correct 3D model has been generated. Although shadowing areas could not be scanned due to the statue height, missing parts of the Bismarck statue could be supplemented computationally with appropriate software. However, different software packages (LaserControl, RealWorks Survey, AutoCAD/PointCloud, Geomagic, Micro-Station) were in use for the production of the final product, since still today no program can cover all substantial work procedures optimally. The object recording and modelling of further monuments and historical buildings in Hamburg are planned, in order to increase the attractiveness of Hamburg's city models by the integration of such detailed 3D models.

Acknowledgments. The project support of Klaus Mechelke (HCU Hamburg) for scanning, Antje Tilsner (Bachelor student at Jade University of Applied Sciences) for data processing, Walter Sieh (Agency for Geo-Information and Surveying Hamburg) and Ingrid Jaquemotte (Jade University of Applied Sciences) for the additional supervision of the project is gratefully acknowledged.

References

1. Sternberg, H., Kersten, T., Jahn, I., Kinzel, R.: Terrestrial 3D Laser Scanning - Data Acquisition and Object Modelling for Industrial As-built Documentation and Architectural Applications. In: The International Archives of Photogrammetry, Remote Sensing and Spatial Information Sciences, vol. 35(7), pp. 942–947 (2004)
2. Ioannidis, C., Demir, N., Soile, S., Tsakiri, M.: Combination of Laser Scanner Data and Simple Photogrammetric Procedures for Surface Reconstruction of Monuments. In: 20th CIPA XX Symposium, Torino, Italy (2005),
   http://cipa.icomos.org/textfiles/TURIN/372.pdf
3. Neubauer, W., Doneus, M., Studnicka, N., Riegl, J.: Combined High Resolution Laser Scanning and Photogrammetrical Documentation of the Pyramids at Giza. In: 20th CIPA XX Symposium, Torino, Italy (2005),
   http://cipa.icomos.org/textfiles/TURIN/470.pdf

4. Kersten, T.: Virtual Reality Model of the Northern Sluice of the Ancient Dam in Marib/Yemen by Combination of Digital Photogrammetry and Terrestrial Laser Scanning for Archaeological Applications. International Journal of Architectural Computing, Special Focus on Cultural Heritage 02(05), 339–354 (2007)
5. El-Hakim, S., Beraldin, J.-A., Picard, M., Cournoyer, L.: Surface Reconstruction of large complex Objects from mixed range data – the Erechtheion experience. In: The International Archives of the Photogrammetry, Remote Sensing and Spatial Information Sciences, vol. 37(5), pp. 1077–1082 (2008)
6. Kersten, T., Lindstaedt, M., Vogt, B.: Preserve the Past for the Future - Terrestrial Laser Scanning for the Documentation and Deformation Analysis of Easter Island's Moai. PFG - Photogrammetrie - Fernerkundung - Geoinformation (1), 79–90 (2009)
7. Kersten, T., Büyüksalih, G., Baz, I., Jacobsen, K.: Documentation of Istanbul Historic Peninsula by Kinematic Terrestrial Laser Scanning. The Photogrammetric Record 24(126), 122–138 (2009)
8. Remondino, F., Gruen, A., von Schwerin, J., Eisenbeiss, H., Rizzi, A., Girardi, S., Sauerbier, M., Richards-Rissetto, H.: Multi-Sensor 3D Documentation of the Maya site Copan. In: 22nd CIPA Symposium, Kyoto, Japan (2009), http://cipa.icomos.org/textfiles/KYOTO/131-1.pdf
9. Toubekis, G., Mayer, I., Doring-Williams, M., Maeda, K., Yamauchi, K., Taniguchi, Y., Morimoto, S., Petzet, M., Jarke, M., Jansen, M.: Preservation and Management of the UNESCO World Heritage Site of Bamiyan: Laser Scan Documentation and Virtual reconstruction of the Destroyed Buddha Figures and the Archaeological Remains. In: 22nd CIPA Symposium, Kyoto, Japan (2009), http://cipa.icomos.org/textfiles/KYOTO/185-2.pdf
10. Cieslik, B.: Hamburg in der dritten Dimension. ZfV - Zeitschrift für Geodäsie, Geoinformation und Landmanagement, Heft 4, 254–259 (2003)
11. Kersten, T., Mechelke, K., Lindstaedt, M., Sternberg, H.: Methods for Geometric Accuracy Investigations of Terrestrial Laser Scanning Systems. PFG - Photogrammetrie - Fernerkundung - Geoinformation (4), 301–316 (2009)
12. Kersten, T., Sternberg, H., Mechelke, K., Lindstaedt, M.: Datenfluss im terrestrischen Laserscanning - Von der Datenerfassung bis zur Visualisierung. In: Terrestrisches Laserscanning (TLS 2008), Schriftenreihe des DVW, Band 54, Beiträge zum 79. DVW-Seminar am 6.-7, Fulda, pp. 31–56. Wißner-Verlag, Augsburg (November 2008)
13. Tilsner, A.: 3D-Erfassung und Modellierung des Bismarck-Denkmals in Hamburg durch terrestrisches Laserscanning. Unpublished Bachelor thesis, University of Applied Sciences Ostfriesland, Oldenburg, Wilhelmshaven (November 2008)

Use of Geoinformatics for the Digitization and Visualization of Cartographic Heritage: The Case of an Early 1920s Mytilene Town Map

Evangelia Kyriazi[1,2], Nikolaos Soulakellis[1], Georgios Tataris[1], and Stefanos Lappas[1]

[1] University of the Aegean, Department of Geography, University Hill,
81100 Mytilene, Lesvos island Greece
[2] 14th Ephorate of Byzantine Antiquities, Gianni Deli 11, 81100 Mytilene,
Lesvos island Greece
Evangelia_Kyriazi@yahoo.gr

Abstract. A map series of 1920s Mytilene town, property of Lesvos Archives, had been inaccessible due to its poor condition. One map of this series was restored, scanned, digitised and given a geographical reference system. Geographical coordinates were collected, and geoinformatics technology was used to create a geographically corrected map in GCS-GGRS-1987 Geographical Coordinated System and Greek Grid as a Projected Coordinated System. Comparison of the map to a 1953 map series revealed that the latter is a hand-made copy of the first. Therefore GIS tools were used to digitally visualise missing areas of the authentic map. This project may open new horizons for the Mytilene cartographic heritage through the creation of a digital map library, featuring the history of the town's cartography, and the development and use of new interpretation tools allowing online access for educational and recreational activities.

Keywords: cartographic heritage, geoinformatics, map conservation.

1 Introduction

'Cartographic Heritage' entered officially the glossary of the international cartographic community in 2005, embedded in the immense domain of modern digital information and communication technologies [1]. The impact of the notion of cartographic heritage is a modern, fresh and innovative constituent of the overall cultural heritage resetting cartography and maps in their distinct place as important products of human intellect and skill [2].

The starting point of this study were i) the ideas that cartographic heritage is cultural heritage, ii) that heritage has to be a shared experience and iii) that for cartography the criterion of accessibility is essential, as it marks a condition to meet the demands of cartography, namely to make reality accessible [3].

The subject of this study is an early 20th c. map, property of the Lesvos General State Archives, that for years had been inaccessible to the public. To increase accessibility, the project included conservation of the original object, digitisation, and

M. Ioannides (Ed.): EuroMed 2010, LNCS 6436, pp. 193–205, 2010.

use of Geoinformatics and map visualisation techniques. The project is in accordance to the International Cartographic Association (ICA) Commission on Digital Technologies in Cartographic Heritage [4] aiming to study and research on the possibilities of applying new information and communication technologies (ICT) on issues related to the cartographic heritage, focused on:

1) The transformation of the map into digital form.
2) The application of digital techniques in the study of the map
3) The application of digital support for the preservation and restoration of the map
4) The launching of the first steps to assist the work and functionality of the Lesvos Archives, to increase accessibility to cartographic heritage for future diffusion of the history, cartography and early 20th century maps to the public.

According to the ICA, "a map is a symbolised image of geographical reality, representing selected features or characteristics, resulting from the creative effort of its author's execution of choices, and is designed for use when spatial relationships are of primary relevance" [4].

The first known map was created by Eratosthenes in the late 3rd c. BC, followed by that of Hipparchus in the 2nd c. BC. The 1st c. BC papyrus by Artemidorus is considered to be the oldest saved Greek map. The birth of cartography, as we know it today, is owed in Ptolemy (2nd c. AD). In the Middle Ages (4th-13th c) cartography becomes thematic, with intense ideological content, having Christian symbolism as the main subject. The only exception was the case of the Arabs, especially during the 9th-11th centuries. In the 13th c. Europe rediscovers Ptolemy's cartography which becomes fast spread. In the Renaissance, map creation becomes more artistic. The spread of Ptolemy's cartography and geographical thought, the invention of typography and the great geographical discoveries, determined future developments. With the philhellenic spirit of the following centuries, the Greek territory becomes widely mapped. Cartography flourishes in the 20^{th}c., era of the great wars [5]. The map in this study dates in the early the 20^{th}c., and comprises part of the history of the first decades of possession of the town of Mytilene by the Greeks.

Old maps digitization has been performed in the past [3], [6], [7] and discussion is being made regarding the technique choices and developments [8], [9].

Digitization of the Mytilene map series may assist the Lesvos Archives into expanding their services outside their walls. Digital information is changing the way people learn, communicate and think, and the way that archives work. Digital information is neither final nor finite, it is flexible, easily re-edited, reformatted, reproduced and copied, and can make available powerful teaching materials for students who would not otherwise have access to them.

2   Materials and Methodology

The material and data used were i) an analogue early 20th century Mytilene map, ii) a 1953 Mytilene map series in digital form, and iii) geographical coordinates of 16 ground control points of Mytilene town, collected with a GPS. Methods exploited were coordinate sampling, georeference and mosaic creation of the 1953 map series, conservation, scanning, georeference and mosaic creation of the early 20[th]c. map, and superimposition and comparison of the two maps to create a geo-refered map of the early 20[th]c. with digital addition of the missing parts.

2.1 The Early 20th c. Map

The early 20[th]c. hand-drawn map presents part of the urban structure of Mytilene town, the capital of Lesvos Island, located in the NE Aegean Sea, built on the eastern peninsula of the island. Up to 1995, the map belonged to the Municipality of Mytilene, and then became property of the General State Archives-Lesvos Archives.

It measures 100cm x 98cm and is part of a series comprising of more than 10 maps, some of which are not saved today. It portrays a central area of Mytilene town.

It features part of the castle, the court, the prefecture building, the Yeni Mosque, a military hospital, baths, the Metropolis church and bishop's palace, St Theodore, St Apostles, St Simon and St George churches. Some of the map series features may indicate their creation date. One of the maps contains the Panayia Chryssomallousa church bell tower, built in 1903. Another one contains Kastrelli, a small Byzantine tower demolished in 1922. Therefore, they must have been drawn between 1903-1922. A more detailed study of the maps was not possible, due to restricted access.

The map is made from hard paper stuck on canvas with water-based adhesive. Initially drawn in pencil, it was then inked and coloured. It features buildings and other structures, tachymetric stops, contours, a faint pencil-drawn grid and a North arrow in black ink on the centre of the right side of the map, pointing to the right.

The object is worn due to long-term use (Fig. 1). The paper is yellowed and discoloured due to photo-degradation after exposure to high light levels. Its edges present significant losses of paper and the geographical information that it once presented. The paper and fabric on the edges are detached, folded, bended or curled. Several pinholes penetrate both paper and fabric. Three oxidised pins are attached on the map. Staining includes beverage stains, fingerprints, dirt, domestic fly droppings and iron oxides on the pinholes' areas. Dust, black Indian and blue ink stains are present on the canvas backing. On its upper back side, paper had been applied to support a detached area. Finally, yellowed sticky tape is present on the front side.

Buildings: The outlines of buildings, architectural elements i.e. pillars, staircases and verandas, and structures such as reservoirs, stockyards etc are drawn with black Indian ink. Stockyards and fencings are drawn in a double line, and building walls in a single line. Light grey shading indicates private, and dark grey indicates public buildings (Fig. 1). Most public buildings are pointed out with verbal description of their operation. Some misspelled words indicate that the designer lacked good grammatical knowledge. Small churches or Ottoman panes are pointed out with the symbols of cross or crescent respectively, without verbal description. Circular and square light blue forms represent water tanks and wells. Square yellow-coloured forms may represent sheds or non-permanent structures. Solubility testing revealed that the black ink is water-based, most probably black Indian ink; a black colouring constituting from coal, usually soot from burned timber or resin, dissolved in water. The varying black lines thickness, combined with the presence of several black ink stains, shows the likely use of pen for inking. The use of pens has the disadvantage of not allowing the continuous and uniform ink flow, making staining easy.

Tachymetric stops: Along road lengths, numbers connected in dashed lines are drawn with black Indian ink. These are the topographer's stops and route.

Topographers followed a concrete way, their stops being marked with black dashed lines on the map. Each tachymetric stop is recorded with a small circle and marked with the Greek letter Σ, possibly standing for the Greek word Στάση (Stop), and a number. Next to the circle, the altitude is marked inside a parenthesis. I.e. stop 192 is marked as Σ 192 (2,61). It should be noted that the altitudes have been changed by several centimetres since the map creation, due to maintenance works on the paving. The fact that letters and numbers corresponding to the tachymetric stops and their altitudes are well-written and astonishingly uniform, indicates that stencils had been used. In certain points, red coloured stops are marked with the initials ΣΣ, possibly connected with a military mapping service and may stand for Στάση Στρατού (Army Stop). Red stops appear to be of a later date. Some stops in black have been circled with red ink. In some points, red ink overlaps the black Indian ink. Although quite calligraphic, red fonts lack uniformity in their various appearances, indicating free-hand drawing. The altitude recording in this case uses three decimal digits. Interestingly, in the same stop, the two different topographers have recorded slightly different altitudes, i.e. 2.235 instead of 2.4 and 2.003 instead of 2.3.

Fig. 1. Part of the map before treatment

Contours: Contours have been drawn in cherry red ink. Every 5 contours the line has an intense bold cherry red colour. Contours were drawn based upon the tachymetric stops. The mapping out of the contours was first performed in pencil and later inked; a usual design practice, since drawing in pencil creates a slight ditch in the paper for the ink to flow in. The pencil trace is visible in many areas, overlapping the already inked buildings, proving that the mapping out of the curves is of a later date. Occasionally and due to the designer's carelessness, the contours overlap the buildings. The fact that lines are constant at the full length of the contours, reveals an experienced designer with a steady hand. The line thickness is quite uniform despite their big length, indicating the likely use of rapidographs, which allow the smooth and permanent ink flow, contrary to pens. An additional clue on rapidograph use is the lack of cherry red ink stains. In certain cases of lengthy lines, cherry red coloured contours lack uniform thickness, fact owed to the ink flow, since the rapidograph blunts from paper remains especially in the case of designing on bad quality paper.

Later additions: These include buildings drawn or shaded with pencil, such as the 5th Elementary School, notes and lines in pencil possibly portraying a proposed road layout, and circled areas in coloured pencil, red and blue ink.

2.2   The 1953 Mytilene Map Series

The 1953 map series consists of 26 paper maps, portraying the Mytilene town area before its 1984 expansion. Each of the original maps is in a scale 1:500. The series had been in use from 1953 up to 1984, when Mytilene maps were redrawn at a scale of 1:1.000. The 1953 map series was digitally available by the University of the Aegean Geography Department.

2.3   Methodology

Ground Control Point sampling: For the comparison of the 1953 maps with the early 20th century map, it was of great necessity to transform the first into the GCS- GGRS-1987 Geographical Coordinated System using Greek Grid as a Projected Coordinated System. The first step was sampling ground control points with a GPS. The 29 appropriately selected points were corners of buildings, built before 1920, and consequently very probable to appear in the early 20th century map series as well. These points were scattered in the town, in its surroundings, as this is presented in the 1953 map series, as well as in its centre. For reading stabilisation of each of the points, at least three minutes were allowed, while in many points multiple efforts were attempted until the obtaining of the maximum possible accuracy. The desirable precision was below 10 metres. For each of the coordinates sampling points, a photograph was taken. Data collected included X, Y and Z coordinates, accuracy, date and time. The average accuracy of the 29 control points was 6.24 m.

Transformation of the coordinates in a schematic file: The data were passed into an excel file and transformed into a database file (dbf), to ensure ESRI ArcGIS software compatibility. With the import of the dbf file in ArcGIS, the coordinates also acquired spatial entity and a schematic file of the points (shapefile) was created. The shapefile uses the GCS-GGRS-1987 Geographical Coordinated System and Greek Grid as a Projected Coordinated System.

Geographical correction of the 1953 maps: Based upon these 29 ground control points, the geometric correction of the 1953 maps was then performed. ERDAS Imagine 8.7 software was used to import the 1953 maps and the Ground Control Points (gcp). The points were identified on the map and each of them was referred to the equivalent gcp (Fig. 2). Initially, the exterior points were referred, followed by the points located at the centre of the map series. For the georeferencing of the maps, a transformation of a second order polynomial was chosen, since the area was big and with distortion due to the scanning process. Multiple efforts were performed until the achievement of the minimum possible RMS. The required RMS was below 10 metres. In the final attempt, making use of 16 selected points, the resulting RMS was 3.0047 m. The outcome of the above process was a georefered 1953 map series with GCS- GGRS-1987 Geographical Coordinated System and Greek Grid as a Projected Coordinated System.

Creation of 1953 map mosaics: ERDAS Imagine 8.7 software was used to transform the 26 maps into a mosaic, a united georeferred map. A second mosaic was also made, using the 8 maps that picture the same area as the early 20th c. map.

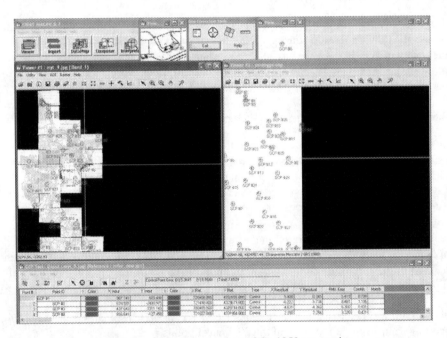

Fig. 2. Georeference procedure of the 1953 map series

Conservation of the early 20thc. map: Solubility tests were performed with deionised water, ethanol and acetone in cotton swabs. The dark red ink proved to be water-soluble, while the black ink proved to be soluble in ethanol and in water. The minimum possible cleaning was performed, in order to prevent losses of ink, pencil and other elements that constitute part of the historical use of the map. In some cases, the stains were not completely removed in order not to wound the paper and other elements during treatment. Mechanical cleaning of the surface dirt was performed using Wishab Hart™ cleaning dust, Wishab™ cleaning sponge, Absorene™ and a paintbrush. The old sticky tapes, insect droppings and beverage stains were removed mechanically with a scalpel. The oxidised pins were removed mechanically with pincers, and their oxidation products were removed with a scalpel. Chemical cleaning was performed with acetone and ethanol on cotton swabs where appropriate. For the flattening of fabric and paper, a preservation pencil, spatula and fasteners were used. The paper was adhered onto the canvas with a solution of acrylic emulsion Evacon R™ 20% v/v in deionised water, or pure Evacon R™ applied by paintbrush and toothpick. The adhered areas where fastened for a minimum of 12 hours. The canvas was cleaned mechanically with Wishab ™ sponge and a paintbrush. The pieces of added paper were removed with a spatula and a scalpel, and the aged adhesive and iron oxides were removed with a scalpel. Finally, the edges were backed with Japanese tissue paper in 6 cm wide stripes, adhered with Evacon R™ 20% v/v in deionised water. The map was then kept flat under pressure for 24 hours.

Scanning of the early 20th c. map: For safety reasons, Lesvos Archives did not allow the removal of the map from their building installations. Photographing the map was impossible, due to the lack of a photographic studio and suitable photographic equipment. Controlled light sources for shadings and reflections obliteration, light measurement instruments and large format cameras with a flat lens for the obliteration of deformity at the edges observed by concave photographic lenses would be needed. Due to these restrictions, it was decided to scan the map, using the table scanner of Lesvos Archives. Multiple overlapping scans were performed, dividing the map in 6 columns and 5 lines, giving a total of 30 A4 size scans. The superimposition of the scanned regions aimed in the restriction of distortion that could be presented by the scanner lens. Each scan was saved as jpg picture format file with a 400 dpi resolution.

Georeference of the scanned images: Each scanned part of the early 20th century map was georeferred using the 1953 georeferred map as a reference. The process was realised with the use of ERDAS Imagine 8.7 software, importing eight 1953 maps coinciding to the early 20th century map area. For their geographical correction, a transformation with a 2nd degree polynomial was executed. In each attempt, a different scanned area was imported and corrected by using at least eight ground control points, from which 4 internal and 4 external (Fig. 3). The final RMS resulting from the georeference of the 30 scanned images was 0.0155m. Upon completion of the georeferencing process, a mosaic was created in order to depict the map in a united form with geographic coordinates. ERDAS Imagine 8.7 software and the corresponding algorithm were used. The algorithm recognises the areas overlapped by two or more scanned pictures, and the final surface results from the picture found in the top of the superimposition. The result was a raster format file portraying the map in digital form and with the GCS-GGRS-1987 Geographical Coordinated System, using Greek Grid as a Projected Coordinated System. The very small RMS resulted in minimum faults in the limits of the pictures, giving a very satisfactory result.

Creation of early 20th c. map mosaic: ERDAS Imagine 8.7 was used to turn the 30 georeferred parts of the early 20th c. map into a mosaic. The final outcome was a georeferred digital map.

Comparison of the 1953 and early 20th c. maps: The mosaic consisting of the 30 scanned parts of the early 20th c. map, and that of eight 1953 maps, were superimposed and visually compared using blending and transparency techniques of the ESRI ArcGIS and ERDAS softwares. This process would be practically impossible without the use of Geoinformatics technology. Visual inspection aimed at identifying similarities and differences between the two maps (Fig. 4). Map 1 shows the correlation between the 1953 map series and the 1920s map. ESRI ArcGIS software was used to visualize maps from the available and acquired data (Map 1) and to determine the early 20th c. map scale.

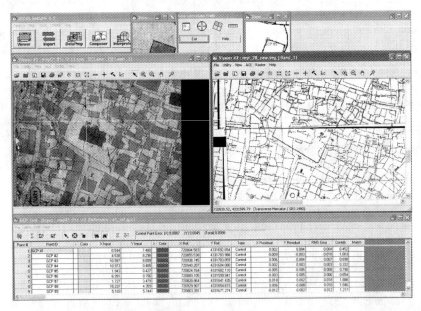

Fig. 3. Georeference procedure of the early 20th c map

Recomposition of the missing parts of the early 20th c. map and map dating: Visual observation proved that the two maps were identical. Therefore, using the image resulting from the superimposition of the two mosaics, ERDAS Imagine 8.7, ESRI ArcMap and PhotoShop softwares were used to digitally recompose the missing 1920s map areas (Fig. 5-6). Since the two maps were identical, the 1953 map series was further studied, in order to identify the featured buildings. It was found that houses known to be built up to 1920 were present on the map; however, houses built in 1922 and later were not present on the map.

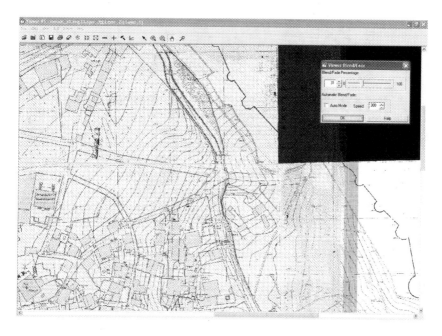

Fig. 4. Comparison of the two maps and reconstruction of missing areas

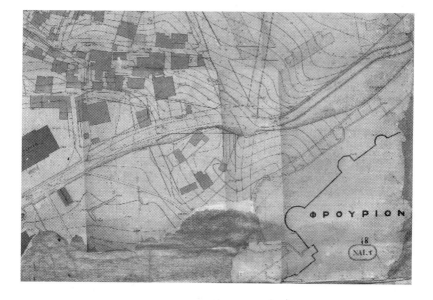

Fig. 5. Part of the map with losses of geographical information

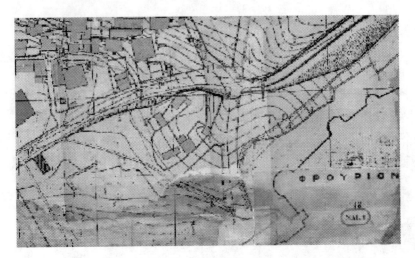

Fig. 6. The same area after digital reconstruction of the missing information

3   Results and Discussion

The early 20[th]c. map was found to have been designed between 1920-1922. The dating is very significant and may explain the presence of a military hospital on the map. It is likely that the map was created by the Greek army in the years of the Greco- Turkish War of 1919 – 1922, to serve military purposes.

Visual comparison of the two maps revealed that they were nearly identical. Buildings, topographer's routes, and even decorative map elements such as trees were identical. Even though the 1953 maps are at a different orientation of the 1920s map, elements, such as trees, were not redrawn to the correct orientation. However, all fonts have been redrawn into the correct orientation. Elements appearing in the 1920s map but do not appear in the 1953 map are: i. the North arrow, ii. the pencil-drawn buildings and iii. the pencil-drawn road network proposal. This leads to the conclusion that the 1953 map series is a hand-made copy of the 1920s series on different paper size, and with a different orientation. The 1953 map series is actually a representation of Mytilene in the years between 1920-1922 and may be used for digital recomposition of the missing areas of the 1920s map series (Map 1).

ERDAS Imagine 8.7 software was a very useful tool, and has also been used in the past in similar cases Type [3]. Not only does it join the images after providing reference points, but it also assists in the map geographical reference in the selected reference system. In addition, colour alterations due to the scanning process are corrected automatically, giving the map homogeneity in colour and brightness.

Digitisation facilitates access to information without handling the original object and therefore eliminates wear-and-tear of the original. However, preventive conservation of the original map is of fundamental value, in order to prolong its expected life span. The map should be stored flat at the following conditions:

Map 1. Superimposition of the 1953 and 1920s maps

Relative Humidity (RH) 55-65 %, Temperature (T) 15 °C, maximum visible light levels at 50 Lux and maximum UV levels at 10 µW/Lumen. The storage area should be kept clean and gloves should be used while handling.

Digitization affects the map material, its content and its communication properties. Questions arise concerning the vulnerability of the map under digitization, the dimensions of the digitization carrier with respect to those of the map, the geometric deformations induced by the digitization process, the scale alterations of the digital copy, the difficulties and problems in stitching, the necessity for preserving the colour reliability of the digital copy and the final digitization cost Type [1].

Digital information is dependent on machines to decode and re-present the bit streams in images on computer screens. Without machines, and without active human intervention, those data will not last. The benefits of making underused objects more accessible should be viewed in conjunction with factors such as compatibility with other digital resources and the collection's intrinsic intellectual value [10].

The work presented in this paper may open new horizons for the Mytilene town cartographic heritage. The project may well be continued, uniting all known town maps into a digital map library featuring the history of Mytilene cartography. New interpretation tools may be used and developed to assist in the understanding of the historic development of the town. Users may access the maps online for learning and recreation, while new educational activities may be developed.

4 Conclusions

Old town-maps should be viewed both as geographical data as well as part of our cultural heritage and as such, paper conservators and archivists can take advantage of geoinformatics in their own field areas. In certain cases digital reconstruction of missing parts of authentic maps may also be achieved by exploiting geoinformation methods and techniques.

The present study focused on two map series (early 1920s and 1953) portraying Mytilene town. Both maps were found to have been drawn at a scale of 1:500.

Bibliographical research revealed that the early 20th c. map was designed between 1920-1922, possibly by the Greek army, in the years of the Greco-Turkish War (1919– 1922) in order to serve military purposes.

Visual comparison of the two digitally processed and fused maps leads to the conclusion that the 1953 map series is a hand-made copy of the early 1920s series redrawn on different paper size, and with a different orientation. The latest series is actually a representation of Mytilene town in the years between 1920-1922 and as such it may serve for digital recomposition of the missing areas of the oldest map series. The outcome of the digital processing and fusion was a new map at a scale of 1:500, consisting mainly of the 1920s map, and the missing parts from the 1953 map series which can be further exploited through a digital library of the General State Archives.

Geoinformatics open new horizons in the preservation of cartographic heritage, by digitising, georeferencing, visualising and comparing data, and provide powerful tools for data interpretation, educational activities and access to information. Future research will focus on these fields, examining their application into historic town maps of Mytilene.

Acknowledgements

Special thanks to Mrs. Katerina Karagiannopouloy, directress of the Lesvos Archives for providing access to the early 1920s maps.

References

1. Livieratos, E.: The challenges of Cartographic Heritage in the digital world. In: ICA Commission on Digital Technologies in Cartographic Heritage Third International Workshop Digital Approaches to Cartographic Heritage, Barcelona, June 26-27 (2008)
2. Livieratos, E., Tsorlini, A., Boutoura, C., Pazarli, M.: How the Cultural Heritage of Cartography and Maps may Positively Influence the Development of a Small Society: The Kozani experiment (2008-2010). Presented at the 24th International Cartographic Conference, Santiago, Chile, November 15-21 (2009),
   http://icaci.org/documents/ICC_proceedings/ICC2009/html/nonref/25.html
3. Hruby, F., Plank, I., Riedl, A.: Cartographic heritage as shared experience in virtual space: A digital representation of the earth globe of Gerard Mercator (1541). e-Perimetron 1(2), 88–98 (2006); International Cartographic Association 1995, ICA Mission, Adopted by the 10th General Assembly of the International Cartographic Association, Barcelona, Spain (September 3, 1995), http://icaci.org/mission
4. Livieratos, E.: Commission on Digital Technologies in Chartographic Heritage (2009), http://icaci.org/commissions
5. Livieratos, E.: Comments upon cartography, maps and their Greek "complications". Geografies, 43–72 (Spring 2001) (in Greek)
6. Hongye, B.: Digitization of Ancient Maps Based on GIS Technology: The Yu ji tu Map. In: World Library and Information Congress: 75th IFLA General Conference and Assembly "Libraries Create Futures: Building on Cultural Heritage", Milan, Italy, August 23-27 (2009)
7. Chias, P., Abad, T.: Visualising Ancient Maps as Cultural Heritage: A Relational Database of the Spanish Ancient Cartography. In: 12th International Conference Information Visualisation, vol. IV, pp. 453–457 (2008)
8. Daniil, M., Tsioukas, V., Papadopoulos, K., Livieratos, E.: Scanning Options And Choices In Digitizing Historic Maps. In: Proc. of CIPA 2003 International Symposium, Antalya, Turkey, September 29-October 4 (2003)
9. Adami, A., Fregonese, L., Guerra, F., Livieratos, E., Tsioukas, V.: Digital representations and analysis of deformations induced in map supporting materials. In: XXI International CIPA Symposium, Athens, Greece, October 01-06 (2007)
10. Smith, A.: Why Digitize? Council on Library and Information Resources. Commission on Preservation and Access (1999)

An Emblematic Bronze from Cyprus the Idalion Project

Patrick Callet[2,3], François–Xavier de Contencin[4], Anna Zymla[5], Philippe Denizet[6],
Thibaut Hilpert[1], Kesuke Miyazawa[1], and Bertille Robin[1]

[1] ECP, Ecole Centrale Paris, grande voie des vignes, Châtenay-Malabry, France
{thibault.hilpert,kesuke.miyazawa,
bertille.robin}@student.ecp.fr
[2] MAS lab, ECP
[3] Centre Français de la Couleur
[4] GI Lab., ECP
[5] LGPM, ECP
[6] Atelier Audiovisuel ECP
{patrick.callet, francois-xavier.de-contencin,
anna.zymla,philippe.denizet}@ecp.fr

Abstract. The Idalion Tablet, an antique bronze (480-470 BC) found around 1850 in the antique city of Idalion in Cyprus is the main purpose of the presented interdiciplinary work. The tablet is the property of the Bibliothèque Nationale de France (BNF) since 1862, and is absent from collections of the Idalion Museum (Cyprus). Our final goal is to realise an accurate copy of the Idalion Tablet (scale 1, with no patina) as a donation to the Mayor of Dhali on behalf of the "Local History Society – Kypros". As the Tablet has an important cultural and historical value, we were not allowed to handle it directly neither to realise a mould by physical contact. Therefore, we used 3D digitization to create a virtual and accurate replica of the Tablet shape. By rapid prototyping a physical copy of the Tablet was obtained for casting with bronze. The simulated tablet, thanks to a very accurate 3D digitization, was obtained with the Virtuelium free software. With the elementary composition of the alloy, the complex index of refraction of the alloy was calculated and compared to spectroscopic ellipsometry measurements. A didactic movie is also in progress and will be translated first into greek and later into several languages.

Keywords: 3D Digitization, Spectroscopic Ellipsometry, Virtual Metallurgy, Rapid Prototyping, Rendering, Lost-Wax Casting Technique.

1 Introduction

Following some important results previously obtained [1], we realised a virtual copy of an antique bronze from Cyprus, the Idalion tablet. The same visual aspect as the original was required and obtained by spectral simulation using the Virtuelium free software. This work is part of a most important project, which aims at realising a perfect physical copy in bronze of the Idalion tablet, using 3D digitization, rapid prototyping and casting.

M. Ioannides (Ed.): EuroMed 2010, LNCS 6436, pp. 206–224, 2010.
© Springer-Verlag Berlin Heidelberg 2010

We first present the historical context of the project, and its goal. Then we explain how we digitized the Idalion tablet and how we got the necessary data for the spectral simulation: elementary composition of the bronze in order to determine its complex index of refraction. The last part is dedicated to the metallurgical work for obtaining a physical replica of the famous tablet.

2 The Idalion Project

The Idalion tablet is named from the antique city where it was found in Cyprus. In this section we explain why it has an important historical value for Cyprus, and what the goal of our project is.

2.1 The City and Kingdom of Idalion

Idalion was an antique city of Cyprus (near the current town of Dali). According to the legend, Chalcanor, an Achaean hero of the War of Troy, funded it. The Kingdom of Idalion was at the top of its cultural and economic power during the 7th century BC and until the conquest of the town by the Phoenician Kings of Kition during the 5th century BC. Idalion is now one of the most important archaeological sites in Cyprus. The site contains two acropolis and a town. Very few buildings remain and the main one is the temple of Athena at the top of the west acropolis.

2.2 The Idalion Tablet

The Idalion tablet is made of bronze (Fig. 1). Some illegal excavators at the archaeological site of Idalion discovered it around 1850. It used to be hanged in the temple of

Fig. 1. The Idalion tablet (Face A) in its actual state. Thin corrosion or intentionally patinated surface?

Athena. A French collector, Honoré d'Albert, Duke of Luynes, bought it. In 1862, the Duke gave the tablet to the *Bibliotheque Nationale de France*, with all his collection. The dimensions of the tablet are: (X: 14.2; Y: 21.5; Z: 1.1 cm) while its weight is 2 247.22 g.

Cyprus syllabary writing covers the tablet on its two sides. The Idalion tablet is the oldest testimony known of this writing [2]. It is also its longest and richest corpus. The knowledge of the existence of Cyprus syllabary writing was permitted by the discovery of the Idalion tablet. The text was written in 480-470 BC. It is an agreement between the King of Idalion Stasikypros (probably the last king before the fall of Idalion) and the doctors Onasilos and his brothers. The doctors commit themselves to cure the wounded after the siege of the city by the Persians and the Phoenicians of Kition. In exchange of their help, they will be given lands near the city (the Kingdom of Idalion was certainly very rich).

3 Digitization

As the tablet has an important cultural and historical value, we were not allowed to handle it directly neither to realise a mould by physical contact. Therefore, we used 3D digitization to create a virtual and accurate (spatial resolution of 50 µm) replica of the today tablet shape.

3.1 Principle

To make a highly precise replica of the tablet, the first step was 3D digitization. For doing this, we used a structured light scanner from Breuckmann company (Figure 2), made up of a projector and a digital camera. The projector emits a structured light on the object. The shape of the light and shadow fringes is transformed by the relief of the object. During this time, the digital camera captures a large number of images corresponding to various types of projected fringes and analyzes their transformations. This system enables us to construct 3D graphics of the object with the triangulation principle. The accuracy in 3D coordinates is about 50 µm all over the surface (Figure 3). Recent experiments and low cost devices based on the use of structured light is exposed in [3].

3.2 3D Sensors and Data Processing

The aim of the digitization was to get 3D image data, to be able to make a physical replica of the tablet. The digitization was done in collaboration with the Eotech company. The Ecole Centrale Paris supported the financial needs of this step. Even if the Idalion tablet is a small object, the main difficulty of this step was the amount of data necessary to guarantee a good precision (Figure 3) for the reproduction of the tablet by casting. For the rendering by optical simulation with *Virtuelium* such an amount of data is not required. A total of about 5 Gb was then collected and dispatched in 63 views.

Fig. 2. The structured light used in 3D digitization without any contact with the tablet

Fig. 3. A high quality and density 3D cloud of points

4 Metallurgical Analyses of the Alloy

The goal of this project is to create an accurate copy of the Idalion tablet. The replica will then appear as the original in its shape, writing, and the composition of its alloy will be as close as possible to the original one. We wanted to see the tablet in its original aspect without the patina. This project will therefore give us the opportunity to see how the tablet looked like at the time it was made.

Fig. 4. Detail of the writing on the original Idalion tablet

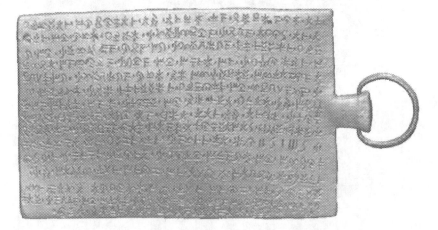

Fig. 5. 3D copy of the Idalion tablet rendered with the CAD software CATIA (non spectral rendering)

Fig. 6. Detail of the recorded writing on the 3D copy of the tablet with the software Rapidform. The almost periodic surface waviness, probably due to the initial clay tablet, is quite visible

4.1 The PIXE Method

The *Centre de Recherche et de Restauration des Musées de France* (C2RMF) analysed the alloy of the tablet for us. The *PIXE method* thanks to the *AGLAE* particle accelerator was used for the elementary composition (see Table 1). The PIXE   method [4] is based on the principle of the X-ray emission induced by charged particles. The physical principle of this technique is an atomic process in four stages:

1- a proton beam is emitted towards the analyzed object.
2 - ionization in deep layer of the targeted atom by the proton beam.
3 - an electron of an external layer fills the created gap.
4 - the release of extra energy by emission of a characteristic X-ray.

The energy of this characteristic X-ray is used to determine the nature of the element of the atom by using the Moseley's law. Thus by analyzing all the X-ray emissions, this method obtains all the different elements that composed the analyzed object and their own proportions.

4.2 Experimental Conditions

For the tablet analysis, the C2RMF used a beam of protons of 3 MeV and of about 0.5 mm of diameter, with a scanning of the surface on 0.5 mm x 0.5 mm. The analysis was done until 50 μm deep into the alloy. A filter of 100 μm of Al was placed in front of the detector of high energies. To be sure that no layer of alteration disrupts the measurements, a RBS spectrum (Rutherford Backscattering Spectrometry) was acquired at the same time. The analyses were done on metallic shavings taken by microborehole (with a rapid drill in steel) near the suspension ring, that were laid out on an adhesive sheet of carbon.

4.3 Results

The composition of the Idalion tablet is shown in the Table 1 below. It is mainly composed of copper (96.5%), tin (2.4%) and lead (0.8%).

Table 1. Elementary composition of the alloy

Element	Mn	Fe	Co	Ni	Cu	Zn	As	Ag
Mass (%)	<0.05	0.3	0.05	<0.03	96.5	<0.08	0.04	<0.09
Element	Cd	Sn	Sb	Te	Au	Pb	Bi	
Mass (%)	<0.06	2.4	<0.9	<0.4	<0.1	0.8	<0.06	

As expected for a bronze, the main elements in the alloy are copper and tin. In this alloy the ratio of copper is very high. This is probably due to the fact that there was a lot of copper available in Cyprus, which was very famous for its copper fields. We cannot compare those results with the composition of other antique objects from Cyprus, as the data on this subject are rare.

5   Virtual Copy of the Idalion Tablet

In addition to casting the tablet, one of the goals of our project is to create a virtual copy of the Idalion tablet for several purposes. In a few months the historical building "Richelieu" of the *Bibliothèque Nationale de France* is going to be renovated leading the museum where the Idalion tablet is to be closed for an unknown time. Thus, we decided to realise a virtual copy of the Idalion Tablet which could be shown on the BNF website and accessible to all even during the renovation of the museum. To do that, we used the Virtuelium open-source software [5]. Different levels of detail are shown in Figures 4, 5 and 6 for comparison with the original view.

5.1   Virtuelium

Virtuelium is an open-source software developped by a research team of the Ecole Centrale Paris laboratory called MAS (Applied Mathematics and Systems). This software can be download at http://virtuelium.free.fr. Virtuelium is a software that renders physically realistic images. It differs from other renderers because it combines the most fundamental material properties in its algorithm. In addition, it is able to consider many optical phenomena, usually ignored by common rendering softwares such as spectral dispersion due to a translucent material with variable indices of refraction, or polarization transport of light. This software is a renderer and not a modeler. Thus, it renders the 3D scenes described in XML format that links the exported shapes from other software (OBJ format) and materials to use.

Some of the main characteristics of Virtuelium are:

1. Spectral rendering with a parametrable wavelength sampling for all elements (viewer, materials, illuminants, propagation media).
2. Polarization effects accounted for all steps of the computations.
3. XML formalism for 3D scenes and data descriptions.
4. Multithreading and/or grid computing.
5. Multilayered materials (macroscopic layers of paints or multiple thin films assembly).
6. High Dynamic Range Imaging.

A special photon-mapping algorithm according to Jensen specifications is also implemented in Virtuelium software and used here for realistic rendering.

To run, the software needs the computation of the following elements: the 3D file of the digitized tablet and complex indices of refraction of the tablet material. To get these complex indices, we first did a lineary interpolation of between the complex indices of copper and tin which are the main elements that give the colour of a bronze. This computation is based on previous work done at the Ecole Centrale Paris. Given the fact that we have the elementary composition of the tablet thanks to the analysis made by the C2RMF, we took a sample of the alloy of the Tablet made during the casting of the physical copy. We then measured the complex indices by spectroscopic ellipsometry and we compare the results with the indices computed by interpolation. All the computations involved a CIE colorimetric standard observer (CIE 1964 – 10°) and CIE-D65 normalized illuminants ; the last image (Figure 16) in this article shows the obtained results due to the whole chain of knowledge developed during the project.

5.2 Spectroscopic Ellipsometry

The spectroscopic ellipsometry is an optical technique for surface analysis based on the measure of the change in the polarization state of light after reflection on a flat surface (Figure 7). The measurement is performed on all visible spectrum and more. Such a device is shown in Figure 11. It consists in a monochromator, a unit command for filtering, two mobile arms supporting the rotating polarizers, a scientific software for the data management and exportation. In addition a small pump create a depression for fixing the sample to study in a vertical plane.

5.2.1 Measurement Principle

Considering a plane electro-magnetic wave arriving on a flat and smooth surface. A part of the wave is transmitted or absorbed through the surface, another part is reflected out from the surface.

The electric field E_i (Figure 7) of the incident wave can be decomposed on two axes: one E_{pi} parallel to the incidence plane, the other E_{si} perpendicular to the incidence plane. The reflection coefficients are here for a parallel polarization r_p and for a perpendicular polarization r_s:

$$r_p = \frac{E_{pr}}{E_{pi}} \quad \text{and} \quad r_s = \frac{E_{sr}}{E_{si}} \tag{1}$$

These coefficients are complex. In practice, we measure the ratio of these two coefficients:

$$\frac{r_p}{r_s} = \tan(\alpha)\exp(i\Delta) = \rho \qquad (2)$$

with $\tan(\varphi) = \dfrac{r_p}{r_s}$ ratio of modulus and Δ the phase difference introduced by the reflection. For a bulk and isotropic sample, the refraction angle φ_1 is governed by the Snell-Descartes' law:

$$N_0\sin(\varphi_0) = N_I\sin(\varphi_1) \qquad (3)$$

with N_0 index of the external medium, $N_1 = n_1 + jk_1$ (n_1 being the refractive index (real) and k_1 its extinction coefficient, here equal to 1), φ_0 the angle of incidence, φ_1 the angle of refraction. The Fresnel reflection coefficients (r_p, r_s) can be deduced from the continuity of the tangential components of the electric field $\mathbf{E}$ and magnetic field $\mathbf{H}$ at the interface:

$$r_p = \frac{N_1\cos(\varphi_0) - N_0\cos(\varphi_1)}{N_1\cos(\varphi_0) + N_0\cos(\varphi_1)} \qquad r_s = \frac{N_0\cos(\varphi_0) - N_1\cos(\varphi_1)}{N_0\cos(\varphi_0) + N_1\cos(\varphi_1)} \qquad (4)$$

Thanks to the Snell-Descartes' law we deduce r_p and r_s in terms of N_0, N_1 and φ_0. Then by reversing these relationships and by using eq. (4) above we have the equation:

$$\frac{N_1}{N_0} = \sin(\varphi_0)\sqrt{1 + \left(\frac{1-\rho}{1+\rho}\right)^2 \tan^2(\varphi_0)} \qquad (5)$$

5.2.2 Measurement Technique

The measurements are made by an ellipsometer with rotating polarizer [6] in about 20 mn for a wide spectral band from 250nm to 2000nm. It consists of the succession of a lamp, a polarizer, the sample, an analyzer and a detection device as shown in (Fig. 8).

The amplitude of the electromagnetic field is splitted along two orthogonal axes S and P. The action of each element can be represented by a 2x2 matrix with complex coefficients.

This allows by measuring ρ to calculate the complex index of refraction of the alloy:

$$N_1(\lambda) = n_I(\lambda) + ik_I(\lambda) \qquad (6)$$

polarizer, analyzer:
$$P = A = \begin{pmatrix} 1 & 0 \\ 0 & 0 \end{pmatrix} \qquad (7)$$

(in the system of eigen axes of the polarizer or analyzer) sample:

$$E = \begin{pmatrix} r_p & 0 \\ 0 & r_s \end{pmatrix} \quad \text{and a rotation} \quad R(A) = \begin{pmatrix} \cos A & -\sin A \\ \sin A & \cos A \end{pmatrix}$$

(8)

A being the rotation angle of the analyzer (A) or of the polarizer (ωt).

For an isotropic lamp diagram: $L = \begin{pmatrix} E_0 \\ E_0 \end{pmatrix}$. On the detectors, the amplitude of the detected field is:

$$E_d = A.R(A).E.R(-\omega t).P.L$$

(9)

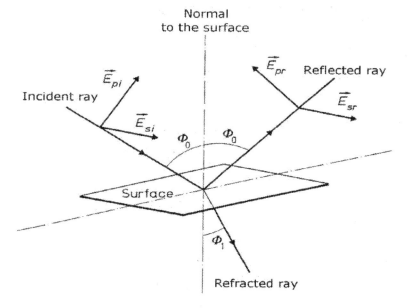

$\vec{E}_{pi}$ Component, in the plane of incidence, of the incident electric field

$\vec{E}_{si}$ Component, perpendicular to the plane of incidence, of the incident electric field

$\vec{E}_{pr}$ Component, in the plane of incidence, of the reflected electrique field

$\vec{E}_{sr}$ Component, perpendicular to the plane of incidence, of the reflected electric field

Φ_0 Angle of incidence

Φ_1 Angle of refraction

Fig. 7. Reflection of the polarization axis at the surface of the sample ; definition of angles and fields

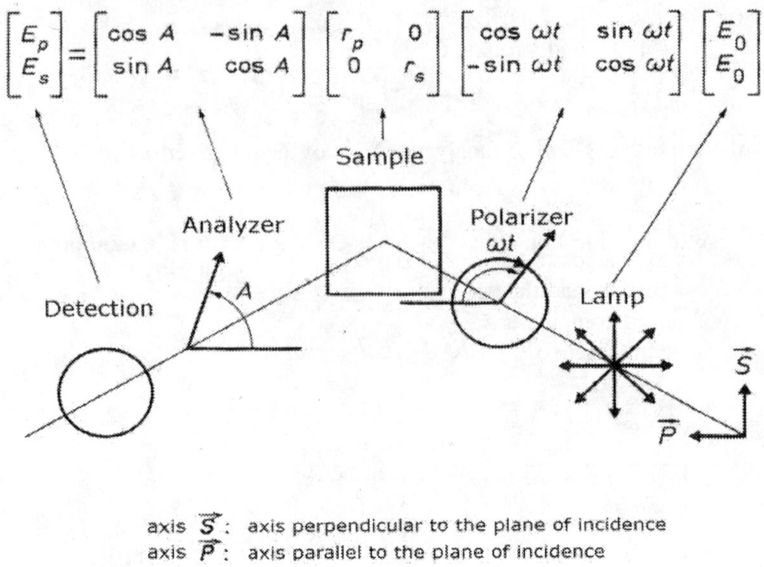
$\begin{bmatrix} E_p \\ E_s \end{bmatrix} = \begin{bmatrix} \cos A & -\sin A \\ \sin A & \cos A \end{bmatrix} \begin{bmatrix} r_p & 0 \\ 0 & r_s \end{bmatrix} \begin{bmatrix} \cos \omega t & \sin \omega t \\ -\sin \omega t & \cos \omega t \end{bmatrix} \begin{bmatrix} E_0 \\ E_0 \end{bmatrix}$
Sample
Analyzer
Polarizer
ωt
A
Lamp
Detection
S
P
axis S: axis perpendicular to the plane of incidence
axis P: axis parallel to the plane of incidence

Fig. 8. Influence of the different elements on the polarization of the beam in an ellipsometer with rotating polarizer

This gives the intensity: $I=|\vec{E_d}|^2$. Then after linearization of the sine and cosine~:

$$I = I_0\left[\alpha\cos(2\omega t)+\beta\sin(\omega t)+1\right] \quad (10)$$

where :

$$\alpha = \frac{\tan^2(\wp)-\tan^2(A)}{\tan^2(\wp)+\tan^2(A)} \quad (11)$$

$$\beta = 2\cos(\Delta)\frac{\tan(\wp)\tan(A)}{\tan^2(\wp)\tan^2(A)} \quad (12)$$

$$I_0=\frac{|r_s|^2|E_0|^2}{2}\cdot\frac{\cos^2(A)}{\tan^2(\wp)+\tan^2(A)} \quad (13)$$

The coefficients α and β don't depend on the lamp intensity; this allows us not to do any baseline measurement of the beam intensity. Using α, β and A we formulate tanφ et cosΔ. The practical implementation of this technique is mainly beam collimation and alignment of optical components. The next step is to retrieve data from tanφ and cosΔ on a computer for different wavelengths.

5.2.3 Results

Previous works were used to calculate by linear interpolation of the real and imaginary parts of the index of refraction of the alloy. The lead influence was not taken into account for calculating the complex indices, because it has no impact on the visual aspect of the alloy for a so weak amount (less than 1%, see Table 1).

The figures 9 and 10 show the comparative results for the real part N and the imaginary part K. The colour of a metallic body mainly depend on the imaginary part of its complex index of refraction. The ellipsometric measurements, driven at INSP (Institut des Nano Sciences de Paris) are in a good agreement with our predictive values. With those results, and thanks to the 3D copy of the Idalion tablet, we were able to use Virtuelium to compute the final virtual copy of the tablet. The result is shown on the last image in (Fig. 16).

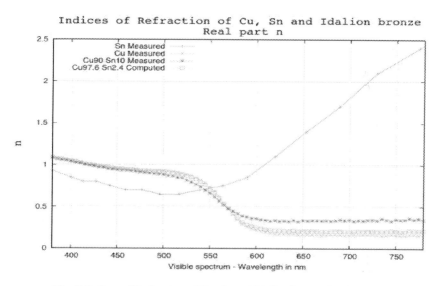

Fig. 9. Indices of Refraction of Cu, Sn and Idalion bronze, Real part N

5.3 The Original State of Surface

The natural or intentional patina of the Idalion tablet remains an opened question. Many further developments and analyses have to be led not only for optical simulation but for characterizing the origin of many cypriot artefacts. The term patina can refer in the widest sense [7].

Patina connotes a specific colour and continuous surface layer. **Patina** is a film on the surface of bronze or similar metals (produced by oxidation over a long period in the soils or outdoor (natural patina) or by a chemical process (**synthetic artificial or applied patina**) or any such acquired change of a surface through age and exposure. On metal, patina is a coating of various chemical compounds such as oxides or carbonates formed on the surface during exposure. The origin of the word *patina* comes from the Italian term, *patena,* used to denote a shiny dark varnish applied to

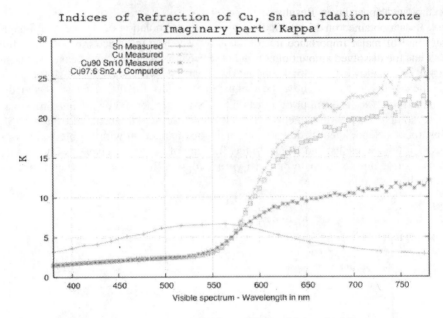

Fig. 10. Indices of Refraction of Cu, Sn and Idalion bronze, Imaginary part κ

shoes, and the first known printed definition of the word in Baldinucci's *Vocabolario* of 1681. The use of the word *patina* as a term predominately associated with the green corrosion crust found on buried bronzes that form during long exposure seems to have developed in the 18th. Morphology of patina of bronzes can be smooth and shiny, dense, uniform (and then called **noble patina**), or rough, and destroyed. When including an important damaged coating, the pulveraceous and/or with cracks create an unattractive aspect and is called **virulent patina.** Their colour is very typical, green, bluish-green, but could also appear grey pale or black. The colour of patina depends on many factors. For example, green or greenish-blue colour that the green compound has produced consisted primarily of brochantite or basic copper sulphide, (urban environment) copper carbonates, malachite and azurite (on buried bronzes). Ancient Greek bronze vessels have an unusually attractive and stable patina containing green basic copper carbonates produced from burial conditions and could serve here to illustrate a "noble patina". Another example on outdoor bronze sculpture is the very attractive oxide layer that typically forms at the lowest layer of the corrosion crust formation of first layers by internal tin oxidation. The second phenomenon is copper selective dissolution from solid solution and formation of cuprite layer [8]. This structure is a semiconductor and can act as a membrane for transport of ions with cations (Cu^{2+} and Cu^+) outward and anions (Cl^-, O^{2-}), migrating inward. As a result, the oxygen and other compounds present in the environment come in contact with the alloys and could interact with it according to the following process.

Cuprous species such as Cu_2O can be later oxidized to cupric compounds CuO and the other part is dissolved into the environment and can precipitate onto the surface as cupric compounds (hydroxycarbonates, hydroxychlorides, sulphides) forming porous precipitated upper layer. Results of Robbiola [9] established on the basis of 44 analytical data obtained on 15 artefacts show that soil elements incorporated in the outer layer are of major importance in the achievement of the final colour of the surface whereas the dissolved amount of copper is not characteristic of the given colour to the patina.

Fig. 11. The Woollam Ellipsometer used for optical constants acquisition (n and κ) at INSP (Paris)

Here, after some non-destructive optical observations, it was concluded that the thin corrosion layer supposed to be the original one developed inside the soil during centuries. The metallic surface was probably smooth enough for developing a thin corrosion layer defined in the meaning of the Cook-Torrance modelling of roughness as $m = 2\sigma/T = 0.3$ (mean height over mean correlation distance). Dorsey [10] studied a physical but non-spectral modelling of metallic patinas for using in computer graphics. The future of our project will consider in a more experimental way, all these aspects of corrosion, either natural or not.

Fig. 12. The metallic and polished sample of bronze, with the measured composition, replicated at LGPM for ellipsometric measurements (diameter : 15 mm)

6 Physical Copy of the Idalion Tablet

The technique which was used to make the Idalion Tablet is currently unkown but several details show that it might have been made using the lost-wax casting technique. Thus, in order to get close to the antique technique, we decide to make the physical copy of the Idalion Tablet using the lost-wax casting technique.

6.1 Rapid Prototyping

This stage was realized by the *Centre Technique des Industries de la Fonderie* (CTIF). In order to use the lost-wax casting technique, we have to make a copy of the Idalion Tablet in wax (Fig. 13). To do so, we use the 3D file which was acquired during the 3D digitization, to make a wax copy by rapid prototyping. This step is realized using a 3D printer. The printer makes the prototype layer by layer. Each layer has a thickness of several microns. The lower layers of wax, that support the prototype, are not as precise as the upper ones. There fore, it was not possible to real-ise the prototype of the tablet in one block: the writings on the lower face would not have been enough precise. This stage was particularly difficult, as the tablet is very thin and as its shape is curved. The two parts were then separated from the support wax, and assembled together. Then, the CTIF in partnership with the *Ecole Supérieure de Fonderie et de Forge* (ESFF), realised the spruing of the wax copy. The wax prototype is sprued with a treelike structure of wax that will provide paths for molten casting material to flow and air to escape. The carefully planned spruing begins at the top with a wax "cup," which is attached by wax cylinders to various points on the wax copy.

Fig. 13. One of the two folds of the prototype in wax of the Idalion tablet, printed at the CTIF

6.2 Mould Manufacturing

The second step – the realisation of the mould - was also realised by the CTIF. The sprued wax copy is dipped into a slurry of silica, then into a sand of controlled grain size. The slurry and grit combination is called ceramic shell mold material, although it is not literally made of ceramic (Fig. 14). This shell is allowed to dry, and the process is repeated until at least a half-inch coating covers the entire piece (Fig. 15). Then the mould is placed in a kiln, whose heat hardens the silica coatings into a shell, and the wax melts and runs out. The melted wax can be recovered and reused, although often it is simply burned up. Now all that remains of the original artwork is the negative space, formerly occupied by the wax, inside the hardened ceramic shell. The feeder and vent tubes and cup are also hollow.

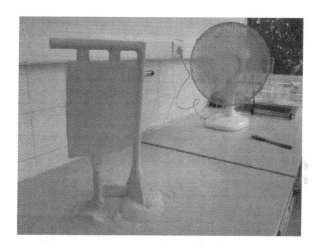

Fig. 14. The first silica-sand ceramic thin layer recovering the wax replica

Fig. 15. The last coarse ceramic coating forming the final shell with the casting feeder and air evacuation cones and tubes

6.3 Casting of the Idalion Tablet

The third and last step which is the casting of the Idalion Tablet was done by the
CTIF. The mould is reheated in the kiln to harden it. To realise the physical copy, we
use the same alloy as the Tablet that was determined with the analysis of the composition. The metal is melted in a crucible in a furnace, then poured carefully into the
shell. The spruing, which are also faithfully recreated in metal, are cut off, to be reused in another casting. Just as the wax copies were chased, the casting is worked
until the telltale signs of the casting process are removed, and the casting now looks
like the original model. Pits left by air bubbles in the casting, and the stubs of spruing
are filed down and polished.

Fig. 16. The virtual restitution by photon-mapping of the Idalion Tablet rendered with
Virtuelium (4000 x 3000 px²) in 24h on a grid of 6 CPUs at about 2GHz each. CIE D65 illuminants, CIE 1964 (10°) colorimetric observer and ellipsometric data acquired on a physical
sample of the alloy.

7 Conclusions

Many scientific fields met together for this international project was a success. We
created a very complete chain of knowledge with historians, curators, metallurgists,
computer scientists, engineer students, chemists and video-makers. So exciting this

project is, still now, we have many things to do for enhancing the results in each discipline. The study of patinas, even restricted to bronzes, makes a new challenge for rendering with physical and chemical parameters involving analysis, non-contact methodologies, spectrophotometric measurements, colour analysis and surface distribution using textures and images (UV-Visible-IR) as information sources. Diplomatic relations between countries and cultural institutions could find some new ways of collaboration using 3D tools adapted for virtual restoration, physical replication and communication purposes.

Acknowledgements

This project started in Cyprus (VSMM 2008) when we met Kyprianos Kountouris[1] in during the visit at the Dali Museum and discussed about bronzes with a great reciprocal enthusiasm. We also thank the Medals and Coins department of the *Bibliothèque Nationale de France* and especially Mrs. Avisseau-Broustet for allowing us to digitize the Idalion tablet, M.-F. Monanges for realizing the documentary film on our work, and D. Bourgarit from the *Centre de Recherche et de Restauration des Musées de France* (C2RMF) for analysing the elementary composition of the tablet alloy. This work would not have been possible without the financial support of the *Ecole Centrale Paris*. Bruno Gallas and Jacques Lafait from Institut des Nano-Sciences de Paris, help us in ellipsometric measurements. We also want to mention that nothing would have been possible without the partnership with the *Centre Technique des Industries de la Fonderie* (CTIF) and the *Ecole Supérieure de Fonderie et de Forge* (ESFF).

References

1. Callet, P., Zymla, A.: Rendering of binary alloys – Example and validation with bronze. In: Kozera, R., Noakes, L., Paulus, H., Skarbek, W., Smolka, B., Wojciechowski, K. (eds.) 2nd International Conference on Computer Vision and Graphics, ICCVG 2004. Springer, Warsaw (2005)
2. Masson, O.: Les inscriptions chypriotes syllabiques: recueil critique et commenté. Boccard, Paris (1983)
3. Rocchini, C., Cignoni, P., Montani, C., Pingi, P., Scopigno, R.: A low cost 3D scanner based on structured light. In: Chalmers, A., Rhyne, T.M. (eds.) Proceedings of EuroGraphics 2001, vol. 20. Blackwell publisers, Malden (2001)
4. Grassi, N., Migliori, A., Mandò, P.A.: Differential PIXE Measurements For The Stratigraphic Analysis Of The Painting "Madonna Dei Fusi" By Leonardo Da Vinci. In: 10th International Conference on Particle Induced X-ray Emission and its Analytical Applications, PIXE 2004, Portorož, Slovenia, June 4-8, pp. 843.1–843.3 (2004)
5. The virtuelium project, http://virtuelium.free.fr
6. Ellipsometry principle and elliposmeters, http://www.jawoollam.com

---

[1] Local history Society.

224 P. Callet et al.

7. Quaranta, M., Sandu, I.: Micro-Stratigraphy of Copper-Based Archaeological Objects: Description of Degradation Mechanisms by Means of an Integrated Approach. In: 9th International Conference on NDT of Art, Jerusalem, Israel, pp. 1–8 (2008)
8. Sandu, I., Marutoiu, C., Sandu, I.G., Alexandru, A., Sandu, A.V.: Acta Universitatis Cibiniensis, Seria F Chemia, vol. 9, pp. 39–53 (2006)
9. Robbiola, L., Blengino, J.-M., Fiaud, C.: Morphology and mechanisms of formation of natural patinas on archaeological Cu-Sn alloys. Corrosion Science 40, 2083–2111 (1998)
10. Dorsey, J., Hanrahan, P.: Modeling and rendering of metallic patinas. In: Proceedings of the ACM-SIGGRAPH (1996)

Scotlandsplaces: Accessing Remote Digital Heritage Datasets Using Web Services

Ashley Beamer[1,3] and Mark Gillick[2,3]

[1] ScotlandsPlaces Project Manager, RCAHMS
ashley.beamer@rcahms.gov.uk
[2] IS Operational Manager, RCAHMS
mark.gillick@rcahms.gov.uk
[3] RCAHMS - The Royal Commission on the Ancient and Historical Monuments of Scotland,
16 Bernard Terrace, Edinburgh, EH8 9NX

Abstract. The ScotlandsPlaces project is an official, permanent website found at www.scotlandsplaces.gov.uk. It exhibits a very novel and exciting way of searching across cultural heritage information. It uses geography to discover relevant records and lets the public sift through the results using geographic-based technologies. The ScotlandsPlaces website has seen the development of innovative technologies including the redevelopment of open-source geo-middleware, the ScotlandsPlaces XML schema for data transfer and the use of dynamic map interfaces for user querying. Although these technologies that sit behind the site are innovative and cutting edge, the website itself has a simple design and is easy to use. System developments such as the digital volumes management system allow different partner organisations to include resources in a standard format, efficiently disseminating information to the public.

Keywords: Web services, Geography, Archives, Heritage, Gazetteer, XML, Remote Databases.

1 Introduction

The ScotlandsPlaces project is a partnership between, currently, two of Scotland's foremost national collections, the Royal Commission on the Ancient and Historical Monuments of Scotland (RCAHMS) and the National Archives of Scotland (NAS). ScotlandsPlaces (http://www.scotlandsplaces.gov.uk) is a web project established in 2008 and was beta launched in October 2009. It allows the public to search from information from each of the partner organisation's databases. This means that although the relevant information is being provided to the user in the ScotlandsPlaces website, the data itself remains in the databases of the host institutions. The site was launched by the Scottish Culture Minister and was re-released in April 2010 to include further functionality.

The significance of the ScotlandsPlaces project is as follows:

- The retrieval of information is based upon geographical location. The site uses mapping for both searching and sorting, and the ScotlandsPlaces

M. Ioannides (Ed.): EuroMed 2010, LNCS 6436, pp. 225–239, 2010.

gazetteer was developed for place name searching. The ScotlandsPlaces gazetteer may form part of a wider Scottish National Gazetteer. The internal broker, based on CYGnus, has been developed to request, receive and present the datasets as both a tabular XML listing or a plot-able KML file.

- The project has seen the development of a bespoke ScotlandsPlaces XML to bring together the datasets from the different partner domains.
- ScotlandsPlaces uses web services, and the aggregation of disparate record types exhibits joined up government and provides an example front end for a UK Spatial Data Infrastructure (SDI). In March 2010 ScotlandsPlaces was named an official Scottish pilot for the EU INSPIRE Directive which aims at providing the technical underpinnings for an EU SDI.

These technical and political significances will be addressed throughout this paper.

The ScotlandsPlaces website is designed to be extensible with simple technical joining rules. The project aims to see the collaboration of different organisations in bringing together geographically indexed information for the benefit of the public. The website demonstrates organisations working together to efficiently amalgamate and present heritage datasets.

2 Partners and Resources

2.1 RCAHMS

The resources available from the Royal Commission on the Ancient and Historical Monuments of Scotland incorporate a multitude of datasets including archaeological and architectural records from the numerous collections held in the RCAHMS *Canmore* database.

The national collection provides invaluable knowledge and is a rich resource for the study of Scotland's built and historic environment. RCAHMS has been collecting data and archiving information for over 100 years. This data has been gathered through RCAHMS' own field surveys and research programmes as well as from outside collections deposited for long term care. The datasets held at RCAHMS describe archaeological and building work throughout Scotland and include some 300,000 sites recorded in the database and 3 million related items of archive, many of which have been digitised. The website provides access to these digitised images for ordering or download, and gives information on the content and extent of the non-digitised collections. The digitisation program is on-going and collection items currently only available in paper format may be requested for digitisation.

The collections materials include:

- The National Collection of Aerial Photography
- Photographic Collections
- Drawings Collection
- Digital Collections
- Book Collection
- Manuscript Collection
- Map Collection
- Framed Material Collection

The Canmore records are indexed to site level by both place name as well as by National Grid Reference (NGR) and Lat/Long.

2.2 The National Archives of Scotland

The National Archives of Scotland provide a series of records called the *Register House Plans* (RHP). These contain approximately 150,000 topographical plans, marine charts, architectural and engineering drawings. The NAS have provided access to the Register House Plans which are geographical referenced by place name and many are indexed to coordinate level. The RHP collection is extremely diverse and includes plans received from government departments and agencies, as well as industries, the courts, churches, private organisations, landed estates and families. Most of the RHPs are unique and many are engraved and lithographed. The collection contains photographic reproductions or original plans. The plans are largely topographical in nature and the National Archives of Scotland has the largest collection of original maps and plans of Scotland from 1750 onwards (NAS, 2007).

Many of the RHPs have been digitised and are available to view in the website using software called Zoomify. Zoomify allows the user to render the image full-screen and examine the details of these often rather large resources allowing for outstanding off-site access to the materials.

2.3 The Digital Volumes

The NAS have also provided a resource invaluable to genealogical and local history researchers. There resources are "digital volumes" or e-books, the pages of which can be viewed in the site using Zoomify. These digital volumes currently include:

- *Royal Commission on the Owners of Lands and Heritages from 1872-1873* (NAS library reference GA149/560) – This report of a parliamentary commission into land ownership gives the names of every owner of land (of one acre or more) in each county.
- *Farm Horse Tax rolls, 1797-1798* (NAS library reference E326/10) - When the Crown collected taxes it collected information about its subjects. Most taxation was levied from landowners until the late 18th century when the government sought to broaden the tax base by taxing other forms of property. A by-product of this is a useful series of records for historians, listing different types of people in each of Scotland's parishes and burghs. The farm horse tax rolls from 1797-1798 can be viewed on the site, listing the owners of work-horses in each place. More tax volumes will be added shortly. The Farm Horse Tax rolls list the names of the owner and number of horses and mules used in husbandry or trade in 1797-1798. In some rolls the tax inspectors made repeat visits to track down non-payers, which explain why some parishes and burghs are repeated.
- *Medical Officer of Health Reports, 1891* (NAS library reference HH62) - From 1890 onwards, a full-time Medical Officer of Health was appointed in each county in Scotland with a remit to report on the state of health of the county and its various parishes and towns. The annual reports of the Medical Officers give an objective view of the living conditions, diseases and major

health issues in different parts of Scotland. Information on the individual parishes and towns are found within the 'registration districts' headings found in these volumes. The NAS has an incomplete set of the published reports from 1891 onwards.

- *Hay Shennan, Boundaries of Counties and Parishes in Scotland, 1891-* The website currently offers the pages of "Boundaries of Counties and Parishes in Scotland as Settled by the Boundary Commissioners under the Local Government (Scotland) Act, 1889" in PDF format. This book was published by William Green and Sons in Edinburgh, 1892. Here, researchers can locate information on the boundary changes that took places in Scotland in 1889. Such changes affected the boundaries of counties, parishes, and burghs.

  When a boundary line is drawn between places, it can have a huge impact on the everyday life of the people who live there, as many modern Council boundaries do today. These lines can affect how much local tax must be paid, who provides local services, which school children go to and where, and who owns what. Consequently boundaries are often disputed and have to be redrawn. For the historian, the boundaries between parishes, burghs and counties are important in determining where to find information about those places. Changes to boundary lines are therefore an issue. There were many changes to parish boundaries in the 16th and 17th centuries. In 1889, many parish and county boundaries, based on an out-of-date pattern of landownership, had to be revised to meet the needs of local government. More boundary changes were made in 1900 and 1929. On this site you can read how the widespread boundary changes in 1889 affected towns, villages and individual houses in Scotland.

The above descriptions have been taken from the ScotlandsPlaces site at: http://www.scotlandsplaces.gov.uk/digital_volumes/types.php.

A database has been built to house the image references for these e-books and the images are called on demand by the user from the NAS server. As the above digital volume resources are in the form of e-books and not catalogued records, a *Digital Volume Content Management* system, or DVMS, has been developed to allow ScotlandsPlaces partners to easily add new digital volume resources into the website, connecting the books to place names from the ScotlandsPlaces gazetteer. The DVMS allows entries to be edited and modified by the partner organisation giving them full control over the presentation of their own data. Each partner is provided with an administrative-side username and password and a set of guidelines for entering the digital volumes material into the site. The descriptive side of a digital volume makes up the wordage seen on the ScotlandsPlaces digital volume pages and each digital volume book is allocated a XML file location and individual image locations on the server of the partner organisation. This XML file is imported into the website's MySQL database where the image references can be found and requested. Any changes to the partner's XML file flags up in the system and the affected XML file if re-imported. The DVMS also accepts resources in PDF format for increased accessibility. Overall it is an excellent facility for partners to enter materials held in book format and provides invaluable remote access for users.

Although the DVMS requires that information is added in a particular way, many different types of information can be added including books, journals, diaries, parliamentary papers, rolls, registers and more.

As the digital volume information is retrieved on the fly using web services and held on the server of the host organisation, each organisation is able to maintain their own DVMS resources including associated metadata and image references. They are also able to provide their resources out elsewhere if they wish.

3   A Brief Overview of Functionality

The site enables the user to enter a place name or conduct a co-ordinate search, thus making *location* the common thread for record retrieval.

3.1   Place Name Searching

The homepage of the site provides a county map and listing to allow the user to easily enter the site based on a broad place name search.

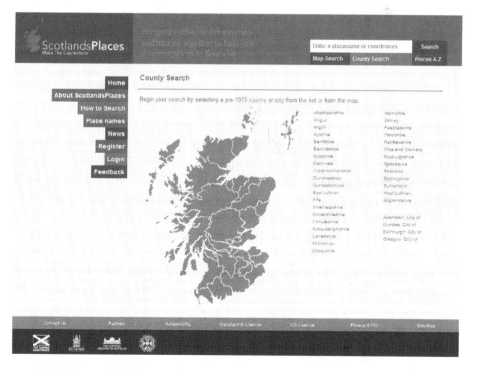

Fig. 1. Image of the ScotlandsPlaces homepage (http://www.scotlandsplaces.gov.uk)

The user is able to return to the homepage from anywhere in the site by clicking on the ScotlandsPlaces icon at the top left hand corner, by clicking "Home" in the menu or by clicking on "County Search" under the search box.

Once the user selects a county from the map or list, they are taken to a county results page. County results pages provide information about that place from the ScotlandsPlaces gazetteer (discussed below), a map of the place showing its location in
Scotland as well as heritage datasets from the partner organisations:

Fig. 2. Example of Aberdeenshire results page

Clicking on the county map on the top right of the results page allows users to select a parish and narrow down the results by location. The user is then taken to the
parish results page of their choosing which allows them to filter the number of results

retrieved at the county level. On each results page the user is also able to filter results based on organisation as well as keyword.

Each page of the site also provides a search box where the user is able to search on a more specific place name. When a place name is entered, it is sent to and compared against the place name listings in the gazetteer (discussed below).

3.2 Coordinate Searching

If a user decides to search by coordinate/extent they may enter the following into the search box according to the formats outlined in the "How to Search" section of the menu:

- Decimal Degrees
- Degrees, Minutes and Seconds
- National Grid References
- Eastings/Northings

Users are also able to access the OpenLayers functionality in the site. This allows users to zoom into the map, pan around, zoom in and out, and drag the red search pin onto the map to conduct a coordinate/extent search. This type of search efficiently pulls together the heritage records that are indexed by coordinates - a strong tool in information search and retrieval. If the user knows the exact location they wish to search, the OpenLayers search facility can be utilised to circumvent the retrieval issues relating to place names; issues like primary/variant names and misspellings.

4 Mapping in ScotlandsPlaces

As the website is geographically-based, a number of different mapping elements have been incorporated. Each results page provides a location map to show where the administrative area or particular place is located in Scotland. These maps are generated on-the-fly using the coordinates from the gazetteer (discussed below) for each place name. The homepage provides a county "roll-over" map and such maps are also available for parishes within each county on the respective county results pages.

The site also provides mapping for both search and retrieval as well as record sorting.

4.1 OpenLayers and KML

As mentioned above, OpenLayers is a piece of open source software that allows developers to include dynamic map layers into a website. In ScotlandsPlaces OpenLayers is available under "Map Search" on each page of the website and lets the user conduct searches based on coordinate and extent. This coordinate and extent information is then sent to the gazetteer and appropriate databases to extract information of sites and records that fall within the selected boundary. By sending these coordinates to the gazetteer, the system is able to provide information on the parish boundaries that the search hit upon.

The ScotlandsPlaces internal broker (discussed below) provides the results in a tabular listing in the webpage. However, users have the option to see the results in a different manner. On each results page the user is given the option to "plot the results on a map". This allows the user to see their results spatially using the OpenLayers facility:

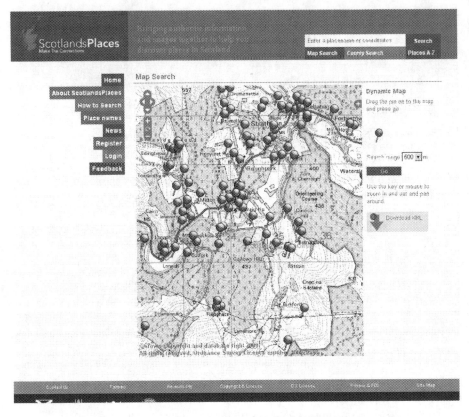

Fig. 3. Example of OpenLayers plotting in the ScotlandsPlaces website

Once the records have been plotted, the user can click on one of the pins that represent a site or a record and they are presented with the title and location of the record as well as a link to the fully individual record within the ScotlandsPlaces site.

The user can also "download the KML file" and plot the results in a popular external geobrowser such as Google Earth. Thus, if records are indexed to co-ordinate level, records can be displayed visually on a map to allow the user to sift through their search results based on location, rather than from a tabular listing. This is very useful functionality for individuals who are searching for information where they know the location associated with a site or record but not its name or any other keywords that could be associated with it.

OpenLayers provides Ordnance Survey map layers and county and parish boundary layers as web map services. It is in the future plans of the project to develop the

OpenLayers functionality further to include historic map layers, base layers, and more administrative boundary layers showing boundary changes over time.

5   The Technical Aspects of ScotlandsPlaces

5.1   Platform

The ScotlandsPlaces project endeavours to use open source software whenever possible. As mentioned in the previous section, OpenLayers was implemented to allow both user coordinate/extent searching and also as a means of displaying results. Other Open Source elements include the internal broker, (developed in PHP from the middleware CYGnus, the MySQL database which sits behind the website and controls results pages and the DVMS, the Joomla content management system and the Apache server platform.

Both CYGnus and the MySQL (namely the DVMS) are discussed in detail below.

5.2   The Gazetteer

The ScotlandsPlaces project included the development of a comprehensive historical place names gazetteer for Scotland. The gazetteer is utilised in two ways. Firstly it intercepts a user query for the purpose of clarifying and refining the user search. Secondly, it acts as an information database by providing relevant data to populate a search results page. When a user enters a place name into the search box this name is firstly sent to the gazetteer to see how often that term occurs. If the search term is found more than once the user will be asked to clarify which place they intended. Once a single geographic place has been determined this place name is sent to the partner organisational databases for querying.

The gazetteer currently holds counties, parishes, modern councils, regions, districts, burghs, major cities, islands, and "populated places". Populated places are towns and cities with a populated of 100 people or more up until 1982.

If a search term is entered that is not found in the gazetteer, that keyword term is sent to the partner databases and a "free text search" is conducted.

The gazetteer has spatial, temporal, hierarchical and cross-searchable elements, tracking place name and boundary changes over time. It holds primary and variant place names and has the capacity to include other languages such as Gaelic. It was developed following the International Alexandria Digital Library standard for gazetteer development and is therefore interoperable with other database gazetteers.

The gazetteer developed for ScotlandsPlaces sits outside of the system as a separate service module and can therefore be used in other projects. Importantly, the gazetteer is likely to be included as the historical place names index listing in a wider Scottish government endeavour to develop a national gazetteer.

5.3   The Internal Broker

The website was developed around a piece of open source geo-middleware, developed as a proof-of-concept system by an MSc GIS student at the University of Edinburgh. This middleware was called CYGnus and exhibited a lightweight solution to providing results from separate information providers into one application (Carter & Gittings, 2009).   CYGnus was redeveloped and strengthened by the ScotlandsPlaces team to handle the queries it would receive through ScotlandsPlaces.   This middleware, or "internal broker", makes sense of the queries by communicating with the ScotlandsPlaces gazetteer and sends the search requests (whether place names or coordinates) to the separate remotely hosted databases of the partner organisations.   The internal broker uses geography as the "glue" for information retrieval.   It then amalgamates and ranks the results in order of relevance to the user, and presents them in the ScotlandsPlaces website.

The key to the internal broker is efficiency.   The importance of the broker is that it retrieves data from the separately held database and displays the results in a single interface.   It does this by using web services.

5.4   Web Services

The overall significance of the ScotlandsPlaces project is it does not host data, but instead offers an access point to a realm of data connected by geography.   The system allows datasets to be maintained by the host organisation or institution thereby removing the necessity for the duplication of data in providing information to the public.   Results are provided from the hosting database as the query is made, where smaller amounts of data are requested on demand, on the fly, in real time, via web services.

This allows organisations to provide a live, up-to-date feed from their database directly to the website using web services in the form of URL parameterised pairs.

As there is no need to duplicate information, host organisations are able to maintain, update, delete and modify their own database without having to repeat these efforts elsewhere.   The website therefore relies on live web services so that information is called upon when requested by the user and is always up-to-date.

Importantly by using web services, all contributing organisations maintain ownership and control over their own data.

The primary concept in using web services is the notion of 'hold the data once, and use it many times'.   Organizations who have set up their system to respond to web service queries are therefore able to provide their data out as a service to as many other queries as they choose.   They are able to provide their data to multiple locations, thereby making their data more efficiently available to the public.

In ScotlandsPlaces web services are carried out using simple URL/parameter pair calls, chosen so as not to put too high a technical barrier to joining the project, for those organisations without formal Simple Object Access Protocol (SOAP) web service skills.   As explained below, once the EU INSPIRE Web Feature Services (WFS) have been published, the ScotlandsPlaces team will be implementing these WFS alongside the parameter pairs to act as a testbed for the INSPIRE Directive (European Commission, 2010).

5.5   The ScotlandsPlaces XML

As the project is extensible and ongoing, it is very difficult to foresee the many possible partners who may join the site in the future.   The project is not domain specific and the only 'join' criteria is that the information to be included is indexed spatially;

either by place name or, preferably, by coordinates. Aside from the indexing requirements, the only other stipulation is that joining partners have their data held in a database and visible to a web server for querying.

Although the project currently holds largely historical datasets and is currently speaking with heritage institutions to join in the project, it does not restrict joining partners to particular domains. As discussed above, the project relies on web services to amalgamate the data and pulls relevant data into the site to display for the user. During the planning phases of the project it was decided that as domain data interoperability could be an issue, a ScotlandsPlaces XML schema would be developed in order to avoid XML mapping (Beamer & Gillick, 2009). Therefore the project does not specify a pre-developed existing standard for data sharing but rather defines the XML format that partner organisations need to return the appropriate datasets. In short, mapping between pre-existing XML formats was not an option due to the multi-domain nature of the project and the complexities of the data that could be integrated into the website.

When using web services to bring information together, data can be supplied in one of three ways:

- The agencies can provide their data in a pre-defined XML standard stipulated by the project and which would have to be mapped to the standard used by the site. This is a soup bowl concept for data sharing by XML. This aspiration would be feasible in larger XML based projects however was not an option for ScotlandsPlaces due to the maintenance overhead needed for processing speeds of on-the-fly translations.
- The agency provides their data in any format they wish. The data broker then maps these formats into either a chosen existing XML standard or a bespoke project based XML standard.
- A compromise; a simple, published bespoke XML necessary to make a particular project work quickly, as a lightweight solution, preparing only the XML tags needed to attain the desired information.

This third option was the one selected by the ScotlandsPlaces team. It was deemed the most suitable solution for two reasons. Firstly, mapping between both known as well as unknown XML standards would have been time consuming for a project programmer with no expertise in XML schemas. This would therefore consume considerable resources in development and operation. Secondly, such mapping would impede future partners from joining the project quickly.

The site makes two web service calls to each of the partner organisations. The first call is to provide the user with a finite amount of information about a record. It provides just enough information to allow the user to determine if they want to click into that result to receive the full record. The second web service call retrieves the full record information.

The first call XML tags are shared across each partner organisation. These include tags for name, UID, record name/title and thumbnail URL. A few other tags are currently specified as <other1>, <other2>, and <other3>. This allows each partner to add a few other pieces of information that may be specific to their records. RCAHMS currently fills these tags with parish and counties names as well as the number of images associated with the record. The NAS currently uses only two of these <other>

tags in providing an image count and the date corresponding to the record. The XML used to respond to the first database call is therefore fairly standard, and as new organisations include custom data in these <other> tags, the XML may become more well-defined.

The XML for the second calls shows how very different the retrieved datasets can be as few tags are used for both organisations. As new partners will be joining the site with a variety of different datasets, the ScotlandsPlaces XML will grow to fit the elements of the data that require new XML tags. Therefore, new partners to ScotlandsPlaces will either use pre-existing tags to transfer their data or new code will be introduced for the inclusion of these datasets.

Making the decision to create a bespoke XML schema or use a pre-existing XML standard which may need to be customised, depends on the breadth and diversity of potential partners and the scope of the project in the future. In 2000, O'Brien reminded readers that "XML is concerned with the quick and easy creation of metadata rather than establishing fixed and standardised metadata structures" (O'Brien, 2000). This pragmatic approach is the position taken in the ScotlandsPlaces project.

With the current ScotlandsPlaces partners normally using two different heritage XML schemas for data transfer (MIDAS XML and EAD), a published ScotlandsPlaces XML was created. As we shall see below, wider geographic strategies mean that future partners may well go beyond the heritage and archives sectors to include partners from a range of sectors of government and beyond.

6 Government Strategies

In using web services the ScotlandsPlaces site demonstrates the efficient use of data and shared services in government. The project is in line with various government initiatives including the One Scotland, One Geography strategy which aims to see government organisations working together for the benefit of the public (Scottish Government, 2005). As mentioned above, project also aims to be in line with the EU INSPIRE Directive which is currently developing a technical infrastructure for a spatial data infrastructure for Europe (European Commission, 2010).

One Scotland One Geography is a strategy to develop a more systematic and effective means of delivering geographic information to the public. The strategy is particularly interested in the development of efficient public services using the most efficient and up-to-date resources available. An ultimate goal of this strategy is to create a spatial data infrastructure for geographic-based information. The INSPIRE Directive offers a technical means of bringing the appropriate datasets together to reach this goal.

The EU INSPIRE directive sets out standards for interoperability for both public and private organisations across the UK and Europe to share their geographic data and for the public to access these datasets via a central hub using formal web feature services. The hub will hold the metadata catalogue for retrieving relevant datasets, the national gazetteer and the internal client software to combine and deliver the requested data. A modern address gazetteer has been developed by the Scottish Government called the One Scotland Gazetteer ScotlandsPlaces which marks the beginnings of a comprehensive spatially enabled national Scottish place name and address gazetteer.

The INSPIRE (Scotland) regulations came into effect by the Scottish Government on December 31st 2009 stipulating that particular government organisational domains will be INSPIRE compliant over the next few years.

ScotlandsPlaces has been developed alongside the INSPIRE directive and is an example front end to a potential INSPIRE-based spatial data infrastructure for Scotland. ScotlandsPlaces plans on implementing the INSPIRE Web Feature Services to sit alongside the URL parameter pairs currently used in the site for querying. New organisational partners will have the option of selecting which service they wish to use as some organisations may wish to be INSPIRE compliant and some may not. The project will ultimately illustrate what may be done by using the underpinning IN-SPIRE infrastructure to retrieve data from different sources and presenting this data to the public.

In late April 2010, ScotlandsPlaces was announced the winner of the annual AGI (Association for Geographic Information) conference competition for "Most Beneficial Information Service".

7 Future Developments

The website is currently being used by both national and international user groups including archaeologists, genealogists, architects, local history researchers, archivists and disparate Scots interested in discovering more about their ancestors and the places associated with them. In the first six months of going live, the ScotlandsPlaces website has seen over 350,000 hits and is used internationally. Analytics shows that ninety percent of the traffic coming into the site is via place name searches inside the search engine. This means that the website is very visible to search engines such as Google and users are being taken straight to the website's individual results pages within the site, essentially using the search engine as the search box within the site.

The project was developed to be an ongoing fully supported endeavour and as such is under fairly continuous technical development. The 'technical joining documents' for the project have recently been completed and the project team are now pursuing new partners in the site. The project will be welcoming a new national project partner by the end of 2010.

Overall website developments for 2010 may include a subscription system for the inclusion of new digital volumes made available at a charge. These newly released digital volumes will be regarded as added-value to the site and will not replace the concept of free digital volumes or other site resources in the future. More free volumes will be moved over to the site later in the year. These volumes will include more historical tax information.

The project team would also like to see further development in terms of the gazetteer and place name information in the site. Over the years various other Scottish historical place name resources have been developed including the Gazetteer for Scotland (University of Edinburgh, 2010). It is possible that web services will pull through place name descriptive information of this online gazetteer, or the user will be able to link out to it, providing the user with more background knowledge of the place they are interested.

7.1 Scalability

The ScotlandsPlaces project was designed to be easily scalable. Although the "join" work for the first two partners took several weeks in order to iron out bugs and issues with the web service queries, the technical join document prepared by the ScotlandsPlaces team estimates that a straightforward join would take approximately 1 week of development time.

The join documentation stipulated the XML used, the types of parameter pairs a new partner can expect to receive by the system and also provides information on using Zoomify, querying their database and ranking for search results returned to the infrastructure. Joining partners with technical requirements above and beyond the scope of the infrastructure thus far, will be discussed by the project governance board and suggestions and recommendations will be made on how the project can be designed to include the new partner.

ScotlandsPlaces provides this joining documentation and also the personnel and guidance needed for a successful join. The nature of the project means that new partners need to adhere to a simple method of making their data available and providing it out for consumption. The benefit of providing this data in such an efficient manner through the ScotlandsPlaces infrastructure and out to the general public far outweighs the minimal amount of join work needed to adapt to the system.

8   Conclusions

The ScotlandsPlaces project demonstrates shared services and information, as well as government organisations effectively working together to efficiently disseminate information to the public. It is, and will remain, in accordance with larger UK and EU government initiatives to share geographic data.

The project exhibits a new and exciting way for the public to search across heritage records and sites by using geography as the underlying element in data retrieval and sorting. It demonstrates that information can be provided in a fun, efficient and easy to use manner and will be a source of more exciting national and local collections in the future.

References

1. Beamer, A., Gillick, M.: ScotlandsPlaces XML: Bespoke XML or XML mapping? Program: Electronic Library and Information Systems (2009),
   http://www.emeraldinsight.com/Insight/viewContentItem.do;
   jsessionid=FE34D11C2ADF45D68C559447345376B4?
   contentType=Article&contentId=1839191s
2. Carter, N., Gittings, B.: Getting Beyond the Silos (2009),
   http://www.geoconnexion.com/uploads/beyond_silos_ukv7i1.pdf
3. European Commission, European Commission – Inspire Directive (2010),
   http://inspire.jrc.ec.europa.eu/
4. NAS, Topographical, architectural and engineering plans in the NAS (2007),
   http://www.nas.gov.uk/guides/plans.asp

5. O'Brien, M.J.: Creating data exchange standards with XML: a waste? In: First International Conference on Web Information Systems Engineering (WISE 2000), Wise, vol. 2 (2000), http://www2.computer.org/portal/web/csdl/doi/10.1109/WISE.2000.882856
6. Scottish Government, Building Better Services, Open Scotland (2005), http://www.scotland.gov.uk/Publications/2005/08/31114408/44098
7. University of Edinburgh, Gazetteer for Scotland Homepage (2010), http://www.geo.ed.ac.uk/scotgaz/

Assessing the Socio-economic Impact of 3D Visualisation in Cultural Heritage

Jaime Kaminski, Jim McLoughlin, and Babak Sodagar

University of Brighton Business School, Mithras House, Lewes Road, Brighton,
United Kingdom, BN2 4GJ
j.kaminsk@brighton.ac.uk

Abstract. Despite the multitude of impact measurement techniques available to heritage site managers there is a case for the bigger strategic picture to figure more strongly in impact measurement decision making for ICT and 3D applications in the heritage sector. Discussions with heritage mangers raised the need for a holistic practical social impact model, one which combines impact measurement with overall strategic decision making considerations, accommodating internal and external dimensions of impact, as well as mission (and vision) and stakeholder perspectives; and one that embeds impact as a dynamic issue for management in heritage organisations. The 3D-ISF approach is broadly divided into two complementary elements. The left side of the framework considers the strategic perspective of the organization, while the right side encapsulates the impact measurement. The two elements combine to form a holistic vision of the interaction between the site strategy, 3D deployment and its relationship to impact.

Keywords: Socio-economic impact, economics, 3D visualisation.

1 Introduction

3D technology is becoming an increasingly widely used in the entertainment and consumer spheres. Understandably, many heritage sites wish to exploit 3D technologies in their presentation of the past to the public. However, when it comes to adoption of technology the heritage sector tends to be cautious [1]. Many organisations are seeking data regarding the impact and outcomes of 3D deployments in order to furnish both individual sites and the sector with information than can be used for strategic decisions about adoption. Even very basic data such as financial returns and revenues are not available. Furthermore, establishing the causality of the link between the 3D asset and the long-term impact is particularly problematic.

Impact measurement is a mechanism for demonstrating the benefit of the application of 3D technology through evidence of outcomes and impacts. If the results of impact assessment are integrated with the strategic decision making of the organisation this information can then be used to deliver an improved service or product; or offer better value (in the wider social sense) to their target beneficiaries.

A detailed evaluation of the existing impact measurement and valuation tools was undertaken in which it was concluded, that despite the range of "off the shelf" methodologies available that no existing impact tool or measure precisely met the requirements of the heritage sector when it came to assessing the impact of the deployment of 3D technology.

M. Ioannides (Ed.): EuroMed 2010, LNCS 6436, pp. 240–249, 2010.

It is clear that there is a fundamental need to develop a coherent and robust methodology for the assessing and measuring the impact and outcomes of 3D applications at heritage sites and other contexts that would provide the conceptual and practical bases for training and embedding. The 3D-ISF approach fills a gap as a tool for holistic impact thinking that offers tried and tested accessible steps, with robust measures.

Therefore, the challenge is to develop a holistic impact measurement model that would work at the conceptual level but also, and most importantly, at a practical level to build the capabilities of heritage site managers to introduce their own impact measurement systems that could assess the impact of 3D assets and technology.

The team drew from the results of a needs assessment and the impact tools evaluation survey to develop the 3D-ISF as tool to comprehensively conceptualise the impact problem, and provide an effective practical methodological basis for impact measurement training, help managers to demonstrate the value of their 3D assets to society, to support improved operational performance, business planning, and strategic decision making.

The 3D-ISF (3D Impact and Strategy Framework) approach was specifically designed to develop capabilities to systematically measure impacts of 3D technology in heritage organisations and also be used at a deeper level to support operations management and strategic decision making. The 3D-ISF approach helps heritage site managers to conceptualise the impact problem; identify and prioritise impacts for measurement; develop appropriate impact measures; report impacts and to embed the results in management decision making.

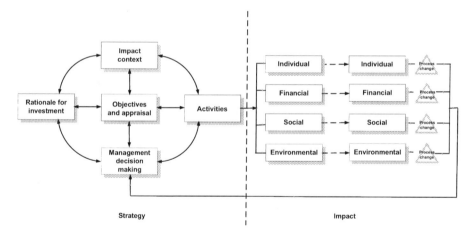

Fig. 1. A summary version of the 3D-ISF approach

The ISF approach shown in Figure 1 represents the synthesis of two impact assessment models: the holistic site model developed by the University of Brighton Business School's CUBIST Research Group, for the cultural heritage sector [2]. And a holistic impact measurement model for social enterprises, developed by the CUBIST Research Group and Social Enterprise London, called SIMPLE (Social Impact for Local Economies). The SIMPLE impact model and methodology has been tried and tested on over 40 social enterprises through a series of three day training courses [3]. Together the models have been tested at over 60 organisations.

Neither of these models could however be directly used to capture the impact of 3D technology at a heritage site. However, both sets of models had been proven and applied to actual organisations and so it was decided to integrate elements of the various models, and add other components to create an impact model that was focused on the application of 3D technology to heritage sites.

2   3D-ISF: An Impact Measurement Tool for Business and Strategic Planning

Despite the multitude of impact measurement techniques available to heritage site managers there is a case for the bigger strategic picture to figure more strongly in impact measurement decision making.

Discussions with heritage mangers raised the need for a holistic practical social impact model, one which combines impact measurement with overall strategic decision making considerations, accommodating internal and external dimensions of impact, as well as mission (and vision) and stakeholder perspectives; and one that embeds impact as a dynamic issue for management in heritage organisations.

In other words, there is a case for a total systems approach to impact which delivers from conceptualization to detailed implementation; right through to integrated strategic decision making. One that also can easily accommodate, if appropriate, other more specific measurement methods (e.g. Return on investment, contingent valuation or choice experiments). While, at the same time, such a model should be practical, flexible and robust which gives heritage site managers ownership over their impact measures and develops the capabilities to implement a professional measurement and reporting system.

The approach is broadly divided into two complementary elements. The left side of the framework considers the strategic perspective of the organisation, while the right side encapsulates the impact measurement. The two elements are complementary and combine to form a holistic vision of the interaction between the site strategy, 3D deployment and its relationship to impact.

A more detailed verison of the ISF model is shown in Figure 2. Here the backward feedback loop highlights the linkage between impact measurement and ongoing organisational planning and strategic management processes to achieve continuous improvement and maximize desired social impacts and minimize negative impacts.

2.1 Conceptualising Impact and Understanding the Drivers

The model is composed of two elements. The left side (SCOPE IT) is designed to enable heritage site managers to gain an understanding of the impact problem and impact drivers. Before embarking on the initial scoping exercises it is vital to clarify terminology and motivations. Key preliminary questions an organization should answer, before embarking on a formal measurement process, are: What is meant by impact? And more importantly, why measure impact? A clear rationale is needed to justify the time and resources for undertaking this challenging process. For example, is the assessment being conducted in order to assess the financial return on investment or is it looking at the social impact of 3D technology, or some combination of these factors. If impact assessment is not a priority, then there is a risk of poor outcomes.

Turning to the four key dimensions of the SCOPE IT stage – that is the key impact drivers: strategic rationale for technology investment; External drivers (the Heritage site impact context); Internal drivers (The organizational context and management decision making) and Stakeholder drivers. Each impact driver is briefly explained below.

2.2 Strategic Rationale for Technology Investment

There has to be a strategic rationale for technology investment. This is usually closely linked to the mission and vision for the site. Strategy needs to underpin the management decision making at a heritage site. For example is 3D the right solution? While 3D technology is a powerful medium for communicating heritage to the public and has numerous research implications, it may not be the appropriate solution for all heritage sites and organisations at a particular moment in time. Therefore, prior to deployment organisations need to make a strategic decision as to the viability of 3D technology in their particular context. Two principal considerations are suitability and feasibility.

Vision for investment. All investment decisions usually involve some intended innovation to enhance the cultural product offer. The vision is eventually a strategic view of where the site should be and what it should offer. Once this is clearly defined the exploration of the appropriate ICT for the vision can take place.

Suitability. There must be a strategic logic for the deployment of ICT. At its simplest a heritage site's strategy revolves around three questions: where is the site positioned

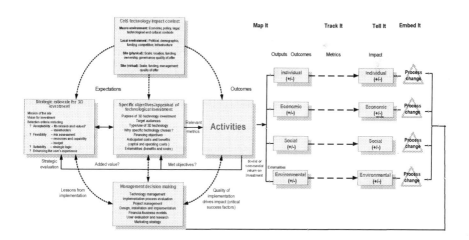

Fig. 2. The 3D-ISF holistic impact model –"deeper" strategic version

now, where does it want to be positioned and how will it achieve that goal. A 3D-based solution may, or may not, be the most effective use of resources for achieving that goal. While 3D technology is a powerful medium for communicating heritage to the public and has numerous research implications, it may not be the appropriate

solution for all heritage sites and organisations at a particular moment in time. Therefore, prior to deployment organisations need to make a strategic decision as to the
viability of 3D technology in their particular context.

Questions that need to be considered include:

- Does it fit with the objectives and mission of the site?
- Is financial sustainability required and if so what is the potential ROI?
  (techniques that could be applied include: Return on investment predictions,
  payback method)
- Is there user demand for 3D technology at the site in question? (techniques
  that could be applied include: questionnaires, choice experiments)
- Site mission: another key question is does the particular use of 3D fit with
  the mission and values of the site? The mission can be thought of as a heritage site's overriding purpose and normally is an explicit expression of the
  values of the organisation. Mission of an organisation outlines the broad
  general directions that an organisation should and will follow. Questions that
  need to be asked include: What is the site there for? Whom is it serving?
  Whom should it serve? Why is it being funded? Some organisations have a
  mission that is explicitly tied in with 3D content such as the 3D Museum
  (http://www.3dmuseum.org). However, most museums have a mission that
  is more general such as education, which partly reflects the impact context
  (the culture, the national system, and corporate governance and legal system)
  and also the power and interest of the stakeholders. As a process, not least to
  guide an impact evaluation, it is useful to know who decides the mission and
  how it is decided.

The objectives of an organisation represent a more specific commitment, often over a
specified time period, consistent with the mission (this may be quantified, but this can
be inappropriate in some circumstances). Objectives take the generalities of the mission and turn them into more specific commitments: Usually this process will cover
what is to be done and its timing. While trade-offs may arise in objective setting,
prioritisation of objectives should be based on the fundamental mission and values of
the heritage site.

An organisation's explicit mission/objectives will create a list of intended impacts
and, is therefore the central driver of impact measurement selection, strongly influenced by stakeholder analysis. All investments involve opportunity costs. The potential funds that may be devoted to an ICT project can alternative uses. It is therefore
essential that stakeholders support the deployment of resources.

2.3 Feasibility

- *Risk assessment*: The installation of 3D could potentially represent a risk
  for heritage sites. For many it is an area beyond their traditional sphere of
  experience so they are reliant upon external sources of consultancy and services. A typical risk factor is cost outweighing the benefits.
- *Budget*: Sites have to consider if they have the budget for 3D installation and
  maintenance and/or the resources and capability to support such an installation.

- *Resources and capability*: The introduction of 3D requires numerous new skills. Heritage sites need to establish what resources and capabilities they have for such a deployment. Do they have any skills in house or will the entire project (or part of the project) need to be outsourced?

2.4 Management Decision Making

The management decision-making element is another key component that influences impact. There are three components within this element; technology management, the financial and business models, and the technology and marketing strategy.

Technology strategy. Cultural heritage sites should have a continuous review of technology strategy (e.g. Web strategy) that can support the cultural offer.

Technology management. Technology management is a multi-faceted area:

- *Technology project management*: There are numerous considerations to be made when managing a 3D technology project. For example does the project meet the heritage site's vision? Is there a clear objective? As (Soren 2005) notes "clear objectives and values help curators take ownership of a project, and feel responsible for whether it succeeds or fails." It is necessary to liaise with external partners and with internal players (i.e. using human resource management for managing change). Not all heritage sites have the luxury of having full-time staff devoted to ICT management. Some have to share IT staff between sites or have staff that do IT-related tasks in addition to other jobs. These sites may have to purchase these skills from outside consultants. If the heritage site is for some reason unable or unwilling to maintain their ICT deployment then its impact may change from a positive to a negative. Furthermore, deploying ICT at a heritage site is not the end of the story. Information technology, as with all technology requires maintenance. Many sites do not have the skills to keep ICT projects running if the technology breaks down. This of course then requires external consultancy to fix any problems – but, needs to be factored into the running costs of the original business and sustainability model. The following factors are also integral with technology management:
- *Management 'buy-in'*: Much work has been conducted in the commercial business sector that shows that the lack of senior management buy-in is one of the biggest reasons for the failure of technology projects. This is extremely important in the cultural heritage sector because there can still be reticence to the use of information technology in what is still a sector with traditional origins. Without management buy-in projects could fail before deployment or could have insufficient resources for successful deployment, leading to negative impressions by visitors.
- *Leadership*: Closely related to the above is leadership. Leadership for an ICT deployment at a heritage site exists at two levels; the strategic leadership that drives the overall conceptualization, and the IT project leadership that manages the actual day-to-day running of the project. Strong strategic and project leadership can greatly enhance its chances of success.

- *Design, installation and implementation*: When visitors come face-to-face with front-of-house 3D at heritage sites their first impression is a function of the design, implementation and installation of the technology. The design of ICT applications is a complex area that is usually beyond the experience of heritage site personnel because so many different skill-sets are required (ICT development, graphic design, ergonomics, etc).
- *The quality of the implementation drives the potential impacts*: An exceptional use of technology can be let down by poor design, location, and implementation (both at a physical site and over the internet). Alternatively, lack of funding may result in poor design because shortcuts were made. This is important because considerable evidence points to cultural tourists as being increasingly sophisticated visitors.

Financial and business models. In the past many heritage sites have been caught out by the lack of coherent, sustainable business models. Capital funds and grants have been devoted to projects but less consideration has been devoted to the sustainability of the project. There is evidence that this is slowly beginning to change – many funding bodies now require evidence of sustainability and business planning before they grant capital funds to projects. For example, in the UK funders such as the Heritage Lottery Fund and English Heritage now require sustainability plans for the projects they fund. There are numerous considerations for financial and business models, such as charging for specific exhibitions, developing exhibitions with the potential to tour and so gain extra revenue, or more imaginative models such as sharing development costs in return for a percentage of the revenue.

2.4.1 Marketing Strategy and Target Audiences

- *Marketing strategy*: ICT deployments do not exist outside of a business system. If visitors are not motivated to go to the physical or virtual heritage site in the first place then the impact of the ICT deployments can be reduced. A significant investment in 3D might form the basis of a marketing campaign. This certainly increases the awareness and can have a considerable influence on the scale of the impacts and outcomes.
- *User evaluation and research*: Heritage sites have a long tradition of conducting research on their visitors to determine user satisfaction. Visitor surveys or interviews are and well understood by heritage sites. There is also considerable external consultancy available to sites. There is therefore a well-established mechanism that heritage sites can use to determine the socio-economic impact of technology at heritage sites. Furthermore, user evaluation can be used to support marketing research.

2.5 Specific Objectives and Appraisal of the Technology Investment

This is fundamental for understanding the impact of 3D deployments. 3D investment reflects cultural product innovation and can provide a basis for a 'new offer'. There can be a wide range of reasons for the deployment of visitor-facing ICT at heritage sites. These can include:

- Enhancing the user's experience
- Increase visitor numbers
- Enhancing educational impact, or
- Some combination of the above.

A key question that sites often want answered is 'has the investment achieved this aim?' The objectives of a project are key to determining what impacts should be assessed.

The essence of appraisal is the anticipation of costs and benefits. The initial capital cost outlay can be estimated as can the potential social returns and benefits. The anticipated costs may be assessed through the use of Return On Investment (ROI), and Net Present Value (NPV) calculations. It is essential to consider both the capital and operating costs for a deployment. These assessments can then be compared to the potential anticipated benefits that the use of ICT may entail. Once a project is running the impact measures can be used to provide data on the actual return.

3 Impact Categorization

A key innovation introduced in this 3D-ISF model is to re-classify impact categories, moving from the commonly termed triple bottom line to the quadruple bottom line (4BL). The triple bottom line typically includes the financial (including in this case economic) performance plus the social and environmental impacts. The quadruple bottom line shown in the figure below emphasises the role of the individual in the appreciation of 3D technology.

3.1 Mapping Impact: Applying the Logic Model

Mapping impacts helps to more precisely and systematically identify the linkages between outputs, outcomes and impacts of heritage sites. This approach utilises an organizational impact mapping methodology derived from the long-established Logic Model [5].

This method provides a graphical representation of multiple outputs, outcomes and eventual impacts as a practical basis for developing impact measures. It is a chain of connection which logically states how an organisation's activities are expected to achieve desired results. Mapping (Logic Model) is presented in the logical flow diagram shown in Figure 3:

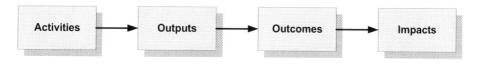

Fig. 3. Mapping impacts using a Logic Model

The key four components of the MAP IT process are explained below:

- *Activities*: What are the products, projects or processes that allow the heritage site to fulfil your objectives?
- *Outputs*: What is produced as a direct result of these actions? Generally depict completion of activity

- *Outcomes*: What benefit or change is accomplished, in the short term, as a direct result of the output?
- *Impacts*: What the organisation is able to achieve over the long-term as a result of combined outcomes.

It should be noted in the standard logic model resources are also included, to precede activities but this is already covered in the SCOPE IT analysis. Prioritisation of impacts for measurement will be influenced by the Stage 1 analysis, SCOPE IT, as through analyzing the drivers of mission, stakeholders, external and internal drivers.

3.2 Measuring Impact Using Impact Indicators

The users draw up a checklist of desired/perceived impact measures which emerge from the conceptual and strategic analysis. Impacts have been divided into groups in order to make their assessment more coherent. This 'bottom line' comprises individual, economic, social, and environmental impacts. Managers need to prioritise the impact categories for measurement. For example, if economic impact is not a priority then there is no need to devote resources to measuring it.

All heritage sites (and all businesses in general) generate impact, positive or otherwise, in each of the four impact areas. A Key Impact Indicator or KII is a quantifiable metric that an organisation can develop to help understand and gauge its performance and impact.

Key Impact Indicators (KIIs) are used to 'value' difficult-to-measure activities such as the engagement with beneficiaries, service level standards, and satisfaction with the product or service.

Collect the data (track it). This step revolves around the collection of the data and how to do it. The methods used should be decided on (such as internal records/questionnaires/surveys, etc). This would also be an appropriate time to review management systems in regard to the collection of data in the future. Systems and procedures need to be established for data collection. Responsibility for collection of data needs to be set, in conjunction with time targets.

Comprehend and communicate (Tell it). Comprehension is achieved through the analysis of the impact data. This is also an appropriate time to review the indicators chosen and assess their usefulness. It is also essential that the lessons learnt from the analysis are communicated in a targeted way to the relevant stakeholders. The results should also be compared with past performance benchmarks.

Change (Embed it). The framework involves the feedback of the analysis of impact data into the strategic, operational and business processes of the site. This crucial component is so often omitted. This is the most important reason for sites to conduct impact analysis – to see if the organisation can be improved.

Consideration should also be given to questions such as is the mission is being met? Are perceived/desired impacts being achieved? Are the stakeholders satisfied? With all this information it should be possible to conduct a strategic/operations review, and propose changes for the future.

Consider new strategies, business processes, systems and organisation. The potential for new investment in areas such as technology should also be evaluated.

4 Conclusions

The 3D-ISF holistic impact measurement model provides a both a conceptual and practical approach to measuring impact. The model offers those in the heritage sector a practical methodology for developing impact measures specific and relevant to their own organization. It guides them through the thought processes of conceptualising impact; identifying and prioritising impacts for measurement; developing specific measures, reporting impacts and embedding the process in management decision making. The model initially formed the basis of the EPOCH holistic site impact model for cultural heritage and the SIMPLE training methodology for social enterprise and which together have been tested on over 60 organisations. This has shown that the underlying principals of the 3D-ISF methodology can be adapted to all organizational sizes and enterprise sectors and is an enabling model in that the specific measures are selected by each organization.

Furthermore, this paper has guided impact measurement, through the various steps to tailored indicator design which are most relevant and practical for managers to implement. However, being a holistic, non-prescriptive tool, 3D-ISF can easily accommodate other measurement methods (such as Contingent Valuation or Return on Investment) depending on a heritage site's priorities, purpose, resources, and capabilities.

The 3D-ISF method could in the future form the basis of an integrated strategic management, impact training and consultancy for the heritage sector, which would require slight adaptations to the model, for example through addressing feedback loops and adapting other conventional management tools.

Acknowledgments. The authors wish to thank the museums' curators and managers who kindly took part in the research required to develop this model. The work presented in this paper has been supported by the European Commission's 3D-COFORM integrated project, which has received funding from the Community's Seventh Framework Programme (FP7/2007-2013) under grant agreement no. 231809 (www.3d-coform.eu).

References

1. Arnold, D., Geser, G.: Research Agenda for the Applications of ICT to Cultural Heritage, 2nd edn. Budapest, Archaeoloingua (2009)
2. McLoughlin, J., Kaminski, J., Sodagar, B.: Assessing the socio-economic impact of heritage: From theory to practice. In: McLoughlin, J., Kaminski, J., Sodagar, B. (eds.) Technology Strategy, Management and Socio-Economic Impact, pp. 17–42. Budapest, Archaeoloingua (2007)
3. McLoughlin, J., Kaminski, J., Sodagar, B., Khan, S., Arnaudo, G., Harris, R., McBrearty, S.: A strategic approach to social impact of social enterprises: The SIMPLE methodology. Social Enterprise Journal, 154–178 (2009)
4. Soren, B.J.: Best practices in creating quality online experiences for museum users. Museum Management and Curatorship 20, 131–148 (2005)
5. Wholey, J.: Evaluation: Promise and performance. Urban Institute Press, Washington, D.C. (1979)

Comparative Study of Interactive Systems in a Museum

Despina Michael[1], Nectarios Pelekanos[2], Isabelle Chrysanthou[2], Panagiotis Zaharias[3], Loukia L. Hadjigavriel[4], and Yiorgos Chrysanthou[3]

[1] University of Nicosia, Cyprus
michael.d@unic.ac.cy
[2] A.R.M.E.S. Ltd, Nicosia, Cyprus
{nectarios.pelekanos,isabelle.chrysanthou}@armes-tech.com
[3] University of Cyprus, Cyprus
{zaharias,yiorgos}@cs.ucy.ac.cy
[4] The Leventis Municipal Museum, Cyprus
Loukia.Loizou@nicosiamunicipality.org.cy

Abstract. Museums research new ways to offer positive experience to the visitors and encourage them to return, using modern communication and learning tools. To the effect, technologically advanced interactive ICT systems, are placed in modern-day museums. In this paper we describe and compare six different types of museum exhibits, one traditional and five interactive ICT exhibits. The five interactive ICT systems offer different types and level of digital information, different interaction constraints and different types of activities. The exhibits, which are located in the Leventis Municipal Museum in Nicosia, are the following: a traditional map learning activity, a virtual tour projection, a multi-touch table application and three different augmented reality applications. We evaluated the experience of young users with the exhibits and conclude that the experience scores top marks for the interactive ICT systems.

Keywords: Interaction, Museum, Comparative Study, Video Projection, Multi-touch Table, Augmented Reality.

1 Introduction

Traditionally, museums conveyed information to their visitors through the exhibit of real objects. During the last couple of decades, the new trend is toward active involvement through the installation technologically advanced interactive ICT systems. The systems are installed within the physical space of a museum as a communication and learning tool and as an additional material next to the original objects.

Those interactive ICT exhibits includes applications like VR systems (Roussou, 2001), Augmented Reality systems (Wojciechowski, 2004), haptics displays (Loscos, 2004), multi-touch tables (Averkiou, 2009; Geller, 2006), etc. Generally they allow reality-based interactivity of the user with a virtual 3D representation of objects within virtual or real worlds.

In this paper we present a comparative study between five different types of interactive user interface exhibits (VR tour, touch table, three augmented reality exhibits)

M. Ioannides (Ed.): EuroMed 2010, LNCS 6436, pp. 250–261, 2010.

and a traditional exhibit (real maps). The study has been conducted in a museum with children between the ages of 9 and 11 years of age. We are quantifying high-level interaction qualities such as enjoyment, satisfactions and desire to perform again. Subjective data has been collected through questionnaires targeted to this young age group.

Further we attempt to explain the results. To that effect we classify the interactive systems using previously proposed taxonomy of interactive user interfaces in a broader sense. We classify the interactive systems according to three parameters: First, the digital information that is linked to the interface (2D still/dynamic or 3D still/dynamic). Second, the interaction constraints of the system (3D free interaction in space, 2D interaction on a surface, 1D interaction with touch buttons). And third, the type of activity promoted (open ended, game like, exploratory or passive). Based on this classification and on the results of this experiment, we discuss their effectiveness in providing satisfaction and desire to perform again.

Given the novelty of the investigated interactive user interfaces as a research field, existing literature is limited in providing a specific evaluation method for such a study investigation for a specific age group. Generally, proposed evaluation methods are objective quantitative methodology, for example task completion time, error rate, and memorization time (Jacob, 2002). Those experiments are run usually in laboratory environment. Further studies, which have been evaluated in the field, have been reported to quantify more high-level interaction qualities such as enjoyment, engagement and legibility of actions (Pedersen, 2009). Another adopted evaluation method is interaction analysis from video as used in the field of HCI (Sharp, 2007).

This paper is organized in 6 sections out of which Section 1 is the introduction. Section 2 describes the exhibits, which have been used for comparisons in this paper. Section 4 analyses the preliminary results of the study. Section 5 discusses the results and takes conclusions.

2 Systems Description

In this section we describe the systems that have been used in this comparative study. The authors of this paper have been involved in the development of the ICT systems described below.

2.1 Projection: Virtual Tour

The installation "Virtual Tour in Nicosia of the 19th Century" uses a single wall, front-projection setup and it allows the visitor to get a glimpse of how the city might have looked like around the middle of the nineteenth century, (Fig. 1). The scenario is built on the description given by an un-named English traveler who visited the island at the time and published his report in a British Magazine called "The Home Friend" (Anonymous, 1850). The traveler entered the Old Town at one of the 3 gates, most likely Famagusta Gate, since he was coming from Larnaca, and left again from the same Gate returning to Larnaca. Along the way he crossed the city going through different neighborhoods, poor and rich, points of interest, bazaars, a hammam (Turkish Baths) , administrative quarters etc. Along the way he crossed the city going through different neighborhoods, poor and rich, points of interest, bazaars, a hammam, administrative quarters etc.

Since our application is placed in the museum where many visitors go through every day, we had to maintain the total time spent by each visitor to less than 5 minutes and therefore it was not possible to "walk" through all the streets described in the report. Rather we selected the most representative. In our tour, after entering through the city gate, the visitor goes to a desolated street where the houses are falling down and they are only inhabited by donkeys and cows, if at all. Second stop is the Serai, a rich nicely paved square hosting the administration buildings, mosques, coffee shops and big houses. Then it's the Bazaar, or street market followed by the hammam (steam bath). Exiting from the hammam, the visitor walks to the house of Kornesios, a rich local functionary, where he is hosted, and finally as he exists the city from the Famagusta Gate. Some images from the tour are shown in Fig. 2.

Fig. 1. The virtual tour installation. Projection wall and touch screen serving as user interface for navigation of the 3D graphics.

For certain parts of the route, it was very challenging to be recreated realistically using real-time graphics, so they were filmed using conventional methods. One such part is the Bazaar which is crowded with people. The two others were the house of Kornesios and Famagusta Gate, which they have not been destroyed and still exist in a good condition, therefore they could be filmed. In the current implementation shown at the museum, the video footage alternates with computer graphics (see Fig. 1).

The user of the application in the museum is able to navigate within the virtual world in real time and is allowed to interact with the application in certain pre-defined areas of the tour. An automated navigation with predefined paths occurs from one point of interest to the next, giving the opportunity to the user to watch the route and exterior of the buildings as a passive viewer. At the parts of the route that are done using computer graphics the user is allowed to change the viewing direction, the zoom, and navigation speed using touch buttons on the touch screen mounted next to the projection wall. In Fig. 1, we see on the right of the wall the touch-screen which is used for the navigation.

Fig. 2. Screenshots from the virtual tour system

2.2 Multi-touch Table: The Walls of Nicosia

The installation "The Walls of Nicosia" (Averkiou, 2009) is an interactive application that allows the user to have a virtual tour through the fortifications of Nicosia across the centuries. The target was to explain and present the development of the area and the history of the development of the fortifications of the city – From a Roma and Byzantine Castle to a Medieval Royal Capital and a Venetian Fortified city. The application runs on a multi-touch table (see Fig. 3) which allows for a natural interaction. Three dimensional models of the fortifications of the city, Fig. 4, as well as the most important landmarks are demonstrated for five historical periods: pre-Roman (villages with no fortification), Roman castle, Byzantine castle, Lusignan Walls and Venetian Walls. The users can navigate through time with the help of a menu that appears on the top of the screen of the table. They can then interact and study the 3D models of the historical period they choose using intuitive gestures. The users are able to zoom in/out, pan and tilt the virtual camera. A helping menu exists on the interface of the application, describing how each of these operations can be performed. A compass, on the top-right corner of the interface, assists the users with orientation. Traditional music is played for each historical period, in order to immerse the user (see Fig. 3 and Fig. 4).

Fig. 3. A group of students using the multi-touch table

Fig. 4. Screenshot from the multi-touch table application

The multi-touch table hardware is based on back projection. A projector, connected with the host computer resides inside the table. The final image on the top surface is produced with the use of a mirror that reflects the projector image. This technique is used in order to virtually increase the space within the table and allow us to use a standard DLP project (not a short throw one). The gestures of the user's fingers are tracked using infrared light. 300 LEDs and an infrared camera have been mounted inside the table for the finger tracking. LEDs emit light towards the table surface. When a user touches the surface the infrared light is reflected back and the infrared camera captures that light. Each frame that is captured by the camera is processed in order to detect the position of the user's fingers on the screen.

2.3 Augmented Reality (AR) Exhibits

Places, monuments and buildings of Nicosia that have played or are playing an important role in the development of the history and the social life of the city, are the main idea of these three augmented reality applications.

All the applications are based on circular marker tracking technology with the use of a PS3 Eye camera to capture the real scene. The software system is using Open-SceneGraph for the construction of the augmented scene and the rendering of the 3D models. The augmentation of the real scene is displayed on wide 42" LCD screen hanging on the wall of the exhibition room. In order to achieve accurate tracking, appropriate lights were setup and adjusted to illuminate the markers yet not affecting the visibility on the LCD screens.

AR Puzzle. The AR Puzzle application is using four markers and the user interacts with all of them sliding them over the table. Four photos of the same landmark at different time periods have been cut into four pieces and have been mounted onto four cubes linked to the four markers. By physically displacing and rotating a marker on the 2D surface of the table, the user displaces and rotates the digital 3D cube seen on the LCD display on the wall. The user has to put together the correct pieces to create the picture.

There are four columns, one on each marker with one piece of a different photo on each side. The user finds the four pieces of the picture and then puts them in the correct order to solve the puzzle. This can be repeated for all the four pictures of the application. There are two AR exhibits with this puzzle application, one with the Famagusta gate photos and one with the Eleftheria square photos (see Fig. 5).

Fig. 5. The AR Puzzle installations

AR Map. In the second AR application the user explores the location of four monuments in the city of Nicosia. With the use of a printed map and four markers he tries to place the monuments on the correct location on the map by sliding the marker onto the 2D surface of the map. Each of the four markers corresponds to one specific monument. In order to see the 3D model of a monument the marker must be placed on the correct position on the map. The application uses models of the Phaneromeni church, the City Hall, the Leventis museum and the Pankiprio gymnasium (see Fig. 6).

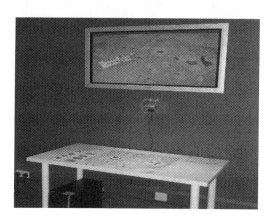

Fig. 6. The AR Map installation

Touch History. The last application uses only one marker and by presenting that marker to the camera a 3D object appears on it. In our case the 3D object is a 14th century chalice with engraved decoration. The user can move the marker freely in all special dimensions and see the object from all the perspectives, inside and outside (see Fig. 7).

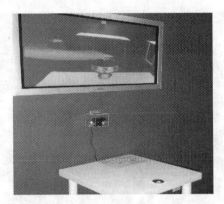

Fig. 7. The Touch History installation

Real Maps. A control group was given a tour of one of the more traditional exhibits of the museum, the room with the maps of Nicosia (see Fig. 8). The teacher used the maps, some of them several hundred years old, to provide the group with information about the fortifications of Nicosia over the centuries.

Fig. 8. A group of students at the maps room

3 Method

This paper evaluates the subjective user experience of the children and more specifi-cally aspects of fun such as engagement, endurability and returnance (Read & MacFarlane, 2000). 36 children participated for each exhibit except for the touch table and real maps where the number of participants was 25. The age range of the children was 9-11 years.

As already mentioned there are several evaluation methods with interactive exhibits; here the main emphasis was to compare the user experience of the children while interacting with the exhibits. Therefore we employed the Smileyometer and the Again-Again table, which are tools of the FunToolkit method. The latter is a well-known and validated tool for assessing user experience with technology when the users are children (Read, 2008). Right after the interaction of the children with the exhibits, children were asked to tick one face in the Smileyometer and fill in the Again –Again table. These tools are presented in the Fig. 9.

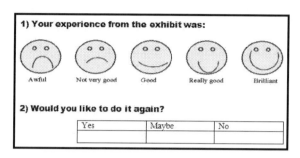

Fig. 9. Questionnaire to estimate subjective satisfaction from exhibit

The interactive ICT systems and traditional way of exhibition (real maps) have been classified as shown in Table 1. The rational was to illustrate the similarities and differences within the investigated systems using interactive interface taxonomy (Shear, 2009). In the table, the column digital information refers to the type and amount of content in each application.

Table 1. Systems classification

	Digital information	Interaction constraints	Type of activity
Touch History	3D still, low	3D free	exploratory, non-challenging
AR puzzle	2D still, low	2D free	game like, challenging
AR map	3D still, medium	2D free	game like, highly challenging
VR tour	3D dyn, very high	1D buttons	passive
Touch table	3D still, high	2D free	exploratory, challenging
Real Maps	2D still, medium	N/A	passive

4 Preliminary Results and Analysis

Preliminary results, Fig. 10, reveal that the interactive ICT exhibits have been rated higher and that they are very popular with this age group of children. We note though that within a similar group of application, namely here AR, the scores differ greatly.

258   D. Michael et al.

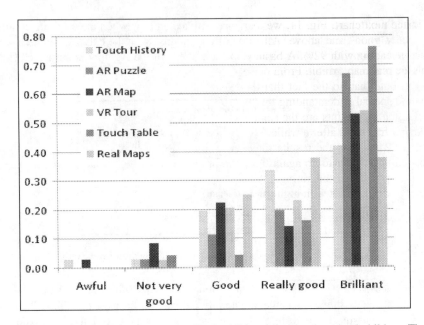

Fig. 10. Results for the smileyometer for the 6 exhibits visited by the school children. The y-axis shows the percentage of children giving a certain answer.

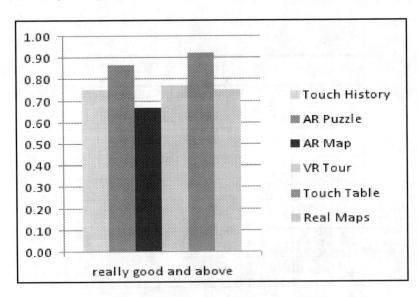

Fig. 11. Summarizing the cumulated results having scored above very good

The AR puzzle scores over 67% while Touch History scores only 42% in brilliant score category. Overall the touch table is leading with 72% of children giving it a brilliant score.

In the next chart, Fig. 11, we show the cumulated results having achieved a score of "really good" and above. All the exhibits score above 67% and again the touch table is leading with 92%. A basic remark here is that the AR map scores even lower than the real map exhibit. From our observation of the children during the experiment, we attribute that, to the fact that the AR map application requires knowledge of the city and special understanding that most of the children did not possess. Although the interaction constraints are the same as the highly popular AR puzzle, they would get tired and frustrated after a while.

Fig. 12 presents the results of the Again-Again table which is about returnance. Most children want to do again the several activities. AR puzzle and Touch table are the most popular in this rating. On the contrary the traditional way of exhibition (real maps) has been rated with high scores in "no" responses.

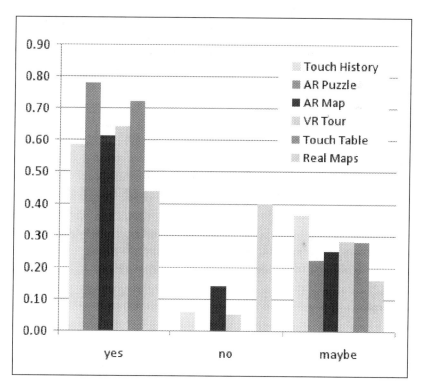

Fig. 12. Results of the questions asking if the school children would like to repeat or not the activity

5 Discussion and Conclusions

In this paper we present a comparative study of interactive museums exhibits with main emphasis on assessment of user experience. Preliminary results have shown that interactive ICT exhibits have been rated higher than the traditional teaching methods (real map) and that most of the school children would want to do it again, especially for the interactive ICT exhibits. Similar findings have been reported by other studies (Wrzesien 2010, Pujol 2007, Pujol 2009). When cumulating the "really good" and "brilliant" scores together, it is evident that there is less discrimination between all the exhibits.

According to the preliminary results it seems that the puzzle game initiates the wish to repeat the same type of interaction. The VR tour does score high on the Again-Again table, which might be due to its enjoyable entertainment similar to a movie theatre.

If we assess the augmented reality exhibits alone, we see that the experience of the children varies considerably across the three exhibits. The AR puzzle is most appreciated, even if the content was 2D images mounted on a 3D cubes and even if the interaction was constraint to a 2D surface. It would thus seem that it is the type of activity rather than the level of detail of the information or the degrees of freedom of the interaction that governs experience with schoolchildren. Touch history, with its detailed models of 3D objects and 3D interaction scored much lower, possibly due to its non-challenging type of activity. To this end, it seems that the type of activity promoted by the exhibit seems to be the main factor when assessing the wish to repeat the experience with the exhibit, here game like puzzle activity scored highest. This result supports the work proposed by (Marshall, 2003) to categorize frameworks for interfaces in this domain according to the types of activities they promote.

A limitation of this study is that only one traditional method of exhibition has been assessed, limiting the validity of the claims that interactive ICT exhibits are better than traditional methods. A future study will have to address this issue by including other traditional methods of exhibition as well. In addition, it is quite interesting to investigate for further correlations between the classification of the exhibits and the user experience results.

There is also a need for a macro-type of a comparative evaluation, since perceived novelty of technology sometimes wears thin after time. Accordingly a future study can address issues regarding an evaluation of multiple experiences of the same ICT exhibits vs traditional activities over an extended period of time.

References

1. Averkiou, M., Chrysanthou, Y.: Evaluating a multitouch interface for 3d navigation inside the virtual world of a museum exhibit. In: VAST 2009 (2009)
2. Anonymous, A Visit to Cyprus VI, The Home Friend; A Weekly Miscellany of Amusement and Instructions, Vol. 86, 1850
3. Ang, K., Wang, Q.: A case study of engaging primary school students in learning science by using active worlds. In: Proceedings of the First International LAMS Conference 2006: Designing the Future of Learning, pp. 5–14 (2006)
4. Chittaro, L., Ieronutti, L., Ranon, R.: Navigating 3d virtual environments by following embodied agents: a proposal and its informal evaluation on a virtual museum application. PsychNology Journal Special Issue on Human-Computer Interaction 2, 24–42 (2004)
5. Gaitatzes, A., Christopoulos, D., Roussou, M.: Reviving the past: cultural heritage meets virtual reality. In: VAST 2001: Proceedings of the 2001 Conference on Virtual Reality, Archeology, and Cultural Heritage, pp. 103–110. ACM, New York (2001)

6. Geller, T.: Interactive tabletop exhibits in museums and galleries. IEEE Comput. Graph. Appl. 26(5), 6–11 (2006)
7. Hut, P.: Virtual laboratories. Progress of Theoretical Physics 164, 38–53 (2007)
8. Karoulis, A., Sylaiou, S., White, M.: Usability evaluation of a virtual museum interface. Informatica 17(3), 363–380 (2006)
9. Jacob, R.J.K., Ishii, H., Pangaro, G., Patten, J.: A tangible interface for organizing information using a grid. In: Proceedings of CHI 2002, pp. 339–346. ACM, NY (2002)
10. Loscos, C., Tecchia, F., Frisoli, A., Carrozzino, M., Widenfeld, H.R., Swapp, D., Bergamasco, M.: Themuseum of pure form: touching real statues in an immersive virtual museum. In: VAST, pp. 271–279 (2004)
11. Marshall, P., Price, S., Rogers, Y.: Conceptualizing tangibles to support learning. In: Proceedings of IDC 2003, pp. 101–109. ACM, NY (2003)
12. Nijholt, A.: Agent-supported cooperative learning environments. In: Kinshuk, I., Jesshope, C., Okamoto, T. (eds.) International Workshop on Advanced Learning Technologies (IWALT 2000), pp. 17–18. IEEE Computer Society Press, Los Alamitos (December 2000)
13. Pedersen, E.W., Hornbæk, K.: mixiTUI: A tangible sequencer for electronic live performances. In: Proceedings of TEI 2009, pp. 223–230. ACM, NY (2009)
14. Pujol, L., Economou, M.: Exploring the suitability of Virtual Reality interactivity for exhibitions through an integrated evaluation: the case of the Ename Museum. Online International Museology Journal 4, 84–97 (2007); Department of Cultural Technology and Communication, University of the Aegean
15. Pujol, L., Economou, M.: Worth a thousand words? The Usefulness of Immersive Virtual Reality for Learning in Cultural Heritage Settings. International Journal of Architectural Computing 7(1), 157–176 (2009)
16. Read, J.C.: Validating the fun toolkit: an instrument for measuring children's opinions of technology. Cogn. Technol. Work 10(2) (2008)
17. Read, J.C., MacFarlane, S.J.: Measuring Fun. Computers and Fun 3, York, England (2000)
18. Roussou, M.: Immersive interactive virtual reality in the museum. In: Proc. of TiLE (Trends in Leisure Entertainment) (2001)
19. Shaer, O., Hornecker, E.: Tangible User Interfaces: Past, Present, and Future Directions. In: Human–Computer Interaction, vol. 3(1-2), pp. 1–137 (2009)
20. Sharp, H., Rogers, Y., Preece, J.: Interaction Design. John Wiley, Chichester (2007)
21. Tzanavari, A., Vogiatzis, D., Zembylas, M., Retalis, S., Lalos, P.: Affective aspects of web museums. Studies in Communication Science, for the Thematic Section User- Centered Communication Design for Interactive Applications 5(1) (2005)
22. Wrzesien, M., Raya, M.A.: Learning in serious virtual worlds: Evaluation of learning effectiveness and appeal to students in the e-junior project. Computers and Education 55(1), 178–187 (2010)
23. Wojciechowski, R., Walczak, K., White, M., Cellary, W.: Building virtual and augmented reality museum exhibitions. In: Web3D 2004: Proceedings of the Ninth International Conference on 3D Web Technology, p. 135. ACM, New York (2004)

Communication of Digital Cultural Heritage in Public Spaces by the Example of Roman Cologne

Matthias Trapp[1], Amir Semmo[1], Rafael Pokorski[2], Claus-Daniel Herrmann[2], Jürgen Döllner[1], Michael Eichhorn[2], and Michael Heinzelmann[3]

[1] Hasso-Plattner-Institut, University of Potsdam, Germany
{matthias.trapp,amir.semmo,juergen.doellner}@hpi.uni-potsdam.de
[2] KISD, University of Applied Sciences Cologne, Germany
{rafael.pokorski,daniel.h,michael.eichhorn)@kisd.de
[3] Archaeological Institute, University of Cologne, Germany
michael.heinzelmann@uni-koeln.de

Abstract. The communication of cultural heritage in public spaces such as museums or exhibitions, gain more and more importance during the last years. The possibilities of interactive 3D applications open a new degree of freedom beyond the mere presentation of static visualizations, such as pre-produced video or image data. A user is now able to directly interact with 3D virtual environments that enable the depiction and exploration of digital cultural heritage artifacts in real-time. However, such technology requires concepts and strategies for guiding a user throughout these scenarios, since varying levels of experiences within interactive media can be assumed. This paper presents a concept as well as implementation for communication of digital cultural heritage in public spaces, by example of the project Roman Cologne. It describes the results achieved by an interdisciplinary team of archaeologists, designers, and computer graphics engineers with the aim to virtually reconstruct an interactive high-detail 3D city model of Roman Cologne.

Keywords: High-detail 3D Models, Virtual Reality, Real-Time 3D Visualization, Museum, Roman Cologne.

1 Introduction

With the beginning of the digital revolution in the second half of the 20th century, a new era heralded for all information-related activities, redefining how information is retrieved in economic, social and technological systems today. The communication of cultural heritage is one of these areas that experienced a continuous growth during this time, where it leveraged from the digitalization for a long-ranging preservation and efficient communication of context-sensitive information.

With major interest, the reconstruction of archaeological excavation sites emerged as a powerful tool to communicate archaeological features and cultural knowledge, not only to experts, but also to broad audiences of exhibitions or museums. A continuation of this trend for these public spaces involves digitized cultural heritage, in order to enable people an immersive exploration [13] of "collections for inspiration,

M. Ioannides (Ed.): EuroMed 2010, LNCS 6436, pp. 262–276, 2010.

learning and enjoyment". With the ongoing advancements on the field of virtual reality over the last decades [22], the coupling with digital cultural heritage has evolved as a promising application for an effective and immersive communication of this context-sensitive information. Here, the visualization with interactive 3D applications opens a new degree of freedom beyond the mere presentation of static visualizations. They allow a user to directly interact with 3D virtual environments and enable the depiction and exploration of digital cultural heritage artifacts in real-time.

However, these scenarios mostly induce highly complex and massive data, as being true to the original is one of the ultimate goals. Consequently, visualization concepts and strategies are required that do not only permit an effective communication of these context-sensitive information, but also guide a user throughout these scenarios, since varying levels of experiences within interactive media can be assumed. Therefore, visualization techniques are required on both, technical level in order to allow a real-time visualization of the reconstructions, and conceptual level for allowing users to interactively explore the environment and perceive this information intuitively.

Fig. 1. Exhibition of Roman Cologne at the Roman-German Museum in Cologne. This project is used as feasibility study for the general concepts described in this work.

In this paper we present general concepts and implementations of visualization techniques for interactive 3D reconstructions of digital cultural heritage in public spaces, by example of the project Roman Cologne (Fig. 1). It describes the results achieved by an interdisciplinary team of archaeologists, designers, and computer graphics engineers with the aim to virtually reconstruct an interactive high-detail 3D city model of Roman Cologne. It can be read as a guideline for similar future projects, e.g., to setup a collaborative content creation process, select appropriate data exchange formats, or to apply the presented visualization and optimization techniques to other domains of virtual archaeology [20].

To summarize, this paper makes the following contributions to the scientific community:

1. We propose a concept for the communication of digital cultural heritage in public spaces, such as museums or exhibitions. This basically comprises the identification and justification of different visual presentation modes.
2. We further present the research results for a prototypical application and implementation of a client-server model for information communication and human computer interaction in public spaces.
3. We furthermore present the application of these concepts to the project Roman Cologne that is currently and successfully presented as a permanent exhibition in the Roman-German Museum in Cologne.

The remainder of this paper is structured as follows: Section 2 reviews related work of the field virtual reality and digital cultural heritage. Section 3 presents the concept of three presentation modes suitable for communicating digital cultural heritage in public spaces using 3D virtual environments. Section 4 describes a client-server model and concepts for guided navigation and interaction. Section 5 explains the implementation of the previously described concept. Section 6 evaluates and discusses the preliminary results of the research project Roman Cologne and presents ideas for future work. Section 7 concludes this paper.

2   Related Work

Subsequently, we briefly summarize related work that evolved in the areas of virtual reality and communication of digital cultural heritage in the past.

2.1   Virtual Reality for Digital Cultural Heritage

Numerous projects have been proposed that involve the   modeling and rendering of digital cultural heritage in 3D virtual environments. Examples are the virtualization of the great inscription of Gortyna (Crete, Greece) for 3D documentation and structural studies [30], a reconstruction of ancient fresco paintings for a revival of life in ancient Pompeii [24], the reconstruction of Peranakans and their culture [26] and the reconstruction of 19th century Koblenz (Germany) as a case study for a 4D navigable movie [15].

However, only few projects have been presented so far that facilitate users to freely roam inside these virtual worlds, i.e. exploring digital cultural heritage in real-time and being fully navigable. In [9] the project Virtual Reality Notre Dame (VRND) is presented that builds on a gaming-based 3D engine for facilitating a virtual tour guide at real-time rates. With respect to the VRND project, [23] describe methodologies how to use widely available standard programming languages and APIs to not base on proprietary commercial 3D game engines, but still achieving visually compelling results. In [21] 3D real-time virtual simulations of the populated ancient sites of Aspendos and Pompeii have been proposed, that facilitate from virtual reality and simulated dynamic virtual humans for an immersive experience.

Beneath the mere reconstruction of virtual heritage in these environments, other research dealt with rendering techniques for enhancing the immersion aspect and increasing realism. In [12] light scattering is modeled including participating media for enhancing the perception of sites by the example of the ancient Egyptian temple of Kalabsha. Goncalves et al. make use of high dynamic range (HDR) imagery in order to enhance viewing experiences and depicting environments towards a predictive ancient lighting [10]. Furthermore, crowd simulation has been done to enhance realism regarding the population of these environments. In [28], a rule behavior system is used to model such specific and complex behavior.

2.2 Communication in Public Spaces

The reconstruction of archaeological excavation sites, used in combination with an interactive visualization in 3D virtual environments, emerged as a powerful tool to communicate archaeological features and cultural knowledge, not only to experts, but also to broad audiences of exhibitions or museums. Here, virtual reality offers new communication channels, whose use statically increased in these environments over the last years.

In 1994, a first application using virtual reality for heritage has been presented, that allowed the audience to interactively explore a 3D reconstruction of Dudley Castle (England) [4] on a regular screen. More sophisticated installations made use of the CAVE system [8], where the illusion of immersion is sustained by the projection of visuals on display screens of a cube and the audience positioned in the middle. Examples are the Dunhuang caves [18] and a reconstruction of an ancient greek temple in Messene [7]. A third installation possibility is panoramic screens of cylindrical shape, e.g. used in the Virtual Sculpture Museum of Pietrasanta (Italy) [6].

One of the most challenging issues when using these systems in public spaces is, however, the installation of interaction devices that are on the one hand intuitive and consistent, and on the other hand allow visitors to explore application-specific content they should experience without restrictions. A variety of evaluations of interaction devices for these environments exist, from regular 2D (mouse) and 3D (spacemouse) input devices [25, 16] to tactual explorations [2] and visionary interaction techniques like brain-computer interfaces [17].

3   Presentation Modes

This section describes the different presentation modes provided for the effective communication of 3D digital cultural heritage in interactive 3D virtual environments. Fig. 2 exemplifies the visualization of the following three modes: the *reconstruction, comparison,* and *findings* mode.

3.1   Reconstruction Mode

The visualization of possible virtual reconstructions or artifacts can be considered as main purpose for a system that communicates digital cultural heritage. It forms the basis for the remaining two presentation modes. Such reconstruction visualization is

Fig. 2. Presentation modes for the communication of digital cultural heritage by the example of Roman Cologne at a single hot spot: (A) reconstruction mode, (B) findings mode, and (C) comparison mode that uses 360° horizontal panoramic views of the ancient and today's Cologne

the result of numerous projects that deal with interactive 3D virtual environments. Fig. 2(A) shows such visualization by the example of Roman Cologne [19]. Basically, there are two possibilities for the images synthesis of this visualization mode: photo-realism vs. abstract visualization. For example, in the case of Roman Cologne people often wish to have more realism in texturing and lighting, but archaeologist concerns that this would imply a "finished" reconstruction to the user. We choose an abstract, non-photorealistic, and simple coloring schema to communicate that the visualized reconstruction is only one out of many realities.

3.2 Comparison Mode

Based on the reconstruction mode, the comparison mode enables the comparison and dissemination of structural changes over time, i.e., between the reconstruction and today's state. We further observed, that this mode enable visitors with a local background a certain degree of entertainment.

There are several computer graphical approaches and rendering techniques of different implementation complexity to enable the image synthesis for such modes, e.g.

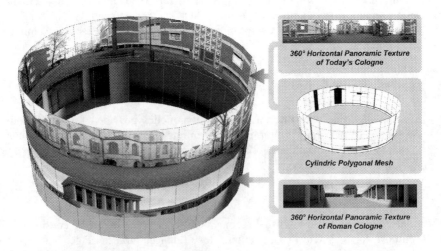

Fig. 3. Components for rendering the comparison mode of Roman Cologne

3D magic lenses [3] can be used to combine different geometries within a single view. Another possibility constitutes the usage of multiple viewports that contain images or screenshots using the same or similar camera configuration.

For the visualization framework of Roman Cologne, we apply a simple image-based approach that allows the side-by-side comparison of locations between the modern Cologne and the ancient version (Fig. 2 (C)). Instead of planar images, we create 360° horizontal panoramic images which are mapped onto two cylinders, each rendered using a virtual camera with an orthographic projection (Fig. 5). To navigate within this setup, the user can rotate both panoramic cameras at the same time.

3.3 Findings Mode

The purpose of this mode is the communication of the findings at their respective locations, which lay the basis for the actual reconstructions. Our goal was to enable a user to understand the relation between artifact and proposed 3D reconstructions performed by archaeologists and designers. As an example, Fig. 3 shows screenshots for the reconstruction mode of the Dionysus villa within Roman Cologne. Approaches for the communication of finding information embedded in reconstruction visualizations have to deal with the following challenges:

1. Multiple findings for a single reconstruction require interaction concepts and rendering techniques for the selection and highlighting of an instance or a group of finding objects.
2. The approaches require a concept that enables the communication of different reconstructions that can be derived from a set of findings.
3. It is necessary to handle different graphical representations for a finding object: 2D photographs, hand-drawn or digital images, as well as 3D polygonal meshes or point clouds, which are obtained from laser scanning.
4. Textual descriptions likely the medium that conveys and communicates the most context information. However, the depiction of text is limited by the available screen space and rendering quality.

In contrast of the geometric models of the reconstructions, the finding geometry has no textures assigned. Instead, we are using non-photorealistic lighting [11] in combination with unsharp masking the depth buffer [29] in order to support shape and depth perception. In addition thereto, a grid is displayed that approximates the underlying terrain (Fig. 3 (A)). It eases the perception which finding object was originally located above or below the ancient terrain. To distinguish between selected and unselected objects, simple color highlighting is used.

Fig. 4 (B) and (C) shows different reconstructions for a single set of findings. These different versions can be mutually blended with the rendering of the highlighted findings. Here, the user can control the blending factor as well as the blending speed. We experimented with an automatic decrease of the blending values over time, but believe that this rather distracts the user. With respect to the textual descriptions of findings, we choose not to embed these within the 3D visualization [19] but depict them on an additional viewport. This functionality is described in the next section.

Fig. 4. Finding mode of the visualization of Roman Cologne: (A) depiction and highlighting of different findings at a hot spot, (B) blend-in of a reconstruction based on Fremersdorf, and (C) the reconstruction of Precht. They differ, e.g., with respect to the number of floors.

4 Exhibition Concept

This Section describes the application of the proposed presentation concept by the example of Roman Cologne. The permanent exhibition is located at the Roman Germanic Museum in Cologne and is a constituent part. The main requirements comprised the interactive exploration as well as guided interaction of the virtual 3D reconstruction.

4.1 Conceptual Overview

Fig. 5 shows a conceptual architectural overview of the presented client-server system. The basic museum setup is shown in Fig. 1. It mainly consists of the following two components:

Server: The server performs real-time image synthesis of the 3D content or scene, which is then projected on a vertical surface. Depending on the scene complexity, this can be computational costly and thus requires corresponding rendering hardware.

Client: The client offers the user control over the servers viewing configuration (e.g., the presentation modes) via a touch-based user interface and a 3D mouse. It displays additional information about the scene projected and is adapted to the presentation modes respectively (Fig. 6).

The separation between server-side rendering/visualization and client-side interaction/visualization has two major advantages for systems that provide interactive installations within public places:

1. The two viewports of the server and client provides more physical space to display various types of information that can be presented with an optimal screen real-estate.
2. It enables guided interaction and navigation with the 3D virtual environment using 2D touch events and an additional 3D mouse to control the virtual camera and server state.

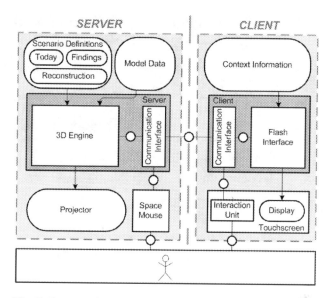

Fig. 5. Conceptual overview of the proposed client-server system

4.2 Concepts for Interaction and Navigation

This Section focuses on the user interface of the client (Fig. 6) and the control of server's virtual camera. As a basic functionality, the touch interface enables the switching between the three proposed presentation modes (Fig. 6 (d)).

The avoidance of "getting lost situations" [5] in 3D virtual environments is the major goal of the proposed interaction and navigation metaphors. This comprises a trade-off between navigation aids or constraints and the total freedom to interact with the system. The orientation of the user is enabled by an overview map (Fig. 6 (e)) that contains a camera glyph indicating the position and orientation of the virtual camera within the 3D scene. This map alters slightly in each presentation mode: an aerial screen shot of the complete reconstruction visualization (Fig. 6 (1)(e)), a combined abstract map of the ancient and modern Cologne (Fig. 6 (2)(e)), and an aerial image of today's Cologne (Fig. 6 (3)(e)). The 3D virtual camera and the camera glyph are synchronized (Section 5.3).

To ease the access to specific locations in the 3D virtual reconstruction, the touch interface presents a number of hot spots (Fig. 6 (b)), which can be selected from a scroll menu at the bottom. After selecting a hot spot the server's virtual camera automatically approaches it by using automatic camera control, which is an important feature for interaction within 3D virtual environments. It is applied for moving the 3D virtual camera between hot spots and between different findings in the scene. Instead of explicitly modeling more than 100 camera paths we decided to derive these paths automatically.

Given the start and target camera settings, and the path duration, our system creates the camera path in the following manner: 1) to avoid possible collisions with buildings, the camera positions are interpolated on a parabolic path; 2) the viewing directions of

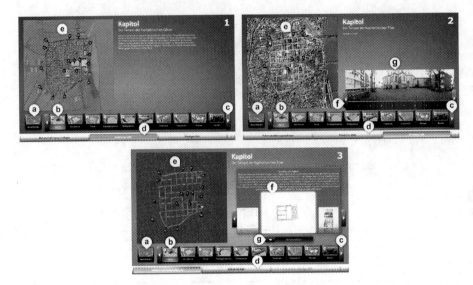

Fig. 6. Structure and organization of the client-side user inferface for the reconstruction mode (1), the findings mode (2), and the comparision mode (3) by the example of Roman Cologne

the virtual camera are interpolated linearly; 3) non-linear speed is used, which results in a slow path start and end.

With respect to the interaction possibilities, we distinguish between two basic types of hot spots: 1) an overview hot spot (Fig. 6 (a)) and local hot spots (Fig. 6 (b)). The local one allows user interaction using an orbital camera model only, while the global hot spot enables free navigation of six degrees-of-freedom via a 3D mouse. If in comparison mode, the 3D mouse can be used to rotate the panorama. In addition thereto, the user can control the rotation via a slider (Fig. 6(3) (f)) on the touch interface. If switching to the findings mode, the user faces a flow-menu from which he/her can select an active finding (Fig. 6 (2)(f)). Successively, the server moves the camera closer the findings and highlights it. A slider (Fig. 6 (2)(g)) can be used to blend-in the available reconstructions for the respective hot spot. To avoid collisions between the virtual camera and the scene objects, designers created an explicit collision model for the complete scene. In contrast to derived bounding approximations, this gives maximum control to the physics designer (Section 5.4).

4.3 Presentation Setup

We divide the presentation setup into two parts: A client and a server. These two computers communicate with each other via a LAN (Fig. 1). The client is connected with a touch screen by inputech (1920x1080px) based on Nextwindow technology and runs a Core2Duo 3 GHz with 2 GByte RAM and a ATI Radeon 4650 (1 GByte RAM). It is used for both, the display of context-specific information as well as terminal for controlling the server. The server runs a Core i5 750 2.66 GHz with 4 GByte RAM and a NVidia GTX 285 (2 GByte RAM) and is connected with a beamer (1280x800 pixels) for displaying the 3D reconstruction on a vertical surface in front of the terminal.

5 Implementation

This Section briefly describes the implementation of the previously described concepts, with the main focus on the server-side image synthesis, content management, and messaging. The client was implemented on Adobe® Flash® using object-oriented action script.

5.1 Real-Time Image Synthesis

The server-side image synthesis can be performed in real-time using modern consumer graphics hardware [1]. Since the optimized geometric model (Table 1) fits into the video memory, we use in-core rendering techniques instead of out-of-core rendering techniques. The complete process of mesh optimization is described in [20]. We use a custom scene graph, shader programs [14] and a compositing pipeline for rendering. Therefore, each presentation mode represents a specific scene graph configuration. At loading time the geometric models are loaded and the scene graph is constructed. The client commands (Section 5.3) triggers the respective reconfiguration of the scene graph.

5.2 Content Management and Content Creation

Since we have a separate data basis for 2D content of the client visualization and 3D content of the server, special care is required for the synchronization between these two. For the communication between client and server (Section 5.3), we use unique global textual identifiers for modes, hot spots, and findings that are mapped by the client and server individually to the respective local content repositories.

In addition to the content creation pipeline described in [20], the geometric representations of the finding meshes are explicitly modeled or triangulated point clouds derived from laser scan data of the original findings. We choose a fixed aspect ratio (16:10) for 2D content creation of the client to minimize sampling artifacts, which would be introduced by rescaling the content otherwise. Both, client and server use a XML data-based file format that allows for easy maintenance and extension. This approach is also suited for a possible data-base binding later on.

The images required for the comparison mode can be obtained by photographs and application screen shoots. In the case of Roman Cologne, we use panoramic images with 360 degrees horizontal field-of-view. After relevant positions are determined within the reconstruction, a photographer acquired real-world images, which are aligned and stitched using Adobe Photoshop®. Our visualization system can acquire panoramic images using a rendering technique described in [27].

5.3 Client-Server Communication

For the communication between the client and the server we implemented a simple text-based protocol that can be easily extended and maintained. The textual messages are exchanged via TCP/IP sockets, whereas the client controls state consistency and initiates hand-shakes and resynchronization. The following messages are exchanged:

Client-Side: The Adobe® Flash® interface performs the initial hand-shake, transmits mode-changes, hot spot changes, the rotation angle of the panorama, as well as the blend factor for the reconstruction and the active finding. It further issues the demo mode after a defined idle time span.

Server-Side: The rendering server confirms the execution of sent commands, and sends the position of the virtual camera at a fixed interval, as well as automatically breaks a demo mode on user interaction.

All interactive controls, such as sliders or the flow-menu element, are sampled at a user defined frequency in order to handle possible network latency and socket congestion correctly. In our implementation we achieve best result using a frequency of 70ms within LAN.

5.4 User Interaction and Collision Handling

A central component for implementing the user interaction is collision detection and handling. It is used to preserve the intrusion of the virtual camera into buildings and to compute intersection points required for the orbit navigation metaphor. For implementing collision handling we use the Bullet physics engine, which is an open source software project. To increase the performance of the collision detection, we decided to use explicitly modeled collision geometry consisting of 57,840 vertices and 95,409 faces (Fig. 7). This approach has the advantage of providing maximal control to design the collision bodies, but requires a complete update of the collision model if only parts of the graphical model changes.

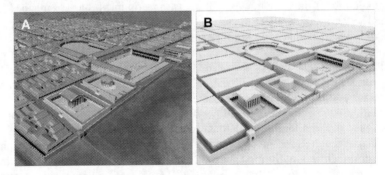

Fig. 7. Comparison between the geometry representation for visualization (A) and the collision handling (B)

6 Results and Discussions

This Section describes the results and evaluation of the proposed system. We start with a performance analysis and then describe preliminary observations with respect to the users. The performance of a 3D reconstruction is an important issue when a smooth and real-time experience for a user is aspired. The majority counts any application a real-time application, as soon as it renders more than 30 frames per second in average. Table 1 summarizes basic statistics for each of the three modes presented in Section 3.

Table 1. Statistics for the modes: reconstruction (Roman), comparison (Modern), and findings

Mode	Mesh	Vertices	Faces	Texel
Roman	372	15.465.030	21.132.616	1.307.049.984
Modern	2	136	128	12.987.912
Findings	64	327.842	291.988	4096

We measured the performance for the mode "Roman Cologne" on the setup described in Section 4.3. For the benchmark, we enabled view frustum, and backface culling, and disabled vertical synchronization. As basis for measuring, we used four different camera paths: Two paths that cover a bird's eye perspective and two paths that cover a pedestrian perspective. Table 2 summarizes the performance for different screen resolutions.

The results in Table 2 show that our system setup allows rates at real-time. We furthermore observe a higher frame rate of approximately 8% in pedestrian areas. A third observation allows classifying our implementation regarding a limiting factor. As the frame rate decreases with higher resolutions, the GPU can be seen as limiting device. As a summary, our application is fill-limited, showing an increase of 15% when using a resolution of 800x600 pixels instead of 1920x1200 pixels (Full HD).

The evaluation of the proposed system comprises two main steps: a test phase and a reviewing phase. During the test phase, the systems setup is tested thoroughly offline. This includes the tuning of sensitivity parameters of the input device and the physics engine. In the reviewing phase, the system is installed in the Roman-German Museum and is tested by staff and visitors. The results of that phase (one month) are then incorporated in the system. The preliminary observations during that phase basically yield positive response by the users, even if only a single user can interact with the system, while others are watching or waiting. We observed that the modern mode was very popular among most of the visitors.

Table 2. Performance evaluation for the mode "Roman Cologne" in frames-per-second (fps)

Resolution	Bird's Eye View [fps]			Pedestrian View [fps]		
	Avg.	Min	Max	Avg.	Min	Max
1920 x 1200	65.2	46	72	70.0	61	77
1600 x 1200	68.9	57	75	73.0	64	79
1024 x 768	72.7	43	81	78.8	70	84
800 x 600	74,7	40	83	80.5	71	85

7 Conclusions and Future Work

This paper presents a concept and implementation for the interactive communication of digital cultural heritage in public spaces by the example of the research project Roman Cologne. The proposed concept makes use of a client-server architecture, consisting of a 3D real-time rendering server and 2D touch sensitive user-interface to enable guided user exploration of a 3D virtual environment and knowledge communication. We generalized the approach towards a visualization tool for digital cultural heritage. The systems turns out to be a success, thus, other cities are eager to install similar approaches.

In order to enhance the usability of our system, we incorporated an additional statistics module that collects user data with respect to selected hot spots and the amount of time spent within these. We hope to identify remaining possibilities for get-lost situations and to rank features based on the importance to the users. We further strive towards making the existing content interactively available via the world-wide-web by using the recently standardized web-perspective view service (WPVS). In this context, we furthermore plan to evolve the existing system into a framework, which then can be used by third parties. Therefore, a data-base binding as well as out-of-core rendering techniques in combination with level-of-detail approaches are required to enable the interactive image-synthesis of geometrically even more complex data sets.

Acknowledgements

This work has been partially funded by the German Federal Ministry of Education and Research (BMBF) as part of the InnoProfile research group '3D Geoinformation' and RheinEnergie foundation Jugend/Beruf/Familie. Among many others, we especially like to thank the following people for their support and commitment: Johannes Bäuerlein, Henner von Hesberg, Fabian Kampa, Simone Lamberts, Janine Lehmann, Christian Leuenhagen, Stefan Maass, Silvio Mölter, and Leif Rumbke.

References

1. Akenine-Möller, T., Haines, E.: Real-Time Rendering, 2nd edn. AK Peters Ltd., Wellesley (2002)
2. Bergamasco, M., Brogni, A., Frisoli, A., Salvini, F., Vignoni, M.: Tactual Exploration in Cultural Heritage. In: XIV Round Table Computer-Aided Egyptology, Pisa, July 8-10 (2002)
3. Bier, E.A., Stone, M.C., Pier, K., Fishkin, K., Baudel, K., Conway, M., Buxton, W., DeRose, T.: Toolglass and Magic Lenses: The see-Through Interface. In: CHI 1994, pp. 445–446. ACM Press, New York (1994)
4. Boland, P., Johnson, C.: Archaeology as computer visualisation: 'Virtual tours' of Dudley Castle c. 1550. In: Higgins, T. (1997)
5. Buchholz, H., Bohnet, J., Döllner, J.: Smart and Physically-Based Navigation in 3D Geovirtual Environments. In: 9th International Conference on Information Visualization, pp. 629–635. IEEE Computer Society Press, Los Alamitos (2005)
6. Carrozzino, M., Evangelista, C., Scucces, A., Tecchia, F., Tennirelli, G., Bergamasco, M.: The virtual museum of sculpture. In: Proceedings of the 3rd International Conference on Digital Interactive Media in Entertainment and Arts DIMEA 2008, Athens, Greece, September 10-12, vol. 349, pp. 100–106. ACM, New York (2008)
7. Christou, C., Angus, C., Loscos, C., Dettori, A., Roussou, M.: A versatile large-scale multimodal VR system for cultural heritage visualization. In: Proceedings of the ACM Symposium on Virtual Reality Software and Technology VRST 2006, Limassol, Cyprus, November 01-03, pp. 133–140. ACM, New York (2006)

8. Cruz-Neira, C., Sandin, D.J., DeFanti, T.A.: Surround-screen projection-based virtual reality: the design and implementation of the CAVE. In: Proceedings of the 20th Annual Conference on Computer Graphics and interactive Techniques SIGGRAPH 1993, Anaheim, CA, August 02-06, pp. 135–142. ACM, New York (1993)
9. DeLeon, V., Berry Jr., R.: Bringing VR to the Desktop: Are You Game? IEEE MultiMedia 7(2), 68–72 (2000)
10. Gonçalves, A., Magalhães, L., Moura, J., Chalmers, A.: High dynamic range—a gateway for predictive ancient lighting. J. Comput. Cult. Herit. 2(1), 1–20 (2009)
11. Gooch, B., Gooch, A.A.: Non-Photorealistic Rendering. AK-Peters, Wellesley (2001)
12. Gutierrez, D., Sundstedt, V., Gomez, F., Chalmers, A.: Modeling light scattering for virtual heritage. J. Comput. Cult. Herit. 1(2), 1–15 (2008)
13. Heim, M.: Virtual Realism. OUP, Oxford (1998)
14. Kessenich, J.: The OpenGL Shading Language, Version: 1.20 Document Revision: 8, Manual (September 2006)
15. Laycock, R.G., Drinkwater, D., Day, A.M.: Exploring cultural heritage sites through space and time. J. Comput. Cult. Herit. 1(2), 1–15 (2008)
16. Lepouras, G., Katifori, A., Vassilakis, C., Charitos, D.: Real exhibitions in a virtual museum. Virtual Real. 7(2), 120–128 (2004)
17. Lotte, F., Van Langhenhove, A., Lamarche, F., Ernest, T., Renard, Y., Arnaldi, B., Lécuyer, A.: Exploring Large Virtual Environments by Thoughts using a Brain-Computer Interface based on Motor Imagery and High-Level Commands. Presence Teleoperators & Virtual Environments / Presence Teleoperators and Virtual Environments 19(1) (2010)
18. Lutz, B., Weintke, M.: Virtual dunhuang cave; a cave within a CAVE. In: Eurographics 1999 (1999)
19. Maass, S., Döllner, J.: Seamless Integration of Labels into Interactive Virtual 3D Environments Using Parameterized Hulls. In: 4th International Symposium on Computational Aesthetics in Graphics, Lisbon, pp. 33–40 (2008)
20. Maass, S., Trapp, M., Kyprianidis, J.E., Döllner, J., Eichhorn, M., Pokorski, R., Bäuerlein, J., Hesberg, H.v.: Techniques For The Interactive Exploration Of High-Detail 3D Building Reconstruction Using The Example Of Roman Cologne. In: Loannides, M., Addison, A., Georgopoulos, A., Kalisperis, L. (eds.) 14th VSMM, Archaeolingua, pp. 223–229 (2008)
21. Magnenat-Thalmann, N., Foni, A.E., Cadi-Yazli, N.: Real-time animation of ancient Roman sites. In: Proceedings of the 4th International Conference on Computer Graphics and Interactive Techniques, GRAPHITE 2006 in Australasia and Southeast Asia, Kuala Lumpur, Malaysia, November 29-December 02, pp. 19–30. ACM, New York (2006)
22. Mazuryk, T., Gervautz, M.: Virtual Reality History, Applications, Technology and Future. Technical Report TR-186-2-96-06 (1996)
23. Papagiannakis, G., L'Hoste, G., Foni, A., Magnenat-Thalmann, N.: Real-Time Photo Realistic Simulation of Complex Heritage Edifices. In: Proceedings of the Seventh International Conference on Virtual Systems and Multimedia (VSMM 2001), October 25-27, p. 218. IEEE Computer Society, Washington (2001)
24. Papagiannakis, G., Schertenleib, S., O'Kennedy, B., Arevalo-Poizat, M., Magnenat-Thalmann, N., Stoddart, A., Thalmann, D.: Mixing virtual and real scenes in the site of ancient Pompeii: Research Articles. Comput. Animat. Virtual Worlds 16(1), 11–24 (2005)
25. Petridis, P., White, M., Mourkousis, N., Liarokapis, F., Sifiniotis, M., Basu, A., Gatzidis, C.: Exploring and Interacting with Virtual Museums. In: CAA 2005: The World in Your Eyes, Tomar, Portugal (2005); Remondino, F., Girardi, S., Rizzi, A., Gonzo, L.: 3D modeling of complex and detailed cultural heritage using multi-resolution data. J. Comput. Cult. Herit. 2(1), 1–20 (2009)

26. Song, M., Elias, T., Müller-Wittig, W., Chan, T.K.: Interacting with the virtually recreated Peranakans. In: Proceedings of the 1st International Conference on Computer Graphics and Interactive Techniques, GRAPHITE 2003 in Australasia and South East Asia, Melbourne, Australia, February 11-14, p. 223. ACM, New York (2003)
27. Trapp, M., Döllner, J.: A Generalization Approach for 3D Viewing Deformations of Single-Center Projections. In: Braz, J., Nunes, N.J., Pereira, J.M. (eds.) International Conference on Computer Graphics Theory and Applications (GRAPP), vol. (3), pp. 162–170. INSTICC Press (2008)
28. Ulicny, B., Thalmann, D.: Crowd simulation for virtual heritage. In: Proceedings of First International Workshop on 3D Virtual Heritage, pp. 28–32 (2002)
29. Luft, T., Colditz, C., Deussen, O.: Image enhancement by unsharp masking the depth buffer. In: Proc. of the ACM SIGGRAPH Conference 2006, pp. 1206–1213 (2006)
30. Remondino, F., El-Hakim, S., Girardi, S., Rizzi, A., Benedetti, S., Gonzo, L.: 3D Virtual reconstruction and visualization of complex architectures - The 3D-ARCH project. In: International Archives of the Photogrammetry, Remote Sensing and Spatial Information Sciences, Trento, Italy (on CD-Rom), vol. 38(5/W1) (2009)

Architectural Heritage Online: Ontology-Driven Website Generation for World Heritage Sites in Danger

Elham Andaroodi[1] and Asanobu Kitamoto[2]

[1] University of Tehran, University College of Fine Arts, Faculty of Architecture,
Enghelab Street, Tehran, Iran
andaroodi@ut.ac.ir
[2] Research Organization of Information and Systems, National Institutes of Informatics,
2-1-2, Hitotsubashi, Chiyoda-ku, Tokyo, Japan
kitamoto@nii.ac.jp

Abstract. We introduce an online knowledge base for semantic representation and annotation of a world heritage site in danger. For this purpose we designed ontology inside the protégé tool with multiple metadata-based schemas to represent a knowledge base for heritage buildings and to annotate heterogeneous data sources. The ontology schema also references multiple bibliographies so it can gather the complex history of each building, or multiple coordinated locations of each building. We built an ontology-driven Website generation system "Bam3DCG" based on the Resource Description Framework graph exported from Protégé, and discuss practical problems for this type of system.

Keywords: Ontology Knowledge Model, Architectural Heritage, Heterogeneous Data Resources, Ontology-Driven Website Generation.

1 Introduction

In cultural heritage Websites, the quality of data and the level of reliable information it represents has an important role in increasing knowledge and proper awareness of tangible or intangible heritage sites. Complex historical background, various physical attributes, and different local and environmental characteristics give multiple-domain-related features to cultural heritage sites. The questions are how to effectively represent such complex knowledge of cultural heritage sites in an online database.

Architectural heritage data, as part of tangible heritage, contains information on heritage buildings. Historical background, constructional attributes, and location features represent information of a building. To represent such sophisticated information online, it is important to recognize different categories of data and conceptualize them in a standard schema. We introduce a metadata-based ontology knowledge model and a generated Website that conceptualizes a world heritage site (Citadel of Bam) by providing information of the site online.

The rest of the paper is structured as follows: Section 2 describes the attributes of heritage buildings and characteristics of our ontology knowledge model. Section 3 introduces the metadata-based ontology knowledge model, Section 4 discusses the generation of a Website for our target case study based on the ontology, and section 5 concludes the paper.

M. Ioannides (Ed.): EuroMed 2010, LNCS 6436, pp. 277–290, 2010.

2 Semantic of Heritage Buildings

To capture the semantics of a heritage building, it is important to verify major topics to precisely describe the building, such as its history, physical attributes, function, location, ownership, and preservation process. We introduce three of these categories that greatly influence the conceptualization of a knowledge model.

2.1 History and Dating

The first category, history, starts with a chronology of a particular building. An inscription can specify the construction date of a building, but in several cases such information is not available. Studying the architectural style or reviewing historical records can fulfill this goal. Type of decorations, constructional elements (arches or vaults), material (bricks), or organization (presence of a courtyard) can provide the necessary information to estimate the history of the building or its related period of construction. A record in a travelogue manuscript, such as a description by Ibn Hawqal [4] (travelled 943-969 AD) of the Citadel of Bam is another way to uncover the history of a building. In many cases a building does not represent a short period of time, but continues to change over different historical periods in different layers of construction or areas of expansion. The Citadel of Bam has a history starting from 500 B.C. until 1925 A.D. The chronology of such sites is a challenge that requires a multiple referencing approach.

Based on the above explanation, the history and dating of a building in a knowledge base has two characteristics: it must be able to give multiple dates or multiple historical descriptions to a building and it needs to link each historical record to its reference (both bibliographic or on site surveys) to validate the dating.

2.2 Physical Attributes

The type of building elements and structural components are important attributes for specifying the physical appearance of a heritage building. For the Citadel of Bam, these features represent desert architecture of the middle region of Persia. Most of the walls are load bearing. The characteristic feature of building components is types of coverings such as barrel, cloister or arched vaults. The type of arches also has a key role in representing different historical periods. Other components consist of floors, roofs and openings such as doors or windows.

Material and decoration are another subcategory and reflects the environmental characteristics of the site or historical background. The major wall and coating material of the Citadel of Bam is mud brick, mud-straw or chalk. Decorations are important attributes for distinguishing buildings (such as the house of a commander) or religious buildings such as mosques. The knowledge model for conceptualizing different categories of physical attributes of heritage buildings must provide a complete list of elements in a systematic way based on metadata standards.

2.3 Heterogeneous Data

Architecture is a type of visual knowledge. Its language corresponds more with drawings and images than with texts. Each database or knowledge base related to architectural heritage has a considerable amount of visual data with various data types. Architectural drawings made using Auto CAD or Micro Station, 3D models made by 3ds Max or Sketch Up, photogrammetric material made using Photo Modeler, different kinds of images such as on-site, landscape, aerial, and satellite photos, and different kinds of videos, such as Quick Time Virtual Reality, walk through, and aerial views result in heterogeneous datasets.

Such heterogeneous data require proper management in a knowledge base. They must be annotated by a standard attribute-set. Each piece of visual data needs to be connected with the textual descriptions representing information of the building in the knowledge model to disambiguate and validate it.

2.4 Knowledge-Based Schema for Heritage Buildings

We introduced different information aspects of heritage buildings needed for an advanced online web page. Any model for conceptualizing the above-mentioned aspects must have these major characteristics:

1. Provide multiple schemas to cover different attributes such as history, physical features, environment, management, and preservation.
2. Provide multiple bibliographic referencing.
3. Use metadata standards to describe building attributes or annotate the dataset.
4. Link every textual entity with visual data, such as images, movies, or architectural drawings, to validate the textual descriptions.

When a target building is selected, it is important to connect the different schemas mentioned above together with the visual dataset to easily navigate between various topics and acquire as much information of the building as possible. Weaving cultural heritage information into knowledge, which helps to develop an advanced knowledge model proper for the semantic web [1], is accomplished using advanced knowledge models. An ontology provides semantic relations between different topics in a hierarchical manner [3] and is appropriate enough to conceptualize information of heritage buildings.

3 Ontology for Heritage Buildings

To acquire semantic of the Citadel of Bam, we designed an ontology knowledge model called Bam 3D CG ontology using three major schemas: metadata-based schema, which is conceptualized using different metadata standards, referencing-based schema, which provides location or bibliographic attributes, and lexical-based schema, which provides terminological specifications for each heritage building. The architecture of the Bam 3D CG ontology is described in Figure 1. In the target ontology designed using the Protégé knowledge acquisition tool [15] as an RDF file [13], every piece of information or visual data is an entity connected to other entities by semantic links. These links are descriptive attributes of entities. Each homogeneous group of information is hierarchically categorized in classes with subclasses [10].

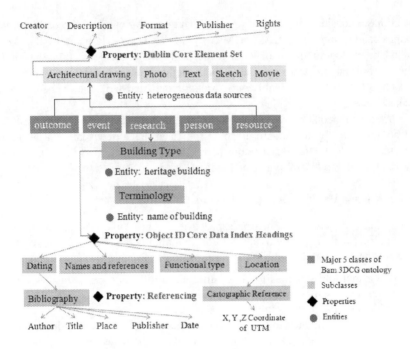

Fig. 1. Architecture of Bam 3D CG Ontology

3.1 Metadata-Based Schemas of the Ontology

Metadata standards provide a widely accepted list of elements to describe an object or data. A complete list of elements of metadata standards can help to precisely survey data in heritage sites because collecting data at such sites is complicated. It is important not to miss any information during a field survey by using a complete list of required information and an appropriate metadata standard. It is important to note that metadata standards are domain-based and focus on a specific field. If the target topic requires multiple domains for complete annotation and description, it is necessary to study different standards and select the desired topics and map between various metadata standards. For the heritage-building domain, we used part of the Core Data Index of Object-ID standard and the Dublin Core metadata standard to annotate visual data such as photos or videos. We describe how the schemas are modeled and connected in our ontology.

Metadata of Heritage Buildings and Integration inside Bam 3D CG Ontology. To describe the attributes of heritage buildings, we selected the Core Data Index, which is part of the Object ID standard. "Object ID is an international standard for describing cultural objects as a metadata standard containing specific items." [5,6]. The Core Data Index to Historic Buildings and Monuments of Architectural Heritage is a part of Object ID that focuses specifically on buildings.

The Core Data Index template inside the ontology provides the structure of data input and is conceptualized as follows. Each of the nine headings, such as Names and References, Location, Functional Type, and Dating, which are obligatory headings, is a class. Subclasses are those sub headings in the Core Data Index that have attributes in the third sub level, such as Administrative Location, Address, and Cartographic Reference, as subclasses of location. Every subheading that has attributes is a property or slot in the ontology. Each of the nine headings is defined as slots and takes instances from the class with the same name from the template. The template class provides the schema and structure, and the property class provides connections between different headings by using instances to weave every piece of information together.

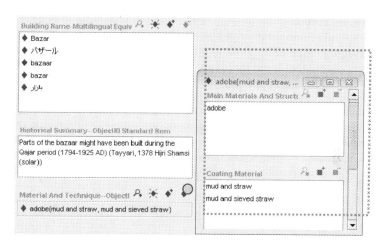

Fig. 2. Interconnected instances of Core Data Index template of Bam 3D CG ontology, bazaar

In conceptualizing properties or slots inside the schema, it is important to note which kind of information will be collected under it. If it is an explanation, then the *slot value* will be a *string*, and data is directly input (such as *coating material* in Figure 2). If several pieces of information with different attributes are available, the *slot value* will be an *instance*. This instance will be a link to connect different pieces of attributes. The form on the left side of Figure 2 is connected to the slot *Material and Technique* by an instance. This instance specifying *main material and technique* is adobe and *coating material* is mud and straw. Instances can connect several pieces of attributes and their information in the schema and can be freely selected from different classes. We integrated the Core Data Index schema inside the Bam 3D CG ontology. We modified the complete schema of the Core Data Index and selected those headings that had available information, as shown in Figure 2.

Metadata of Buildings Digital Data and Integration inside Bam 3D CG Ontology.
To describe and catalogue visual data, consisting of photos, videos, architectural drawings, and sketches, we used the Dublin Core Metadata Element Set, which is a standard vocabulary of fifteen properties for use in resource description [14]. The Dublin Core element set is less complicated to conceptualize inside the ontology schema than the Core Data Index of Object ID since one level of headings is available. We defined a class named Dublin Core, and each element, such as Contributor and Creator, is a slot with a value-type string and directly gathers information about the data.

Figure 3 shows integration of the Dublin Core element set inside the Bam 3D CG ontology. We had several images taken of the Citadel of Bam before and after the earthquake. Each photo is annotated using the Dublin Core schema as presented in the first box. It is important to note that we modified the slot values of the Dublin Core schema for those attributes that are related to the names of persons from slot value *string* to *instance* since they take instances from another schema related to people inside the Bam 3D CG ontology, as shown in properties of "Rights" in Figure 3. All data is restored in the repository and linked with the ontology schema as a file path in the local file system (slot image in Figure 3).The schema resolves syntactic differences between different distributed heterogeneous data sources. The Resource Description Framework (RDF) converts all types of data into RDF data using the reference ontology [8].

3.2 Referencing Schemas of Ontology

For online representation of the information of each heritage site, two major references are necessary. The first one specifies the location of the target site using the standard Spatial Referencing Systems. The second one that provides referencing to multiple bibliographies is necessary to validate historical research.

Geo reference of Heritage Buildings. As part of the ontology schema from the Object-ID Core Data Index, we provided the X, Y, and Z coordinates of each building located in the Citadel of Bam according to the Universal Transverse Mercator (UTM) Spatial Referencing System (Figure 4). For each property, a string slot is created and the complete schema is connected by an instance to the main body of the ontology by the slot that takes its name from the Core Data Index sub heading, named Cartographic Reference, as part of the heading Location. For each building one location is proposed as the middle point of the courtyard (as shown in Figure 4), or middle point of major dome on the roof. If the building is linear, such as the surrounding wall, several points on the edges are proposed.

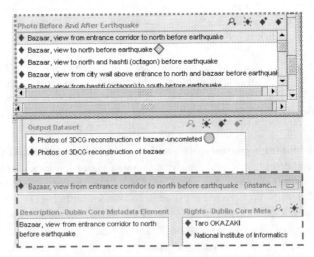

Fig. 3. Part of ontology for annotation of photo using the Dublin Core Element Set

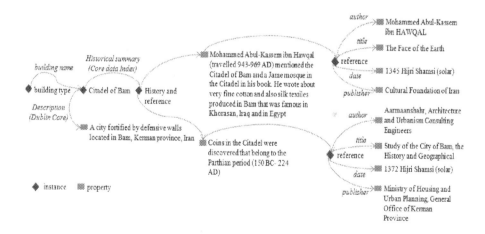

Fig. 4. Instances of coordinate referencing of building, commander's house

The location schema of Bam 3D CG ontology provides the UTM coordinates for around 52 buildings inside the Citadel of Bam (provided by the 3D Cartographic Map as IFCA project between (CNRS) and (NCC)). In the Website generated using this ontology, each location instance is referenced on the Google earth satellite images of the Citadel of Bam before and after the earthquake, as shown in Figure 4.

Fig. 5. Historical summery linked with multiple references

Multiple Historical References Bibliographic Attributes. We previously described the conceptualization process of bibliographic schema of the ontology [7]. Its main characteristic is the ability to provide multiple referencing to historical material to determine the dating and history of each building by defining different instances, as shown in Figure 5. The bibliographic schema is linked to the body of the ontology together with the lexical schema that gives semantics to each building type.

3.3 Lexical Schemas of Ontology

The multilingual lexical schema of the ontology provides the semantics of each building in different languages. We previously described this schema and its constraints in detail [7]. In the Bam 3D CG ontology for each building type, the multilingual equivalents accompanied by their lexical information are provided as shown in Figure 6.

4   Ontology-Driven Website Generation

To browse the RDF graph created on Protégé, we designed a Website generation and maintenance system so that people can browse knowledge bases using a standard Web browser. The Website "Bam3DCG" (http://dsr.nii.ac.jp/Bam3DCG/) has been open to the public since December 2008.

Fig. 6. Instances of multilingual building name in Bam 3D CG website

4.1 Architecture of Website

Referring to the model proposed in Intelligent Information Presentation System (IIPS) [9], we divide our system into three components, an ontology editor, ontology manager, and Website generator. For the ontology editor, we decided to use Protégé off the shelf to reduce the cost of developing a new system. A Web interface for managing ontology, such as WebProtégé and Ontowiki, were still premature at the time of system development, so we decided to use a stand-alone version of Protégé. This raises the problem of synchronizing ontology between the client and the server.

Insert, update, and delete actions on the knowledge base are done in the client side, and they have to be reflected on the server side to update the knowledge base on the Website. The update of the ontology can only be done offline, and users cannot update the ontology on the Web interface to avoid inconsistencies of the ontology. This is not a problem in our case because the Website is mainly designed for browsing, but

Web-based ontology management should be considered in a future version of Bam 3D CG as a portal to improve the usability of the system.

For the ontology manager and Website generator, we designed our ontology-driven Website generation system in a hierarchical layer structure, as depicted in Figure 7. The base layer is the Web application server, Tomcat, and we installed Web application frameworks, namely Apache Click and Velocity, on top of Tomcat. The RDF is managed using the semantic Web framework, Jena, and the RDF graph is stored in PostgreSQL. This architecture was chosen because of the ease of integration of various tools. We manage the data using the following steps. First the RDF graph exported from Protégé is uploaded to the system. The RDF graph is then parsed by Jena, and after applying some pre-processing steps, RDF triples are stored in PostgreSQL.

The problem is that the RDF graph cannot manage binary objects, such as images and videos, and can only maintain pointers to binary objects such as a file path in the local file system. This means that we need a separate uploading interface for binary objects in addition to the RDF graph. Currently, we use Secure Copy (SCP) for uploading binary objects and Hypertext Transfer Protocol (HTTP) for uploading the RDF graph. After pre-processing of the RDF graph and binary objects, they are stored in the database to support on-the-fly generation of HTML pages from stored data.

This uploading process, however, is not fully automated, and deletion or update sometimes requires administrator's intervention to manage existing data. Hence, we may need dedicated uploading software in the future that can manage both the RDF graph and binary objects using protocols such as Web-based Distributed Authoring and Versioning (WebDAV).

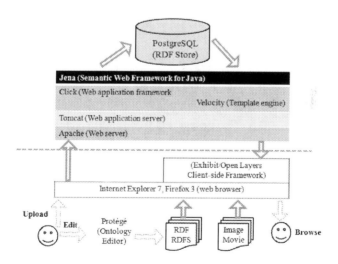

Fig. 7. Architecture of Website

The Web interface is designed using Cascading Style Sheets (CSS) and Javascript. The interface has five classes (Fig. 1) and four views, list (class), instance, hierarchy, and map. Instance view displays binary objects on the HTML page when it needs to display images and videos. Map view uses Google Maps to render spatial location of instances whenever they have spatial coordinates. We also introduced two satellite image layers into Google Maps so users can compare the Citadel of Bam before the earthquake, just after the earthquake, and the current status (default). Finally we also provide two searching interfaces, 1) search by terms for general users and 2) search by SPARQL (SPARQL Protocol and RDF Query Language) for advanced users. These functions also help users obtain resources directly from other resources.

4.2 Discussion

Representation of Resources. RDF is defined as a link of resources, so the natural unit of representation is a resource. We discovered, however, that this strategy does not produce intuitive representation in terms of HTML page generation. This is especially true for binary objects such as images and videos.

On the RDF graph, an image or a video is a resource that is linked from another resource. Hence, the representation of a non-binary resource may have a link to a binary resource, and traversing a link to a binary resource displays the binary object. This is not what a user expects, however. For example, the resource of a building and image resources of that building refer to the same real-world building (entity), so a user expects to see images and videos of the building on the HTML page of a building. If we follow the one-resource-per-HTML-page principle, however, a user needs to traverse links each time to see images and videos of the building.

Our solution to this problem is pre-fetching and embedding of resources that are linked from the resource in focus. That is, we do not just show a link to the resource, but actually fetch (upon request) the resource and embed it with a simple description. Figure 8 is an example of a resource page, on which users can see the image resource without traversing to the image resource page. From our experience this method is especially effective for multimedia resources such as images and videos.

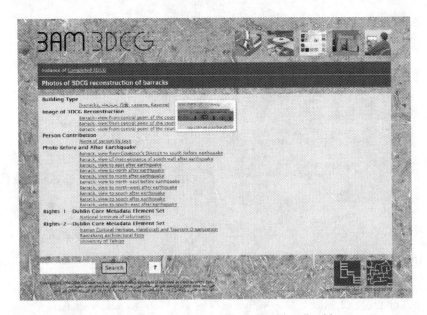

Fig. 8. Pre-fetching and embedding of multimedia objects

This can be explained by the problem of entity identification. Photographs of a building and the description of the building actually describe the same real-world building using different representation forms. Another explanation is that photographs and videos are "appearance" variants of the entity specified by the resource. Hence, we feel that they should be viewed in the same HTML page to facilitate comparison and interpretation of the real-world entity. To support this idea, we need to differentiate the relationship of appearance variants from the general links that represent different entities.

Representation of Spatial Objects. Spatial objects are now represented with a point in a spatial coordinate. As a spatial reference system, we used both UTM coordinates, obtained from the 3D cartographic map (IFCA project between NCC and CNRS), and World Geodetic System 84 (WGS84), obtained by identifying buildings on Google Earth. We discovered, however, that WGS84 and UTM coordinates do not represent the same point on earth. The reason may be 1) UTM coordinates depends on a domestic datum, 2) coordinates on Google Earth (so-called Google Earth datum) are different from WGS84. We have not investigated this reason, but we decided to keep both coordinates, and use Google Earth coordinates to represent the point of buildings on Google Earth/Maps, as illustrated in Figure 9.

Another problem with spatial objects is the specification of regions. Currently, buildings are represented with points, but this is not enough, especially when representing a large building. A more problematic case is the surrounding walls of the citadel, because the wall surrounding the whole site cannot be represented by a single point. The system should support a mechanism to specify the geometry of an object on the map. One possible solution is to use Scalable Vector Graphics (SVG) to represent spatial objects. By providing an interface for drawing the boundary of spatial objects with polygons or polylines, and exporting the geometry into a SVG file, we can render the boundary of a geometric object on the map as a clickable element.

Practical Problems with Protégé. We used Protégé as the ontology editor. Here we discuss the problems we had with version 3 of the protégé. The first problem was on making the multilingual version of RDF. This is not a limitation of RDF as a specification but a limitation of Protégé, which does not support multilingual labels for instances. This problem may be solved using a Web Ontology Language (OWL) plug-in for Protégé, which supports multilingual labels. This solution is not easy, however, because we need to transform RDF to OWL. The second problem was, as already stated, the issue of binary objects. There are no built-in mechanisms to maintain the consistency of pointers to binary objects, so we use filenames of binary objects as one property of a resource. This is obviously not a good design, however, because this process is error-prone and tends to be inconsistent. One possible solution is to use a separate data management system, which maintains the Uniform Resource Locator (URI) and an access method of the object. The third problem was that Protégé treats the collection of properties as a bag of properties, but a user actually needs a sequence of properties because properties often have an intuitive order of importance. There are no mechanisms to support this requirement, so we implemented mechanisms to manage the order of properties when generating HTML pages. Another limitation involves the description of classes and properties because the RDF created on Protégé does not have a simple mechanism to do this.

Navigation for Browsing RDF Graph. The purpose of the Bam3DCG Website is to help users browse the RDF graph. The simplest implementation of the Website is to render each subject as one HTML page in which links to objects or literals are shown with predicates. This design is not easy to use, however, because information is fragmented into too small pieces, preventing users to understand information in a broader context. For the same reason, this interface design requires users to traverse links several times back and forth, and users gradually feel lost in the complex structure of the RDF graph. We tried to design a proper graphic site view specially for five major classes (digital reconstruction, reference, research, outcome, people). Each class is presented by a photo in the main page that is repeated on top of every page so the user can recognize the main category of information that is browsed (upper part of figure 9). Another solution is the pre-fetching and embedding approach described previously.

Fig. 9. Displaying spatial objects on Google Maps

4.3 Toward Linked Data

The current RDF graph is specially designed for our project. However, on the concept (class) level, we introduced domain ontologies developed in other communities to enhance interoperability between communities, as described in the previous sections. The next step is to enhance interoperability on the data (instance) level to integrate our knowledge base with a global information space called linked data. Linked data refers to a set of best practices for publishing and connecting structured data on the Web, leading to the creation of a global data space containing billions of assertions – the Web of Data [16]. For this purpose, we need the following four steps [12].

1. Use URIs as names for things.
2. Use HTTP URIs so that people can look up those names.
3. When someone looks up a URI, provide useful information, using the standards.
4. Include links to other URIs, so that they can discover more information.

In our case, task 1 is satisfied by using the ontology editor. Task 2 is superficially fulfilled, but still has an essential problem from the viewpoint of cool URIs [16]. The current URIs contains irrelevant information, such as date created and sequential numbers, which are not related to "things" as introduced in the step 1 of cool URIs. Hence they do not satisfy the policy of cool URIs such as simplicity, stability, and manageability. Task 3 is not satisfied because the current Website returns information only in HTML format, but not in RDF format. Finally, Task 4 is still in a preliminary stage. We incorporated some ID systems into our ontology, but we have not started linking with other linked data initiatives such as DBpedia. More important future contribution is to open our Website so that other people can link to our URIs.

5 Conclusion and Future Work

We introduced ontology-driven Website generation for semantic representation of knowledge of a World Heritage Site in Danger, the Citadel of Bam. We discussed multiple schemas of the ontology designed using different metadata standards or referencing systems and the interconnected entities linked with properties of each schema. We discussed the architecture of the ontology-driven generation of our target Website, Bam 3D CG, and the constraints in the process of converting the RDF file of the ontology linked with binary objects, such as photos, to HTML pages that a user can browse easily. The metadata schema designed in Bam 3D CG ontology is extensible to collect knowledge of other architectural heritage buildings. Our ontology-driven Website generation software is based on open source software libraries, so it is extensible to other heritage Websites. Our software was not designed as a general framework for heritage Websites, but some components are domain independent and allow reuse for such Websites. Finally, scalability of the Website largely depends on the RDF store shown in Figure 7. We are currently using PostgreSQL for the RDF store. PostgreSQL is a relational database management system (RDMBS), and it is well known that RDF, which is a collection of triples, does not match with the data model of a relational database, which is a collection of tuples. We can replace the RDF store to one optimized for triples, and this will improve the performance of the system to achieve scalability.

The Bam 3D CG Website presents information on the Citadel of Bam in an advanced knowledge model and links it with visual data such as photos or maps. We still have several studies to conduct regarding linked data, which is an important future step in making our infrastructure valuable to researchers and people around the world. We will also investigate how to extend ontology-based approach from a Website to a portal to which heritage-building experts can contribute and annotate data of cultural heritage by a web server for managing the ontology.

Acknowledgements. The supporting research project, 3D CG reconstruction of the Citadel of Bam is a collaborative project between the Digital Silk Road project of NII and Iranian Cultural Heritage, Handicraft and Tourism Organization (ICHHTO) lead by Prof. Dr. Kinji Ono. We would like to thank Associate Professor Dr. Frederic Andres for his support in developing the ontology. We also thank Mr. Tomohiro Ikezaki for developing the Website generation and management software and assistant professor Mohammad-Reza Matini for site view graphic design. This work was conducted using the Protégé resource.

References

1. Berners Lee, T., James, H., Ora, L.: The semantic web, a new web content that is meaningful to computers will unleash a revolution of new possibilities, Scientific American.com, Feature Article (2001)
2. Bizer, C., Heath, T., Berners-Lee, T.: Linked Data – The Story So Far. International Journal on Semantic Web & Information Systems 5(3), 1–22 (2009)
3. Gruber, T.R.: Toward principles for the design of ontologies used for knowledge sharing. International Journal of Human and Computer Studies 43(5-6), 907–928 (1995)
4. Ibn e Haugal: Surat-ol-Arz, Translated by J. Sho'aar, Tehran (1345 solar)
5. Thornes, R., Bold, J.: Documenting the Cultural Heritage, The J. Paul Getty Trust (1998)
6. Thornes, R., Dorrell, P., Lie, H.: Introduction to Object ID, Guidelines for Making Records that Describe Art, Antiques, and Antiquities. The J. Paul Getty Trust (1999)
7. Andaroodi, E., Ono, K., Kitamoto, A.: Metadata-Based Terminology Ontology for Knowledge Management of an Architectural Heritage in Danger. In: Proceeding of Conference on Virtual Systems and Multimedia Dedicated to Digital Heritage (VSMM-Full papers), ARCHAEOLINGUA, Hungary, Budapest (2008)
8. Jin, Y., Decker, S., Wiederhold, G.: OntoWebber: Model-Driven Ontology-Based Web Site Management. In: The 1st International Semantic Web Working Symposium (SWWS 2001). Stanford University, Stanford (2001)
9. Lei, Y., Motta, E., Domingue, J.: An Ontology-Driven Approach to Web Site Generation and Maintenance. In: EAKW 2002: Proceedings of the 13th International Conference on Knowledge Engineering and Knowledge Management, pp. 219–234. Springer, Heidelberg (2002)
10. Noy, N.F., Fergerson, R., Musen, M.: The knowledge model of Protégé 2000: Combining interoperability and flexibility. In: Dieng, R., Corby, O. (eds.) EKAW 2000. LNCS (LNAI), vol. 1937, pp. 17–32. Springer, Heidelberg (2000)
11. Mehriar, M.: The history of citadel of Bam, report of archaeological studies, Bam recovery office, Iranian Cultural Heritage and Tourism Organization (2003)
12. Berners-Lee, T.: Linked Data – Design Issues (2006),
    http://www.w3.org/DesignIssues/LinkedData.html
13. Brickley, D., Guha, R.V. (eds.): Resource description framework (rdf) schema specification, Note: World Wide Web Consortium, W3C Candidate Recommendation, CR-rdf-schema-20000327, March 27 (2000)
14. Dublin Core Metadata Element Set, Version 1.1,
    http://dublincore.org/documents/dces/
15. The Protégé editor and knowledge acquisition system,
    http://protege.stanford.edu/
16. W3C, Cool URIs for the Semantic Web, W3C Working Draft (2007),
    http://www.w3.org/TR/2007/WD-cooluris-20071217/

The DAF DDI Profile, a Metadata Set to Address Digital Curation and Preservation Issues in Cultural Heritage Institutions

Ruggero Lancia

Humanities Advanced Technology and Information Institute (HATII),
George Service House, 11 University Gardens,
University of Glasgow, Glasgow, G12 8QH, Scotland, UK
R.Lancia@hatii.arts.gla.ac.uk

Abstract. This investigation, funded by the Digital Curation Centre (DCC) and conducted in the Humanities Advanced Technology and Information Institute (HATII) of the Glasgow University, is part of the activities within the Data Asset Framework (DAF) to provide research organisations with an online tool to identify, locate, describe and assess how they are managing their research data assets. This research has produced a metadata set fitted for the implementation of curation and preservation policies in small research institutions. In this paper, the DAF DDI profile will be exposed and explained. Further, it will be discussed, the advantages this metadata set offers to the small Cultural Heritage institutions for supporting curation and preservation policies. The DAF DDI profile is the first example of a DDI 3.1 implementation in a general curatorial context, that is not disciplinary specific, and its integration with PREMIS 2.0 is the first published mapping of PREMIS to DDI.

Keywords: DAF Interactive Tool, DCC, Metadata, DDI, PREMIS, *Digital Curation and Preservation.*

1 Introduction

This investigation, funded by the Digital Curation Centre (DCC) and conducted in the Humanities Advanced Technology and Information Institute (HATII) of the Glasgow University, is part of the activities within the Data Asset Framework (DAF) to provide research organisations with an online tool to identify, locate, describe and assess how they are managing their research data assets.

This study was aimed at developing a metadata set to ease the satisfaction of the requirements attached to the DAF interactive tool redevelopment, that is a) the possibility for the users to extend and customize its audit forms, b) the improvement of the analysis tools, such as for example implementing automatic recommendations facilities, c) and the interoperability with the DRAMBORA tools, available at http://www.repositoryaudit.eu/ (accessed 14 June 2010). In particular, the need for extensible and customizable audit forms has been interpreted here as the need for a metadata set flexible, modular and extensible, while to address the interoperability

M. Ioannides (Ed.): EuroMed 2010, LNCS 6436, pp. 291–305, 2010.
© Springer-Verlag Berlin Heidelberg 2010

and reuse of data across the DCC framework, the researched metadata set has been expected to be interoperable and pertinent to the entire curatorial lifecycle of digital assets.

Featuring all these characteristics, the DDI 3.1 metadata set has been chosen as a basis for this study. In effect, from DDI 3.0, this metadata set supports a lifecycle model, the "Combined Lifecycle Model", including as curatorial steps the conception, creation, ingestion, storage, access and reuse. Further, the DDI 3.1 offers a modular structure made of 21 XML namespaces, which can be assembled without restrictions but maintaining the consistence of the hierarchical relationships among their schemas, and allows for external extensions as long as the general DDI profile is not altered. This characteristic makes the DDI 3.1 easily interoperable with other metadata sets, for example the DCMI elements have been integrated in the DDI documentation within a specific namespace and mappings to other sets have been already released by the DDI developers.

So, at the beginning of this study the DDI structure has been analysed evaluating its use to document the curation and preservation practices This investigation has demonstrated a weakness of the DDI set managing the assets' preservation and its need for the integration with a metadata set specifically designed for preservation purposes. For this reason, a mapping of the PREMIS 2.0 core elements to DDI 3.1 has been developed to compensate these shortcomings: a major accomplishment of this research since it is the first mapping between these metadata set to be so far completed and published. Then, the researched metadata set has been designed as a DDI profile resulting from the selection of DDI elements accomplishing the objectives of this investigation.

In this paper, the DAF DDI profile will be exposed and the selection process of its elements will be explained giving prominence to the mapping of PREMIS to DDI. Further, it will be discussed, the advantages this metadata set offer to the small Cultural Heritage institutions for supporting curation and preservation policies.

2 DDI 3.1 as Basis for the DAF Metadata Set

Looking in this study for a metadata set modular, customizable and extensible, the DDI 3.1 set appeared to be the fittest option. That assumption was comforted by its wide adoption in prestigious institutional archives; nevertheless, because of its disciplinary specialisation, this metadata set was expected to cause difficulties being implemented in a general framework such as the one of the DAF methods and tools.

Thus, in this study, the implementation of the DDI 3.1 as basis for the researched metadata set has been assessed against its shortcomings serving the curation and preservation purposes of a repository from a research institution.

2.1 DDI Shortcomings Serving the Curation and Preservation Purposes

The DDI set is claimed by its creators to support the productive lifecycle of the digital assets rather than its archival part and, in effect, from the "Combined Life Cycle Model" proposed in the "Overview" a lack of attention for all the curatorial processes but the access and reuse of assets is evident: the "Data Archiving" step in this lifecycle model is just accessed through an alternative path on the way from "Data Processing" to "Data Distribution" and in this way the management duties of repositories are completely obliterated [1].

Thus, the DCC Digital Curation Lifecycle model, because of its general and holistic approach to curation [2], has been chosen as methodological background to analyse the DDI shortcomings recording a complete curatorial lifecycle disciplinary unspecific.

In more detail, the classification of the metadata has been limited to the sequential actions of the DCC lifecycle model, that is the curatorial steps "Create and Receive", "Appraise and Select", "Ingest", "Preservation Action", "Store", "Access Use and Reuse" and "Transform" since the full time and the occasional ones appeared to be respectively too general and too specific for the purposes of this study.

From this analysis emerged, firstly, a bias toward few specific functions and events affecting the digital assets resulting in the insufficiency of descriptions for general curation purposes in the "Ingest", "Store", "Access Use and Reuse" and "Transform" sections, and second, the lack of concentration on preservation issues.

In effect, while many DDI descriptors allow to record, aiming at their reuse, the structure of statistical data and to reference their data structures and collection procedures, the element <LifecycleInformation> is the only descriptor available to describe the relevant events of the curatorial steps "Ingest", "Store" and "Preservation action". In a similar fashion, DDI offers just <FundingInformation> and <LifecycleInformation> to record the appraisal and the disposal of the assets in an unspecific curatorial context while a more accurate technical appraisal of the digital objects' quality is possible just for statistical data through the descriptors of <ProcessingEvent> and <CollectionEvent>. Similarly, at the "Access Use and Reuse" step, the DDI set offers many administrative and structural metadata especially related to quantitative analysis for social sciences to manage accessibility and reuse of the assets but no descriptors to record their reuse apart from referencing elements such as <source>, <OtherMaterial>and <Comparison>.

On the preservation's side, the descriptors of <LifecycleInformation> allow a listing of events in the lifecycle of a data set or collection but do not offer specific descriptors to facilitate the automation of this kind of report, nor the sufficient guide for a human being to relate his description to preservation levels and curatorial policies, that is to assess his activity on the repository and to scale his efforts according to feasibility considerations.

2.2 The DDI 3.1 as a Basis for the Researched Metadata Set

The disciplinary specialisation of this metadata set is evident also considering its structure.

Offering 6 specific namespaces to allow the computational reuse of quantitative social sciences data, the structure of the DDI metadata reflects its main application's field. In effect,

"ddi:physicaldataproduct_ncube_normal:3_1",
"ddi:physicaldataproduct_ncube_inline:3_1",
"ddi:physicaldataproduct_ncube_tabular:3_1",

"ddi:physicaldataproduct_proprietary:3_1",   "ddi:logicalproduct:3_1"   and
"ddi:datacollection:3_1" describe coding and variables of the assets supporting verification and reuse of quantitative researches.

Similarly, this set of metadata aims at being interoperable with other metadata
standards such as Dublin Core, MARC, ISO11179 (metadata registries), SDMX (data
exchange), and geographic standards such as FGDC (Federal Geographic Data Committee) and ISO 19115 which are widely diffuse in the social sciences archives.

Nevertheless, the DDI set's interoperability depends on its modularity, which allows also the creation of metadata registries, the import of external namespaces and
the grouping and versioning of both data and documentation. Further, the modular
approach of this metadata is due to the adoption of a data lifecycle model which, although defective dealing with the preservation management, offers these advantages
for a curatorial framework: a) to allow the capture and preservation of metadata generated by different agents at different points in time; b) to track changes and updates
in both data and documentation; c) to enable investigators, data collectors and producers to document their work directly in DDI; d) to benefit data users who need information from the full data lifecycle for optional discovery, evaluation, interpretation
and reuse of data resources [3].

In this way, the DDI 3.1 allows also a strong customization adopting its descriptors
through the identification of a profile, that is a selection of descriptors common to a
collection or group, and at the same time enough flexibility to render compliant also
incomplete records, supporting the feasibility of its implementation. Moreover, the
DDI content can be integrated in digital repository systems, such as DSpace, e-Prints
and Fedora, into data search system allowing queries across multiple modules, and
into data search and manipulation tools, in doing so fostering the implementation of
automated curatorial procedures.

For these reasons, considering the benefits offered by DDI complementing its
shortcomings, DDI 3.1 has been chosen in this research as basis for the researched
metadata, which has been designed as a DDI profile.

3   Integrating PREMIS in DDI

Since the researched metadata set has been considered mainly intended for small research institutions in a very early stage of their curatorial procedures' implementation,
the DDI profile resulting from this research was expected to be a light metadata
model aiming less at the completeness of the recorded information than at the feasibility of its implementation. Thus, despite the modular structure of DDI allows external
extensions, a mapping to other metadata sets with a specific curatorial interest has
been considered the fittest option to obtain a DDI profile retaining the adequate information to support curatorial procedures in small contexts. Otherwise, the extension
would had caused expansive redundancies of the information that if resolved, for example selecting the metadata elements to be imported as DDI extension in a separate
namespace, would had caused partial validations of the metadata records.

In particular, since the release of DDI 3.0, the PREMIS standard has been reported
to have been analysed for mapping to the DDI model in order to face the preservation
issues arising in research repositories [4]. Encouraged by this previous attempt, in this
research it has been decided to integrate the PREMIS semantic units in the DAF DDI
profile through a mapping.

3.1 Difficulties Integrating PREMIS Semantic Units in DDI

The structural differences between PREMIS and DDI cause many difficulties mapping the one into the other. In effect, the linking among the five core entities proposed by the PREMIS model, that is "Intellectual Entities", "Objects", "Events", "Rights" and "Agents", compared to the horizontal description offered by DDI, implies a considerable loss of information in the translation.

Further, despite the stated limit of the PREMIS 2.0 to offer descriptive metadata, the granularity this set offers by individuating the entities' "typologies" as "representations", "files" and "bitstreams" is not repeated in DDI 3.1 (PREMIS, 2008). As suggested in a draft of the mapping of PREMIS 1.0 to DDI 3.0 released in December 2007 in the ICPSP online forum [5], the asymmetry between those metadata set is best controlled by considering the entire information on the assets related just to the "file" typology.

Similarly, also significant information for the long-term preservation of the assets is inevitably lost through the integration of PREMIS in DDI, that is the semantic units "1.3 preservationLevel", "1.5.1 compositionLevel" (especially "1.5.2 fixity", "1.5.3 size" and "1.5.6 inhibitors"), "1.8 environment" (a part from its sub-unit "1.8.4 dependency") and "1.9 signatureInformation". In effect, these descriptors record respectively the information indicating the policy on the set of preservation functions to be applied to an object, the context in which the policy was made, the technological environment supporting the use of the object and the authoritative quality of the assets.

Because of the limited preservation policies small research institutions are likely to apply, this kind of information's incompleteness concerning the digital assets' preservation has been considered tolerable for the researched DDI profile. For this reason, the selection of the PREMIS semantic units to be mapped to DDI has been narrowed down to the elements declared mandatory by the PREMIS XML schema.

The vast majority of the information requested by this schema concerns the entity "Objects" and is repeated, if applicable, for the files, the files compound and the bitstreams in order to obtain a granular curatorial description of the intellectual entities' components. The basic description of each file includes its identifier and its format through the elements <format> of <objectCharacteristics> and <objectIdentifier>, as it could be noticed reading the relative selection of units from the PREMIS XML schema featured below, see http://www.loc.gov/standards/premis/premis.xsd (accessed 14 June 2010):

```xml
<xs:complexType name="file">
<xs:complexContent>
<xs:extension base="objectComplexType">
<xs:sequence>
<xs:element ref="objectIdentifier" minOccurs="1"
maxOccurs="unbounded"/>
<xs:element ref="objectCharacteristics" minOccurs="1"
maxOccurs="unbounded"/>
</xs:sequence>
<xs:attribute name="xmlID" type="xs:ID"/>
</xs:extension>
</xs:complexContent>
</xs:complexType>
```

```
<xs:complexType name="objectIdentifierComplexType">
<xs:sequence>
<xs:element ref="objectIdentifierType" minOccurs="1"
maxOccurs="1"/>
<xs:element ref="objectIdentifierValue" minOccurs="1"
maxOccurs="1"/>
</xs:sequence>
<xs:attributeGroup ref="xlink:simpleLink"/>
</xs:complexType>
<xs:complexType name="objectCharacteristicsComplexType">
<xs:sequence>
<xs:element ref="format" minOccurs="1"
maxOccurs="unbounded"/>
</xs:sequence>
</xs:complexType>
<xs:complexType name="formatComplexType">
<xs:sequence>
<xs:choice>
<xs:sequence>
<xs:element ref="formatDesignation" minOccurs="1"
maxOccurs="1"/>
</xs:sequence>
<xs:element ref="formatRegistry" minOccurs="1"
maxOccurs="1"/>
</xs:choice>
</xs:sequence>
</xs:complexType>
<xs:complexType name="formatDesignationComplexType">
<xs:sequence>
<xs:element ref="formatName" minOccurs="1"
maxOccurs="1"/>
</xs:sequence>
</xs:complexType>
<xs:complexType name="formatRegistryComplexType">
<xs:sequence>
<xs:element ref="formatRegistryName" minOccurs="1"
maxOccurs="1"/>
<xs:element ref="formatRegistryKey" minOccurs="1"
maxOccurs="1"/>
</xs:sequence>
<xs:attributeGroup ref="xlink:simpleLink"/>
</xs:complexType>
```

Although in the PREMIS 2.0 data dictionary <storage> is listed erroneously as mandatory, in the PREMIS XML schema this element is not considered fundamental, thus, it has not been mentioned here. The absence of the mandatory element <compositionLevel> is motivated by the assumption that since in this mapping the digital objects are described just at the file level there is little need to indicate if the object is subject to processes of decoding; indeed, its default value, 0, indicates that the object described is a base object not subject to further decoding, and that could really be more often the case of the assets the DAF prototype is intended to deal with.

The "Rights" entity has a slightly less complex description concentrated on the copyright, licenses, and statute description of each object aimed at determining whether a repository has the right to perform a certain action on its assets in an automated fashion:

```
<xs:complexType name="rightsComplexType">
<xs:choice minOccurs="1" maxOccurs="unbounded">
<xs:element ref="rightsStatement"/>
</xs:choice>
<xs:attribute name="xmlID" type="xs:ID"/>
</xs:complexType>
<xs:complexType name="rightsStatementComplexType">
<xs:sequence>
<xs:element ref="rightsStatementIdentifier" minOccurs="1"
maxOccurs="1"/>
<xs:element ref="rightsBasis" minOccurs="1"
maxOccurs="1"/>
</xs:sequence>
</xs:complexType>
<xs:complexType
name="rightsStatementIdentifierComplexType">
<xs:sequence>
<xs:element ref="rightsStatementIdentifierType"
minOccurs="1" maxOccurs="1"/>
<xs:element ref="rightsStatementIdentifierValue"
minOccurs="1" maxOccurs="1"/>
</xs:sequence>
<xs:attributeGroup ref="xlink:simpleLink"/>
</xs:complexType>
```

The "Agent" and the "Event" entities have structures far more simple than the previous entities: the first offers just one mandatory element, <agentIdentifier>, while the second adopts the elements <eventType>, <eventDateTime> and <eventIdentifier> as minimum describers:

```
<xs:complexType name="agentComplexType">
<xs:sequence>
<xs:element ref="agentIdentifier" minOccurs="1"
maxOccurs="unbounded"/>
</xs:sequence>
<xs:attribute name="xmlID" type="xs:ID"/>
</xs:complexType>

<xs:complexType name="eventComplexType">
<xs:sequence>
<xs:element ref="eventIdentifier" minOccurs="1"
maxOccurs="1"/>
<xs:element ref="eventType" minOccurs="1" maxOccurs="1"/>
<xs:element ref="eventDateTime" minOccurs="1"
maxOccurs="1"/>
</xs:sequence>
<xs:attribute name="xmlID" type="xs:ID"/>
</xs:complexType>
```

3.2 Cross-Walk from PREMIS Core Elements to DDI

The following table (Table 1) summarise the proposed mapping of the PREMIS mandatory elements to DDI:

Table 1. Cross-walk from PREMIS core elements to DDI

PREMIS 2.0 core semantic unit Name	DDI 3.1 – Complex Element	DDI 3.1 – Element/ attribute	Value
(1.1) objectIdentifier	<DDI Instance>	@id	xs: string
(1.1.1) objectIdentifierType			
(1.1.2) objectIdentifierValue			
(1.5) object Characteristics			
(1.5.4) format	<Item>	<Format>	xs: string
(1.5.4.1) format Designation			
(1.5.4.1.2) formatName			
(1.5.4.2) formatRegistry	X	X	X
(1.5.4.2.1) formatRegistryName	X	X	X
(1.5.4.2.2) formatRegistryKey	X	X	X
(2.1) eventIdentifier	<Lifecycle Event>	@id	xs: string
(2.1.1) eventIdentifierType			
(2.1.2) eventIdentifierValue			
(2.2) eventType	<Lifecycle Event>	<EventType>	xs: string
(2.3) eventDateTime	<Lifecycle Event>	<Date>	xs: string
(3.1) agentIdentifier	<Agency Organization Reference>	<ID> or <URN>	xs: string or URN
(3.1.1) agentIdentifierType			
(3.1.2) agentIdentifierValue			

Table 1. (*continued*)

(4.1) rightsStatement			
(4.1.1) rightsStatementIdentifier	\<Citation\> and \<DCElements\>	\<Copyright\> and \<rights\>, respectively	xs: string
(4.1.1.1) rightsStatementIdentifier Type			
(4.1.1.2) rightsStatementIdentifier Value			
(4.1.2) rightsBasis			

But, the mapped elements are not structurally equivalent, as it is particularly evident considering the elements describing the file formats and the rights statement associated to the instances.

In effect, PREMIS, taking into account the use of extensions to apply descriptive, structural and administrative metadata, adopts a system of external references and pertinent descriptors for each of its five core entities. In this way, the "formatRegistry" unit identifies the format of an instance by reference to an entry in a format registry and the "rightsStatementIdentifier" locates the rights statement within a preservation repository system. Nevertheless, these units are options of a mandatory selection and their partners, "formatDesignation" and "rightsBasis", can be effectively expressed through the values of \<Format\> and \<rights\>. In particular, this latter would supplement the information recorded by the entity \<Copyright\> that might be used to express thoroughly the rights statement that would be usually referenced by "rightsStatementIdentifier".

Similarly, the units "objectIdentifier" and "eventIdentifier" can be mapped to the identifier attributes of the entities \<DDIInstance\> and \<LifecycleEvent\> despite the flattening of the information in the passage from PREMIS to DDI. The unit "agentIdentifier" can be mapped to the elements \<ID\> or \<URN\> of the entity \<AgencyOrganizationReference\> narrowing down the possibilities for the unit "agentIdentifierType" to either ID or URN.

4 The DAF DDI Profile

The DDI, at its minimum configuration, does not demand any other element than the "id" attribute of the \<DDIInstance\> and the entity \<UserID\>, other elements become mandatory in a specific DDI profile as consequence of the selection of other elements they are hierarchically bound with.

Thus, the elements selected for the DAF DDI profile depended both on the characteristics this study decided in advance to attribute to the researched metadata set and on the very DDI structure.

4.1 Selecting the DDI Elements for the DAF DDI Profile

Since the first objective of this research was designing a metadata set allowing the management of a complete general curatorial lifecycle model, the fist elements which have been included in the researched DDI profile have been the mandatory PREMIS units previously mapped to DDI, that is the complex elements <Item>, <LifecycleEvent>, <AgencyOrganizationReference> and <Citation>. In particular, since the system of URN references appeared too ambitious for the expected users of the DAF tools, the element <ID> has been chosen as unique descriptor for <AgencyOrganizationReference>. Further, the inclusion of <LifecycleEvent> and <Item> in the DAF DDI profile implied that, on the one hand, their containers, the complex elements <Group> and <Archive>, were added to the selection and, on the other, that the elements <LifecycleInformation>, <Description>, <Date>, <ArchiveOrganizationReference> and <OrganizationScheme> would have been inserted to complement the description of the one, while, the elements <ArchiveSpecific>, <ArchiveOrganizationReference> and <OrganizationScheme> to refine the description of the other.

Then, aiming at improving the compatibility of the first DAF interactive tool with the data from future audits, since 11 elements out of 16 of its set are borrowed from the DCMI but the element <Purpose>, the entities of the complex <DCElements> have been added to the DAF prototype's profile as complementary descriptors for the entity <Citation> and the element <Purpose> has been inserted among the descriptors of <DDIInstance>.

But, where the DDI schemas did not influence the selection of the descriptors, some conceptual refinement were applied to specify the use of the selected elements in the researched DDI profile.

That was the case of <OrganizationScheme>, which would be validated by a parser even if not containing further descriptors but its "id" attribute; thus, the elements <OrganizationSchemeReference> and <Description>, bearing the ideal minimum information describing the organisation acting as archive, have been added to the selection.

Similarly, the descriptors contained in <DCElements>, as it is stressed in the DDI technical specifications, are not sufficient to obliterate identical DDI elements from <Citation> since the Dublin Core is not used as main citation mechanism in DDI and its use is aimed just at supporting applications which do not understand DDI; for this reason, within <Citation> have been included also <Creator> and <Copyright> while within <Item> the element <Format>. To ease the research of text documents it has been included also the element <Abstract> of <Citation>.

Other elements have been included being pertinent to the curatorial procedures implemented within research institutions and to their needs for more adequate curation and preservation policies. In effect, the elements <LocationInArchive> and <ArchiveModuleName> have been selected to complement the records concerning the ingestion process when this takes place on movable media physically stored in the repositories, as it happens in many institutions [6] In the same way, the elements <AccessTypeName>, <AccessPermission>, <Restrictions> and <AccessRestrictionDate> have been selected to offer a support for the implementation of formal procedures, while the element <EventType> of <LifecycleEvent> has been inserted to support the use of vocabularies corresponding to formal curatorial procedures. The elements <CollectionCompleteness>

and <OriginalArchiveOrganizationReference> of <Collection>, and <FundingInforma-
tion> have been selected to encourage the implementation of selection and disposal
procedures through the assessment of the digital assets value.

4.2 The DAF DDI Profile

Given these premises, below is transcribed the XML resulting from the researched
DDI profile:

```
<?xml version="1.0" encoding="UTF-8"?>
<DDIInstance xmlns="ddi:instance:3_1"
 xmlns:xsi="http://www.w3.org/2001/XMLSchema-instance"
 xsi:schemaLocation="ddi:conceptualcomponent:3_1
   file:/your_location_for_the_DDI_schema/instance.xsd"
 id="">
<UserID xmlns="ddi:reusable:3_1" type=""></UserID>
<Citation xmlns="ddi:reusable:3_1">
<Title></Title>
<Creator></Creator>
<Copyright></Copyright>
<DCElements xmlns="ddi:dcelements:3_1">
<title xmlns="http://purl.org/dc/elements/1.1/"></title>
<creator
xmlns="http://purl.org/dc/elements/1.1/"></creator>
<type xmlns="http://purl.org/dc/elements/1.1/"></type>
<format
xmlns="http://purl.org/dc/elements/1.1/"></format>
<date xmlns="http://purl.org/dc/elements/1.1/"></date>
<source
xmlns="http://purl.org/dc/elements/1.1/"></source>
<identifier
xmlns="http://purl.org/dc/elements/1.1/"></identifier>
<rights
xmlns="http://purl.org/dc/elements/1.1/"></rights>
<relation
xmlns="http://purl.org/dc/elements/1.1/"></relation>
<subject
xmlns="http://purl.org/dc/elements/1.1/"></subject>
<description
xmlns="http://purl.org/dc/elements/1.1/"></description>
</DCElements>
</Citation>
<Group xmlns="ddi:group:3_1" id="">
<Abstract id="">
<Content xmlns="ddi:reusable:3_1"></Content>
</Abstract>
<Purpose id="">
<Content xmlns="ddi:reusable:3_1"></Content>
</Purpose>
<Archive xmlns="ddi:archive:3_1" id="">
<ArchiveModuleName></ArchiveModuleName>
<ArchiveSpecific>
<ArchiveOrganizationReference>
<URN xmlns="ddi:reusable:3_1"></URN>
```

```
</ArchiveOrganizationReference>
<Item>
<LocationInArchive></LocationInArchive>
<Format></Format>
<Access id="">
<AccessTypeName></AccessTypeName>
<AccessPermission></AccessPermission>
<Restrictions></Restrictions>
<AccessRestrictionDate>
<SimpleDate xmlns="ddi:reusable:3_1">xxxx-xx-
xx</SimpleDate>
<User xmlns="ddi:reusable:3_1"></User>
</AccessRestrictionDate>
</Access>
</Item>
<Collection>
<OriginalArchiveOrganizationReference>
<URN xmlns="ddi:reusable:3_1"></URN>
</OriginalArchiveOrganizationReference>
<CollectionCompleteness></CollectionCompleteness>
</Collection>
<FundingInformation xmlns="ddi:reusable:3_1">
<AgencyOrganizationReference>
<ID></ID>
</AgencyOrganizationReference>
<Description></Description>
</FundingInformation>
</ArchiveSpecific>
<OrganizationScheme id="">
<OrganizationSchemeReference>
<URN xmlns="ddi:reusable:3_1"></URN>
</OrganizationSchemeReference>
</OrganizationScheme>
<LifecycleInformation xmlns="ddi:reusable:3_1">
<LifecycleEvent id="">
<EventType></EventType>
<Date>
<SimpleDate>xxxx-xx-xx</SimpleDate>
</Date>
<AgencyOrganizationReference>
<URN></URN>
</AgencyOrganizationReference>
<Description></Description>
</LifecycleEvent>
</LifecycleInformation>
</Archive>
</Group>
</DDIInstance>
```

5   The DAF DDI Profile for Cultural Heritage Institutions

Apart from supporting the adoption of policies and the implementation of procedures for the curation of digital assets, the DAF DDI profile can significantly benefit small

Cultural Heritage institutions, such as museums and government agencies, by contributing to both the enhancement of the repositories' information quality and the sustainability of the Digital Curation and Preservation practices.

5.1 Metadata Quality

DDI satisfies all the characteristics that are commonly attached to quality metadata in regards to their semantic and syntactic structures, to their data values, and to their context of use.

These characteristics concern a) the completeness of the information, b) its accuracy, that is its coherence, c) the provenance of the metadata set and its logical consistency, d) its synchronization with the instances and its maintainability, e) and the accessibility of the information in respect to its context of use. As explained above, the DDI modular structure allows for coherence control in the records, versioning and access management, and, despite being designed for the quantitative researches in social sciences, its application in a general context is still adequate because of the relatively exhaustive information conveyed. In effect, the completeness of a metadata set for the Cultural Heritage institutions should be assessed against the needs of the growing federation of digital resources in this field [7].

It has been reported that immediate local needs, such as for example disciplinary ones, have often taken priority over the needs of interoperability in Cultural Heritage institutions [8]. As a result, a tension between efficient cataloguing and quality cataloguing has become particularly evident in this context undermining the integration of resources, for example, harvested adopting the OAI protocol. The difficulties suffered by the aggregator and the service providers maintaining metadata consistency in a federated environment demonstrate that shareable metadata are crucial for the data accessibility and very detailed records are not the results of quality metadata.

The discipline unspecific approach to curation of the DAF DDI profile, the integration of DCMI elements within its descriptive metadata, and the lightness of the records produced facilitate the interoperability of this set. In adjunct, the semantic structure of the DDI DAF profile is fostered by its predisposition to implement controlled vocabularies while its syntactic consistency by the very structure of the DDI set which avoids ambiguities and incoherence in the data values.

Furthermore, the versioning control granted by DDI is particularly valuable for the institutions aiming at employing their resources in digital academic practices, such as for example the emerging non-linear scholarly publications and the e-learning initiatives.

5.2 Contribution to the Sustainability of Curatorial Practices

The digital Cultural Heritage initiatives tend to trigger preoccupations about their sustainability in small institutions; as a result the main focus of information and communication technology development in the Heritage sector concentrates on medium to larger institutions [9] The nature of this problem is mainly organisational and depends on a frequent lack of business plans and other planning tools that exposes small institutions to failure rendering operational digital cultural projects because of the resulting inadequate resources and untenable staff workloads [10].

The DAF DDI profile promotes and eases curatorial planning for the entire lifecycle of digital assets and in doing so helps improving also the internal business processes. In effect, adopting this DDI profile, small institutions would be led to create an accurate curatorial planning involving in particular the assessment of the economical value of the digital assets stored in their repositories, especially through the information recorded by <FundingInformation>, and the evaluation of the benefits obtainable from their exploitation, through the management of the intellectual rights. In this way, and taking advantage of the DDI control on data versioning, the small institutions could also implement formal practices of disposal of their obsolete and not profitable assets.

Further, the integrability of DDI in the major DMS improve the feasibility of the implementation of curatorial procedures in small institution since its users in this way can have recourse to robust products, easy to use, well serviced and stable, that is cheap to be implemented and maintained.

6 Conclusions

Reconstructing its design process, the DAF DDI profile has been demonstrated being a quality metadata for the integrated management of digital assets, that is the management along their entire lifecycle, and especially fit for the framework of federated digital resources.

A part from serving the redevelopment of the DAF interactive tool, the DAF DDI profile has been shown facilitating, in the context of the small Cultural Heritage institutions, the adoption of preservation and curation policies, of business plans, and the implementation of curatorial procedures, also through its integration in the major DMS.

Further, the DAF DDI profile is the first example of a DDI 3.1 implementation in a general curatorial context, that is not disciplinary specific, and its integration with PREMIS 2.0 is the result of the first published mapping of PREMIS to DDI.

Acknowledgments. The author would like to thank all the colleagues from HATII which offered guidance, suggestions and support for this research, and in particular Dr Ian Anderson, Patrick McCann, Joy Davidson, and Sarah Jones.

References

1. Thomas, W., Gregory, A., Gager, J., Kuo, I.-.L., Wackerow, A., Nelson, C.: Data Documentation Initiative (DDI), Technical Specification, Part 1: Overview, Version 3.1, DDI Alliance (2009)
2. Higgins, S.: Draft DCC Curation Lifecycle Model. IJDC 2(2), 82–87 (2007)
3. Martinez, L.: The Data Documentation Initiative (DDI) and Institutional Repositories (2008), http://www.disc-uk.org/docs/DDI_and_IRs.pdf
4. DDI: Data Documentation Initiative, Technical Specification, User Guide version 3.0, DDI Alliance (2008)

5. Thomas, W.: [DDI-SRG] DDI 3.0 Questions - preservation, fwd (2008),
   http://www.icpsr.umich.edu/pipermail/ddi-srg/
   2008-January/002695.html
6. Jones, S., Ross, S.: DAFD Final Report (2009),
   http://www.data-audit.eu/docs/DAFDfinalreport.pdf
7. Shreeves, S., Riley, J., Milewicz, L.: Moving towards shareable metadata. First Monday,
   8(11) (2006),
   http://www.firstmonday.org/issues/issue11_8/shreeves/
   index.html
8. Shreeves, S., Knutson, E., Stvilia, B., Palmer, C., Twidale, M., Cole, T.: Is 'quality' metadata 'shareable' metadata? The implications of local metadata practice on federated collections. In: Proceedings of the Twelfth National Conference of the Association of College
   and Research Libraries, pp. 223–237. Association of College and Research Libraries,
   Minneapolis (2005)
9. Geser, G.: Assessing the readiness of small heritage institutions for e-culture technologies.
   Digi. CULT. info. 9, 8–13 (2004)
10. Zorich, D.M.: A Survey of Digital Cultural Heritage Initiatives and Their Sustainability
    Concerns. Council on Library and Information Resources, Washington D.C. (2003)

Annotation of Cultural Heritage Documents Based on XML Dictionaries and Data Clustering

Zenonas Theodosiou[1], Olga Georgiou[1], Nicolas Tsapatsoulis[1], Anastasis Kounoudes[2], and Marios Milis[2]

[1] Dept. of Communication and Internet studies, Cyprus University of Technology,
31 Arch.Kyprianos, P.O. Box 50329, 3603, Limassol, Cyprus
{zenonas.theodosiou,olga.georgiou,
nicolas.tsapatsoulis}@cut.ac.cy
[2] SignalGeneriX Ltd, Arch.Leontiou A' Maximos Court B', 3rd floor,
P.O. Box 51341, 3504, Limassol, Cyprus
{tasos,marios.milis}@signalgenerix.com

Abstract. Cultural heritage forms the local and national identities. It shapes relationships between neighbors and other communities around the world. The sweet wine named "Commandaria" is part of Cypriot heritage and currently holds a protected destination of origin within European Union, USA and Canada. In the framework of the Commandaria project we managed to gather an enormous amount of data, related to Commandaria wine, corresponding to photographs, scanned documents and videos. The need of a method for efficient retrieval of these data based on their actual content was mandatory. The data were appropriately indexed through a multilevel labeling scheme allowing access from various modalities and for a variety of applications. Despite the huge efforts for automatic characterization and classification human intervention is the only way for reliable multimedia data annotation. Manual data annotation is an extremely laborious process and efficient tools developed for this purpose can make, in many cases, the true difference. In this paper we present the CulHIAT, a cultural heritage item annotation tool, which uses structured knowledge, in the form of XML dictionaries, combined with a hierarchical classification scheme, to attach semantic labels to image and video segments at various levels of granularity. Finally, XML dictionary creation and editing tools are available during annotation allowing the user to always use the semantic label she/he wishes instead of the automatically created ones.

Keywords: Cultural Heritage Documents, Video Annotation, Hierarchical Classification, XML Dictionaries, Data Clustering.

1 Introduction

Cultural heritage is the legacy of physical artifacts and intangible attributes of a group or society that are inherited from past generations, maintained in the present and bestowed for the benefit of future generations. The heritage that survives from the past is often unique and irreplaceable. Commandaria wine, is for many years one of most important Cypriot cultural heritage items. In the context of the Commandaria project

M. Ioannides (Ed.): EuroMed 2010, LNCS 6436, pp. 306–317, 2010.

[1] huge amounts of literature work have been scanned, true stories, relics, tools and related items were recorder or animated, and agriculture photographs were captured to provide better access to researchers in the area of Humanities, to primary and secondary school teachers, to university students and the great public in general.

No more than twenty years ago we faced the problem of information unavailability or inaccessibility; today we face issues related to data overflow and information filtering, which make users' investigation for relevant information cumbersome [2]. The growing amount of digital video and images are driving the need for more effective methods for indexing, searching, and retrieving of video and images based on their content. While recent advances in content analysis, feature extraction, and classification are improving capabilities for effectively searching and filtering digital video content, the process to reliably and efficiently index multimedia data is still a challenging issue. Besides, in order to learn audio-visual concept models, supervised learning machines also require ground truth labels being associated with training videos [3].

In consistency with the broader digital multimedia domain, manual annotation is the predominant way of attaching description and indexing information to digitized cultural heritage items [4]. Manual annotation, however, is a laborious, time consuming and expensive task. Furthermore, the terminology and description of cultural heritage are often too technical and difficult for nonprofessional users of the domain [5]. Thus, annotation based on a dictionary according to the different knowledge levels of users is a critical aspect of annotation enhancement. The use of an integrated system which can provide the dictionary creation and data annotation can greatly simplify the process.

In this paper we present the CulHIAT cultural heritage item annotation tool which is based on MPEG-7 standard [6], [7], [8]. It supports image, video and digital data annotation though a highly interactive panel. Video annotation at lower levels of granularity is supported through automatic video segmentation into shots while shots are combined into scenes through clustering with the aid of a Genetic Algorithm scheme. A new XML dictionary based on the Commandaria taxonomy was created to attach semantic labels to an enormous amount of images, videos and other digitized or digital documents related to the Commandaria wine with the aid of this tool. Although many annotation tools are publicly available, few of them can be used to annotate data in multiple levels of granularity as required, for example, for audiovisual documents.

Annotation can be performed in several manners, ranging from completely manual to tool-assisted to fully automatic. *VideoAnnEx* MPEG-7 annotation tool is implemented by IBM for collaborative multimedia annotation task in distributed environment [3]. *MovieTool* is developed by Ricoh for creating video content descriptions conforming to MPEG-7 syntax interactively [9]. *Multimodal Annotation Tool* is a release of IBM's Multimedia Mining Project, which is derived from an earlier version of VideoAnnEx with special features with audio signal graphs and manual audio segmentation functions [10]. *Microsoft Research Annotation System (MRAS),* which is a web-based system for annotating multimedia web content [11]. Synchronous *Multimedia and Annotation Tool (SMAT)* is used to annotate images and there is no granularity for video annotations nor controlled-term labels [12]. *A4SM (Authoring System for Syntactic, Semantic and Semiotic Modelling)* developed a semi-automated annotation tool for audio-visual media in news [13]. *The European Cultural heritage*

Online (ECHO) is developing a multimedia annotation tools which allows people to work collaboratively on a resource and to add comments to it [14].

While the majority of the above tools are very well-developed and efficient they emphasize on a particular medium, usually video. Furthermore, the annotation lexicons that are used to attach labels to the data are predefined and non-editable. Modifications to these lexicons or creation of new ones cannot be done in "context" (during the annotation process) and require the use of external tools. This is clearly a limitation since the annotator rarely stops the annotation process to modify the lexicons (even if we assume that he/she is allowed to do so). Lexicon enrichment, on the other hand, is an important facility and must be preserved because it leads to more effective data indexing and data retrieval.

The remaining of this paper is organized as follows: Section 2 gives a brief description of the Annotation Tool, while the dictionary creation and annotation procedure are described in Section 3. In Section 4 we present the algorithm that is used for shot clustering. Finally, conclusions are drawn and further work hints are given in Section 5.

2 CuLHIAT Annotation Tool

The CulHIAT annotation tool was developed based on MPEG-7 standard using MAT-LAB. The tool boasts a user-friendly Graphical User Interface allowing the management of multimedia content (images, videos or any other digital or digitized document), video segmentation into shots and scenes, video and image annotation, image watermarking and creation of XML dictionaries. Any PC or workstation can be used as far as the hardware is concerned, although as expected, the more computing power the better performance level it will reached. In particular, a large amount of RAM memory will help to improve the performance of video segmentation and classification.

The GUI consists of three major panels. The *Video Panel* provides the video or animation segmentation and annotation while the *Image Panel* provides the image (or scanned documents) annotation and watermarking. The dictionaries used for annotation are created via the third panel named *Dictionary Panel*. A brief description of each panel follows.

2.1 Video Panel

An example screen of *Video Panel* is shown in Fig. 1. The Panel consists of three tabs. The first and second ones provide the manual and automated segmentation respectively, while the third accords the video annotation.

Video Segmentation: Video segmentation is required to split a video sequence into smaller video units. As shown in Fig. 1, the user can select one of two available modes for video segmentation: manual and automated. The video sequence displayed in the window on the upper left-hand corner during manual segmentation. The user can explore it and set the shots boundaries by specifying the first and last frame of each shot. Then she/he might choose and set key-frames. Key-frame are representative images of the video shot, and offer an instantaneous recap of the whole video shot. The shot frame boundaries and key-frames of each shot along with any other annotation information are saved in an XML-file related with the particular video sequence.

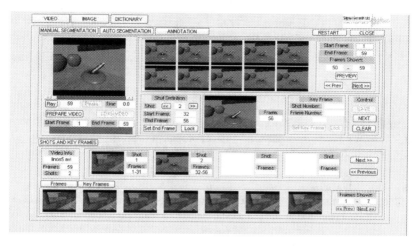

Fig. 1. Video Segmentation panel. The frames shown present a segment from an animated video clip created to present a production phase of Commandaria. It represents real Commandaria production procedure at LINOS, a renovated wine press located at Lania village in Cyprus.

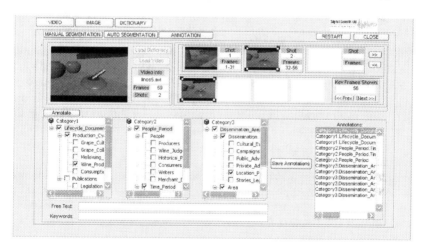

Fig. 2. Video Annotation panel. This figure presents the annotation of a frame shot, taken from Commandaria production phase, video. The dictionary panel was defined based on Commandaria taxonomy structure.

Automated shot detection is also supported with the aid of the Color Histogram Differences algorithm [15]. The algorithm is one of the most trustworthy variants of histogram-based detection algorithms and is based on the idea that the color content rapidly changes across shots. So, hard cuts and other short-lasting transitions can be detected as single peaks in the time series of the differences between color histograms of contiguous frames or of frames a certain distance k apart.

Let $p_i(r, g, b)$ be the number of pixels of color (r, g, b) in frame I_i of N pixels. Each color component is discretized to 2^B different values, resulting in $r, g, b \in [0, 2^B - 1]$.

Usually B is set to 2 or 3 in order to reduce sensitivity to noise and slight light object as well as view changes. Then the color histogram difference CHD_i between two color frames I_{i-1} and I_i is given by:

$$CHD_i = \frac{1}{N} \cdot \sum_{r=0}^{2^B-1} \sum_{g=0}^{2^B-1} \sum_{b=0}^{2^B-1} |p_i(r,g,b) - p_{i-1}(r,g,b)| \tag{1}$$

If within a local environment of radius I_c of frame I_i only CHD_i exceeds a certain threshold, then a hard cut is detected. As presented in [15], for particular type of hard cut which consists of one transitional frame, in a pre-processing stage double peaks (i.e. groups of $S_c=2$) contiguous CHD_i exceeding threshold were modified into single peaks at the higher CHD_i.

A video clip can simply annotated by describing its content in its entirety. However, when the video sequence is large, indexing particular video segments is invaluable. Smaller video units might correspond to video shots or a collection of similar video shots usually referred to as scene. Shot detection has already been described earlier while scene construction is performed using shot clustering as described in Section 4.

Given the shot boundaries, the annotations are assigned for each video shot by using the *Video Annotation* Tab. The tool uses a specific type of dictionaries based on MPEG-7 descriptions made via the *Dictionary Panel*. To be more precise the video annotation is performed through the following three steps.

Video Annotation: First, the annotation dictionary (XML) that will be used to annotate the key-frames of each shot is loaded. Annotation dictionaries can be created using the *Dictionary Panel* as will be explained in Section 2.3. Each dictionary can be divided up to three main categories, as illustrated in Fig. 2, usually corresponding to different annotation contexts or annotation perspectives. This choice was made for space fitting purposes since every main category can be further divided to any number of subcategories and any subcategory to any number of nodes and so on, providing a hierarchical annotation tree.

Second, the segmented video resulted from the video segmentation procedure is loaded and its shots are shown in shot axes at the upper right-hand corner. After choosing a shot, its key-frames are shown in the four axes below the shot axes. The user can choose a key-frame in order to annotate it. The chosen key-frame can be seen in the axes at the left-hand corner.

Third, the key-frame annotation can be implemented using the dictionary categories presented in list-boxes on the bottom left corner of the video annotation panel. The user ticks the boxes of the most representative labels and adds if needed free text and key-words using the corresponding edit boxes. Annotations are shown in the list-box on the bottom right corner and are saved into an XML file in the video directory.

2.2 Image Panel

CulHIAT provides the capability of annotating and embedding information into an image, scanned document or digital item via the *Image Panel*. A screen shot of the *Image Panel* is shown in Fig. 3. The input image and its features are presented on the top left corner of the panel. The user can choose between *Image Annotation* and *Watermarking*.

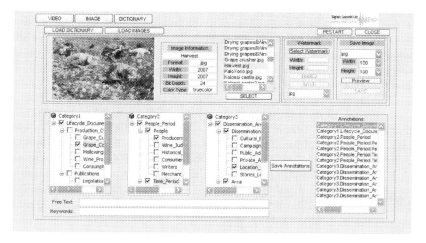

Fig. 3. Image Annotation. The image shown presents the grape collection procedure during grape collection season, which is usually starts early September and ends late October.

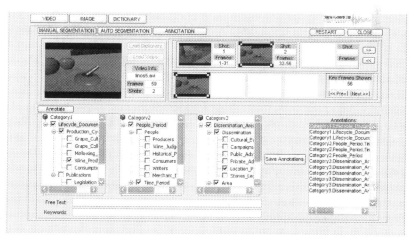

Fig. 4. Dictionary Panel. The shown dictionary was created based on Commandaria taxonomy and involves six main sections.

Image Annotation: An image can be simply annotated following the three steps described in the previous section. The three categories of the annotation dictionary are presented in the list-boxes (under left-hand) and the chosen image is shown at the upper left-hand axes. The user can annotate the image by ticking the most appropriate annotation boxes of the three lists. Free text and keywords edit boxes can be used for a more detailed annotation. The saved annotations are shown in the list-box on the right-hand corner and are saved into an XML file.

Image Watermarking: The selected image can be watermarked and saved in any image format and in any scaling using the *Watermark* tab. After the watermark selection, the user defines the wanted width and height. The watermarked image can be

312   Z. Theodosiou et al.

seen in the left-corner axes and can be saved in any image format. The chosen image also can be rescaled and saved in any format, without being watermarked using the *Save Image* tab.

2.3 Dictionary Panel

Dictionaries used for annotation via the CulHIAT are created using *Dictionary Panel*. As mentioned earlier each dictionary consists of three different categories as presented in Fig. 4. Categories can be divided in subcategories, subcategories into nodes, nodes into subnodes, etc, providing an hierarchical structure. The user can create a new dictionary from scratch or add/delete a node at any level in the hierarchy. During the annotation process any number of node-labels at any level can be used to characterize the data. However the selection of a node-label implies also the selection of its ancestor node-labels. Dictionaries are saved in an XML file.

3 Cultural Heritage Data Annotation

An enormous amount of data was collected in the framework of Commandaria project. Some of these data date back Homer's era indicating the historical value of Commandaria wine. Proper annotation of collected data items was an absolute requirement in order to allow efficient information retrieval related to Commandaria for various categories of users including students, tourists, scientists, wine producers, etc.

The Commandaria data collection consists approximately of 7500 files. The 3500 files are digitized manuscripts and scanned papers from books, journals and official legislating documents, while the remaining 4000 files are images and videos. Most of the images are taken using a digital camera, from visits towards the Cyprus agriculture and well known wine villages. Video files correspond to interviews with experienced wine producers as well as recordings of Commandaria production cycle steps. Additionally, project archives consist of short clips presenting agriculture tools and places, used for wine production. Some of the Commandaria production cycles were modeled using 2D and 3D animations.

Currently the size of data collection is around 35 GB but it continuously grows. The value of the collected information is priceless for Cyprus heritage, therefore the collection, proper preservation and easy access to this information is a task of tremendous importance [1]. Efficient indexing and retrieval of this information requires accurate and rich annotation of data; this annotation was done with the aid of CulHIAT. For example, an important evidence discovered during the data collection process, is the interview with a resident of the Cypriot village Kornos (Fig. 5(a)) who found at his grandfather's house (Fig. 5(b)) a substance in almost solid form which is probably Commandaria in concentrated form (Fig. 5(c)-5(i)). The condensed substance, which, as reported by the resident, dates more than one hundred years, was generated from a natural evaporation of alcohol and water. The Commandaria existed for many years in wooden barrels until 1976, when the majority was sold and a small part was transferred to glass bottles, preserved until today.

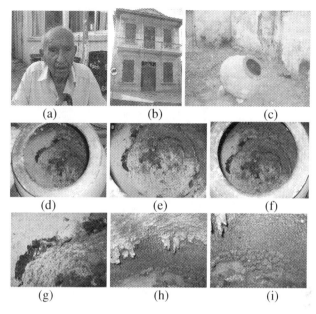

Fig. 5. Photographs taken from the Cypriot village Kornos during the interview with the resident found the 100 years old wine. (a) Mr. Sergides is the person that owns the old wine, (b) family house where the solid wine found. (c) The traditional wine making tool, so called "Pithari", which stored the wine for so many years. (d), (e), (f) present the internal content, taken from different angles. (g), (h), (i) show the solid situation of the wine, after so many years kept in a big jar.

It is clear that the observing the images shown in Fig. 5, the overall story and the important of this evidence cannot be understood. Proper annotation of these images allows not only the classification and indexing according to the Commandaria devised taxonomy [1] but also the attachment of free text description which enables and deeper appreciation of the discovered item.

As mentioned earlier, the CulHIAT annotation tool was used to characterize the Commandaria documents. For this purpose a new XML dictionary based on the Commandaria taxonomy was created using the tool, as described in section 2.3. An example of this dictionary is shown in Fig. 6.

The dictionary includes all the possible sources of the collected data, the users or producers of these data, the related historical period, production cycle or any other related information. In the production cycle we annotate images related to the production of Commandaria, starting from the grapes cultivation wine consumption. A large number of images were related to wine producers' interviews, places of Commandaria region and people working during the Commandaria production. All the collected data fall into a specific time period, therefore a relevant category was created to help us separate the corresponding information based on the historical period they belong to.

314 Z. Theodosiou et al.

```
- <root>
  - <Lifecycle_Documentation>
    - <Production_Cycle>
        <Grape_Cultivation />
        <Grape_Collection />
        <Mellowing_Draining />
        <Wine_Production />
        <Consumption />
      </Production_Cycle>
    - <Publications>
        <Legislation />
        <Books />
        <Research />
        <Wine_Review_Results />
      </Publications>
    </Lifecycle_Documentation>
  - <People_Period>
    - <People>
        <Producers />
        <Wine_Judges />
        <Historical_People />
        <Consumers />
        <Writers />
        <Merchant_Dealer_Trader />
      </People>
    - <Time_Period>
        <Ancient_Times />
        <Middle_Times />
        <Modern_Times />
      </Time_Period>
    </People_Period>
```

Fig. 6. An XML dictionary example

4 Shot Clustering Using Genetic Algorithm

In this section we present a genetic algorithm which is used for shot clustering in order to create scenes. Scenes are composed of conceptually similar shots. Shots belonging to the same scene must be abutted each other. The algorithm assumes that the input data is divided into a desired number N_c of clusters. We assume also that the input data is already annotated with aid of method presented in the previous section.

We define the set $\mathbf{K} = \{K_1, K_2, ..., K_{N_k}\}$ of data points with a data point K_i corresponding to cluster C_i. Let us define a vector of integer values in increasing order:

$$Idx^{(i)} = \left\{ Idx_1^{(i)}, Idx_2^{(i)}, ..., Idx_{N_{c-1}}^{(i)} \right\} \tag{2}$$

with $1 < Idx_j^{(i)} < N_k$, $j = 1, ..., N_{c-1}$. Each vector $Idx^{(i)}$ defines a partition $P^{(i)} = \{P_1^{(i)}, P_2^{(i)}, ..., P_{N_c}^{(i)}\}$, of set $\mathbf{K}$ with $P_j^{(i)}$ corresponding to a set of data points $\{K_{Idx_{j-1}^{(i)}}, ..., K_{Idx_j^{(i)}-1}\}$, while $P_1^{(i)} = \left\{ K_1^{(i)}, ..., K_{Idx_1^{(i)}-1} \right\}$ and $P_{N_c}^{(i)} = \left\{ K_{Idx_{N_{c-1}}^{(i)}}^{(i)}, ..., K_{N_K} \right\}$. Given that each data point corresponds to a cluster, the partition $P^{(i)}$ defines a possible division of input data into N_c clusters. The task of the genetic algorithm described next is to find a partition $P^{(\xi)}$ which creates the optimum division of input data into N_c clusters given a properly defined metric.

4.1 A Genetic Algorithm for Shot Clustering

Genetic Algorithms are adaptive optimization methods that resemble the evolution mechanisms of biological species [16]. Feature selection is one of the areas that GAs present excellent performance. The main advantages of GAs are:

- They do not require the continuity of parameter space and,
- They are able to efficiently search over a wide range of parameters /parameter sets.

In a GA, the search begins from a population of P_N possible solutions (in our case strings corresponding to integer vectors $Idx^{(i)}$, $i = 1,..., P_N$ of length $N_c - 1$, with integer values limited to the interval [1 N_k], and not just one possible solution. Solution refers to a partition $P^{(i)}$ as explained in the previous section. A population of solutions guarantees that search will not be trapped in a local optimum, especially if significant diversity exists among the various solutions. The population of solutions tends to evolve toward increasingly better regions of the search space through the use of certain randomized processes, called genetic operators. Typical genetic operators are the *selection, mutation* and *recombination*. The *selection* process chooses strings with better objective function value and reproduces them more often than their counterparts with worse objective function value. Thus, a new population is formed consisting of the strings that perform better in their environment. The *recombination* (crossover) operator allows for the mixing of parental information, which is then passed to their descendants. The initial population is randomly acquired; this means that the first and major degree of diversity is introduced in this stage of the GA. The second and lesser degree of diversity is introduced when *mutation* operator acts upon each string of the population. The whole evolution process stops after a predefined maximum number of iterations (generations) is reached or the variation among population of solutions is too small.

Once the initial population has been created the process of creating new generations starts and consists, typically, of three stages:

- A fitness value (measure of optimality) of each string in the random population is calculated.
- Genetic operators, corresponding to mathematical models of simple laws of nature, like reproduction, crossover and mutation are applied to the population and result in the creation of a new population.
- The new population replaces the old one.

In our case the fitness function F is a metric of similarity between data points corresponding to the same cluster divided by the similarity of data points corresponding to different clusters. Equation 3 gives the mathematical notation of the fitness function F_i corresponding to the string $Idx^{(i)}$ ($\| . \|$ refers to the second norm of a multidimensional matrix):

$$F_i = \sum_{j=1}^{N_s} \left(\frac{\sum_{K_l, K_m \in P_j^{(i)}, l \neq m} \|K_l - K_m\|}{\sum_{K_l \in P_k^i, k \neq j} \|K_l - K_p\|} \right) \tag{3}$$

The objective is to find the string that maximizes the fitness function F. The realization of the genetic operators (reproduction, mutation and crossover) is as follows:

Reproduction. The fitness function F is used in the classical "roulette" wheel reproduction operator that gives higher probability of reproduction to the strings with better fitness according to the following procedure:

1. An order number, say q, is assigned to the population strings. That is q ranges from 1 to P_N, where P_N is the size of population.
2. The sum of fitness values (F_{sum}) of all strings in the population is calculated.
3. The interval $[0 \ F_{sum}]$ is divided into P_N sub-intervals each of one being $[SF_{q-1} \ SF_q]$ where

$$SF_{q-1} = \sum_{i=1}^{q-1} F_i, \quad q > 1 \tag{4}$$

$$(SF_{q-1} = 0 \text{ for } q = 0 \text{ and } q = 1)$$

$$SF_q = \sum_{i=1}^{q} F_i, \quad \forall q \tag{5}$$

F_i is the value of fitness function for the $i - th$ string (see equation 3).

4. A random real number R_0 lying in the interval $[0 \ F_{sum}]$ is selected.
5. The string having the same order number as the subinterval of R_0 is selected.
6. Steps (4) and (5) are repeated P_N times in order to produce the intermediate population to which the other genetic operators will be applied.

Crossover. Given two strings (parents) of length N_{c-1} an integer number $1 < r < N_{c-1}$ is randomly selected. The two strings retain their gene values up to gene r and interchange the values of the remaining genes creating two new strings (offspring). Obviously the integer numbers in offspring must be reordered so as to correspond to vectors of integer values in increasing order.

Mutation. This operator is applied to each gene of a string and it alters its content, with a small probability. The mutation operator is actually a random number that is selected and depending on whether it exceeds a predefined limit it changes the value of a gene. If gene r is to be mutated, the allowable values $Idx_r^{(i)}$ for it are those in the interval ($Idx_{r-1}^{(i)} \ Idx_{r+1}^{(i)}$).

5 Conclusions and Further Work

In this paper we presented an annotation tool for Cultural Heritage documents named CulHIAT. CulHIAT can be used for annotation of digital or digitized data, including video and animations, at various levels of granularity. XML dictionaries are used as predefined lexicons while the tool provides an easy to use interface to modify these or create new dictionaries. An enormous amount of data related to the sweet Cypriot wine Commandaria was annotated using this tool with the aid of newly created XML dictionary based on the Commandaria taxonomy.

CulHIAT allows for semantic labeling using structured knowledge in the form of XML dictionaries and provides a powerful algorithm for shot detection algorithm which minimizes the human intervention for video segmentation at lowest level. In addition, with the aid of an intelligent clustering algorithm shots are grouped together to form conceptually similar video units, called scenes. Our future work includes ontology support, incorporation of key-frame selection methodologies and the automatic creation of a list of semantic labels which will be proposed to the user, for the annotation of key-frames and shots, based on machine learning processes.

Acknowledgements. This work was undertaken in the framework of The History of Commandaria: Digital Journeys Back to Time project funded by the Cyprus Research Promotion Foundation (CRPF) under the contract ANTHRO/0308(BE)/04.

References

1. Papadopoulos, K., Tsapatsoulis, N., Lanitis, A., Kounoudes, A.: The History Of Commandaria: Digital Journeys Back To Time. In: 14th International Conference on Virtual Systems and Multimedia (VSMM 2008), Limassol, Cyprus (2008)
2. Benjamins, V.R., Contreras, J., Blázquez, M., Niño, M., García, A., Navas, E., Rodríguez, J., Wert, C., Millán, R., Dodero, J.M.: ONTO-H: A collaborative semiautomatic annotation tool. In: 8th International Protégé Conference Collaborative Development of Ontologies and Applications, Madrid, Spain, pp. 69–72 (2005)
3. Lin, C.Y., Tseng, L., Smith, R.: Video Collaboration Annotation Forum: Establishing Ground-Truth Labels on Large Multimedia Datasets. In: NIST Text Retrieval Conference, TREC (2003)
4. Schreiber, A.T., Dubbeldam, B., Wielemaker, J., Wielinga, B.: Ontology-Based Photo Annotation. IEEE Intelligent Systems 16(3), 66–74 (2001)
5. Fujisawa, S.: Automatic Creation and Enhancement of Metadata for Cultural Heritage. Bull. IEEE Tech. Committee on Digital Libraries (TCDL) 3(3) (2007)
6. ISO/IEC 15938-3:2001 Information Technology - Multimedia Content Description Interface - Part 3: Visual, Version 1
7. ISO/IEC 15938-4:2001 Information Technology - Multimedia Content Description Interface - Part 4: Audio, Version 1
8. ISO/IEC 15938-5:2003 Information Technology - Multimedia Content Description Interface - Part 5: Multimedia Description Schemes, First Edition
9. Ricoh Movie Tool, website
   http://www.ricoh.co.jp/src/multimedia/MovieTool
10. Adams, W.H., Lin, C.Y., Iyengar, B., Tseng, B.L., Smith, J.R.: IBM Multimedia Annotation Tool. Technical report, IBM Alphaworks (2002)
11. Bargeron, D., Gupta, A., Grudin, J., Sanocki, E.: Annotations for Streaming Video on the Web: System Design and usage Studies. In: ACM 8th Conference on World Wide Web, pp. 1139–1153. Elsevier, North-Holland (1999)
12. Steves, M.P., Ranganathan, M., Morse, E.L.: SMAT: Synchronous Multimedia and Annotation Tool. In: 34th Hawaii International Conference on Systems Sciences (2001)
13. Nack, F., Putz, W.: Semi-automated Annotation of Audio-Visual Media in News. GMD Report 121 (2000)
14. Cultural Heritage Online (ECHO), http://www.mpi.nl/echo/
15. Lienhart, R.: Comparison of Automatic Shot Boundary Detection Algorithms. In: SPIE Storage and Retrieval for Image and Video Databases VII, San Jose, CA, USA, vol. 3656, pp. 290–301 (1999)
16. Goldberg, D.: Genetic Algorithms in Search, Optimization, and Machine Learning. Addison-Wesley, Reading (1989)

Hyperspectral Ground Truth Data for the Detection of Buried Architectural Remains

Athos Agapiou[1], Diofantos Hadjimitsis[1], Apostolos Sarris[2],
Kyriacos Themistocleous[1], and George Papadavid[1]

[1] Department of Civil Engineering and Geomatics, Faculty of Engineering and Technology,
Cyprus University of Technology, 3603, Limassol, Cyprus
{athos.agapiou,d.hadjimitsis,k.themistocleous,
g.papadavid}@cut.ac.cy
[2] Laboratory of Geophysical - Satellite Remote Sensing and Archaeo-environment, Institute for
Mediterranean Studies Foundation for Research & Technology, Hellas (F.O.R.T.H.), 74100,
Rethymno, Crete
asaris@ret.forthnet.gr

Abstract. The aim of the study is to validate hyperspectral ground data for the detection of buried architectural remains. For this reason spectro-radiometric measurements were taken from an archaeological area in Cyprus. Field spectro-radiometric measurements were undertaken from March to May of 2010. Spectro-radiometric measurements were taken over the previously detected magnetic anomalies using the GER 1500 spectroradiometer and they were found to be in a general agreement with the geophysical results. The results of the subsequent excavations which took place in the area verified partially the geophysical and spectro-radiometric measurements. However, the results obtained from the in-situ spectro-radiometric campaigns were found very useful for detecting spectral vegetation anomalies related with buried features. This is an issue which the authors will continue to investigate since it has proven that local conditions of the area, such as geology, is a key parameter for the detection of buried architectural remains.

Keywords: Spectro-radiometric measurements, hyperspectral data, detection of architectural remains.

1 Introduction

Remote Sensing techniques, including ground spectro-radiometric data, offer new perspectives in archaeological research [1-3]. High multispectral resolution satellite images indicate that changes of the spectral signature of vegetation may have occurred due to the presence of buried architectural remains. Lasaponara and Masini [4] in their study have successfully identified subsurface monuments from high multispectral resolution satellite images using spectral signature anomalies (Fig. 1). The use of hyperspectral satellite data has been applied successfully in different studies in order to identify architectural remains [5-8].

M. Ioannides (Ed.): EuroMed 2010, LNCS 6436, pp. 318–331, 2010.
© Springer-Verlag Berlin Heidelberg 2010

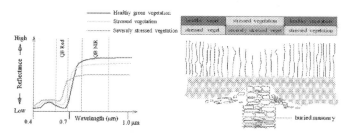

Fig. 1. Spectral signature of vegetation under certain conditions (Lasaponara R., Masini 2007, fig. 1)

However Parcak [9] noted that if soil cover is not uniform then the use of satellite hyperspectral data can be problematic. Such problems are presented from Crete in the study of Rowlands and Sarris [10].

This can be avoided if ground hyperspectral data are provided. The use of ground spectro-radiometers can minimize such errors including atmospheric absorption, scattering a.o.

The use of spectro-radiometer in not a recent development. However the novelty of this paper is based on the fact that field spectroscopy has been widely used for research in different scientific fields and applications (e.g. agricultural monitoring), yet the use of field spectroscopy for archaeological applications is still an open research question.

The first use of field radiometry was carried out by Penndorf [11] in order to study human vision. During the 1960s, many applications were carried out for the study and understanding of photosynthesis [12]. Some of these instruments were designed to capture a range of wavelength [13, 14 and 15] while other investigations were focused on specific regions of wavelengths [16].

Scientific interest later shifted to studying geological rocks [17]. Similar studies were presented by Hunt [18-19] who classified various rocks using spectral signatures. At this time the first airborne scanner was developed for monitoring vegetation and vegetation stress based on wavelength variations in the red edge range [20].

Spectroscopy fluctuations from different angles are a special case of radiometer. One such case is the PARABOLA system, which investigates the characteristics of angle- radiation in vegetation areas. A historical overview of such systems is presented in detail in Milton et al. [21].

Research by Kriebel [22] in spectral signature of vegetation indicates there is a distortion of the radiation by 1% change in the change of 1° of the zenith angle (of the sun) and also 1% change for every 10% change of the aerosol optical thickness. Robinson and Bielh [23] found a difference of about 3% of radiation at 0.5 - 0.6 mm in a hazy day (visibility = 8 Km).

Recently spectroscopy is used for taking accurate real spectral signatures which are necessary for the radiometric calibration of satellite and airborne scanners [21]. Although there are several applications which investigate the correlation of the spectral signature of an object, in the majority of the applications the aim is exactly the opposite: the study and identification of "unknown" targets through the spectral signature [12]. This process, however, requires special attention, particularly in vegetation since two different types of plants can have identical spectral signatures due to other factors [24].

2 Case Study Area

The Kouklia Palaepaphos site was selected as the case study area for application of ground spectro-radiometric measurements. It is located on the SW coast of Cyprus (Fig. 2) and is an extensive yet insufficiently defined archaeological landscape. Kouklia Palaepaphos is considered an important archaeological site since it contains many important monuments. Its few visible secular and sepulchral monuments and its famous open-air sanctuary to an aniconic deity, who was to become known as Aphrodite, are scattered over an area of two square kilometres.

In the last few years systematic archaeological investigations are carried in Palaepaphos area, following the results of geophysical surveys that were carried out in different sections of the site [25-26].

Fig. 2. Palaepaphos archaeological site (Google Earth©)

The results of the geophysical surveys identified areas of interest which contain potential subsurface monuments. One such area is in the locality of Arkalon in Kouklia, just east of the village (Fig. 3). The results showed the presence of architectural remains identified as a rectangular structure with high magnetization. Linear features appear to be aligned in N-S and W-E directions delineating a rectangular structure that extends for more than 70 m.

Fig. 3. Magnetic anomalies near Arkalon, Kouklia (Iacovou et al., 2009)

3 Methodology

In situ spectroscopy measurements were held in Arkalon during the life cycle of cereals (October to May) which are grown in the area and they were taken in locations where the geophysical anomalies were detected.

Spectro-radiometric measurements were carried out along transects above the detected anomalies (Fig. 4). The first three visits were performed when cereals were still in flower while the other two when the cereals had already begun to dry. The visits covered a two months period, from March to May of 2010. Each date is recorded in a database and a short description of weather conditions, photographs of the cereals a.o. The spectro-radiometric results are presented as spectral signatures diagrams were at the X axis is plotted the wavelength from visible to near infrared spectrum and in Y axis is the reflectance given in percentage.

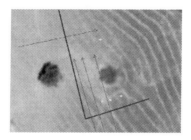

Fig. 4. Location of the transects (indicated with arrows) in which spectroscopic measurements were taken over the magnetic anomaly (indicated with lines) (background image Google Earth ©)

For the exact location of the magnetic anomalies a Global Positioning System (GPS) was used. The characteristic points indicating the possible architectural remains were identified with a precision of ± 2cm.

The radiometric instrument that was used to register the spectral signature was the GER 1500 (Fig. 5). This instrument can record electromagnetic radiation between 350 nm up to 1050 nm. It includes 512 different channels and each channel cover a range of about 1.5 nm. The field of view (FOV) of the instrument is 4°. The instrument was recently calibrated and the accuracy provided from the manufacturer of radiometric measurements was: 400nm: ± 5%, 700nm: ± 4% and 1000nm: ± 5%.

Fig. 5. GER 1500 used in this study with its calibration target

4   Spectro-Radiometric Results

4.1   In Situ Measurements 05/03/2010

The first visit was carried out in 05/ 03/2010. In this day four transects, as shown in Fig. 6, were carried out. The sections A - C were applied in the southern anomaly from west to east and the section D was performed in the N-S anomaly.

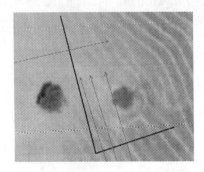

Fig. 6. Sections in 05/03/2010

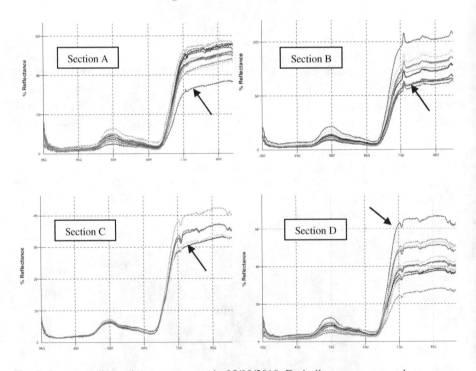

Fig. 7. Spectro-radiometric measurements in 05/03/2010. Each diagram corresponds to a cross section (A-D) while the spectral signature indicated with an arrow corresponds to the subsurface geophysical anomaly.

The spectral signatures of the sections (A-D) results are shown in Fig. 7. The measurement which corresponds to the subsurface anomaly is indicated with an arrow in the diagrams.

The results were very encouraging since in all cases a high or low reflectance was recorded which is particularly evident in the infrared wavelength (750nm). In sections A-C, which cover the southern architectural feature, the spectral radiation, tends to be lower from the surrounding area at 750 nm. Contrary to section D, related to the architectural N-S feature, spectral radiation is higher than the rest measurements along the transect.

4.2 In Situ Measurements 12/03/2010

The next visit was at 12/03/2010 and three sections were carried out (E-G). In the first section (section E) measurements were taken perpendicular to the southern anomaly, while in section F measurements were taken along the direction of subsurface anomaly. Finally, in the third section (section G) measurements were taken perpendicular to the N-S anomaly (Fig. 8).

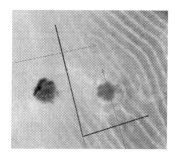

Fig. 8. Sections in 12/03/2010

The spectro-radiometric results of the sections (A-C) are shown in Fig. 9. The measurement which corresponds to the subsurface anomaly is indicated by arrow in the chart (except for section B).

An anomaly at about 750 nm was detected in section E and G where the measurements were over the magnetic anomaly. At this area the reflectance is lower than in the surrounding area. The measurements in section F, which were taken along the subsurface architectural remains, showed different variations.

Moreover, an infrared thermometer (Fluke 62 Mini) was used in order to measure the temperature of the soil (Fig. 10). The idea of this application is based on the differences of temperature that may occur due to sub-surfaces anomalies. The measurements showed that the temperature over the anomaly was one of the largest one obtained in the area of interest (Fig. 11).

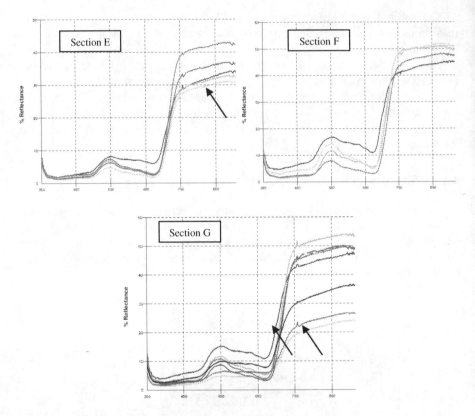

Fig. 9. Spectro-radiometric measurements in 11/03/2010. Each diagram corresponds to a cross section (E-G) while the spectral signature indicated with an arrow corresponds to the subsurface geophysical anomaly.

Fig. 10. The infrared thermometer Fluke 62 Mini

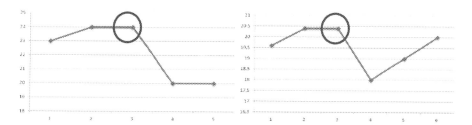

Fig. 11. Ground temperature. The measurement which corresponds to the subsurface anomaly is circled.

4.3 In Situ Measurements 24/03/2010

In the next visit to Arkalon on 24/03/2010, six spectro-radiometric measurements were carried out in cross sections (H – M) perpendicular to the southern anomaly. The diagrams of these sections are shown in Fig. 12.

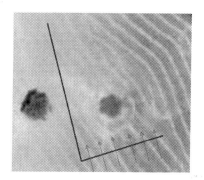

Fig. 12. Sections in 24/03/2010

The results of the spectro-radiometric measurements are shown in Fig. 13. The measurement which corresponds to the subsurface anomaly is indicated by arrow in the chart.

Five of the six spectroscopic measurements (sections H-I and sections K-M) showed that vegetation had the highest or lowest reflection in vegetated areas over the magnetic anomaly (at 750 nm). In section J, the reflectivity was greater than other measurements except one.

Infrared thermometer was also used for measuring the temperature of the ground. Five cross sections were performed over the anomaly and the measurements showed that the temperature over the anomaly was the lowest one (Fig. 14).

4.4 In Situ Measurements 28/04/2010

Subsequent measurements were conducted in 28 /04 /2010. In this period the cereals were already yellowing and measurements were made in order to determine whether the spectral signature anomaly could still be detected.

326   A. Agapiou et al.

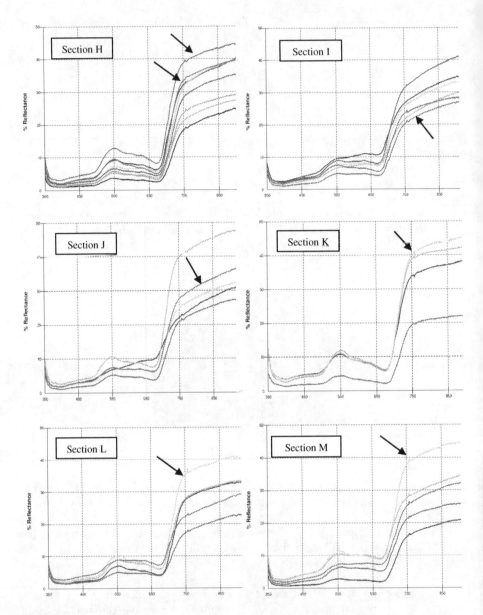

Fig. 13. Spectro-radiometric measurements in 24/03/2010. Each diagram corresponds to a cross section (H-M) while the spectral signature indicated with an arrow corresponds to the subsurface geophysical anomaly.

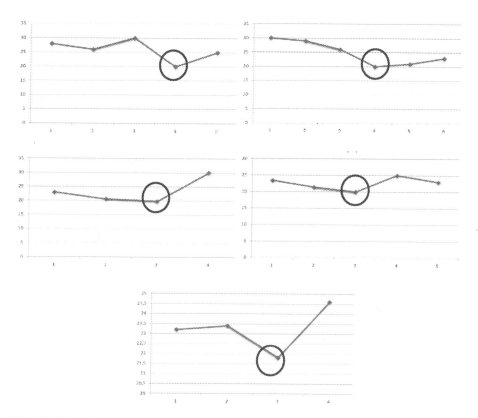

Fig. 14. Ground temperature as measured by the infrared thermometer. The measurement which corresponds to the subsurface anomaly is circled.

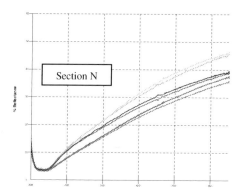

Fig. 15. Spectro-radiometric measurements in 28/04/2010. The characteristic vegetation curve in the infrared band is not apparent.

Spectroscopic measurements showed that barley had no longer the characteristic curve in the near infrared (NIR), which occurs in plants with healthy vegetation (Fig. 5).

4.5 In Situ Measurements 04/05/2010

The last measurements were made on 04/05/2010. While previous measurements (28/04/2010) had not shown encouraging results it was considered appropriate to make another visit and take more spectro-radiometric measurements since the previous days (02-03/05/2010) it was raining in the area. As it was found from the literature the days after a rain are the most appropriate for investigating an archaeological site through remote sensing techniques (Lasaponara and Masini 2007).

From the measurements (Fig. 16) it appears that in the last part of the cereal life cycle the distinction of the subsurface features was relatively difficult.

From the measurements (Fig. 16) it appears that the subsurface defection was difficult to find based on the spectral signature in the last part of the cereal life cycle.

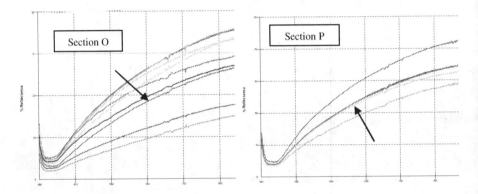

Fig. 16. Spectro-radiometric measurements in 04/05/2010. Each diagram corresponds to a cross section (O-P) while the spectral signature indicated with an arrow corresponds to the subsurface geophysical anomaly.

5 Archaeological Excavations

Archaeological excavations in Arkallon locality were carried out in June of 2010 by the Archaeological Research Unit of the University of Cyprus. Excavations squares (4 x 4 m) were carried out over different parts of the magnetic anomaly as indicated in Fig. 17.

The archaeological excavations did not confirm either the magnetic anomalies or the spectro-radiometric measurements. However in area A (Fig. 17) a small architectural remain was found. In the eastern excavation square of area B (Fig. 17) –where the spectro-radiometric measurements were taken- loose stones were found in a depth of 0.50 m. This could explain the differences occurred in the spectral signatures of the cereals.

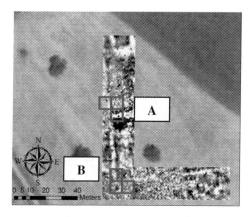

Fig. 17. Excavation squares at *Arkalon* locality

6   Conclusions

The paper aimed to introduce the ground spectroscopy capabilities for detection of buried architectural remains. It was found that spectroscopy was able to confirm the results of the geophysical surveys that have been carried out in the region. Field spectroscopy can be an alternative tool for monitoring spectral signature anomalies over vegetated areas where subsurface archaeological architectural features may exist. Moreover, field spectroscopy can support post-processing techniques intended to enhance satellite images. Ground spectro-radiometric measurements may combine with time-series multispectral satellite images and geophysical surveys in order to provide auxiliary information. However the real benefit of the use of ground spectro-radiometric data is the fact that in this way it will be able to find a "window" in the spectrum were vegetation anomalies, occurred form buried architectural remains, can be recognized. In this way satellite hyperspectral and multispectral satellite images can be used for vast archaeological areas and not only in Cyprus.

Ground infrared thermometer had shown similar results as the spectro-radiometric measurements. However the main target of the methodology applied is still open and more experiments are needed. Ground spectroscopy measurements and geophysical surveys were not verified by the archaeological excavations. This is an issue which the authors will continue to investigate since it has proven that local conditions of an area are a key parameter for the detection of buried architectural remains.

Acknowledgements

The authors would like to express their appreciation to the Remote Sensing Laboratory of the Department of Civil Engineering & Geomatics at the Cyprus University of Technology (www.cut.ac.cy). Also thanks are given to Professor Maria Iacovou, Archaeological Research Unit, University of Cyprus.

References

1. Kaimaris, D., Georgoula, O., Karadedos, G., Patias, P.: Aerial and Remote Sensing Archaeology in Eastern Macedonia, Greece. In: 22nd CIPA Symposium, Kyoto, Japan (2009) (in press)
2. Aqdus, S.A., Hanson, W.S., Drummond, J.: A Comparative Study for Finding Archaeological Crop Marks using Airborne Hyperspectral, Multispectral and Digital Photographic Data. In: 22nd CIPA Symposium, Kyoto, Japan (2009) (in press)
3. Altaweel, M.: The use of ASTER Satellite Imagery in Archaeological Contexts. Archaeological Prospection Archaeol. Prospect. 12, 151–166 (2005)
4. Lasaponara, R., Masini, N.: Detection of Archaeological Crop Marks by using Satellite QuickBird Multispectral Imagery. Journal of Archaeological Science 34, 214–221 (2007)
5. Alexakis, D., Sarris, A., Astaras, T., Albanakis, K.: Detection of Neolithic Settlements in Thessaly (Greece) Through Multispectral and Hyperspectral Satellite Imagery. Sensors 9, 1167–1187 (2009)
6. Bassani, C., Cavalli, R.M., Goffredo, R., Palombo, A., Pascucci, S., Pignatti, S.: Specific Spectral Bands for Different Land Cover Contexts to Improve the Efficiency of Remote Sensing Archaeological Prospection. The Arpi case study. Journal of Cultural Heritage 10, 41–48 (2009)
7. Masini, N., Lasaponara, R.: Investigating the Spectral Capability of QuickBird Data to Detect Archaeological Remains Buried under Vegetated and Not Vegetated Areas. Journal of Cultural Heritage 8, 53–60 (2007)
8. Cavalli, R.S., Colosi, F., Palombo, A., Pignatti, S., Poscolieri, M.: Remote Hyperspectral Imagery as a Support to Archaeological Prospection. Journal of Cultural Heritage 8, 272–283 (2007)
9. Parcak, S.H.: Satellite Remote Sensing for Archaeology. Routledge, Taylor and Francis Group, London, New York (2009)
10. Rowlands, A., Sarris, A.: Detection of Exposed and Subsurface Archaeological Remains using Multi-Sensor Remote Sensing. Journal of Archaeological Science 34, 795–803 (2007)
11. Penndorf, R.: Luminous and Spectral Reflectance as Well as Colors of Natural Objects. U.S. Air Force Cambridge Research Center, Bedford (1956)
12. Milton, E.J.: Principles of Field Spectroscopy. Remote Sensing of Environment 8(12), 1807–1827 (1987)
13. Adhav, R.S.: Wide Angle Spectroradiometer. Journal of Scientific Instruments 40(9), 455–456 (1963)
14. Brach, E.J., Wiggins, B.W.E.: A Portable Spectrophotometer for Environmental Studies of Plants. Laboratory Practise 16, 302–309 (1967)
15. Bulpitt, T.H., Coulter, M.W., Hamner, K.C.: A Spectroradiometer for the Spectral Region of Biological Photosensitivity. Applied Optics 4(7), 793–797 (1965)
16. Birth, G.S., McVey, G.R.: Measuring the Colour of Growing Turf with a Reflectance Spectrophotometer. Agronomy Journal 60, 640–643 (1968)
17. Goetz, A.F.H.: Portable Field Reflectance Spectrometer. JPL Technical Report. Pasadena, California Jet Propulsion Laboratory, California Institute of Technology, 183–188 (1975)
18. Hunt, G.: Spectral Signatures of Particulate Minerals in the Visible and Near Infrared. Geophysics 42(3), 501–513 (1977)
19. Hunt, G.: Near-infrared (1.3-2.4 pm) Spectra of Alteration Minerals- Potential for use in Remote Sensing. Geophysics 44(12), 1974–1986 (1979)

20. Milton, E.J., Schaepman, M.E., Anderson, K., Kneubühler, M., Deering, D.W.: A Sphere-Scanning Radiometer for Rapid Directional Measurements of Sky and Ground Radiance. Remote Sensing of Environment 19, 1–24 (1986)
21. Milton, E.J., Schaepman, M.E., Anderson, K., Kneubühler, M., Fox, N.: Progress in Field Spectroscopy. Remote Sensing of Environment 113, 92–109 (2009)
22. Kriebel, K.T.: Average Variability of the Radiation Reflectedby Vegetated Surfaces due to Differing Irradiations. Remote Sensing of Environment 7, 81–83 (1978)
23. Robinson, B.F., Biehl, L.L.: Calibration procedures for measurement of reflectance factor in remote sensing field research. Society of Photo-optical Instrumentation Engineers 196, 16–26 (1979)
24. Price, J.C.: How unique are spectral signatures. Remote Sensing of Environment 49, 181–186 (1994)
25. Sarris, A., Kokkinou, E., Soupios, P., Papadopoulos, E., Trigkas, V., Sepsa, U., Gionis, D., Iacovou, M., Agapiou, A., Satraki, A., Stylianides, S.: Geophysical Investigations at Palai-paphos, Cyprus. In: 36th Annual Conference on Computer Applications and Quantitative Methods in Archaeology, Budapest (2008) (in press)
26. Iacovou, M., Stylianidis, E., Sarris, A., Agapiou, A.: A Long-Term Response to the Need to make Modern Development and the Preservation of the Archaeo-Cultural Record Mutually Compatible Operations. The GIS Contribution. In: 22nd CIPA Symposium, Digital Documentation, Interpretation & Presentation of Cultural Heritage, Kyoto, Japan (2009) (in press)

Environmental and Human Risk Assessment of the Prehistoric and Historic Archaeological Sites of Western Crete (Greece) with the Use of GIS, Remote Sensing, Fuzzy Logic and Neural Networks

Dimitrios Alexakis and Apostolos Sarris

Laboratory of Geophysical – Satellite Remote Sensing & Archaeo-environment,
Institute for Mediterranean Studies, Foundation for Research & Technology,
Hellas (F.O.R.T.H.), Rethymno 74100, Crete, Greece
alexakis@chania.teicrete.gr, asaris@ret.forthnet.gr
www.ims.forth.gr

Abstract. The island of Crete is an area with continuous habitation for more than 6 thousand years consisting of a variety of archaeological sites. The vulnerability of those archaeological sites is extremely high due to the changing land-use practices and various natural disasters. The use of modern technologies such as Geographical Information Systems (GIS), Remote Sensing (RS), and Global Positioning Systems is considered to provide a valuable tool for the protection of cultural heritage from human and environmental threats. Additionally, sophisticated classification methods based on fuzzy and neural networks theory contribute to a more detailed and precise mapping of the archaeological regime of the island.

Keywords: GIS, Crete, Archaeological Sites, Fuzzy Logic, Neural Networks.

1 Introduction

Nowadays it is well known that the conservation of the archaeological heritage is endangered by different environmental and human factors such as landfills, fires, seismicity, land use practices and urbanization [2, 18]. Thus, Geographical Information Systems (GIS) are used to combine several different factors in order to proceed to the construction of a risk assessment model. The use of GIS provides the most effective methodology for such kind of integrated analysis based mainly on spatial information [1].

2 Study Area, Data and Methodology

The study area covers the western part of the island of Crete and especially the prefectures of Chania and Rethymno. It is an area with a rich record of prehistoric and historic archaeological sites. The climate of study area is sub – humid Mediterranean with humid cold winters and rather warm summers [17].

M. Ioannides (Ed.): EuroMed 2010, LNCS 6436, pp. 332–342, 2010.

Initially, digitization of 1:50,000 scale topographic and geological maps of the Geographic Service of the Hellenic Army and of the Institute of Geological and Mineral Exploration were accomplished respectively. The original Digital Elevation Model (DEM) of the study area with 20m pixel size was based on SPOT satellite stereoscopic images. The geological formations of the geological maps were reclassified and all the geomorphologic attributes and details of the above maps, such as rivers, lakes, faults and modern villages were also digitized and superimposed on the particular background layers.

3 Analysis of Environmental and Human Factors in GIS Environment

The risk assessment model was separated to two different parts regarding the environmental and the human factors. Initially, each agent was analyzed separately and at the end they were combined to provide a final risk assessment model.

3.1 Environmental Factors

The main environmental factors that were used to the risk assessment model were seismic risk, erosion risk, landslide risk, and distance from the coast. These agents have been proved to cause major problems to the archaeological relics.

3.1.1 Seismic Risk of Archaeological Sites

Crete is located on the apex of the Hellenic arc and it is characterized from the often occurrence of earthquake [9-11]. Thus, the seismic activity has been selected as one

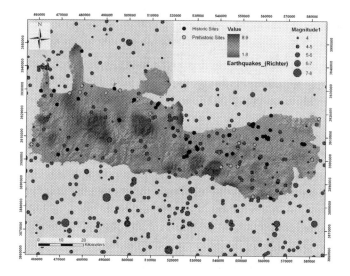

Fig. 1. Regional seismicity of Crete and application of spline interpolation method to the seismic intensity parameter

of the most crucial natural hazards that could cause severe damages to the archaeological sites of western Crete. The seismological data of the specific research were collected from the digital archives of the Aristotle University of Thessaloniki and the Geodynamic Institute of Athens. These data concerned the last century's seismic activity focusing in the wider region of Crete since May 2005. The data regarded the epicenters of earthquakes of magnitude larger than 4R and its corresponding density. The following equation was used to relate intensity with magnitude [12]: $Io = a + bM$, where a =1.23 and b=1.1 for the surficial earthquakes in the area of Greece.

In order to present the intensity factor through a continuous raster image the spline interpolation method was used (Fig. 1). In the end of the process, a sigmoidal membership monotonically increasing function based on fuzzy theory was applied to the final interpolated image to classify the values from 0 to 1 indicating a continuous increase from non membership to complete membership. Examining the statistics it was obvious that most of the archaeological sites fall inside a moderate earthquake risk zone.

3.1.2 Landslide Risk Assessment of Archaeological Sites

Landslides are considered to be extreme natural hazards worldwide, causing human losses and severe damages to the modern facilities [3, 6]. The specific study used the landslide model derived from the work that has been carried out during the course of the EMERIC project [5, 16]. Different environmental data such as geological data from the unified geological map of IGME, slope data derived from stereoscopic SPOT satellite images, hydrolithological data, average precipitation and a database of geological and tectonic faults were used for the construction of the final landslide risk assessment model.

The geologic regime of the study area is quite complicated. All the formations were digitized in GIS environment and the final map was simplified to 12 main geological formations. The great majority of archaeological sites was established on carbonate formations.

The average rainfall data of 65 meteorological stations of the National Meteorological Service and the Ministry of Agriculture for the period of 1991 – 2000 were obtained and recorded. Average annually rainfall maps were created through the use of interpolation methods to create final continuous raster maps. At the end 3 main categories of rainfall data were considered: 224-600mm, 600-1000mm and >1000mm of rain.

The landslide risk assessment model was based on a three different synthetic agent model. The first model was related with hydrolithology, precipitation and slope (M1) of the study area. Hydrolithology-precipitation relation was established by giving an increasing weight factor from gypsum and karst formations and relatively high to medium hydropermeability and low precipitation levels to non permeable formations with relatively low permeability and high levels of precipitation. Slope inclination-rainfall interaction was established by assigning a rising weight factor from lower inclination and low levels of precipitation to higher inclinations (>50 degrees) and high levels of precipitation. The algebraic multiplication of the two weighted surfaces provided the first category of landslide agents (M1).

The second agent was based on the relation between geology and inclination (M2) and the third agent was based on the relation between geology and distance from fault areas (M3). A low weight factor was applied to areas with low inclination. Medium to high weight factors were assigned to neogene formations and quaternary deposits with a relative average inclination (~30-70 degrees), while large weight factors were assigned for almost all formations (except carbonates and plattenkalk) belonging to high sloping areas. Regarding the third agent, buffer zones of 1000m and 500m were created around each active and non active tectonic fault correspondingly and the geologic regime of each buffer zone was weighted accordingly. All the fault buffer zones that were located within neogene and quaternary deposits, flysch and phyllites received a high weight risk factor.

The final landslide risk model was computed by using the below equation (Eq. 1).

$$Risk_{landslides} = a_1*M1+a_2*M2+a_3*M3 .$$ (1)

All the coefficients were specified based on past landslide occurrences in the island of Crete. In the final model, the landslide risk map was classified to three main categories, from 1 to 3, indicating the increasing landslide susceptibility (Fig. 2). At the final results, 76 sites fall within the moderate landslide risk zone and only 5 historic and 4 prehistoric sites fall inside high risk zone.

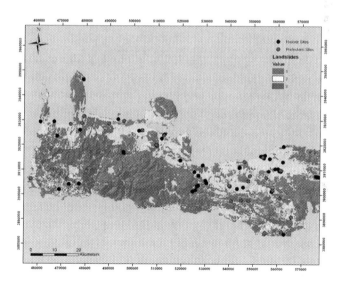

Fig. 2. Landslide risk assessment model

3.1.3 Distance of Archaeological Sites from Coast

The archaeological sites that are established along the coastlines environments are always threatened by shoreline erosion, sea wave storms, tsunamis and sea level rise [14]. In the case of the western Crete many different types of archaeological relics are close to the coast. In order to search the regime for the risk of the coastal environment, a buffer zone of 500m with a risk value of 1 was created around the coastline of western Crete with direction to the inlands (Fig. 3). Examining the statistics, 17 archaeological sites were found within this buffer zone.

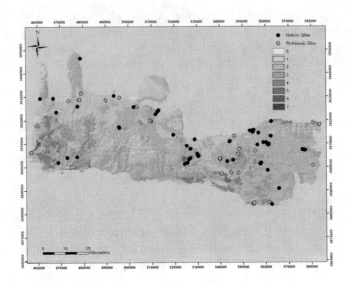

Fig. 3. Erosion risk assessment model

3.1.4 Affection of Soil Erosion to Archaeological Sites

Regarding soil erosion, the specific phenomenon should never be ignored because of its importance in affecting landscape sustainability [6, 19, 20]. However, at Crete terracing has contributed from the ancient times to decrease soil erosion rates.

Regarding the data for the specific study, all were digitized in GIS environment and the final maps were reclassified to 7 erosion rate classes (Fig. 4). The vast

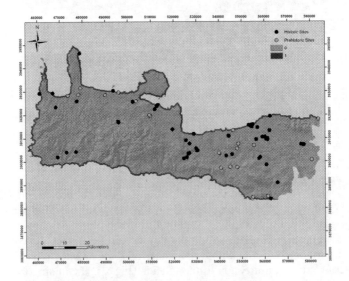

Fig. 4. Coastline risk assessment model

majority of both historic and prehistoric sites are established in low erosion risk areas. At the final raster archive, a fuzzy logic algorithm was applied to normalize the values from 0 to 1.

3.2 Human Factors

Considering the treat of cultural heritage, various parameters can be attributed to the human driven agents. The continuously expanding cities and villages, the industrialization and development works, the agricultural fires, the land use and cultivation practices, the proximity to landfills and other waste disposal areas and air pollution can be attributed as main human risk factors. In the specific model, four agents were considered, namely agricultural fires, proximity to landfills and urban and tourist centers and land use.

3.2.1 Agricultural Fires Risk Assessment

The estimation of agricultural fires risk assessment was based on the results of EMERIC project [15, 16]. Satellite imagery was used (9 Landsat-5 thematic mapper and Landsat-7 enhanced thematic mapper images period of 1985to 2003) to provide information regarding the changing vegetation patterns for the last 20 years. The images were classified to highlight changing patterns of land use, followed by an object-oriented classification to produce a digital image of vegetation types based on more than 1000 ground-control points.

The final fire risk assessment model was based on a classification of risk based on the evaluation of certain parameters such as the vegetation distribution (based on the reflectance of Landsat TM5 images at the NIR (0,76 - 0,90μm), the vegetation type (based on the object-oriented classification of the Landsat images), the fire potentiality of the major types of vegetation, the historical registries of fires (area extent and frequency) and the Digital Elevation Model (DEM). All these parameters were applied on specific training sites and three categories (low, moderate and high) of fire risk assessment were derived. These categories were further expanded to the rest of the satellite image through supervised classification algorithms. The final fire risk model was derived for the year 2010 based on the changes of the land use practices, the logarithmic increase of population, the percentages of moisture and temperature and the altitude and slope of the terrain. Finally, about 50 historic and 16 prehistoric sites were found to be located within regions with a high fire risk (Fig. 5a).

3.2.1 Proximity of Archaeological Sites to Landfills

It is well known, that landfills are seriously affecting the degradation of the landscape. However, except the national or municipal controlled landfill areas, there are also a number of illegally operating landfills that endanger the archaeological reserves and parks.

After an extensive GPS survey 55 legal or illegal landfills were registered in the prefectures of Chania and Rethymno. According to the Greek legislation, a landfill site should not be located within a distance of 500m from an archaeological site. The final landfill impact zone was created by applying a buffer zone of 500m around each landfill. At the final results, only 3 archaeological sites were found inside the specific buffer zone (Fig. 5b).

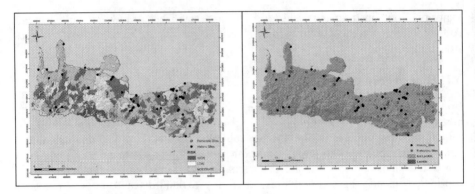

Fig. 5. (a). Fire risk assessment model. (b). Landfills risk assessment model.

3.2.3 Urbanization and Land Use Practices

During the last centuries, urbanization and agricultural cultivation seem to have an important impact on the preservation of the archaeological sites. A buffer zone of 1500m was created around towns and villages to identify the areas under urbanization pressure. About 19 sites were found to fall within these regions (Fig. 6a).

The land cover regime of the study area was examined through the use of the Corine Land Cover (CLC) database. The cartographic layers of CORINE were re-projected to the Greek Geodetic Reference System (GGRS'87) and the land use categories were reclassified to 3 levels of low, moderate and high risk. Most of the registered archaeological sites were found within the moderate risk cultivated lands (Fig. 6b).

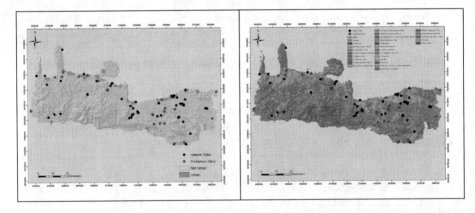

Fig. 6. (a) Urbanization risk assessment model. (b) Corine land use classification scheme.

4   Application of Fuzzy and Neural Network Algorithms to the Final Maps

After having applied a specific rating to the subcategories of each agent, the weights of significance of the variables were specified based on the statistical analysis of the risk agents in terms of the location of the archaeological sites. The environmental parameters constructed the first category including seismic activity (Se), erosion (Er), landslides (Ls) and distance from the coastline (Co), while the second category included agricultural fires (Fi), proximity to landfills (Lf), land use practices (Lp) and urban pressure (Ur). The intermediate steps involved the construction of maps (Fig. 8a and Fig. 8b) presenting the above mentioned risks, by summing up through the use of Boolean algebra the product of each category with the corresponding weight of significance (Eq. 2).

$$Environmental\ Model = 0.3*Se+0.2*Er+0.4*Ls+0.1*Co \ .$$

$$Human\ Model=0.3*Fi+0.2*Lf+0.4*Lp +0.1*Ur \ . \tag{2}$$

The final risk assessment model was computed by the sum of the environmental and anthropogenic risk maps. However, two models were created, one calculating an equal participation of the agents (50 – 50%).

In the final stage, a neural network algorithm was applied to all risk maps to provide a finer tuning of the classification. Artificial neural networks are non linear mapping structures that are mainly based on the structure of human brain [8]. A major advantage of the neural networks is that they are independent of the statistical distribution of the data used [13]. For this study, a neural network that is based on ART

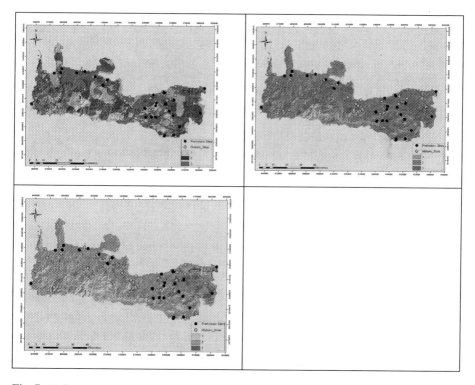

Fig. 7. (a) Environmental risk assessment model. (b) Anthropogenic risk assessment model. (c) Final risk assessment model.

Table 1. Statistical Results of the Risk Assessment of the Archaeological Sites of West Crete after the application of Neural Networks Classification Method

	Number of Prehistoric Sites	Number of Historic Sites	Sum of Sites	Risk Area (km^2)	Percent of Risk Area (%)
Environmental (Env)					
High	10	24	34	1034.5	27
Moderate	9	20	29	1482.7	39
Low	15	38	53	1296.3	34
Anthropogenic (Anthr)					
High	9	12	21	929.4	24
Moderate	11	30	41	1890.7	50
Low	14	40	54	991.6	26
0.5*(Env) + 0.5*(Anthr)					
High	11	20	31	756.1	20
Moderate	9	31	40	1647.8	43
Low	14	31	45	1407.8	37

architecture (Adaptive Resonance Theory) named fuzzy ART&ARTMAP neural network was used [9, 21]. An unsupervised fuzzy ART&ARTMAP method was applied so as the final network to be composed from 2 different layers: The input layer (F1) that receives the input data and the recognition layer (F2) that stores the final classes (clusters). The number of F2 neurons is automatically determined so as the F2 layer can begin with few layers and can grow in greater number during the learning procedures [4].

After applying several different vigilance parameters to each image, ten different classes were produced. The first 4 classes (0-4) were categorized to low risk rate, the three next (5-7) to moderate risk rate and the final 3 (8-10) to high risk rate (Fig. 7a Fig. 7b, Fig. 7c). The final results of the classification regarding the risk areas and their relationship to archaeological sites are demonstrated in Table 1.

5   Conclusions

This study brought out the fact that human and environmental factors can contribute with equal or different percentage to the degradation of archaeological monuments. Human factors such as agricultural fires and urbanization expansion may contribute to the degradation of the cultural landscape. On the other hand environmental factors such as earthquakes and landslides can provoke violent and severe damages to the sites. Regarding the final results, the environmental risk model recorded most of the high level risk areas to be located mainly in the plain regions of western Crete. However, there was not any clear demarcation of the areas with high level of human driven risk.

The results of this study can be used as a road map for taking specific actions regarding the protection of the archaeological monuments in the island of Crete. The application of fuzzy ART&ARTMAP algorithm proved to be really efficient, making the final classified results more unbiased for archaeological interpretation.

Additionally, it is really important to mention that a high percent (more than 50%) of the archaeological sites are established to moderate high risk areas. The GIS module used in this study provides the opportunity to the researchers to enter flexible more and different parameters to the final model.

Acknowledgements

This research made use of data obtained from the scientific projects "Digital Crete: Mediteranean Cultural Itineraries" and " Development of an expert system for the Monitoring, Management and Protection of the Natural Landscape and Environmental Resources of the Island of Crete (CRINNO EMERIC I)" that were funded by the Prefecture of Crete and the European Union.

References

1. Canuti, P., Casagli, N., Catani, F., Fanti, R.: Hydrogeological hazard and risk in archaeological sites: some case studies in Italy. Journal of Cultural Heritage 1, 117–125 (2000)
2. Carlon, C., Marcomini, A., Fozzati, L., Scanferlal, P., Bertazzon, S., Bassal, S., Zanovello, F., Stefano, F., Chiarlo, R., Penzo, F.: ArcheoRisk: a Decision Support System on the Environmental Risk for Archeological Sites in the Venice Lagoon. In: Proceedings of the 1st Biennial Meeting of the iEMSs, Lugano, Switzerland (2002)
3. CEOS DMSP Report.: Earth Observation for Landslide Hazard Support. In The use of Earth Observing Satellites for Hazard Support: Assessments & Scenarios: Final Report of the Committee on Earth Observation Satellites - Disaster Management Support Group (2002), http://disaster.ceos.org/DMSGFinalReport.cfm
4. Eastman, R.: IDRISI Andes Guide to GIS and image processing. Clark Labs, Clark University, Worcester, USA (2006)
5. Fassoulas, C., Georgila, K., Sarris, A., Kokkinaki, M.: Geohazard Risk Assesment based on the evaluation of Cretan faults, Crete-Greece. In: The 6th International Symposium on Eastern Mediterranean Geology & The 9th International Conference of Jordanian Geologists Association, Amman, Jordan (2007)
6. IGOS GEOHAZARDS: GEOHAZARDS theme report: For the Monitoring of our Environment from Space and from Earth. European Space Agency (ESA) publication (2004)
7. Jiao, J.Y., Tzanopoulos, J., Xofis, P., Mitchley, J.: Factors affecting distribution of vegetation types on abandoned cropland in the hilly-gullied Loess Plateau region of China. Pedosphere 18(1), 24–33 (2008)
8. Mas, J., Puig, H., Palacio, J.L., Lopez, A.: Modelling deforestation using GIS and artificial neural networks. Environmental Modelling and Software 19, 461–471 (2004)
9. Lopes, M., Minussi, C., Lotufo, A.: Electric load forecasting using a fuzzy ART&ARTMAP neural network. Applied Soft. Computing 5, 235–244 (2005)
10. Monaco, C., Tortorici, L.: Faulting and effects of earthquakes on Minoan archaeological sites in Crete (Greece). Tectonophysics 382, 103–116 (2004)

11. McKenzie, D.: Active tectonics of the Mediterranean region, Geophys. J. R. Astron. Soc. 30, 109–185 (1978)
12. Papaioannou, Ch. A.: Attenuation of seismic intensities and seismic hazard in Greece and surrounding area, PhD thesis, University of Thessaloniki (1984)
13. Pradhan, B., Lee, S., Buchroithner, M.: A GIS based back-propagation neural network model and its cross application and validation for landslide susceptibility analyses. Computers Environments and Urban Systems 34, 216–235 (2010)
14. Robinson, M., Alexander, C., Jackson, C., McCabe, C., Crass, D.: Threatened Archaeological, Historic and Cultural Resources of the Georgia Coast: Identification, Priorization and Management Using GIS technology. Geoarchaeology 25(3), 312–326 (2010)
15. Sarris, A., Vallianatos, F., Georgila, K., Karathanasi, V., Kokkinaki, L., Lazaridou, O., Mertikas, S., Papadakis, G., Papadopoulos, N., Papazoglou, M., Pyrintsos, S., Savvaidis, A., Soupios, P., Trigkas, V., Fassoulas, C.: Δια-δικτυακή Πύλη των Φυσικών Διαθεσίμων της Κρήτης. In: Karanikolas, N. (ed.) Proceedings of the 9th National Conference on Cartography: Cartography of Networks – Cartography through Networks, pp. 321–340. Ziti (2006) (in Greek)
16. Sarris, A.: Management of Landscape & Natural Resources through Remote Sensing & GIS. In: The International Society for Optical Engineering, SPIE Newsroom (2007), http://newsroom.spie.org/x6173.xml
17. Soupios, P., Kouli, M., Vallianatos, F., Vafidis, A., Stavroulakis, G.: Estimation of aquifer hydraulic parameters from surficial geophysical methods: A case study of Keritis Basin in Chania (Crete – Greece). Journal of Hydrology 338, 122–131 (2007)
18. Taboroff, J.: Cultural Heritage and Natural Disasters: Incentives for Risk Management and Mitigation. In: Managing Disaster Risk in Emerging Economies. Disaster Risk Management, vol. 2, pp. 71–79. World Bank, Washington (2008)
19. Wang, K., Wang, H.J., Shi, X.Z., Weindorf, D.C., Yu, D.S., Liang, Y., Shi, D.M.: Landscape analysis of dynamic soil erosion in Subtropical China: A case study in Xingguo County, Jianxi Province. Soil and Tilage Research 105(2), 313–321 (2009)
20. Wilson, G.V., McGregor, K.C., Boykin, D.: Residue impacts on runoff and soil erosion for different corn plant populations. Soil & Tillage Research 99, 300–307 (2008)
21. Xu, Z., Jianping, X., Tielin, S., Wu, B., Hu, Y.: Application of a modified fuzzy ARTMAP with feature-weight learning for the fault diagnosis of bearing. Expert Systems with Applications 36, 9961–9968 (2009)

The Digital Archive of Sculptures of Tien-Shen Poo in Early Taiwan History

Ying-Hsiu Huang

Department of Industrial Design, Tung-Hai University, Taichung, Taiwan
yinghsiu@thu.edu.tw

Abstract. The traditional sculptures with posture and beauty are created by the fingers of sculptors, and these traditional techniques cannot be replaced by contemporary computer technologies. However, based on the development of 3D scanning technology, computers have more influences on sculptures. In terms of preservation, the sculptures can be permanently preserved in the form of a computer triangular mesh surface, which could be stored and distributed in any digital formats, and also can be replicated by rapid prototyping or computer automatic cutting. The aim of this project intends to permanently preserve four serious sculptures of a famous sculptor, Mr. Tien-Seng Poo, from the early Taiwan history. In addition, this project is not only proposing a standard process from 3D scanning to texture mapping, but also demonstrating some applications of exhibition, such as virtual reality, augmented reality, and rapid prototype, at the end of this project.

Keywords: Digital Archives, 3D Scanning, Virtual Reality, Augmented Reality, Poo Tien-Seng.

1 Introduction

In the past decade, there are more and more organization of governments and educational institutes interesting in preserving historical and cultural heritages around the world by varieties of methods and devices. The major methods and equipment for documenting and surveying of historical and cultural heritages are: traditional manual methods, topographic methods, photogrammetric methods, and scanning methods [1]. Real 3D objects can be reconstructed automatically by using 3D scanning methods with the significant advantages of their high accuracy in geometry measurements [2]. Moreover, Blais [3] has evaluated various commercial range scanning systems. In General, most of the scanning methods demand a series of sequent steps for object geometric and texture acquisition and registration.

Due to the well-developed of 3D scanning technologies in contemporary computer graphics [4], a variety of 3D scanning methodologies have proposed major solutions for generating realistic detailed 3D replicas. Real objects or elements usually could be scanned and formatted by using triangulated meshes, supported by all commercial 3D graphics hardware and software. On the other hand, in the process of texture acquisition, Bernardini and Rushmeier [5] have addressed some mapping techniques onto the

M. Ioannides (Ed.): EuroMed 2010, LNCS 6436, pp. 343–355, 2010.
© Springer-Verlag Berlin Heidelberg 2010

geometric model. By doing so, their method not only could exploit images of the object acquired by digital camera from different angles of viewpoints, and reconstruct the geometric model by using photogrammetry, but also is a low-cost and useful method when direct access to the object is not allowed.

Although several methods for 3D digitization could archive high geometric resolution of cultural artifacts, there are still some weaknesses of mapping high textural resolution on complicated historical objects, such as sculptures, for digital preservation and virtual exhibition. This project attempts to form a stand process from 3D scanning to high textural mapping for historical sculptures of a famous sculptor in early Taiwan history. Therefore, a complete process from 3D scanning of real sculptures to texture mapping of multiple-angle of viewpoints, and to virtual museum and their applications, will also be proposed at the end of this project.

2 Mr. Tien-Seng Poo

Mr. Tien-seng Poo is a famous deceased sculptor from the early periods in Taiwan. He is mainly famous his bronze sculptures of half-length portraits, such as the sculptures of the Father of Chinese, Dr. Sun Yat-sen, in front of Zhongshan Hall, the late president, Chiang Kai-shek, on Dunhua Road, Wu Feng in Chiayi, etc. By cooperating with Professor Hao-ming Poo (the eldest son of Tien-seng Poo), this projects uses 3D technology to digitalize and preserve the works of Mr. Poo. In addition, the "Virtual Sculpture Gallery of Mr. Tien-seng Poo" is constructed to exhibit the works of Mr. Poo, via virtual space.

Mr. Tien-seng Poo was born in Chiayi, Taiwan in 1912. At the age of 19, he went to Japan to learn sketching and painting Nihonga (one kind of old Japan drawings), and he eventually transferred to the division of sculpture. He was one of the earliest Taiwanese artists to study abroad in Japan. He created more than 200 pieces of sculptures in his life. The works in his early days, such as "Wife" (Fig. 1, left), created in 1941 for his wife in their second year of marriage, which presented simplicity and soft outlines textured in mud, and expressed his love for his wife.

Fig. 1. Left: Wife (1941, bronze 24×11×10cm); Right: Child Carrying A Dog (the third son carrying a dog, 1956, bronze 35×19×20cm)

Some of his works were inspired by his life, for example, Child Carrying A Dog (Fig. 1, right) was created during a leisure afternoon when Mr. Poo asked his third son, who was carrying a Pekingese, to remain still, and used mud to create the sculpture. Although it was an improvisation, the sculpture revealed good posture and smooth lines.

In 1996, at the age of 85, Mr. Poo completed his last piece of art, a memorial bronze statue of teacher Ching-chuan Lin. He spent four years, five months, and 15 days to create the work, which is now erected in Zhingshan Art Park nearby the Taipei Fine Arts Museum. Mr. Poo died of gastric cancer at the National Taiwan University Hospital on May 31 at the age of 85. He created as many as 223 pieces in his life, including the categories of family, personage, animal, outdoor memorial statues, a gymnastic series, and memorial head statues. The processes of the digitalization of 3D scanning required a great deal of labor and equipment; therefore, a total of 56 small-scale sculpture pieces were scanned first, including 11 pieces of family sculptures, 19 pieces of personage sculptures, 16 pieces of animal sculptures, and 10 pieces of the gymnastic serial sculptures.

Table 1. Statistical table of the works of Tien-seng Poo (arranged by Hao-ming Poo and Yi-chun Poo in July, 2006)

No.	Categories	Number
1	Family	11
2	Personage	19
3	Animal	16
4	Gymnastic	10
	Subtotal (1+2+3+4)	**56 scanned in this project**
5	Outdoor	14
6	Body	63
7	Head	90
	Total	223 total

The project for building the digital archive of Tien-seng Poo includes three stages. The first stage is the 3D scanning and digitalization of sculptures. The second stage is the 3D texture mapping. The final stage is the presentation and application of digitalized sculptures. The procedures of the project are arranged as follows: (Fig. 2)

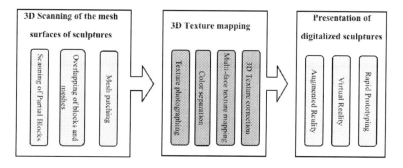

Fig. 2. Arrangement of the project procedures

3   3D Scanning of the Mesh Surfaces of Sculptures

The main purpose of the first stage is to employ 3D scanning technology to convert the sculptures into triangular mesh surfaces in the computer, which are permanently preserved, undamaged by time or environment. As for the process and technology of 3D scanning of sculptures, there are different operating procedures for different scanners. In terms of the project, the 3D scanning of mesh surfaces could be divided into four steps, namely, the scanning of partial blocks, adjustments of relevant positions of the blocks and meshes, automatic overlapping of blocks and meshes, and mesh patching.

3.1   Scanning of Partial Blocks

The 3D scanner utilizing in this project is Desktop 3D Scanner, made by NextEngine Inc. (http://www.nextengine.com) (Fig. 3). The scanning field is ranging from 5.1" x 3.8" (Macro) with 400 DPI to 13.5" x 10.1" (Wide) with 150 DPI. The dimensional accuracy are ±0.005" in Macro Mode, and ±0.015" in Wide Mode. In addition, there is no limitation on the size of sculpture by using composite-captured software, ScanStudio™.

Fig. 3. Desktop 3D Scanner by NextEngine Inc. (http://www.nextengine.com)

Therefore, the difficulty in 3D scanning sculptures is that one sculpture cannot be entirely scanned in one step because it is a 3D object. Moreover, there is a restriction on the scanning area of the scanner itself. Therefore, in the scanning step of partial blocks, a sculpture would be divided into three or four layers in order to conduct a preliminary scan (Fig. 4, left). In addition, a single circle scan of each layer must be conducted prior to continuing with the next step of adjustments of positions. However, at present, some scanners are equipped with a mechanical device to rotate the object being scanned, which achieves the completion of scanning 3D mesh surfaces in one step. However, such scanners are very expensive.

After completing the scanning of three or four layers, there remained many faces that could not be scanned, such as the hindbrain and mandible of Fig. 4 (left), and many parts had to be rescanned alone by adjusting the scanning angles. After obtaining the mesh data, and the meshes of specific parts by multilayered scanning, the adjustment of positions are conducted in the next step.

3.2 Overlapping of Blocks and Meshes

The second step in constructing the 3D mesh surfaces is to adjust the 3D spatial positions of the meshes of different partial blocks, and assembling them (Fig. 4, Right). The more advanced 3D scanning equipments, as mentioned above, could automatically assemble layers of mesh surfaces. However, the scanning equipment used in this project required more time to adjust the mesh surfaces prior to the automatic overlapping of computer formed circles of mesh surfaces.

Fig. 4. Left: Scanning of three-layer mesh model; Right: Adjusting and assembling meshes

3.3 Mesh Patching

After the automatic connection of mesh surfaces by the computer, many meshes still lacked mesh data, which are known as broken meshes. Therefore, the major purpose

Fig. 5. Digitalized sculpture after the completion of scanning

of the final step of 3D scanning of sculptures is to patch the broken meshes. The deficiency in the mesh surfaces could be calculated by the mesh data surrounding the broken surface; however, meshing patching can only be used to patch the smaller broken surfaces. If a broken surface is too large, Step 1 must be re-initiated to conduct rescanning, readjusting, and repeat the overlap by computer. The entire triangular mesh of the sculpture is completed (Fig. 5).

4   3D Texture Mapping

After scanning of geometric mesh in previous section, the next step is to match high-resolution texture on the digitalized sculptures. However, all the relevant scanning equipment at present fails to deal with texture integration with different viewpoints during or after scanning mesh surfaces. Therefore, in this project, another 3D software application, Maya, is used to conduct texture mapping, as different 3D editing software has different procedures and effects for texture processing. According to the test results of this study, the effects of Maya software were the best. Therefore, Maya software is used for the stage of texture mapping, which includes the steps of texture photographing, model import, color separation, texture mapping of six faces, and texture correction of 3D painter.

4.1   Texture Photographing

In the first step of texture mapping, in a studio with good lighting, the five cube faces of the sculpture are photographed first, namely, front, back, left, right, and top, respectively (Fig. 6), which are photographed under the simulated lighting of the actual exhibition space, with a high resolution professional digital camera. In order to reduce the weight of the sculpture, most of the sculptures are hollow; therefore, there is no need to photograph the bottom of the face.

Fig. 6. Photographs of the front, back, left, right, and top face surfaces from a front view

4.2   Color Separation of the Model

After taking pictures of the five faces of the sculpture, the high-density mesh model from the previous step is changed to a more appropriate mesh number. The file is converted to the .obj file format and imported to the Maya software to conduct the texture mapping of the five faces. During the process of texture photography, the front plane projections of the x, y, and z axis are used as a baseline, in order to facilitate the use of texture mapping in the current step. Therefore, prior to the mesh model being imported to the Maya software, the color separation of textures is first conducted. The blocks for color separation are determined by the shooting angle of the front, back, left, right, and top faces (Fig. 7).

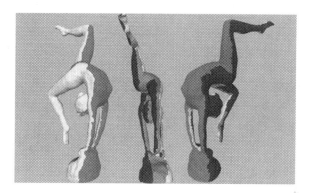

Fig. 7. Blocks for color separation of the model

4.3 Multi-face Texture Mapping

After completing the color separation of the model, the texture mapping from the five photographed faces is imported to the 3D software in order to conduct multi-face texture mapping. During the mapping, the texture mapping of the five faces is set for different textures and properties, and is mapped to different colors according to the color separation model of the previous step. However, it takes time to adjust the mapping in this step as the computer cannot automatically determine the relationships between textures and mesh surfaces (Fig. 8, left). It could be inferred that it requires the human eyes to determine and adjust the mapping texture to the position of the mesh surfaces. After each multi-face texture is adjusted, the multi-face texture mapping step is complete (Fig. 8, right). However, there could be problems with uneven lighting or seams among the different textures, which are solved in the next step.

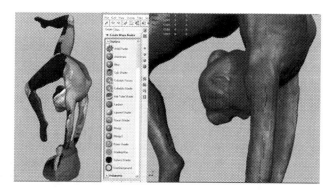

Fig. 8. Left: Mapping textures of different properties to different mesh surfaces; Right: Completed graph of multi-face texture mapping

4.4 Texture Correction of 3D Painter

During the texture photography of 4.1, multi-angle pictures are taken from the front view without changing the light source, which is in an attempt to simulate the exhibition. However, in 3D software, after different pictures mappings are imported, there remains an unevenness of multiple textures or significant seams (Fig. 9, left). The 3D painter of the 3D software can patch unevenness and seam textures of similar colors by using the spray gun. The final step is the completion of the texture mapping of the entire sculpture (Fig. 10).

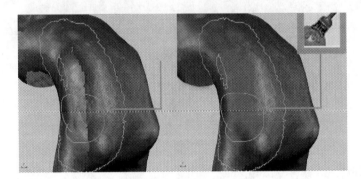

Fig. 9. Left: Unevenness and significant seams among different textures; Right: Textures after correction

Fig. 10. Completion of the texture mapping of the entire sculpture

5 The Digitalized Sculptures

In this project, we have completed 56 pieces of sculptures by 3D-scanning process in previous section. There are four series of sculptures, including Family, Personage, Gymnastic, and Animal series. All oh them have been scanned in this 3D-scan project. The following sections are representing them after 3D-scanning and texturing in 3D software.

5.1 Family Serial

There are 11 pieces of sculptures in the Family serial (Fig. 11), which are about family members of Mr. Tien-Seng Poo, including his wife, mother, father, sons, daughters…etc..

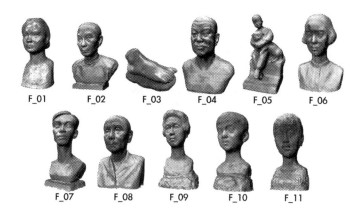

Fig. 11. The 3D-scanned and texture mapped sculptures of Family serial

5.2 Personage Serial

In this Personage serial, there are several famous people in Taiwan and China histories (Fig. 12), such as Dr. Sun Yat-Sen (P_10, the Father of R.O.C.), Confucius (P_11), Wang Chen-chu, (P_12, the first Taiwanese playing baseball in Japan)…etc..

Fig. 12. The 3D-scanned and texture mapped sculptures of Personage serial

5.3 Gymnastic Serial

Mr. Tien-Seng Poo was familiar in expressing the details of human postures (Fig. 13), and animals (Fig. 14). In this project, there are 10 pieces of Gymnastic serial and 16 pieces of Animal serial (next section), respectively.

Fig. 13. The sculptures of Gymnastic serial

5.4 Animal Serial

Fig. 14. The 3D-scanned and texture mapped sculptures of Animal serial

6 Presentation of Digitalized Sculptures

In terms of the presentation of sculptures after digitalization, different technologies have different presentation methods [7]. Three different technologies are used to present the sculptures of Mr. Tien-seng Poo, including augmented reality, virtual reality, and rapid prototyping. However, this project is focusing on the introduction of digitization process from 3D scanning to high solution texture mapping. We only briefly illustrate the results of three kinds of presentations, but not the details of them.

6.1 Augmented Reality (AR)

In an augmented reality environment, users can use the Head-Mounted Display (HMD) to watch the digitalized sculptures in a real environment. In addition, users can change visual angles and distances to watch the digitalized sculptures. The exhibition of augmented reality is constructed based on the augmented reality environment software "ARToolKits" developed by "HIT Lab" of the Washington University. The digitalized 3D sculptures are presented through stereo glasses, with the training of image identification and real-time 3D display [8]. In this way, users can freely change the visual angles to watch sculptures at different angles. With the changes in distance between users and images, the details of the sculptures can be observed. Therefore, as opposed to general exhibition environments, users can closely interact with the sculptures.

Fig. 15. Exhibition environment of augmented reality (AR)

6.2 Virtual Reality (VR)

In the virtual reality of the big screen, after computer-generated imagery is utilized to digitalize the actual exhibition scenes and sculptures, the computer-simulated exhibition space of the actual environment enables users to feel "immersed" [9]. Two projectors simulate two images of binocular disparity, which it projects onto a 210cm x 300cm large-scale screen. Then, wearing polarized 3D glasses, users can manipulate a wireless remote control of the virtual reality system environment to move freely within the virtual exhibition area, for a feeling of being immersed in the virtual space with the 3D sculptures.

Fig. 16. Exhibition space of virtual reality

6.3 Rapid Prototyping (RP)

Current reverse engineering is introduced by the field of product design, and has considerable applications in different design fields, such as architectural design and accessories design. In addition to digitalizing the sculptures of Mr. Poo, another major purpose of this project is to promote the art of sculpture through digitalized sculptures. Therefore, in addition to exhibitions in real and virtual spaces, another approach, called rapid prototyping, is used to replicate the full or reduced size of digitalized sculptures in order to achieve the effects of promotion.

In addition, during the process of creating sculptures, each piece of work is unique, and even when a sculptor replicates a work, the replication cannot be the same as the original. However, with the technology of rapid prototyping, identical sculptures can be replicated, in both reduced and full-sized sculptures for different needs.

Fig. 17. Rapid prototyping

7 Conclusions

Consequently, in order to digitally archive of the sculptures of Mr. Poo through 3D scanning technology, the standard procedure for 3D geometric scanning and high-resolution texture mapping are presented in this project. Although the 3D scanning technologies are well-developed for commercial purpose, digital preservations of historical and cultural heritages are still labor and time consuming works depending on varieties of target heritages. Moreover, three different technologies in this project are used to present the digitalized sculptures.

Furthermore, with the release of new scanning technologies and equipments, the efficient and accuracy can easily be promoted, and updated software functions may make it more convenient to operate the software. Such new technologies, platforms of virtual reality, software, and presentation methods may be more suitable for exhibiting virtual sculptures, and present research directions for aggressive future investigation.

Regarding future research directions, in addition to constructing the virtual gallery for the digitalized sculptures of Mr. Poo, presented via the internet platform of virtual reality (e.g. Secondlife), this study aims to enable the global neighborhood to observe and appreciate the sculptures of Mr. Poo, under a variety of preferred circumstances, such as hosting a simultaneous global press conference.

Acknowledgements

This project is supported by National Science Council in Taiwan - NSC 99-2631-H-029 -001. The authors of this project would like to thank the family of Mr. Tien-seng Poo, Professor Hao-ming Poo, and Mr. Hao-chi Poo for their support, and provision of the works of Mr. Poo for 3D scanning.

References

1. Scherer, M.: About the synthesis of different methods in surveying. In: XVIII International Symposium of CIPA, Potsdam, Germany, pp. 423–429 (2002)
2. Pavlidis, G., Koutsoudis, A., Arnaoutoglou, F., Tsioukas, V., Chamzas, C.: Methods for 3D digitization of cultural heritage. J. Cult. Herit. 8, 93–98 (2007)
3. Blais, F.: Review of 20 years of range sensor development. J. Electron. Imaging 13, 231–240 (2004)
4. Blais, F., Beraldin, J.-A.: Recent developments in 3D multi-modal laser imaging applied to cultural heritage. Mach. Vis. Appl. 17, 395–409 (2006)
5. Bernardini, F., Rushmeier, H.: The 3D model acquisition pipeline. Comput. Graph. Forum. 21, 149–172 (2002)
6. Shiaw, H., Jacob, R.J.K., Crane, G.R.: The 3D vase museum: a new approach to context in a digital library. In: Proceedings of ACM/IEEE Conference on Digital Libraries (JCDL 2004), Tucson, Arizona, USA, pp. 125–134 (2004)
7. Huang, Y.H., Wang, P.S.: The comparisons of interactive demos and cognitive behaviors in the virtual environments by representing 3D artifacts. In: Proceeding of 26th 2008 eCAADe Conference, Antwerpen, Belgium, pp. 375–382 (2008) ISBN 978-0-9541183-7-2
8. Prince, S., Williamson, T., Cheok, A., Farbiz, F., Billinghurst, M., Kato, H.: 3-D Live: Real-Time Interaction for Mixed Reality. In: Proceedings of the ACM Conference on Computer Supported Collaborative Work, CSCW 2002 (2002)
9. Cruz-Neira, C., Sandin, D.J., DeFanti, T.A.: Surround-Screen Projection-Based Virtual Reality: The design and Implementation of the CAVE. In: Proceedings of ACM SIGGRAPH 1993 Conference, pp. 135–142 (1993)

E.Stone, an Archive for the Sardinia Monumental Witnesses

Giorgio Verdiani[1] and Stefano Columbu[2]

[1] Dept. Architettura: Disegno - Storia - Progetto, Facoltà di Architettura, Firenze, Italy
giorgio.verdiani@unifi.it
[2] Dept. Scienze della Terra, Facoltà di Scienze Matematiche Fisiche e Naturali,
Università di Cagliari, Italy
columbus@unica.it

Abstract. The "E.Stone" project is based on the survey, documentation investigation and physical, geochemical and petrographic characterisation of the great zoomorphic and phytomorphic stones of Sardinia. The name chosen to indicate this project means the full value of these stones, standing before the beginning of human history. The main task of this project is to survey and to document, with an accurate laserscan survey, supported by topographical survey and integrated by GPS tracing and photographic and photogrammetric survey and supported by specific investigations on the rock characteristics. The further development of the collected data will be aimed to the definition of a digital "state of the knowledge" about the stone. This research will produce two main benefits: the creation of a clear and stable archive of these monuments and on the second hand will create the possibility to reply at any distance, a copy in any material of the original item.

Keywords: Stones, Sardinia, Landscape, Laserscan, Survey, Geology, Decay, Modelling, Documentation.

1 The E.Stone Archive

1.1 Background

In the world of humanity there are two kinds of processes which are always present: the natural processes and the anthropic processes. These manifestations taken different times and conditions to evolve; some of these mutations are clearly visible in a human lifetime, others take few instants, while certain requires millenniums or even millions of years to complete their cycle. In this way if we think to a stone on a seaside, sculpted by the sea and by the wind, it comes immediately clear how long it will remain at its place and in its conditions if compared to a bare foot impression left by a man on the sand: the simple human sign will have a duration of some seconds or maybe of some minutes, the first wave will erase the trace. But even with this meaningful difference, in our time we are able to damage or even completely demolish the whole patrimony of monumental rocks which is richly present in the Sardinia Island. Sardinia is the larger Island in the Mediterranean Sea and is the place some meaningful natural masterpieces, in some

M. Ioannides (Ed.): EuroMed 2010, LNCS 6436, pp. 356–372, 2010.

cases this curious and fascinating stones are enriched by the work of men (like it is for the Elephant Stone where some "Domus de Janas"/"Fairy House", a specific kind of ancient tombs, were carved in the prehistoric age). The fact that Sardinia Island shows very ancient rocks, with some formation coming from an age far more then 500 millions of years from our time, create a great emphasis about these stones, giving to the observer a great impression which goes far behind the simple surprise happening in front of some natural wonder.

The name chosen for this project is "E.Stone, an Archive for the Sardinia Monumental Witnesses", the reason for this choice are first of all linked to the specific approach to the research, which is based on advanced digital tools, so the "E" of "Electronic" is placed in front of the word "Stone" written in English also in the Italian version of the name to underline the intention to share and to disseminate these contents at an international level. The term "Witnesses" is used according to the word often used in geology to refer to the rocks testifying a previous condition. The use of the term "monuments" should be understood in its value described in the definition of the Treccani vocabulary: "[...] to indicate what, for its size, is giving an impression of grandeur and solemnity [...]".

Fig. 1. The stone and the footstep, two different times

1.2 Documentation and Dissemination

To allow the preservation of these monuments the first step is knowledge, but not only as a theoretical work ending in itself but as a passage of awareness based on a dissemination process. The tools available today make it easier and more versatile than ever before. In this way, this particular monument will be treated like they deserve, like any other monument from the earth heritage, giving to the "monumental witnesses" their right value and preserving their memory from the risk of deterioration and decay, creating the right conditions for knowledge and protection.

The digital survey tools and the advanced investigation solutions combined with high-tech multimedia presentation may found in three-dimensional modelling the right place to be focused, with the opportunity to realize different levels of learning. The creation of a repository of knowledge based on accessible criteria and three-dimensional access, will in time allow to repair or even to rebuild, if necessary, even when the monument should be seriously damaged.

Procedures based on a wide digital approach, from a massive use of laserscan survey to the digital modelling aimed to produce multimedia contents, can simultaneously be a process of effective disclosure of this environment, allowing users from all over the world to view, study, explore these monuments and learn more about the territory that they have all around.

The possibility to use both the current prototyping techniques to produce partial or total reproduction of these items in different material can operate in three main areas: the creation of "spare parts" for the monument, the reconstruction of the monument, and the easy and effective deployment in museums, exhibition areas or schools where the visitor will be able to touch the shapes of the monument. (and this will be a great occasion for the blind or visually impaired as well as for the people with normal sight), in this way, developing well oriented models, it will be possible to disassemble, to understand, to build innovative learning paths based on digital/physical models.

1.3 Decay Analysis for the Monumental Witness

Through the study of the geomaterials which are the natural constituents of the monuments of high historical and cultural significance examined here, it will be possible to evaluate the state of alteration and the causes that may have led the chemical and physical alteration. The intent will be to further investigate these issues, trying, on the basis of the results, to propose strategies for the conservation operating before then any catastrophic issue can take place. Operationally, all the monuments will be studied in detail about their minero-petrographic and physical characteristics, including various forms of macroscopic alterations and their distribution in the same monuments.

1.4 The E.Stone Project

If adequate resources will be found, the project will develop a first program of one year, at the starting phase of the project it will be immediately activated an Internet space to allow collaboration between the research teams. Within the first six months of activity the main campaigns of survey and documentation will start, inclusive of sampling and study of geomaterials from the monuments, the archive will begin to be formed immediately and simultaneously, together with the progress of the treatment and study of the collected data.

A first task in the survey campaign will be the completion of the documentation about some of the main witnesses of Sardinia, including: Elephant Stone near Castelsardo (surveyed in 2006), the Bear stone in Palau, the remains of the turtle stone and of the other stones with zoomorphic or phytomorphic shapes around San Teodoro, the remains of the Columns and Mushroom stone (this one surveyed in 2010) on the island of San Pietro (Carloforte), the red rocks of Arbatax, the "Pipe organ" of Guspini, Punta Goloritzè (Baunei), S'Archittu (the small arch) near Santa Caterina Pittinuri (Cuglieri), the monolith (also know as "the shaped cake") on the Pulchiana Mountains in the Gallura area, the San Giorgio's staircase in Osini. For each of these natural monuments it will be also catalogued and stored all the data on the compositional characteristics, state of alteration and possible methods of restorative intervention in case of the presence of strong chemical and physical deterioration.

As told before, the survey will be operated with the use of laserscan units, the use of phase-shift or time of flight technology, will be choose according to the specific survey condition, certain monuments will require long range scanner to be completely documented, other will require an high level of detail from the close range, the vantage of the phase shift solution, which is capable to measure a range equal to a full dome (320 vertical degree and 360 horizontal degree) with an accuracy up to four millimetres collecting up to 200.000 points for each operative second, make this kind of laserscan very interesting a reduce the operative time, but when the operative range will need to operate from a meaningful distance, a slower, but more reliable time of flight solution will be used. The entire survey, conducted using even different tools will allow the full coverage of the investigated object. The survey will be linked to a specific topographic network, and then referenced on the national map, this will allow a solid archiving of the collected data and fully useful for all subsequent stages of processing and analysis. The main steps of processing the data will be made up by the development of traditional two-dimensional representations, views zenith, plans, elevations, sections, useful to present the object using representation solutions which will be easily understandable and communicable. After this phase, the survey data will be used to develop a three-dimensional digital surfaces model, with a procedure aimed to preserve the greatest correspondence between the collected points and the final result. These models will be useful for the analysis and the study about the surfaces and the shape of the object, they will be used to study specific functions and, when mapped with photographs, to create images of graphics rendering.

Starting from these models, a complex process of treatment of the data will produce a new series of three-dimensional digital models, designed for online viewing and implementation of multimedia products.

The stage of treatment completion will include the implementation of digital models for the 3D printing of physical models, produced with additive or subtractive processes with 3D printers which are becoming more common with. In this sense, the models allow users to access downloadable versions of the scaled digital model, using specific machines, to print and create scaled versions of these monuments.

The models will allow reproducing a copy in resin, PVC or other economical materials, depending on the technology available. The production process of a physical model can be very simple, and in most cases it is very economical. In this way, it will be possible to envisage the possibility of reconstructing an entire remote collection of the monumental witness. Any school or association in the United States, South America, Australia or Japan, will be able to receive digital data a start to build scale models or even real-sized models. This solution will allow also the access to this kind of monument to blind and visually impaired people, they will be able to experience and understand the shapes of these stones thanks to tactile models.

Considering the fact that three dimensional printing may still result a difficult operation to many users, the models will be prepared in a sort of "assembly kit" based on a sequence of sections, laser engraved with specific machines or simply printed with a common printer on paper to be transferred to appropriate thickness and then cut manually. So, starting from the digital model and following simple installation instructions, everybody will be able to get a scale models absolutely affordable and accessible to all.

E.Stone project, step 1: Setting up an Internet space for data sharing. At the beginning an Internet space will be activated on the network for sharing and collaboration between the research groups. In this way the data previously collected, bibliographic references, iconographic, photographic, geographic references manuals and all information useful for the development of the project, will be kept continually updated. In this collaborative space, based on classical protocols for remote sharing and video-conferencing will be possible to solve the main participation trouble among the groups. At this stage, only active members of research teams, will access to the complete materials under development. However a small part of the whole research, set up as a "preview" of the site will be activated to facilitate the dissemination of information about the ongoing activities.

E.Stone project, step 2: Defining a catalogue about the state of knowledge on the elements of the research. This important step will have a rapid development in the first phase of the project so it will be used to plan the survey and documentation campaign. This phase will be based on the development of an online database.

The creation of this catalogue will determine the complexity, scientific interest, conservation status, risk status and accessibility or each monumental witness.

E.Stone project, step 3: Starting the survey and documentation campaign, on-site sampling and analysis of geomaterials. During this phase an intensive campaign of survey will start. The operations program will bring the survey units to operate on various monumental witnesses. Regarding the study of geomaterials in the monumental witnesses, it is expected to develop individual campaigns, with duration up to some days for each of the monumental witnesses; in this time the study about the macroscopic characteristics of lithological materials will be done, the material samples will be collected and the forms of alteration detection will be performed. When one of the monuments of major importance will be the subject of the survey, a specific workshop / seminar will be organized, it will be opened to the local technical operators who handle land management (municipalities, provinces, Soprintendenze), scholars, students of schools and the professionals who work in Cultural Heritage and Landscape, as architects, engineers, geologists, archaeologists, surveyors, etc..

The operations of this phase will collect a huge volume of data and wide dissemination of the ongoing works.

E.Stone project, step 4: First morfographic data processing, information sharing. Once the phase of collecting information will be completed and treated to create an early accessible and "cleaned up" set of models, three-dimensional models laserscan, printouts, photographic and textual data will be made homogeneous according to common standards for the research groups, structured in accessible formats. In this phase, data collection will enrich the catalogue database of monumental testimony, with a substantial increase in the state of knowledge about these elements.

E.Stone project, step 5: The second stage of data processing (advanced models, physical model development). At this stage the treatment of data collected will be in its advanced phase, with the production of the first models aimed to multimedia broadcasting and public access through the project site. The production structure for the models will be organized around three main lines of development models: for online viewing with photorealistic features; models for specific information viewing (decay, thematic maps, etc ...); for 3D printing process solutions.

E.Stone project, step 6: Interpretation of data about geomaterials processes of change and proposals for the preservation of monumental witnesses. The handling and analysis on the collected data going to store them into the database system of E.Stone. In detail, all geomaterials which are in the selected monuments will be studied in detail, the geochemical characteristics (fluorescence, spectrometry, X-ray), mineral-petrographic (optical microscopy and X-ray diffraction) and physical characteristics. The analysis of materials will be mainly done on the outcropping geological parts which formed the area around and not directly on the witness. This study will define the causes and processes of ongoing deterioration in the each monument. A proposal about intervention strategies for restoration and preservation will be based on the results of this phase.

E.Stone project, step 7: Dissemination of Information. A version for easy reference catalogue of monumental testimony will be posted on the site of E. Stone. The section dedicated to access to three dimensional models and the section about multimedia materials will be inaugurated. The models will be set available for users of E.Stone, with the ability to request access to the specimens and recording. The information and the progress of research will be disseminated through the traditional forms of research and discovery of information from the Internet.

E.Stone project, step 8: Consolidation and management of the Internet dedicated space. At the end of the phase 7, the site of E.Stone will continue its growth by implementing a structure to make possible to access the Web geography resources (Google Earth and similar systems). The areas dedicated to individual monumental witnesses will enrich the discussion forum with the participation of users outside the project that this will contribute by adding their own images, reports, information about the "large stones of Sardinia" in this way users will be more involved in the site and will also give the opportunity to ensure a continuous update about the condition of the monuments, forming a sort of "public" monitoring.

E.Stone project, step 9: When the E.Stone website will arrive to complete the main tasks and to present exhaustive set of information about the monuments a series of seminars and workshops in the area. Will take place, the techniques, procedures and technologies used for the E.Stone research will be shared with activities on the Sardinia Island and with Internet based learning, the online seminars will be structured in such a way as to ensure maximum usability by different users (students, scholars, professionals, technicians). The double activity about learning, with direct workshops and online seminars will be done to allow the better dissemination of the results.

1.5 Expected Results

- Creation of an online documentation centre about the "monumental witnesses of Sardinia" that will determine the methods and a reference for the management and processing of this data.

- Creating an archive based on the logic of sharing and the continuous enrichment of the catalogue, integrating it with the continuity of training experiences like degree Thesis and Ph.D.
- Sharing and dissemination of knowledge; networking with other groups of scholars, to promote and enhance the state of knowledge and the state of the art in dealing with this category of heritage subject.
- Creating the conditions to allow a better approach to conservation and restoration of this particular stones.

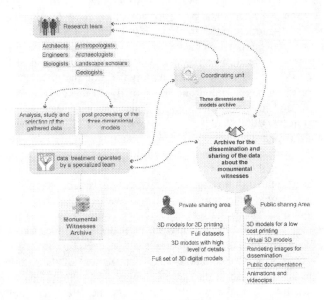

Fig. 2. Schematic view of the E.Stone archive project

2   What Was Done Until Today

At the time for this project/work two stone monuments were examined: the Elephant of Castelsardo (Anglona, north Sardinia) and the Mushroom of Carloforte (north of San Pietro Island, southwest Sardinia). For the first stone operations in the following activities were set up: 1) laserscan technology complete survey 2) study of various forms of macroscopic alterations and their distribution in the same stone; 3) removal of small sample from the stone monument; 4) experimental determination of physical, geochemical and petrographic characteristics of geomaterials by laboratory analysis, using many instruments: helium pycnometer, polarized microscope, electronic microscope (SEM), X-ray diffractometer (XRD), X-ray fluorescence spectrometer (XRF), etc.; 5) interpretation of first data of laserscan survey and laboratory analysis; 6) evaluate the grade decay and the causes of chemical and physical alteration of geomaterials. For the second stone, the work activities were limited only to the following points: 1), 2), 3) and 5). The end of this study, based of the results obtained, will be proposed strategies for the conservation of stone monuments.

2.1 Geomaterials and Geologic Settings

Planning The Elephant and the Mushrooms stones are big blocks of ignimbritic rocks of the Sardinian Cenozoic volcanism that forms a magmatic arc running along the western margin of Sardinia and southern Corse microplates (Lecca et al. 1997 and references therein).Volcanic activity, with a calcalkaline affinity l.s., began in Oligo-Miocene (around 32.4 My ago; Beccaluva et al. 1985, Savelli 2002 and references therein) producing basaltic and andesitic lavas and ended about 13 11 My ago, showing a climax between 23 and 17 My. From 23-22 My onwards (Beccaluva et al. 1985 and references therein), highly explosive ignimbritic fissural emissions with dacitic-rhyolitic composition occurred simultaneously and with alternating basaltic and andesitic lavas in various parts of the island, mainly along the western graben. This volcanism, whose products crop out in vast areas of Sardinia, is generally related with a subduction of oceanic lithosphere in a N-NW direction along the European continental paleomargin that produced the Oligocene rift between Sardinia and Provence (Cherchi & Montadert, 1982). The volcanic activity preceded and partly accompanied the opening of the western Mediterrean sea through the formation of the Provençal Balearic and Algerian basins. This lead to a 60° counterclockwise rotation of Corsica-Sardinia blocks around a pole located at 42.7° N and 9.6° E (Gueguen 1995).

2.1.1 Anglona Area

The crop out of Elephant ignimbrite is located in the northern of the Oligo-Miocene Sardinian Rift, in Anglona (north Sardinia). In this area three extensional phases can be recognized in this area during a fifteen million year period which spanned Corsica–Sardinia continental microplate separation and Western Mediterranean back-arc basin opening (Sowerbutts, 2000). The first phase, initial late Oligocene extension created a half-graben geometry with syn-rift clastic deposits shed locally from fault-bounded highs, passing laterally to lacustrine marlstones. Calc-alkaline volcanic activity subsequently predominated as volcanic centres developed along one half-graben bounding fault, producing voluminous pyroclastic and epiclastic material. Second phase mid-Aquitanian–early Burdigalian extensional faulting, recognized from localized clastic syn-rift stratal wedges, truncated and subdivided the half-graben. The syn-rift sediments were sealed by a regionally correlated ignimbrite that in turn was offset by late second-phase faulting. Third phase extensional fault movement, which reactivated the original fault trend then occurred. The pyroclastic rocks of Anglona show a strong heterogeneity, as the result of different eruption conditions and emplacement temperatures (high- to medium- to low-grade ignimbrites). Scatter also depends on the different incidence of pumice, crystal and lithic fragments and matrix. Based on their volcanological the pyroclastic rocks were divided into two main groups: 1) pyroclastic flow deposits with high- to medium-welded grade (including lava-like ignimbrites), from poorly to medium porous; 2) pyroclastic fall deposits with low-welded grade (e.g. cineritic products), from medium to strongly porous.

2.1.2 Volcanic Island of San Pietro

The crop out of Mushroom pyroclastic rocks is located on the San Pietro Island (southwestern of Sardinia), completely formed by volcanic rocks belonging to the Cenozoic Sulcis complex (Garbarino et al. 1985; Garbarino et al. 1990). During the final phases of Cenozoic magmatism (Arana et al. 1974), three important episodes of volcanism occurred in the area of San Pietro, characterized by the eruption of a peralkaline rhyolitic lavas and ignimbritic complex, interlayered in the products of a regionally extended calc-alkaline activity. In a first, has a calc-alkaline volcanism (older than 15 My) with a character fissural and led to the formation of lavas and ignimbritic deposits to regional extension. In the second phase, there is a type of comenditic volcanism, with the formation of lavas and peralkaline ignimbrites. The last phase will have a calc-alkaline volcanism, with the emplacement of products with textural aspects typical of pyroclastic flow.

The volcanic outcrops in the 'Punta delle Oche' (north island), where the mushroom stone is located, are ignimbritic rocks (with a calc-alkaline affinity l.s.,) formed in the latter phase.

2.2 The Elephant Stone

Until laserscan technology, this monument was not really surveyable, the strange shape, the huge massive structure was a real problem for anyone who would try to realize a serious survey of the whole stone. Thanks to the laserscan technology this work became as easy as a complete photographical campaign. The older survey, published years before, was about the tombs and was a good work, but it was a simple, classical bidimensional set of drawings, moreover it was aimed to document only the ancient graves, and gave no information about the stone in itself. To face this work we choose to use a Leica HDS 3000 panoramic scanner, based on the time of fly technology. This was done for two reasons: for first this scanner is capable to gather a very accurate set of points from a very short distance and this was a very important feature to allow the survey of the inner parts of the graves. Secondly this scanner is also capable to gather a very accurate result from a long distance, so it was possible to place the scanner in the upper parts of the hill in front of the stone and take the survey of the upper parts with the same quality of the all the rest of the monument. To allow an high quality result in the overall operation the laserscan survey was supported by a complete topographical survey, aimed to build a specific network of all the special targets placed on the monument and absolutely necessary for a clean reconstruction of the single scans. It is important to remember that the use of a topographical survey is not only fundamental because of the high level of accuracy in the registration process and for the better and easier scanning planning; it is important because when the topographical network is planned, a series of permanent points are placed on the ground around the monument. Those special points can remain placed in the site for many years; so if there is the need for a new survey, for example if it happens that a part of the monument is damaged, or for simple monitoring needs, it is possible to have a really accurate comparing of the two surveys according to points which are external to the monument. In facts it would be possible to reply a new survey from any new position of the laserscan and there will be no need to have a complete new survey while also a single part of the monument can be measured again.

The new survey can be placed exactly on the old one according to the topographical survey, based on some of the old points left on the area during the first digital survey. In this way, having a reference system based on the general environment, allows to monitor any change not only in the shape of the stone but also in its position on the ground. The survey was completed in two single days, twelve scan stations were operated, and the whole work was organized in three main development paths, one going around the stone, one for the long distance stations and a final one crossing inside the system of the lower tombs. In this way a good, almost complete coverage of the stone was produced and a large amount of the landscape around the monument was also taken. The overall pointcloud is made of almost twenty five millions collected points. The accuracy obtained was around six millimetres for each scans. When the scanner was placed inside the graves the use of a wireless access point was very useful to have a remote control of the scanner from the outside.

The topographical network was based on six topographical stations and took the survey of the almost forty targets applied on the stone and completely removed at the end of the whole scanning session.

2.2.1 First Data Treatments (Digital Survey Dataset)

The first step in the treatment of the collected data was, as usual, the registration of all the single scans in a unique digital model. This was done following two classical criteria for this kind of survey: for first the single pointclouds were registered over the topographical survey, then they are geometrically compared (using the "cloud constrain" function in Leica Cyclone) to improve the alignment of each pointcloud over the other.

After the registration, the first operation taken on the resulting pointcloud were aimed to produce some simple sections all around the monument and a first, simplified, surface model with almost all the occlusion holes fixed.

The whole first treatment was aimed to produce a massive, basic model of the monument. This was a first surface model useful to verify the quality of the collected data. On the surface digital model a first texturing treatment was applied to have a better evaluation of the result.

Bringing this model to generic rendering software like Maxon Cinema 4D allowed testing how was versatile the obtained model. Inside this software it was possible to produce a series of rendering view of the digital model and it was possible to use this environment to develop some 3D interactive simulations to allow a better sharing of the first result without the need to share the heavy and hard to manage surface 3D model. The 3D interactive simulations were developed using the Quicktime VR output, a pre-compiled system of visualization capable to bring the perception of a full virtual space, with a visualization based on a pre-calculated series of frames. The overall effect is quite good, allowing a good sight on the whole model and a quick exploration of the shape of the monument without any need of complex navigation systems. Obviously this was just a simple, first test to verify the quality of the survey, while the whole project is planned to achieve a more complex structure.

All the process is aimed to produce three main results, each result integrates the other:

- The first result is to have a very high quality survey of the monument, useful as a precious documentation of the conditions of the stone in the November 2006.
- The second result is to produce a set of popular and interpretative models to enhance the possibility of using and sharing of the knowledge about this important monument.

- The third result is to build a rich set of information, which will be available as a starting point for the enhancement of the knowledge of this ancient patrimony and as an incentive to the research about this awesome theme.

2.2.2 Final Data Treatments (Digital Survey Dataset)

The first part of the work over the data treatments clearly showed that an approach developed in a small simplification of the model can give a good looking result, but it is interesting only for shape analysis and monitoring purposes.

The time consuming rendering and the impossibility to use the high resolution model for real time access creates the need to face the modelling process in a new and specific way. So a different approach was chosen, no more direct modelling from the pointcloud, but a process starting from a new rebuilt and optimized polygonal model and then a reconstruction based on the subdivision surface modelling.

The following steps in modelling produced a variable resolution model, capable to switch gradually from a full resolution representation to a lower polygon representation, crossing all the intermediate steps of the representation.

The keywords for this process of variable simplification were: edge loop modelling, Re-Topology modelling. To greatly enhance the representation two advanced digital modelling and texturing solutions were adopted, the classical texture Unwrap procedure based on the photographical documentation campaign of the stone and a specific Normal Mapping procedure based on the information coming from the high resolution model in itself. In this way a whole new model was produced, not aimed to monitoring or accurate information extraction, but greatly suitable for multimedia and representation.

The software workflow for the developing of this new multimedia oriented model was based on Pixlogic Zbrush and Maxon Cinema 4D.

A The whole process was aimed to develop a specific solution for this kind of items, to produce a method to face and develop high performance models of rich shaped stones and natural monument, the case study operated on the Elephant Stone demonstrate the full opportunity offered by the method, capable to produce a high

Fig. 3. Rendering view of the three dimensional digital model of the elephant stone

level documentary model, useful to create an accurate memory of the real shape of the item and a versatile multimedia model, capable to adapt its level of detail to the representation scale and to the environment in which it will be inserted to. The points of strength that link the procedure to the monuments the stone of the elephant represent are the natural shape, the human artefacts producing smooth parts in the stone carving, the impossible task to define a regular geometric pattern as real solution to the description of the monument; the real need to have a continuous variation of the level of details while changing the representation scale.

2.2.3 The Volcanic Rocks of Elephant Stone

On the geological front of the analysis for this monument the some meaningful sample collection is just completed and the geological research unit is working on the materials study. All the collected and treated information will be then linked to the pointcloud model to create specific visualizations of the decay conditions of this particular and unique stone.

The Elephant stone are pyroclastic rocks with welded from high- to medium-grade and a strong heterogeneity, due to variable presence of lithic fragments, lithoclast (with various size, until to decimetre) and pumice into the matrix of stone. These rocks have an open porosity ranging about from eight to 25% (in litho-clasts and lithic fragments of lava-like ignimbrites with strongly welded); the matrix of these pyroclastic rocks, characterized from low- to medium-welded grade, the open porosity varies about from 15% (into unaltered matrix) to 45% (in altered matrix). In some sample strongly altered, the porosity comes to 50%.

What happens inside the vitreous matrices, already characterized by poor welding original (Macciotta et al. 2001). Microscopic analysis indicated that the ignimbrite of Elephant stone have a porphyritic structure (with porphyritic index between 10÷15%) with phenocrysts of opaque minerals (magnetite and/or titanomagnetite), plagioclase, ± clinopyroxene and rare quartz. Actually, further analyses are in progress.

2.3 The Mushroom Stone

About the Carloforte Mushroom Stone it is possible to say "we just arrive too late" a large part of the stone remembering the "umbrella" of the mushroom collapsed in March 2010, while a survey was planned for the end of may 2010. The mushroom is an ancient stone completely developed by the action of the atmospheric agents (e.g. wind with marine aerosol, meteoric water, thermoclastism, etc.; see paragraph 2.4 Decay of stone witnesses) over a very articulated volcanic stone.

A particular alteration process has produced a kind of "umbrella" over a more solid rock. The reasons of the fall are probably due to a natural issue, but this simply underlines how urgent is a survey of these fragile system. So, even if in its hardly damaged shape, the survey was done in June 2010.

The complex shape of this stone and the demanding walk needed to reach it with all the instruments, made us prefer to operate with a light phase-shift scanner like the Cam2 Faro Photon 80. The survey was based on spherical target system, to allow the reconstruction of each single scan into a unique model.

Fig. 4. The digital survey of the mushroom stone

The scans were taken in three series, a first series with the scanner placed directly on the ground, a second series with the scanner on the tripod at medium elevation and a third series with the scanner on the tripod at the maximum elevation.

In this way it was obtained a very good coverage of the whole stone and of the fallen fragment, mainly too large and heavy to try to turn them on the other side to try a scan of the opposite side, it was preferred to avoid this fearing to produce any further damage. A complete collection of sample and a first geological documentation of the whole stone and of the area around it was made.

A study about the various forms of macroscopic alterations was made on site with the gathering of small samples from monument stone.

All the digital survey data and all the geological data (physical, geochemical and petrographic characteristics of geomaterials) are now under development and analysis, in the next months it is planned to investigate what is effectively happened to cause the collapse of the umbrella and to define a clear picture of the state of decay of this stone.

2.4 Decay of Stone Witnesses

Aside from the late-stage syngenetic alteration processes, the pyroclastic rocks of Elephant and Mushroom stones are greatly affected by epigenetic alteration.

Decay processes are mainly concentrated in the vitreous matrix of pyroclastites, characterized by a higher porosity and low degree of welding, and carry on two different ways: (a) geochemical and mineralogical alteration and (b) physical degradation. In the first case (a), late-stage chemical alteration processes transformed partially the original paragenesis to a greater or lesser extent, altering the mineral assembly and the glass (with incipient devitrification) with the formation of new secondary minerals. In the second case (b), the mechanisms of physical degradation are principally related by: 1) presence of soluble salts (from soil or atmosphere) that exert a crystallization pressure into open porous of stone; 2) differential thermal dilatation induced by normal day range of temperature and solar radiation; 3) absorption/desorption in the stone of meteoric water (Columbu et al. 2008) or water from soil or air moisture; 4) water hydration/dehydration of hygroscopic mineral (e.g. salts). Nevertheless, the decay mechanisms of these two stone witnesses are different.

This depends, on the one hand, by different microclimatic conditions and exposure of stone surface to atmospheric agents and, on the other hand, by different physical and mineral-petrographic characteristic of geomaterials.

In fact, the Mushroom stone is located near to the sea (about 200 metres), while the Elephant stone is located about 3.3 kilometres from the sea. Moreover, the pyroclastic rocks of Elephant have different petrographic features and then are more heterogeneous, due to the greater presence of lithic fragments, lithoclast into the matrix. In the Elephant and Mushroom monuments there are diverse macroscopic forms of physical decay (decohesion, exfoliation, alveolation, differential degradation) and presence of crypto- and ef-florescence.

These macroscopic forms are distributed differently in them extern surface of each stone. In the Elephant the decay processes are mainly concentrated: 1) in the basal part of the big block of stone (that rests directly on the soil and is characterized by presence of circulating water solution by capillarity), with strong backward vertical profile of stone; in this zone differential degradation, with enucleation of lithic fragments and lithoclast, and exfoliation are the principal alteration macroscopic forms; 2) on the top and median parts of Elephant stone that exposure to the SE-S-SW-W and where there is more frequent the solar radiation; in these zones strong alveolation processes and physical degradation are more present, due to the differential thermal dilatation and diurnal cycles of moisture absortion/desorption; the alveolation is present mainly under the 'proboscis' of Elephant and into the outer room of 'domus de janas'. In the other outer parts of the monument with exposure to the NE-N, there are bio-deterioration agents (e.g. musk, lichens, etc.). In the Elephant stone, oxidation processes were observed. XRD analysis performed on the collected samples take on extern surface of parts of monument exposed to south and to west, indicated the presence of hematite, consequently to alteration of Fe-Mg minerals.

Diffractometric analysis on other samples taken on the outer crust of precipitation indicated the considerable amounts of gypsum.

It is planned to investigate which is the origin of this phase; probably, it come partially from meteoric precipitations because these have often a small quantity of gypsum; this is formed by interaction of sulphur dioxide, acidic rainwater and atmospheric particles of $CaCO_3$.

Inside the 'domus de janas' of Elephant stone, precipitation crust are present in surface of wall and ceiling of the small rooms. These crusts will be studied for determination the composition of secondary phases.

Fig. 5. Macroscopic alteration form of alveolation on the surface under the proboscis of Elephant stone of Sedini with the presence of salts within to the vitreous matrix of volcanic rock

In the Mushroom stone the decay (that produced a particular kind of "umbrella") shows: 1) exfoliation in the stem of the mushroom; this alteration form is concentrated: a) where there are mechanisms of water wash-out, that remove constantly thin flakes produced by other alteration processes, b) on face of stem exposed to the north-wind come from the sea. The meteoric water run along the stem by fractures and fissures present into the top head of mushroom; on the base of first macroscopic

Fig. 6. Physical decay of stem of Mushroom stone of Carloforte with exfoliation processes by mechanisms of absorption/desorption and wash-out of meteoric water

Fig. 7. Macroscopic alteration form of alveolation under the head of Mushroom stone of Carloforte

observation, probably parts of head collapsed due to the presence of these fissures; 2) articulated alveolation (that penetrated until about 8 cm from surface below) under head where coexist two important factor of decay: a) physical decohesion of stone, therefore to continue mechanisms of absorption/desorption of meteoric water or humidity, containing a small quantities of seawater (with salt), (note: the thickness of head of mushroom is about maximum 30 cm), b) turbulence induced near to the mushroom by the sea-wind, which can frequently remove the thin flakes of stone weathered.

In the near future it is planned to investigate what is happened to cause of collapse of the "umbrella" (with determination of properties of resistance physical-mechanics of stone under stress of own lithostatic load) and to define actually state of decay of this natural stone monument.

Acknowledgements

The survey of the elephant stone was made in 2006 in collaboration with Area3D s.r.l., Livorno, the survey team was coordinated by Giorgio Verdiani and composed by Francesco Tioli, Federico Piras, Sergio Di Tondo and Giovanni Guccini.

The geological survey of the elephant stone was made in 2010 and coordinated by Stefano Columbu. The research group is also composed by Prof. Giampaolo Macciotta, Prof. Marco Marchi, Dr.ssa Anna Maria Garau.

The survey of the Mushroom Stone was made in 2010 in collaboration with Area3D s.r.l. Livorno, the survey team was coordinated by Giorgio Verdiani and composed by Stefano Columbu, Alessandro Peruzzi, Filippo Fantini, and Gaia Lavoratti.

The geological survey of the Mushroom Stone was made in 2010 and coordinated by Stefano Columbu and composed by Federico Piras and Giorgio Verdiani.

A special thank to Antonio Cipollina from Carloforte for the support and indications.

References

1. Araña, V., Barberi, F., Santacroce, R.: Some data on the comendite type area of S. Pietro and S. Antioco islands, Sardinia. In: Bulletin of Volcanology, vol. 38(2). Springer, Heidelberg (1974)
2. Beccaluva, L., Civetta, L., Macciotta, G., Ricci, C.A.: Geochronology in Sardinia: results and problems. Rend. Soc. It. Min. Petr. (1985)
3. Cherchi, A., Montadert, L.: Oligo-Miocene rift of Sardinia and the early history of the Western Mediterranean Basin. Nature 298(5876), 736–739 (1982)
4. Columbu, S., Franzini, M., Garau, A.M., Gioncada, A., Lezzerini, M., Macciotta, G., Marchi, M.: Degrado fisico indotto da assorbimento d'acqua in rocce vulcaniche usate per costruire la chiesa di Nostra Signora di Otti. ulteriori dati e nuove considerazioni. V° Congresso Nazionale di Archeometria – Scienza e Beni Culturali (A.I.A.R.), Sardegna Nord Occidentale, Italia, Siracusa, Italy (2008)
5. Contu, E.: La Sardegna preistorica e nuragica. Carlo Delfino Editore, Sassari (2006)
6. Garbarino, C., Maccioni, L., Salvadori, I.: Carta geo-petrografica dell'Isola di San Pietro (Sardegna). Selca, Firenze, scala 1:25.000 (1985)
7. Garbarino, C., Lirer, L., Maccioni, L., Salvadori, I.: Carta vulcanologica dell'Isola di San Pietro. Selca, Firenze, scala 1:25.000 (1990)
8. Gueguen, E.: Le bassin Liguro-Provençal: un véritable océan. PhD thesis, Brest Univ. (1995)
9. Lecca, L., Lonis, R., Luxoro, S., Melis, E., Secchi, F., Brotzu, P.: Oligo-Miocene volcanic sequences and rifting stages in Sardinia: a review per mineral, vol. 66 (1997)
10. Macciotta, G., Bertorino, G., Caredda, A., Columbu, S., Franceschelli, M., Marchi, M., Rescic, S., Coroneo, R.: The S.Antioco of Bisarcio Basilica (NE Sardinia, Italy): water-rock interaction in ignimbrite monument decay. In: Cidu, R. (ed.) Proc. WRI-10, Balkema, Rotterdam (2001)
11. Melis, P.: La Domus dell'Elefante, Sardegna Archeologica (15), Carlo Delfino Editore, Sassari (1991)
12. Murroni, F.: La Sardegna preistorica e Mediterraneo Antico. Storia e movimento di popoli. Grafica del Parteolla (2007)
13. Puddu, M.: La Sardegna dei megaliti. Megalitismo, miti e simboli nell'area del Mediterraneo. Iris editore (2005)
14. Savelli, C.: Time-space distribution of magmatic activity in the western Mediterranean and peripheral orogens during the past 30 Ma (a stimulus to geodynamic considerations). J. Geodyn. (2002)
15. Sowerbutts, A.: Sedimentation and volcanism linked to multiphase rifting in an Oligo-Miocene intra-arc basin, Anglona, Sardinia. Geological Magazine 137(4), 395–418 (2000)
16. Verdiani, G., Piras, F., Guccini, G.: The Elephant Stone, tracing a new path for the digital approach to unsurveylable monuments. In: Proceedings of the 15th International Conference on Virtual Systems and Multimedia, VSMM 2009, Vienna, September 9-12. IEEE Computer Society, Los Alamitos (2009) CPS, ISBN 978-0-7695-3790-0

3D Modelling of the A Famosa Fortress in Melaka, Malaysia

M. Izani[1,*], A. Bridges[1], P. Grant[1], A. Razak[2], and A. Rafi[3]

[1] Department of Architecture, University of Strathclyde, 131 Rottenrow G4 0NG UK
{mohamad.zainal-abidin,a.h.bridges,
barnabas.calder,p.m.grant}@strath.ac.uk
[2] FIT, Multimedia University, Cyberjaya, 63100 Malaysia
aishah@mmu.edu.my
[3] FCM, Multimedia University, Cyberjaya, 63100 Malaysia
ahmadrafi.eshaq@mmu.edu.my

Abstract. This paper presented our approach to developing the 3d model of A Famosa Faortress in Melaka, Malaysia. As the physical remnant of the fortress are minimal, a traditional 3D modelling technique based on collected data has been adopted. This method has been adopted based on case studies of three comparable reconstruction projects namely Michelsberg synagogue, The Jewish Quarter in Regensburg and Reconstruction of the old main church in Curitiba, Brazil. In this paper we discussed the 3D modeling technique used and presented some output of the model.

Keywords: Fortress, 3D model, A Famosa, conjectural layout, visual data.

1 Introduction

Historically, the A Famosa Fortress is one of the oldest partially extant European buildings in Malaysia. Its origins may be traced back to a fortress built by the Portuguese in 1511. The fortress is located in the city of Melaka and was largely destroyed during the British occupation of 1824 and the remains are currently as shown in Figure 1. Throughout the 300-year period of occupation it went through several architectural developments and changes. Recently Melaka has been listed in the UNESCO World Heritage list and Malaysian government have put significant resources into preserving this old heritage. A large amount of money has been allocated for excavation and conservation work as an effort to preserve this historical relic. Within the last few years, the conservation team has started to reconstruct some of the found areas. Most of these areas are locations for the bastions. However, work to uncover more of the buried wall, despite its historical significance and potential to draw more tourists into the area, may not be feasible as it would involve tearing up the major road that links the old town with the new commercial area, which has been reclaimed since the days of British occupation.

---

* Corresponding author.

M. Ioannides (Ed.): EuroMed 2010, LNCS 6436, pp. 373–380, 2010.
© Springer-Verlag Berlin Heidelberg 2010

Fig. 1. Remains of old Portuguese fortress, Porta de Santiago gate in Melaka

With the complex logistical condition and geographical factors of Melaka city to-day, it is undesirable to fully reconstruct this fortress in its physical context. Considering all these factors, it is believed that rebuilding the fortress in the form of a 3D model is the most practical solution. As the physical remains of the fortress is minimal, advanced 3D modelling techniques such as photogrammetry and 3D laser scanning are not applicable.

To identify the appropriate technique to be used, 3 projects which have similar situations has been selected and studied namely Michelsberg synagogue, The Jewish Quarter in Regensburg and Reconstruction of the old main church in Curitiba, Brazil. Table 1 compares the findings of these 3 projects with A Famosa. In general, the main similarities between this reconstruction of A Famosa and the three case studies are the very limited data resources and minimal physical remains of the building available. However in terms of available data, Lost Jewish Heritage and The Old Main Church of Curitiba have some advantages over the A Famosa and Jewish Quarter in Regensburg since the buildings were still available until the 19th century. Therefore, they provide more reliable evidence through photographs of the original buildings as compared to drawings or paintings. The architectural drawings produced in this era are also more accurate and advance compared to those of previous eras. In the case of A Famosa and the Jewish Quarter in Regensburg, extensive data verification has had to be done due to very old, inconsistent records and insufficiently reliable data.

Based on these findings it was decided to use a traditional 3D modelling techniques to reconstruct A Famosa. To accomplish this modelling process, 3D Studio Max has been chosen for the entire process of 3D visualisation such as polygonal modelling, texturing, lighting and rendering.

2   The 3D Modelling Process

Prior to the 3D modelling process, extensive data collection and verification has been conducted [4,5,6]. Once all the data has been verified, the 3D modelling process commences through several stages. First is the modelling of the fortress elements followed by the modelling of the fortress wall. Then the process is completed with texturing, lighting and rendering.

Table 1. Comparison of the elements in case studies

Project \ Elements	Lost Jewish Heritage [1]	Jewish Quarter in Regensburg [2]	The Old Main Church of Curitiba, Brazil [3]	A Famosa
Building's year	1869-1938	9th century - 1519	1714-1875	1511-1807
Project's Year	1998	1998	2004	2007
Conservation	No	No	No	Partial
Who	University of Applied Sciences, Germany	University of Applied Sciences, Germany, research agencies and other institutions	Master thesis by Jose Manoel Kozan	Strathclyde University and Multimedia Univ.
Purpose	To preserve and reconstruct in digital medium (3D)	To preserve and reconstruct in digital medium (3D)	To preserve and reconstruct in digital medium (3D)	To preserve and reconstruct in digital medium (3D)
Available physical remains	No physical remains at all. The site has been converted into a highway	No physical remains except some foundations from the excavation	No physical remains except tower clock	Only a gate and some bastions from excavation data
Available data	Some old photographs and water colour drawings Historian records	Limited drawings and excavation data Copperplate engravings	Photos of the original building, old paintings, drawings and maps, similar buildings	Old report, inconsistent drawings with old measurement units, similar fortresses
Method	Traditional 3D modeling process based on available data No data verification involved	Traditional 3D modeling process based on available data Data analysis and interpretation done by curators	Single image photogrammetry based on tower clock and photos	Traditional 3D modeling process based on available data. Conducted extensive data verification process on available data
Output	3D computer animated film	3D presentation in video, CD and picture	3D model and rendered images	3D model and rendered images
Applications	Presented to public and won some awards for the film	Presented in the museum for public	Education and research purpose	Potential application for education and tourism in Malaysia

2.1   Modelling of the Fortress Elements

In this process, the A Famosa plan in Figure 2 is divided into several sections. For each section, three sketches were made presenting a perspective view, internal wall view and external wall view. The sketches have been drawn based on the findings which have been gathered using two approaches:

1) Defining the fortress elements through detailed study on the features of medieval fortress and fortress architecture
2) Matching the elements to the surviving fortresses from the Dutch and the Portuguese eras. This is done through site visits to three selected fortress which are:

   - Aguada fortress, Goa, India
   - Galle fortress, Sri Lanka
   - Rotterdam fortress, Indonesia

These sketches are then presented to three identified persons who have been the main figures in the excavation and reconstruction of Middelburgh bastion on site for evaluation and feedback. Based on the feedback received, any required modification and adjustment is made. This pre-visualisation process is very important before commencing with the 3D modelling stage. This is to ensure that only finalised elements of the fortress will be modelled in 3D model. Based on these sketches the modelling of fortress elements in 3D were done accordingly.

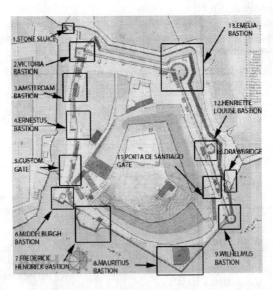

Fig. 2. Sections of the drawing transformed into sketches

2.2   Modelling of the Fortress Wall in 3D

To start the modelling of fortress wall process, the statistically-verified conjectural layout of A Famosa has been mapped onto the satellite image from Google Earth.

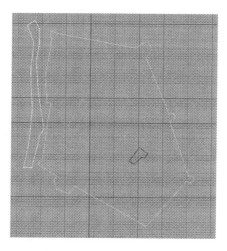

Fig. 3. Extracted line drawing of the conjectural layout of A Famosa

This is to match the location of the layout with the existing topology and mark the location of surviving buildings from the Portuguese and the Dutch era such as St. Paul's church and the Stadhuys. The information is then exported to a line drawing as shown in Figure 3 to be used in a 3D application.

Figure 3 has been used as the basis for the modelling process which started with the construction of the fortress site topology. This involves modelling the river, the seaside of the fortress and the land. After that the fortress line is extruded to become the wall and the 3D model of the fortress elements such as the bastion, gates, walls, ramps and passageways are then included. Since the fortress elements are modelled individually, any further detailed development and amendment can be done separately. Polygonal modelling has been fully used to model the entire 3D model.

To complete the 3D visualisation of this fortress, mock-up building models have been included inside the fortress. These buildings are not part of this research scope, and have been added for illustration purpose only. Figure 4 show the top of the 3D model of A Famosa.

2.3 Texturing

Once the modelling process is completed, textures are mapped onto polygonal surfaces. To control textures individually, each element is divided into several polygonal surfaces. Each polygonal surface has a specific texture. To avoid repetitive textures and to create a realistic look, textures have been created with various tones, patterns and styles. All of these textures were collected during the research fieldtrip to Sri Lanka and India. Manipulation of these textures is performed in Adobe Photoshop.

2.4 Lighting and Rendering

To create the finished 3D model, lighting and rendering must be applied. With the advancement of lighting and rendering technology today, photorealistic rendering output can easily be achieved by using minimal 3D lighting. This method is known as physical based lighting. It mimics the real lighting based on the real world. To accomplish this, a rendering method known as Mental Ray has been used. It uses a global illumination approach to create a photorealistic output. Besides a realistic lighting output it also produces a very soft shadow. This combination has given a very promising result to projects that require a realistic rendering output. Final rendering outputs are based on the framing of the 3D camera. Generally these framings are positioned at the most significant locations such as the bastions, gates, walls and overall views of the fortress.

3 The Rendered Output

In this section we presented some rendered images of the significant elements of the fortress such as bastion, gate and wall.

Fig. 5. Emelia bastion

Fig. 6. Frederick Hendrick bastion

Fig. 7. Drawbridge at Porta de Santiago gate

Fig. 8. Overall look of the fortress from the sea

4 Conclusion

This project paper presented our attempt to model A Famosa fortress in 3D. Based on the comparison with some selected similar 3D reconstruction projects, it is decided to use traditional 3D modelling techniques using 3D Studio Max for the modelling of this fortress. Prior to the modelling process, extensive data collection and verification has been done to gather all the required data on the fortress since the physical remain of the fortress are very limited. The 3D modelling process commences through several stages which are the modelling of the fortress elements, the fortress wall, texturing, lighting and rendering. The output of this project are some rendered images of the important fortress elements such as the bastions, gates and walls. By modelling this fortress in 3D, we hope to digitally preserve this important heritage and search for possible application of the model in the education and tourism industry.

Acknowledgments. Our special thanks to British Council for sponsoring this research under PM2 initiative grant.

References

1. Krebs, F., Bruck, E.: The potential and useful applications of digital tools for the memory and preservation of Jewish Heritage. In: Gruber, S.D. (ed.) The Future of Jewish Heritage in Europe, Prague (2004)
2. Krebs, F., Brück, E.: 3D-Visualisation of lost Jewish heritage (2002),
   http://www.memo38.de/root_IE/main/d/d_01/
   3d-visualisation_of_lost_jewish_heritage.pdf
3. Kozan, J.M.: Virtual heritage reconstruction the old main church of Curitiba, Brazil Department of Architecture. University of Cincinnati, Ohia (2004)
4. Izani, M., Bridges, A., Razak, A.: Determination of the plan of the A Famosa Fortress, Malaysia. In: Proceeding of International Conference on Computing and Informatics, Kuala Lumpur, pp. 292–297 (2009)
5. Izani, M., Bridges, A., Razak, A.: 3D Modelling Of A Famosa Fortress, Malaysia Based on Comparison of Textual and Visual Data. In: 6th International Conference Computer Graphics, Imaging and Visualization, pp. 491–496. Conference Publishing Services, Tianjin (2009)
6. Izani, M., Bridges, A., Razak, A.: Using procrustes analysis to determine verifiable conjectural layout of A Famosa fortress, Malaysia. In: Proceeding of International Conference on Software Technology and Engineering, Chennai, pp. 291–295 (2009)

3D Digitization and Its Applications in Cultural Heritage

Renju Li, Tao Luo, and Hongbin Zha

Key Laboratory of Machine Perception (Ministry of Education)
Peking University, Beijing, China
{lirenju,luotao,zha}@cis.pku.edu.cn

Abstract. 3D digitizing technology has a variety of applications including reverse engineering, quality control, virtual reality and digital heritage. Recently, great development in 3D digitizing technology facilitates archaeology and digital preservation of cultural heritage. In this paper, we introduce a 3D digitizing pipeline for cultural heritage. By using 3D technology, both geometry and texture can be recovered with high precision. Four main applications including digital archiving, 3D line drawing, virtual restoration and virtual display are introduced. The technology has been successfully implemented in many digital heritage projects such as Longmen, Xiangtangshan, Maijishan, Nanyuewang museum and so on. These projects demonstrate that 3D digitization greatly facilitates archeology and plays an important role in cultural heritage protection.

Keywords: 3D digitization, 3D scanning, 3D line drawing, Geometric modeling, Texture mapping, Cultural heritage.

1 Introduction

Digital heritage and archaeology have attracted a lot of attention of researchers in computer vision and computer graphics. A large number of cultural heritage objects are being destroyed due to natural weathering, eroding or disaster. Capturing digital representation of these heritage objects can be used for the preservation, restoration, access, and scholarly study. Recently, great development in 3D digital technology facilitates archaeology and digital preservation of cultural heritage. Representative examples include the Great Buddha Project [1], Stanford University's Michelangelo Project [2], Columbia University's French cathedral Project [3], etc.

China is an ancient civilization country with a long history and there are many world cultural heritage sites. During the past several years, we have carried out several digital heritage projects including some grottoes such as Longmen, Maijishan, Xiangtangshan, Huangzesi and some museums such as Nanyuewang Museum, Henan Museum, etc. The heritage objects were destroyed to some extent. It's urgent for us to protect the cultural heritage and preserve, study and display them using new technology.

By using 3D technology, both geometry and texture can be recovered with high precision. The 3D models can be used in digital archiving, 3D line drawing, virtual restoration and virtual display. To obtain the high precision 3D models, we use a global registration method based on feature points. We also design a 3D database management system to effectively manage 3D data, 2D photos and relevant texts for

M. Ioannides (Ed.): EuroMed 2010, LNCS 6436, pp. 381–388, 2010.

different levels ranging from large scenes to a single statue. For 3D line drawing, we propose a multiscale approach to detecting the feature lines on the noisy meshes automatically. Different display methods are also proposed to display the cultural relics of different size.

2 3D Digitizing Pipeline

The pipeline of 3D digitization includes 3D data capturing, 3D registration, geometric modeling and texture mapping. For capturing 3D data, we can use different methods to obtain the range data from several views. Then the multi-view 3D raw data need to be registered and merged. The geometric modeling process includes polygonizing the point cloud, filling the holes, decimating the mesh and some other postprocessing procedures. The output of geometric modeling process is a mesh which can represent the geometric property of the object. For realistic rendering, texture mapping is needed to map high resolution photos onto the geometric models.

2.1 3D Scanning

There are several types of scanners available now in the market. For large scenes, time of flight scanners can be used to obtain the 3D data. Time of flight scanners can capture the 3D information of a large scene very fast. But as the measurement is based on finding the distance of a surface by timing the round-trip time of a pulse of light, so the accuracy is not so high, usually several millimeters. If high accuracy measurement is needed, structured light scanner based on triangulation is a good choice. Fig. 1(a) and Fig. 1(b) show the scanning of a cave using time-of-flight scanner HDS6000 and structured light scanner OKIO respectively. Fig. 1(c) and Fig. 1(d) show the comparison between a Buddha head scanned by the two scanners. We can see clearly that the details are well captured using structured light scanner.

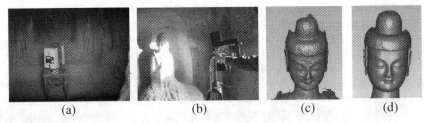

| (a) | (b) | (c) | (d) |

Fig. 1. 3D Scanning. (a) 3D scanning using a time of flight scanner. (b) 3D scanning using a structured light scanner. (c) Data scanned using a time of flight scanner. (d) Data scanned using a structured light scanner.

2.2 3D Data Registration

When we scan a large scene using structured light scanner, it may need several hundreds of scans to cover the entire surface. A serious problem for the registration of so many views is the accumulated error, such as the cave data shown in Fig. 2(a, b), where the red circle shows the accumulated error.

3D data registration is the process of aligning 3D data in different positions to one coordinate system using rigid transform [4, 5] or non-rigid transform [6]. One popular method of registration is to get a rough match among the data and use ICP [7] to refine the registration result. For multi-view registration, several methods have been proposed aiming at reducing the accumulated error [4].

In this paper, we use a practical method of multi-view registration using feature points based on the structured light scanner composed of two CCD cameras and one projector, which is memory and time efficient and easy to implement.

The global registration method includes the following steps:

(1) Obtain the 3D coordinates of the feature points in each scan. The feature points can be man-made markers or image features such as SIFT feature.

(2) Build the global frame for all the feature points.

(3) Register each point cloud to the global frame, as shown in Fig. 2 (c).

The global frame for the feature points is the optimized coordinate for the points of each scan by considering error accumulation. The transformation matrix for the feature points to the frame can also be calculated. We use the same transformation matrix to transform the point cloud. By removing the overlapping data, we can get the point cloud as shown in Fig. 2(d, e). We can see that the registration error caused by the accumulation is eliminated.

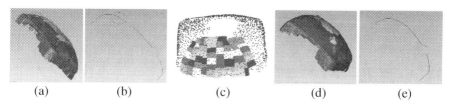

(a)   (b)   (c)   (d)   (e)

Fig. 2. Global registration method. (a) Error accumulation shown in 3D mesh. (b) Error accumulation shown in one cross section. (c) Registering each point cloud to the global frame. (d) Registration result shown in 3D mesh. (e) Registration result shown in one cross section.

2.3 Geometric Modeling

As the 3D data obtained by the 3D scanners are discrete 3D points without any neighbourhood relationship, meshes can be constructed from the point cloud by connecting neighbouring points to polygons. The polygon model can represent the object very well, which is much easier to be postprocessed and rendered than the point cloud. Several polygonization methods can be applied such as Marching Cubes [8], Delauney triangulation and so on.

With the rapid development of the 3D scanners, the 3D model can represent the object with high resolution and accuracy. Meanwhile, the data storage is increasing rapidly, which makes a big challenge for rendering, viewing and editing. Polygon decimation is the data reducing process that tries to use fewer polygons to represent the original object while preserving the features. Because of the complicated structure of the scene, occlusion or the special reflective property of the object, it's inevitable that the 3D data of some parts can not be captured and there will be holes on the model. The holes need to be filled to make the model watertight. Distance field based method [9], method using symmetry, method using RBF and so on can be used to fill the holes of objects.

2.4 Texture Mapping

Texture is as important as geometry for realistic 3D digitizing. Texture mapping is the process to map high resolution photos onto the geometry model. Each vertex on the mesh not only has its 3D position but also has a texture coordinate corresponding to the texture image.

The steps of texture mapping are as follows:

(1) Capture high resolution photos from multiple views under proper light conditions.
(2) Segment the mesh into several parts.
(3) Recover the projection relationship between each part of the 3D model and the photos to obtain the correspondence between the vertex on the 3D models and the pixels in the images.
(4) Blend the color between the corresponding points on different photos.
(5) Generate the texture images for different parts of the model.

3   Applications in Cultural Heritage

3.1   Digital Archiving

The 3D data of cultural heritage can be preserved permanently using the 3D digitizing technology described in the previous section. With the fast development of 3D scanning technology, multi-resolution 3D data of the objects in which we are interested can be captured. The geometry and texture can be recovered with high precision.

The heritage objects are of different type and size and the 3D models are of different resolution. Therefore, how to manage, search and display the information is a critical problem. We design a 3D database management system to handle 3D data, photos and relative texts. The database is based on Microsoft Access database. The features of the system are as follows:

(1) Manage the data in multiple levels ranging from large scenes to a single statue.
(2) 3D models, photos and texts can be included in the system and they can be switched to each other.
(3) The user can view any details of the object freely.
(4) Some analysis functions are also provided such as measuring and sectioning.

Fig. 3 shows the interface of the 3D database management system with 2D photos, 3D models and 3D measurement.

(a)   (b)   (c)

Fig. 3. 3D database management. (a) 2D photo. (b) 3D data. (c) 3D measurement.

3.2 3D Line Drawing

In archaeology, line drawings are essential components of archaeological reports [10], which depict the shapes and structures of heritage objects. Specifically, the measurements are recorded in the line drawings. Therefore, they can be utilized in archaeological illustration and restoration of heritage objects. Traditionally, the archaeological line drawings are made manually by archaeologists. However, the procedure is expensive and time consuming.

In order to generate 3D line drawing, we present a multi-scale approach, which can capture shape features at multiple scales and be robust to noise [11,12]. We construct the discrete 3D multi-scale representation based on random walks and select local scales with a probabilistic method based on the minimum description length (MDL) principle. Finally, the line drawing is generated by detecting ridges and valleys on the mesh model with selected scales.

Fig. 4(a) is a Buddha in LeiGutai in Longmen grottoes, which is about 1.8 meters wide and 3 meters high. The 3D model is shown in Fig. 4(b). The distribution of local scales is illustrated in Fig. 4(c), which is piecewise constant and discontinuity adaptive. Combining curvature information with selected scales, the ridges are traced by connecting the zero-crossing points of first-order derivatives of maximal principal curvatures. Compared with the manual drawing in Fig. 4 (d), the 3D line drawing in Fig. 4(e) captures the main shape of the Buddha.

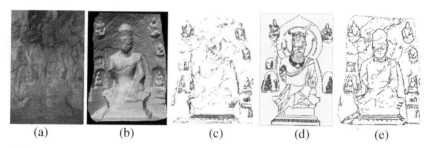

| (a) | (b) | (c) | (d) | (e) |

Fig. 4. 3D line drawing for a Buddha in Longmen grottoes. (a) Photo of the Buddha. (b) 3D model. (c) Local scales. (d) Manual drawing. (e) Multi-scale ridge detection.

3.3 Virtual Restoration

In China, many cultural relics are broken or stolen, so restoration is a very important part of protection and study of cultural relics. Compared with the restoration on real objects, there is no damage to the cultural relics by virtual restoration and different restoration strategies can be applied to obtain a reasonable repairing result.

For different types of missing parts, digital restoration can be classified into the following categories:

(1) The missing parts can be found. The body and the missing parts can be scanned respectively and be merged together virtually. Several such projects in Longmen grottoes and Xiangtangshan grottoes have been carried out. In Longmen grottoes, two Buddha heads were back to China in 2005 and the archeologists found the bodies in the caves. Using 3D digitizing technology, we merge the missing parts with the body.

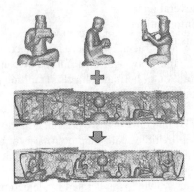

Fig. 5. Virtual merging of sculptures with the body from Xiangtangshan cave

In Xiangtangshan grottoes project, the archeologists from Chicago University scanned over twenty heads, hands or other parts outside China and the cave was scanned in China. The missing objects and the bodies are merged virtually. Fig. 5 shows the merging results of some sculptures with the body from Xiangtangshan cave. Fig. 6(a) shows the merging results of a Buddha head with the body from Huodingdong cave in Longmen grottoes.

(2) The missing parts are not found but can be inferred from the existing parts. The missing parts can be reconstructed based on the neighbourhood information. Fig. 6(b) shows the statue before repairing, and the repaired results based on the neighbourhood are shown in Fig. 6(c). From the general knowledge, we can see that the necklace should be a complete one and the bead should be similar and the curve on the clothes should be smooth. Based on these knowledge, the original appearance of the Bodhisattva can be restored.

(3) The missing parts are large. If there are old photos or any historic record, the restoration can be performed based on these evidence and the 3D models can be constructed manually. If there is no supporting material for the restoration, the restoration can be based on the statues of the same period but sometimes the restoration results will be very controversial.

(a)   (b)   (c)

Fig. 6. Virtual restoration. (a) Restoration pipeline. (b,c) Enlarged view of the part before and after repairing.

3.4   Virtual Display

We know that there is a conflict between the cultural heritage protection and display. For example, when a visitor goes to a cave, usually he can only see the sculptures outside the cave with several meters away from the statues to avoid any damage to the sculptures. Thus, the information that he can obtain is very limited. Virtual display can effectively solve this problem. The audience can enjoy the digital model from any viewpoint without any damage to the cultural relics.

For different scenes, different display strategies should be used. We design a virtual roaming system for large scene in which the user can roam in the scene and view any details of the scene. A stereo display system, consisting of a high frequency projector, stereo glasses and an infrared emitter, is also constructed so that the audience can be fully immersed into the 3D scene. Fig. 7(a, b) show some of the rendered scenes of Longmen grottoes. For small objects, an interactive viewing system is designed so that the viewer can rotate, move or zoom the object to any position and see the details. Fig. 7(c, d) show the interactive display of small cultural relics in the museum.

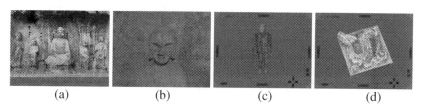

| (a) | (b) | (c) | (d) |

Fig. 7. Virtual display of heritage scenes. (a, b) Display of large scenes. (c, d) Display of small objects in the museum.

4 Conclusions

In this paper, we present a 3D digitizing pipeline for cultural heritage. The pipeline includes 3D scanning, 3D registration, geometric modeling and texture mapping. Different kinds of scanners can be used to obtain the 3D point cloud. For high quality scanning, we use an automatic global registration algorithm based on the registration of feature points. The global registration method is time and memory efficient. The resulting 3D model is of high precision with enough details. Based on the 3D model, we introduce the geometric modeling and texture mapping methods.

3D digitization has many applications in archeology and cultural heritage protection. Four main applications are introduced in this paper, which include digital archiving, 3D line drawing, virtual restoration and virtual display. The technology has been successfully implemented in many digital heritage projects. These projects show that 3D digitization greatly facilitates archeology and plays an important role in cultural heritage protection.

Acknowledgments. This work was supported in part by the NHTRDP 863 Grant No. 2009AA01Z329 and the NHTRDP 863 Grant No. 2009AA012105. Thanks for the cooperation of Longmen grottoes Academy, School of Archaeology and Museology, Peking University and Center for East Art, Chicago University.

References

1. Ikeuchi, K., Oishi, T., Takamatsu, J., Sagawa, R., Nakazawa, A., Kurazume, R., Nishino, K., Kamakura, M., Okamoto, Y.: The Great Buddha Project: digitally archiving, restoring, and analyzing cultural heritage objects. Int. Journal of Computer Vision 75(1), 189–208 (2007)
2. Levoy, M., Pulli, K., Curless, B., Rusinkiewicz, S., Koller, D., Pereira, L., Ginzton, M., Anderson, S.E., Davis, J., Ginsberg, J., Shade, J., Fulk, D.: The Digital Michelangelo Project: 3D scanning of large statues. In: Proc. SIGGRAPH, pp. 131–144 (2000)
3. Stamos, I., Allen, P.: Automatic registration of 2-D with 3-D imagery in urban environments. In: Proc. Int. Conference on Computer Vision, pp. 731–737 (2001)
4. Gelfand, N., Mitra, N.J., Guibas, L.J., Pottmann, H.: Robust global registration. In: Proc. Symp. Geometry Processing, pp. 197–206 (2005)
5. Hou, F., Qi, Y., Shen, X., Yang, S., Zhao, Q.: Automatic registration of multiple range images based on cycle space. The Visual Computer: International Journal of Computer Graphics (5), 657–665 (2009)
6. Brown, B.J., Rusinkiewicz, S.: Non-rigid range-scan alignment using thin-plate splines. In: Int. Symposium on 3D Data Processing, Visualization and Transmission, pp. 759–765 (2004)
7. Besl, P.J., Mckay, N.D.: A method for registration of 3-d shapes. IEEE Trans. on Pattern Analysis and Machine Intelligence 14(2), 239–256 (1992)
8. Lorensen, W.E., Cline, H.E.: Marching cubes: A high resolution 3d surface construction algorithm. Computer Graphics 21(4), 163–169 (1987)
9. Sagawa, R., Ikeuchi, K.: Hole filling of a 3d model by flipping signs of a signed distance field in adaptive resolution. IEEE Transactions on Pattern Analysis and Machine Intelligence 30, 686–699 (2008)
10. Ma, W., Zha, H.: Surveying and mapping caves by using 3d digital technologies. In: Proc. 12th Int. Conf on Virtual Systems and Multimedia, pp. 368–376 (2006)
11. Luo, T., Wu, H.-Y., Zha, H.: Crease detection on noisy meshes via probabilistic scale selection. In: Aisan Conference on Computer Vision (2009)
12. Luo, T., Li, R., Zha, H.: 3d line drawing for archeological illustration. In: IEEE Workshop on eHeritage and Digital Art Preservation (2009)

Interactive Itinerary of Heritage Houses in Beirut: Walking Back to the Future

Nada El-Khoury[1] and Giovanni De Paoli[2]

[1] School of Architecture & Design, Lebanese American University and Faculty of
Environmental Design, University of Montreal, Canada
[2] Faculty of Environmental Design, University of Montreal, Canada

Abstract. The aim of this project paper is to explore the opportunities and challenges of using ICT in the understanding, representation, preservation, management, interpretation of cultural heritage and its Man initiated deconstruction. Aggressive urban development and the rampant growth of tourism pose major problems to world heritage sites. Of particular interest for this project paper are issues related to the specific town of Beirut through interactive virtual reality, and making virtual reality user-friendly and available resources for the general public. A virtual Platform is presented in order to explore and map the challenges and opportunities of using ICT in cultural heritage. This virtual Platform provides a forum to examine and discuss current practices and future directions in the representation, documentation and communication of cultural heritage using ICT. It aims to provide an occasion to share and exchange experiences and research findings, to stimulate more ideas and useful insights regarding the uses of ICT in cultural heritage.

Keywords: ICT, web, interactive virtual reality, Beirut.

1 Introduction

This research project deals with the use of information and communication technologies (ICT) in the enhancement of historical cities, particularly in the case of the city of Beirut in Lebanon. Located in Lebanon, Beirut is at a crossroads between the Orient and the Occident. Beirut is at the centre of an amalgamation of cultures, which shows unique architectural land-marks boasting a number of lively ancient neighbourhoods. Beirut's history goes back more than 5000 years. Excavations in Beirut have unearthed layers of Phoenician, Hellenistic, Roman, Byzantine, Arab, Crusader and Ottoman remains.

The idea for this research arose from the study of certain ancient cities, of which sometimes only few old spaces remain, but that are important enough to merit further exploration: these spaces represent an architectural heritage. There are multiple definitions of heritage, and this a subject of ongoing debate among the various disciplines involved in its conservation. In our case, we define it as the know-how arising from the construction methods and ways of life that characterize a place through history. The goal is to reconstruct the "memory" of a place through the use of new

M. Ioannides (Ed.): EuroMed 2010, LNCS 6436, pp. 389–398, 2010.

information and communication technologies (ICT). Heritage is a constantly evolving concept, particularly since 1989 when UNESCO introduced the notion of intangible heritage, the importance of which was confirmed by the "Convention for the Safeguarding of the Intangible Cultural Heritage" of 2003. The concept of intangible heritage is increasingly gaining currency. According to M. Petzet [12], "The preoccupation with what we try to de-fine as intangible heritage may also contribute to a broader emotional basis of conservation practice, which can help us in the daily fight against the progressive world-wide destruction and decay of our cultural heritage." [12] Intangible heritage is not a static value, but an evolutionary concept: "The notion of intangible heritage must not be fixed at a particular point in time – it is dynamic and evolves and it is the evolving intangible heritage which is important." [2]

It is also important to note that the concept of heritage was brought to Lebanon in the 19th century by European missionaries, explorers, archaeologists and other scientists interested in identifying and describing monuments from Antiquity and the Middle Ages in the Mediterranean. Since then, the notion of heritage in Lebanon has evolved and now refers to a specifically Lebanese heritage, with ideological undertones directly linked to national identity. Lebanon is composed of several social and denominational identities, which means that heritage is perceived differently according to one's background. Without belabouring these nuances, suffice it to say that heritage and its preservation is a major issue in the world today, and is beginning to gain importance in Lebanon.

These new approaches to tangible and intangible heritage have guided our experimentation in developing new digital devices to protect and promote the architectural heritage through ICT. Beirut is loosing its heritage assets and its traditional houses (Figure 1) to make way for monumental concrete and glass buildings that rise up to the clouds. Old houses representing the culture, history and memories of many generations are being destroyed.

In a paper published recently presenting this research project [4] and understand why these buildings aren't protected since they are officially classified as historic monuments we explained that the only existing law for the protection of architectural heritage dates back to 1933. In fact according to Article 1 of decree 166 issued in 1933 on old buildings: "what are considered as ancient remains are all things made by human hands before the year 1700 (...)". The second paragraph of the same article states as follows: "(these buildings) are considered similar to ancient ruins and are subject to the rules of this resolution" (and there-fore benefit from legal protection due to their classification). This also applies to all immovable things built after the year 1700 having historical and artistic value that respond to conservation needs and support the common well-being of the people. This law mainly protects buildings dating before 1700, although newer buildings may also be added to the list by the government.

In 1993, the High Planning Council appealed to a group of architects who had analyzed a number of ancient buildings and had established a list of buildings to be protected. At that time, 1 016 buildings were listed. In 1997, the list was reduced to only 520 buildings, representing only 2.5% of all buildings in Beirut. In 1999, the number decreased to 220. Mona Hallak, who sits on the board of the Association for the Protection of Ancient Sites and Residences (AP-SAD), argues that the list has only aggravated the situation by classifying buildings A through to E according to their state.

Fig. 1. Examples of threatened ancient neighbourhoods in Beirut

"A means that the house is in good condition whereas E means that it is in very bad shape," she says. This list implies that only the dwellings classified as A, B or C should be protected, while the others are left to demolition.

In 2007, Tarek Mitri, Minister of Culture at the time, proposed a law encouraging owners of old houses to maintain them through financial aid. The Council of Ministers adopted the law, however citizens are still waiting for the law to be ratified by Parliament. On April 12, 2010, the Cabinet adopted a decision to stop the demolition of heritage buildings in Beirut classified as A, B and C according to the consultancy study completed in July 1998 by "Khatib and Alami".

Promoters as well as owners suffer from a lack of financial resources with regards to heritage conservation. Both owners and developers want to make profits while saying they contribute to the growth of the country. However old buildings are in bad shape and threatened, and a lot of them have already been demolished. What one should be asking is whether the tourists will come to Beirut to visit the towers of concrete and skyscrapers. The disappearance of old homes in Beirut represents both an economic and cultural loss, a part of the history and culture of a country which is disappearing. [10] [13]

The city of Beirut characterized by threatened heritage is therefore relevant, and these issues encourages one to think about ways to contribute to the preservation of the heritage value of old sites while rampant urbanization continues." [4] (Figure 2)

Fig. 2. Examples of rampant development (photo workshop Gemmayzé, 2005-2007- ALBA)

2 Methodology

In the case of this research project, it is a question of developing a knowledge-sharing space whilst referring to the use of ICTs (Information and communication technologies) and the main objective has been to gain an understanding of heritage in order to demonstrate how, using new methods of representation, management and reuse of content and knowledge, we can attempt to virtually represent the tangible and the intangible: what is and what used to be. ICTs allow for an exploration involving the simultaneous use of simulation and experimentation, while respecting the guidelines set forth in UNESCO's charters on the safeguarding of heritage. [4]

With regard to techniques of representation, it should be noted that in the twentieth century architectural heritage was illustrated by means of drawings, plans, cross-sections and elevations produced by architects and archaeologists. Three-dimensional reconstructions of spaces were often created as well. Graphic reconstitution in the form of drawings is still widely used today for the enhancement of archaeological heritage. [3]

"The restoration of ancient monuments is another way in which architectural heritage can be enhanced. Restoration, according to Pérouse de Montclos, involves a number of different areas. These include "consolidation", which is done to ensure a building's durability, without modifying it; "reassembly", the reconstruction of a building whose parts are still available on-site; "re-constitution", the collection and reassembly of authentic elements that have been dispersed; and "repair", the replacement of deteriorated parts with new, identical elements. The physical reconstitution of monuments is now regulated. The Venice Charter, which preceded the one adopted in Victoria Falls in 2003, states "that architectural heritage must be considered within the cultural context to which it belongs, that conservation and restoration of architectural heritage re-quires a multidisciplinary approach, and that the latter is not an end in itself but a means to an end, which is the building as a whole." [4]

Finally, it should be recalled that, as with life-size reconstructions, scale models also are potential tools for enhancing architectural heritage. They can be used to depict a building, but of-ten provide no information on the factors related to its construction history. Such models are limited to three-dimensional reconstitution of forms that are, in certain cases, hypothetical. They are often used as teaching aids, and also as tools to inform and entertain cultural tourists. ICTs can contribute as unifying elements in a collaborative and multidisciplinary environment. [7]

In our previous research we noted that "more than ever heritage is a subject of international concern and it would be appropriate to create collaborative spaces where one could share knowledge relating to threatened or even missing heritage; this collaborative workspace is an inter-connected environment in which all the participants can access and interact with each other. However the context of heritage is very broad: its concepts are difficult to define, particularly with the complexity of the themes considered. It will therefore be necessary to restrict the field of study to a specific example which is representative of heritage at risk, in other words, the selection of a case study. The example of Beirut in Lebanon is relevant because some neighbourhoods having historic character are disappearing in favour of rampant urbanization. In these neighbourhoods, we do not have many traces left, however, a study of the urban plan of Beirut is underway at the Lebanese Academy of Fine Arts (ALBA) as part of research activities related to heritage based on multiple data. It is therefore appropriate to develop as a first step documentation methods in order to later integrate information concerning heritage at risk in a knowledge sharing space accessible from anywhere via the Web. On the basis of our research data, we propose an initial digital space. This digital space allows the user to clearly identify cultural heritage spaces at risk in Beirut. Subsequently, a final interface is proposed which would meet the designer's target requirements more adequately. The project would be published on the Internet and its promotion of threatened heritage will raise awareness among different stakeholders. An important outcome of the research is to show that the threat of heritage loss is common to many countries where there are often cases of economic development at the expense of heritage conservation." [4]

Based on the presented approach above, experiments have been developed and performed within the context of heritage preservation which deal with the protection and preservation of a building whilst considering its heritage value, using the new information and communication technologies (ICT) currently available. The results of our recent research shows that the roles of these new technologies are not limited to simple communication and representational tools. Increasing amounts of research have shown that they are also used as information tools to understand values, thereby allowing the users to take into account a number of different factors during the demolition of heritage buildings and traditional houses. Therefore the research work attempts to demonstrate that the appropriation of the heritage value of a heritage space is possible and can lead to its preservation. [4] [5]

3   Experimentation

During the presentation of this project at the 2nd International Conference on Heritage and Sustainable development (Evora, Portugal, June 2010) we said that "Today, many strategies are developed in favour of sustainable development. "The Brundtland report entitled Our Common Future, published in 1987, put forward the idea that "sustainable development answers to the needs of the present without compromising the ability of future generations to answer to their own". Five years later the EU

Commission improved this formulation by stating that sustainable development was "both a policy and a strategy to ensure continuity of economic and social development while respecting the environment and without compromising the natural resources indispensable to human activity". [6] In nearly each of our actions, we need to systematically take account of environmental aspects. There are also environmental challenges arising from the themes of the present article which should hopefully contribute to the preservation and protection of environmental and heritage issues. [14]

It is important to remark that, as outlined, in Heritage2010 program: "Nowadays, sustainable development was brought much forward than the concept expressed in the book "Our Common Future", commonly known as "The Brundtland Report". The role of culture and social aspects enlarged the initial statement where environment and economics took the main role, guiding the earliest research on sustainable development." [16]

Efforts are currently being deployed around the world to preserve the spirit of places through the safeguarding of tangible and intangible heritage, which is regarded as an innovative and efficient way to ensure sustainable and social development throughout the world. [9] [11] Urban development is, among other issues, inducing transformations and creating disruptions within societies and there is a need to more fully understand these threats so as to prepare preventative measures and sustainable solutions. Developing ways of preventing degradation and destruction of heritage buildings is an urgent matter. Using ICTs for communicating and preserving such a heritage could contribute to the safeguarding of the spirit of place and better protect them from the threats of a changing world. [5]

In order to test models that could play a role in communicating places that represent examples of heritage in danger, we selected the city of Beirut, which includes streets characterized by heritage buildings. As a first step, we organized and described approaches for the transfer of knowledge (Figure 3) that allowed us to exploit representations of spaces with the help of digital modelling software. We then developed the information structure necessary to validate strategies for defining an informative representation interface, using software applications that enabled us to create web-based interactive digital devices. Starting with the modelling of the street, we tried to identify buildings within this space by including text data and images. This itinerary proposes web content where the user can interact with the proposed interface and find out in real time where the threatened places are located depending on the action selected. This interface can display the various layers and forms of a place so as to allow the user to learn through interaction with the digital modelling systems and by experiencing friendly interfaces. [15] Our method aims to provide new architectural solutions using technological means, with an emphasis on information gathered on heritage sites at risk. By using this approach, we hope to present a cognitive and interactive device, which enables the users to identify the heritage at risk. This system has the advantage of providing information on the site's location, its shape and future threats in order to stimulate action leading to its protection.

On the basis of our research results, we propose an initial digital model. This model allows the user to clearly identify cultural heritage sites at risk. Subsequently, a final computer model is proposed which would meet the designer's target requirements more adequately. This computer model attempts to simulate a model of a particular heritage site. (Figure 4).

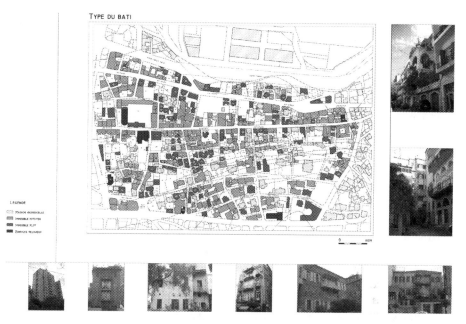

Fig. 3. Gathering data on buildings in Beirut. (workshop Gemmayzé, 2005-2007- ALBA)

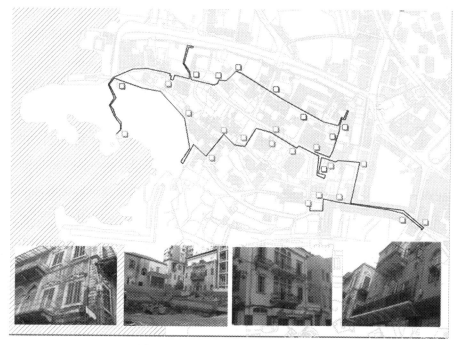

Fig. 4. Itinerary tracing heritage at risk

The results we propose lead us to believe that we can rely on computer tools to communicate heritage spaces at risk. Subsequent research contributes to the development of digital devices that can enable the communication of these heritage sites and contributes to the development of digital knowledge tools. In addition to the potential of simulation, virtual space opens new possibilities of expression and experience. It also helps to re-create and remould a monumental complex without having all the information and to test hypotheses that we would otherwise be unable to validate without compromising the heritage values of a site by physically reconstructing it. This was the case of Beirut, which we used as a case study.

4 Conclusion

This conclusion reiterates the remarks already made when presenting the project at the 2nd International Conference on Heritage and Sustainable Development [16], and following the recommendations of experts who point out that will be important to create a virtual-collaborative platform to enable effective exchange between project participants. In fact as we noted in our previous article "Over the last few years, a remarkable increase has occurred in the use of Information and Communication Technology (ICT) for the e-Documentation of the Past, how to preserve and manage Cultural Heritage, whether books, drawings, architectural and archaeological and discuss future methologies and plans for the local and global cooperation in this area. This has drastically transformed the way we create, reuse and manage knowledge. Visualisation techniques, computer animations for Cultural heritage applications employed have evolved from standard surveying and CAD tools into interactive environments, laser scanning, virtual reality and fully automated video-based techniques. It is often heard that Virtual heritage tend to pre-sent value-free content and thus are inefficient in suggesting cultural and symbolic meanings. Virtual Heritage, as any other expression, tend to preserve, document, manage, present/visualise and disseminate the rich and diverse Cultural Heritage of Mankind. Thus the issue of using (ICT) for cultural heritage is by no means a simple one and must be considered from different angles.

More than ever before, the subject of heritage is of international interest. It would therefore be relevant to create collaborative spaces to unify diverse knowledge on threatened or extinct heritage. However the heritage field is extensive and complex: its notions are difficult to define and at times, to understand, thereby questioning the ambitions of the work proposed. The example of Beirut (Lebanon) a city characterized by threatened heritage, is pertinent as some of its neighbourhoods having heritage value are in the process of disappearing due to rampant urbanization, leaving little trace of their former character. Therefore it is important to establish documentation methods relevant to these disappearing traces, which can be integrated into these pro-posed knowledge-sharing spaces accessible on the Web. Through the development of an environment based on communication, this research project can be implemented in many countries, such as Canada, where certain heritage sites are in peril and many have already disappeared.

Furthermore, by putting the project on the Web, it allows for different players implicated in heritage and in particular, threatened heritage, to better understand the issues relevant to this field. One of the primary benefits of this research project is to make clear that the threat of losing heritage is common to many countries where economic development is prioritized over heritage conservation. Future possible work which furthers the work proposed in this paper involves developing a portrait of different world heritage sites in peril so as to allow those concerned with the future of these sites to communicate the information they have garnered through this knowledge-sharing space and propose solutions for the site's conservation so as to best protect it.

This research work tries to offer an opportunity to raise public awareness concerning the diversity of Lebanon's heritage and the efforts that are required to protect and conserve it, as well as to draw attention to its vulnerability. The proposed work is essentially an exchange between people and established results, where the increased use of ICT offers a renewed use of the Web that improves information management and proposes a system of knowledge management. Let us consider the value of heritage buildings and houses in our lives and join in the effort to protect those sites which are threatened by neglect, destruction and degradation. In a small way, this research work is a contribution to this consideration." [4]

References

1. Anders, P.: Envisioning Cyberspace: Designing 3D Electronics Spaces. McGraw-Hill, New York (1998)
2. Bumbaru, D.: Patrimoine matériel et immatériel, devoir et plaisir de mémoire. In: La mémoire des lieux: préserver le sens et les valeurs immatérielles des monuments et sites, Actes du Symposium Scientifique International, ICOMOS, Victoria Falls (2003)
3. De Paoli, G., El-Khoury, N.: ICT and the Ancient City of Byblos: A new Direction for the Communication of Intangible Heritage. In: Augmented Heritage, Europia Production (2005)
4. El-Khoury, N., De Paoli, G.: A knowledge-sharing space to document the spirit of place: A case study of neighbourhoods in Beirut, Heritage 2010, Evora, Portugal (2010)
5. El-Khoury, N., Meyer, E., Grussenmeyer, P., De Paoli, G.: Projet de création d'un espace-mémoire pour des sites historiques à l'aide des TIC, dans L'esprit du lieu, sous la direction de L. Turgeon, Les Presses de l'Université Laval (2009)
6. Emery, M.: Innovations durables, une autre architecture française, Appropriate sustainabilities, New Ways in French Architecture. Birkhäuser, Berlin (2002)
7. Gillot, C.: La restitution du patrimoine archéologique bâti, aux moyens des technologies de l'infor-mation et de la communication, État de l'art In Rapport de recherche GRCAO, Contribution d'un moyen informatique à la validation d'hypothèses de restitution architecturale dans le domaine du patrimoine bâti ancien. University of Montreal, CRSH Canada (2006)
8. Hook, K., Benyon, D., Munro, A.: Designing Information Spaces: The Social Navigation Approach. Springer, Berlin (2003)
9. Larsen, K.E.: Nara Conference on Authenticity in relation to the World heritage Convention. In: Proceedings of UNESCO World Heritage Center, ICOMOS, ICCROM (1995)
10. Mawad, D.: Le béton menace le vieux Beyrouth, Courrier International (2009)

11. Nourissier, G.: Quel savoir-faire pour entretenir un patrimoine? In: dans Actes du Symposium Scientifique, La mémoire des lieux: préserver le sens et les valeurs immatérielles des monuments et des sites, Victoria Falls, Zimbabwe (2003)
12. Petzet, M.: La mémoire des lieux:préserver le sens et les valeurs immatérielles des monuments et sites. In: Proceedings of the Place, Memory, Meaning: Preserving Intangible Values in Monuments and Sites (2003)
13. Sfeir, R.: Le béton remplace le caractère patrimonial des anciens quartiers de Beyrouth, Al-Nahar, 30/04/2010, Beirut (2010)
14. Williamson, T., Radford, A., Bennetts, H.: Understanding sustainable architecture. Spon Press, London (2003)
15. Zreik, K., Reza, B.: Augmented Heritage: A Sustainable ICT Challenge. In: Zreik, K., Beheshti, R., Fakouch, O. (eds.) dans Augmented Heritage, New Era for Architectural Design, Civil Engineering and Urban Planning, Europia, France (2005)
16. http://www.heritage2010.greenlines-institute.org/H2010website/home.html

Cultural Heritage and Sustainable Valorization in the Governorate of Tartous with Reference to the Euromed IV Project: The Contribution of Geomatics

Grazia Tucci, Francesco Algostino, Laura Bucalossi,
Alessandro Conti, and Alessia Nobile

University of Florence, Faculty of Architecture
Department of Construction and Restoration
via P.A. Micheli 8, 50121 Florence, Italy

Abstract. Six Mediterranean countries are participating in the "Mare Nostrum" project: "A Heritage Trail along the Phoenician maritime routes and through the historic port cities"; the goal of this project is to valorize the cultural heritage of the sites involved by promoting and supporting sustainable tourism. WP4 concentrates on the port cities of Tyre and Tartous, chosen as pilot sites. The on site research was conducted in accordance with the WP4 objectives: on the one hand a survey campaign was set up to acquire metric and qualitative data on the structures chosen as samples; on the other hand an enormous amount of photographic and video documentation was collected for the 3D models that were produced in the first phase. The paper will describe how the disciplines involved in Geomatics can provide important contributions to all four phases of the Heritage and Development framework.

Keywords: Cultural Heritage, Laser scanning, Virtual Tour, Cultural Mapping.

1 Cultural Heritage and Sustainable Valorization

Six Mediterranean countries (Syria, Lebanon, Greece, Italy, Malta and Tunis) are participating in the "Mare Nostrum" project: "A Heritage Trail along the Phoenician maritime routes and through the historic port cities"; the goal of this project is to valorize the cultural heritage of the sites involved by promoting and supporting sustainable tourism.

This goal is being achieved by: raising public awareness of the importance of preserving and promoting sites; valorizing and promoting the Cultural Heritage of the different Mediterranean basin cultures in a more communicative way; promoting effective management plans to reduce the marginalization of archaeological sites and to enhance the centuries-old port-city relationship; defining management plans for target sites that will promote sustainable tourism.

WP4 concentrates on Syria and Lebanon where the port cities of Tyre and Tartous (including the nearby Arwad Island which is already on the World Heritage Tentative List) have been chosen as pilot sites. In both cities WP4 has to: identify

M. Ioannides (Ed.): EuroMed 2010, LNCS 6436, pp. 399–408, 2010.
© Springer-Verlag Berlin Heidelberg 2010

archaeological/urban sites and proposed re-qualification projects that will enable these sites to be better used; design two kinds of itineraries in a sort of "cultural map": an urban map that includes the waterfront/city connection and a Mediterranean map that connects all the port cities involved in the project; place explanatory panels on site to provide information for tourists.

The concept of sustainability has a double meaning when it is applied to cultural heritage management: in the physical sense it means that excessive concentrations of tourists have to be avoided to ensure that the conservation of the cultural heritage is not compromised; in the economic sense it means limiting the cost-benefits differential and thus increasing the capacity for promoting development. Conservation management planning and the model for sustainable valorization can be integrated to evolve a new model wherein heritage serves as the core of the development process. This process moves through four phases: *Awareness*- Development begins with the identification of resources which have to be documented and studied to harness their potential use; *Appreciation*- Development emphasizes public participation in cultural heritage activities; *Protection*- The tools of reference are heritage charters (concepts, policies and practices) and conservation guidelines (technical standards); *Utilization.*

2   The Contribution of Geomatics

The contribution of geomatics does not only consist in the application of the latest information technology procedures but creates a new methodological behavior within the data acquisition and management process. Geomatic techniques can play a central role because they provide innovative and more complete ways of describing reality which, in their turn, allow approaches at different levels:

1. Geomatic techniques can manage enormous quantities of data relating to a single geographic location but generated at different times;
2. Extra features can be added to the representation field during the research phase using processing to reconstruct modifications that have taken place over time;
3. Georeferencing of data makes possible to lin the existing relationship between cultural heritage objects;
4. The knowledge acquired can be widely disseminated on-line;
5. The information can also be transferred to external databases and web sites.

To sum up, the research for this project uses geomatic techniques to propose innovative ways of using case studies, allowing diverse analogous elements (the port cities linked to each other in the Phoenician commercial maritime routes system) to be considered simultaneously. In this sense it is possible to propose hypotheses for valorizing these heritage objects which take into account a series of conditions such as accessibility, current transformations within the area, relations between the more important monuments which profoundly effect their use. The use of these heritage objects should be seen as an opportunity for increasing our understanding of them.

The disciplines involved in Geomatics provide important contributions to all four phases of the Heritage and Development framework: awareness, appreciation, protection and utilization.

On the one hand the acquisition and manipulation of data for studying and conserving sites: preparing geometric and thematic surveys, setting up maintenance programmes and simulating models for predicting the impact of the tourist flow. On the other a powerful tool for communication. To provide the cultural heritage with such a powerful system for learning, enriched by information technologies, is certainly a first step towards a better understanding of the sites and an essential step towards their appropriate valorization.

3 Description of the Places

Tartous was founded in the 2nd millenium B.C. as a coastal settlement on land belonging to Aradus (the present day Arwad), a small island 3 km away and one of the most important Phoenician city–states. It expanded as an independent city under the Emperor Constantine and his son Costanzo II. The city was conquered by Arabs in 636 and was of little importance until it was taken by Raymond de San Gilles during the First Crusade. In the second quarter of the 12th Century the Cathedral of Our Lady of Tortosa, one of the best preserved Crusader religious buildings, was built. Its fortified structure makes it unique among the Latin churches of the Near East.

In 1152 Tartous became one of the main settlements of the Knights Templar who built the Citadel in the north-west corner of the city. This Citadel was built with double concentric walls and a double moat. Although dwellings were later built within

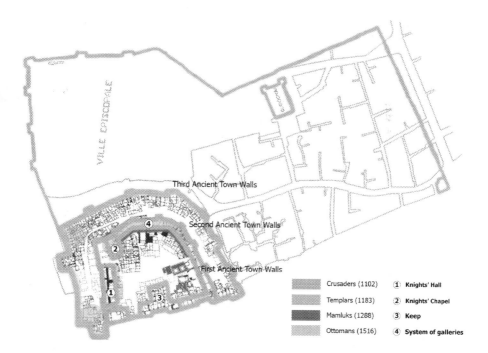

Fig. 1. Historical phases of the Citadel of Tartous. The numbers indicate the most important examples of Crusader architecture that are still recognizable.

the Citadel the remains of its walls and the most important Knights Templar buildings (the Keep, the Banqueting Hall and the Chapel) and the later Ottoman additions such as the galleries along the walls, are still clearly visible (Figure 1).

Tartous is currently the second most important city on the Syrian coast and is the main centre of a network of important points of interest for culture and tourism. The relationship with Arwad has now been reversed: the island is only a small town that depends mainly on local daily tourism. There are significant remains of the Phoenician Aradus on the island including the imposing remains of the walls facing the sea. The importance of Arwad during the Crusades is testified by the presence of two castles, one built by the Crusaders on the highest point of the island, the other built by the Arabs by the sea.

There are other important archaeological remains 7 km from Tartous at Amrit. The temple known as Maabed, is a basin carved into the rock surrounded by blocks of stone with an altar in the centre, which holds water from a nearby spring. Nearby there is a necropolis with underground tombs and two monuments called Meghazil.

There are also the remains of the docks of a port and a stadium from the Hellenistic period. Further from Tartous there are other important sites of cultural interest. One of the most interesting is the Hosn Suleiman archaeological area (the ancient Baetocece), a sanctuary dating from Phoenician times with a well preserved sacred enclosure and the remains of two temples dedicated to Zeus and Astarte. There are numerous castles in the area which date back to the Crusades. The White Castle at Safita, the Al-Marqat Castle and the Krak des Chevaliers, the most famous and best preserved of the castles of the Crusade period, were all inspected during the mission.

4 Goals and Methodological Choices

During previous WPs, graphic, cartographic, iconographic and bibliographic material was gathered for pilot sites and so, after an inspection, it was possible to define the area on which to concentrate the on-site research. Studies by G. A. Neglia and M. Bouteflika were used as references for the urban analysis of Tartous and the surrounding area; the "Memorandum on Sustainable Urban Development in Syria" and the "Workshop on the preservation and development of the old city of Tartous" held by GTZ and the Syrian Ministry of Local Administration and Environment, provided information on guiding principles and programmes in the important areas of urban policy and management.

The on site research was conducted in accordance with the WP4 objectives: on the one hand a survey campaign was set up to acquire metric and qualitative data on the structures chosen as samples; this provided the necessary information for the systematic analysis (chronological phases, construction techniques, state of preservation) required for preparing conservation guidelines; on the other hand an enormous amount of photographic and video documentation was collected for the 3D models that were produced in the first phase; this documentation is being used for multimedia popularization and communication of the most interesting sites: architectural heritage, landscape and archaeological sites.

In particular: integrated topographic and laser scanning techniques were used to provide a metric survey of the Knights' Chapel and the urban spaces inside the Citadel; the most interesting parts of Tartous (the Citadel and the Cathedral/Museum) and the surrounding areas (Arwad Island and the archaeological site at Amrit) were photographed for modelling for communication projects (virtual tours, integrated video and multimedia products).

4.1 Metric and Thematic Survey

The metric surveys and the studies of the materials and construction techniques were mainly carried out in the old city of Tartous. The urban fabric has a complex structure because of its pronounced vertical stratification. The Knights' Chapel and the cross-vaulted galleries, both situated in the inner circle of the city walls, and a part of the wall circle (Figure 1) were chosen because they have best preserved the peculiar characteristics of Crusader architecture. Three-dimensional metric surveys were carried out to obtain the disposition of masses on an urban scale as well as the detail required for analyzing wall textures. A topographical network with 7 vertices was defined to measure, 59 topographical targets which were necessary for the alignment and referentiation of the range maps acquired. An HDS6000 phase-based scanner was used for the detail survey. The shooting geometry and the scanning resolution were modulated to better adapt them to the morphological characteristics of the spaces. Data was acquired from different view points to ensure uniform data coverage and to minimize any possible "shadow areas". Documenting the Chapel's morphometric characteristics, the building techniques used, the extrados of the vaults, the fallen down parts and the thickness of the walls was a complex business partly because it was difficult to obtain access to the adjacent private spaces but also because it was difficult to transfer the reference system around the building. A total of 43 scans were carried out: 20 for the Knights' Chapel, 7 for the Ottoman galleries, 5 for the portion of the town walls and 11 to document the urban fabric in which these structures are inserted.

In the parts that have been studied it is possible to measure the size of the ashlars, their shape, the workmanship involved and the construction criteria used. A wide variety of wall building techniques has been documented. As an example: portion of wall from the Chapel is made up of perfectly squared parallelepiped blocks, the norm for important buildings; portion of wall from the service galleries, is composed of small blocks of rather irregular shape in a homogeneously textured wall surface.

4.2 Image Recording

All the sites that are part of WP4 – the Cathedral/Museum of Tartous, the Citadel, the Amrit site and Arwad - have been documented using the most innovative digital techniques available to produce spherical panoramas, high resolution image mosaics and digital stereo images. More than 14.000 photos were taken to cover the different aspects of the mission: they show the places, the architecture, the landscapes, the residents and the local handicraft production as well as documenting the different stages of the work. A panoramic head, combined with a 15 mm fish-eye lens, was used for photographing complex or particularly wide spaces that could not be covered by a single photo and panoramas were elaborated using cylindrical equirectangular projection. The individual photos were mounted using software so they could be visualized as 2D files and explored as immersive environments. About 70 panoramas were mounted: each one was made up of an average of 21 photos and a maximum of 60 photos. Up to 3 stop bracketing was used for every single photo: these multiple shots also make it possible to obtain images with a colour depth of 16 bits and to recover under or over-exposed details. This process is fundamental for 360° external photography where the exposure differences are particularly strong and to obtain HDR (high dinamic range) images.

5 Graphic Output

The total points model obtained after the alignment and referentiation of the range maps is an extremely versatile 3D database as it allows graphic output to be modified to meet specific requirements. Extracting information from the data gathered by the scanning systems is a complex time-consuming post-processing operation that requires special software and skilled personnel. The following information can be obtained from the range maps: plans, elevations and vertical sections; 2D images of the range map; 3D static and dynamic digital models. Further information can be obtained from the photographic archive: spherical panoramas; high resolution image mosaics; digital stereo images.

Table 1. Summary table of metric survey and image recording data

METRIC SURVEY DATA (Tartous Citadel)	
Tartous Citadel total area	about 31.000 mq
Survey area	about 6.900 mq
Surveyors	4
Topographic survey	
Total station	Leica TCR 303
Closed traverse	1
Open traverse	1
Vertices	7
Least-squares adjustment (stdev)	80^{cc}, 11 mm
Laser scanner survey	
Laser scanner	Leica HDS6000
Laser scanner stations	43
Acquired targets	59
Acquired spatial coordinates	185.018.130
Registration mean absolute error	0.006 m
IMAGE RECORDING DATA (Tartous and surroundings)	
Photographers	2
Cameras	Nikon D3, D90 and D700
Fixed lenses	15mm f/2.8, 24mm f/2.8, 50mm f/1.4
Zoom lenses	18-200mm f/3.5-5.6, 18-55mm f/3.5-5.6, 24-70mm f/2.8
Image resolution	D90: 4288x2848 - D3 and D700: 4256x2832
Photographed locations	16
Avg. number of photos in panoramas	21
Shots for each picture	3
Avg. panorama resolution	360°x80°: 6.000x3.200
Max panorama resolution	360°x40°: 72.000x3.600
Texture pictures	160
Camera and video shooting time	42'33"

Repeated elaboration of the data collected makes it possible to extract a wide range of graphic output whose complexity and articulation depends on the goal desired and to experiment ways of representing this output that have enormous communication potential: 3D digital modelling as a method for checking the historical reconstruction; 3D and kinetic digital modelling as a tool for understanding and for education and communication; 3D digital modelling for representing morphological transformations. The preliminary results of the surveying campaign undertaken in the Tartous area during WP4 of the Mare Nostrum project are presented below.

A. Plans, Elevation and Vertical Sections The following drawings have been produced:

Fig. 2. Integration of the existing plan of the present situation and the plan extracted from the points cloud

− A plan (Figure 2) which was realized by integrating a previous survey of the Citadel with the survey undertaken by our working unit. This mixed plan was completed with an orthogonal image of the range maps of all the connecting areas (lanes and the main square) in order to show the extension of the on-site data acquisition.

− Vertical sections (Figure 3) to analyze the urban morphology and the relationship among the buildings.

B. Bidimensional Images Obtained from the Range Map. A precise digital model can simulate 2D images so well that the human eye cannot distinguish these images from perspective photographic representations. The 2D image shown in Figure 4 is example of the remarkable levels of detail that can be obtained using scanning systems. Obviously, temporal information i.e. the condition of the object at the time it was surveyed, is collected along with the geometric information.

This peculiarity, intrinsic to laser scanner data, has many positive uses for both research and for setting up multimedia instruments for popularizing, promoting and explaining the project to different user categories).

Fig. 3. Transversal section BB' passing through the Knights' Chapel

406   G. Tucci et al.

C. Static and Dynamic 3D Models. The capacity of 3D models to remain unaltered over time and their interactivity, which allows users to extract information (2D and 3D), makes such models ideal instruments for setting up virtual museums which popularize and explain the museums' contents. But this is only one of their possible applications. As these models possess the fourth dimension, time, they introduce a dynamic element to both representation and comprehension.

Fig. 4. 2D image of the total points model of the Knights' Chapel

This factor is extremely important as it provides a method for checking historical reconstructions and for representing morphological transformations.

D. Panoramic Images. The images were organized in a database managed by Adobe Lightroom 3. This software allows the images to be catalogued using metadata, i.e. series of information connected to the files containing the images. Some of this information is memorized when the photo is taken, such as the date, the type of camera used, the lens focus, the time and the diaphragm. Other information can be defined subsequently by designing a suitable thesaurus. About 60 keywords have been identified for cataloguing the images belonging to this project which means it is now possible to undertake detailed research within the database. This method of management has made over 30 GB of photographs accessible to the various members of the work group and will also make it possible for researchers outside the WP4 group to rapidly find images. The position from which the photos were taken is also known thanks to the GPS system connected to the camera. This type of information, known as geotagging, facilitates the use of these images allowing them to be managed in innovative ways such as classifying them on the basis of geographic proximity. The elaborated panoramas (Figure 5) can be used in various ways: to enable the use of inter-connected virtual spaces on the internet or on CDs; to integrate chromatic information with the points cloud; in pairs for photogrammetric restitution (spherical photogrammetry).

Fig. 5. Spherical panorama inside the vaulted galleries (Citadel of Tartous)

The panoramas of the most important archaeological and cultural sites in Tartous will be connected and put on line and, in the future, meta-nodes will be used to do the same for the principal Phoenician Mediterranean ports.

6 Towards a "Shared Cultural Mapping"

There has always been a direct relationship between tourism and cartography: maps of travel routes and general information about the areas to visit are used in selecting the destination and in planning travel and stay. Today cartography is numerical and is used on line. Geographically referred data can be questioned, cross-checked, up-dated and it can be a valid tool for understanding and valorizing planning activities as well as informing and preparing visitors. Cultural mapping is a process of collecting, analyzing and synthesizing information in order to describe the cultural resources, networks, links and usage patterns in a community. The technological revolution has had an enormous impact on the information content available on-line and has given rise to the phenomenon known as user-generated content (UGC). Photos, films, audio and text comments are placed on blogs, podcast guidebooks, social network sites, shared content multimedia sites and Wiki at an uncontrollable rate, allowing an undefined audience to access contents that would not have previously been available unless the places described had been visited in person. This enormous amount of content helps to form opinions among internet users regarding tourist destinations and services offered and in fact influences the choices made by future travelers. These technological innovations are opening the way for so-called virtual tourism which lets potential travelers anticipate their travel experience thereby stimulating their curiosity and increasing their interest in the areas visited.

Making a cultural mapping involves many different categories in a participatory approach: residents, administrators, schools, tourist operators, and generates new perspectives and prepares the ground for effective cultural planning. A map has much greater potential than an inventory; it communicates a rapidly increasing amount of information and appreciation, it draws attention to the cultural area identifying previously unknown resources and activities, it provides the possibility of looking at data from different perspective thereby gaining objectivity and overview and of locating gaps, needs and overlaps. The work to be undertaken, in the EuroMed Mare Nostrum project, will contribute to programming sustainable development by helping transform tourism into an element that valorizes the environmental and cultural qualities of a given territory as well as consuming them. The future of the tourist industry depends on the conservation of the environment in which it takes place. The first steps required are: to increase the awareness of the population regarding the cultural heritage of their own country, to sensibilize visitors and to train tour operators. A series of innovative and experimental measures should also be taken in order to identify strategies and instruments for reducing the pressure of tourism on the environment and for improving the quality of the environment in areas that will remain mass tourism destinations (for example the Island of Arwad where the visible degradation is due to the large numbers of visitors).

408   G. Tucci et al.

Acknowledgement

We would like to thank: Dr. Eng. Maher Hazar (Ministry of Culture of Syria), Dr. Michel Maqdissi and Dr. Bassam Jammous (Directorate General Of Antiquities And Museums) and Dr. Maruan Hassan, Arch. Alaa Hammoud (DGAM Department of Tartous) for their support and cooperation in the project.
Special thanks to arch. Davide Guerra for the photographical campaign on site.

References

1. Bouteflika, M.: PhD thesis: Tartous, Syrie: lecture stratigraphique et restauration urbanine. Tutor: Attilio Petruccioli. Polytechnic of Bari, 17th cycle (2004)
2. Neglia, G.A.: Digital Reconstruction as Part of Urban Renewal Projects: the Case of the Citadel of Tartous, Syria. In: Digital Media and its Applications in Cultural Heritage, pp. 161–175
3. Saidi, M.: PhD thesis: Les forms et le fonctionnement du paysage de Tartous (Syrie): du modele de projettation. Tutor: Attilio Petruccioli. Polytechnic of Bari, 17th cycle (2001-2004)
4. Coquais, J.P.R.: Arados et sa Pérée aux époques Grecque, Romaine et Byzantine. Beyrouth (1974)
5. Deschamps, P.: Les chateaux des croisés en terre sainte. Paul Geuthner, Paris (1934)
6. Folda, J.: Crusader art in the Holy Land. Cambridge University Press, New York (2005)
7. Barber, D., Mills, J.: 3D Laser Scanning for Heritage. English Heritage Publishing (2007)
8. El-Hakim, S., Beraldin, J.-A., Picard, M.: Detailed 3D Reconstruction Of Monuments Using Multiple Techniques. In: Proceedings CIPA WG 6: International Workshop On Scanning For Cultural Heritage Recording, Corfu, Greece, September 1-2, pp. 58–64 (2002)
9. Guarnieri, A., Vettore, A., El-Hakim, S., Gonzo, L.: Digital photogrammetry and laser scanning in cultural heritage survey. International Archives of Photogrammetry and Remote Sensing 35(5), 154–158 (2004)
10. Haggrén, H., Junnilainen, H., Järvinen, J., Nuutinen, T., Laventob, M., Huotarib, M.: The use of panoramic images for 3D archaeological survey. International Archives of Photogrammetry and Remote Sensing 35(5), 958–963 (2004)
11. Reulke, R., Scheibe, K., Wehr, A.: Integration of digital panoramic camera and laser scanner data. In: Proc. International Workshop on Recording, Modeling and Visualization of Cultural Heritage, Centro Stefano Franscini, Monte Verità, Ascona, Switzerland, May 22-27 (2005)
12. Torniai, C., Battle, S., Cayzer, S.: Sharing, Discovering and Browsing Geotagged Pictures on the Web. HPL-2007-73 (2007), http://www.hpl.hp.com/techreports/2007/HPL-2007-73.html {19-08-2010}
13. Tucci, G., Bonora, V., Nobile, A.: Innovative survey methods for the digital documentation of vernacular architectural Heritage in Syria. In: 22nd CIPA Symposium, Kyoto, Japan, October 11-15 (2009)
14. Tucci, G., Bonora, V., Nobile, A., Tokmakidis, K.: Geomatic methods of surveying. In: Villages of Northern Syria. In: Mecca, S., Dipasquale, L. (eds.) An architectural tradition shared by East and West - Earthen Domes and Habitats, pp. 157–162. ETS, Pisa (2009)

VISMAN-DHER Project: Integrated Fruition of Archaeological Data through a Scientific Virtual Model

Antonella Coralini[1], Antonella Guidazzoli[2], Daniela Scagliarini Corlàita[1],
and Elena Toffalori[1]

[1] Università di Bologna, Via Zamboni 33, 40126 Bologna, Italy
{antonella.coralini,daniela.scagliarini}@unibo.it,
elena.toffalori@studio.unibo.it
[2] VisITLab, Cineca, Via Magnanelli 6/3, 40033 Casalecchio di Reno (BO), Italy
a.guidazzoli@cineca.it

Abstract. This paper presents a Virtual Archaeology application realized using ViSMan (Cineca), an open-source framework for visualization and interaction with scientific 3Dmodels connected to digital archives of data. The source for data was research project (survey and documentation, study and communication) carried out by the University of Bologna in the archaeological sites of Pompeii and Herculaneum. Through a collaboration with Cineca VisITLab - experienced in virtual environments design for research and education purposes - virtual models were used as 3D archive for management and visualization of this huge amount of relevant data, thus developing a spatially structured interface for data retrieval and contextualization. The implemented application - ViSMan-DHER - allows navigation through several reconstructed Scenarios; access is provided to a rich archive of data, related to the whole region territory as well as pertaining to a single wall-painting. Some remarks and hints for future development are listed in the conclusive section.

Keywords: Herculaneum, Pompeii, Roman Houses, Scientific Visualization, Virtual Archaeology, Virtual Models.

1 Introduction

Virtual models in archaeological and historical research - provided that they are realized with philological accuracy and clear cut procedures - can perform a variety of functions, like the management of documentary material (as, for instance, in reconstructing a stratigraphic sequence of an archaeological site), providing graphic support for analyses, setting tools for museum and educational purposes as well. A well-structured virtual model can be used as a 3D archive for visualization, organization and analysis of heterogeneous data [12].

New features have been introduced in scientific VR application according to this perspective: hyperlinks from the model to external datasets (including sources and related documents), integration with relational databases, metadata management, better user interaction, multi-channel communication projects, sharing through educational platforms or ePublishing through online archives.

M. Ioannides (Ed.): EuroMed 2010, LNCS 6436, pp. 409–421, 2010.

Providing access to metadata and external information is a key point in making 3D models useful and reliable tools for research - not only for communication - in Cultural Heritage. Of course the data collected have to be made uniform, and connected to the model or to its parts, that is often a time-consuming activity and requires interdisciplinary skills.

3D models have not so far experienced the expected widespread use, especially within the scientific community, which still doesn't consider them valuable tools of research. Hopefully, in the next few years 3D models are set to be shared storage and exchange formats for data, both in the internet and outside it.

This paper analyses an ongoing Virtual Archaeology project, starting from the archaeological study that originated it and from previous similar experiences of the main institutions involved. In order to manage a rich archive of heterogeneous data, a set of 3D virtual environments was chosen as a metaphor for representing and exploring data while keeping spatial relationships and context. For this purpose a dedicated application (ViSMan-DHER) was developed, based on an open-source framework for virtual scenarios visualization and management called ViSMan [4], [24]. Structure and concept of the application are briefly described, together with lessons learned and some future perspectives.

2   Previous Experiences in Virtual Archaeology at VisITLab

Cineca [18] is a Consortium of Italian universities, and the largest Italian computing centre. In 1988 it was equipped with a Virtual Theatre and created a dedicated Laboratory, the VisITLab (*Visual Information Technology Lab*), that in the last decades carried out experimental projects in various fields of research, promoting the use of Computer Graphics and Virtual Reality applications for scientific data visualization and management. Many projects concerned Cultural Heritage and were developed in collaboration with the University of Bologna [13], [15].

With the massive diffusion of Computer Graphics, Virtual and Augmented Reality, mostly encouraged by the videogame market - and recently by geo-information industry - new possibilities and new needs have arisen from the scientific community, above all the needs of easy-to-use tools for the visualization and management of virtual environments, specifically designed for Virtual Heritage and providing users with the possibility not only to navigate 3D models, but also to extrapolate information about reconstructed objects. External data, related to a scientific model, are often necessary in order to attest the huge research activity preceding reconstruction, to ensure correct methodology and data reliability, and to certify its authors and origin. Of course this applies both to metadata and to heterogeneous datasets, spatially or contextually related to the reconstructed structures, such as pictures, drawings or texts. 3D data, on the other hand, can act as an intuitive and spatially structured interface for a better exploration and organization of connected data, contextualizing and showing the objects to which they relate.

Of course video-game hardware and software focus on reconstructed words without allowing management of external references; scientific tools such as GIS (*Geographical Information Systems*) and CAD (*Computer Aided Design*) software do manage complex databases but they don't support interactive navigation of complex virtual environments. Moreover, these tools require users a remarkable learning curve and they need high license fees.

2.1 The Development of ViSMan Software

In order to fill this specific gap, Cineca developed ViSMan (Virtual Scenarios Manager) [4], [24], an open-source framework based on OpenSceneGraph [21] graphic libraries and written in C++ language. ViSMan tends to use open source libraries and resources for every functionality, and presents an open, modular and thus extensible architecture that allows flexibility, integration of new modules and easy updating.

ViSMan is basically a visualization software for virtual environments, provided with an intuitive "video-game like" browsing interface. During navigation it is possible to create relevant points of view, to assign names and create automatic paths between saved points. The 3D world supports ground and surface collision, thus allowing to follow uneven terrain or stairs in an enhancing first-person perspective.

When different models need to be compared or superimposed, switching between Scenarios is possible. This "switch" feature is particularly important to historians and archaeologists, who often deal with reconstruction of landscapes or structures changing over the time, or with alternative hypothesis that need to be compared, or just differentiated according to their reliability degree.

Still, we think the most important feature in ViSMan is the connection between 3D objects and relational databases, just like a GIS does with geo-referenced 2D data; by simply clicking an object or part of it on the stage the user accesses a hyperlink to an archive of multimedia content, such as HTML, texts, images, videos, audio tracks, web-pages and even the results of dynamic scientific visualizations and simulations [14]. Data can be visualized in a custom format and connected to remote databases through the Internet. Starting from a query performed into external data, on the other hand, it is possible to generate polygonal writings or labels into the scene starting from database records (exactly as happens in a traditional 2D GIS), to search objects in the 3D model by selecting them from a list, or just to perform queries in the data-system.

Features of the software are currently being updated, along with the evolution of Virtual Reality into a tool for research and analysis of data.

Examples of Cultural Heritage projects where ViSMan proved its efficacy are Museo Virtuale della Certosa - developed for the municipality of Bologna [19], and VisArq. 1.0. on the archaeological area of Zaragoza (Spain) ([10]; see more case studies in [15], [11]).

The former is a database of images, letters, pictures and witnesses relative to citizens buried in the monumental cemetery of Bologna, that can be queried through an interactive map on a website, through a detailed virtual model of the monumental complex, or simply browsed on a website.

The latter instead is an online catalogue of heterogeneous data coming from a great number of archaeological sites in the Province of Zaragoza, Spain. During real-time (off-line) navigation of a Digital Elevation Model of the territory, relevant sites can be selected and connected data visualized through a HTML web interface and queried in a structured database.

Fig. 1. Virtual model of the Certosa explored with ViSMan

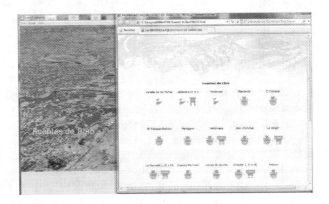

Fig. 2. A screenshot in VisArq 1.0 application; territory DEM inside ViSMan and HTML interface for online database

2.2 Towards Multichannel Communication

As stated above, VisITLab tested different solutions for scientific visualization employing Virtual Reality applications and especially ViSMan software.

However, the same virtual environments, realized by and for researchers, were used for communication and educational purposes as well, e.g. providing high quality renderings as contents for exhibitions and multimedia communication products. Well-built, interdisciplinary teams had to be employed in order to realize these experiences. The starting philological virtual models were declined into narrative contents for applications to be distributed over different media, ranging from palmtop devices to the Internet and from immersive real-time navigation experiences to video recording in a Virtual Television Set (see below).

Fig. 3. Prof. Scagliarini interviewed in a Virtual Set for the "High-Tech Pompeii" documentary (2000), with the virtual House of Centenary as background

Fig. 4. Philological model of the Parma Cathedral, and video installations showing use of models in a Virtual Set, populated with life

The virtual model of the House of the Centenary, originally set as a support for data and a test bed for reconstruction hypothesis by the University of Bologna, was then used as a Virtual Set where real actors seemed to interact within the model; actors are actually playing in a special television Studio in front of a blue screen, and the video recording is composed in real-time over rendering images from the model. A documentary titled "High-tech Pompeii"was realized for the Italian Public Television (RAI).

A museum exhibition, "Living in the Middle Ages. Parma at the time of the Cathedral" was also realized employing a Virtual Set: real actors animated the philological models of the cathedral and the main square of the city. Videos were later used to realize three immersive multimedia installations that took the public on an imaginary journey through time, allowing understanding of daily life in medieval times.

These experiences, besides creating synergies and collaborations among different specialists, highlighted the possibility to transform philological models into didactic spaces and into engaging narrative for the general public. Virtual models - initially built with philological care but paying little if any attention to communication - developed into narrative and didactic spaces, with the introduction of characters and the use of storytelling techniques.

3   The Work of the University of Bologna at Pompeii and Herculaneum

The University of Bologna and Cineca VisITLab have been collaborating since 1990, in many Virtual Archaeology projects, like NUME (*Nuovo Museo Elettronico della città di Bologna*) [3] [22], MUVI (*Museo Virtuale della Vita Quotidiana*) [9] [16] [20], Pompei - Insula del Centenario (IX, 8) and DHER (*Domus Herculanensis Rationes*) [5].

Among these, Pompeii - Insula del Centenario (IX, 8) and DHER are part of the Vesuviana Project, that the University started in 1997 in collaboration with the Soprintendenza of Pompeii and Naples [6] [8] [23].

The Pompeii project (1997-2005) consisted in a detailed and manifold system of documentation, analysis and publication, carried out in Pompeii's Insula IX [5] [7], while DHER (2005-2010) is extended to a whole urban center, the archaeological site of the ancient Herculaneum [8].

The focus of the Herculanensis project is on the study of domestic architecture and housing culture, through two main lines of action: a new campaign of documentation of the decorations (pavements and walls) and the complete analysis and publication of case studies. As starting step, Insula III and its main buildings (especially the so-called House of the Skeleton, House of the Bronze Herm and House of the Wooden Partition...) were studied in detail, and with a multidisciplinary approach.

Fig. 5. Archaeological area of Herculaneum [17]

Such a complex field work ended up with the generation of a huge amount of material, partly recorded on site and partly retrieved from archives by an interdisciplinary team that flanked the archaeologists: specialists in archives, in archaeometry, materials, topography, geology, conservators, structural engineers and multimedia technology specialists, even filmmakers and communication experts.

This amount of data had eventually to be organized and structured in order not to be lost or dispersed. An easily accessible mean for visualization, consultation and even comparison among heterogeneous data had to be implemented, while keeping complexity and relationships between external data, analyzed structures and archaeological context.

4 The ViSMan-DHER Application

4.1 Purposes and Methods

An application based on ViSMan was developed at Cineca VisITLab for the DHER Project. The framework aimed at allowing not only archeologists who had been working on it, but also external researchers, students and specialists to obtain visualizations and to query into the archive created throughout the DHER project, [1] [2].

Since collected data referred to very different contexts (starting from the whole territory and getting to the detail of a single wall-painting) the metaphor chosen for visualization was the creation of some whole virtual environments (called **Scenarios**) with growing level of detail. Each different Scenario gives access to a dedicated section of the database, so that information detail varies according to the reconstructed level that the user is exploring.

In documentation as well as in the virtual models it was necessary to set a "unit" for data visualization: the extent of this unit changes according to the context that is being explored.

In a whole urban area Scenario units are constituted by Insulae and houses, while inside detailed reconstructions of houses rooms or single wall-surfaces were preferred.

These elements were was marked as **Nodes** in the OSG file - and linked to the available types of data.

Different Scenarios are interconnected through the *switch* feature of ViSMan (see above) and according to a logic and spatial hierarchy.

A standard navigation session in the application should involve the following steps: navigation through the territory Digital Elevation Model, choice of one archaeological area (Pompeii or Herculaneum), visualization of the representation of the city, including some Nodes (Insulae and houses), query to the database to know which data are available for a certain Node, visualization of the data (e.g. images), switch to a new Scenario (a reconstructed house), query and visualization of data associated with single walls or rooms.

4.2 Application Structure

Virtual models were realized in OSG format and grouped into few **Scenarios** (Territory of Campania region, Archaeological areas of Pompeii and Herculaneum, and some detailed reconstructions of roman houses).

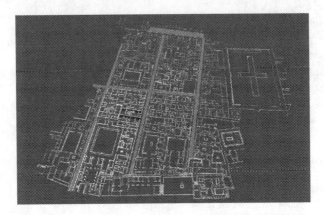

Fig. 6. Scenario "Archaeological area of Herculaneum" with Nodes representing houses and Insuale

In order to connect reconstructed objects to items in the database, the **Nodes** have been devised: a Node is a virtual model or a group of geometries inside a Scenario that has been associated and linked to one or more items or records in the dataset.

A relational database was implemented, containing reference to Nodes and to the corresponding items in an archive of images, texts and documents.

Each type of data pertains to a distinct table in the database, while each single document is a record. Most of them only consist in text, or image and caption, but some are more complex and for each one a simple visualization interface was developed in ViSMan.

The following categories of data were included:

- Photomaps of wall decoration
- Analytic description of wall decoration
- Excavation journals
- Photographs of findings
- Analytic description of findings
- Graphic documentation from the Archive of the Soprintendenza
- Photographs (by Foglia, 1992) from the Archive of the Soprintendenza
- Historic photographs from the Archive of the Soprintendenza
- Restoration journals (1996)
- Survey data: Masonry Stratigraphic Units (USM)
- Survey data: Photomap of the walls

Data formats are JPEG images, TXT text files and PDF documents, but more format are supported by ViSMan and might be included in the future.

Two specific solutions were found for the reconstruction of Roman houses.

Fig. 7. Realistic virtual reconstruction of the House of the Skeleton as it looks today was used as a spatial interface to access survey and archive data

The so-called House of the Skeleton, in Herculaneum, showed a particular situation, with the most rich and complete dataset coming from architectural survey and masonry analysis. The structure had been carefully geo-referenced, surfaces and volumes had been documented through survey, monoscopic and strereoscopic photogrammetry of walls, Masonry Stratigraphic Units with restorations and modern integrations had been mapped. Furthermore, a detailed and realistic 3D model was also included, realized from survey and textures photogrammetric images.

In order to exploit this wealth of data, the model was modified with AutoDesk 3D Studio Max (later with the open source modeler Blender) to optimize it for real-time navigation and integrated into ViSMan-DHER application, thus becoming at the same time the visible representation of the survey and photogrammetric data, and an intuitive spatially organized interface to reach other data.

Other houses, instead, smaller and simpler than the former, presented interesting archive and field data, but no previously built virtual model. In this case undertaking the realization of a detailed 3D model only as support for data visualization seemed to make little sense. Furthermore, it has to be stressed that for research purpose first any virtual model should be functional and effective as a representative model, while realism and completeness comes second, provided that spatial and context information and relationships are conserved.

For these less complex buildings a meaningful level of detail for data organization and visualization was set to the single room, instead of the single wall surface.

This is of course the most common situation for the studied structures in Herculaneum and Pompeii, so a simple and flexible solution had to be thought out to allow future application to further case-studies.

Eventually the choice was to model simplified representations of buildings, just extruding their plan, and keeping division into rooms as different Nodes.

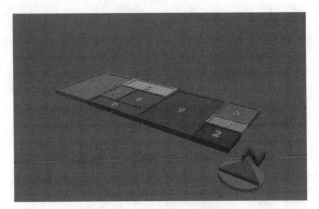

Fig. 8. The House of the Bronze Herm was represented through a schematic model of its room distribution

4.3 Lessons Learned and Perspectives

Once that experiments have been performed to verify the feasibility of this product, that is applying it to the specific case study of the DHER project, the second phase has been started. This still ongoing phase involves the team at work as well as all the other équipes.

Such a "sustainability" assesment goes along with new data acquiring.

At present the product shows to be an essential tool in the procedure system of the DHER project. In particular, it has proved to be a valuable tool to the interpretation of the documentary basis. This is a further proof of the role that 3D visualization, connected to searchable as well as verifiable databases, can play in archaeological research enhancing the potential for understanding the evidence. It has to be stressed that particular operating and methodological choices, that we believe to have rightly made in conducting the experiment, have revealed to be of fundamental importance for its success. Among these we can say that data sharing enables full and potentially endless examining of the documentary basis, both with the team at work and, in perspective, to the whole scientific community.

Successful implementation of ViSMan-DHER application shows how Virtual Environments can evolve into a research tool for archaeologists, as it allows visualization and simulation of concepts and context relationships that would otherwise be theoretical and hardly communicable, at the same time ensuring scientific accuracy of historical reconstructions through documentation [1] [2].

Anyway, while the software architecture, the dataset and the back-side of data management by researchers are firmly established, more work is required on the front-side of final users fruition and interface.

For instance, navigation is currently controlled through keyboard or through a simple navigation bar, but it can be made substantially more user-friendly. Actions such as querying available data types for Nodes or switching between models and data are controlled through a mouse-controller, but could as well be made far more intuitive with the use of instructions or popup labels.

Moreover, direct access to software settings, editing of paths, point of view, and ground collision, while very useful during assemblage, could be preset and thus removed from end-user interface or substituted with few defined options, in order to simplify the navigation experience.

Data visualization is now managed through a very simple frame, that could be improved e.g. by implementation of new functions (such as more complex queries in the database), or greater freedom for the researcher/user on data display.

Target users, as stated above, should include not only the DHER Project team, but also external specialists and students, with different levels of skills both on 3D navigation and on this specific archaeological area. For this purpose a strong work on software documentation and graphical interface is being carried out by ICT specialists at Cineca, together with archaeologists.

Distribution and fruition of contents developed with ViSMan is also a major aspect to be fixed in the next months. Initially, a temporary solution proposed for display to the public was a double monitors: one was used interactively through keyboard and mouse-controller for interactive navigation of the three-dimensional models, the other one was simply joined to automatically display images and other data recalled by queries to the database.

The whole system is currently accessible off-line on performing Personal Computers, and in immersive environments, such as the Virtual Theatre at Cineca.

Fig. 9. A screenshot of data and model navigation inside Scenario "House of the Skeleton"

Future development in distribution publication will probably be a stand-alone application distributed on CD-Rom, but testing of new channels for distribution is also scheduled: above all, other projects realized with ViSMan have shown that on-line hosting of the 3D models, database and contents are an effective channel for communication, allowing great personalization of the interface, and integration or linking to existing projects and institutions [16].

As far as contents are concerned, further progress can be either quantitative growth in information, with the integration of more items in the already existing types of data (e.g. data pertaining to new houses), or creation of new typologies.

5 Conclusions and Remarks

New technologies in Cultural Heritage data management and visualization are valuable assets both for research activity and for data sharing and dissemination, as long as they are included in research projects from the very beginning. At the same time, strong attitude towards interdisciplinary work, flexibility and basic communication and IT skills are required for archaeologists and researchers who want to move in this direction.

Finally, previous experiences carried out by VisITLab in the field of Virtual Reality applications took us to the conclusion that we should start evaluating educational effectiveness of these tools with the support of cognitive psychology methodologies. Also in this sense, a migration of the application to the Web would provide access to a much richer range of tools for user profiling and usage evaluation.

References

1. Alvisi, C., Delli Ponti, F., Diamanti, T., Diarte Blasco, P., Guidazzoli, A.: Scenari virtuali e dati archeologici: il Progetto DHER. Notizie dal Cineca 61, 9–12 (2008)
2. Alvisi, C., Delli Ponti, F., Diamanti, T., Diarte Blasco, P., Guidazzoli, A.: Scenari virtuali interattivi e dati multi-dimensionali per il progetto DHER. In: Coralini, A. (ed.) Domus Herculanensis Rationes, I - Sito archivio museo, AnteQuem, pp. 411–427 (2009)
3. Bocchi, F., Bonfigli, M.E., Ghizzoni, M., Smurra, R., Lugli, F.: The 4D Virtual Museum of the City of Bologna - Italy. In: ACM SIGGRAPH 1999, Los Angeles (1999)
4. Borgatti, C., Calori, L., Diamanti, T., Felicori, M., Guidazzoli, A., Liguori, M.C., Mauri, A.M., Pescarin, S., Valentini, L.: Databases and Virtual Environments: a Good Match for Communicating Complex Cultural Sites. In: ACM SIGGRAPH 2004 (2004)
5. Coralini, A., Guidazzoli, A., Malavasi, M., Raffa, G., Roffia, L., Salmon Cinotti, T., Scagliarini Corlàita, D., Sforza, F., Taboni, C., Vecchietti, E.: Archeologia virtuale e supporti informatici nella ricostruzione di una domus di Pompei. Archeologia e Calcolatori 14, 237–274 (2003)
6. Coralini, A., Scagliarini Corláita, D. (eds.): Ut Natura Ars. Virtual Reality e archeologia. Atti della giornata di studi, Bologna 22 aprile 2002. University Press Bologna (2007)
7. Coralini, A., Vecchietti, E.: L'archeologia attraverso un 3D Virtual Model. In: [6], pp. 17-39 (2007)
8. Coralini, A.: Vesuviana, Archeologie a confronto. Atti del Convegno Internazionale, Bologna 14-16 gennaio 2008. Ante Quem (2009)
9. Delli Ponti, F., Liguori, M.C., Musiani, E.: Abitare il quotidiano: il progetto MuVi prosegue il suo cammino. Storia e Futuro 22, 2–27 (2010)
10. Delli Ponti, F., Diamanti, T., Diarte Blasco, P., Guidazzoli, A., Sebastián López, M.: VisArq. 1.0.: Interactive Archaeology and 3D Data. In: Javier Melero, F., Cano, P., Revelles, J. (eds.) Proceedings of Fusion of Cultures, CAA 2010, Granada, April 6-9 (2010) (in press)
11. Felicori, M., Gaiani, M., Guidazzoli, A., Liguori, M.C.: Frameworks OS per la comunicazione storica e archeologica. In: Open Source, Free Software e Open Format nei processi di ricerca archeologica, IV Workshop Italiano Roma, April 27-28 (2009)
12. Forte, M., Beltrami, R.: A proposito di Virtual Archaeology: disordini, interazioni cognitive e virtualità. Archeologia e Calcolatori 11, 273–300 (2000)

13. Guidazzoli, A.: Experiences of Immersive Graphics for Cultural Heritage. In: Niccolucci, F. (ed.) Proceedings of the VAST Euroconference on VAST 2000, Arezzo, November 24-25. BAR International Series, vol. 1075, pp. 89–92 (2000)
14. Guidazzoli, A., Bisson, M., Calori, L., Cavazzoni, C., Delli Ponti, F., Diamanti, T., Erbacci, G., Esposti Ongaro, T., Gori, A., Imboden, S., Menconi, G., Neri, A., Pareschi, M.T.: An Interactive Virtual Environment to communicate Vesuvius eruptions numerical simulations and Pompeii history. In: ACM SIGGRAPH 2006, Boston (2006)
15. Guidazzoli, A.: L'esperienza del Cineca nel campo della Virtual Archaeology. In: Coralini, A., Scagliarini Corláita, D. (eds.) Ut Natura Ars. Virtual Reality e archeologia. Atti della giornata di studi, April 22, pp. 81–89. University Press Bologna, Bologna (2007)
16. Liguori, M.C.: Museo virtuale della vita quotidiana nel secolo XX, evoluzione di un progetto. Storia e futuro 18, 1–17 (2008)
17. Maiuri, A.: Ercolano, I nuovi scavi (1927-1958), vol. I. Roma (1958)
18. http://www.cineca.it/
19. http://www.certosadibologna.it/ (accessed August 20, 2010)
20. http://muvi.cineca.it/ (accessed August 20, 2010)
21. http://www.openscenegraph.org
22. http://www.storiaeinformatica.it/nume/italiano/ntitolo.html (accessed August 20, 2010)
23. http://www.vesuviana.info/ (accessed August 20, 2010)
24. http://www.cineca.it/resources/pagina/visman.htm (accessed August 20, 2010)

Teleimmersive Archaeology: Simulation and Cognitive Impact

Maurizio Forte[1], Gregorij Kurillo[2], and Teenie Matlock[3]

[1] School of Social Sciences, Humanities and Arts, University of California, Merced
[2] Dept. of Electrical Engineering and Computer Sciences, University of California, Berkeley
[3] School of Social Sciences, Humanities and Arts, University of California, Merced
mforte@ucmerced.edu, gregorij@eecs.berkeley.edu,
tmatlock@ucmerced.edu

Abstract. In this paper we present the framework for collaborative cyber-archaeology with support for teleimmersive communication which aims to provide more natural interaction and higher level of embodiment. Within the framework we create tools for exploration, interaction and communication of archaeologists in a shared virtual environment. Users at different geographical locations are captured by a set of stereo cameras to generate their real-time 3D avatars. The proposed framework is intended to serve as a virtual simulation environment where advanced behaviours, actions and new methodologies of research and training in archaeology, cognitive science and computer science could be tested.

Keywords: Cyberarchaeology, Teleimmersive Remote Collaboration, Shared Virtual Environments, Cognitive Impact.

1 Introduction

Teleimmersive Archaeology is a joint research project between the University of Berkeley (Teleimmersive Lab) and the University of California, Merced (Virtual Heritage Lab), supported by a CITRIS grant. The scope is the creation of virtual collaborative systems using teleimmersive technologies for real-time performances in the interpretation and reconstruction processes in archaeology. The methodological approach is based on the simulation process, in other terms on the idea that cyber-archaeology constitute the core of the interpretation capabilities in the digital simulation of the past (Forte, 2008).

One of the key issues in the collaborative-participatory activities is the role and the behaviours of all the actors involved in the process. Therefore factors such as the sense of presence, embodiment, gestures, interaction, motion capture, spatial sharing, 3D design and virtual tools influence deeply the level of learning and communication.

In the last decade several projects can be counted in this field: ARCHAVE (Acevedo et al., 2001); VITA: Visual Interaction Tool for Archaeology (Benko et al., 2004); SHAPE (Hall et al. (2001), LAVA, Laconia Acropolis Virtual Archaeology (Getchell et al. 2009). In addition other projects have explored the educational potentialities of the virtual communities such as Second Life (Nie, 2008). Further applications

M. Ioannides (Ed.): EuroMed 2010, LNCS 6436, pp. 422–431, 2010.

have been focused on the 3D Web collaborative systems such as the case of the FIRB project (Forte and Pietroni, 2008), using Virtools DEV and Virtools Mutiuser Pack© by linking three different archaeological sites. In this case, all collaborative activity was online and with pre-determined 3D graphic libraries.

Although the massive multi-user environments seem appealing for such applications, they are currently unable to provide users with truly immersive experience or sufficient flexibility to construct the type of complex framework that we propose. The users of the former technologies were mainly observers of virtual replicas of ancient worlds, not active participants contributing to the reconstruction and interpretation processes.

2 Teleimmersion

Achieving an immersive experience in collaborative environments requires providing a visual experience similar to that delivered by reality. Traditional immersive virtual reality systems often use avatars, to represent human users inside the computer generated environments. Pre-modeled avatars, however, have several limitations with respect to body movement dynamics, gestures, eye contact and other subtle communication via body language and facial expressions. Likewise, the existing video conferencing technologies fail to properly preserve the eye gaze which has been shown to be an important factor for remote video-based communication (Fullwood and Doherty-Sneddon, 2006).

In our work we move further from the avatars and apply stereo reconstruction to capture 3D representation of users in real time to facilitate visual experience similar to reality (e.g. face-to-face meetings), where users are able to establish eye contact and use their body to communicate and interact (e.g. pointing at objects). The developed 3D reconstruction framework has been successfully used previously in remote dancing applications and learning of Tai Chi movements (Bailenson et al. 2008).

Fig. 1. Two users are interacting with a laser scanned statue in a shared virtual environment. Integrated 3D video provides a virtual position of each user, allowing users to point at different features of a 3D model as if they were sharing the same physical space.

3   Framework Overview

Our cyberarchaeology framework seamlessly combines computer vision and virtual reality (Fig. 1). The prototype application supports rendering and interaction with various 3D models, real-time interaction with different input devices, exchange of multi-media data streams for communication (i.e. audio, video and 3D video). The collaborative framework is built upon Vrui VR Toolkit, developed by Kreylos (2008) at University of California, Davis, which can run on a wide range of virtual reality hardware with support for different display and input device technologies.

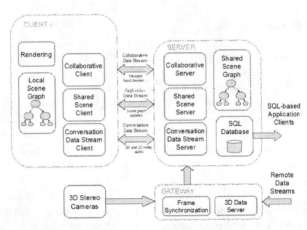

Fig. 2. A simplified block diagram of the 3D teleimmersive application for collaborative interaction in a shared virtual environment

3.1   Shared Scene Graph

The collaborative virtual environment is based on shared scene graph to describe the spatial relationship of objects and facilitate interaction between remote users. The scene graph is maintained on a central server which can connect to a spatial database. Whenever changes are made to the scene (e.g. adding/deleting objects, moving objects etc.), the clients receives the updates for their local scene graph representations. The scene graph also allows for efficient rendering. Current implementation with vertex buffer objects allows for display of 1 million triangles with the frame rate of 60 FPS (GeForce GTX 8800 graphics card).

The scene graph encodes different properties of the scene (e.g. geometry, texture, metadata) through a hierarchical scheme of inter-connected nodes of different types as follows:

Transformation Node defines position and orientation of its child nodes with respect to the other transformation nodes higher in the hierarchy. The transformation is described with six parameters. Nested nodes allow objects to be linked together.

Geometry Node describes object geometry through a list of vertices and a list of indices of the corresponding triangles. The data is used for building vertex buffer objects (VBO) which allow for efficient rendering. The geometry node also encodes the object bounding box, which is used for the collision detection.

Texture and Material Nodes are comprised of object textures and material properties. Several high resolution texture file formats are supported in the application. The textures can also be dynamically switched, for example to alternate between the original and reconstructed surface of a wall painting. We implemented the surface material properties defined by the OpenGL standards.

Object Node is a group node that can incorporate several geometry and texture/material nodes defining a particular object. The clients currently support only OBJ/Wavefront 3D file format with the ability to use several different texture formats. The object node can be easily extended to support other 3D formats by modifying the file loading function.

Grid/Height Map Node is used to render surface grids for emphasizing different surfaces or creating a height map that defines the landscape of the archaeological dig. The map can be texture mapped with the images of the landscape to create more realistic rendering.

Metadata Nodes support rendering of images and text that can be attached to different artefacts in the virtual environment. The metadata can contain information on object geometry, location, short description, and images. Currently the metadata cannot be edited within the application.

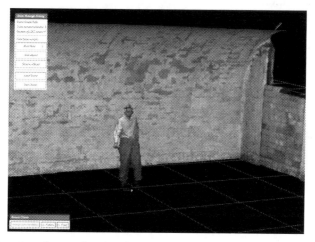

Fig. 3. Locally, users observe the virtual world in the first person perspective. Remote users are represented by their 3D avatars captured by one or more stereo cameras.

3.3 Navigation and Interaction

To explore the virtual environment, users navigate and interact with 3D models in the first person perspective. The presence of the remote users is accomplished through the rendering of their 3D avatar generated by the stereo cameras. The location of their avatar corresponds to the current location of the user's virtual view point.

At any time, individual users can switch to the other user's point of view or select face-to-face mode for direct conversation. The latter functionality will bring the local user in front of the remote user to facilitate a view similar to a video conferencing. Remote users can, however, work independently in the shared virtual environment. To prevent inconsistencies any two users cannot move the same object at the same time. A lock is placed on the node and its children if another user is already interacting with the object. The lock is assigned on first-come-first-serve basis.

The framework in connection with Vrui VR Toolkit features a wide selection of tools for interaction with the environment:

Navigation Tools provide a variety of ways to move around the virtual environment (e.g. flying, surface navigation).

Measurement Tool can be used to perform dimensional and angular measurements to capture the geometry of scanned objects. The measurement tools can also be used to measure spatial relationships between the objects. Fig. 4(a) shows the measurement of features on a small statue from a Western Han Chinese tomb.

Lighting Tool incorporates a virtual flashlight which can be used to relight parts of the 3D scene or point at salient features. The relighting can enhance underlying details of the scanned artifacts. Fig. 4(b) demonstrates the use of a virtual flashlight to enhance spatial details of a laser scanned model of a mask from Mayan city of Copan. In the future we will add ability to place static lights along the scene to more precisely control the illumination of the objects.

Annotation Tool allows users to draw 3D curves to mark different geometrical features and communicate them to the remote users. The annotation tool can also be used to quickly acquire a 2D or 3D sketch of patterns or objects. Fig. 4(c)(d) show an example of sketching the pattern on a scanned tile of a Western Han Chinese tomb and the corresponding geometry.

Dragging Tool is used to move objects in the 3D space. Object picking action is determined through a collision detection algorithm between the dragging tool selection ray and pre-calculated object bounding box. User can interact with an object only if another user has not already picked the same object. Movement of objects in different direction can be controlled independently through a dialog (when using a mouse) or through direct device interaction (when using 6 DOF input device). If the input device tracking and the stereo cameras are aligned, the hand of the avatar will be in contact with the object while it is being manipulated by the user.

Object Selector Tool is used to select objects and perform different actions related to the local functionality, such as changing object rendering style (e.g. texture, no texture, mesh only), retrieving object metadata, focusing current view to object principal planes etc. The selector tool allows selection of several objects simultaneously while different actions can be performed on selected objects.

3.4   3D Video Capture and Rendering

The avatars of users integrated with the virtual environment are created in real-time by the 3D stereo algorithm (Vasudevan et al., 2010). This algorithm performs accurate and efficient stereo computation by employing fast stereo matching through an adaptive meshing scheme. The output of the stereo reconstruction is a 3D mesh which is compressed and sent from each stereo camera to the local gateway. The achievable

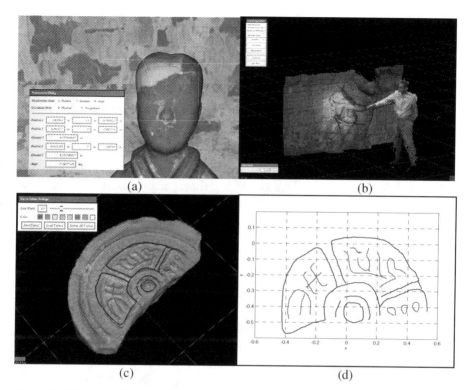

Fig. 4. (a) Dimensional and angular measurement can be performed on the virtual artefacts to capture their geometry. (b) Remote user is interacting with a virtual flashlight to enhance the underlying details of the laser scanned model of a mask from Mayan city of Copan. (c) Annotation tool is applied to mark important features and communicate them remotely to other collaborators. (d) Data from the annotations can be extracted in a form of a 3D sketch for subsequent analysis.

frame-rate is about 25 FPS on images of 320x240 pixels and about 12 FPS on images of 640x480 pixels. The accuracy of the reconstruction and is typically between 1 cm to 3 cm. To increase the fidelity of the reconstructed users, we also apply dynamic texture mapping. Several stereo views can be combined through calibration and blending to increase the workspace of the interaction and to provide 360-degree capturing.

3.5 Results

In this paper we present results from two different experimental setups (Fig. 5) connected over the internet. For the first setup, we used the teleimmersion platform at University of California, Berkeley (Vasudevan et al., 2010), which has several stereo clusters, each connected to a four core server, to perform 360-degree stereo reconstruction. The system is integrated with a tracking system (TrackIR by NaturalPoint) that tracks position and orientation of a Wii Remote (Nintendo). The Wii Remote is used as a 6 DOF input device for interacting with the virtual environment. The second setup consisted of a single Bumblebee 2 stereo camera (Point Grey, Inc.) positioned above 65" LCD screen. Users were able to interact with the environment with a 3D mouse. Users can change the hardware platform by simply modifying a configuration file.

At this stage, we did some preliminary experiments with the 3D archaeological data coming from a monumental Chinese Western Han Tomb (beginning of the first millennium AD). We recorded and documented the tomb with 3D scanners in the summer 2008 at Xi'an, China. The tomb, now closed to the public (because of serious problems of conservation) after the excavation, is now accessible only virtually. For the teleimmersive system, the tomb was reconstructed by laser scanner data and by the integration of high res textures of mural painting and 3D models of funeral goods (recorded by laser scanning), then re-contextualized in their original positions (Fig. 3). Even the corridor and the three chambers of the tomb have been studied in the collaborative systems, especially the architectural elements, the organization of the space and the relation between iconography, the funeral chambers, and the 3D model. The use of lighting and measurement tools with the capacity to move, share and compare the objects in the cyber space, to add visual layers and outlines in the wall paintings have considerably increased the simulation factors and the faculties for data interpretation. The involvement of different interactors in the cyberspace yielded new perspectives in the dialectics of the interpretation process and its multivocality.

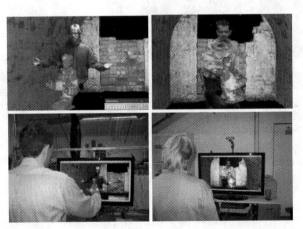

Fig. 5. Two different teleimmersive platforms for interaction with the virtual environment (below) and their corresponding view in the virtual environment

3.6 Cognitive Impact

Cognitive scientists are studying how users interact and manipulate objects in this system. They will track the use and development of the system with various methods of investigation. In the end, the results will be used to develop robust learning tools and to improve the design and use of the system. In one line of cognitive research, the eye movements of multiple users will be tracked as they discuss objects and manipulate objects. Of interest will be how language directs the attention of users. In another line of exploratory research on users, the utility of a pure first person view (no avatar) and a pseudo-first person view (with avatar) will be tested. Here trade-offs related to allotment of attention, ease of use, and awareness are expected. For instance, because of limitations due to cognitive load, users may visually attend to objects less when they are using an avatar to represent themselves. This will of course have implications for how well users learn material in the environment. However, ease of communication may be better with an avatar because users can point and use other gestures for disambiguating the speech stream. In yet another line of research, we will investigate how and when users point at objects (and locations of objects), including the consistency of their pointing and the spatial characteristics of their pointing.

3.7 Learning Process

Teleimmersive environments afford many learning opportunities because they allow users to collaborate remotely on many different types of projects. One obvious issue to study is how easily users can learn new information presented in the environment, and how to simplify or optimize the learning process. Setting up a robust environment that enables shared learning will allow users to collaborate more efficiently and to collectively learn further new material more readily in the future (for excellent discussion of scaffolding in technological learning environments, see Pea, 2004).

For the first cognitive study, we will use the Chinese Western Han Tomb, which was mentioned above, as learning environment. We will begin with a simple study that offers users either a first person view (no avatar to represent the self) or a third person view (avatar to represent the self). In each of these conditions, we will run 10 participants; each will randomly be assigned to either a director role or to an observer role. After they enter the tomb and get used to the environment, directors will be told to reconstruct funeral objects while the observer watches. To accomplish this task, the director will use a set of tools provided in a separate window. In the first person condition, the director will move his or her avatar to the objects, pick them up, and assemble them. In the second person condition, the director will simply touch the objects, pick them up, and assemble them. In this case, no avatar will be visible (to anyone in the environment). To learn how to successfully put the objects together, the director will look at a diagram that shows how the objects go together but no written text (so there is no explicit order of actions).

The task will intentionally be difficult to engage and challenge the users, and to adequately test for differences in performance. Directors will have as long as needed to complete the task. The director will let the observer know when he or she is finished. At that point, the observer will have to put the object together. Various methods will be used to test the success of learning in the avatar versus no avatar instructional phase.

One prediction is that the first person condition, directors will take less time to construct objects because the director will have a direct embodied experience and not have to worry about how the avatar appears. In turn, the observer who worked with the director in this condition should also perform the task more quickly. We also predict there will be fewer errors with the first person condition because there will not be an avatar to distract the visual attention from the objects and how they are assembled. Yet another prediction is that directors, and in turn, observers, will remember details about the task better in the first person condition because more of their attention will have been allotted to the objects and strategies involved in putting them together. Together, these results will provide valuable information about the utility of the system for learning, and cognitive impact.

Follow-up studies will be developed from this initial study. In one, we will cross the avatar/no avatar condition with user. This will enable us to study efficiency of learning with no avatar under any circumstances versus learning an avatar that can be seen only by the director or only by the observer. We will also extend the initial study to situations with multiple users, and in some cases, multiple users constructing an object together. This will be important to developing a system that takes multiple views and mental models into account. We will also test novice versus expert users of the system to determine optimal modes of instruction given learning stages.

4 Conclusions

The system is in prototypal phase and needs significant work to improve the tools, user interfaces and rendering. This learning platform will teach users how to interpret, reconstruct and communicate archaeological datasets using all the information available in a virtual participatory form, for instance, photos, movies, maps, 3D models, spatial data and texts. In the future, we will study the utility of interactions with avatar/no avatar versus first person interaction. In later lines of research, the eye movements of multiple users will be tracked as they discuss objects and manipulate objects. Of interest will be how language directions attention. Finally we will investigate how and when users point at objects (and locations of objects), including the consistency of their pointing and the spatial characteristics of their pointing. We will also study how well users remember materials they have learned in the environments and how well this information is retained over time.

Finally, the study and analysis of a virtual reconstruction process in archaeology will help the virtual community to re-contextualize and reassemble spatial archaeological data sets, from the first draft version (data not yet interpreted) to the final communicative level. The research activity will involve a bottom-up approach, i.e., the analyses of the archaeological remains as they were found on site, and a top-down approach, i.e., the reconstruction/interpretation of the data by cultural comparisons (for example architectural features, artefacts, frescos, styles, materials, shapes, and others).

Acknowledgements. We wish to thank Ram Vasudevan and Edgar Lobaton, University of California, Berkeley, for contribution on the stereo reconstruction and Zhong Zhou, University of Beijing, for texture compression. We also thank Tony Bernardin and Oliver Kreylos, University of California, Davis, for the implementation of the 3D video rendering. For the models related with the Mayan city of Copan, we thank Fabio Remondino, B. Kessler Foundation, Trento, and Jennifer von Schwerin, Department of Art and Art History, UNM/ Research Fellow, International Institute for Advanced Research "Morphomata", University of Cologne, Germany. The project Teleimmersive Archaeology is supported by a CITRIS grant.

References

1. Acevedo, D., Vote, E., Laidlaw, D.H., Joukowsky, M.S.: Archaeological data visualization in VR: Analysis of lamp finds at the great temple of Petra, a case study. In: Proceedings of IEEE Visualization Conference, San Diego, CA, pp. 493–497 (2001)

2. Bailenson, J.N., Patel, K., Nielsen, A., Bajcsy, R., Jung, S., Kurillo, G.: The effect of inter-activity on learning physical actions in virtual reality. Media Psychology 11, 354–376 (2008)
3. Benko, H., Ishak, E.W., Feiner, S.: Collaborative mixed reality visualization of an archaeo-logical excavation. In: Proceedings of the International Symposium on Mixed and Aug-mented Reality (ISMAR 2004), Washington DC, pp. 132–140 (2004)
4. Forte, M., Pietroni, E.: Virtual reality web collaborative environments in archaeology. In: Proceedings of the 14th International Conference on Virtual Systems and Multimedia (VSMM 2008), Cyprus, pp. 74–78 (2008)
5. Forte, M.: Cyber-archaeology: an eco-approach to the virtual reconstruction of the past. In: Proceedings of International Symposium on Information and Communication Technolo-gies in Cultural Heritage, Ioannina, Greece, pp. 91–106 (2008)
6. Fullwood, C., Doherty-Sneddon, G.: Effect of gazing at the camera during a video link on recall. Applied Ergonomics 37(2), 167–175 (2006)
7. Getchell, K., Miller, A., Allison, C., Sweetman, R.: Exploring the Second Life of a byzan-tine basilica. In: Petrovic, O. and Brand, A. (eds.), Serious Games on the Move, pp. 165–180. Springer Vienna (2009)
8. Hall, T., Ciolfi, L., Bannon, L.J., Fraser, M., Benford, S., Bowers, J., Greenhalgh, C., Hellström, S.O., Izadi, S., Schnädelbach, H., Flintham, M.: The visitor as virtual archae-ologist: explorations in mixed reality technology to enhance educational and social interac-tion in the museum. In: Proceedings of Virtual Reality, Archaeology, and Cultural Heritage (VAST 2001), New York, pp. 91–96 (2001)
9. Kreylos, O.: Environment-independent VR development. In: Bebis, G., et al. (eds.) ISVC 2008, Part I. LNCS, vol. 5358, pp. 901–912. Springer, Heidelberg (2008)
10. Nie, M.: Exploring the past through the future: a case study of Second Life for archaeology education. In: Proceedings of 14th International Conference on Technology Supported Learning and Training, Berlin, Germany (2008)
11. Pea, R.D.: The social and technological dimensions of scaffolding and related theoretical concepts for learning, education, and human activity. Journal of the Learning Sciences, 423–451 (2004)
12. Vasudevan, R., Zhou, Z., Kurillo, G., Lobaton, E., Bajcsy, R., Nahrstedt, K.: Real-time ste-reo-vision system for 3D teleimmersive collaboration. In: Proceedings of IEEE Interna-tional Conference on Multimedia & Expo (ICME 2010), Singapore (2010)

Accuracy Verification of Manual 3D CG Reconstruction: Case Study of Destroyed Architectural Heritage, Bam Citadel

Mohammad Reza Matini[1] and Kinji Ono[2]

[1] Faculty of Art & Architecture, Yazd University, Emam St., Yazd, Iran
`matini@yazduni.ac.ir`
[2] National Institute of Informatics, 2-1-2, Hitotsubashi, Chiyoda-Ku,
Tokyo 101-8430
`ono@nii.ac.jp`

Abstract. We explain our approach for verifying the accuracy of 3D CG manual modeling of the Citadel of Bam, which is an architectural heritage site destroyed by an earthquake in 2003. We attempted to control both the architectural quality of the 3D models with different methods and the technical 3D CG aspects since the 3D models of the Citadel of Bam need to be presented in a realistic virtual reality environment and also for research of buildings and spaces. Accuracy verification of 3D models was conducted through instructions and evaluation reports prepared by experts for modeling teams and different discussions between experts and 3D modelers.

Keywords: 3D CG reconstruction, 3D modeling, Evaluation, Quality Control, Cultural Heritage in Danger, Citadel of Bam.

1 Introduction

The Citadel of Bam is a huge complex of adobe architecture in the historical city of Bam in Iran. The city of Bam grew from the silk and cotton trade along the Silk Roads [2]. The Citadel is a collection of different architectural typologies with an historic Persian style in an area of around 180,000 square meters.

1.1 3D CG Reconstruction of Bam Citadel

The Citadel of Bam was destroyed in an earthquake in December 2003. The destruction was so severe, making physical reconstruction a great challenge. We proposed a faster and low-cost 3D Computer Graphics (CG) reconstruction, which could also help experts in the process of physical reconstruction. Since 2005, we have been constructing a three-dimensional model for a virtual reality (VR) presentation of the Citadel as part of the Digital Silk Road (DSR) Project of the National Institute of Informatics (NII) in Tokyo [1].

The most important areas, consisting of the most important buildings that were completely renovated before the earthquake, are being modeled manually [6]. For this

M. Ioannides (Ed.): EuroMed 2010, LNCS 6436, pp. 432–440, 2010.

paper, we focused on the accuracy-verification process of the 3D modeling of the most importance areas, which we nearly completed [1].

1.2 Accuracy-Verification Process of 3D CG Reconstruction

It is evident that 3D CG reconstruction of a building must precisely replicate that building. However several limitations, such as destruction of the buildings and lack of precise and adequate documentations, make the ordinary approach of modeling a challenge. The Citadel of Bam suffered massive destruction and documentation on the Citadel before its destruction was scarce; therefore, the original shapes of many buildings cannot be recognized from 2D drawings, and complementary information should be derived from other heterogeneous data such as photos or sketches [3]. In many cases, it was necessary to make 3D models based on interpretation of relics [8].

The originality of shapes, the preciseness of proportions, the correct geometry of domes, vaults and arches of mud brick structures, and the high level of detail were some of the items we considered in the accuracy-verification process and quality control of 3D CG reconstruction the Citadel of Bam's buildings to ensure the quality of 3D models of the Citadel. This goal was not only to achieve an attractive virtual reality demonstration for attracting non-experts but also to support experts, particularly those involved in the physical reconstruction of the site, to do research, and analysis of the buildings and spaces of the 3D model

In the following sections, we explain three important accuracy-verification stages of the 3D CG reconstruction of the Citadel of Bam.

2   Management of 3D CG Teams

Our 3D CG teams are architectural students (from Espace Virtuel de conception en Architecture et Urbanisme (EVCAU), Ecole Nationale Supeieure d'Architecture Paris-Val de Seine (ENSAPVS)), with expertise in 3ds Max, computer graphics students (from the Global Information and Telecommunication Institute (GITI), Waseda University, Tokyo) with no knowledge of architecture, and professional 3D modellers (Razahang, University of Tehran, Iran). The 3D models made by each team must be merged in a unified final model. The most important instructions given to the modelers by the management team are listed below.

2.1   Scale of 3D Models

The 3D models of the different teams must have the same scale; therefore, each team must choose metric system with similar units and scale as defined in the instructions.

2.2   Coordinates of Elements

The X, Y and Z coordinates of any element must be drawn in global UTM. For this reason, 3D modelers have to use 3D cartographic map of the area[1], which is a

---

[1] This Photogrammetric material was made available under the Irano-French 3D Cartographic Agreement on Bam (IFCA) and the Iranian National Cartographic Centre (NCC).

434   M.R. Matini and K. Ono

photogrammetric material reconstructed from aerial photos taken in 1994. This map is
a wire frame 3D model developed using Micro Station. It can be imported as an Auto-
CAD file with the "dwg" extension and easily used in a 3ds Max environment.

2.3 Layer Naming

The 3D model of the most important areas of the Citadel of Bam consists of buildings with different architectural components. These components were constructed
based on one or several heterogeneous data sources. The chosen 3D modelling tool
neither supports the design of an advanced schema with a hierarchy of classes, attributes of classes, and instances (like ontology schemas) [1] nor proposes a standard
way of naming layers or components. Hence, we devised a simple methodology
similar to linguistic morphology by defining affixes to name different layers as a
single string.

With our layer naming system it is possible to display the name of buildings and
recognize the reference data that the 3D model is built. Also, each model can be separated into its corresponding components that help us to easier and faster analyze,
represent, and control. With the ability to hide and unhide layers, we can see and
study building components separately or together. Each layer name consists of three
parts in our models: a prefix to name the building, an infix to indicate the type of
resources that have been used for 3D modeling, and a suffix to specify the type of
architectural component forming the building, as shown in Table 1 [1].

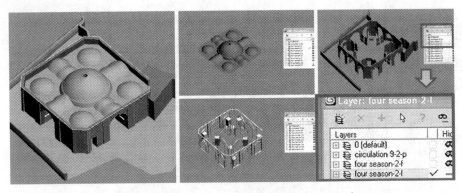

Fig. 1. 3D model and its components under layer naming

With help of this kind of layer naming, the 3D models of the different teams can be
merged without changing or mixing the layers. The layers are listed in alphabetical
order and can be used very easy in a highly complex model with many buildings and
constructional elements.

To unify the heterogeneous data in the second phase of 3D modeling, a preliminary
AutoCAD 3D model was developed. This data could be imported into a 3ds Max
environment for completion. In these cases, the layer naming was created in Auto-
CAD and imported directly into 3ds Max.

Table 1. Layer management abbreviations for development of 3D models

Type of Layer Name	Abbreviation	Full Name	Description
Prefix		bazaar, mosque, …	name of building identifying its function
		"vague"	The building doesn't have a name, there is a lack of data on the building, or the building is small or less important
		circulation	The component is part of a circulation element like a street.
		topography	topography of ground
		landscape	green spaces and natural scenery
		wall	city or defensive walls
Infix		1	imprecise maps
		2	precise maps
		3	photos
		4	sketches by skilled experts
		5	maps of similar style
		6	laser scan
		7	3D cartography maps
Suffix	r, l, f, w, d	roof, wall, floor, window, door	Following a number in case the component is numerous
	t	topography	topography inside the area of the building
	o	ornament	
	g	green space	small gardens inside the houses
	Suffix+ i	interior component	component below the ceiling of a closed space
	Suffix+ e	exterior component	

3 Architectural Quality Control

The 3D models of the Citadel of Bam are being developed in two phases. The data used by the 3D modelers and the quality of their work were completely different in these two phases.

3.1 First Phase of 3D CG Modeling and Problems

The first phase of developing the 3D models, from 2005 to 2007, revealed problems related to simultaneous use of heterogeneous data by 3D modelers [1], [4]. The most important problem for modeling teams in the first phase of the project was proper comprehension of the architectural data and the shortage of domain knowledge about traditional adobe constructions. Therefore at each period of completing the 3D models, architectural experts in the managing team of the DSR evaluated the architectural quality of the models and verified errors, and prepared a report. The reported errors should be corrected by modifying or remodeling the target building. The accuracy-verification process of the 3D models and error correction was repeated until every problem was solved and the accuracy of the 3D model was evident. Most of architectural problems are discussed below.

Geometrical Problems. Finding the original geometry of spaces and also adobe constructions in the Citadel of Bam was an important challenge for the 3D modelers. There are few spaces with 90 grade angle edges and almost there are no flat surfaces of building elements. Most edges are not sharp, and adjacent surfaces have soft joints. The wall surfaces are not exactly vertical and the lower sections are thick and the upper sections are thin. 2D drawings are not precise enough to represent these geometrical aspects; therefore, the 3D modelers had to use on-site photos taken before the earthquake. They needed to superimpose the plan on the 3D cartographic maps (provided by IFCA project headed by Prof. Dr. Adle) to correct errors

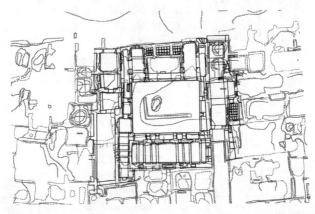

Fig. 2. Control of plan errors through superimposing with 3D cartography map, case of house of west of saabaat

Structural Problems. Due to destruction of most of the interior spaces and facades, modeling particular shapes of structural elements, such as arches, vaults, and domes, was a challenge.

Modelers needed to guess the type of element, such as a barrel or a cloister vault, by using aerial photos or some images from interior spaces and make the 3D model with accurate dimensions by using a limited number of 2D drawings and the 3D cartographic map (IFCA project). This process required domain expertise and was difficult for modelers.

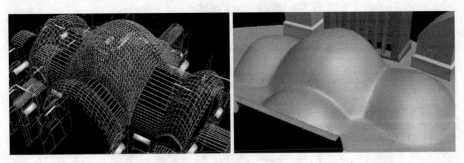

Fig. 3. Vaults in 3D model, the ceiling and the roof

Proportional Problems. The correct thickness, height, angle, and other dimensions of the buildings and spaces, the harmony between the inside and outside surfaces of architectural elements, and the correct position of elements combined are the main proportional aspects the 3D modellers must consider. By manually calibrating photos, the proportions of these building elements could be defined and used for 3D modeling. The 3D cartographic map (IFCA project) also helped to correct dimensions.

Fig. 4. Left: Difference between proportion of 3D model and 3D cartographic map (white lines), Right: ornaments that were not modeled (defined by red lines)

Detail Problems. Special details like chalk bands, ornaments like muqarnas and brickworks, combination elements of doors and windows, column edges, niches and arches were necessary for a highly detailed 3D model.

There were few high-resolution photos or 2D drawings precisely taken from these details, and 3D reconstruction was not possible for modelers without sketches or investigation and guidance from experts.

3.2 Second Phase of 3D CG Modeling and Problems

The modeling process in the first phase of the project was relatively slow and the models had several errors that had to be modified or remodelled. To overcome these problems in the second phase (since 2007), we prepared unified and precise data by combining all the heterogeneous data. These data consisted of information on the correct geometrical and structural character and correct proportions and details of the spaces and buildings. In particular, we developed an AutoCAD 3D wireframe model as a basic unified drawing of the Citadel. As we discussed in a previous publication [6], this model was prepared by complementary application of heterogeneous data and it can easily be imported into a 3ds Max environment and completed by 3D modellers who have little domain knowledge.

The architectural experts in the managing team developed unified data (3D wireframe model). Because of their familiarity with the content and chronology of the data and the original shapes of the mud brick buildings, the problems that were explained in the previous phase did not appear in the second phase. In the first phase, the tasks of the experts included controlling the correctness of 3D models, reporting errors or problems, and controlling the modification or remodeling process. This situation

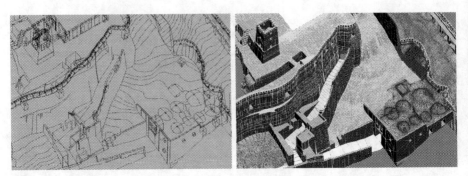

Fig. 5. Ramp and surrounding walls of Governor's Section in Bam Citadel drawn with help of wireframe model

required constant discussion between the modelers and architects, and the domain experts were overloaded with tasks. The 3D wireframe in the second phase decreased the dependency of modelers and domain experts and reduced the task load of both sides, which lead to easier and faster quality control by the experts and fewer remodeling and modifications by modelers.

4   3D CG Quality Control

Level of Detail. The 3D models of the Citadel of Bam are large and consist of several buildings, surrounding walls, topographies, and circulations. We need these models for VR presentation. The models can be seen from a normal distance (the nearest distance is around 25 cm) in a VR environment; therefore, we need to control the detail to an acceptable level. If we increase the number of polygons to more than what we need, the output 3D file will be very heavy, which will lead to over complexity and slow navigation, rendering, movement, and other presentation aspects when different buildings are combined. On the other hand, the number of polygons should not be decreased in such a way that the curved architectural elements lose their smoothness.

Appropriate Method of Surface Modeling. A realistic representation of the free form surfaces of an adobe construction of the Citadel of Bam is not easy and directly related to selection of the appropriate surface-modeling method for these elements inside the tool. For example Patch is appropriate for curved surfaces of buildings without complexity or parts that can be seen from a distance. NURBS is appropriate when a wire frame model of the space is available because the border lines of the architectural elements can be used for creating NURBS surfaces. Polygons are appropriate for surfaces with ornaments and complex curves, such as on roofs, that can be seen up close.

Interference or Incoherent parts. In the 3D models of the Citadel of Bam represented in the early stages of 3D modeling, there was interference, incoherence and forgotten surfaces, and parts that appeared due to inobservance. Seams between roofs and parapets, irregular lines between surfaces of vaults and chalk bands, intersection of roofs and ceilings, and incorrect intersections between windows and doors with walls were major 3D modeling errors reported for correction.

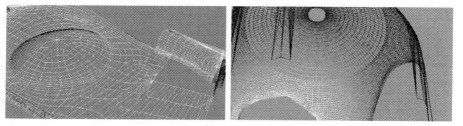

Fig. 6. Left: Example of exterior roof in Governor's House, Right: example of ceiling in Four Season building

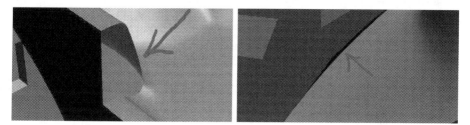

Fig. 7. Left: Example for forgotten surface,   Right: example of two incoherence surfaces

5 Conclusion

We explained the accuracy-verification process of manual 3D CG modeling of heritage buildings, especially when such buildings have been destroyed and the documents for 3D CG reconstruction are incomplete or incorrect. In making the 3D CG reconstruction of the Citadel of Bam, we used three important accuracy-verification stages for achieving precise, reliable, and realistic 3D models based on the original constructions prior to destruction.

The first step focused on management between 3D modeling teams. Experts defined a guideline to harmonize the work of the teams and provided them a basis for coherent 3D modeling. The layer naming system is a key for coherent and semantic 3D modeling. The second step concerned the architectural aspects of the 3D models. We summarized all the architectural aspects of the 3D models in four groups: geometrical, structural, proportional, and details. The 3D modelers had to learn how they should use these architectural aspects after several accuracy-verification processes of 3D models by experts and correction of 3D CG errors. The third step concerned the technical aspects of 3D CG modeling.

Every error found in the three steps discussed above was specified and reported by taking snapshots of the 3D model, annotating the snapshots, and comparing them with photos or any other explanation to make them clear to the 3D modelers. The process of correcting the errors was observed carefully by experts to ensure the accuracy of the models.

This approach can be extended as a key process for large-scale high-precision manual 3D modeling, especially for projects that consist of different types of buildings with different 3D modeling teams in different places. For most of the archeological sites where the original buildings were destroyed, proper application of heterogeneous information is key for precise 3D CG reconstruction. We discussed how each piece of information is applied and how it is modified or completed using other data. We proposed a management strategy in both phases of our project to provide an opportunity for different groups of modelers to work coherently and with fewer errors.

Acknowledgments. The 3DCG reconstruction and virtual reality of the Citadel of Bam is a collaborative research project between the Iranian Cultural Heritage and Tourism Organization (ICHTO) and the Digital Silk Road(DSR) project of the National Institute of Informatics (NII). The authors would like to express their sincere gratitude to Assoc. Prof. Dr. Asanabu Kitamoto from NII, Prof. Chahryar Adle from CNRS, Asst. Prof. Elham Andaroodi from University of Tehran (UT), Assoc. Prof. Dr. Alireza Einifar from UT, Assoc. Prof. Dr. Olivier Bouet and Mr. Franc Chopin from EVCAU, Prof. Takashi Kawai from Waseda University and M.Sc. Saeed Einifar (head of Razahang Architectural Firm). Special thanks go to the 3D modellers of EVCAU in France, GITI of Waseda University in Japan, and Razahang Architectural Firm in Iran,

References

1. Ono, K., Andaroodi, E., Einifar, A., Abe, N., Matini, M.R., Bouet, O., Chopin, F., Kawai, T., Kitamoto, A., Ito, A., Mokhtari, E., Einifar, S., Beheshti, M., Adle, C.: 3DCG reconstitution and virtual reality of UNESCO world heritage in danger: the Citadel of Bam. National Institute of Informatics, Progress in Informatics (5), 99–136 (2008)
2. Mehriar, M.: The history of Citadel of Bam. Iranian Cultural Heritage and Tourism Organization, Tehran (2003) (in Persian)
3. Andaroodi, E., Matini, M.R., Abe, N.: 3-D Reconstitution and virtual reality of the world heritage in danger, Citadel of Bam. In: Fellner, D. (ed.) 13th Eurographics Symposium on Virtual Environments, Proceeding of short papers and posters IPT- EGVE, pp. 43–44. Weimar (2007)
4. Andaroodi, E., Matini, M.R., Abe, N., Ono, K., Kitamoto, A., Kawai, T., Mokhtari, E.: Simultaneous implementation of heterogeneous data for 3-D reconstitution of the UNESCO world heritage in danger: Arg-e-Bam. In: IPSJ Symposium Series, Jinmonkon, Kyoto, vol. (15), pp. 265–270 (2007)
5. Beqqali, M., Bouet, O., Chopin, F., Matini, M.R., Andaroodi, E., Ono, K.: Three-dimensional formalization from heterogeneous data of mud brick caravanserai on the site of Bam (Iran)- Applications to the northern wing and the roof. In: Caravanserais and Caravan Routes State of Knowledge and Inventories Symposium, Paris (2009)
6. Matini, M.R., Andaroodi, E., Kitamoto, A., Ono, K.: Development of CAD-based 3D Drawing as Basic Resource for Digital Reconstruction of Bam's Citadel – UNESCO World Heritage in Danger. In: 14th International VSMM Conference, Limassol, pp. 51–58 (2008)
7. Matini, M.R., Andaroodi, E., Kitamoto, A., Ono, K., Abe, N., Yoon, H.Y., Kawai, T.: Virtual 3DCG of the Citadel of Bam. In: Wada, T., Huang, F., Lin, S. (eds.) PSIVT 2009. LNCS, vol. 5414. Springer, Heidelberg (2009)
8. Matini, M.R., Einifar, A., Kitamoto, A., Ono, K.: Digital 3D Reconstruction based on Analytic Interpretation of Relics: Case Study of Bam Citadel. In: 22nd CIPA Symposium, Kyoto (2009)
9. Dissemination of Bam3DCG research results, http://dsr.nii.ac.jp/Bam3DCG/

Complementary Approach for Vernacular Wooden Frame Structures Reconstruction

Laurent Debailleux

Faculty of Engineering, Department of Architecture, University of Mons,
Joncquois str. 53, 7000 Mons, Belgium
laurent.debailleux@umons.ac.be

Abstract. The research is focused on traditional timber frame structures (TFS) situated in rural areas. Often neglected, remaining examples embody our build Heritage. However, architects have few tools to manage a conservation project in respect to the structural authenticity of these constructions. Therefore, providing a complementary tool able to automatically recognize and reconstruct traditional rural timber walling which have been structurally transformed is the major function of our research. The tool should automate as much as possible the procedure in two steps. Firstly, record the available examples of gables and identify their typologies. Secondly, formulate transformations hypothesis of a given wooden structure through time. The recording procedure is made by analyzing pictures with image processing in order to extract the wooden structures from colored pictures. The typology recognition is based on a statistical approach where' as structural approach will help to achieve reconstruction hypothesis. Structure recording and typology recognition will be presented in this paper.

Keywords: Timber framed structures, Conservation, Image processing, Features extraction, Reconstruction.

1 Introduction

1.1 Motivation

Studies and researches are more and more focused on reconstruction of ancient or vernacular architecture in a digital environment. This interest may be certainly explained by the progressive loss of our rural built heritage. For several authors (Pesez, 1983; Laslett, 2004), timber walling can be seen as part of a world we have definitely lost. However, if we pay more attention to our build environment, it can be argued that European countryside's still present several examples of vernacular wooden constructions. The reasons are various and can be resumed in three main points. Firstly, rural buildings were seldom assigned to respect town-planning laws which, for example, prescribed fireproof materials for the roofs and façades. Secondly, compared to rural areas, we can assume that the city houses have been much more transformed over ages. Finally, constructions localized in the countryside benefit from their geographical isolation. All these facts helped to preserve some vernacular buildings from disappearance until now. Nevertheless, this kind of architecture is fragile and hardly

M. Ioannides (Ed.): EuroMed 2010, LNCS 6436, pp. 441–449, 2010.
© Springer-Verlag Berlin Heidelberg 2010

resists to carelessness of the owners. In a restricted area, vernacular constructions often show similarities to each others due to construction habits of their creators who reproduced a particular existing canvas based on their experience and culture. However, if the constructions still exist, structures may have been strongly transformed to respond to social and economical needs. As a result, despite a global homogeneity of their architecture, each house has something particular in its construction which explains the adjustment of the traditional way of building applied to a particular context. From our concern, we assume that the particularities also reflect more structural transformations/adaptations rather than ornamentations of the façades. We assume that socio and economical context, functional and dimensional requirements are main factors which influence the wooden frame structures design. The influence of the socio and economical context is expressed in the various typologies expressions which reflect a regional belief, the construction style of a carpenter or a lack of particular building materials. In the regions where wood is easily available, timber-framed houses are made of larger beams. At the opposite in the farming regions, constructions have been developed to spare wood as much as possible. As a consequence, structures are often more complicated, using shorter span. Often, constructions have been also transformed due to laws which have forbidden flammable materials such as thatch which obliged to modify the slope of the roof to be adapted to slate.

In several countries such as Belgium, theoretical studies have been published on traditional wooden architecture (Genicot, 1989; Genicot & Butil, 1996; Hoffsummer, 2002; Houbrechts, 2008). Past studies identified that these transformations are more visible in the gable structures. Since the researches carried out in the 90's, it is assumed that timber-framed gables are particularly expressive and distinguishable into typologies according to the architecture and design characteristics of their structures. In the French-speaking part of Belgium, five typologies have been roughly localized taking into account that an exact division of regions is impossible due to intercultural influence between neighbouring regions (fig. 1).

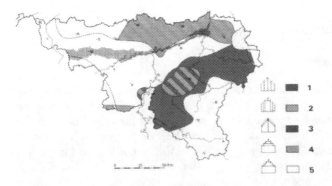

Fig. 1. Localisation of (TFS) in south Belgium by Genicot

This mapping has been used as a reference in order to classify pictures of remaining examples. Type 1: king post and posts rising from a timber sill to the edge, type 2: posts rising from a timber sill to the edge with a rail in the upper part of the gable, type 3: wall plate supporting two posts with a rail in between, type 4: tie-beam and collar-beam supported by braces, type 5: king post rising from a timber sill to the ridge (fig. 2). The richness, the variety but also the fragility of these structures justify to provide to the architects and historians a way to evaluate their quality.

Fig. 2. Referenced gable structures from fig. 1

1.2 Aims

The study has two aims. Generate an automatic tool which firstly, record the available examples of gables and identify their typologies. Secondly, formulate transformations hypothesis of a given wooden structure through time. The recording procedure is made by analyzing pictures with image processing in order to extract the wooden structures from pictures. The typology recognition of the structures is based on a statistical approach. Reconstruction hypothesis are based on shape grammar analysis.

2 Methodology

2.1 Wooden Structure Extraction

The acquisition of data has to be straightforward, avoiding special computing knowledge of the user. An orthophoto of a gable is required for the processing. In order to record, compare and reconstruct the hypothetical structures, we first need to extract the relevant information from the photography. The ability we have to visually isolate the different parts of the image is due to our knowledge of materials and perception of colors (Tucker & Ostwald, 2007). In our context, everyone is able to easily distinguish the wooden parts of the structures at first glance because we all know how wood looks like. The major difficulty in an automatic feature extraction process is to characterize the wooden material to be extracted. Thresholding techniques have been applied. Basically, thresholding methods turn all pixels below some threshold to zero and all pixels over that threshold to one. As a result, we get binary images from the grey-level ones (figure 3).

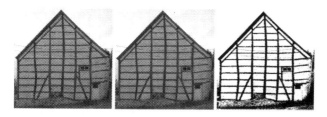

Fig. 3. Thresholded picture. Type 1 example. (RGB/gray/level/BW).

However, using gray levels pictures never provided satisfactory results for the wooden beams extractions. Therefore, in our research, features extractions of the wooden structures have been based on chromatic peculiarities. For this reason, RGB colored pictures has been used for the thresholding. Because we want to compare some existing drawings from past surveys, we decided to extract the edges of the beams from the thresholded image. As a result, these representations can be compared with drawings of existing or even disappeared buildings.

2.2 Typology Recognition

The statistical approach aims to express the different structures examples by means of numerical parameters coming from their Euclidian (length, width) dimensions. In addition, the concept of fractal geometry is used to express the visual complexity of the gable structures in order to calculate for each example, a number called its fractal dimension. Fractal geometry has been exposed in the 80's by Benoit Mandelbrot (Mandelbrot, 1983). Literally, the word fractal, coming from Latin *fractus* means "broken". Therefore, a fractal form is fragmented, geometrically torn, divided into parts from which each is approximately a smaller copy of the whole. In architecture, when we look closer and closer to a building façade, this never ending progression of self similar parts is never infinitely refineable. However, some forms and details can be reproduced from large to small scales. In 1995, Carl Bovill developed these concepts and proved it was possible to express the visual complexity of an architectural conception by calculating a number called its fractal dimension which measures the mix between order and surprise (Bovill, 1995). Fractal geometry in architectural composition is related to the formal study of the progression of interesting forms, from the distant view of the façade to intimate details. As Bovill mentioned rural architecture shows natural detail progression from a large to a small scale. These details can be expressed by ornaments or complexity resulting from the structures. Therefore, from this point of view, all architecture is fractal at certain scales. However, if the fractal dimension of an object refers to the visual complexity of its structure it cannot be related to its esthetical value. In order to calculate the fractal dimension of objects, Bovill proposed the box-counting method.

The method applies an iterative procedure:

- Superimpose a range of different scale grids (*s1, s2*) over the picture you want to study (*s1* is the first grid size).
- Count the number of boxes $N(s1)$ that overlay parts of the image.
- Repeat the procedure, changing *s1* to *s2* with *s1<s2*. The number of boxes containing details of the picture will change with the grid size (fig. 4).

As a result it is possible to obtain a log-log linear correlation between the number of boxes counted and the associated size of the grid. The slope of the regression line is an estimation of the fractal dimension D_b of the picture (fig. 5). N(s) is the number of boxes in each box grid which contains part of the structure and 1/s is the number of boxes across the bottom of the grid.

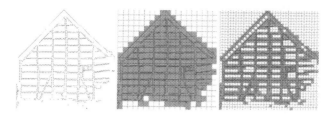

Fig. 4. Applying box-counting method to gable structures

$$D_b = \frac{\left[\log\left(N(s_2)\right) - \log\left(N(s_1)\right)\right]}{\left[\log\left(N\left(\frac{1}{s_2}\right)\right) - \log\left(N\left(\frac{1}{s_1}\right)\right)\right]}$$ (1)

Fig. 5. Box-counting dimension D_b formula

High fractal dimensions ($D_b > 1,5$) mean high visual complexity. As it has been illustrated (Lorenz, 2002; Zarnowiecka, 1998), box-counting method can be used to measure the visual complexity of a vernacular features. Consequently we believe it can highlight an architectural transformation of its structure. Studies proved that box-counting method is also an effective way to evaluate the complexity of our environment (Tucker, Ostwald, Chalup, Marshall, 2005) or artifacts (Elizondo, 2001). It has been proved that ornament subdivides building facades on many different scales and the most effective hierarchical scaling creates a fractal geometry (Moughtin, Tanner, Tiesdell, 1999; Salingaros, 1999).

2.3 Structural Reconstruction

The structural approach is often used when the patterns have a definite structure which can be expressed in terms of composition rules of the form A→B (Stiny, 1980), where A and B are shapes made up of solids, planes, lines or points. The patterns are viewed as being composed of simpler subpatterns which are themselves composed of simplest elements. As a consequence, if a set of rules is able to express the generation of a kind of form, then it is possible generate new forms based on the language which has been created (Colakoglu, 2005; Cagdas, 1996; Flemming, 1987). Therefore, each typology has been expressed through several rules of construction. The combination of these rules allows generating existing examples of wooden frame structures as well as disappeared or still unrecorded structures. The rules parametrization is compulsory in order to avoid absurd reconstruction. A decision tree based on statistical observation is used to guide the user. For each region, width and height of the façades as well as the ratio (W/H), the slope of the roofs, the dimensions of the panels, height of the bases are parameters which help to restrict and improve the reconstruction. As a matter of fact, the panel dimensions are related to the gable dimensions which are themselves linked to the geographical area.

3 Results

3.1 Image Processing

Images processing has been mainly achieved with Matlab. In a picture, a construction is never isolated from its backgrounds. Often, vegetation, artifacts or other constructions have to be removed from the photography. As shown in fig.3, segmentation using grayscale pictures did not give satisfactory results. We decided to work on RGB pictures by using the algorithm "find_color" developed by Ikaro Silva on Matlab. Several other steps have been also added to this algorithm in order to be more adapted to the contexts. Working on colored pictures, the algorithm successively extracts the pixels which have the same color and turn them to black. Then, the boundaries of the structure can be extracted (figure 6).

Fig. 6. Segmented picture (RGB/segmentation/edges)

3.2 Pattern Recognition

12 pictures and 34 drawings founded in the literature have been analyzed. All are 1:200 scale representations. Keeping the same scale representation is compulsory if we want to compare the fractal dimensions of the various gables analyzed within a same range of different scale grids. Two typologies are presented in this paper (type 1 & type 4). Both are divided in two groups: intact and transformed structures. Each typology has been distinguished in two groups in order to identify the original structures ($1_{original}$ and $4_{original}$) and the structures which have been transformed through time ($1_{transformed}$ and $4_{transformed}$). The results conclude that original structures are rather represented by extreme values of the ratio (width/height). Structures of type 1 have rather high ratio expressing their squatness. At the opposite, structures of type 4 are rather slender. On the order hand, transformed structures can be identified by an extreme value of their fractal dimension (D), expressing that structures of the type $1_{transformed}$ are mainly more complex than type $4_{transformed}$ (figure 7).

The number of studied examples is of course relevant if we want to achieve statistical recognition. That is the reason why the data base must be enlarged. However, lots of gables have been hidden under a cladding or even included in new constructions. In some cases, artifacts do not allow access. In order to quickly enlarge our data base, we also propose to use a two-dimensional shape grammar able to generate existing but also unreferenced structures. This knowledge-based approach must help to design wooden constructions that satisfy formal and structural observations.

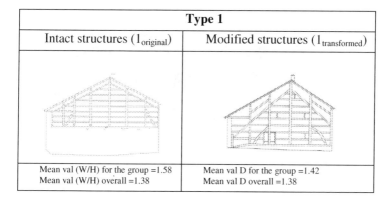

Type 1	
Intact structures ($1_{original}$)	Modified structures ($1_{transformed}$)
Mean val (W/H) for the group =1.58 Mean val (W/H) overall =1.38	Mean val D for the group =1.42 Mean val D overall =1.38

Fig. 7. Statistical results for type 1

3.3 Reconstruction Hypothesis

The parametric rules aim to create idealized two-dimensional representations of typologies structures. At first, it is necessary to analyze the typologies particularities in order to generate a vocabulary able to explain the structural language of the wooden gables. Then, the language has to be transformed into a shape grammar capable of proposing existing or innovative designs.

The language of the timber-framed houses is defined by the beam layouts inscribed within the gable geometries. The vocabulary elements in the shape grammar are an initial shape with constrained parameters. Five simplistic typologies are used to characterize each gable structures. At first, the gable envelope and its base are generated. Then, the façade is transformed by successive rules which (re)construct the intact wooden structure (figure 8). Depending on statistics coming from case studies, several reconstruction possibilities are proposed to the user (figure 9).

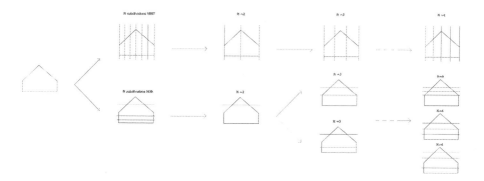

Fig. 8. Iterative rules for type 1 and type 4 reconstruction

Fig. 9. Incorrect (left) and correct (right) reconstruction of a gable

4 Conclusions

Traditional timber frame structures embody particular ways of building. These particularities are illustrated by means of different structural typologies geographically localized.

In this paper, a method able to make architectural recognition of wooden frame structures has been illustrated. It constitutes a work in progress. A statistical approach is based on geometric concerns as well as the evaluation of the visual complexity of wooden frame structures. First results proved that intact and transformed structures examples can be distinguished within the same typology. These first conclusions must be considered with caution due to the little amount of examples. Nevertheless, fractal dimension and geometrical proportions (W/H) have proved to be relevant for vernacular wooden structures distinction. Despite few examples, the statistical approach shows encouraging results. An extended data base should confirm and refine the actual results. A shape grammar adapted to traditional timber framed structures is developed. Wooden constructions seem particularly adapted to this kind of analysis. The creation of existing and unknown structures based on generated rules is a way of studying architecture styles, particularly if the represented examples are difficult to survey. These two approaches will be used as a basis to develop a reconstruction methodology.

References

1. Cagdas, G.: A shape grammar model for designing row-houses. Design Studies 17, 35–51 (1996)
2. Colakoglu, B.: Design by grammar: an interpretation and generation of vernacular hayat houses in contemporary context. Environment and Planning B: Planning and Design 31(1), 141–149 (2005)
3. Elizondo, G.B.: Fractal geometry in Mesoamerica. Symmetry: Culture and Science 12, 201–214 (2001)
4. Flemming, U.: More than the sum of parts: the grammar of Queen Anne houses. Environment and Planning B: Planning and Design 14(3), 323–350 (1987)
5. Genicot, L.-F.: Préliminaire à une géotypologie du pan-de-bois en Wallonie. Nouvelles du patrimoine 27-28, 13–15 (1989)
6. Genicot, L.-F., Butil, P.: Le Patrimoine rural de Wallonie, DGATLP (1996)

7. Hoffsummer, P.: Les charpentes du XIe au XIXe siècle. In: Typologie et évolution en France du nord et en Belgique, Editions du Patrimoine, Paris (2002)
8. Houbrechts, D.: Le logis en pan-de-bois dans les villes du bassin de la Meuse moyenne (1450-1650). Dossier de la Commission Royale des Monuments, Sites et Fouilles, vol. 12 (2008)
9. Laslett, P.: The world we have lost: Further Explored. Routledge, London (2004)
10. Lorenz, W.E.: Fractals and Fractal Architecture. Vienna University of Technology (2002)
11. Mandelbrot, B.: The Fractal Geometry of Nature. W.H. Freeman, New York (1983)
12. Bovill, C.: Fractal Geometry in Architecture and Design. Birkhäuser, Boston (1995)
13. Salingaros, N.: Urban space and its information field. Journal of Urban Design 4, 29–49 (1999)
14. Salingaros, N.: Hierarchical cooperation in architecture and the mathematical necessity for ornament. Journal of architectural and Planning Research 17, 221–235 (2000)
15. Stiny, G.: Introduction to shape and shape grammars. Environment and Planning B: Planning and Design 7, 343–351 (1980)
16. Tucker, C., Ostwald, M., Chalup, S., Marshall, J.: A method for the visual analysis of the streetscape. Paper presented at the Space Syntax 5th International Symposium, Delft, Nettherlands (2005)
17. Tucker, C., Ostwald, M.: Using algorithms to analyze the visual properties of a building's style. In: 4th International Conference of the Association of Architecture schools of Australasia, Sydney (2007)
18. Zarnowiecka, J.C.: Chaos, Databases and Fractal Dimension of Regional Architecture. In: 16th ECAADE Conference, Paris (1998)

CARARE: Connecting Archaeology and Architecture in Europeana

Henrik Jarl Hansen[1] and Kate Fernie[2]

[1] Kulturarvsstyrelsen, H.C. Andersens Boulevard, 1553 Copenhagen V, Denmark
hjarlh@kulturarv.dk
[2] MDR Partners, 2b Fitzgerald Road, London, United Kingdom, SW14 8HA
kate.fernie@mdrpartners.com

Abstract. CARARE is a best practice network funded by the European Commission's ICT Policy Support Programme. The network brings together heritage agencies, organisations, archaeological museums, research institutions and specialist digital archives to establish a service that will make digital content for Europe's unique archaeological monuments and historic sites interoperable with Europeana. As well as bringing 2D images and text documents to Europeana, CARARE will bring a mass of geo-referenced content to Europeana and adds 3D and Virtual Reality as new content types. This paper looks at the activities of the CARARE project in establishing and aggregation service for the archaeology/architecture domain including work to mediate the rich metadata held by the domain for presentation in the Europeana Data Model, the use of semantic web technologies such as SKOS, and work on the documentation and preparation of 3D and VR content for online publication and discovery via the Europeana search service.

Keywords: CARARE, Europeana, Archaeology, Architecture, Heritage Data.

1 Introduction

CARARE is a Best Practice Network, funded under the European Commission's ICT Policy Support Programme, which started on 1 February 2010 and will run for three years. It is designed to involve and support Europe's network of heritage agencies and organisations, archaeological museums and research institutions and specialist digital archives in making the digital content for the archaeology and architectural heritage that they hold available through Europeana, and will establish an aggregation service for the archaeology/architecture heritage domain. CARARE is one of a suite of projects which have been funded by the European Commission to help develop Europeana, and builds on the work of earlier projects which have helped to establish a framework for interoperability within the domain.

1.1 Background and Related Work

From the 1980s there has been work at international level to establish core standards for inventories of historic buildings, archaeological sites and cultural landscapes with

M. Ioannides (Ed.): EuroMed 2010, LNCS 6436, pp. 450–462, 2010.

the aim of improving their management through inclusion in planning and sustainable development processes. The Core Data Index to Historic Buildings and Monuments of the Architectural Heritage established by the Council of Europe was rapidly followed by the CIDOC Core Data Standard for Archaeological Sites and Monuments [1][2]. These standards have been implemented in information systems by heritage agencies across Europe to fulfil the obligations of the Granada and Valletta conventions [3][4] and thus providing a starting point for interoperability and information access. The establishment of the European Heritage network (HEREIN) by the Council of Europe has played an important role in promoting the exchange of information on heritage policies across Europe also contributing to the development of multilingual terminology resources [5].

Two projects have been important in terms of their work on interoperable portals for the cultural heritage and multilingual terminology. AQUARELLE (1996-1999) was funded by the European Commission's telematics programme to demonstrate resource discovery across distributed data sources from the museums and heritage domain; it also developed a multilingual thesaurus server to enable user browsing. [6][7]. ARENA (2000-2004) was funded by the Culture 2000 programme project to digitise archaeological archives from six countries and make them accessible to users via the ARENA portal. The ARENA project has been described as a "path finding" project which set out to investigate and demonstrate the reality of using ICT to enable archaeologists to communicate and share data throughout Europe [8][9][10].

More recently DARIAH (Digital Research Infrastructure for the Arts and Humanities) has been funded by the European Commission's FP7 programme to investigate, develop and maintain infrastructure to support ICT-based research practices across the humanities and arts. In its preparatory phase the project is building on work by the earlier ATHENA project to provide a demonstrator of service oriented architecture enabling access to electronic archives [11].

The EPOCH Network of Excellence, funded through the EC's Sixth Framework programme focussed on the development of open source tools and service to support 3D visualisations and the flows of information from archaeological discovery to education and dissemination [12]. Of particular relevance to CARARE are the open source tools such as ARC 3D, MeshLab, CityEngine and InMan which have become available to cultural institutions to use in the 3D visualisation and interpretation of historic buildings, archaeological monuments and landscapes as a result of the project. SCULPTEUR, an earlier project supported by the EC's 5th framework programme is also of interest for its work demonstrating the potential to navigate, search and retrieving 2D images and 3D models using a combination of metadata and content-based searching.

1.2 Cultural Heritage without Borders

These projects and others (such as the Pathways to Cultural Landscapes Project [13]) illustrate the desire amongst researchers and heritage professionals for cooperation across national borders and to embrace the possibilities offered by information technology to improve search and discovery of digital content.

Europe has a common cultural heritage in which present national borders have little relevance for "cultures" through prehistory and early historic periods. There has been a long-term ambition amongst archaeologists of sharing heritage information across borders through interoperable information systems able to query data from several nations at once and present the result in a meaningful way to users. The potential for cross-border research was discussed by Dam and Hansen in their review of the Arena project [14].

This ambition is very much in line with the initiative to establish Europeana as a single point of access to Europe's cultural heritage and makes entry to Europeana a logical next step for heritage information.

2   Introduction to CARARE

CARARE has been established as a Best Practice Network with funding through the European Commission's ICT Policy Support Programme to involve Europe's network of heritage agencies and organisations, archaeological museums and research institutions and specialist digital archives in the Europeana initiative.

Fig. 1. CARARE project logo [15] © CARARE 2010

The project started on 1 February 2010 and will run for three years. It is designed to:

- Support its member organisations in making the digital content for the archaeology and architectural heritage that they hold available through Europeana,
- aggregate content and deliver services,
- and enable access to 2D, 3D and Virtual Reality content for heritage objects for the users of Europeana.

2.1 Archaeology and Architecture in Europeana

The major objective of CARARE is to increase the quantity and quality of digital content for the archaeological and architectural heritage that is available to users of Europeana. Such content is particularly relevant to Europeana having great potential to support services for cultural tourism and users with interests in local history, family history and humanities research.

Analysis of the content of Europeana in summer 2009, following the initial ingest of 5 million items to support the launch of the prototype service, concluded that that there was a need and demand to increase the available content for the archaeological and architectural heritage.

CARARE proposes to meet this demand by enabling an estimated 2 million items for 1 million unique monuments, buildings, landscapes and heritage sites to be included in Europeana. Including content from heritage organisations in Europeana alongside material from museums, libraries, archives and audio-visual collections will enable sources to be brought together and researched in ways that have rarely been possible previously. It will become possible to bring together distributed collections which have been scattered as a result of long ago boundary changes or the activities of different researchers and institutions.

2.2 Adding a New Dimension to Europeana: 3D and VR

In addition to bringing 2D images and text material to Europeana, CARARE will have a special focus on the 3D and virtual reality models created by archaeologists and architectural historians to record, analyse and present heritage sites and objects. The project aims to solve issues concerning the harvesting and presentation of these formats for Europeana and for other domains.

One issue that is particular to 3D is that users are often required to install browser plug-ins in order to view 3D content. As 3D formats and viewers are relatively unstandardized there is a risk that Europeana users could be directed to install many different plug-ins, this is particularly the case as it is intended that the 3D content will remain on the original content provider's web-servers. To simplify matters for Europeana users, CARARE will make recommendations to content providers on best practices including a set of visualisation technologies for Europeana which are multi-platform, multi-browser and (if possible) do not require the installation of plug-ins.

2.3 Place and Geographic Information

CARARE will also make a positive contribution to Europeana by bringing a critical mass of content which includes spatial coordinates as well as place names, and also the expertise of the heritage community in working with geographic information and geographic information retrieval.

The work by CIDOC and the Council of Europe in establishing Core Index data for monuments and historic buildings included specifications for place information. This work provided the starting point for the widespread implementation of GIS by heritage agencies as technologies became available. Place is one of the most frequent starting points for enquiries about the archaeology and architectural heritage of an area. Importantly the inclusion of spatial coordinates in record sets enables archaeology and architecture data sets to be included in geo-portals alongside other datasets used in planning, development control, tourism and other map-based services.

Differing map projections, coordinate systems and standards cause issues when bringing together spatial data sets from different regions. The 2007 INSPIRE Directive seeks to solve this issue for environmental datasets by establishing an Infrastructure for Spatial Information in the European Community [16]. Many heritage agencies are currently working towards implementing the INSPIRE directive and this is an area where CARARE can contribute expertise to Europeana.

3   Content

CARARE is contributing to the expansion of Europeana both in terms of involving new content providers from the archaeology/architecture domain in Europe and in terms of the content being made accessible. More than 2 million digital objects have been identified in the initial survey by partners. The actual content that these partners will make available to Europeana via CARARE includes:

- archive items created by local citizens, visitors, scholars and scientists who have explored, described and depicted heritage sites since the earliest times, and
- photographs, measurements, drawings, reports, plans, maps, 3D and virtual reality models created by heritage agencies in support of their mission to manage and promote understanding of the heritage sites within their area.

3.1   3D, Virtual Reality and Virtual Reconstructions

3D and virtual reality models are increasingly used in the archaeology/architecture domain to record, analyse and present complex monuments and buildings (see figure 2). The initial content to be made available through CARARE includes 3D and virtual reality models of sites that are of high heritage interest at international, European, national and local level and includes:

- 3D model of the Pompeii civic forum
- Virtual reality model of Ta' Hagrat Temple, Malta
- 3D scan of the fortifications at Gdańsk, Poland
- SVG plan of Silchester Roman town, UK
- 3D models and virtual reality reconstructions of the Paphos theatre, Cyprus and also
- 3D models of ceramic vessels

This content type is not yet represented in Europeana. The initial focus in establishing the Europeana Service was on building a critical mass of textual and image based content with moving image and audio content being added more recently through projects such as the European Film Gateway, EU Screen and Europeana Connect. The first prototype of the Europeana service (www.europeana.eu) was designed around four major content types: images, text, audio, moving image. One of CARARE's activities will be to define the functional specifications to establish both the workflow and a new search facet for 3D and VR content.

Fig. 2. Middle Byzantine Church,1200 A.D., Episkopi Manis, Hellas © The Ministry of Culture and Tourism - 5th Eforate of Byzantine and Post-Byzantine Antiquities (3D Digitization by CETI, Athena Research Centre)

4 Metadata

CARARE will establish an aggregation service for archaeology/architecture organisations. This service will harvest metadata from its content providers, providing data mapping tools to enable the metadata to be transformed into Europeana friendly formats. This transformed metadata will in turn be made available by the CARARE service for harvesting and ingest by Europeana. The aim is to provide the necessary guidance, standards and infrastructure to establish a channel which improves the interoperability of digital content from the archaeology/ architecture domain with Europeana.

4.1 Achieving Semantic Interoperability

Achieving syntactic and semantic interoperability across the metadata sets and the different media formats that exist in heritage organisations is the largest challenge for CARARE. To achieve interoperability between the different native metadata formats, CARARE is exploring the use of the CIDOC CRM to mediate between the semantics of the original data and the standards and schemas defined by Europeana.

The CIDOC CRM (Conceptual Reference Model) represents an 'ontology' for cultural heritage information and describes in a formal language both explicit and implicit concepts and relations which are relevant to the documentation of cultural heritage. The CRM provides the basis for mediating cultural heritage information and the semantic "glue" needed to transform local information sources into coherent global resources [17].

4.2 Mapping and Transformation

CARARE will ask its content providers to map their native metadata schema to an implementation of the CIDOC CRM which will in turn be mapped to the Europeana

Data Model (EDM) [18]. This approach provides flexibility, allowing for development both by Europeana in its data model and the metadata that it maintains to support the main function of search and discovery and also allowing for the maintenance and development by content providers of richer descriptions of heritage objects.

An early decision for CARARE has been selecting an implementation of the CIDOC CRM for use in the mapping tool which will be made available to CARARE content providers. Both RDF and XML implementations of the CRM have been made available and are published on the CIDOC website. Early discussions with CARARE content providers revealed that there were barriers to the implementation of the full RDF schema which would increase the training requirement for heritage professionals who would be undertaking the data mapping. XML implementations of the CRM were found to be more user friendly and to offer the potential for customization for the heritage domain.

4.3 MIDAS Heritage

MIDAS Heritage is a data standard for information about the historic environment which was developed for use in the UK and Ireland and is maintained by the Forum on Information Standards in Heritage [19]. MIDAS builds upon the following sources:

- The development of international data standards for the cultural heritage sector, including the Core Data schemes for historic buildings and archaeological monuments and the CIDOC CRM;
- A first edition of the MIDAS standard [20];
- The experience of the members of the Forum on Information Standards in Heritage in its application (FISH).

MIDAS covers three major areas:

- the individual assets that form the historic environment (buildings, archaeological sites, shipwrecks, archaeological areas of interest and artefacts);
- the work that is undertaken to understand, protect and manage change to those assets (events);
- sources of further information (archives).

In addition to the published documentation, presentations and training materials available for the MIDAS standard, the Forum on Information Standards in Heritage has developed an interoperability toolkit to assist in the process of moving information between information systems with funding from English Heritage and the National Trust [21]. The tools include:

- MIDAS XML
- INSCRIPTION controlled vocabulary and identifiers
- Tools to validate the contents of MIDAS XML files.
- Historic Environment Exchange Protocol (HEEP), a web service protocol to standardise remote querying on heritage data

After a review of the MIDAS heritage standard alongside other implementations of the CIDOC CRM and the CRM itself, CARARE concluded that the standard was of interest for use in the project. The fact that MIDAS builds on the work by CIDOC and the Council of Europe on Core Data for archaeology and architecture gives the schema a European relevance as it covers concepts that are familiar to most heritage agencies in Europe that maintain monument inventories. Mapping between MIDAS and the CIDOC CRM also facilitates its use by CARARE as a schema to mediate between the native metadata held by CARARE partners and the Europeana Data Model.

English Heritage are now working with the CARARE project to internationalise MIDAS, which includes updating the standard to conform to the INSPIRE directive on geographic information.

4.4 Europeana Data Models

Europeana has developed metadata specifications to support the functionality of its search portal and interoperability with the numerous metadata schemes in use by its content providers. The Europeana Semantic Elements (ESE) was published in summer 2008 to support the first prototype portal [22]. There have been minor revisions to the ESE schema since its first publication and it will continue to be used in the new release of the Europeana portal due in summer 2010. But the Europeana v1.0 project has been working on the Europeana Data Model (EDM), based on Semantic Web principles, to enable additional functionality to be incorporated in future releases of the Europeana portal due in summer 2011.

The ESE schema was based on Dublin Core Metadata and, while it supported item level retrieval in the first Europeana prototype portal well, it did not differentiate between temporal and spatial coverage sufficiently well for the archaeological or architectural heritage. The EDM schema is a semantically richer schema which takes into account concepts from the CIDOC CRM and in making clear distinctions between the concepts of time-span, place, agents and events (see figure 3) is more suited to archaeological and architectural heritage objects. For this reason the CARARE project has elected to provide data to the 2011 Europeana release in EDM format.

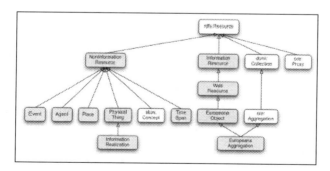

Fig. 3. The EDM class hierarchy © Europeana 2010

An important development in the current version of the EDM is its re-use of concepts from ORE, RDF and SKOS opening the potential for exploitation of semantic web technologies. CARARE plans to benefit from these capabilities and is looking at the SKOSification of multilingual terminology resources for the heritage and at the potential for establishing linked data for use within the domain.

5   Harvesting and Aggregation

Europeana is based on a distributed architecture with aggregation services such as CARARE harvesting and aggregating metadata from content providers and then being targeted for harvesting Europeana itself.

CARARE will establish a network of repositories amongst its content providers which are interoperable with its harvester. The OAI-PMH communication protocol [23] is the preferred method for metadata delivery to CARARE although other web-services may be considered with individual content providers. From the perspective of content providers, the use of OAI-PMH has benefits as it can be implemented on many systems using Open Source software and is increasingly being implemented by vendors of repository systems. It is one of the key standards that have been promoted to culture sector stakeholders and the resultant availability of tools means that the barriers to entry for stakeholders, especially those who are creating new repositories, are relatively low.

5.1   CARARE Workflow

To enable the aggregation of quality metadata into Europeana, CARARE is implementing an ingestion workflow, which centralises some processes in the CARARE repository and enables content providers to be involved in controlling the quality of the metadata produced for the Europeana environment. The stages of the workflow are as follows:

1) Metadata will be harvested from each content provider and to the CARARE repository where it will be indexed and stored in an XML data format. Content providers will be able to declare the harvest as either complete (new, updates or deletes) or partial (new or updated or mixed).
2) Content providers will complete a mapping of the data fields in their native metadata to CARARE's implementation of the CIDOC CRM, MIDAS Heritage using a web-based metadata mapping tool provided by the National Technical University of Athens for the CARARE project.
3) CARARE will complete a mapping of the CRM implementation to the Europeana Data Model (current version).   It is important to note that the EDM schema is still evolving as new functionality and content types are identified for Europeana. By asking content providers to map their data to an intermediary schema (step 2) and then mapping this schema to the EDM, CARARE aims to avoid asking its content providers to do repeat mappings.
4) CARARE will convert selected multilingual thesauri identified by CARARE content providers to SKOS using automated tools.

5) Content providers will be able to view their metadata transformed in Europeana's format in a test environment to check and resolve any data issues which might include:

    i)   Refining the data mapping

    ii) Mapping their terminology to selected lists

    iii) Normalizing the data to Europeana standards, e.g. adding the language of the metadata, content type etc.

    iv) Linking terms to SKOS thesauri

6) CARARE will run a quality control check, for example to check for any missing values or malformed data and report back on the content providers data.

7) Once the checks are completed validated Europeana metadata will be made available in the CARARE OAI-PMH repository for harvesting by Europeana. The SKOS thesauri created and used in CARARE will also be made available to Europeana.

CARARE's workflow is illustrated below in figure 4.

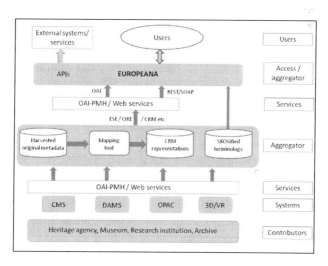

Fig. 4. CARARE's harvesting and aggregation service © CARARE 2010

6 3D Content

CARARE has a specific work package which is focussing on the issues around making 3D and VR content accessible to Europeana. The content survey will help to identify in more detail the formats that are held by CARARE content providers, initial feedback indicates that there is a wide range which includes simple models of museum objects, complex reconstructions of major archaeological sites, virtual tours, CAD data files (useful for students and professional users), and 3D models associated with large related 2D archives, with different levels of granularity and considerable variation in the metadata that is currently available.

The metadata needed to support the description, preservation and discovery of the 3D/VR models produced in the archaeology/architecture domain is one area that is under discussion. On a professional level it is important to document the methods and techniques used in capturing 3D models of real-world archaeological and architectural objects, and in creating virtual reconstructions of these sites as they appeared at various times in the past. Such information may be less immediately important to a general user of 3D models, who may rely on descriptions of the site, its associations and characteristics (who, what, when) and location for resource discovery, and on technical metadata describing the format of the model in order to view the model itself. CARARE is looking at these metadata requirements in order to make recommendations to its content providers and to Europeana.

Another aspect of the metadata for 3D which is under review is the relations between the parts of complex models (which may comprise of a series of linked 3D objects) and between 3D models and linked information sources. 3D and Virtual Reality models increasingly include links to external digital content such as text documents and images, which enhance their educational value. These complex relationships between objects and metadata also increase the complexity of ingesting 3D collections into a repository. The 3D-COFORM project, with funding from the European Commission's 7th Framework programme, is carrying out a programme of research in this field, looking in particular at 3D documentation and the deployment of affordable, practical and effective technologies for use in the cultural heritage sector [24]. At the technical level, it is helpful that 3D-COFORM is investigating the relationships between the CIDOC-CRM and METS as ontologies, provenance data encoding and standard geometric representations (X3D, Collada). CARARE is following the research activities of the 3D-COFORM project consortium with interest and will take its results into account when making practical recommendations to the archaeology/architecture community.

One more aspect of 3D which is under consideration in the CARARE project is the rendering of 3D models online for general users. 3D digitisation of large buildings or monuments often results in very large volumes of data and heavy-weight models, which are too large for presentation on the web. Such models may be made available off-line on standalone systems, or they may be converted (simplified) for presentation on the web. Current best practice guidance recommends the use of VRML, X3D and Collada as standardised formats with longevity [25] [26]. These are very good choices for digital preservation but viewing models in these formats still involves users in installing browser plug-ins, and as the plug-ins are not browser independent different plug-ins need to be offered by content providers. Embedding 3D models into PDF documents may offer a cross-platform solution that enables this content to be viewed without the need to install plug-ins. CARARE plans to make recommendations to Europeana content providers on the selection of suitable visualisation technologies which offer users a satisfying experience of 3D content.

7   Getting Started

The CARARE project started on the 1st February 2010 and, at the time of writing, the project start-up phase is underway. Working groups are meeting to discuss and make recommendations on metadata and vocabularies, and work is in progress to establish the CARARE repository and technical architecture.

A survey has been initiated to gather information from CARARE content providers about the content that they will be making accessible to Europeana and about their technical situations. We know that our partners are starting from different points, with a few already having advanced interoperable and remotely accessible online services while others need to set up their OAI-PMH repositories from scratch. Over the coming months as the survey brings more information about the situations of individual partners, CARARE will develop the advice, guidance and support needed to prepare for harvesting.

The CARARE aggregator will be implemented and tested during 2010, with trial harvesting from our content providers beginning towards the end of the year. Live harvesting will commence in 2011 with CARARE's first set of 2D contents becoming accessible to Europeana users with the Danube release in summer 2011.

8 Conclusions

With CARARE we are at the beginning of an exciting project which constitutes the next step on a journey towards realising the dream of bringing together Europe's archaeological and architectural heritage in a single access point which enables research across borders. We are building on previous work on data standards, terminology and technical infrastructure, and the efforts of heritage organisations, museums and research institutions to digitise the historic environment.

Acknowledgements. CARARE is a project in which 28 organisations participate. The authors gratefully acknowledge the contributions of Rob Davies of MDR Partners, Lena Inger Larsen and Christian Ertmann-Christiansen of Kulturarvsstyrelsen, Vassilis Tzrouvaras of the National Technical University of Athens, Dimitris Gavrillis and Christos Papatheodorou of the Digital Curation Unit, Athena Research Centre, Oliver Mamo of Heritage Malta, Sven Ole Clemens of the Deutsche Archaeologishes Institut, Maria Emilia Mascii of the Scuola Normale Superiore and all the members of the CARARE metadata working group.

References

1. Thomas, R., Bold, J. (eds.): Documenting the Cultural Heritage, J. Paul Getty Trust (1998), http://icom.museu/objectid/heritage/index.html
2. CIDOC Archaeological Sites Working Group, http://cidoc.mediahost.org/wg_archaeological_sites(en)(E1).xml
3. Council of Europe, Convention for the Protection of the Architectural Heritage of Europe (Granada 3.10.1985), http://conventions.coe.int/treaty/en/Treaties/Html/121.htm
4. Council of Europe, European Convention on the Protection of the Archaeological Heritage (Revised) (Valetta 16.1.1992), http://conventions.coe.int/Treaty/en/Treaties/html/143.htm

5. Council of Europe, European Heritage Network,
   http://www.european-heritage.net/sdx/herein/index.xsp
6. Michard, A., Christophides, V., Scholl, M., Stapleton, M., Sutcliffe, D., Vercoustre, A.:
   The Aquarelle Resource Discovery System. In: Computer Networks & ISDN Systems,
   vol. 30(13). Elsevier Science, Amsterdam (1998),
   http://www.ics.forth.gr/isl/publications/paperlink/
   Aquarelle_Ressource/html/comnetv2.html
7. AQUARELLE, Sharing Cultural Heritage through Multimedia Telematics,
   http://www.ercim.eu/activity/projects/aquarelle.html
8. ARENA, Archaeological Records of Europe - Networked Access,
   http://ads.ahds.ac.uk/arena
9. Kenny, J., Richards, J.D., with a contribution from Waller, S.: Pathways to a Shared European Information Infrastructure for Cultural Heritage. Internet Archaeology 18 (2005),
   http://intarch.ac.uk
10. Kenny, J., Kilbride, W.G.: Europe's Digital Inheritance, ARENA archives launched. In:
    CSA Newsletter, vol. XV1(1) (Spring 2003),
    http://csanet.org/newsletter/spring03/nls0302.html
11. DARIAH, Digital Research Infrastructure for the Arts and Humanities,
    http://www.dariah.eu
12. EPOCH, European Network of Excellence in Open Cultural Heritage,
    http://www.epoch-net.org
13. Pathways to Cultural Landscapes, http://www.pcl-eu.de
14. Dam, C., Hansen, H.J.: The European Digital Resource in Archaeology: Sites and Monu-
    ments Data as a Common European Web Resource. Internet Archaeology 18 (2005),
    http://intarch.ac.uk
15. CARARE, http://www.carare.eu
16. European Commission, INSPIRE Geoportal,
    http://www.inspire-geoportal.eu
17. CIDOC CRM The CIDOC Conceptual Reference Model (CRM),
    http://cidoc.ics.forth.gr
18. Europeana, unpublished, Europeana Data Model, Version 5.1
19. English Heritage, MIDAS Heritage,
    http://www.english-heritage.org.uk/publications/
    midas-heritage
20. MIDAS - A Manual and Data Standard for Monument Inventories (First edn.), Royal
    Commission on the Historical Monuments of England, London (1998)
21. FISH, Forum on Information Standards in Heritage,
    http://www.fish-forum.info
22. Europeana Semantic Elements Specifications, Version 3.2.2,
    http://group.europeana.eu/web/guest/technical-requirement
23. Open Archives Initiative, http://www.openarchives.org
24. 3D-COFORM, http://www.3dcoform.eu
25. MINERVA Technical Guidelines for Digital Cultural Content Creation Programmes,
    http://www.minervaeurope.org/interoperability/
    technicalguidelines.htm
26. Fernie, K., Richards, J.D. (eds.): Creating and Using Virtual Reality: A Guide to Good
    Practice for the Arts and Humanities, AHDS, London (2002),
    http://vads.ahds.ac.uk/guides/vr_guide/index.html

AEgArOn – Ancient Egyptian Architecture Online

Ulrike Fauerbach[1], Willeke Wendrich[2], Salma Khamis[1], Martin Sählhof[1],
Bethany Simpson[2], and Angela Susak[2]

[1] German Archaeological Institute Cairo, AEgArOn-Projekt, 31 Sh. Abu el-Feda,
11211 Cairo-Zamalek, Egypt
[2] University of California, Los Angeles, Los Angeles, CA 90095-1511
aegaron@kairo.dainst.org
http://www.dainst.org/aegaron

Abstract. AEgArOn is an international three-year project striving for the open
access online publication of high-quality plans and architectural drawings of
ancient Egyptian buildings. These will give a globally accessible and reliable
overview of the Pharaonic architecture including all major ancient Egyptian periods and building types. Moreover, the information is researched in detail, collected from the best available sources, combined in redrawn CAD-plans,
checked on-site, and accounted for in extensive metadata. As a rule, actual
state- and reconstruction-plans are provided, often complemented by plans of
building-phases. Newly developed drawing conventions allow for immediate
understanding and comparison between monuments. Long term sustainability
and maintenance is ensured by incorporation into the UCLA Digital Library.
Since starting in October 2009, and after six months eighteen PDF-files of five
buildings have been completed and published online.

Keywords: Architecture, Digital Library, Documentation, Egypt, Metadata,
Standards, Visualization.

1 Introduction

Architectural drawings of buildings dating to the Pharaonic period are often hard to
find or have not been published adequately. It is therefore difficult to get an overview
of the built environment of this time. AEgArOn, a three year project funded by the
DFG and the NEH, aims at improving the present state of architectural representations
by developing an open-access online archive of vetted plans. Published and in some
cases unpublished plans of approximately 150 ancient Egyptian buildings are being
collected and critically assessed, important details are checked in the field, and the
plans are then redrawn in CAD according to a newly developed visual standard. The
sources of the information are being made available in detail. The German Archaeological Institute Cairo (DAIK) and the University of California, Los Angeles (UCLA)
are cooperating in this project[1]. The data are collected in Los Angeles, transferred to

---

[1] Primary Investigators: Ulrike Fauerbach, Willeke Wendrich, Stephan Seidlmayer; staff at
DAI Cairo: Salma Khamis, Martin Sählhof; staff at UCLA: Bethany Simpson, Angela Susak.

M. Ioannides (Ed.): EuroMed 2010, LNCS 6436, pp. 463–472, 2010.

new plans in Cairo, checked in the field, and published online and maintained in Los Angeles. The plans will be published through the web pages of the DAI and UCLA Encyclopedia of Egyptology (UEE) in various formats to ensure long term sustainability for different types of users: as AutoCAD-files (dwg), Acrobat-files (PDF), and pixel images (tiff). Eighteen PDF-files of five buildings are at this moment available at http://www.dainst.org/aegaron.

2 The Essentials

The goal of the project is to provide a comprehensive overview of Pharaonic architecture. The selected buildings should represent a balanced cross-section of ancient Egyptian architecture that takes into account the different types of buildings and monuments. Houses and palaces, small and monumental tombs, provincial-and nationally important temples, magazines, workshops, etc. are represented similarly, without limitation to or focus on the 'classical' era of Egyptian culture. In order to collect and present as much information as possible, all of the existing plans of a chosen building are checked and assessed. A selection of drawings is made, based on the quality of first hand information comprised. These are scanned on a flatbed scanner, and loaded into AutoCAD for redrawing. The most important measurements, especially the main dimensions, are compiled from the publications or measured from the original plans so that the inevitable distortion created by the scanner can be compensated. Each building has to be examined in detail so that the information given in the plan can be transferred to a standardized visual language. Whenever personal communication with the excavator or architectural historian cannot be established, this process will be accomplished through the published descriptions of the buildings, photographs, and, if possible, field checking (see below).

3 Visualization

3.1 Drawing conventions

Plans of historic buildings show considerable disparity in the evident standards of accuracy and visualization, e.g. a partly preserved wall in a floor plan may be indicated by hatching or solid black, representing a section view resulting from "cutting", or the wall may be shown from a top view with details of its masonry or brick pattern. This makes it more complicated to understand and compare the buildings and thus hampers architectural research—irrespective if it is in the field of Egyptology, building archaeology, or art history. All of the plans compiled in AEgArOn will display the same clearly outlined drawing conventions. The use of specified line thickness, types, and colors will enable immediate optical understanding of the building (fig. 1). Despite the attention to detail, it is inevitable that features are rendered abstract. For example, in the floor plans stone-by-stone renderings of walls are represented merely as a surface, which is then coded with the appropriate hatching representing the material; this also facilitates comparison with other buildings for which there are only less-detailed images. Initially, the drawings were rendered black and white, currently standardized color codes are being developed.

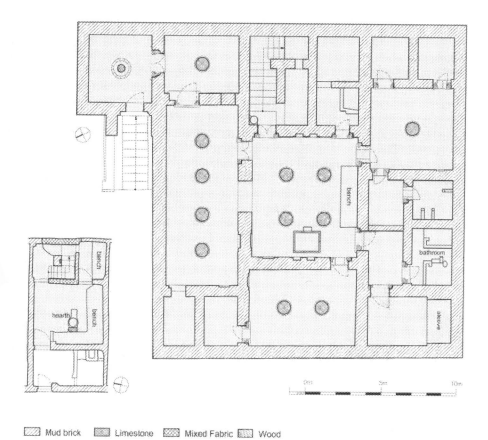

Mud brick   Limestone   Mixed Fabric   Wood

Fig. 1. Glimpse of the social stratification of a town in the 14th century B.C.: The reconstruction plans of two contemporaneous houses in Amarna on the same scale and with the same visual standards are placed side by side. The ground floor of the villa of general Ramose had a floor space of ca. 400 m² and consisted of a central hall, a large access area, and more than eight rooms and a bathroom. The numerous columns are indicators of not only a roofed area that was usually utilized for communal activity but also of an upper room. Furthermore, a number of outbuildings, a well, and a garden of ca. 694 m² belonged to the estate. The inhabitants of the house "Gate Street No. 8", which was located within a walled-in exclave, were probably workmen in the necropolis of the town. They had at their disposal ca. 43 m² on the ground fl oor, which included a hearth in the front court. Here, too, we can assume that an upper room lay above, or at least an upper floor which was either unroofed, or contained shelters made from mats. Both houses were built of mud brick; the varying thickness of the walls must have had great influence on the indoor climate. Redrawn by S. Khamis after El-Saidi & Cornwell (1986, fig. 1.1) and Borchardt & Ricke (1980, plan 23).

3.2 Types of Plans

Often times, archaeological publications do not distinguish between actual state- and reconstruction-plans, e.g. by depicting destroyed parts of a building as existing in a plan which pretends to give the actual state. To call attention to this problem, actual state- and reconstruction-plans of each building are produced as a rule in AEgArOn to compare (fig. 2). There may be exceptions if a reconstruction is not possible or a reconstruction plan is the only evidence of a destroyed building. Grossmann (1974, pp. 108-110) described the problem that many publications only contain reconstructions and that actual state drawings are ignored; he postulated to cease publishing reconstructions. Although his argumentation is convincing, the effect would probably be that outdated reconstructions are published instead of the actual state plans. If a building shows evidence of numerous reconstruction- or use-phases, the online publication will facilitate the publication of further drawings without high costs. For this a layer structure composed of 89 layers (Table 1) was developed, which is the basis of every drawing. The large amount of layers was generated due to the necessity to distinguish

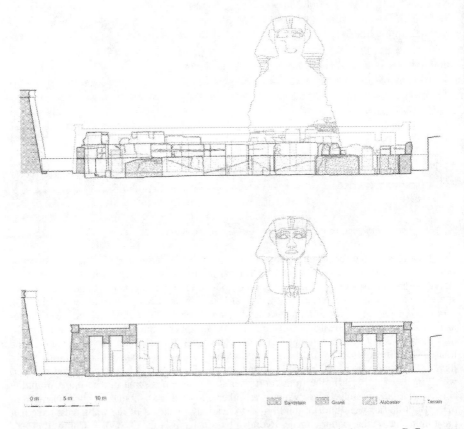

Fig. 2. Giza, Harmachistemple and Sphinx, 4th Dynasty, twenty-sixth century B.C., cross section with view towards the west, actual state and reconstruction. The drawings are compiled out of 80 layers in AutoCAD in a standardized layer structure, cf. fig 3. The cross sections are augmented by three floor plans, which display actual state, reconstruction, and building phases. For the first time, the temple and Sphinx have been drawn together in this form, which visualizes the combined effect of both monuments. The section lines through the temple, which deviate in the actual state- and reconstruction plan, are copied from Ricke (1970). Redrawn by S. Khamis after Ricke (1970, plan 3) and Lehner (1992, figs. 2 and 9).

different materials, actual state, building stages and reconstructions visually. Thus a distinction is made between reconstruction according to building archaeological findings (stage 1) versus reconstructions based on comparisons (stage 2) or reconstructions based on conjectures, which cannot be verified by the actual state (stage 3).

3.3 Why 2D?

A considerable part of documentation of cultural heritage today is done 3D, e.g. by laser scanning, and virtual 3D-reconstructions are becoming more and more popular. So why does AEgArOn stick to 2D drawings? Since it is the projects aim to give a well balanced overview over a large number of sites and building types, it is based on existing publication, which is almost entirely 2D. Sections are rarely published, and even several sections, floor plans and elevations are hardly sufficient to create an accurate 3D model without surveying the monument itself, especially when the building has irregular surfaces as partly destroyed structures usually have. Furthermore, 3D models are less able to represent details of construction, are less user-friendly due to the larger file size and cannot be included in printed works. 3D is a useful addition to the documentation of architecture, but will never replace 2D drawings. When presenting comparable material for a representative number of examples, there is at this time no alternative to 2D drawings.

4 Methods

4.1 Lessons Learned

Published plans of historic architecture display a surprisingly high number of discrepancies, which is particularly evident when there are numerous drawings of one building such as the Roman Temple at the Island of Philae (fig. 3a/b). Astonishingly it is the plans of the most famous buildings which are the most erroneous. This is probably due to them being copied more often for republication, while each copy adds new faults and errors. Therefore it is essential not only to republish drawings online, but to compare the available information and to verify it. Furthermore users of drawings will be enhanced to retrace the steps AEgArOn took when producing the individual plans.

4.2 Field-Checking

Each accessible building that is being published in AEgArOn is field checked during the drawing phase. Observations are recorded in a sketch, but measurements are not taken. Survey work in Egyptian monuments requires a permit, which must be requested three months in advance and contain the papers of all of those involved. The administrative efforts for 150 buildings cannot be met within the scope of this project. Relative to the time and effort spent, the increase in knowledge based on such sketches (fig. 3c) is significant. Most of the new findings are related to doors, blocking of openings, ceiling construction, and indications of structural changes. In order to record them in a plan, taking measurements would be desirable, but not necessarily essential. An approximate

Table 1. The layer structure compiled of 89 layers is the basis for all of the project's drawings. The layers are either frozen [o] or unfrozen [✓] in the various types of plans, actual state [A], building phases [B], and reconstruction [C], which are managed in AutoCAD-Layouts.

Layername	A	C	B
Auxilary lines (1)	o	o	o
Auxilary lines (2)	o	o	o
Axes	o	o	o
Layout (Plot)	o	o	o
Section lines	(✓)	(✓)	o
Plan 01	o	o	o
Plan 02	o	o	o
Plan x	o	✓	✓
Actual state elem. in section	✓	✓	o
Actual state destruction in section	✓	o	o
Actual state buildg. joint in section	✓	(✓)	(✓)
Actual state buildg. joint in elev. (1)	✓	(✓)	(✓)
Actual state buildg. joint in elev.(2)	✓	(✓)	(✓)
Actual state older elem.	✓	o	o
Actual state later edition in section	✓	(✓)	(✓)
Actual state later edition in elevation	✓	(✓)	(✓)
Actual state elem. in elevation (1)	✓	✓	✓
Actual state elem. in elevation (2)	✓	✓	✓
Actual state elem. in elevation (3)	✓	✓	✓
Actual state elem. above section line	✓	✓	✓
Actual state hidden edges	✓	✓	✓
Actual state sill	✓	o	o
Actual state stairs	✓	✓	✓
Actual state door jamb	✓	o	o
Actual state flooring	✓	o	o
Actual state depression	✓	✓	o

Layername	A	C	B
Actual state object	✓	o	o
Actual state damage floor (1)	(✓)	o	o
Actual state damage floor (2)	(✓)	o	o
Actual state destruction in elev. (1)	✓	o	o
Actual state destruction in elev. (2)	✓	o	o
Actual state destruction in elev. (3)	✓	o	o
Completition elem. in section	✓	o	o
Completition elem. in elevation (1)	✓	o	o
Completition elem. in elevation (2)	✓	o	o
Reconstruction elem. in section (1)	o	✓	✓
Reconstruction elem. in section (2)	o	✓	✓
Reconstruction elem. in section (3)	o	✓	✓
Reconstruction elem. in elevation (1)	o	✓	✓
Reconstruction elem. in elevation (2)	o	✓	✓
Reconstruction elem. in elevation (3)	o	✓	✓
Reconstr. elem. above section line	o	✓	✓
Reconstruction hidden edges	o	✓	✓
Reconstruction sill	o	✓	✓
Reconstruction stairs	o	✓	✓
Reconstruction doors (definite)	o	✓	✓
Reconstruction doors (suggested)	o	✓	✓
Reconstruction door jamb (definite)	o	✓	✓
Reconstruction door jamb (suggested)	o	✓	✓
Building Phase I	-	-	✓
Building Phase II	-	-	✓
Building Phase III	-	-	✓

Table 1. (*Continued*)

Layername	A	C	B
Building Phase I Reconstruction	-	-	✓
Building Phase II Reconstruction	-	-	✓
Building Phase III Reconstruction	-	-	✓
Building Phases Roofing	-	-	✓
Hatching Act. state elem. in section	✓	(✓)	(✓)
Hatching Act. st. later addit. in section	✓	(✓)	(✓)
Hatching Actual state Limestone	✓	(✓)	(✓)
Hatching Actual state Sandstone	✓	(✓)	(✓)
Hatching Actual state Hardstone	✓	(✓)	(✓)
Hatching Actual state Mud brick	✓	(✓)	(✓)
Hatching Actual state Burned brick	✓	(✓)	(✓)
Hatching Actual state Wood	✓	(✓)	(✓)
Hatching Actual state Roofing	✓	(✓)	(✓)
Hatching Reconstr. elem. in section (1)	o	✓	✓
Hatching Reconstr. elem. in section (2)	o	✓	✓
Hatching Reconstr. Limestone	o	✓	✓
Hatching Reconstr. Sandstone	o	✓	✓
Hatching Reconstruction Hardstone	o	✓	✓
Hatching Reconstruction Mud brick	o	✓	✓
Hatching Reconstr. Burned brick	o	✓	✓
Hatching Reconstruction Wood	o	✓	✓
Hatching Reconstruction Roofing	o	✓	✓
Header 200 Actual state Text	✓	o	✓
Header 200 Reconstruction Text	o	✓	✓
Header 200 Building Phases Text	o	o	✓

	A	C	B
Header 200 Compass & Scale	✓	✓	✓
Room Number	(✓)	(✓)	(✓)

Layername	A	C	B
Label (1)	(✓)	(✓)	(✓)
Label (2)	(✓)	(✓)	(✓)
Height Indication (1)	(✓)	(✓)	(✓)
Height Indication (2)	(✓)	(✓)	(✓)
Coordinates (1)	(✓)	(✓)	(✓)
Coordinates (2)	(✓)	(✓)	(✓)
Original plan indistinct	o	o	o
Topography	✓	✓	✓

Key Legend	
Frozen Layer	o
Unfrozen Layer	✓
Layer frozen or unfrozen	(✓)
Layer not used	-
Actual State	A
Reconstruction	C
Building Phases	B

470   U. Fauerbach et al.

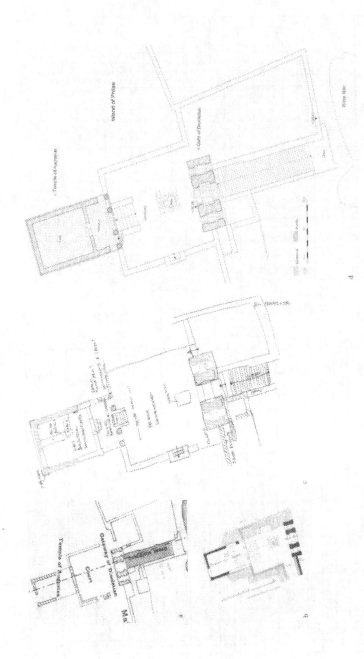

Fig. 3. Roman temple and gate, first and third centuries A.D. a) Actual state plan, detail from Lyons 1908, plate 1, floor plan. b) Actual state plan, Borchardt 1903, fig. 3, floor plan. c) Sketch after Lyons 1908, with mapping of actual state. d) New drawing M. Sählhof 2010, reconstructed floor plan (M 1:400). The plan is a synthesis of the older actual state plans, which were checked in a field survey of the building and were augmented by additional information.

record is better than an unpublished one. This step is indispensable also for well documented buildings especially when producing reconstruction plans. Buildings which are inaccessible due to lack of permission, state of excavation or preservation are checked by using photographs.

4.3 Metadata

In order to make the different steps in the development of the plans comprehensible, metadata are added to the drawings. As a critical apparatus they document authorship as well as the origin and the reliability of the information. This is contrary to the customary method of copying plans without checking the original or without any reference to their origin, during which the sum of errors increases and a wrong sense of up-to-dateness is conveyed since authorship is disregarded.

Fig. 4. Philae, Roman temple from southwest, 13-12 B.C., Photo by M. Sählhof 2010   **Fig. 5.** Philae, Roman gate from the east, ca. 300 A.D., Photo by U. Fauerbach 2009

5 Conclusion

AEgArOn aims at making a representative selection of ancient Egyptian buildings more accessible through detailed research and standardized visual language. The developed standards benefit Egyptology as well as architectural research, art history, and public interest. The project gives a broad overview of ancient Egyptian architecture and through original research in addition to comparisons of existing plans and elevations, contributes an important resource, which will form the basis for architecture as an important scholarly source.

References

1. Borchardt, L.: Der Augustustempel auf Philae. Jahrbuch des Kaiserlich deutschen Archäologischen Instituts 18, 73–90 (1903)
2. Borchardt, L., Ricke, H.: Die Wohnhäuser in Tell El-Amarna. Gebr. Mann, Berlin (1980)
3. El-Saidi, I.M., Cornwell, A.: Work inside the Walled Village. Amarna Reports 3, 1–33 (1986)

4. Großmann, G.U.: Einführung in die historische Bauforschung, Darmstadt (1993)
5. Grossmann, P.: Standardisierung der Darstellung. Diskussionen zur archäologischen Bauforschung 1, 100–112 (1974)
6. Lehner, M.: Documentation of the Sphinx. In: 1st International Symposium on the Great Sphinx, vol. 1, pp. 55–107. AUC Press, Cairo (1992)
7. Lyons, H.G.: A Report on the Island and Temples of Philae. Waterlow and sons, London (1896)
8. Lyons, H.G.: Report on the Temples of Philae. National Printing Department, Cairo (1908)
9. Ricke, H.: Der Harmachistempel des Chefren in Giseh. Franz Steiner, Wiesbaden (1970)

A Sustainable Repository Infrastructure for Digital Humanities: The DHO Experience

Donald Gourley[1] and Paolo Battino Viterbo[2]

[1] Digital Initiatives Consultant, 310 Melvin Avenue, Annapolis, MD, USA
donald.gourley@gmail.com
[2] Royal Irish Academy, 19 Dawson Street, Dublin, Republic of Ireland
p.battino@dho.ie

Abstract. The Digital Humanities Observatory was created to support the long-term management of electronic cultural heritage resources for the digital humanities in Ireland. However, the project grant was for three years and the economic downturn has diminished opportunities for continued funding. The challenge is to demonstrate the importance and value of maintaining these e-resources, and to make it feasible for the resource owners to do so without the DHO if necessary. ICT systems can support cost effective and value-adding access and management of resources in a way that might be sustained in the short-term by organizations and projects that lack the funding, staffing, and skills to build and operate a digital preservation environment. In this project paper we describe how the DHO uses technology to promote the value of preservation and interoperability of e-resources, and to provide a means for achieving these goals in the face of significant sustainability risks.

Keywords: Digital Humanities, repository, Fedora Commons, Drupal, metadata, Europeana, sustainability.

1 Introduction

The Digital Humanities Observatory (DHO) [1] was established in 2008 as part of the Humanities Serving Irish Society (HSIS) [2] consortium to manage and co-ordinate the increasingly complex e-resources created in the arts and humanities throughout the Republic and Northern Ireland. Part of the mission of the DHO project is the provision of data management, curation, and discovery services supporting the long-term access to, and greater exploitation of, digital resources.

The DHO was funded for three years; in 2011 there is hope that the project can gain continuing funding in order to maintain its services, but this is far from certain. We are in the awkward, but not uncommon, position of promoting and supporting long-term access and preservation of digital resources in a potentially short-term context. The Blue Ribbon Task Force Report (2010) described the common economic and financial issues that impede implementation of digital preservation strategies, and identified three "technical actions" to overcome them: building capacity, lowering costs, and making operational an *option strategy* to hedge against irreversible loss.[3] The DHO response has been to build system sustainability and exit strategies into the information technology infrastructure that we provide our partner projects.

M. Ioannides (Ed.): EuroMed 2010, LNCS 6436, pp. 473–481, 2010.

2 The DHO Repository

A key requirement to support the DHO mission is a central e-research repository for resources developed by HSIS. The wide variety of e-resources that are candidates for the DHO repository, and the uncertainty regarding the requirements of that content, demanded digital asset management software that is flexible and extensible. As a resource intended to provide services and support to a variety of scholarly and digitization projects concerned with cultural heritage, the DHO repository must support heterogeneity across several dimensions:

- *Variety of resource types.* The repository is required to manage various media, such as images (manuscripts, historic pictures, etc.), encoded texts, audio recordings, and videos.
- *Variety of project goals.* Digital humanities projects vary in size, scope, and final aims; for example, while some projects need a comprehensive web site with user authentication, advanced search features, comment posting, and so on, others neither need nor can afford the development of those interfaces and thus require a more lightweight approach.
- *Variety of project abilities.* The DHO's involvement in the development of final deliverables varies according to the skills and resources available within the projects; some need support in all phases of development, while others may have the resources and expertise for in-house development and only avail of the DHO infrastructure for storage, indexing or interoperability.
- *Variety of long-term sustainability plans.* While some projects can afford the maintenance and update of their final deliverable, others face funding uncertainty themselves and have few options to keep their cultural heritage resources accessible in the long-term.

No single repository or digital asset management system can support the various resources and project requirements that we anticipate. We recognized the need for a modern service-oriented framework on which specific web applications could be easily built as needed. The foundation of such a framework is a repository platform that is open, based on web services, able to handle a variety of data and metadata models, and easy to extend.[4] Without the resources to develop a custom platform, we needed repository software that was mature and had a strong and dynamic set of tools being developed around it. The Fedora Commons [5] open source repository was the only system that met all these requirements. Fedora Commons supports a number of front-end solutions to access the e-resources stored in the repository, so we would not be locked into one set of tools for all the ways we would be publishing the resources on the web.

A key requirement of DHO web site development is the need to support both the development of thematic research collection project web sites, led by our partners and focusing on a single collection of resources, and the need to provide a generic cross-collection interface to discover and re-use resources across the whole repository. For this reason, the repository infrastructure has to be flexible and support different ways of implementing various features. Fedora Commons meets this challenge by being very modular and pluggable. For example, Fedora Commons does not have a built-in indexer and search engine, but comes with a generic easy-to-configure search service that is based on Apache Lucene [6]. This service can be replaced or extended and the DHO (and many other Fedora repository projects) have added Solr, Lucene's enterprise search platform, to implement powerful full-text search, hit highlighting, faceted search, dynamic clustering, and other modern search features.

2.1 Front-Ends for Thematic Research Collections

After evaluating various classes of tools, including rich Internet application (RIA) and asynchronous JavaScript and XML (AJAX) frameworks, the DHO settled on integration with content management systems (CMS) as the most effective way to develop front-ends to the repository for thematic research collections. Although RIA and AJAX frameworks provide tools for accessing the Fedora API and could be used to develop front-end web sites, several factors led us to select CMS integration:

- The extant development skills and experience available in the DHO and partner projects.
- The primary focus that our partners have on publishing text-based resources rather than publications that require advanced graphics and animation.
- The flexibility and efficiency of server-side discovery and delivery for large data sets, as compared to client-based on-line exhibition solutions.

Our investigation into CMS integration looked at PHP-based Drupal [7] and Python-based Django [8]. Although Django offers many technical benefits with its object-oriented model-view-controller architecture, Drupal was selected for the sustainability that its large development and hosting community provides. Drupal is one of the most popular CMS, which means there are a very wide user base, ample choice of modules, and many hosting solutions for web sites. Human resources for developing Drupal modules and user interfaces are readily available. Because of the uncertain future of the DHO, technology sustainability is a more urgent requirement than technical elegance.

Integration with the CMS was achieved by means of the Fedora REST API Drupal module developed by the DHO and now available as open source software [9]. The Fedora REST API module is based on metadata harvesting, which adds some complexity to the process of ingesting and updating e-resources. In contrast, the Islandora [10] Drupal module, developed at the University of Prince Edward Island for integrating Drupal and Fedora, accesses the metadata in the repository and uses a Lucene index for searching, so new and updated resources don't have to be harvested to show up in Drupal. However, the Fedora REST API module has a flexible mechanism for mapping Fedora object structure and description to Drupal nodes, so it can work with the numerous core and contributed modules that operate on nodes, such as Search, Taxonomy, Views, Workflow, and the like. We felt this was a reasonable trade-off for cultural heritage resources that don't change much after they have been stored in the repository, but would benefit from new presentations and visualizations that take advantage of Drupal functionality.

The Fedora REST API module provides a programming interface to invoke Fedora Commons REST methods, including a PHP class that encapsulates all the REST API methods so they can be easily invoked from other Drupal modules. It also defines a type of content node ("fedora_object") that represents a digital object in the repository. One can define a new content-type in a custom module that invokes the Fedora

REST API module's hook implementations to add the Fedora object attributes to a node and, in an object-oriented sense, "extend" and "inherit" from the "fedora_object" content-type. A template module file is included to simplify the process of creating modules that extend the "fedora_object" content-type. Thus the Fedora REST API module, along with the Drupal framework, comprise a rapid application development environment that minimizes the procedural and SQL programming required to create web sites to publish digital cultural heritage resources stored in a Fedora Commons repository.

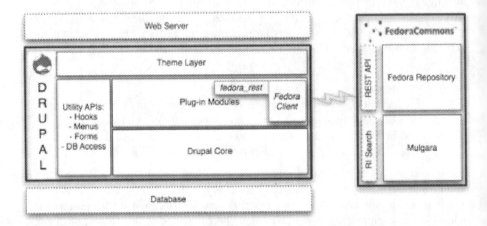

Fig. 1. Drupal-Fedora integration using the Fedora REST API module

We are also developing a mechanism for content to be imported and integrated into Drupal, so discontinuation of the DHO repository need not pose a threat to the preservation of each individual project. Their resources can be completely packaged in a Drupal web site that is hosted on any of the numerous hosting sites that support Drupal, and maintained by developers in the broad Drupal community. The content imported into Drupal using this mechanism will be structured as digital objects using the BagIt [11] format, so they can be easily ingested into future repositories as the opportunity arises. This supports our worst-case exit strategy: if the DHO is not funded and no repository solution is available for migration, a project can host a Drupal site with minimal effort and cost so their resources remain accessible, and the resources are also safe and verifiable (if not optimally re-usable).

A CMS solution provides a separation between the e-resources (stored in the repository) and supplementary content (like posted comments and resource tags to customise grouping and browsing) that is not inherently part of the e-resources themselves. It also offers opportunities to empower partners to customize their projects' websites with minimal intervention from DHO staff. Drupal user interface, user authentication, and search/browse facilities are provided by the CMS and configurable with simple administration web forms. And by levering Drupal's support of input filters, the Fedora REST API module offers additional levels of customization and empowerment:

- At a basic level, each page (more precisely, each Drupal "node", whose body can include any XML metadata file imported from the digital object) can be filtered using a configurable XSL style sheet, allowing for complete control of the design and layout of the main body of the page without relying on Drupal's theme system.
- At a more advanced level, additional XSL style sheets can be applied to transform and extract any fragments of the XML files in the object and expose them to the Drupal theme system, allowing for more sophisticated customizations.

2.2 DHO:Discovery – A Cross-Collection Repository Interface

To demonstrate the value of and ability to create resources that could be accessed and remixed, and are generally interoperable, the DHO needs a user interface for searching and browsing the repository across all the thematic research collections. We recognized that meeting this requirement relied more on the Solr index than on the Fedora API for discovering and accessing e-resources, and would be easier to implement and maintain if it was, in fact, completely independent of the repository source of content. So for this requirement our investigation focused on interfacing with the Solr index, rather than with the Fedora API.

After evaluating various front-end development tools, we selected AJAX-Solr [12], a framework-agnostic JavaScript library for creating user interfaces to Solr indexes. AJAX-Solr requires many calls to the server to display search results, typically one call for every page reload, but the queries retrieve only a limited amount of data in the

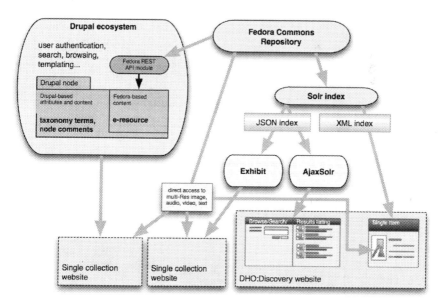

Fig. 2. The architecture of the DHO repository system with loosely coupled and individually sustainable components

very compact JSON format, making it more responsive than a pure server-based web application and less resource-intensive than an exhibit that must be loaded in its entirety into the browser.

While we were designing the search index for the cross-collection repository interface (known as DHO:Discovery), the DHO was working with the Irish Manuscripts Commission [13] to aggregate metadata describing digital content from national cultural institutions for the European cultural heritage portal Europeana [14]. We were able to lever the Europeana project's extensive experience reconciling heterogeneous metadata for cross-collection searching in our design for the DHO:Discovery index. Since the DHO repository contains a variety of metadata schemas, we are developing the DHO Repository Interface Metadata (DRIM) schema as a common denominator schema that can be used for DHO:Discovery. This schema is based on the Europeana Semantic Elements [15] (ESE v3.2.1) schema, which is a flexible metadata standard that allows heterogeneous resources to interoperate while presenting a very low barrier to projects that want to be included in the portal. The current draft of DRIM adds four additional elements to ESE v3.2.1, for linking to resources and browsing by facets. These extensions are given in Table 1.

Table 1. DRIM extensions to Europeana Semantic Elements v3.2.1

Element name	Attributes	Description
dho:collection	dho:url	Name of the thematic research collection(s) that the resource is a part of.
dho:datastream	dho:url dho:mime	An unambiguous URL and label for retrieving part or all of the content of the digital object.
dho:partner		Name of the DHO partner providing the resource.
dho:year		Date of creation of the original analogue or born-digital object.

We are creating crosswalks for deriving DRIM from any kind of metadata that is deposited in the DHO repository. The DRIM is then indexed using Solr to create a coherent cross-collection search facility. By following the ESE specification and the Metadata Mapping & Europeana Normalisation Guidelines for the Europeana Prototype v1.2 [16], the DHO is also ensuring that the metadata in the repository can be easily transformed and contributed to the Europeana digital library.

3 Current Status

The first thematic research collection based on the DHO Fedora repository and Drupal, The Doegen Records Web Project [17], went live in November 2009. This digital archive of recordings in Irish-language dialects, made during 1928-31, comprises an important audio collection of stories, songs and other material. The collection includes 137 Gaelic speakers from 17 Irish counties. The Doegen Records Web Project web site is fully bilingual, with both English and Irish language versions built with Drupal internationalisation and translation features. It offers a unique resource for linguists, social historians, anthropological researchers, educators, musicologists, genealogists, local communities, and anyone interested in Ireland's cultural heritage. The materials provide a fascinating and priceless legacy of now extinct Irish-language dialects. Users can browse and listen to these recordings and appreciate the spoken record of the early twentieth century in rural Ireland. During the first four months of 2010, the website received over 2,000 visits.

4 Future Work

The Doegen Records web site will be greatly enhanced during the Summer 2010 with the addition of information about the speakers, and transcriptions and translations of the audio files. The project team is adding this additional content to the repository through a management interface built with Drupal and the Fedora REST API module. The project is also considering allowing mediated comments for scholars and the general public to annotate recordings, something that is easily implemented with Drupal and the Fedora REST API module.

At the time of writing, two other thematic research collections have been ingested into the repository, and their websites are being developed using Drupal and the Fedora REST API module. Additional collections will be ingested into the repository and their websites will be developed in the following months. This will be a test-bed for the rapid application development and customisation features of the Fedora REST API module, as the different collections will require quite distinct front-end web presentations. Ingestion of further collections will also greatly increase the quantity and utility of items accessible through DHO:Discovery.

We are continuing to refine the DRIM schema, informed both by our DHO: Discovery implementation experience and developments in the Europeana project. We are currently verifying compatibility with the latest version of the Europeana Data Model [18]. DHO:Discovery will offer faceted browsing and full-text search on some of the DRIM elements, a video/audio player, and a multi-resolution image viewer. Additionally, a key aspect of the interface is to provide a link to each item in the thematic collection web site where the item is shown in its original context. DHO:Discovery is currently in a prototype stage. At the time of writing, initial user testing is planned within the next month and a first release is scheduled to be launched in September 2010.

5 Conclusion

The political and economic context in which the DHO project was created and operates presents a dilemma: How do we support and promote best practices and technology for the long-term access and re-use of digital resources in a short-term project?

From a technology perspective, the DHO has met this challenge by creating systems that are exemplary and sustainable:

- Rather than describing our digital repository as a preservation archive, it is promoted as an exemplar repository for storing, managing, discovering and delivering digital humanities resources.
- Rather than developing a few highly customized web sites for cultural heritage collections, we created a rapid web site application development environment that levers the Drupal content management framework to empower projects to do as much customisation as they are able using a range of skills from web admin forms to XSLT to PHP programming.
- Rather than enforcing strict consistent metadata requirements on all projects, we deployed a low barrier of entry metadata schema that can be used to demonstrate the value and importance of conforming to minimal standards in order to make project outputs interoperable.
- Rather than locking projects into a technology infrastructure dependent on the DHO's sustainability, we created infrastructure that is easily sustainable on its own, using commodity hosting and development resources.

None of these solutions are ideal; all involve trade-offs that must be considered with regard to project goals and risks. But significant risks to project funding and sustainability are prevalent in all initiatives that endeavour to research, manage, preserve, and disseminate the rich and diverse cultural heritage of the world. At the DHO, the current environment has forced us to find a balance between the immediate need to publish scholarly results and the imperative that these results be accessible for future uses and investigation.

Acknowledgments

The Digital Humanities Observatory and the work described in this paper are funded by the Irish Higher Education Authority (HEA) under the Programme for Research in Third Level Institutes Cycle 4 (PRTLI-4). The DHO was established under the auspices of the Royal Irish Academy. Additional support for repository hosting and programming is provided by the Dublin Institute for Advanced Studies (DIAS) and the Irish Centre for High-End Computing (ICHEC). The authors would like especially to acknowledge the contributions of Bruno Voisin (ICHEC) for his work designing the repository and indexing architecture, and Kevin Hawkins (University of Michigan) for his work specifying the first draft of the DRIM schema.

References

1. Digital Humanities Observatory, http://dho.ie/
2. Humanities Serving Irish Society, http://hsis.ie/
3. Blue Ribbon Task Force: Sustainable Economics for a Digital Planet: Ensuring Long-term Access to Digital Information. Final Report of the Blue Ribbon Task Force on Sustainable Digital Preservation and Access (2010)

4. Zhang, A., Gourley, D.: Creating Digital Collections: A Practical Guide, Chandos, Oxford (2009)
5. Fedora Commons repository software, http://www.fedora-commons.org/
6. Apache Lucene, http://lucene.apache.org/
7. Drupal content management platform, http://drupal.org/
8. Django web framework, http://www.djangoproject.com/
9. Fedora REST API Drupal module, http://github.com/dongourley/fedora_rest/
10. Islandora Drupal module, http://islandora.ca/
11. BagIt file packaging format, https://wiki.ucop.edu/display/Curation/BagIt
12. AJAX Solr JavaScript library, http://wiki.github.com/evolvingweb/ajax-solr/
13. Irish Manuscript Commission, http://www.irishmanuscripts.ie/
14. Europeana Project, http://www.europeana.eu/
15. Europeana v1.0: Europeana Semantic Elements v3.2.1. Europeana Project (2009)
16. Europeana v1.0: Metadata Mapping & Normalisation Guidelines for the Europeana Prototype v1.2. Europeana Project (2009)
17. Doegen Records Web Project, http://dho.ie/doegen/
18. Europeana v1.0: Europeana Data Model v4.11. Europeana Project (2010)

A Simple Approach to Link 3D Photorealistic Models with Content of Bibliographic Repositories

W. Moussa and D. Fritsch

Institute for Photogrammetry (ifp), University of Stuttgart, Geschwister-Scholl-Str.,
24D 70174 Stuttgart, Germany
{wassim.moussa,dieter.fritsch}@ifp.uni-stuttgart.de

Abstract. Linking 3D photorealistic and virtual reality models with contents of bibliographic repositories and resources is needed for archeological and historical analyses, public understanding of ancient settlements, and simple common sense studies using web content. As the Web 2.0 is used more and more by the community, it will help to deepen the knowledge of many interested internet users. Within this paper, a combination of 3D photorealistic modeling and content of bibliographic repositories, which describes the history of the Hirsau Abbey, Germany, is presented. In particular, it will serve for the special needs of the Verein "Freunde Kloster Hirsau e.V." which is a registered association for taking care of the Hirsau Cultural Heritage site. The 3D photorealistic models have been acquired by means of static LiDAR and HD close range photogrammetry.

Keywords: 3D Photorealistic Model, Virtual Reality Model, Bibliographic Repository, Cultural Heritage, LiDAR, Close Range Photogrammetry.

1 Introduction

Up to now, there are two worlds of representing and maintaining cultural heritage objects: the geometry world and the semantics world. An efficient and direct link is missing. A more advanced approach would be to build software agents which snoop the Web just to find out references describing the single cultural heritage object. Thus, an effective procedure to build a bridge across the two worlds is extremely required. This bridge allows finding sources and references related to the desired cultural heritage object.

As a matter of fact the Web 2.0 is frequently used and easily obtainable to a larger and larger degree by the community. This indicates that simple approaches are needed to combine 3D photorealistic models with contents of bibliographic repositories and resources. Moreover, many interested internet users prefer to deepen their specific knowledge. Additionally, many fields of study and different applications such as archeological analyses, historical findings, public understandings of ancient settlements and simple common sense studies using web content need such a link. Quite similar ideas have been introduced already. On the one hand, it was proposed in the field of archaeology by the Information Centre for Archaeology (ArcheoInf), Bochum/Germany. ArcheoInf directs at having a combination between primary acquired data from different archaeological excavations and 2D field surveys. On the other

M. Ioannides (Ed.): EuroMed 2010, LNCS 6436, pp. 482–491, 2010.

hand, this basic idea is also presented in the FOCUS K3D project. This project works towards promoting the usage of semantics in 3D content modeling and processing and focusing at virtual product modeling and cultural heritage.

Moreover, the current 3D COFORM project hides similar ideas and aims at advancing the cutting edge in 3D digitisation and 3D documentation as a common choice for digital preservation in the cultural heritage domain. This work will contribute to the European Digital Library (EDL) Project. The goal of the EDL project is to integrate the bibliographic catalogues and digital collections of several national libraries in Europe.

In our application, this link will, on the one hand, contribute to the needs of the "Verein Freunde Kloster Hirsau e.V.", which is a registered association for taking care of the Hirsau Abbey site. On the other hand, it will offer Internet users to get the right bibliographic content associated with parts of the corresponding 3D virtual reality model.

The paper deals with a basic approach using simple web technologies to overcome this gap between the two worlds. This approach is considered as a first and simple step to provide the desired information and references. Our next challenge will be to build software agents (or Internet "bods") as a more advanced technology.

In a first pilot project we have implemented the link of a 3D photorealistic model of one of the buildings of the ruins of the Hirsau Abbey, which is called the "Hunting Lodge", with content of bibliographic repositories. Therefore, the work in this paper is a starting point and serving for the special needs of the complete project, which is aiming towards a complete digital preservation of the whole area of the Hirsau Abbey. In addition to that, this project contributes to the CyArk 500 Project which aims to digitally preserve 500 of the most important heritage sites in the whole world [1].

2 Data Collection and Preparation

The data collection, which has been used for our application, was performed in cooperation with the "Friends Association Monastery Hirsau (Verein Freunde Kloster Hirsau e.V.)", Calw/Germany and the Public Office for Historical Monuments' Care (Landesamt für Denkmalpflege), Stuttgart/Germany. The overall goal of the project is to generate a 3D virtual reality model of the Hirsau Abbey, Germany (as depicted in Figure 1).

2.1 Hirsau Abbey

Hirsau, a village in the northern part of the Black Forest, today a suburb of Calw/Germany, has a great history. In particular, the Hirsau Abbey, once known as the Hirschau Abbey (most probably because of the Swabian dialect or may be because of many deers around) was one of the most prominent Benedictine abbeys of Germany. Founded around 830 AD by Count Erlafried of Calw, it served as an abbey until it was destroyed by French soldiers in 1692. By the way, the famous William of Hirsau, abbot from 1069 to 1091, introduced the Astrolabe for measuring latitude positions. Therefore, the Hirsau abbey served already more than one

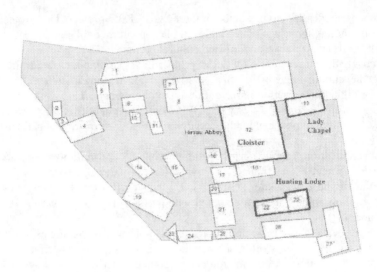

Fig. 1. Hirsau Abbey buildings (ground plan information)

millennium ago for geodetic purposes, a fact not well-known to the geodetic community. Today, just ruins are found - one can see the Cloister, the ruins of the Hunting Lodge, the Lady Chapel and some other Hirsau Abbey Buildings, which are demonstrated in Figure 2.

2.2 3DPhotorealistic Modeling of the Hunting Lodge

3D photorealistic models play a fundamental part in case of risk, damage and archiving and they serve for cultural, touristic and advertising purposes. Those models are increasingly demanded in many fields of application. One of the most important applications is the 3D preservation of cultural heritage sites.

For this purpose, both static LiDAR and close range photogrammetry have been employed successfully for the precise documentation of our cultural heritage study [2,3,4]. Terrestrial laser scanning has been used for collecting highly accurate 3D geometric models. The Leica Scanstation HDS 3000 has been used for data acquisition. Moreover, the 3D virtual reality models are obtained by means of data fusion linking static LiDAR with High Definition (HD) close range photogrammetry. Here, to perform the texturing of the 3D models and for the photogrammetric reconstruction, a digital metric camera, Nikon D2X has been employed. More details can be found in [5].

Figure 3 describes the methodology used from the data acquisition (3D laser scanning and photogrammetric techniques) to the final generation of the 3D virtual reality model using the Google SketchUp program. This chart illustrates the process followed to transform the 3D laser scanning data (point clouds) to a virtual reality model. Using Leica's Cyclone program, registration, georeferencing and modeling of point clouds are achieved. Then, corrections and texturing processes of the previous model are followed, using the Google SketchUp program to get a complete 3D virtual reality (VR) model in the end.

Fig. 2. (a) Hirsau Abbey (© Große Kreisstadt Calw und Oberfinanzdirektion Karlsruhe Copyright 1991). (b) The Hunting Lodge. (c) The Lady Chapel. (d1,2) The Cloister.

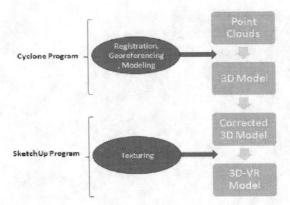

Fig. 3. Workflow for the generation of 3D-VR Models in Google SketchUp

In this paper, we deliver a 3D photorealistic model of one of the biggest parts of the ruins of the Hirsau Abbey, which is called the Hunting Lodge (Figure 4).

Fig. 4. The Hunting Lodge, snapshot for the model in SketchUp [5]

This work is the first step of a complete project, which is running at the Institute for Photogrammetry (ifp), University of Stuttgart, since July, 2009. By the way, the ifp has a very good experience regarding cultural heritage documentation, more information is given by [3,6,7,8]. The overall aim is to deliver a complete 3D photorealistic model of the whole Hirsau Abbey site. The photorealistic model will serve for cultural, archiving and touristic aims.

Figure 5 depicts two examples of our ongoing work, where the 3D virtual reality models of the Cloister and the Lady Chapel are generated. In the near future these models will be available for free in Google Earth.

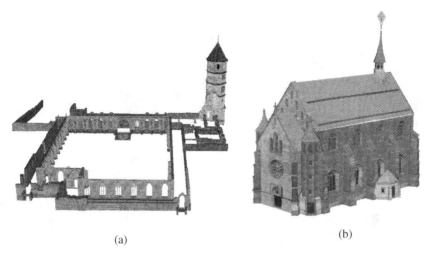

(a)   (b)

Fig. 5. (a)The Cloister [9]. (b) The Lady Chapel [10].

3 Linking Two Worlds in Digital Preservation – Geometry and Semantic

The idea of our approach is to find an easy way linking an uploaded, web-accessible 3D photorealistic model of any Cultural Heritage site with web-accessible content of bibliographic repositories. Our focus is to use open and free-of-charge sources just to maintain the demands of the public. Moreover, these simple technologies were selected due to the fact of wide public usage.

To do so, we combined successfully the community-based Wikimapia and the Google 3D Warehouse, first to find the site using Google Maps and secondly, to watch the site in three-dimensions by means of Google Earth with a provided link to bibliographic resources and related texts.

3.1 Integration of the 3D Virtual Model in Google Earth

To link the 3D virtual reality model with bibliographic resources and because of the large and open usage of virtual globes, the first step is integrating the 3D virtual reality model with Google Earth. Concerning this step, we could use the Leica Virtual Explorer Architect (LVE), but we decided to use Google Earth to have more options regarding visualization and 3D scene generation. More information can be found in [11].

To integrate the 3D photorealistic model with Google Earth, we first have used the Google SketchUp software to place the model and export it to Google Earth with KMZ format, which is the standard exchange style to integrate 3D photorealistic models into Google Earth. After that, we created an account in the Google 3D Warehouse to have the opportunity to upload our KMZ file to Google Earth. The Google

3D Warehouse is a free online repository where you can find, share, store, publish, and collaborate on 3D models. As a result of this, the 3D photorealistic model of the Hunting Lodge becomes open for the public and can be visualized freely and easily as in Figure 6.

Fig. 6. The Hunting Lodge in Google Earth

Uploading the 3D virtual reality models into the Google 3D Warehouse is considered the easiest way to share any model of a site with millions of internet users. To watch our 3D virtual reality model you may visit the Google 3D Warehouse website and type in the name, the Hunting Lodge, and then you will get the webpage which is shown in Figure 7. Through this webpage, we have the opportunity to view the model in 3D or install the model's KMZ file to be visualized using Google Earth. Furthermore, it provides an external link to Wikimapia where you can find the desired references and sources that describe the Hunting Lodge.

3.2 Wikimapia Website

Wikimapia is an online map and satellite imaging resource that combines Google Maps with a wiki system allowing users to add information, in the form of a note to any location on Earth. The Wikimapia project, created by Alexandre Koria-kine and Evgeniy Saveliev, was launched on May 24, 2006 and is aiming towards "describing the whole planet Earth".

As a matter of fact, there is no other option to add a direct link between a 3D model integrated in Google Earth and bibliographic resources. So, using Wikimapia, we used a 2D shape, which refers to the footprint of the 3D model, to link it to the 3D model which is already stored in the Google 3D Warehouse. We prepared the web

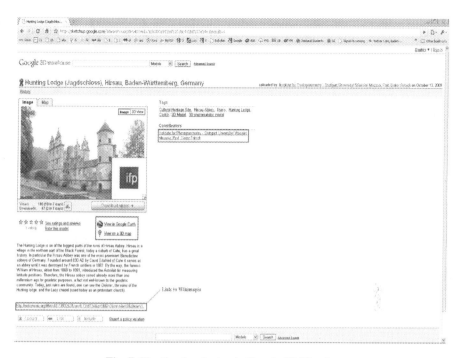

Fig. 7. The Hunting Lodge in Google 3D Warehouse

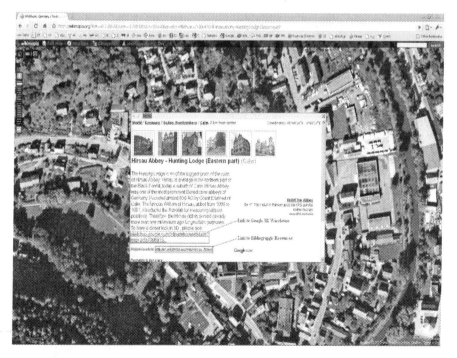

Fig. 8. The Hunting Lodge in Wikimapia

page which relates to our model, the Hunting Lodge, by adding information about the site and uploaded few pictures collected by us. Moreover, explicit links between the 3D model and the bibliographic resources were allocated.

By typing in the Wikimapia homepage and the desired name (Hunting Lodge) will lead to the Wikimapia page. It shows all the above mentioned information and guides the interested user to get answered any enquiries about the Hunting Lodge, Hirsau Abbey. Figure 8 demonstrates the web page and its possible options and deliverables.

4 Conclusions

The combination by linking 3D photorealistic models with content of bibliographic resources, which describe the history of the cultural heritage sites, is highly needed. We presented a simple idea which is considered as a starting point to connect both the geometry and the semantics worlds. This link was missing for a long time. Our next step is to have an advanced approach which aims to build software agents for getting information about references describing each single cultural heritage object. We hope that our work in this paper together with our contribution to the CyArk project will not only gather both, 3D photorealistic models and their bibliographic resources, but will also help in globally preserving our collective history.

References

1. Kacyra, B.: CyArk 500 – 3D Documentation of 500 Important Cultural Heritage Sites. In: Fritsch, D. (ed.) Photogrammetric Week 2009, Wichmann, Heidelberg, pp. 315–320 (2009)
2. Guidi, G., Tucci, G., Beraldin, J.-A., Ciofi, S., Ostuni, D., Costantini, F., El-Hakim, S.: Multiscale archaeological survey based on the integration of 3D scanning and Photogrammetry, Intern. In: Workshop on Scanning for Cultural Heritage Recording - Complementing or Replacing Photogrammetry, Corfu, Greece, September 01-02, pp. 58–64 (2002), NRC 44914
3. Alshawabkeh, Y.: Integration of Laser Scanning and Photogrammetry for Heritage Documentation. Dissertation, Universität Stuttgart (2006)
4. Böhm, J.: Terrestrial LiDAR in Urban Data Acquisition. In: Fritsch, D. (ed.) Photogrammetric Week 2009, Wichmann, Heidelberg, pp. 169–178 (2009)
5. Moussa, W.: Digital Preservation of the Hirsau Abbey by Means of Static LiDAR and HD Close Range Photogrammetry, Master Thesis, TU-Berlin (2010) (not published)
6. Alshawabkeh, Y., Haala, N., Fritsch, D.: Range Image Segmentation Using the Numerical Description of the Mean Curvature Values. In: The International Archives of Photogrammetry, Remote Sensing and Spatial Information Sciences. ISPRS Congress 2008, Beijing, China, vol. XXXVII, Part B5, Commission 5, p. 533 (2008) ISSN pp. 1682-1750
7. Alshawabkeh, Y., Haala, N., Fritsch, D.: A New True Ortho-photo Methodology for Complex Archaeological Application. Archaeometry Journal 52(3), 517–530 (2010)
8. Abdelhafiz, A.: Integrating Digital Photogrammetry and Lasr scanning, PhD Thesis, Deutsche Geodätische Kommission, München (2009)
9. Khosravani, A.M.: Digital Preservation of the Hirsau Abbey by Means of HDS and Low Cost Close Range Photogrammetry, Master Thesis, Stuttgart University (2010) (not published)

10. Heng, Z.: Digital preservation of the Hirsau Abbey by means of automated HDS and close range photogrammetry, Master Thesis, Stuttgart University (2010) (not published)
11. Dubravka, B., Srđan, P., Miro, G.: Site View Reconstruction Using 3D Modeling Techniques, Faculty of Technical Sciences, Novi Sad, Serbia (2009)
12. Herrbach-Schmidt, B., Westermann, C.: Klostermuseum Hirsau: Führer durch des Zweigmuseum des Badischen Landesmuseums, pp. 16–24. Badisches Landesmuseum, Karlsruhe (1998) ISBN 3-923132-69-7
13. Teschauer, O.: Kloster Hirsau, Ein Kurzführer, Calwer Druckzentrum, pp. 6–22 (1991) ISBN 3-926802-10-3
14. Würfel, M.: Lernort, Kloster Hirsau, pp. 4–38. Einhorn-Verlag, Eduard Dietenberger GmbH (1998), ISBN 3-927654-65-5

http://www.archeoinf.de (accessed June 5, 2010),

http://en.wikipedia.org/wiki/Hirsau_Abbey (accessed January 20, 2010),

http://www.focusk3d.eu/ (accessed August 20, 2010),

http://www.3d-coform.eu/ (accessed August 20, 2010),

http://sketchup.google.com/intl/en/3dwh/index.html (accessed May 28, 2010)

A Working Environment for Management and Exploitation of Audiovisual Archives – ASA-SHS Project

Francis Lemaitre

Fondation Maison des Sciences de l'Homme (FMSH)
Equipe Sémiotique Cognitive et Nouveaux Médias (ESCoM)
54 bd Raspail, 75006 Paris, France
lemaitre@msh-paris.fr

Abstract. This document describes the working environment developed by ESCoM laboratory (Equipe Sémiotique Cognitive et Nouveaux Médias, Fondation Maison des Sciences de l'Homme) during the ASA-SHS project (Audiovisual Semiotic Workshop for Human and Social Sciences). ASA-SHS is a R&D project financed by the French National Research Agency (ANR, Programme Blanc 2008) and targets to develop strategies of indexing and semiotic description for audiovisual resources in Social and Human Sciences. The environment developed by ESCoM is a complete environment for managing, describing and publishing audiovisual documents for research and learning. It consists more particularly in tools, resources and distant services for: 1/Management of audiovisual documents, 2/ Management of ontological resources, 3/Semiotic description of documents, 4/Publishing of documents in web portals, 5/Exploitation of documents in the form of publications dedicated to specific uses.

Keywords: *ASA-SHS*, Semiotic Audiovisual Description, Controlled Vocabulary, Ontologies, Description Template, Publication Template.

1 Introduction

ASA-SHS Project (*Audiovisual Semiotic Workshop for Human and Social Sciences, http://www.asa-shs.fr*) is a R&D Project, chosen and financed by the *French National Research Agency* (*ANR, "Programme Blanc Edition 2008", http://www.agence-nationale-recherche.fr*). *ASA-SHS* is developed by *ESCoM* (*Equipe de Sémiotique cognitive et nouveaux medias*). It officially started on 1st of January 2009 and last for 36 months (Expected end on 31th of December 2001).

The audiovisual material used on *ASA-SHS* Project comes from the diversified and important (5000 hours of videos) collections of the *Audiovisual Research Archives* (*ARA Program, http://www.archivesaudiovisuelles.fr*), also developed by *ESCoM*.

The working environment developed for *ASA-SHS* Project is the result of thinking made since 2001 for the *ARA Program*. In consequence, it is an evolution of an existing environment, combining improvements of existing tools and new technologies, specifically developed for the project.

M. Ioannides (Ed.): EuroMed 2010, LNCS 6436, pp. 492–503, 2010.

This environment should answer 2 complementary contexts of use of audiovisual documents:

- The standard context of production/publication as experienced for the *Audiovisual Research Archives Program* – whose results are the bases of *ASA-SHS* Project.
- The context of *ASA-SHS* Project, based on complex problematic of semiotic description of audiovisual documents and specialized publications, which constitute a great re-exploitation and promotion for an important collection such as the *ARA* collection.

2 General Overview of the Environment

2.1 User Roles

We can distinguish 5 kinds of roles in this working environment (cf. *Fig. 1*):

- *Cogniticians* configure the environment by editing controlled vocabulary, types of medias, description templates, but also parameters and templates of publication of the web portal.
- *Producers* register new audiovisual productions, via the web portal.
- *Analysts* describe the audiovisual documents.
- *Translators* translate the environment vocabulary.
- *Authors* manage the publications on the web portal.

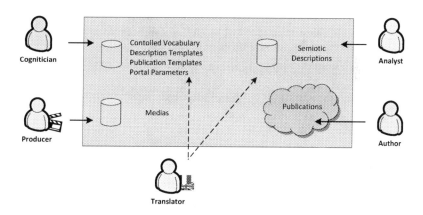

Fig. 1. Roles in *ASA-SHS* Environment

2.2 Interfaces

The environment is composed of 3 main interfaces (cf. *Fig. 2*):

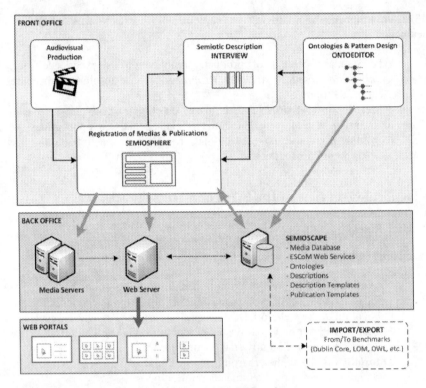

Fig. 2. Interfaces of *ASA-SHS* environment

1/ Semioscape: the heart of the system. This is the server with which the tools communicate. It contains all the resources of the system:

- A database storing every information about medias, controlled vocabulary, descriptions, etc.
- Business libraries that provide all necessary methods for reading, insertion, modification, transformations of data, and methods for rights control.
- Web services providing necessary resources and methods to user tools.

2/ User tools: two user tools are used during the pre-publication phase:

ESCoM OntoEditor:
This is a controlled vocabulary editor which provides an interface for the configuration of the system: ontologies, description and publication templates, translations, benchmarking, etc.

ESCoM-INA Interview:
This is the audiovisual semiotic workshop, co-developed with *French National Audiovisual Institute* (INA). It enables the cutting of the video clip and a very rich description of each sequence.

3/ Semiosphere: the web portal, developed on *ASP.Net* framework, on which audiovisual documents are published. An administration interface enables the authors to manage the media database, and the publications on the portal.

2.3 Semioscape

The architecture of *Semioscape* is composed of 3 main layers (cf. *Fig. 3*)

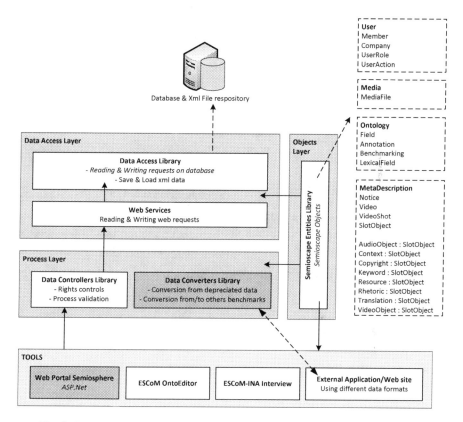

Fig. 3. *Semioscape* Architecture. In gray, parts which are still under development

1/ Objects Layer

The *Semioscape Entities Library* contains every object (in a proprietary format) used by the system, tools and web applications:

- *Ontology* object represents a controlled vocabulary. It is defined as a *Field* object, which contains a list of fields (this defines the structure of the vocabulary) and a list of *Annotation* objects which define the content of a field in any language.
- *MetaDescription* object is defined by a list of *Video* objects, which are defined by a list of *VideoShot* objects (corresponding to a sequence of video). Both video and video sequences are defined by a set of *SlotObject* objects

corresponding to the different elements that describe the video or video sequence (keywords, translations, audio objects, etc.).

2/ Data Access Layer

The *Semioscape Data Access Library* contains every method used for data handling:

- Requests on database (reading and writing requests)
- Load and save methods for data stored as files (mostly controlled vocabulary, stored both in database and file repository)
- These methods are called by web services. Tools access to data by calling the web services, enabling distant uses.

3/ Process Layer

The *Semioscape Controllers Library* contains every method used for checking the validity of any requested process:

- Check the validity of sent data
- Check if user has sufficient rights for any requested process (writing and reading request on every object)

The *Semioscape Converters Library* contains methods used for the transformation of data:

- Methods for transforming data saved in depreciated format (after a critical update of *Semioscape Entities* objects, this ensures that old data will still be usable)
- Methods that should convert data from/to others formats (MetaDescription / Mpeg-7; Ontology / OWL; etc.)

3   Semiotic Workshop

3.1   Controlled Vocabulary

ESCoM OntoEditor enables to register the system parameters, in a proprietary xml format. Thus, the cognitician has a visual tool that enables him to define:

- Video formats (wmv, flash, etc.)
- Modes of video diffusion (streaming, progressive download, mobile, etc.)
- Video definitions (low, high definition, etc.)
- Description templates (cf. next chapter)
- Publication templates
- Benchmarks for data transformations, in order to reuse data in other technological contexts.

This controlled vocabulary is described in a hierarchical manner in the xml format. Beyond the internal name, user can define for each element of the hierarchy:

- Public name, abbreviation, locution,
- Definition, descriptions, examples,
- Link, picture,

- Its reference in every benchmark (LOM, Dublin Core, DEWEY, MPEG7, etc.)
- Information relative to description templates (cf. next chapter)

Finally, we can notice that each kind of this information can be translated in any language. More, *ESCoM OntoEditor* offers automatic completion functionalities, helpful for translator tasks.

3.2 Description Templates

The tool *ESCoM OntoEditor* enables habilitated users ("cogniticians") to define and create dynamically the descriptive schemas (the "description scenarios") by the means of which audiovisual clips or corpora of audiovisual clips have to be described and indexed (cf. Fig. 4)

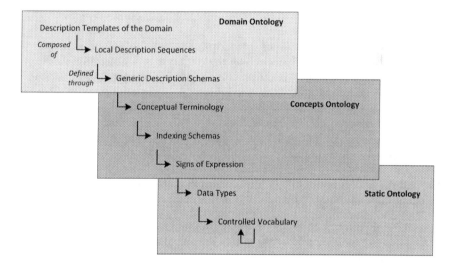

Fig. 4. Description Templates Structure

The specification and development of a set (or "library") of description scenarios relies on three different categories of meta-linguistic resources:

1/ **The category "domain ontology":** it enables the cognitician to define the empirically appropriate description models or scenarios of a selected and circumscribed domain of knowledge (such as the domain "cultural diversity", the domain "literary heritage", the domain "research in archeology", etc.). Principally speaking, a model or scenario of description is composed of a selected set of conceptual terms ("concepts", in short) which have (or which should be) indexed. Each model or scenario of description possesses a functional, a hierarchical and a configurational organization:

The functional organization of a description template
Distinguishes between several canonical functional fields of description of a video source such as:

- The description of the objet or domain of reference (i.e. the description of about what the video or a selected segment of video is);
- The description of the (spatial, temporal and contextual) localization of the object of reference;
- The production of interpretative comments;
- Etc.

The hierarchical organization of a description template
Each model of description is composed of a set of sequences (and sub-sequences) which are specialized in the one or the other functional field of description (description of the domain of reference, description of the localization of a domain of reference, etc)

The configurational organization of a description template
Each sequence is constituted of generic description schemas or objects that define the internal structure of a sequence. Each generic schema or object contains one or more conceptual terms to be indexed. A generic schema or object can belong to many different sequences. For instance, the generic object "Title" is composed of conceptual terms such as "Principal title", "Subtitle" or again "Short title" and it defines – with other generic schemas or objects – each sequence which has to do with the indexing of, for instance, documents, intellectual or artistic works, literature, etc.

2/ The category "concept ontology": it contains the central meta-linguistic resources of a template or scenario of description of video clips or corpora of video clips, i.e.:

The conceptual vocabulary of the ASA-SHS domain
Each template or scenario of description is composed of a selection (a set of) conceptual terms belonging to this vocabulary.

The indexing schemas
These schemas defines how a conceptual term has to be indexed – as a proper noun, as a common noun or nominal expression, in form of a defining phrase, by the means of non-linguistic means such as acoustic or visual images as well as in form of controlled vocabularies, etc.

3/ The category "static ontology": it includes a set of files which are necessary for the technical environment of *ASA-SHS*

- Definition of data types, i.e. basic types (text, numeric, date, etc.) and user-defined types (writer, politician, country, etc.);
- Controlled vocabulary, in which words can be defined into several categories;
- Media configuration (formats, definitions, diffusion modes);
- Ontology versioning;
- Etc.

Example

The figure below (Fig. 5) shows an example of nested schemas. This example was taken from an ontology about Literature called *ALIA*.

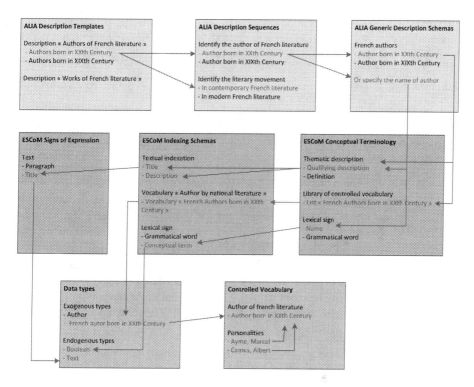

Fig. 5. Example from ALIA ontology

1/ ALIA domain ontology defines specific description templates in literature, such as "Authors of French Literature born in XXth Century", or "Works of French Literature". "Authors of French Literature born in XXth Century" can be described using 2 different sections:

- From the static list of French authors born in XXth Century ;
- By specification of the author (if not included in the static list).

2/ These sections use description templates from the ESCoM's Concepts Ontology. Note that they both have a common resource: "Qualifying description". This resource is defined by a title and a description.

3/ Finally, sections of concepts ontology are finalized when nested with an element of static ontology: this specifies the type of data corresponding to the section. In our example, title is typed as "Text" (then description form will dispose this element as a text box). Conceptual term is defined as a boolean (description form will dispose this element as a check box).

List of French authors is nested with a section of the controlled vocabulary: in this case, description form will dispose a list box. To provide this list of authors, we use a property particular to the controlled vocabulary: sections can be nested with sections inside the vocabulary. This enables to associate a vocabulary with different sections (in our example, we need to define Albert Camus as an author, a philosopher and a journalist). Thus, the list of authors will not only display elements under the "Author born in XXth Century" section, but also elements nested with this section.

3.3 Semiotic Description

The name of the central tool for the concrete segmentation and description of video clips is *ESCoM-INA Interview*, co-developed with *INA* (*Institut National de l'Audiovisuel*) in Paris, France. The concrete description/indexing of a video clip is performed on three levels:

- The production of a kind of "meta-description" of the description itself (title, author, summary, etc.)
- The production of a global description of the video clip as a whole
- The segmentation of the video clips in a set of (user-determined) sequences and the description of each sequence.

The principal tasks of a description/indexing of a video clip and/or its sequences are concerned with the eliciting and structuring of the main features that characterize the content of a video (or of one of its sequences). In this sense, the description of a video or one of its sequences by the means of the previously defined templates or scenarios of descriptions covers:

- The *description of the topic* of a video (or of one of its sequences);
- The *description of the "visualization"* of the topic by the means of audiovisual techniques;
- The *description of the sound level* of a video used for the acoustic expression and communication of a topic;
- The *description of pragmatic aspects* characterizing the specificity of a video clip and/or of one of its sequences (target public, target uses, …);
- The *enriching of a video* or of one of its sequences by the means of comments, explanations, aids, links, references, etc.;
- Etc.

Description forms of the description of topics are displayed according to nested schemas designed in the domain ontology, as explained in the previous chapter:

- The analyst select a description schema in a list depending on the selected domain
- The hierarchy of elements to describe is displayed according to the "definition formats"
- When this hierarchy reaches the lowest level, the level of data types, a form control is displayed, depending on the data type (text input, date select, check box, list of elements from the static vocabulary, etc.) (cf. examples on Fig. 6 & 7. Note that they follow the example presented on Fig. 5).

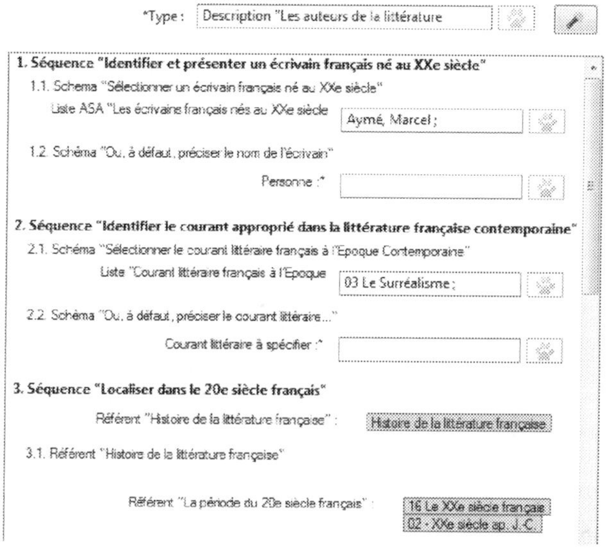

Fig. 6. Example of an ALIA Description Form

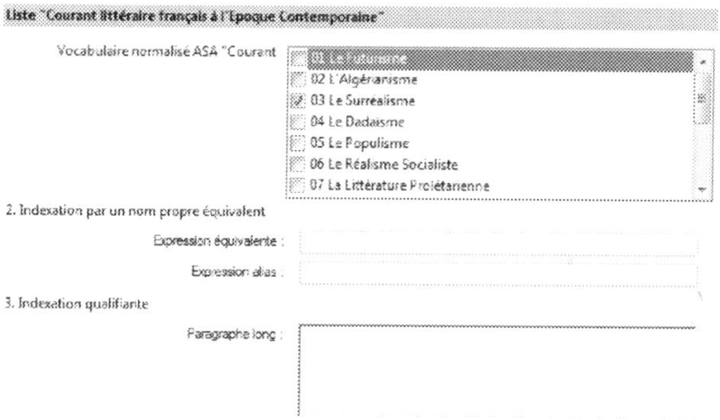

Fig. 7. Example of a Concept Form

4 Semiotic Processing and Publication

At the level of the indexing, the system enables the cognitician not only to configure the global concepts, but also their specialization by domain.

At the level of publication, the philosophy is exactly the same: the system can publish the audiovisual documents - and their corresponding descriptions - on different web portals. Thus, each portal has its own visual identity, its own knowledge domain, its own publication templates, etc. In consequence, the same audiovisual description will be used in various ways on each web portal. In the context of *ASA-SHS* Project, 3 portals have been developed:

- *"Atelier à la Rencontre des Cultures"* (ARC, *http://semioweb.msh-paris.fr/corpus.arc/*)
- *"Atelier Littéraire d'Ici et d'Ailleurs"* (ALIA, *http://semioweb.msh-paris.fr/corpus/alia/*)
- *"Atelier des Arkéonautes"* (ADA, *http://semioweb.msh-paris.fr/corpus/ada/*)

Using the administration interface of a portal, an author can manage different kinds of publications:

4.1 "Standard" Publications

This is the default publication template, which improves the one already existing on the portal of the *Audiovisual Research Archives*. In this case, a publication is organized using a factual point of view: first, the author defines an event, and organizes it hierarchically (for example, a seminary divided in courses). Then, the author associates an audiovisual description to each part of the event, which means that each video clip will be published as an "hypermedia folder":

- General presentation of the video clip, actors, topics, etc.
- Access to each sequence of the video clip from the list of chapters
- A video-lexicon is displayed, offering an access to the sequences associated to each term of the lexicon.
- A list of main topics is displayed, offering an access to the sequences associated to each topic.

4.2 Specialized Publications (or « Re-publications »)

These publications use advanced semiotic descriptions, produced in very specific contexts. They are either associated with an existing publication, as complementary publications, or combined in new fictive events. These republications are displayed from specific templates. Here are some examples of templates developed for *ASA-SHS* Project:

1/ The pedagogical folder: publication adapted to a particular pedagogical exploitation, i.e. a pedagogical level and a topic of the domain very specific ("Reading portfolio for a Persian civilization course in graduate level", "Reading portfolio of the discovery of Persian literature for adults", etc.);

2/ The narrative course: publication that provides "reasoned" courses (chronologically, thematically, etc) through a collection of video sequences coming from various video clips;

3/ The virtual documentary: publication that provides a linear reading of a film composed of sequences, selected from various video clips, following the cutting principles of documentaries;

4/ The bilingual folder: publication adapted to the exploitation of the audiovisual document for the learning of foreign languages;

4.3 Specialized Access

Beyond the access to publications using common search criterions (such as main topics, authors, languages, etc.), the administrator of the portal can elaborate new sections by himself, by selecting his own search criterions. These sections are automatically updated after each new publication, and constitute audiovisual "virtual cuttings", or guided navigation courses (for a pedagogical goal, for example) about very specific topics. Here are some examples of templates developed for *ASA-SHS* Project:

- Selection of video sequences by *knowledge domain* ("the French writers in the 19th century", "the german literature in the 16th century", etc.);
- The *video-lexicon*, access that enables to display every sequence dealing with a particular term (For example, every sequence dealing with the "One Thousand and One Night" tale) ;
- Access to audiovisual resources via *chronological and thematic friezes* (similar to the thematic-temporal friezes used in schoolbooks) ;
- Access to audiovisual resources via *geolocalisation of the content.*

5 Conclusion

The project has finalized very advanced achievements in the fields of ontology design and media description. The developed architecture already followed - and reached - several objectives:

- Upgrade the existing environment and tools developed in previous contexts (ANR Project SAPHIR, European Project Logos)
- Base the architecture on the publishing features we want to develop (*ASA-SHS* is a content project)
- Develop a system that could be exploited in different contexts (of knowledge domains, institutions, projects, etc.) and where developed ontologies could be reusable.

Thus, the main objective of the project – providing specialized publications – is still under development ("*Semiosphere*"). However, we are very optimistic about future results.

Finally, the weakness of our architecture is not to follow any existing standard. We know how we want to solve this issue (using data converters) and important development efforts need to be done.

References

1. Stockinger, P.: Le document audiovisuel. Editions Hermes (2003)
2. Stockinger, P.: Traitement et contrôle de l'information. Editions Hermes (2001)
3. Buresi, C.: Conduire un projet de numérisation. Hermes/Lavoisier (2002)
4. Bachimont, B.: Ingénierie des connaissances et des contenus. Hermes/Lavoisier (2007)
5. ASA-SHS Project, http://www.asa-shs.fr
6. ANR, Agence Nationale de la Recherche, http://www.agence-nationale-recherche.fr
7. ARA, Audiovisual Research Archives, http://www.archivesaudiovisuelles.fr

Ktisis: Building an Open Access Institutional and Cultural Repository

Alexia Dini Kounoudes, Petros Artemi, and Marios Zervas

Library and Information Services, Cyprus University of Technology,
Arch. Kiprianou 31, 3036, Limassol, Cyprus
{alexia.kounoudes,petros.artemi,marios.zervas}@cut.ac.cy

Abstract. The unique value of cultural heritage has long been recognized together with the need for accurate and detailed information in order to preserve and manage cultural heritage material. Any organization whose mission includes promoting access to information is aware of the value of digital collections. For the last few years, digital technology has become very familiar in cultural organizations, providing enhanced access to the content. This paper gives information about Ktisis (http://ktisis.cut.ac.cy), the institutional repository of the Cyprus University of Technology (CUT). Ktisis was developed by the Library and Information Services of CUT. The paper reflects on the technical issues that the Library had to face in the preparation of this project and the strategy that had to be defined in order to tackle them. Such issues, among others, include the file and metadata format, the design and implementation software, etc.

Keywords: Open source software, institutional repository, intellectual rights, open access, cultural.

1 Introduction

As the Information Society is evolving in a very fast manner, the technological growth plays an important part in various sectors of the social life, one of which is culture. The cultural diversity of the existing material and the disposal for the exploitation of its value, in combination with the requirement to preserve the original work, constitute the motivation for many institutions to work on projects in order to digitize content of cultural heritage.

Since the early 1990s libraries have worked on digitization projects to provide access to and to preserve unique materials in their collections. These collections are accessible in an enhanced format that allows searching and browsing via the World Wide Web. Preservation of the original content and wide access to researchers and the public are the major reasons that libraries are undertaking digitization projects. Through digitization, the library is able to provide access to all sorts of materials – text, photographs, manuscripts, audio, and moving image materials. Digitization also allows for the preservation of rare, fragile, and unique materials. Another benefit of digitization is that it raises the profile of the institution as user's worldwide access its collections remotely.

M. Ioannides (Ed.): EuroMed 2010, LNCS 6436, pp. 504–512, 2010.

An important aspect of a digital library involves handling intellectual property rights. When libraries undertake a digitization project, they need to take into consideration whether or not the material to be digitized is protected by copyright law, or whether it is in the public domain.

Cyprus has a rich cultural heritage in the form of monuments, buildings, paintings, manuscripts, coins, etc. Most of these items are publicly available at museums or archaeological sites. However, there are many private collections of important items that are in danger of being damaged or lost. Examples of such items are private collections of old photographs, volumes of newspapers or magazines that are no longer published and whose content is historical or can be considered as a cultural treasure, etc.

In this manner, the Library and Information Services at the Cyprus University of Technology has defined that one of its major priorities is to collect, disseminate and preserve cultural heritage and to contribute to the cultural evolution of Cyprus. Based on this priority, the Library has designed and developed the first institutional repository in Cyprus, named "Ktisis".

2 The Ktisis Project

Ktisis is the institutional repository created by the Library and Information Services at the Cyprus University of Technology. Ktisis's main purpose is to collect and preserve the products of the research of the academic staff and researchers of the university and also to collect, digitize and disseminate cultural content.

One of the main priorities of the Library was to define a strategy for the collection and archiving of cultural heritage material (old photographs, newspapers etc). The objective of this project is to fulfill the Library's mission for collecting, disseminating and preserving cultural heritage.

When Ktisis was at the designing stage, the Library defined the set of goals that Ktisis needed to achieve. These goals were:

- To locate and archive together cultural heritage items from private collections.
- To guarantee long-term preservation and access to the data.
- To promote interest and involvement in the digitization process and preservation of cultural heritage.
- To promote open access at the Cyprus University of Technology.

In order to fulfill the task, Ktisis needed to accomplish these goals by organizing the data in an effective and coherent representation providing easy access to the public.

Ktisis is a member of a world wide system of open access institutional repositories, participating actively in the new shaped model of scientific communication. Currently Ktisis provides its metadata as a data provider applying the OAI-PMH protocol of metadata harvesting to the following service providers: OAIster, OpenDoar, Openarchives.gr, Driver, Openarchives.eu, Scientific Commons, University of Illinois Data Provider.

2.1 Data Selection

Considering the huge volume and heterogeneity of information on the web, the selection and evaluation of the material to be digitized is one of the most difficult tasks when setting up a digital library. The selection of the material for a digital repository involves handling intellectual property rights, legal issues and copyright.

The Library and Information Services has collaborated with the Patticheio Historical Archive Museum and Centre of Studies for the digitization and archiving of cultural heritage material belonging to the Centre.

The Library has also collaborated with the Cyprus Federation of Amateur Track and Field Athletics for the digitization of a collection of photographs. In addition to that, the Library is in contact with various other organizations or owners of private collections in order to review and record the existing material in order to include it in Ktisis.

2.2 Software Selection

Following the directions of DRIVER (Digital Repository Infrastructure Vision for European Research, (http://www.driver-repository.eu), the Library and Information Services decided to set up Ktisis using the open source software DSpace (http://www.dspace.org), an open source software developed by the MIT Libraries and Hewlett-Packard Company that enables open sharing of content.

DSpace follows the national standards such as the Dublin Core (http://www.dublicore.org) and is compatible with the OAI-MPH protocol of metadata harvesting. It enables capturing the data in any digital format – text, video, audio, and data files. DSpace indexes the digital content, so users can search and retrieve the material. DSpace distributes the digital content over the World Wide Web and it preserves the material over the long term.

The long term preservation facility is supported by using three types of data formats: supported, known and unsupported types. For all three types, DSpace does bit preservation, i.e. the preserved file remains exactly the same over time, and not a single bit is changed. For supported types, DSpace does functional preservation as well. The file changes over time so that the material can me immediately usable in the same way it was originally, while the physical media and digital formats change.

DSpace is a community-based, open source software platform that can be downloaded free of charge and used to create a digital repository. Organizations and institutions can more easily share and preserve their scholarly collections with an archiving system that stores digital representations of books, theses, 3-D digital scans of objects, photographs, film, video, research data sets and other forms of content.

Because DSpace repositories are internet-based, it is easy for users to deposit content and browse collections from anywhere in the world. Materials in DSpace repositories are distributed through the Internet and gain exposure through search engines, such as Google. These same items are permanently stored in a non-proprietary format, so researchers can continue to access its contents for decades to come.

2.3 Technical Issues

In a digitization project, even minor decisions may have a potentially large future impact. At the beginning of the project, one of the first challenges was to determine the future size of the digital repository. In order to do that we had to count the amount of documents we had to digitize, to calculate the amount of space they will need at the host server and estimate the data scalability for the following years. After completing this demanding process we realized that we only have sufficient data to make rough estimations. There was no way to predict what kind of material will come into our hands in the future for digitization and preservation in Ktisis.

Ktisis is covering a wide range of originals: newspapers, journals, photographs, etc. The Library is trying to digitize these items in high quality, with 24 bits in colour depth and resolutions from 300 to 600 dots per inch (dpi). These images are registered in JPG format with sizes ranging between 30 and 800 KB.

2.4 Data Processing

Using the appropriate digitization equipment that complies with the materials being digitized is essential for a successful digitization project. Therefore the Library has been equipped with a high resolution scanner suitable for scanning photos and textual material. The scanned images are stored in the JPG image file format. Then the items go through a watermarking procedure in order to protect them and secure them from unauthorized use.

2.5 Ktisis Data Organization

After the items have been scanned and stored in a JPG format, they need to be submitted to Ktisis. The DSpace content is organized around communities which can correspond to administrative entities such as schools, departments, labs and research centers, or digital collections. Within each community there can be an unlimited number of sub-communities and an unlimited number of collections. Each collection may contain an unlimited number of items.

The Ktisis content is organized in two communities, the Academic Publications containing the produce of the academic and research activity of the members of the university, and the Digital Collection containing the digital heritage material that this paper focuses on.

Currently, the Digital Collections community consists of three collections:

- "Satiriki epitheorisi", containing approximately 2800 items (number increases daily as new items are added continuously). This collection contains scanned images of caricatures from the cartoon newspaper "Satiriki Epitheorisi" ranging between 1964 and 1985.
- Photos from the Ports of Cyprus, containing 163 photos. This collection includes photographs taken during the construction of the Famagusta port during the period 1871-1933. The documentation took place in collaboration with the Patticheio Historical Archive Museum and Centre of Studies.

- Photos of Olympia Gymnastics sports club, containing 202 photos. The Olympic Gymnastics Sports Club is the oldest athletic club of Cyprus and the second oldest in the Greek area after the Panellinios Sports club. This collection contains photographs from the Cyprus Track and Athletics games. The whole history of the Cyprus track athletics can be seen through this collection. The photographs were taken from the Cyprus Federation of Amateur Track and Field Athletics photo album "Golden Cyprus Winners" as well as from the photographic archive of the Association of Veteran Track Athletes of Limassol. The documentation of the material was accomplished using the album "Golden Cyprus Winners".

2.6 Data Submission and Registration

The stage of data submission and registration comprises mainly of the creation and registration of the metadata for the resources, and the submission of the resources to the repository. All the items submitted to the repository are structured according to the Dublin Core metadata schema.

The Dublin Core set of metadata elements provides a small and fundamental group of text elements through which most resources can be described and catalogued. Using only 15 base text fields, a Dublin Core metadata record can describe physical resources such as books, digital materials such as video, sound, image, or text files, and composite media like web pages. Metadata records based on Dublin Core are intended to be used for cross-domain information resource description and have become standard in the fields of Library and Information Science and Computer Science. Implementations of Dublin Core typically make use of XML.

DSpace is installed and configured to use the Dublin Core metadata schema by default. Dublin Core is made up of elements, and qualifiers. The Dublin Core basic elements can be seen in Table 1.

Table 1. The Dublin core basic elements

TITLE	The name given to the resource by the CREATOR or PUBLISHER.
CREATOR	The person(s) or organization(s) primarily responsible for the intellectual content of the resource; the author.
SUBJECT	The topic of the resource; also keywords, phrases or classification descriptors that describe the subject or content of the resource.
DESCRIPTION	A textual description of the content of the resource, including abstracts in the case of document-like objects; also may be a content description in the case of visual resources.
PUBLISHER	The entity responsible for making the resource available in its present form, such as a publisher, university department or corporate entity.

Table 1. (*Continued*)

CONTRIBUTORS	Person(s) or organization(s) in addition to those specified in the CREATOR element, who have made significant intellectual contributions to the resource but on a secondary basis.
DATE	The date the resource was made available in its present form.
TYPE	The resource type, such as home page, novel, poem, working paper, technical report, essay or dictionary. It is expected that TYPE will be chosen from an enumerated list of types.
FORMAT	The data representation of the resource, such as text/html, ASCII, Postscript file, executable application or JPG image. FORMAT will be assigned from enumerated lists such as registered Internet Media Types (MIME types). MIME types are defined according to the RFC2046 standard.
IDENTIFIER	A string or number used to uniquely identify the resource. Examples from networked resources include URLs and URNs (when implemented).
SOURCE	The work, either print or electronic, from which the resource is delivered (if applicable).
LANGUAGE	The language(s) of the intellectual content of the resource.
RELATION	The relationship to other resources. Formal specification of RELATION is currently under development.
COVERAGE	The spatial locations and temporal duration characteristics of the resource. Formal specification of COVERAGE is also now being developed.
RIGHTS MANAGEMENT	A link (URL or other suitable URI as appropriate) to a copyright notice, a rights-management statement or perhaps a server that would provide such information in a dynamic way.

DSpace provides the functionality to create different Dublin Core metadata schemas according to the type of the items belonging to a collection. For example, in the case of Ktisis, the metadata describing a collection of photographs is different to the metadata describing a collection of PhD theses.

2.7 Access and Intellectual Rights

Anyone using the internet can access and view the contents of Ktisis without any restrictions. The users can find and retrieve information from the repository easy and fast as Ktisis supports interoperability providing access via multiple search engines and other discovery tools. However, due to copyright issues the items cannot be published or reproduced without the written consent of the owner.

Since its operation, Ktisis provides the capability to choose and apply one of the available Creative Commons licenses. Using the Creative Commons licenses is not obligatory. However, the option to use them is offered in order to be able to define in an easy way the rights that the owner of the item being submitted keeps and the rights that the owner discharges for the use of other creators. A Creative Commons license is a simple way to encourage others to share and reuse your digital content.

Our experience in using the Creative Commons licensing schemes so far has shown that if someone is publishing material of any variety on the web and is interested in spreading this work, then licensing this work under Creative Commons is an effective action as it actively encourages sharing the work with permission and attribution.

Also Creative Commons licenses bridge the gap between full copyright and the public domain, moving content from "all rights reserved" to "some rights reserved." Creative Commons licenses are not a replacement for copyright; rather, they allow you to modify your copyright terms so your work can be shared and reproduced legally. Additionally, everyone can benefit from the Creative Commons as adding such a license to your work can be seen as a marketing tool. Releasing content under a Creative Commons license gives the content creator full control over how the owner would like his/hers content attributed.

In a digital repository it is required that the rights of the creators are being defined precisely, together with the user rights. This information is precisely defined in the Creative Commons licenses. Currently, there has not been any work on adjusting the Creative Commons licenses for the Cyprus law, so Ktisis uses the English version instead. The Library and Information Services has been in contact with the relevant team of Creative Commons in order to start the procedure of implementing the Cypriot version of the Creative Commons licenses. This procedure is still at the early stages.

The licensing procedure in Ktisis consists of two steps: the first step involves the Creative Commons licenses, and the second involves the Library's license of submission and dissemination.

When submitting an item and before completing the submission procedure, the user can choose whether he/she wishes to declare the rights of the item being submitted. If the user wishes to use the Creative Commons license, then Ktisis connects with the Creative Commons website. The choices offered at this stage involve the definition of whether the creator or owner of the item allows the commercial use of the item or not, and also whether the owner/creator allows modifications. Then, the available Creative Commons are being displayed where the user is prompted choose one of them.

2.8 Promotion of Open Access

Ktisis was developed as part of the Library's mission to promote open access at the Cyprus University of Technology. The main reason for universities to have institutional repositories is to enhance the visibility, access and impact of the research product of the university.

Researchers can be actively involved in the promotion of open access by submitting their articles in Open Access journals. Academics can also be more involved in the promotion of Open Access by educating the next generation of scientists in open access. They have to make sure that the new researchers understand the issues of open access and that it increases the impact of research articles.

2.9 Statistics of Use

The Ktisis access statistics show that there is a continuous interest in the content with users visiting Ktisis from all over the world. Analytically, approximately 20000 visitors visited Ktisis in the year 2009. The average number of visitors per month is 1750 from which the 24% are returning visitors.

Approximately 1300 visitors accessed Ktisis directly, 5000 through referring sites and the rest of the visitors found Ktisis through search engines. Ktisis's visitors came from countries such as Greece, Cyprus, the United States, the United Kingdom, India, Germany, Canada, Australia, China, Iran, etc.

2.10 Future Work

As mentioned before, one of the Library's goals is to promote interest and involvement in the digitization process and preservation of cultural heritage. Therefore the Library aims to contribute to the KYPRIANA program(http://www.kypriana.eu/). This program is collaboration between various Cyprus organizations in order to contribute in a coordinated way in the growth of the EUROPEANA (www.europeana.eu) project. KYPRIANA aims to become the digital library of Cyprus.

Ktisis has been created using the open source software DSpace. The default installation of DSpace gives the capability to export the metadata in the Dublin Core standard using the OAI-PMH protocol. The problem is that these data cannot be imported into Europeana as Europeana does not support the Dublin core standard, but the Europeana Semantic Elements (ESE), an application profile based on the Dublin Core. The last year a lot of work has been done in Greece in the basis of the program EuropeanaLocal in order to overcome this problem. The outcome of this work was the creation of a DSpace plugin which has been created and is available to use free of charge in DSpace installations. The Library aims to apply this plugin into the Ktisis installation making the Ktisis data compatible to the Europeana requirements.

2.11 Lessons Learnt

Today Libraries around the world are deeply involved in the task of preserving the intellectual and cultural heritage of their countries. The Library and Information Services of the Cyprus University of Technology is a pioneer in this field in Cyprus being the very first organization that has created an institutional repository.

The barriers that have come across the Library's work during the development of Ktisis have led the team to infer a number of lessons learnt that may be useful to others. First, we have realized that building an institutional repository requires engaging people with different skills and knowledge in the areas of project management, technology, cataloguing, metadata, etc. Additionally, the development of a repository is a procedure that requires a lot of time. The staff working on the development needs to have a balanced workload in order to reach the short and long term goals of the project. Libraries with limited resources need to be creative and persistent when creating a repository as there are many difficulties in the process.

Institutional repositories are still relevantly new but a number of important benefits have already become apparent. First of all, they support the open access movement. They provide a specialized information service by giving access to the academic and research work of the university and to the digital collections of cultural heritage material that the Library has digitized. Today institutional repositories address a very strong need in the academic world and therefore there will be a steady growth of repositories globally.

References

1. Borbinha, J.: An infrastructure for a national digital library. In: Proceedings of the 5th WSEAS Int. Conf. on Simulation, Modelling and Optimization, Corfu, Greece, August 17-19, pp. 146–151 (2005)
2. Harnad, S.: The implementation of the Berlin declaration on open access. D-Lib Magazine 11(3) (2005)
3. Lawrence, S., Giles, C.L., Bollacker, K.: Digital libraries and autonomous citation indexing. IEEE Computer 32(6), 67–71 (1999)
4. Lopatin, L.: Library digitization projects, issues and guidelines. Library Hi Tech. 24(2), 273–289 (2006)
5. Lynch, C., Garcia-Molina, H.: Interoperability, scaling, and the digital libraries research agenda. Microcomputers for Information Management 13(2), 85–132 (1996)
6. Samuelson, P.: Copyright and digital libraries. Communications of the ACM 38(4) (1995)
7. Suber, P.: Removing the barriers to research: An introduction to open access for librarians. College & Research Libraries News 64(2), 92–94 (2003)
8. Hutar, J., Melichar, M., Stoklasova, B.: Czech National Digital Library and Long-term Preservation Issues, CULTURAL HERITAGE on line Empowering users: an active role for user communities, Florence, Italy, December 15-16 (2009)

Realization of a Cartographic GIS for the Filing and Management of the Archaelogical Excavations in the Nelson's Island

Domenica Costantino and Maria Giuseppa Angelini

DIASS - Technical University of Bari - viale del Turismo, 8 74100 Taranto, Italy
(d.costantino,mg.angelini)@poliba.it

Abstract. The island of Nelson is situated around 7-8 miles far from the Egyptian Mediterranean coast, and about 25 km far from Alexandria of Egypt. It has small size, since it doesn't currently overcome the 350 m², even if in the antiquity it was greater: geologic phenomena and activity of cave sensibly reduced the emerged part of it. Campaigns of excavation were carried on that have brought to light important rests related to a fortification and to a military installation, inscriptions of Greek and Byzantine epoch, enormous complexes for the water restocking and a necropolis of late epoch. In the circle of the collaboration in the research CMAIA the geodetic and topographic survey of the island and of the principal structures of archaeological interest are realized. The activities of excavation have not always allowed a perfect synergy with the operations of survey. Nevertheless, the collected results have been integrated with paper maps compiled by draftsmen present on site during the phases of excavation. The activity of survey has been finalized to the cartographic rebuilding of the island and subsequently to the georeferencing of all the findings both through the direct survey and through the integration of the supplied images. An information system has been compiled (database and GIS), once seen the wide massive structure of data and the difficulties of interventions on field; it led to an easier management and cataloguing of the operations of excavation and survey, as well as the accomplishment of an integrated archive of consultation and management of the archaeological, topographic, historical and documentary data.

Keywords: Archaeological site, Map, DTM, Reference systems, GPS, Georeferencing, Data base, GIS.

1 The Archaeological Excavations on the Canopo's Island

1.1 Introduction

The project aims at either preserving the safety of existing and recently discovered documentation and its historical knowledge, or giving a chance to reconstruct the archaeological richness of the Canopo island. The diachronic reconstruction has been accomplished by means of several interconnected activities as archaeological reconnaissance, cartography, analysis of archaeological relics and of historical, epigraphic and iconographic documents. By means of some territorial and archaeological surveys, a

M. Ioannides (Ed.): EuroMed 2010, LNCS 6436, pp. 513–527, 2010.

cartographic documentation of the topographic development of the island has been edited. Integrated methods of geodetic and topographic detection have been employed. Starting from a GPS based method, detailed views of the discovered archaeological sites have been finally carried out through a classical topographic survey and the georeferencing of the pictures provided by the archaeologists. The availability of high quality digital cameras, together with advanced software for calibration and production of photogrammetric pictures, allowed to gain a product of good quality. This is why low cost techniques of survey have been employed, which combine the classical topographic instruments with amateur cameras. Obviously, even if cost is lower, the overall quality of the final result is lower too. For Abuquir site the activity has been carried on following this method basically for two reasons: to work with the aforementioned instruments (if possible) and to supply the archaeologists with an easy-to-use tool. Collecting digital data to be examined both real-time and during post processing and analysis required an ad hoc information system. The method we have adopted is based on building a GIS database which is made of two modules: the former is useful for input, displaying, and graphical querying, and is managed by the software ArcGIS; the latter is an ACCESS database of alphanumerical data. The two modules are linked via SQL connections. In order to get a really profitable system to manage the great mass of records given by the archaeological inspection, which could be also capable of improving the knowledge, the aspects we have dealt with the greatest care are: to create an open architecture, which is easy to be integrated with the novel kind of information raising up from the research; setting a correct level of detail in the treatment of each class of data, combining the needs of specific insights on particular aspects of a research project with the criteria necessary for agility successful use of the data; the possibility to have a differentiated usage of depending on the goals of the project and user's computer skills. Under a merely technical point of view, a great attention was paid to the user interface in the development of the database for managing archaeological data.

1.2 The Archaeological Excavations

The island of Nelson, although small, is covered by ruins of tombs, houses, big cisterns and monumental buildings. No scientific excavation has been carried out on the island before 1997, due to the huge natural and bureaucratic difficulties that the excavations involve. On the peak of the oriental promontory of the island, at around 15 m above sea level., signs of an Hellenistic installation of the end of the 4th century BC have been recovered, constituted by a quadrangular building with a side that maybe was about 40 m long at its origin (Fig. 1).

The mighty stone boundaries of the structure, of which only the foundations and some axes remain today, are 1m thick and they are made with big blocks of local sandstone. The plan of the building and its strategic position make us think of it as a structure realized for practical purposes, as for instance a strengthened defence finalised to the control of the naval traffic to the canopic mouth of the Nile. Along the slope that descends gradually towards the sea, the rests of poor houses, maybe belonged to people preceded to the operation of the neighbour structure on the promontory have been brought to light. It is possible therefore that the island of Canopo has lodged a military garrison in defence of the Alexandrine coast. In the western side of

Fig. 1. Settlement of the 4th century BC

the island several complexes of hydraulic structures have been situated for the collection of the rain water. In this area between 1998 and 2000 three great joined and interconnected rectangular cisterns were found. A further survey made in the centre of the island has shown the existence of a tomb hypogeum room entirely excavated in the friable local rock. The continuous erosion which the southern side of the falesa of the island is submitted to, as well as the scour due to the rains, has shown a collective tomb to precipice on the falesa, where many Egyptian mummies were found (Fig. 2).

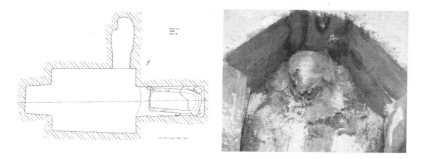

Fig. 2. Sketch of the pharaonic tomb and an Egyptian mummy

1.3 The GPS Survey

The topographic survey of the Nelson's island began with the 1997 campaign during which, using the technique of GPS, the surveys of the island and its detail, as well as the survey of some structures of great archaeological interest, were carried out. A point of reference with a relevant presence of monuments has been chosen on the island. Starting from that point, in the campaigns performed between 1997 and 2000 the monumentation has been executed through a metallic datum nailed in the site denominated FERLA that, nevertheless, for the geologic nature of the island has suffered from a macroscopic move. Insofar, the datum, beginning from the 2001 campaign, has again been monumented by placing it on a pre-existing cement building (whose denomination has been

"85402820"). For both the data and in the different epochs of measurement was performed a connection with the vertex of coordinates notes constituted by the permanent
station CEAlex situated in Alexandria. In 1998, a reference point was installed on the
roof of the building were the premises of the CEAlex are situated within the heart of
Alexandria. After two 24-hours observation sessions, the coordinates were calculated
within the global reference system, ITRF (Table 1).

Table 1. ITRF coordinates of permanent station CEAlex

Geographic Coordinates			Cartesian Coordinates		
Longitude (°)	Latitude (°)	Elev.(m)	X (m)	Y (m)	Z (m)
29°54'39,56536'	31°11'49,43277'	57,995	4733389.059	2723027,730	3284632,234

Since then, this point has served to link all the archaeological excavations into the
one-reference system. At the end of the year 2000, this reference point was turned
into a permanent GPS station with an error of about 2~3 mm. Since 1st December
2001, the resultant data have been available for free downloading from the internet,
which represents a first example in Egypt (Fig. 3).

Fig. 3. Master Station placed on the reference vertex of the island

The connection between the instituted datum and CEAlex has been performed with
GPS measures in static modality with session of around 8 hours and interval of acquisition of 15 seconds. Once the coordinates of arrangement of the datum have been
resolved, the detail survey of the whole emerged surface and the outline of the coastline has been implemented with GPS instrumentation and survey in kinematics modality, enclosing the limits of the submerged barrier, with the purpose to get a DTM,
with contours representation of the Nelson's island (Craig, N., 2000). A total of
around 3500 points inside the island have been relieved, with pass of around 5 m,
whose coordinate have resolved with precision of around 1-2 cm both in planimetry
and in quota (Fig. 4).

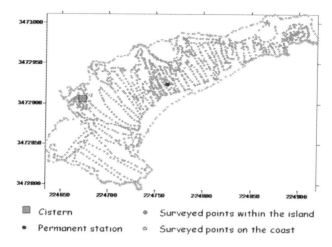

Cistern   ⊛ Surveyed points within the island

• Permanent station   ⊚ Surveyed points on the coast

Fig. 4. GPS points Survey

1.4 The Cartography

The existing cartographic representations of the Nelson's island, have demonstrated
not to be suitable to constitute a complete support to the archaeological activities, due
to the cartographic scale adopted and to the almost exclusively qualitative content,
therefore it was necessary to realize ex novo a cartography of detail of the island
(Fig. 5). To such purpose the post-verification data of survey have been treated with
the two software: Autocad and Surfer. The script Inspoint allows to easily insert a set
of points, in the window of the CAD, once their spatial coordinates are known. In this
way a file in DXF format has been created with the spatial representation of all the
relieved points and of the outline of the coastline. With the Surfer software using the
verified data, and using the interpolation method of Natural Neighbour a regular Grid
of known points has been built, to square stitch of side 3 m (Hageman, J.B. et al.,
2000). The knowledge of the DTM of the island allows to study and to interpret the

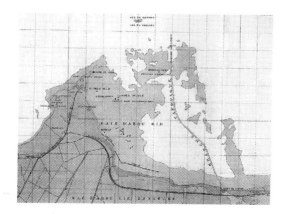

Fig. 5. A part of an already existing map

morphology of the ground to the quest of possible areas of interest for the future excavations; anomalous topographic gradients can, for instance, be located in comparison to the contour, possible indicators of artificial interventions on the ground.

Naturally, to such purpose, it is necessary to choose proper ways of representation of the digital model: the plain map (Contour Map), the three-dimensional one (Wire frame), the shade map (Shaded Relief Map) and the model of surface (Surface), created to represent the island of Nelson, allow to visually interpret the state of the ground in the three dimensions in simple and immediate way (Fig. 6).

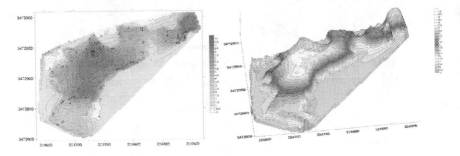

Fig. 6. 3D model of the island

The plain coordinates are expressed in the coordinated UTM-WGS84 system, zone 36, while the quota referred to the level of the sea contextually determined to the surveys. Moreover, the study through time of the coastline will allow to reconstruct, on the base also of the comparison with the historical cartography (if available), the variations in the time of the topography of the emerged part of the island.

1.5 Survey of Archaeological Structures

Using the IRASC software, we effectuated the georeferencing of the sketches of the archaeological excavations of the island of Nelson (Fig. 7), through the individualization

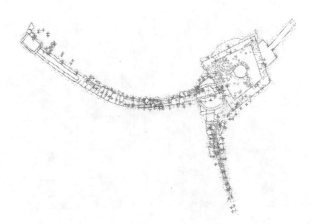

Fig. 7. Overlap of the survey of the main cistern

of a set of coordinates of points acquired on the image (well recognizable and distributed in uniform way) and the relative set of the same relieved points. The georeferencing was obtained using the polynomiais of 1st -5^h order individualizing 21 points, among which, a reference vertex; the best results were obtained using the polynomial 1st. The goodness of the taken operations has been estimated both in terms of differences among the coordinates read on the georeferenced image and the coordinates of survey, and from the comparison of the distances among points measured on the image and the same measured in the survey.

The results of the georeferencing of the image are reported in figure 8.

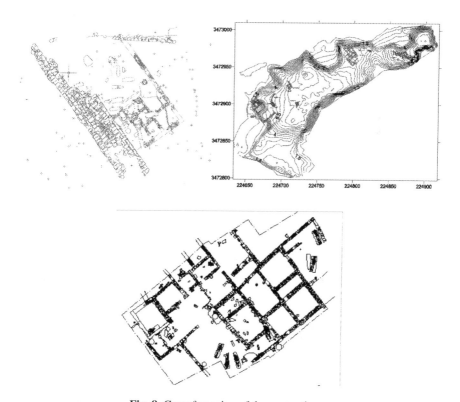

Fig. 8. Georeferencing of the excavations

1.6 The Elaboration and the 3D Analysis

Data acquisition aimed at 3D modeling of layers and structures has been carried on by means of a total electronic station for the measurement of check points, boundaries, and internal points of every US, and with an amateur digital camera (NIKON D40) for zenithal vision (Chiorboli, A., et al., 2005). The calibration of the camera has been performed in the first stage of the post-processing in the Laboratorio di Geomatica. A commercial software, Photomodeler has been used (Gianinetto et al., 2005), which suggests the calibration sequence and calculate the parameters of the camera. A fixed-lens camera has been used to ensure a constant focal length during the calibration and the photogrammetric surveys. The software performs a calibration based on a grid of 100 points marked on a rigid support. Photomodeler identifies the points automatically, determines their coordinates and builds a 3D model of the shots calculating their parameter too (focal length, coordinate of the primary point XC and YC, sensor size, coefficients Ki of the polynomial of radial reversal).

Fig. 9. Parameter of calibration

Once the calibration has been finalized, it was possible to achieve the photogrammetric model through the available digital images and using the GCPs given by topographical survey adding the further geometrical constraint of the distance between two points identified on the model.

Fig. 10. Picture of the wall

Figure 10 shows an example made on a stone wall found during one excavation. 400 topographic points have been identified on the whole surface that has a linear extension of about 100 m.

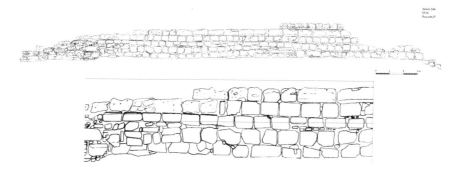

Fig. 11. Prospect W of the Edimon wall

We made such a choice to achieve high accuracy despite not using photogrammetric methods and cameras. Accuracy of the final measurements depends on several factors as the number of available pictures, the angle between them, and the number of points involved in the georeferencing (an increase of which enlarge necessarily the number of CGP which should also be correctly spread on the picture and in the case of a 3D object should also be well representative of picture depth) (Fraser, C. et al., 2006). An accuracy of about some millimeter has been achieved (Brown, D.C., 1971).

All image was orthorectified (Fig. 12).

Fig. 12. Ortophoto of the Edimon wall

2   Geographic Information Systems

2.1   The Nelson's GIS

The objective is to be able to have archive updated for all the activities developed on the field. We needed to create thematic images, fruit of the combination of written, graphic and geographical information, so we used al the potentials offered by the GIS systems. At first a databases is realized, internal to the GIS, customized according to the specific needs.

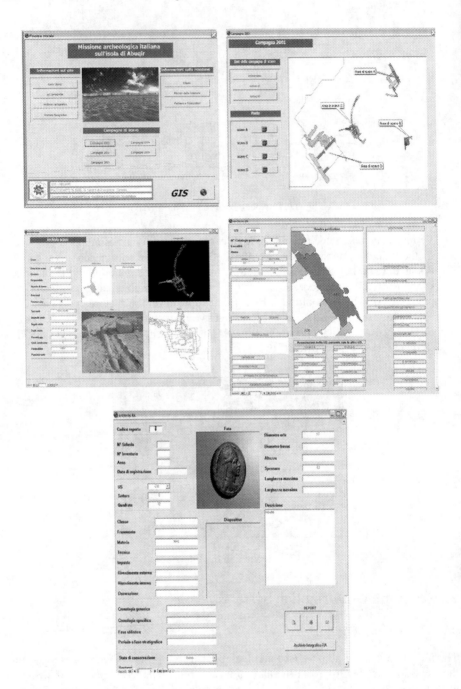

Fig. 13. Database

The informative system has been realized through the building of two modules: one of imission, visualization and graphic-spatial query, managed through the ArcGIS software; the other, connected to the first one through the SQL link, for the management of the alphanumeric data (database), realized in ACCESS. The realization of the GIS was developed through the following steps: the information's coding and structuration of the alphanumeric archive inside a database (DBMS); the formulation of dictionaries and control algorithms to drive the data-entry; the conversion of the plain maps and the single plants of layer in vectorial form, according to levels distinguished for US; the georeferencing of the realized digital cartography and ascription of a numerical code to the graphic objects that define the single unities; the integration of the alphanumeric information and the graphic data through a vectorial GIS engine; the reconstruction of the stratigrafic sediment and of the building structures in 3D, with possibility of spatial analysis and query. The functionality of the system has been guaranteed: by the elaboration of an open and easily integrable architecture (stated the changeable dynamics of the research on the single contexts); by the definition of the degree of detail in the treatment of the single classes data, by conjugating the specific needs of the deepenings on particular aspects with the necessary criterions of agility for a useful fruition of the datum; by the possibility of a diversified use of the solution according to the objectives and of the type of user's computer alphabetization. The database (Fig. 13) allows the access to all the files and to all the information about the Italian archaeological mission to Abuqir, through the initial mask organized in order to allow a rapid access to all the given files, as well as to the information (invariant in comparison to the campaigns of excavation). The relational database is built in such a way as to proceed in the input of the data through the special masks for stratigrafic unity; information of other nature (graphic-geographical) and further details (photographic), as also the other possible cards. From the section "campaigns of excavation" it is possible to access to the files of the single campaigns actually conducted or currently in progress. For each campaign the database is structured in 3 levels: the first, containing the fundamental data inherent the single area of excavation (date of beginning excavation, characteristics of the soil, etc.); the second, related to the stratigrafic data (files US) that reproduces the format of the ministerial ICCD's cards (Central Institute of the Catalog and the Documentation) with the possibility to check the associations between a single US and the others, to define its state of preservation, the dating, the reliability; the last, containing the table of the finds (files RA, ceramic finds, glassy finds, metallic finds, numismatic finds, human osteologic finds, animal osteologic Finds, other finds) with the inherent information, for every recovered find, the classification, the dimensions, the ways of restauration, etc. ICCD and card RA. This relationship happens exactly through the identity code of the US that is used as primary key of connection between the tables, according to a relationship "one to many" are connected to the above database. The cycle is closed with the automatic issuing of a report that, beginning from the introduced data, reassembles the typical card (US e/o RA) we can print and/or send by e-mail (Fig. 14).

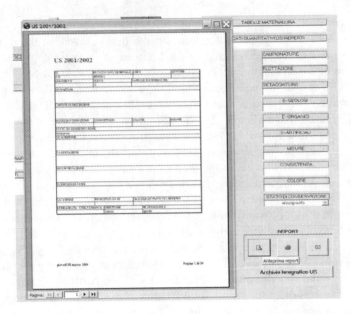

Fig. 14. Export window of the US report according to ICCD's standard and e-mail sending

2.2 The GIS Engine

The GIS system with the visualization of the cartography, including the excavations, and with the connection to the Database in SQL link, represents the real engine of the system (Tripcevich, N., 2004). A theme has been realized related to the different stratigrafic unities (US), proceeding to the attribution of a numerical code for the vectorial objects in order to make the direct connection between the tables of the attributes and those of the Database possible (Costantino, D. et al., 2008), by assigning the US relative number, as attribute (Fig. 15).

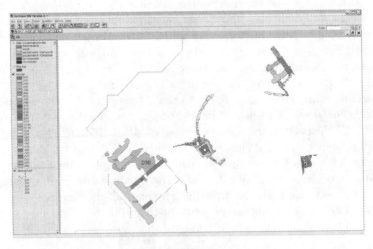

Fig. 15. GIS Structure

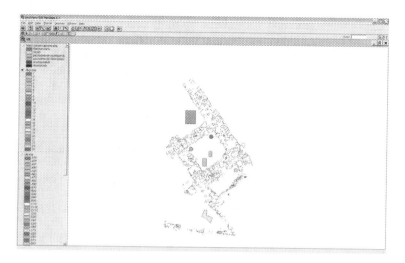

Fig. 15. (*Continued*)

The second theme is related to the unities of find. Different connections (join and link) between the database and the tables of the attributes of the graphic associated entities, have been finally created, taking advantage of the relationship between identity codes, (Fig. 16).

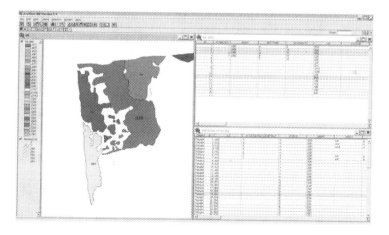

Fig. 16. Example of link between US polygon, RA polygon and relative table of attributes

3 Results

The obtained results have highlighted the efficacy and the applicability of the techniques of topographic and geodetic survey to the goals of a detailed representation of sites of archaeological interest. Of peculiar importance is noticed the methodology of satellite acquisition (GPS) that has allowed the filing of a considerable massive structure of data with high temporal and spatial frequency to the purpose of the automatic generation of the cartography of the island and the georeferencing of the sketches of excavation. The reliability of this last process has furnished precisions with order of greatness comparable to those resultant from the raster images provided. The cartography datum so obtained results necessary for the development of the future activity both for the geographical analysis of the excavations that for an unequivocal location of the same. The employ of amateur cameras has been really interesting, since it gave nice results and is a low cost and easy to use tool. The growing employ of digital cameras permits, once the calibration has been achieved, to get a good geometric accuracy in restitution phase. The accomplishment of 3D models gives accurate and precise depiction of morphological details, especially in the field of closed-range. The acquisition of information data is easier, cheaper and faster by this way. Photoplanes and ortophotos has shown to be very important in the archaeological documentation. The realized GIS has been structured in order to allow the processing of the data from the site of the harvest to the printing, according to ICCD's standard formats, the filing and the updating of the documentation of excavation in continuous and an easy use, in consideration to the simple user interface. The benefit of the realized tool is useful for those who operates on the field (archaeologist, surveyor, draftsman, topographer, etc.) and to those who intend to complete studies or to have a transversal knowledge of the site.

Acknowledgements

The autors would like to thank the Province of Taranto for founding used in this project.

References

1. Brown, D.C.: Close-Range Camera Calibration. Photogrammetric Engineering 37(8), 855–866 (1971)
2. Zeng, Z., Wang, X.: A General Solution of a Closed-Form Space Resection. PE&RS 58(3), 327–338 (1992)
3. Craig, N.: Real-time GIS construction and digital data recording of the Jiskairomuoko excavation. Perù. The Society for American Archaeology Bulletin 18(1), 24–28 (2000)
4. Tripcevich, N.: Flexibility by design: how mobile GIS metts the needs of archaeological survey. Cartography and Geographic Information Science 31(3), 137–151 (2004)
5. Costantino, D., Angelini, M.G., Caprino, G.: Planning of a metric historical and documental archive for the realization of a city's cultural portal. In: The 14th International Conference on Virtual Systems and Multimedia, vol. I, pp. 877–882 (2008)
6. Costantino, D., Rossi, G., Angelini, M.G., Leserri, M.: 3D Modelling for the Urban Area "Porta Napoli". In: CIPA/VAST/EG/EuroMed2006 "The e-volution of Information Technology in Cultural Heritage. Where Hi-Tech Touches the Past: Risk and Challenges for the 21st Century", Project Papers, pp.79-85 (2008)
7. Fraser, C., Remondino, F.: Digital camera calibration methods: consideration and comparisons. In: ISPRS Symposium "Image Engineering and Vision Metrology", Commission V, WG V/1, IAPRS, vol. XXXVI, Part 5, pp. 266–272 (2006)

8. Hageman, J.B., Bennet, D.A.: Construction of Digital Elevation Models for Archaeological Applications, in Practical applications of GIS for archaeologists. A predective modeling kit, 111–127 (2000)
9. Chiorboli, A., Gatti, M.: Low cost techniques for building surveying and their 3D representation. In: Proceedings of ISARC 2005, Paper number 16. Ferrara, September 11-14 (2005)
10. Gianinetto, M., Roncoroni, F., Scaioni, M.: Calibration of Thermal Imagery for Integration into 3D VR Models. In: 3D Digital Imaging and Modeling: Applications of Heritage Industry Medicine and Land, Padova, maggio 17-18 (2005)
11. Costantino, D., Capra, A., Angelini, M.G.: Virtual reconstruction of damaged decorative elements. In: Workshop Italy-Canada 2005 "3D Digital Imaging and Modeling: Applications of Heritage, Industry, Medicine and Land", Padova, Maggio 17-18 (2005)

Seismic Risk Assessment for Historical Town Centers and Their Surroundings Using Geoinformatics: The Case Study of Paphos, Cyprus

Christis Chrysostomou, Diofantos Hadjimitsis, Athos Agapiou,
and Nicolas Kyriakides

Department of Civil Engineering and Geomatics, Faculty of Engineering and Technology,
Cyprus University of Technology, 3603, Limassol, Cyprus
{c.chrysostomou,d.hadjimitsis,athos.agapiou,
nicholas.kyriakides}@cut.ac.cy

Abstract. This paper highlights the importance of using Remote Sensing and GIS for assisting the seismic risk assessment for historical town centres in Cyprus. The selected case study is the Paphos town centre including the archaeological area of Nea Paphos. The authors present their proposed methodology for inventory collection, which is based on the integrated use of aerial photos and satellite imagery and the application of digitisation process. A 3D representation of the area using the heights of the buildings and the orthophotos was produced in the ArcGIS software for a more realistic result. The information produced in this pilot project will be used for the seismic risk assessment of the case-study area.

Keywords: seismic risk assessment, historical centers, land use change detection, building inventory.

1 Introduction

The simulation of earthquake losses is the principal basis for the development and implementation of a wide range of planning, zoning, and building ideas that should provide cities with greater safety protection and lower economic losses in the event of a future earthquake that might affect a city. A key and important question that arises in the planning and development of an urban area is: "If earthquakes present a risk of economic loss to area of a city, what are the characteristics and extent of the losses that might occur?". While seismic hazard studies of urban areas are increasingly more common, it is not so common to apply hazard results to estimate future earthquake losses. Without the estimation of the nature and extent of future losses, it is more difficult to improve emergency relief measures, land use planning, and the seismic provisions of building code in order to mitigate the effects of possible future earthquake losses.

Earthquake loss (risk) assessment consists of three elements: a) an inventory; b) vulnerability relationships; and, c) an earthquake hazard model. Inventory is defined as the geographical distribution and description of things at risk that are included in the study. Vulnerability is defined as the relationships between the hazard assessment

M. Ioannides (Ed.): EuroMed 2010, LNCS 6436, pp. 528–535, 2010.

and the inventory that result in losses. Vulnerabilities may be developed for anything at risk (buildings, lifelines, population, etc), although, in practice, vulnerability may be an exceedingly difficult parameter to determine. The earthquake hazard model or models used depends on the kind of risk simulation or assessment required.

One of the most difficult parts of such studies is the determination of the inventory. This is both time consuming and expensive. A number of researchers have studied the possibility of using satellite images [1 and 2] and synthetic aperture radar (SAR) [3 and 4] for the development of inventory of buildings as well as a tool for post-earthquake reconnaissance. Mansouri et al [5] describe such a methodology for the development of a seismic loss model for Tehran, while Chrysostomou et al. [6] for Nicosia, Cyprus.

In this paper the historical town-centre of Paphos in Cyprus is used as a case-study to show how remote sensing techniques can be used to obtain the inventory to be used for the seismic risk assessment of historical centres.

2   Case Study

The historical town centre of Paphos was selected as the case study area for the seismic risk assessment analysis. The historical town centre of Paphos, can be characterized as of equal importance as it is the area that keeps the historical and cultural continuity of the town from the ancient times till today. Paphos historical centre is located in the SW area of Cyprus and it is very near to important archaeological sites (Tombs of the Kings and Nea Paphos) which are listed as UNESCO World's cultural heritage monuments.

Fig. 1. Historical centre of Paphos (NE) and the archaeological sites of Tombs of the Kings and Nea Paphos (W) (background image Google Earth)

Some of the historical buildings of this area are the first Manor houses of Ktima (dated in the early 20th century), Paphos Holy Bishopric (1910 building), Agios Theodoros Metropolitan Church (built in 1896), Ethnographical Museum (build between the late 19th and early 20th century), Town Hall (built in 1955), the Municipal Library (built during the 1940s) a.o.

Fig. 2. The archaeological sites of Tombs of the Kings

Fig. 3. The first Manor houses of Ktima (left) and the Town Hall of Paphos (right)

3 Methodology

For seismic risk assessment analysis, a detail data collection was carried out. This includes cadastral maps, geological maps, earthquake hazard maps, aerial photographs and orthophotos over the area. Moreover a detail database was created in GIS software (ArcGIS 9.3) where the attributes characteristics of each building were recorded. In situ observations were carried out in order to verify these characteristics regarding the buildings (e.g. height of the building). The overall methodology applied for this study is shown in Fig. 4.

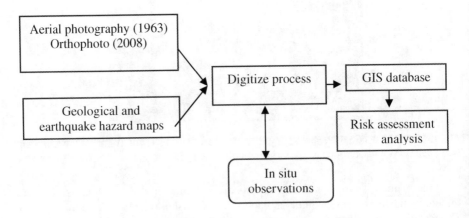

Fig. 4. Methodology applied

4 Data Collection

4.1 Digitization of the Data

In order to observe the changes occurred in the case study area over the last 50 years, nine aerial images (scale 1: 5000) were used dated back to 1963. All these aerial images were georeferenced using an affine polynomial transformation (Fig 5). The digitized procedure was performed in the AutoCAD environment. Distortions due to elevation and geolocation accuracy were considered not be important for the purpose of the study, since the center is located in a flat area. However a more accurate correction of the aerial images is expected to be complete in the future creating an orthophotos mosaic using Digital Elevation Model and Ground Control Points (GCP).

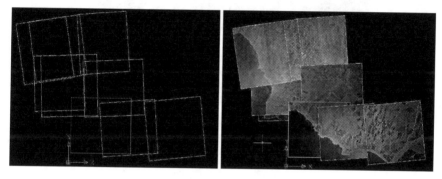

Fig. 5. Georeference of the aerial images (left) and the digitized of the buildings (right)

The same area was digitized using recently obtained orthophotos images of 2008, scale 1: 5000 (Fig. 6 left). The buildings were digitized in AutoCAD software (Fig. 6 right) giving special attention to the area of interest (Fig. 7).

Fig. 6. Orthophoto of the area (left) and digitization procedure of the buildings in the 2008 orthophoto (right)

Fig. 7. Detail digitization procedure of the buildings in the area of interest

Soil types and geological zones were also recorded as it is indicated in Fig. 8. As it was found, the case study area is located in terrace deposits formations while three soil types cover the majority of the area. These are: a) the lithic and epipetric types which cover the coastal area of Paphos (where the Nea Paphos archaeological site is located) and the historical town centre of Paphos, b) the epipetric and leptic-chromic soil type, which cover the southern area of Paphos and c) the calcaric-fluvic and vertic type which are located in the historical town center.

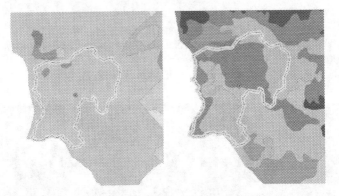

Fig. 8. Geological zones (left) and soil zones (right) in the case study area (polygon)

4.2 GIS Database

Building heights were recorded in a GIS database (ArcGIS 9.3). The data were provided from the Department of Surveys and Cadastral of Cyprus. However in situ observations were carried out in order to complete the entire case study and moreover to verify the data and record any changes. Thematic maps were produced in order to visualize this procedure (Fig. 9).

Fig. 9. Buildings height of the area

A 3D representation of the area using the heights of the buildings and the ortho-photos was made in the ArcScene software for a more realistic result. For this purpose the orthophotos were draped over the DEM of the area (accuracy ± 10m) (Fig. 10).

Fig. 10. 3D terrain of the area

The 3D buildings were also categorized according to their height for better inter-pretation (Fig. 11). The overall area is shown in Fig. 12.

Fig. 11. 3D buildings in the ArcScene software

Fig. 12. The overall area in 3D

5 Seismic Risk Assessment

Figs. 11 and 12 give a clear picture of the distribution of the height of the buildings in the area under study. The height of the buildings is one of the main parameters used for the determination of the seismic vulnerability of buildings. Once the location of the various buildings are established in a GIS database, then additional information regarding the buildings that is very useful for the accurate determination of the vulnerability of these structures, such as construction material, type of construction, structural systems, age of the buildings etc., can be assigned. This will assist in the designation of vulnerability relationships as well as site specific earthquake hazard to each building and site. The presence of this information in a GIS database, will give the opportunity for a graphical representation of the data that can be used both for planning as well as earthquake response purposes, and it will be an invaluable tool for the seismic risk assessment of the case-study area.

6 Conclusions

In this paper the methodology of using aerial photography combined with satellite images and a GIS database for the development of the inventory that will be used for the determination of the seismic risk of a case-study is presented. The combination of the above technologies provides a tool that can be used for the accurate documentation of the required inventory in an economic way. The immense graphical capabilities of the GIS database provide the means for continuous build-up of necessary information along with accurate representation of this information, which is imperative for seismic risk analysis. The same tool can be also used for post-earthquake planning and response. In future work, this tool will be further developed to include the vulnerability and hazard parts that are necessary for the determination of the seismic risk of the case-study area.

Acknowledgements

The authors would like to express their appreciation to the Ministry of Interior of Cyprus and the Department of Land and Surveys for their permission to use cadastral data. Moreover thanks are given to the Remote Sensing Laboratory of the Department of Civil Engineering & Geomatics at the Cyprus University of Technology (www.cut.ac.cy).

References

1. Estrada, M., Matsuoka, M., Yamazaki, F.: Use of Landsat images for the identification of damage due to the 1999 Kocaeli, Turkey earthquake. In: 21st Asian Conference on Remote Sensing, Taipei, Taiwan, pp. 1185–1190 (2000)
2. Matsuoka, M., Yamazaki, F.: Use of Satellite SAR Intensity Imagery for Detecting Building Areas Damaged Due to Earthquakes. Earthquake Spectra. 20(3), 975–994 (2004)
3. Eguchi, R.T., Huyck, C.K., Houshmand, B., Tralli, D.M., Shinozuka, M.: A new application for remotely sensed data: Construction of building inventories using synthetic aperture radar technology. In: 2nd Multilateral Workshop on Development of Earthquake and Tsunami Disaster Mitigation Technologies and Their Integration for the Asia-Pacific Region, Earthquake Disaster Mitigation Research Center, Kobe, Japan, pp. 217–228 (2000)
4. Shinozuka, M., Ghanem, R., Houshmand, B., Mansouri, B.: Damage detection in urban areas by SAR imagery. J. Eng. Mech. 126(7), 769–777 (2000)
5. Babak, M., Mohsen, G.-A., Kambod, A.-H., Reza, N., Mehdi, M.: Building Seismic Loss Model for Tehran. Earthquake Spectral 26(1), 153–168 (2010)
6. Chrysostomou, C.Z., Algermissen, T., Rogers, A., Demetriou, T.: Seismic Risk Assessment of Nicosia, Cyprus. In: World Conference on Earthquake Engineering, Paper No. 3148, Vancouver, Canada (2004)

Monitoring Air Pollution in the Vicinity of Cultural Heritage Sites in Cyprus Using Remote Sensing Techniques

Kyriakos Themistocleous[1], Argyro Nisantzi[1], Diofantos Hadjimitsis[1],
Adrianos Retalis[2], Dimitris Paronis[3], Silas Michaelides[4], Nektarios Chrysoulakis[5],
Athos Agapiou[1], George Giorgousis[6], and Skevi Perdikou[7]

[1] Department of Civil Engineering & Geomatics, Remote Sensing Laboratory,
Cyprus University of Technology, Lemesos, P.O. Box 50329- 3603 Lemesos, Cyprus
{k.themistocleous,argyro.nisatzi,d.hadjimitsis,
athos.agapiou}@cut.ac.cy
[2] Institute for Environmental Research & Sustainable Development,
National Observatory of Athens, I. Metaxa & Vas. Pavlou, Lofos Koufou,
GR 152 36, P. Penteli, Athens, Greece
adrianr@meteo.noa.gr
[3] Institute for Space Applications & Remote Sensing, National Observatory of Athens,
I. Metaxa & Vas. Pavlou, Lofos Koufou, GR 152 36, P. Penteli, Athens, Greece
paronis@space.noa.gr
[4] Cyprus Meteorological Service, Nicosia, Cyprus
smichaelides@ms.moa.gov.cy
[5] Foundation for Research and Technology – Hellas (FORTH),
Institute of Applied and Computational Mathematics
zedd2@iacm.forth.gr
[6] Raymetrics S.A., Lidar Systems, Kanari 5, 15354 Glyka Nera
[7] Department of Civil Engineering, Frederick University, Nicosia, Cyprus
skevi@mail.com

Abstract. Cultural Heritage Sites are in danger of being destroyed due to several factors, such as earthquakes, uncontrolled urbanization and air pollution. The latest, whether it is from industrial, transport or domestic sources, can cause significant degradation and corrosion of cultural monuments. The use of satellite images for monitoring air pollution in different areas has received considerable attention and several related techniques have already been developed. In this study, such techniques are extended to examine air pollution monitoring in areas located in the vicinity of cultural heritage sites in Cyprus. Sun-photometers and Lidar have been used to support the results. The authors incorporate also 3D documentation using a laser scanner for monitoring changes over time. The available technologies and methodologies for digital recording of heritage sites and objects are really promising and the whole heritage community is trying to adopt these approaches for quick, effective, detailed and straightforward 3D reproduction.

Keywords: LIDAR, AOT, Sun-photometers, air quality, cultural heritage, air pollution monitoring.

M. Ioannides (Ed.): EuroMed 2010, LNCS 6436, pp. 536–547, 2010.
© Springer-Verlag Berlin Heidelberg 2010

1 Introduction

Cultural heritage sites are under constant threat from air pollution [1-3]. Europe has one of the largest concentrations of cultural heritage sites in the world [4]. The Mediterranean region is very rich in historical monuments, attracting a significant number of tourists every year, thus the conservation of heritage sites is very important. Studies on air pollution effects on historical monuments in Cyprus have shown high fine and coarse particle concentrations causing particle deposition onto interior vertical surfaces of Asinou church and colour changes perceptible to the human eye within a nine-month period [5]. Assessment of air pollution effects has been performed by different means over the years. In this study, the effects of air pollution on the Medieval Castle of Limassol, which is considered an important cultural heritage site, have been examined using remote sensing techniques.

In order to measure the air pollution in the area, a Lidar and sun-photometer system were established at the Cyprus University of Technology, which is located very near to the study area. Also, an air quality monitoring station that is run by the Department of Labour Inspection (DLI), Ministry of Labour and Social Insurance was available in close proximity.

With the aid of satellite images and ground measurements, the Remote Sensing Laboratory of the Cyprus University of Technology is monitoring pollution at a city-wide level, as well as for a synoptic large cultural area for the cultural heritage sites that are located in urban areas. Satellite remote sensing can be used to assist in air quality monitoring [6-9] and identify the need to protect cultural heritage in urban areas from air pollution. Satellite remote sensing is a valuable tool for assessing and mapping air pollution due to its major benefit of providing complete and synoptic views of large areas in one snap-shot image, on a systematic basis due to the sufficient temporal resolution of various satellite sensors [10-11].

2 The Site

The Medieval Castle, located in the center of Limassol town (Fig. 1), was built in the 14th century on the site of an earlier Byzantine Castle, where Richard the Lionheart, King of England, married Princess Berengaria of Navarre in 1191 and crowned her Queen of England. According to Etienne Lusignan, the original Castle was erected by Guy de Lusignan in 1193 and was surrendered to the Knights of Jerusalem in 1308. Archaeological excavations within the Castle exposed a marble podium from an early Christian basilica and the floor of a Middle Byzantium monument from the 10th or 11th century. In 1373, the Genoese burned down Limassol town after having occupied the Castle. It is likely that the Castle was badly damaged. The Castle was again restored in order to withstand renewed attacks by the Genoese in 1402 and 1408. In 1413, the Castle survived the first attack of the Mamelikes but severe damage resulting from an earthquake led to its capture in 1425 by the Mamelikes in their second attack on the city. At the beginning of the 16th century, extensive reconstruction took place. The gothic arches of the underground chamber and the openings in the side walls can be attributed to this period. The castle is a significant tourist attraction all year round.

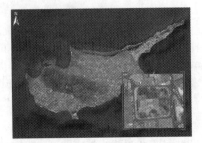

Fig. 1. Area of Medieval Castle

3 Methodology

The overall methodology of this paper is shown in Fig 2. The methodology is based on the integration of several tools for assessing the air pollution measurements determined directly from satellite imagery such as Landsat TM or ETM+ and/or MODerate resolution Imaging Spectroradiometer (MODIS) imagery. Such tools are the sunphotometers, Lidar system and air pollution measurements.

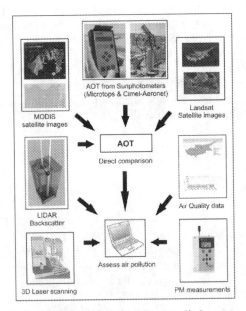

Fig. 2. The methodology applied

3.1 Satellite Based AOT Detection

The use of Earth observation to detect atmospheric pollution in different geographical areas and especially in cities has received considerable attention [6]. All the studies have involved the determination of aerosol optical thickness (AOT) either using indirect methods using Landsat TM and SPOT images or MODIS images in which AOT is given directly. The superior spatial resolution of Landsat and SPOT enable several researchers to develop a variety of methods. For example, Kaufman et al. [7] developed an algorithm for determining the aerosol optical thickness (using land and water dark targets) from the difference in the upward radiance recorded by the satellite between a clear and a hazy day. This method assumes that the surface reflectance between the clear day and the hazy day images does not change. Sifakis and Deschamps [12] used SPOT images to estimate the distribution of air pollution in the city of Toulouse in France. They developed an equation to calculate the aerosol optical depth difference between one reference image (acquired under clear atmospheric conditions) and a polluted image. Their method was based on the fact that after correction of solar and observation angle variations, the remaining deviation of apparent radiances is due to pollutants. Retalis [8] and Retalis et al. [9] showed that an assessment of the air pollution in Athens could be achieved using the Landsat TM band 1 by correlating the aerosol optical thickness with the acquired air-pollutants. Moreover Hadjimitsis and Clayton [13] developed a method that combines the Darkest Object Subtraction (DOS) principle and the radiative transfer equations for finding the AOT value for Landsat TM bands 1 and 2. Hadjimitsis [14] developed a method to determine the aerosol optical thickness through the application of the contrast tool (maximum contrast value), the radiative transfer calculations and the 'tracking' of the suitable darkest pixel in the scene for Landsat, SPOT and high resolution imagery such as IKONOS and Quickbird. Satellite remote sensing is certainly a valuable tool for assessing and mapping air pollution due to their major benefit of providing complete and synoptic views of large areas in one image on a systematic basis due to the good temporal resolution of various satellite sensors [6]. Aerosol optical thickness (AOT) is considered as the main parameter that is used to assess air pollution.

AOT expresses the degree to which aerosols prevent the transmission of light and comprise an indicative parameter for assessing air pollution in the vicinity of cultural heritage sites. AOT is a measure of aerosol loading in the atmosphere. A higher AOT value indicates higher columnar of aerosol loading and hence lower visibility [15]. MODIS on board the Earth Observing System (EOS) Terra and Aqua satellites [16] is a sensor with the ability to measure the total solar radiance scattered by the atmosphere as well as the sunlight reflected by the Earth's surface and attenuated by atmospheric transmission.

The accuracy of satellite-derived AOT is frequently assessed by comparing satellite based AOT with AERONET (AErosol RObotic NETwork – a network of ground-based sun-photometers) or field based sun-photometer [17-18]. The determination of the AOT from the Landsat TM/ETM+ imagery is based on the use of standard calibration targets defined on the image, preferably dark targets. For every grid (30m × 30m) on the Landsat imagery, the aerosol optical thickness is determined using the radiative transfer equation.

Since MODIS has a sensor with the ability to measure the total solar radiance scattered by the atmosphere as well as the sunlight reflected by the Earth's surface and attenuated by atmospheric transmission, the AOT results found by MODIS were compared with the sun-photometer's AOT results [18]. For the MODIS images, despite its low pixel resolution, aerosol optical thickness values were extracted for the 550 nm band. Based on the fact that a Landsat TM/ETM+ almost covers the whole area of Cyprus with sufficient spatial and temporal resolution, it was considered that such images were the most appropriate to be used for monitoring purposes.

3.2 Sun-photometers

In this study, two different sun-photometers were used to retrieve AOT. The Micro-tops II (Solar light Company, USA) hand-held sun-photometer measures the attenuation of the direct sunlight and the total transmittance from which AOT of the atmosphere is derived [19]. In order to achieve measurements with higher accuracy, this sun-photometer was mounted on a tripod at the same location on each occasion. The second sun-photometer used was the Cimel sun-photometer which is a multi-channel, automatic sun-sky scanning radiometer that measures the direct solar irradiance and sky radiance at the Earth's surface. The instrument is calibrated under the supervision of the AErosol RObotic NETwork (AERONET) network [20]. Measurements were taken in the visible and near-IR parts of the spectrum to determine atmospheric transmission and scattering properties. The correlation between the two instruments was determined in order to establish the validity of the AOT levels measured by the sun-photometers.

3.3 Lidar

The findings were triangulated using the Lidar system. The Lidar system is a laser radar using electromagnetic radiation 10000 to 100000 times shorter than those used by conventional radars [21]. For this study, the Raymetrics Backscattered Lidar was used, located in the Limassol area near the Medieval Castle. The Lidar is able to provide aerosol or cloud backscatter measurements from a height beginning from 170m to tropopause height. The Lidar emits a collimated laser beam in the atmosphere and then detects the backscattered laser light from atmospheric aerosols and molecules. The Lidar transmits laser pulses at 532 and 1064 nm simultaneously and co-linearly with a repetition rate of 20 Hz. Three channels are detected, with one channel for the wavelength 1064 nm and two channels for 532 nm. The columnar optical depth is determined from sun-photometers at the wavelength of 500nm, while from Lidar and MODIS at 532nm and 550nm respectively.

3.4 $PM_{2.5}$/ PM_{10}

Air quality in Cyprus is monitored by a network of nine advanced stations (Fig. 3 and 4) by the Department of Labour Inspection (DLI). These data are recorded hourly and are available on the internet. They have been used for comparison and validation purposes. $PM_{2.5}$ and PM_{10} data were recorded in June 2010, around the Medieval Castle, as shown in Fig. 4, using the Partical Handheld Mass Counter (AEROCET 531), which counts individual particles using scattered laser light and calculates the equivalent mass concentration.

3.5 Comparison of Methods

Comparison between the in-situ measurements taken in the centre of the city and the MODIS and Landsat satellite images allows estimation of the air quality levels throughout the city. The method is based on the principle that any changes between the derived atmospheric path radiances from the satellite imagery can be attributed to varying degrees of scattering and absorption by varying concentrations of aerosols

Fig. 3. Photos of Traffic Station used for monitoring air quality in Cyprus

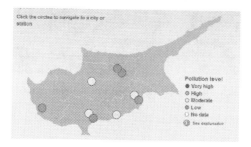

Fig. 4. Direct web-access to retrieve air quality data

(including haze), since molecular scattering is assumed to be constant with time in the same geographical area. The method is applied to the standard calibration targets for determining the atmospheric path radiance in the area under investigation. Indeed, dark and bright objects in the image are selected in the vicinity of cultural heritage sites. Landsat TM satellite image using band 1 is used to identify AOT in a grid format.

3.6 3D Laser scanning

The 3D laser scanner Leica Scan Station C10 was used to document the castle (Fig 5). The specific laser scanner has a maximum scan rate of 50000 points per second, while the accuracy is ±6mm in position (X,Y,Z) at a distance up to 50m. The laser beam diameter is ±7mm, while the field of view of the Scan Station is 360° × 270°. More-over, the laser allows acquiring the reflected beam intensity and RGB colours. The castle will be documented every year with the 3D laser scanner in order to compare the results to determine any deterioration caused by air pollution. To establish that the deterioration is a result of air pollution, areas of the castle which show deterioration on the 3D laser scanner will have samples taken to determine the chemical analysis of the surface to establish if the deterioration was caused by air pollution or natural causes. Photographs of the castle were also taken and applied to the 3D laser scanned point cloud.

Fig. 5. 3D laser scanning of the Castle (left) and Point cloud generated by 3D laser scanner (right)

4   Results

According to the air quality data provided by the Department of Labour Inspection, the majority of daily air pollution concentration values for PM_{10} exceeded the relevant limit, which is 50 $\mu g/m^3$, as prescribed by the European Union (Fig. 6).

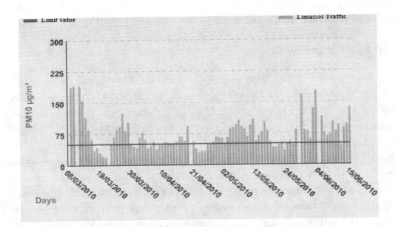

Fig. 6. Daily variance of PM10 for the study area (http://www.airquality.dli.mlsi.gov.cy/)

The AOT measurements with two sun-photometers, CIMEL and MICROTOPSII were taken adjacent to Medieval Castle (34.675° N, 33.043° E) within 40 minutes of the satellite overpass time on each day with full sunshine during the three month period April to June 2010. The high correlation r=0.92, which is derived from the coefficient of determination R^2=0.84, between the two sun-photometers (Fig. 7) ensures a high level of confidence in the measurement of AOT.

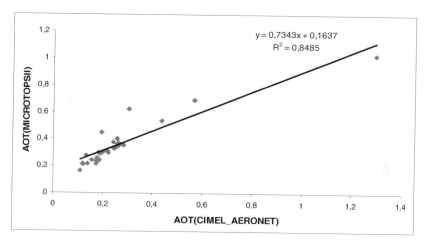

Fig. 7. Sun-photometers AOT correlation

The AOT data retrieved from MODIS and sun-photometer (CIMEL) also provided a high correlation (r=0.9, R^2=0.81) as shown in Fig. 8.

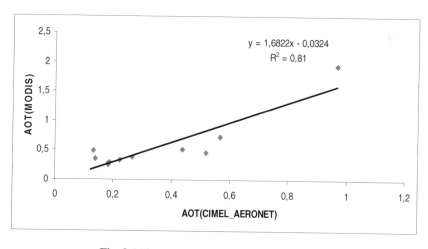

Fig. 8. MODIS and AERONET AOT correlation

Determination of AOT measurements using Landsat images has shown that the centre of Limassol, where the Medieval Castle is located, experiences the highest level of AOT values (Fig. 9).

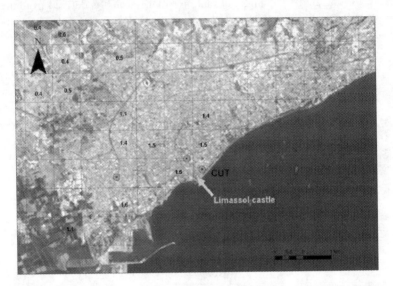

Fig. 9. The AOT distribution in the Limassol area retrieved from LANDSAT images

A PM_{10} /$PM_{2.5}$ field measurement in situ campaign has also been carried out in the area of Medieval Castle using a Particle Mass Counter. Especially on 23rd June 2010 it was found that PM_{10} readings exceeded the limit value (50 $\mu g/m^3$) for all four locations in Medieval Castle with the greatest value in the South part of the area (Table 1). Concerning the $PM_{2.5}$ data, values remained in low concentrations and only in the South part of the Castle the value was close to the limit value (25 $\mu g/m^3$).

Table 1. Concentrations ($\mu g/m^3$) for the study area

Location	Time(UTC)	$PM_{2.5}$	PM_{10}
East	9.10	14	239
South	9.15	22	301
West	9.20	11	164
North	9.25	16	247

The Lidar system provides accurately the spatial and temporal evolution of the aerosols within the troposphere. As shown in Fig. 10 and Fig. 11 (which indicate a high aerosol loading), the vertical profile of aerosol backscatter coefficient and the temporal evolution could be viewed up to a height of 4km.

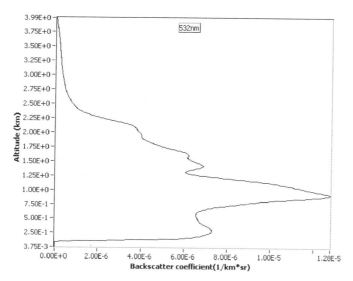

Fig. 10. Vertical distribution of the backscatter coefficient, over the area of Medieval Castle, on the 02/06/2010 (09:00 UTC)

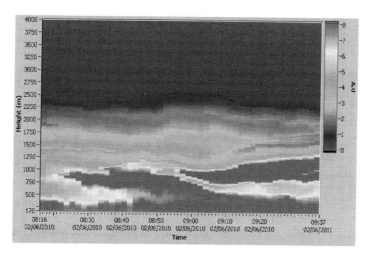

Fig. 11. Temporal evolution of aerosol layer over the area of Medieval Castle, on 02/06/2010 (09:00 UTC)

5 Conclusions

Existing air quality monitoring stations in major cities can provide warning of potential damage to cultural heritage sites, but they typically employ ground-based instrumentation, which restricts the area of land that can be monitored and investigated [22]. Additionally, ground-based monitoring can be expensive, time-consuming and restricts the access of tourists to heritage sites. This paper has shown that satellite remote sensing can be successfully employed together with ground measurements for the purposes of air pollution monitoring near heritage sites.

Satellite remote sensing has been widely used to improve air quality monitoring in urban areas. It comprises a valuable tool for assessing and mapping air pollution due to its major advantage of providing complete and synoptic views of large areas in one snap-shot image on a systematic basis, due to the sufficient temporal resolution of various satellite sensors.

Results from satellite remote sensing have identified that the centre of Limassol contains high levels of air pollution, with values of AOT higher than other surrounding areas. Further investigation will identify the worst hit areas in terms of air pollution at heritage sites in Cyprus and the variability of AOT values over time.

Systematic monitoring of heritage areas, such as the area of the castle, by using the 3D laser scanner will further assist validation of deterioration possibly caused by air pollution. Thus, chemical analysis of deteriorated surfaces will follow for final verification.

Cyprus has a number of cultural heritage sites that are located in the centre of cities, such as Nea Paphos, Tombs of the Kings, and ancient Kition. Areas under threat from natural disasters or anthropogenic effects can be monitored using remote sensing. Monitoring cultural heritage sites in urban areas can also be extended to other major cities in Cyprus that have cultural heritage sites located in urban areas.

Acknowledgements

The authors would like to express their appreciation to the Cyprus University of Technology for funding support. Thanks are given to the Remote Sensing Laboratory of the Department of Civil Engineering & Geomatics at the Cyprus University of Technology (www.cut.ac.cy).

References

1. Brimblecomble, P.: History of air pollution and damage to the cultural heritage of European cities, Science technology and European cultural heritage. In: European symposium, Bolognia, Italy, pp. 51–66 (1991)
2. Metallo, M.C., Poli, A.A., Maurizio, D., Franca, P., Cirillo, M.C.: Air pollution loads on historical monuments: an air quality model application to the marble Arch of Titus in Rome. The Science of the Total Environment 171, 163–172 (1995)
3. Kucera, V., Fitz, S.: Direct and indirect air pollution effects on materials including cultural monuments. Water Air and Soil Pollution 85, 153–165 (1995)
4. Doytchinov, S., Screpanti, A.: European UNESCO Cultural Heritage sites and the air pollution effects. Ecology and the Environment: Air Pollution XIV 86, 645–656 (2006)
5. Salmon, L.G., Cass, G.R., Christoforou, C.S.: Asinou Church, Cyprus World Heritage Site Aerosol Pollutant Study. Air Pollution and Cultural Heritage 1(2), 63–70 (2004)
6. Hadjimitsis, D.G., Retalis, A., Clayton, C.R.I.: The assessment of atmospheric pollution using satellite remote sensing technology in large cities in the vicinity of airports. Water, Air & Soil Pollution: Focus, An International Journal of Environmental Pollution 2, 631–640 (2002)

7. Kaufman, Y.J., Fraser, R.S., Ferrare, R.A.: Satellite measurements of large-scale air pollution: methods. Journal of Geophysics Research 95, 9895–9909 (1990)
8. Retalis, A.: Study of atmospheric pollution in Large Cities with the use of satellite observations: development of an Atmospheric correction Algorithm Applied to Polluted Urban Areas, Phd Thesis, Department of Applied Physics, University of Athens (1998)
9. Retalis, A., Cartalis, C., Athanasiou, E.: Assessment of the distribution of aerosols in the area of Athens with the use of Landsat TM. International Journal of remote Sensing 20, 939–945 (1999)
10. Wald, L., Basly, L., Balleynaud, J.M.: Satellite data for the air pollution mapping. In: 18th EARseL symposium on operational sensing for sustainable development, Enschede, Netherlands, pp. 133–139 (1999)
11. Tulloch, M., Li, J.: Applications of Satellite Remote Sensing to Urban Air-Quality Monitoring: Status and Potential Solutions to Canada. Environmental Informatics Archives 2, 846–854 (2004)
12. Sifakis, N., Deschamps, P.Y.: Mapping of air pollution using SPOT satellite data. Photogrammetric Engineering and Remote Sensing 58, 1433–1437 (1992)
13. Hadjimitsis, D.G., Clayton, C.R.I.: Determination of aerosol optical thickness through the derivation of an atmospheric correction for short-wavelength Landsat TM and ASTER image data: an application to areas located in the vicinity of airports at UK and Cyprus. Applied Geomatics Journal 1, 31–40 (2009)
14. Hadjimitsis, D.G.: Description of a new method for retrieving the aerosol optical thickness from satellite remotely sensed imagery using the maximum contrast value principle and the darkest pixel approach. Transactions in GIS Journal 12(5), 633–644 (2009)
15. Wang, J., Christopher, S.A.: Intercomparison between satellite derived aerosol optical thickness and PM2.5 mass: Implications for air quality studies. Geophys. Res. Lett. 30(21), 2095 (2003)
16. King, M.D., Kaufman, Y.J., Tanré, D., Nakajima, T.: Remote Sensing of Tropospheric Aerosols from Space: Past, Present, and Future. Bulletin of the American Meteorological Society 80, 2229–2259 (1999)
17. Chu, D.A., Kaufman, Y.J., Ichoku, C., Remer, L.A., Tanré, D., Holben, B.N.: Validation of MODIS aerosol optical depth retrieval over land. Geophys. Res. Lett. 29(12), 8007 (2002)
18. Tang, J., Xue, Y., Yu, T., Guan, Y.: Aerosol optical thickness determination by exploiting the synergy of Terra and Aqua MODIS. Remote Sensing of Environment 94, 327–334 (2004)
19. Tsanev, V.I., Mather, T.A.: Microtops Inverse Software package for retrieving aerosol columnar size diustributions using Microtops II data, Users Manual (2008)
20. Holben, B.N., Eck, T.F., Slutsker, I., Tame, D., Buis, J.P., Setzer, A., Vermote, E., Reagan, J.A., Kaufman, Y., Nakajima, T., Lavenu, F., Jankowiak, I., Smirnov, A.: AERONET – A federated instrument network and data archive for aerosol characterization. Rem. Sens. Environ. 66, 1–16 (1998)
21. Sivakumar, V., Tesfaye, M., Alemu, W., Moema, D., Sharma, A., Bollig, C., Mengistu, G.: CSIR South Africa mobile LIDAR- First scientific results: comparison with satellite, sunphotometer and model simulations. South Africa Journal of Science 105, 449–455 (2006)
22. Knobelspiessea, K.D., Pietrasa, C., Fargiona, S.G., Wanga, M., Frouine, R., Millerf, M.A., Subramaniamg, A., Balchh, W.M.: Maritime aerosol optical thickness measured by hand-held sun photometers. Remote Sensing of Environment 93, 87–106 (2004)

Author Index

Printed in the United States
By Bookmasters